Theories of Race and Racism

A Reader

This comprehensive reader brings together foundational works in the study of race and racism by such authors as W. E. B. Du Bois, Frantz Fanon and Robert Park with some of the most exciting contemporary writings in the field by, amongst others, Paul Gilroy, Homi Bhabha and bell hooks. *Theories of Race and Racism* is divided into six main sections covering the following key topics:

- Origins and Transformations
- Sociology, Race and Social Theory
- Racism and Anti-Semitism
- Colonialism, Race and the Other
- Feminism, Difference and Identity
- Changing Boundaries and Spaces

Each section begins with a brief editorial introduction, providing a guide to the readings in that section by historically contextualising them and relating them to other writings in the reader. Cross-national in content, historical in scope and offering a variety of perspectives, *Theories of Race and Racism* will be an invaluable resource for undergraduates across a range of disciplines.

Les Back is Senior Lecturer in Sociology at Goldsmiths College, University of London. **John Solomos** is Professor of Sociology at South Bank University.

Routledge Student Readers

Series Editor: Chris Jenks, Professor of Sociology,
Goldsmiths College, University of London

Forthcoming Titles:

Gender: A Reader
Edited by Stevi Jackson and Sue Scott

Theories of Race

and Racism

A Reader

Edited and introduced by

Les Back and John Solomos

London and New York

First published 2000
by Routledge
11 New Fetter Lane, London EC4P 4EE

Simultaneously published in the USA and Canada
by Routledge
29 West 35th Street, New York, NY 10001

Routledge is an imprint of the Taylor & Francis Group

Typeset in Perpetua and Bell Gothic by
Florence Production Ltd, Stoodleigh, Devon

Printed and bound in Great Britain by
TJ International Ltd, Padstow, Cornwall

British Library Cataloguing in Publication Data
A catalogue record for this book is available from the British Library

Library of Congress Cataloging in Publication Data
Theories of race and racism: a reader/edited by Les Back and
    John Solomos.
        p.   cm.
    Includes bibliographical references and index.
    1. Race.   2. Race relations.   3. Racism.   I. Back, Les, 1962–
II. Solomos, John.
HT1521.T473 1999
305.8—dc21   99–16826
                                                        CIP

ISBN 0–415–15671–8 (hbk)
ISBN 0–415–15672–6 (pbk)

For Nikolas Solomos, Daniel Solomos,
Stephanie Back, Sophie Back and Charlie Back,
in the hope of a better future

Contents

PART SIX
Changing boundaries and spaces

Notes on contributors

Theodor W. Adorno (1903–69) was one of the leading figures in the Frankfurt Institute for Social Research from the 1930s until his death. He published a number of books on various aspects of critical theory, including *Prisms* (1967), *Negative Dialectics* (1973) and *The Culture Industry: Selected Essays on Mass Culture* (1990).

K. Anthony Appiah is Professor of Afro-American Studies and Philosophy at Harvard University. He is also an editor of the journal *Transition*. He has researched and written on the history of ideas about race and on philosophical thought and race. His books include *In My Father's House: Africa in the Philosophy of Culture* (1992) and *The Dictionary of Global Culture* (with Henry Louis Gates Jr, 1997).

Michael Banton is Professor Emeritus of Sociology at the University of Bristol. He is a former President of the Royal Anthropological Institute of Great Britain. He has written widely on race and ethnicity, and his previous books include *Racial and Ethnic Competition* (1983), *Promoting Racial Harmony* (1985), *Racial Theories* (1987 and 1998) and *International Action Against Racial Discrimination* (1996).

Zygmunt Bauman is Professor Emeritus in Sociology at the University of Leeds. He is the author of a wide range of studies in social theory, including *Legislators and Interpretors* (1987) *Modernity and Ambivalence* (1991) and *Postmodern Ethics* (1993).

Ruth Benedict (1887–1948) was a leading American anthropologist and taught at Columbia University in New York. Her books included *Patterns of Culture* (1945) and *The Chrysanthemum and the Sword: Patterns of Japanese Culture* (1947).

Homi K. Bhabha is Chester D. Tripp Professor in Humanities at the University of Chicago. He is one of the most influential theorists in the field of postcolonialism and he has written widely on key issues related to colonialism and postcolonialism. He is the author of *The Location of Culture* (1994) and the editor of *Nation and Narration* (1990).

Chetan Bhatt is a Senior Lecturer in Sociology, Goldsmiths College. He has carried out extensive research on race, ethnicity and new religious movements, including detailed studies of Hindu nationalism and Aryanism in India. He is the author of *Liberation and Purity* (1997) and a number of papers on aspects of Hindu nationalism.

Gargi Bhattacharyya is a Lecturer in Cultural Studies and Sociology at the University of Birmingham. She is the author of *Tales of Dark-skinned Women* (1998) and numerous articles on questions of race, gender and culture.

Avtar Brah is Senior lecturer in Extra-Mural Studies at Birkbeck College in the University of London. She is the author of *Cartographies of Diaspora* (1996) and of numerous articles and reports on aspects of race, gender and identity. She is a member of the editorial collective of *Feminist Review*.

Hazel V. Carby is Chair of African and African-American Studies and a Professor of American Studies at Yale University. She is the author of *Reconstructing Womanhood: The Emergence of the Afro-American Woman Novelist* (1987) and *Race Men* (1998).

Barbara Christian is Professor of African-American Studies at the University of California, Berkeley. She is the author of *Black Women Novelists* (1980) and *Black Feminist Criticism* (1985).

Patricia Hill Collins is Charles Phelps Taft Professor of Sociology in the Department of African-American Studies at the University of Cincinnati. She has written widely on issues of gender, race and social class, especially in relation to African-American women. She has written *Black Feminist Thought: Knowledge, Consciousness, and the Politics of Empowerment* (1990) and *Fighting Words: Black Women and the Search for Justice* (1998).

Oliver C. Cox (1901–74) was born in Trinidad and spent most of his life in the United States. He taught at Lincoln University and Wayne State University. He researched various aspects of the history of capitalism and its evolution, including the history of race and racism. He published a number of studies of the history of capitalism, including *The Foundations of Capitalism* (1959) and *Capitalism as a System* (1964).

Kimberlé Williams Crenshaw is Professor of Law at UCLA and the Columbia School of Law in New York. She is one of the leading scholars in the area of race and law in developing what is called a Critical Race Theory in legal studies. She is a co-editor, along with N. Gotanda, G. Peller and K. Thomas, of *Critical Race Theory* (1995).

W. E. B. Du Bois (1868–1963) was a student at Fisk, Harvard and Berlin and became a leading black sociologist and activist. He was a staff member of the National Association for the Advancement of Colored People (NAACP) and the editor of its journal *The Crisis* from 1910 to 1934. He published a wide range of books during his lifetime, including *The Philadelphia Negro* (1899), *Dusk of Dawn* (1940) and *Black Reconstruction* (1956).

Richard Dyer is Professor of Film Studies at the University of Warwick. He has written on stars, entertainment and representation and on gay and lesbian culture. He is the author of *Heavenly Bodies* (1986), *Only Entertainment* (1992) and *The Matter of Images* (1993).

Frantz Fanon (1925–61) was born in the French Caribbean island of Martinique. He studied medicine and psychiatry in France and worked in a hospital in Algeria between 1953 and 1956. He identified with Algeria's struggle for independence. He was the author of a number of books, including *The Wretched of the Earth* (1961) and *A Dying Colonialism* (1967).

Ruth Frankenberg is Associate Professor of American Studies at the University of California, Davis. She has researched and written on racism, anti-racism and whiteness, and is currently researching spiritual practices in the United States. She is the editor of *Displacing Whiteness* (1997).

Sander L. Gilman is Henry R. Luce Professor of the Liberal Arts and Biology at the University of Chicago. He has researched and written on the history of medicine, sexuality and race. Among his books are *Difference and Pathology* (1985), *Jewish Self-Hatred* (1986) and *Smart Jews* (1996).

Paul Gilroy is Professor of African-American Studies and Sociology at Yale University. He was previously Professor of Sociology and Cultural Studies at Goldsmiths College, University of London. He is one of the leading theorists on questions of race and culture in relation to the African diaspora and his major books include *There Ain't No Black in the Union Jack* (1987), *The Black Atlantic* (1993) and *Small Acts* (1993).

David Theo Goldberg is Director and Professor in the School of Justice Studies at Arizona State University. He has researched and written on the history and contemporary expression of racism and was one of the founding editors of the journal *Social Identities*. He is the author of *Racist Culture* (1993), and he has edited a number of influential collections, including *Anatomy of Racism* (1990), *Jewish Identity* (1993) and *Multiculturalism* (1994).

Stuart Hall is Professor Emeritus in Sociology at the Open University. He was the co-author of the influential text *Policing the Crisis: Mugging, the State, and Law and Order* (1978), the author of *The Hard Road to Renewal: Thatcherism and the Crisis of the Left* (1988) and the editor of numerous volumes, including *New Times: The Changing Face of Politics* (1988) and *Formations of Modernity* (1992).

bell hooks is Distinguished Professor of English at City College in New York. She has written a wide range of essays on racism, feminism and contemporary popular culture. Her numerous books include *Yearning* (1990), *Black Looks* (1992) and *Outlaw Culture* (1994).

Max Horkheimer (1895–1973) was the Director of the Frankfurt Institute for Social Research in Frankfurt from 1930 to 1958. He was the author of a number of books, including *Eclipse of Reason* (1947) and *Critical Theory: Selected Essays* (1972).

Matthew F. Jacobson is Associate Professor of American Studies and History at Yale University. He is the author of *Special Sorrows: The Diasporic Imagination of Irish, Polish and Jewish Immigrants in the United States* (1995).

Winthrop D. Jordan is William F. Winter Professor of History at the University of Mississippi. He has published a number of books on the history of race relations in the United States, including *White Over Black: American Attitudes Toward the Negro 1550–1812* (1968), *The White Man's Burden* (1974) and *Tumult and Silence at Second Creek* (1993).

Michael Keith is Reader in Sociology at Goldsmiths College, University of London. He has carried out research on race and policing, urban politics and the politics of identity. He is the author of *Race, Riots and Policing: Lore and Disorder in a Multi-Racist Society* (1993) and he has co-edited such influential collections as *Place and the Politics of Identity* (edited with Steve Pile, 1993) and *Geographies of Resistance* (edited with Steve Pile, 1997).

Anne McClintock is Professor of English at Columbia University. She has written on gender, race and sexuality in a number of journals, including *Social Text*, *Transition* and *Critical Inquiry*. Her books include *Dangerous Liaisons: Gender, Nations, and Postcolonial Perspectives* (edited with Aamir Mufti and Ella Shohat, 1997).

Kobena Mercer studied at the St Martin's School of Art and Goldsmiths College, University of London. He has worked at the British Film Institute and at the University of California, Santa Cruz. His publications include *Welcome to the Jungle* (1994) and a wide range of articles on the intersection between race and cultural studies.

Robert Miles is Professor of Sociology at the University of Glasgow. He has written widely on various aspects of racism and has carried out extensive research on the history of racism in Britain. Among his books are *Racism and Migrant Labour* (1982), *Racism* (1989) and *Racism After 'Race Relations'* (1993).

Chandra Talpade Mohanty is Associate Professor of Women's Studies at Hamilton College, and Core Faculty at the Graduate School of the Union Institute, Cincinnati. She has worked extensively on questions of feminist theory, pedagogy and democratic culture. Her books include *Feminist Genealogies, Colonial Legacies, Democratic Futures* (edited with M. Jacqui Alexander, 1997) and *Third World Women and the Politics of Feminism* (edited with Ann Russo and Lourdes Torres, 1991).

George L. Mosse (1918–99) was Professor Emeritus of History at the University of Wisconsin, Madison. He previously held academic positions in the UK, South Africa, Holland and Israel. He was involved in the Wiener Library and was co-editor of the prestigious *Journal of Contemporary History*. He has written and researched on a wide range of issues, including studies of modern German and European history. His books include *The Crisis of German Ideology* (1966), *The Nationalization the Masses* (1975) and *Nationalism and Sexuality* (1985).

Gunnar Myrdal (1898–1987) was a leading Swedish economist and sociologist who carried out research on a wide range of social and economic issues. He was commissioned by the Carnegie Corporation to conduct one of the first systematic studies of the position of black Americans. The study was eventually published as *An American Dilemma* (1944) and he also published a number of other influential books, including *Value in Social Theory* (1958) and *Asian Drama* (1968).

Robert E. Park (1864–1944) was one of the leading figures in the Chicago School of Sociology. He, along with his students, made major contributions to the development of urban sociology, and the study of race relations, collective behaviour and social control. He published *An Introduction to the Science of Sociology* (1924) and numerous papers that were published in edited collections after his death, including *Race and Culture* (1950).

John Rex is Professor Emeritus of Sociology at the University of Warwick. He has researched and written widely on theories of race relations and on race relations in Britain. Among his books are *Race, Colonialism and the City* (1973), *Race and Ethnicity* (1986) and *Ethnic Minorities in the Modern Nation State* (1996).

Stephen Steinberg is a Professor in the Department of Urban Studies at Queens College and the PhD Program in Sociology at the Graduate Center, City University of New York. His books include *The Ethnic Myth* (1981) and *Turning Back* (1995).

Ann L. Stoler is Professor of Anthropology, History and Women's Studies at the University of Michigan. She has published widely on race and sexuality in colonial societies, including *Race and the Education of Desire* (1995) and *Tensions of Empire: Colonial Cultures in a Bourgeois World* (with Frederick Cooper, 1997).

Tzvetan Todorov works at the Centre Nationale de la Recherche Scientifique in Paris. He was written a number of books, including *Mikhail Bakhtin* (1977), *The Conquest of America* (1984) and *The Morals of History* (1995).

Patricia J. Williams is a Professor of Law at Columbia University. She also writes a column for *The Nation*, and her books include *The Rooster's Egg* (1995) and *Seeing a Color-Blind Future* (1997).

Howard Winant is a Professor of Sociology at Temple University, Philadelphia. He is the author, with Michael Omi, of *Racial Formation in the United States* (1986 and 1994) and *Racial Conditions* (1994).

Lola Young is a former professional actress and is Professor of Media and Cultural Studies at Middlesex University. She has published widely on questions about race and the cinema, including her book *Fear of the Dark* (1996).

Slavoj Žižek is a researcher at the Institute of Social Sciences at the University of Ljubljana, Slovenia. He has published widely on social theory, psychoanalysis and related issues. His numerous books include *The Sublime Object of Ideology* (1989), *Looking Awry* (1991), *The Plague of Fantasies* (1997) and *The Ticklish Subject* (1999).

Series Editor's Preface

SOCIOLOGY, IN UNIVERSITIES, colleges and schools, remains an attractive and buoyant subject – one with which students find it easy and rewarding to connect, and consequently a high recruiter.

Undergraduate students, often in large classes with limited contact time with lecturers, have not, however, always been well served with accessible and appropriate foundational reading material. The Routledge Student Readers series has been developed to answer that need. It aims to fill the gap between introductory textbooks, which tend to be perspectival in character and are all too often culture-specific and ahistorical, and the truly independent learning which is the goal of all good university education. The series is envisaged as a positive and informative response to the mass audiences and rapidly changing circumstances that increasingly shape initial university education. Books within the series are also intended to stimulate the interest of undergraduates and to engage the critical faculties of the reader in a manner likely to enable a transfer of analytic skill from one context to another. This is to be achieved by directing the student through a series of carefully selected core readings which transcend particular social structures both in space and time. These books are therefore not dedicated to encouraging students in an over-attachment to the detailed retention of particular empirical situations. Their concerns are theoretical, though informative of practice, rather than purely empirical. Sociologists do need to know 'facts' about the social world but primarily they require conceptual frameworks within which all and any social facts can be understood and problematised.

It is not the intention of this series to attempt to produce an orthodoxy or a 'middle-way' for the discipline or its sub-disciplines, nor to recommend an established set of topics for its curriculum and pedagogy. It intends rather to engage the student in a set of oppositions, contradictions and dilemmas that have preoccupied and thus organized sociological thought over the years. Critically the books in this series are organized in the form of readers but readers arranged thematically to combine the ancient and modern (or traditional and fashionable) at a conceptual level. Students of our discipline need to be strongly advised that the sociological tradition is neither a museum nor a series of islands disconnected through heroic epistemological breaks. They need to know, for example, that Foucault would make no sense unless Durkheim had set the problem before, that the nihilism of post-modernity only acquires vitality in response to the formalism of modernity, that modernity and science are and continue to be major human achievements in controlling and organizing the world.

Welcome to the new series, Routledge Student Readers, and I trust that your experience as a reader of this work matches up to our aspirations in compiling the series. I am particularly pleased that our first volume should be on such a timely and critical topic as Race and Racism. It would be hard to imagine, in the wake of the Stephen Lawrence Inquiry in the UK and the Rodney King incident in the US, that any part of our culture or any institution or organization within our society could be untouched by a conscious recognition of issues concerning ethnic integration. However, we are also only too painfully aware of the differentiation and stratifications that race continues to draw, marked out by vicious overt neo-fascist thuggery at one end of the spectrum and, perhaps more dangerously, by unthinking, covert 'institutional racism' at the other.

This is a fine book, brimming with insightful, stimulating and carefully selected pieces of writing on the topic. It also has the advantage of having been diligently edited by John Solomos and Les Back, two of the leading sociological contributors to this area of study with reputations extending beyond national boundaries and beyond academic circles.

Chris Jenks, *Professor of Sociology*
Goldsmiths College, University of London

Preface

THE PRODUCTION OF A READER of this kind is a long and arduous process, and is in many ways more demanding than writing a book on the same topic. As usual we have accumulated a range of debts on the way that need to be acknowledged. In particular we are grateful to the encouragement and advice in one way or another of Martin Bulmer, Chetan Bhatt, David Theo Goldberg, Clive Harris, Michael Keith, Tony Kushner, Marco Martiniello and Liza Schuster at various stages of the project. The comments of the anonymous academic referees used by Routledge to look at a draft of the whole Reader (a thankless task) were also extremely helpful in influencing us to revise it somewhat in ways that have hopefully made it more useful. Even if we did not listen to all the suggestions, we thought about them. Jeffrey Weeks, Dean of the Faculty of Humanities and Social Science at South Bank University, was helpful in facilitating the final stages of work on the project. The help of our publisher, Mari Shullaw, who first suggested to us that we put this Reader together, has been important at a number of stages. Even after all the delays she believed in the project and we hope that the final product justifies her faith. We are also grateful for the hard work of Geraldine Williams in tracking down copyright holders and ensuring that we gained permission to use the extracts that we wanted to use. Liza Schuster diligently searched for some of the less accessible books and articles and made our job easier; she also kindly read a draft of all the introductory material and provided useful suggestions.

Finally, but not least, we are both aware that projects such as this one would not be feasible without the help and indulgence of our families. They put up with the time taken by yet another book with a sense of humour and patience, and provided us with the love and care we needed as well as encouragement. Though this may be a lost cause, we do hope to make up for time lost in the future. For

John Solomos numerous trips to watch the Baggies play the beautiful game and struggle to return to their place in the sun have as usual provided a source of inspiration and a distraction from the pettiness of academic life, helping to put things in perspective. Various London-based Baggies provided good company, a sense of humour and a fair degree of cynicism on our often wasted trips. Our memorable 'retro' trip to Norwich stands out. The struggle continues.

John Solomos, *South Bank University*
Les Back, *Goldsmiths College*
May 1999

Acknowledgements

The publishers would like to thank the following for their permission to reprint their material:

Barbara Christian for permission to reprint 'Diminishing Returns: Can Black Feminisms Survive the Academy?' in *Multiculturalism: A Critical Reader* by David Theo Goldberg, Oxford: Blackwell, 1994, pp. 1–10, 236–8, 238–40, 242–3.

Beacon Press for permission to reprint Stephen Steinberg, 'America Again at the Crossroads', from *Turning Back: the Retreat from Racial Justice in American Thought and Policy*, Boston: Beacon Press, 1995, pp. 205–13, 214–20. *Turning Back* by Stephen Steinberg ©1995 by Stephen Steinberg. Reprinted by permission of Beacon Press, Boston.

Berg Publishers for permission to reprint Avtar Brah, 'Difference, Diversity, Differentiation', in John Wrench and John Solomos, eds, *Racism and Migration in Western Europe,* Oxford: Berg, 1993, pp. 195–9, 200–9, 211–14.

Blackwell Publishers for permission to reprint David Theo Goldberg, 'Racial Knowledge', chapter 7 in David Theo Goldberg, *Racist Culture*, Oxford: Blackwell Publishers, 1993, pp. 149–55, 155–9, 163–6, 168–77; Zygmunt Bauman, 'Modernity, Racism Extermination II', in Zygmunt Bauman, *Modernity and the Holocaust*, Cambridge: Polity Press in association with Oxford: Blackwell Publishers, 1989, pp. 61–70, 72–82.

Carfax Publishing Limited, PO Box 25, Abingdon, Oxfordshire OX14 3UE, for permission to reprint Michael Keith, 'Identity and the Spaces of Authenticity', *Social Identities*, vol. 1, no. 2, 1995.

Chetan Bhatt for permission to print 'The Lore of the Homeland: Hindu Nationalism and Indiginist "Neoracism"'.

Continuum Publishing Group for permission to reprint Max Horkheimer and Theodor W. Adorno, 'Elements of Anti -semitism: Dialectic of Enlightenment', trans. John Cumming, London: Verso, 1976, pp. 168–70, 173–6, 183–6. From *Dialectic of Enlightenment,* by Max Horkheimer and Theodor W. Adorno, Copyright (English translation by Herder and Herder. Reprinted by permission of the Continuum Publishing Company, New York.

Cornell University Press for permission to reprint Zygmunt Bauman, 'Modernity, Racism, Extermination II', in Zygmunt Bauman, *Modernity and the Holocaust,* Cambridge: Polity Press in association with Oxford: Blackwell Publishers, 1989, pp. 61–70, 72–82.

Harvard University for permission to reprint Patricia Williams, 'Race and Rights', *The Alchemy of Race and Rights,* Cambridge, MA: Harvard University Press, 1991, pp. 166–78. Reprinted by permission of the publisher from *The Alchemy of Race and Rights* by Patricia Williams, Cambridge, Mass.: Harvard University Press, ©1991 by the President and Fellows of Harvard College; Tzvetan Todorov, 'Race and Racism', from *On Human Diversity: Nationalism, Racism and Exoticism in French Thought*, Cambridge, Mass.: Harvard University Press, 1993, pp. 90–5, 153–7. Reprinted by permission of the publisher from *Race and Racism* by Tzvetan Todorov, Cambridge, Mass.: Harvard University Press, ©1993, the President and Fellows of Harvard College.

Homi K. Bhabha for permission to reprint Homi K. Bhabha, 'Race, Time and the Revision of Modernity', in Homi K. Bhabha, *The Location of Culture,* London and New York: Routledge, 1994, pp. 236–51.

JAI Press Inc. for permission to reprint Michael Banton, 'The Idiom of Race: A Critique of Presentism', from *Research and Race Relations*, vol. 2, (1980), London: JAI Press, pp. 21–2, 24–30, 32–8, 39–40.

Michael Keith for permission to reprint Michael Keith, 'Identity and the Spaces of Authenticity', *Social Identities*, vol. 1, no. 2, 1995.

Monthly Review Foundation for permission to reprint Oliver C. Cox, 'Race Relations', *Caste, Class and Race,* New York: Monthly Review Press, 1948, pp. 321–2, 331–4, 345–8 © 1948, Oliver C. Cox, printed by permission of Monthly Review Foundation.

Parallax for permission to reprint Gargi Bhattacharyya, 'Black Skin/White Boards: Learning to be the "Race" Lady in British Higher Education', *Parallax 2: 'Theory/Practice'*, edited by Joanne Morra and Marquand Smith, (February 1996), pp. 161–71.

Pluto Press for permission to reprint Frantz Fanon, 'The Fact of Blackness', *Black Skin, White Masks,* trans. Charles Lam Markmann, London: Pluto Press, 1986/1952, pp. 109–22, 130–5.

Princeton University Press for permission to reprint Anthony Appiah, 'Racial Identity and Racial Identification', *Color Conscious,* © 1996, Princeton University Press. Reprinted by permission of Princeton University Press.

Robert Miles for permission to reprint Robert Miles, 'Apropos of the Idea of "Race" . . . again', in Robert Miles, *Racism after 'Race Relations'*, London and New York: Routledge, 1993, pp. 28–34, 35–43, 44–50.

Routledge for permission to reprint Anne McClintock, 'White Family of Man' © 1995. From *Imperial Leather* by Anne McClintock. Reproduced by permission of Routledge, Inc.; Hazel Carby, 'White Woman Listen!', *The Empire Strikes Back: Race and Racism in 1970s Britain,* London and New York: Routledge, 1982, pp. 212, 24, 228–33; Homi K. Bhabha, 'Race, Time and the Revision of Modernity', in Homi K. Bhabha, *The Location of Culture,* Routledge: London and New York; John Rex, 'Race Relations in Sociological Theory', *The Theoretical Problem Stated,* London and New York: Routledge, 1970, pp. 1–6, 13–16, 30; Patricia Hill Collins, 'Black Feminist Thought' © 1990. From *Black Feminist Thought* by Patricia Hill Collins. Reproduced by permission of Routledge, Inc; Richard Dyer, 'The Matter of Whiteness', in Richard Dyer, *White*, London and New York: Routledge, 1997, pp. 1, 2–4, 10–12, 12–14, 39–40; Robert Miles, 'Apropos of the Idea of "Race"... again', in Robert Miles, *Racism after 'Race Relations'*, London and New York: Routledge, 1993, pp. 28–34, 35–43, 44–50; Sander Gilman, 'Are Jews White?' © 1991, from *The Jew's Body* by Sander Gilman. Reproduced by permission of Routledge, Inc.: Kobena Mercer, 'Identity and Diversity in Postmodern Culture', in Kobena Mercer, *New Positions in Black Cultural Studies*, London and New York: Routledge, 1994, pp. 259–63, 265–71, 274–85; Lola Young, 'Imperial Culture', in Lola Young, *Fear of the Dark: Race, Gender and Sexuality in the Cinema,* London and New York: Routledge, 1986, pp. 55–6, 56–62, 62–8, 70–4, 79–83.

Ruth Frankenberg for permission to reprint 'White Women, Race Matters' in Ruth Frankenberg, *White Women, Race Matters: The Social Construction of Racism*, Minneapolis: University of Minnesota Press, 1993, pp. 1–10, 236–8, 238–40, 242–3.

Serpent's Tail Ltd for permission to reprint Paul Gilroy, 'The Dialectics of Diasporic Identification', from *Small Acts*, London: Serpent's Tail,1991, pp. 120–7, 131–42.

South End Press for permission to reprint bell hooks, 'Racism and Feminism', in bell hooks, *Ain't I a Woman?,* Cambridge, Mass.: South End Press, 1981, pp. 119–26, 127–130, 136–9, 144–6, 148–50, 151–2, 153–5, 157–8.

Taylor and Francis Ltd for permission to reprint Gargi Bhattacharyya, 'Black Skin/White Boards: Learning to be the "Race" Lady in British Higher Education', *Parallax 2: 'Theory/Practice'*, edited by Joanne Morra and Marquand Smith, (February 1996), pp. 161–71.

Transaction Publishers for permission to reprint Gunnar Myrdal, 'The Nature of Race Relations', *An American Dilemma*, New Jersey: Transaction Publishers, 1962, pp. 84–8, 88–9, 89–93, 97–9. Reprinted by permission of Transaction Publishers. Copyright 1944, © 1962, by Harper and Row, Publishers, Incorporated; copyright renewed 1972 by Gunnar Myrdal; all rights reserved.

University of Minnesota Press for permission to reprint Ruth Frankenberg, 'White Women, Race Matters', in Ruth Frankenberg, *White Women, Race Matters: The Social Construction of Racism*, Minneapolis: University of Minnesota Press, 1993, pp. 1–10, 236–8, 238–40, 242–3.

University of Minnesota Press for permission to reprint Stuart Hall, 'Old and New Identities, Old and New Ethnicities', in *Culture, Globalisation and the World System: Contemporary Conditions for the Representation of Identity*, ed. Anthony D. King, University of North Carolina Press for permission to reprint Winthrop D. Jordan, 'First Impressions', pp. 3–4, 4–8, 11–15, 20–3, 24–7, 28–32, 32–6, 43, from *White Over Black: American Attitudes to the Negro, 1550–1812* by Winthrop D. Jordan (1968, the University of North Carolina Press. Used by permission of the publisher.

Verso for permission to reprint Theodor W. Adorno and Max Horkheimer, 'Elements of anti-Semitism', *Dialectic of Enlightenment,* trans. John Cumming, London: Verso, 1976, pp. 168–70, 173–6, 183–6.

The publishers have made every effort to contact authors and copyright holders of works reprinted in *The Race and Racism Reader*. This has not been possible in every case, however, and we would welcome correspondence from individuals or companies we have been unable to trace.

Introduction:
Theorising race and racism

■   John Solomos and Les Back

E VEN A FEW YEARS AGO, A COLLECTION of this kind would have
been difficult to put together. This is not because questions about race and
racism were not of importance in either social or political terms. Rather, the major
difficulty would have been in finding the variety of studies that seek to address
questions about how to theorise race and racism and develop conceptual tools for
the analysis of the variety of ways in which they have shaped both past and contemporary societies. This is no longer the case, as is evidenced by the ever-expanding
range of books and journals that address questions about race, racism and related
topics from a variety of disciplinary and conceptual perspectives (for an overview
of some of these developments see Bulmer and Solomos 1999). It is also clear
that there is growing academic and public recognition of the importance of studying
these phenomena and developing conceptual tools for analysing the role and impact
of racial inequality, racist movements and parties and forms of racial and ethnic
violence.

   It is as a result of this growing recognition of the need for greater theoretical clarity and conceptual analysis that we have put together this Reader on
Theories of Race and Racism. In doing so we had two related sets of objectives.
First, to provide for students and the general reader a collection that introduces
them to the key arenas around which theoretical debates have been conducted, and
the range of perspectives that have emerged over the years in this field. We have
consciously tried to reflect different perspectives and avoid the obvious danger of
putting together extracts from texts close to our own theoretical starting point.
This is not to say that we have not been selective in terms of the authors and the
particular extracts we have chosen to include. Given the breadth of material we
had to cover in one volume we have inevitably been selective and in places the
choice of extracts may seem arbitrary. But we hope that whether readers agree

with our choice of texts or not, that they find them of interest and reflective of the range of positions and attitudes that have shaped the study of race and racism in recent times.

Our second objective is closely related to the first, in that we have attempted to use texts that cover a range of disciplines, historical situations and geographical contexts. This arises partly out of our concern to show the diversity of theoretical and empirical work that has been evident in this field. In addition, however, we wanted to provide in one single volume a range of original sources that could be critically evaluated and analysed in some detail in relation to the conceptual issues they seek to explore or the situations they are attempting to understand. Part of the problem with the recent proliferation of textbooks and monographs in this field is that there has been a noticeable neglect of some important texts, along with a lack of historical perspective about the origin of current theoretical debates. It is partly in order to balance this neglect that we have included extracts from works published at various stages of the twentieth century as well as more contemporary texts.

Bearing these objectives in mind, we have also sought, as far as is possible in a single volume, to make the main ideas more accessible by organising them into six interrelated parts and providing introductory material that outlines the main themes. Although all the component parts of the Reader link up, we have divided the main debates around key themes and illustrated them by including extracts from some of the main contributors to each sub-field. Part One explores the question of the origins of race and racism, and includes extracts from the work of some of the main scholars in this field. This is an issue that has in fact attracted much attention in recent times and the various extracts included in this Part address questions that are still the subject of intense scholarly debate. From this starting point Part Two moves on to explore some important facets of social theorising about race and what is often called race relations. Bringing together both classical and more contemporary theorising in this field, the main objective of this Part is to provide an overview of the place of race and racism within social theory. Part Three shifts the focus somewhat by looking at one specific manifestation of racism, but one which has had murderous consequences, namely anti-semitism. Anti-semitism is an issue that tends to be treated somewhat separately from other expressions of racism, and relatively few attempts have been made to include it within the core of contemporary debates about race and racism. But, as we attempt to illustrate in this Part, any comprehensive analysis of racism has to include anti-semitism as a key component. In Part Four the complex linkages between colonialism and constructions of race are explored in some detail. This is an issue that has been at the heart of much contemporary scholarship, both in the social sciences and in the humanities and cultural studies, and the extracts included here highlight the shifting boundaries of race in colonial and postcolonial situations. Part Five includes a number of influential contributions to the development of a feminist, or more specifically a black feminist, perspective on racism. The main concern that holds the somewhat divergent extracts here together is the argument that theories of race and racism need to be re-imagined in such a way that a gendered perspective comes more to the fore. As a number of the contributors to this part emphasise the interplay between race, class and gender can take complex forms in specific situations. The final part of the reader, Part Six, brings together a group of suggestive pieces that explore the changing boundaries and spaces within which contemporary debates about race and racism are being carried out. One of the shared concerns to be found in a number of the contributions to this part is the need to place questions about race and racism within an analytic framework that allows for change and diverse experiences. Another underlying theme in this part is the question of what issues are likely to shape academic and public discourses in this field in the coming period. In addition to these substantive parts we have included an annotated Guide to Further Reading that provides a basis for exploring important themes and debates in an organised manner.

We are aware that many of the linkages in theoretical debates are by no means self-evident or easy to place within the parameters of wider theoretical debates. This is partly because a number of the issues that have been the focus of much recent debate in this field are conceptually difficult. But it is also the case that many of the core texts in this field are written with little concern about their accessibility to students and even less so for the wider public. The fixation with theoretical abstraction has produced a plethora of texts that may in some fashion have something valuable to say, but that in practice are addressed to other scholars in very narrow specialised fields. Some of the difficulties this has given rise to are evident in the readings we have included in this Reader, though we have made an effort to avoid this. Thus, in order to provide a starting point for using this Reader in the most productive manner, we, as editors, have felt it important to include a substantive introductory overview of the main themes covered in this volume. We have done this in the form of this introduction and in brief introductions at the beginning of each Part. In doing so we are not intending to simplify what are often complex scholarly debates, but to provide a map of key themes and terminology that is suggestive and contemplative rather than exhaustive. Elsewhere we have indeed attempted to provide a more detailed theoretical overview of issues covered in this Reader and fleshed out our own analytic framework (Solomos and Back 1996). Our concern here is more basic, in the sense that we have sought to use the introductory overviews as a way of engaging with the main arguments of the chosen authors. It is to this mapping that we now turn before moving on to the substantive parts that make up *Theories of Race and Racism*.

Race and racism in perspective

One of the more reliable, if depressing, predictions about the twentieth century was made by the black American scholar W. E. B. Du Bois back in 1903 when he asserted that 'the problem of the twentieth century is the problem of the colour line — the relation of the darker to the lighter races of men in Asia and Africa, in America and in the islands of the sea' (1903: xx). It is perhaps with Du Bois's words in mind that the black British scholar Stuart Hall asserted a few years ago that 'the capacity to *live with difference* is, in my view, the coming question of the twenty-first century' (Hall 1993: 361). This is because, argues Hall, in contemporary societies we are seeing an increasing diversity of subject positions, social experiences, and cultural identities that cannot be grounded in a set of fixed transcultural or transcendental racial categories and which therefore are constantly evolving and changing (see contribution by Hall in Part Two).

As the next millennium fast approaches, these contrasting statements provide an important point of reference for those of us thinking about the future of race and racism. It is of course not possible to make any sensible comment on the relevance of Du Bois's or Hall's predictions for the next century. But one reason to counterpose the two statements here is that one of the vital questions we have to reflect on is the meanings that are attached to ideas about race and ethnicity in the contemporary social context. One way to see the different language used by Du Bois and Hall is to remember that while for scholars of Du Bois's generation the 'colour line' was an everyday reality based on institutional patterns of racial domination, in recent times questions about race and racism have been refashioned in ways that emphasise cultural difference. This is not to say, of course, that for writers such as Hall questions about race and racism are in any way less important. It is clear that whatever the changing terms of language used to talk about race and ethnicity in the present day environment, we have in practice seen growing evidence of forms of racial and ethnic conflict in many parts of the globe. The shifts in conceptual language that have become evident in the past two decades are symptomatic of wider debates about the analytical status of race and racism, as well as related shifts in political and policy agendas.

The study of race and 'relations relations' as important social issues can be traced back to the early part of the twentieth century, at least in relation to the United States of America. It has to be said, however, that the expansion of research and scholarship in this field is far more recent. It is really in the period since the 1960s, in the aftermath of the social transformations around questions of race that took place during that decade, that we have witnessed a noticeable growth of interest in the theorisation of race and racism and more generally what is called the 'sociology of race relations'. The publication in 1967 of Michael Banton's book *Race Relations* and in 1970 of John Rex's *Race Relations in Sociological Theory* can be seen as symptomatic of wider social trends and of their impact on the course of scholarly research and debate.

Banton's study looked at race relations from a global and historical perspective, concentrating particularly on situations of cultural contact, beliefs about the nature of race, and the social relations constructed on the basis of racial categories. By looking at the experience of changing patterns of interaction between racial and ethnic groups from a historical perspective Banton argued that six basic orders of race relations could be delineated: institutionalised contact, acculturation, domination, paternalism, integration and pluralism (Banton 1967).

It was during the period of the 1960s that what Banton and others have called the 'race relations problematic' became the dominant approach in this field (Banton

1991). While often utilising racial classifications, this literature also incorporated anthropological perspectives on ethnicity and social boundaries. Richard Jenkins, among others, has shown that there are continuities between the methodological and theoretical approach applied to tribal societies and their 'modern' equivalent – *ethnic groups* (Jenkins 1986 and 1997).

John Rex's *Race Relations in Sociological Theory*, along with his subsequent output, represents another important attempt to construct a theoretical framework for the analysis of race relations and racism. Rex's work has exercised a major influence over this field and his contribution remains one of the most ambitious attempts to provide a theoretical grounding for research in this field. According to Rex's analytic model, the definition of social relations between persons as race relations is encouraged by the existence of certain structural conditions: e.g. frontier situations of conflict over scarce resources, the existence of unfree, indentured, or slave labour, unusually harsh class exploitation, strict legal inter-group distinctions and occupational segregation, differential access to power and prestige, cultural diversity and limited group interaction, and migrant labour as an underclass fulfilling stigmatised roles in a metropolitan setting (Rex 1983). From this perspective the study of race relations is concerned with situations in which such structured conditions interacted with actors' definitions in such a way as to produce a racially structured social reality.

What is also interesting about Rex's work is that he has attempted to utilise his conceptual framework in two seminal studies of race relations in Birmingham during the 1960s and the 1970s. In the study conducted by Rex and his associates in the Handsworth area of Birmingham during the mid 1970s (Rex and Tomlinson 1979) the basic research problem was to explore the degree to which immigrant populations shared the class position of their white neighbours and white workers in general. The substance of the analysis goes on to outline a class structure in which white workers have been granted certain rights that have been won through the working class movement, through the trade unions and the Labour Party. For Rex an important feature of the position of migrant workers and their children is that they are located outside the process of negotiation that has historically shaped the position of white workers. They experience discrimination in all the areas where the white workers had made significant gains, such as employment, education, housing. It follows from this that the position of migrant workers placed them outside of the working class in the position of an 'underclass':

> The concept of underclass was intended to suggest . . . that the minorities were systematically at a disadvantage compared with their white peers and that, instead of identifying with working class culture, community and politics, they formed their own organisations and became effectively a separate underprivileged class.
>
> (Rex and Tomlinson 1979: 275)

From this point Rex and Tomlinson develop a model for analysing the changing position of minority communities within the context of class and political relations in societies such as Britain. In the process of this analysis they also explore the differential positioning of minorities, through a comparison between Asian and West Indian communities. Within Asian communities they highlight the concentration on capital accumulation and social mobility. In the West Indian community they point to a pattern of withdrawal from competition altogether, with an emphasis on the construction of a black identity. This all leads to what Rex refers to elsewhere as the 'politics of defensive confrontation' (Rex 1979).

As can be seen from the extracts included in Parts One and Two, the approach adopted by scholars such as Banton and Rex has much in common with the arguments to be found in the work of American sociologists of the time. Quite apart from the classical work of Robert Park, whose early studies of American race relations continue to influence key aspects of contemporary debates, there are important links with the arguments to be found in the work of contemporary scholars. A case in point is the work of William Julius Wilson, whose early theoretical work in this field attempted to outline a historical and comparative framework for the analysis of race relations, focusing particularly on the situation in the USA and South Africa (Wilson 1973). A recurrent theme in the work of Wilson, which was produced in the aftermath of the riots and turmoil that characterised American race relation in the 1960s, was the relationship of the concepts of racism and power and their role in explaining processes of change in the context of race relations.

Rethinking the boundaries of race

The arguments articulated by writers as diverse as Banton, Rex and Wilson were in many ways shaped by the discussion of race relations that was developing during the 1960s and the 1970s in both the USA and Britain. This was a time when social reforms implemented in the aftermath of the Civil Rights Movement, urban violence and unrest, and the development of black power ideas and forms of cultural nationalism helped to reshape the politics of race in America, as well as in other parts of the world.

It became clear, however, that by the early 1980s a number of fundamental criticisms of the whole field of race relations research were emerging. These critiques were influenced to some extent by theoretical arguments that emanated from neo-Marxist, feminist, postcolonial and related theoretical perspectives. Such criticisms were influenced both by theoretical and political considerations, and they helped to stimulate new areas of debate. As a result there has been a rapid expansion of scholarship on race and racism within the social sciences and the humanities, particularly in sociology, political science, philosophy, anthropology, psychology, cultural studies and geography (Rex and Mason 1986; Goldberg 1990). A number of questions have come to the fore in recent times: What kinds of meaning can be given to the category 'race'? How should racism be identified as a political force within European societies, the USA and other parts of the globe? Have we seen a growth of new forms of racist expression in contemporary societies?

While it is clear what questions are being asked, what remains in dispute is exactly how to respond to them. A number of distinct paradigms have emerged in response to these key questions, influenced in particular by changing research agendas as well as by political transformations. In the context of the concerns of this volume we want to focus particularly on the influence of (i) the neo-Marxist approach articulated by Robert Miles, and (ii) the approach associated with the collectively produced volume *The Empire Strikes Back*, that emanated from the Race and Politics Groups of the Centre for Contemporary Cultural Studies (hereafter CCCS) at the University of Birmingham (1982).

The starting point of Miles's critique was his opposition to the existence of a sociology of race, and his view that the object of analysis should be racism, which he viewed as integral to the process of capital accumulation and class relations in capitalist societies (Miles, 1982; 1986). His analysis was first articulated in *Racism and Migrant Labour* and it is perhaps the most sustained attempt to include the study of racism within the mainstream of Marxist social theory. His empirical research has focused specifically on the situation in Britain and the rest of Europe, and has looked at the role of political, class and ideological relationships in shaping our understandings of racial conflict and change in these societies. As can be seen from a number of extracts in Parts Two, Four and Five, in particular Miles was not alone in making these criticisms of the conceptual focus on 'race'. His influence on recent debates can be seen in the way that the status of race as a social and analytical concept has been an important and recurring area of concern.

For Miles the idea of race refers to a human construct, an ideology with regulatory power within society. Analytically race constitutes a paper tiger (Miles 1988) that may be a common term of reference within everyday discourse, but which presents a serious theoretical problem. It is here that Miles diverges from what he sees as the race relations problematic. While Rex is concerned with models of social action (i.e. for Rex it is enough that race is utilised in everyday discourse as a basis for social action) Miles is concerned with the analytical and objective status of race as a basis of action (Miles 1982: 42). Race is thus an ideological effect, a mask that hides real economic relationships (Miles 1984). Thus the forms of class consciousness that are legitimate for Miles must ultimately be seen as shaped by economic relations that are hidden within the process of racialisation.

For Miles the process of racialisation is inter-related with the conditions of migrant communities. Its effects are the result of the contradiction between 'on the one hand the need of the capitalist world economy for the mobility of human beings, and on the other, the drawing of territorial boundaries and the construction of citizenship as a legal category which sets boundaries for human mobility' (Miles 1988: 438). Within the British setting this ideological work, conducted primarily by the state, acts as a means of crisis management and results in racialising fragments of the working class. Race politics are thus confined to the forces of regulation. For Miles the construction of political identities that utilise racial consciousness plays no part in the development of a progressive politics.

Miles's work raises some fundamental questions about the nature of racism and migration in contemporary societies. The most important of these is the degree to which black and minority politics are really distillations of class conflict. If this is true any movements away from class-based political action (i.e. movements towards any notion of black community politics) are doomed to failure (Miles 1988, 1989). If one takes this argument further, class-based political action is ultimately in opposition to any sort of sustained political organisation around a notion of race. For Miles the politics of race is narrowly confined to the struggle against racism. This is neatly captured in the way he uses Hall's (1980: 341) statement on the relationship between class and race. He concludes that it is not race but racism that can be the modality in which class is lived and fought through (Miles 1988).

Miles's insistence that racial differentiations are always created in the context of class differentiation (Miles 1989) is a core feature of his critique of the work of Banton and Rex. One danger of his position, however, is that it can result in a kind of class reductionism that ultimately limits the scope of theoretical work on conceptualising racism and racialised social relations. For example, in some contexts class exploitation may be incidental to the construction of situations of racial dominance (Goldberg 1992). However, the greatest contribution that Miles makes is his insistence that 'races' are created within the context of political and social regulation. Thus 'race' is above all a political construct. It is within this context that the concepts of *racial categorisation* and *racialisation* have been used to refer to what Robert Miles calls 'those instances where social relations between people have been structured by the signification of human biological characteristics in such a way as to define and construct differentiated social collectivities' (1989: 75). His work constitutes an attempt to reclaim the study of racism from an apoliticised sociological framework and locate it squarely in a Marxist theorisation of social conflict.

In contrast to Mile's approach, the arguments articulated in *The Empire Strikes Back* (CCCS 1982) were less concerned with the development of a neo-Marxist analysis of racism than with the analysis of the changing nature of the politics of race and the development of new forms of racial ideology. The theoretical approach of this volume was influenced by the work of Stuart Hall in particular (Hall 1980). This volume attracted widespread attention at the time and it still remains a point of reference in current debates (Bulmer and Solomos 1999). The approach articulated in this volume has also been extended in the work of key authors associated with it, including Hazel Carby, Paul Gilroy and John Solomos.

A major concern of the Centre for Contemporary Cultural Studies Group was the need to analyse the complex processes by which race is constructed as a social and political relation. They emphasised that the race concept is not simply confined as a process of regulation operated by the state, but that the meaning of race as a social construction is contested and fought over. In this sense they viewed race as an open political construction where the political meaning of terms like 'black' are struggled over. Collective identities spoken through race, community and locality are, for all their spontaneity, also a powerful means to co-ordinate action and create solidarity (Gilroy 1987). In some ways *The Empire Strikes Back* shared Rex's concern with social action but it rejected his overall framework as being at best ill-founded and at worst politically spurious.

Within this model of political action a multiplicity of political identities can be held. An inclusive notion of black identity can prevail and at the same time allow heterogeneity of national and cultural origins within this constituency. In his subsequent work, for example, Gilroy argues that the crucial question here is the extent to which notions of race can be re-forged into a political colour of opposition (Gilroy 1987: 236; see also Gilroy 1990). He holds little hope that this process can be developed within the arena of representative democracy. Instead he views pressure group strategies that have evolved out of community struggles and utilise a specifically black political vernacular as the way forward. Gilroy argues for a radical revision of class analysis in metropolitan contexts. He suggests that political identities that are spoken through race can be characterised as social movements that are relatively autonomous from class relations.

It should also be noted that *The Empire Strikes Back* was one of the first books on race relations in Britain to look in any depth at the question of gender and the role of sexism in the context of racialised relations. The contributions of Hazel Carby and Pratibha Parmar to this volume provided a point of reference and discussion in the debates about the interplay of race, class and gender during the 1980s. Along with the interventions of bell hooks and Angela Y. Davis in the USA, they were among the first authors to argue for a specifically black feminist voice. They also highlighted the relevance of looking at this dimension of racial relations in a context where the bulk of research remained gender blind.

In exploring these issues, *The Empire Strikes Back* acted as a catalyst to a politicisation of debates about the role of research in connection with race relations. In a sense the political struggles that were occurring around the question of race during the 1980s were being echoed in the context of the production of knowledge about racism. The sociology of race relations stood accused of being implicitly conservative and unable to articulate the theorisation of racism with an analysis of class divisions and structural inequalities in power. Sociologists of race and ethnic relations were also criticised for letting their theoretical imaginations be coloured by an implicit Eurocentrism. The result was that the sociological literature demonstrated an inability to record the experiences of minority communities in a sympathetic way.

The arguments to be found in the work of Miles and *The Empire Strikes Back* marked an attempt to articulate a theoretical debate about how to understand racism within the political environment of the 1980s, including the ideological challenge of the Conservative New Right. It is quite clear that the preoccupation with prioritising the analysis of racism was linked to a concern to fix the theoretical debate on questions of power and inequality. In this sense the radical critiques of race relations that have become a recurrent refrain in the literature on race and racism during the 1990s were produced in an environment where the main question that interested many researchers was the role of racism in structuring the social and political marginalisation of minority communities. However, in making the conceptualisation of racism a priority, these critiques failed to develop a theoretical framework for an elaborated analysis of the complex ways in which questions about race tie up with wider social cultural processes. As we shall see later on in this Introduction this is an issue that has come more to the fore in recent years.

Racism and anti-semitism

One of the most noticeable gaps in many contemporary texts on race and racism is a failure to examine the question of anti-semitism in a substantive fashion. Yet it should be clear from the whole history of racism over the past two centuries that anti-semitism has been a central theme in racial discourses and in political mobilisations around questions of race. This relative absence is all the more surprising since it seems to be an inescapable fact of our recent history that the experience of the Holocaust and the genocidal policies of the Nazi state are an integral part of any contemporary discussion of race and racism. Although there is by now a very substantial literature on the racial theories and practice of the Nazis and on the Holocaust (Proctor 1988; Weindling 1989; Burleigh and Wippermann 1991), little of this has been fed into broader discussions about race and racism.

This gap is beginning to be filled, particularly through the growing body of work that explores the interrelationship of anti-semitism and racism from both a conceptual and a political perspective (see Guide to Further Reading). It is partly for this reason that we have chosen to focus in Part Three of this Reader on Racism and Anti-semitism, with the inclusion of a set of extracts that explore this dimension in some detail. This concern to link the analysis of racism to discussions about anti-semitism is embedded in our awareness of the important role that the rise of Nazism had on scholarship and research in this field. The actual term anti-semitism came into popular usage at the end of the nineteenth century. But it is widely accepted that as a term it captures the long history of resentment and hatred of Jews. Anti-semitism can be seen therefore as a term that refers to the conception of Jews as an alien, hostile and undesirable group, and the practices that derive from, and support, such a conception. The history of anti-semitism is of course much more complex and of longer historical origin that the racial theories of the Nazis (Poliakov 1974; Gilman and Katz 1991). It has existed in a variety of historical contexts and it has been legitimised by a wide range of beliefs and folklore about Jews. Indeed it seems quite clear that if one looks at all the major European countries they all have quite specific histories of anti-semitism, influenced both by sets of beliefs about Jews and by broader socio-political processes. In the British context, for example, there is evidence of anti-semitism at different historical conjunctures. But it is perhaps in the period of the late nineteenth century that the arrival of a sizeable number of Jewish migrants from Eastern Europe became a focus of political debate, leading to the development of a political anti-semitism in particular localities. The political influence of anti-semitism in France towards the end of the nineteenth century can also be seen as related to the changing political and social relations in French society at the time.

Not surprisingly, in the aftermath of the Holocaust one of the main concerns of research on political anti-semitism has been in relation to Germany. Although the history of anti-semitism in Germany was by no means unique, it is certainly the case that in the aftermath of the Holocaust the German experience has been at the heart of most research. Whatever the limitations of this focus on the German experience, the wealth of research on the social and political context within which various kinds of anti-semitism developed in Germany has provided some important insights into the ways in which racial ideologies and practices are constructed by and through specific political movements. A case in point is Theodor Adorno's and Max Horkheimer's *Dialectic of Enlightenment*, an extract from which is included in Part Three. Adorno and Horkheimer sought, on the one hand, to situate anti-semitism in the broader context of class and political struggles in German society and, on the other, to underline its specific and unique characteristics. Although they sought to locate anti-semitism in the broader framework of capitalist society, they also highlighted the murderous consequences of the fascist construction of the Jews as a 'degenerate race':

> The fascists do not view the Jews as a minority but as an opposing race, the embodiment of the negative principle. They must be exterminated to secure the happiness of the world.
>
> (Adorno and Horkeimer 1986: 168)

The usages of racial theories by the Nazis thus provided not only a basis for the articulation of anti-semitism but a means of justifying the 'final solution to the Jewish question' and the inevitability of a 'race war'. From this perspective the political consequences of Nazi racial theories, with their emphasis on race as a total criterion, provided the basis for the extermination of Jews. The Holocaust itself needs to be analysed in the context of what actually happened during the period of Nazi rule from 1933 to 1945. As a number of studies have shown, a key feature of the Nazi state was precisely its 'racial' nature.

A fascinating discussion of the role that anti-semitism played in German society during the nineteenth and early twentieth centuries is provided by George Mosse's magisterial study on *The Crisis of German Ideology* (1966). Mosse provides perhaps the best insight into the variety of factors that helped to shape the articulation between anti-semitism and racism in the period from the second half of the nineteenth century to the rise of Adolf Hitler. He also illustrates the complex variety of processes that went into the transformation of latent anti-semitism, including the role of educational institutions, youth organisations and political parties. Mosse's rich account of Volkish thought during the nineteenth century provides perhaps the best and most powerful account of the social and political roots of German anti-semitism, highlighting the contrast in images of 'the uprootedness of the Jew' with those of the 'rootedness of the Volk' (Mosse 1966: 27–8). He also provides a detailed analysis of the linkages between the growth of anti-semitism and the rise of national socialism as a mass political movement:

> That the Volkish ideology, wedded as it as to anti-modernity, could be absorbed by the modern mass movement techniques of National Socialism led to its final realisation. To be sure, if it had not been for very real grievances and frustrations, both on a personal level and on the national level, Germany's development in modern times might have taken a different turn. But the most important question is: Why did millions of people respond to the Volkish call?
>
> (Mosse 1966: 317)

In some ways of course Mosse's question has not been fully answered, even when one takes into account the wealth of research on this question. What is clear is that the fact that the Nazis used racial anti-semitism as an important plank of their platform has cast a long shadow over subsequent debates about racism.

This has been highlighted by one of the most challenging recent attempts to rethink the whole experience of the Holocaust, namely Zygmunt Bauman's *Modernity and the Holocaust* (1989). Bauman seeks to reinterpret the meaning of the Holocaust and its role in contemporary history from the perspective of contemporary sociological theory. One of the ironies that he points to is that anti-semitism in Germany at the beginning of this century was weaker than in many other European countries. He points to the ways in which there were many more Jewish professionals and academics then in Britain, France and America. He also cites evidence that popular anti-semitism was not that widespread in Germany, although it grew rapidly in the aftermath of the First World War. Perhaps most controversially, Bauman contends that the Holocaust was not an aberration but an integral feature of modernity:

> The Holocaust was born and executed in our modern society, at the high stage of our civilisation and at the peak of human cultural achieve-ment, and for this reason it is a problem of that society, civilisation and culture . . .
>
> (Bauman 1989: 13)

From this perspective Bauman argues that a core feature of Nazism was its view of the need for 'social engineering' through its racial policies. The use of geno-cide by the Nazis was a means to an end, an element in the construction of the 'perfect society' (Bauman 1989: 91). In this sense Bauman is agreeing with the arguments articulated by historians such as Mosse. But he also wants to go beyond such historical accounts and explore more deeply the implications of the Holocaust for how we think about our societies today.

The Nazi attempt to construct a 'racially pure' society and to use state power to help bring this about has exerted a major influence in discussion about race and racism in the post-1945 period. In particular it helped to emphasise and warn against the destructive and genocidal consequences of racist theorising and political mobilisation. It also helped to highlight the complex forms which racist ideologies can, and do, take in particular historical conjunctures. In addition, it highlighted the genocidal impact of the use of state power as a tool of racial policy (Wolf 1999), an issue that has returned to haunt European societies once again in the 1990s.

Colonialism, race and the other

While much of the literature on racism and on race relations tends to leave the question of anti-semitism to one side, there has been a noticeable growth of interest in the issue of the role of racial ideologies and practices during the colonial period. This has been reflected in important and valuable accounts of the impact of colonialism on our understandings of race and culture. A key point of reference in this discussion has been the work of the psychiatrist Frantz Fanon (1967), along with the work of Edward Said (1978) on orientalism. Among other things this work has helped to highlight, for example, the complex processes of racial and gender identification experienced by the colonised during the colonial and postcolonial periods. Other studies have sought to show that the oppressed themselves have produced their own discourses about race and identity in the context of their own experiences of domination and exclusion.

In much of the literature on the development of racist ideologies and practices an important role is assigned to the ways in which colonialism and imperialism helped to construct images of the 'other' (Mannoni 1964). In particular there have recently been numerous studies of the development of images of colonised peoples and the ways these were popularised and reproduced in British society. There have also been a number of attempts to analyse the ways in which ideas about race were in one way or another the product of attempts to analyse the 'differences' between coloniser and colonised. Such studies have certainly done much to shed light on an issue that has by and large been marginal to the study of race and racism. Part of the problem in discussing the interplay of imperialism and colonialism with racism is the tendency to over-generalise without exploring in any detail the connections between the institutionalisation of imperial domination and colonisation and the emergence of racist ideas and practices. Mosse is surely right when he argues that: 'Imperialism and racism ... were never identical; their interrelationship was dependent upon time and place' (Mosse 1985: x). It is precisely the nature of this relationship that remains to be fully analysed, particularly if we are to understand how and why common-sense images about race were influenced by the role that countries such as Britain played as colonial and imperial powers.

A variety of recent critical research on the politics of colonialism has shown that images of the 'other' played a central role in colonial discourses (Ross 1982; Pratt 1992; Parry 1998). Such images were closely tied to racial stereotypes, but it was also clear that they related to all aspects of the relationship between the colonised and colonisers. Sander Gilman has made this linkage clear when he argues:

> In the nineteenth century, in the age of expanding European colonies, the black becomes the primitive per se, a primitivism mirrored in the stultifying quality of his or her dominant sense, touch, as well as the absence of any aesthetic sensibility.
>
> (Gilman 1991: 20)

From this perspective the linkage of colonised peoples with images of the 'primitive' was the product of complex historical processes and it took different forms in specific colonial situations. A case in point is the impact of the 'scramble for Africa' on images of the peoples of the 'dark continent', and the circulation of these images in the metropolitan societies. While, as we have shown above, European images of Africa had taken shape over some centuries it is also the case that the expansion of colonial power during the nineteenth century helped to invent new images and to institutionalise specific forms of class, gender and racial relations (Mudimbe 1988 and 1994; Appiah 1992; Coombes 1994).

What of the impact of these images on racial ideas and values in the colonial powers themselves? In the British context it seems clear that in the Victorian era the experience of colonialism and imperial expansion played an important role in shaping ideas about race, both in relation to Africa and India. It was also during this period that the question of the Empire become rooted as an integral part of British politics and society. Images of colonial peoples were not the outcome of any singular process. In the context of both Africa and Asia, for example, a number of interlinked processes were at work in the construction of images of both the 'natives' and the 'colonisers' (Dirks 1992; Spurr 1993; Sharpe 1993). We need to remember that most Victorians had no personal contact with the 'exotic' peoples and places that they were assuming responsibility for. Their opinions were formed according to the sources of their information, and these sources were for the most part the popular press and literature. The linkages between colonialism and racism became evident throughout the late nineteenth and early twentieth centuries in the form of the articulation between nationalism and patriotism in the construction of the very definition of 'Englishness' and 'Britishness'.

It would be a mistake, however, to see such racial images in isolation from wider sets of social relations. As a number of commentators have forcefully argued, an important aspect of racial thinking during the nineteenth century was the similarity between discourses about race and those about class. This was evident in both Britain and the rest of the Empire. Douglas Lorimer's study of racial attitudes in Victorian society brings out the parallels between the colour and the class prejudice of middle class Victorians in the clearest manner. He notes the similarities between the attitudes of those middle class travellers whose tourism took them to India, Egypt, and to the East End of London, in order to view the strange, the primitive and the exotic creatures of the world (Lorimer 1978).

It is also clear that during the high point of imperialism in the late nineteenth and early twentieth centuries, racialised notions of national identity were pertinent outside of the colonial context. By the late nineteenth and early twentieth centuries imperialist ideologies had developed a racial notion of national identity to refer to other European nations as well as colonial people. It was during this period that nationalist movements and ideals began to gain a degree of influence in many European countries.

What this process made clear is the variety of ways in which the idea of race could be used to refer to the putative 'racial' differences between competing nations and states. Interestingly enough, in the period before the First World War it was precisely such ideas about 'race' that gained an important role in political discourses of the time. This is not to say that colonialism and imperialism did not also have an important impact on political ideologies, literature and popular culture. Certainly if one looks at literary and cultural output from the period at the end of the nineteenth century, and well into the twentieth, it is redolent with images of the role of Britain as an imperial power and as a source of civilised culture for the colonies. Some of the most interesting research in this field has been about the role that colonialism and imperialism played in influencing political discourses and values through popular culture at this time. In the British context a number of valuable studies have helped to show the depth of the impact that imperialism had on popular cultural expressions through the late nineteenth and early twentieth centuries. John MacKenzie has shown in his interesting studies of imperialism and popular culture both the complexity and the depth of the impact of imperial propaganda on popular culture, education, literature and other cultural forms (MacKenzie 1984, 1986). Other studies of colonial societies have also highlighted the depth of the cultural and political imagery of colonialism and its impact on Western societies (Miller 1990; Pieterse 1992). The important role of sexuality in constructions of the 'native' has also been highlighted by recent research about imperial culture (Hyam 1990; Parker et al. 1992; Young 1995).

Yet it has to be said that one of the major lacunae in the existing literature is that while much has been written about the impact of colonial expansion and imperial domination on racial attitudes there has been surprisingly little comment on the role and impact of anti-colonial ideas and movements. Given the extent of its influence on political and social discourses during this period, it is indeed surprising that we have little knowledge of both the nature of the anti-colonialist movements and the influence that they had on the changing ideas about race in Britain and elsewhere. It is perhaps this absence that has helped to produce a rather monolithic view of the impact of the Empire on domestic British political culture.

It has to be noted here that in practice recent research has tended, if anything, to question the idea of a uniform and unchanging colonial view of 'race' that was prevalent at all stages of colonial history and European expansion. Rather, a number of scholars have shown that in reality colonial societies were by no means static and unchanging in their articulation of racial ideologies and social relations. In summary, while it is important in analysing the history of racism to include the role played by processes of domination and colonisation, it would be misleading to construct a simplistic one to one relationship between the two. It is perhaps understandable in the immediate aftermath of the decline of colonialism that much of the attention of researchers has focused on its role in fostering and spreading racial stereotypes and myths in metropolitan societies. The danger, however, is that in so doing we may lose sight of the complexity and diversity of colonial social relations and blame many of our contemporary mores on the 'experience' of colonial domination.

Feminism, difference and identity

Alongside the increased attention given to colonialism and postcolonialism in recent years, we have seen a proliferation of feminist writings on race and racism from a variety of angles. Indeed it can be said that during the past decade some of the most important contributions to the analysis of racism have come from writers whose work can be seen as deriving from feminism, though often also influenced by some of the perspectives we have touched upon already. From the early 1980s a growing number of studies, chiefly from the USA and Britain, have sought in one way or another to place questions about sexism, gender and sexuality on the agenda of the study of racial relations. This has led to some valuable insights into the everyday social processes that helped to shape the interrelationship between race and gender in particular historical contexts (Hall 1992; Ware 1992). It has also produced a wealth of theoretical interventions by black and minority feminist writers into debates about contemporary racisms and their socio-political contexts (Carby 1987 and 1998; Williams 1991).

As we noted earlier in discussing the British context, for example, *The Empire Strikes Back* was one of the first books on race relations in Britain to look in any depth at the question of gender and the role of sexism in the context of racialised relations. The contributions of Hazel Carby and Pratibha Parmar to this volume provided a point of reference and debate in the literature about the interplay between race, class and gender during the 1980s (CCCS 1982). They also high-lighted the relevance of looking at this dimension of racial relations in a context where the bulk of research remained gender blind. Carby's contribution in partic-ular is a point of reference in discussion within feminism about racism, and led to some heated debates in *Feminist Review*, among other journals.

At the same time a vibrant and critical discussion about the position of black and other minority women in relation to feminism was emerging in the USA. This took a number of forms. The work of writers such as bell hooks addressed the limits of feminist theory in dealing with questions of race and class. The work of other writers questioned the limitations of black nationalist politics when dealing with questions of gender. A particularly controversial example of this trend was the book by Michele Wallace *Black Macho and The Myth of the Superwoman*, that was originally published in 1979, and which sought to explore important aspects of the relationship between black men and women (Wallace 1990). Another influential text was *Ain't I A Woman: Black Women and Feminism* by bell hooks, originally published in 1981, and which was concerned with both establishing the possibility of a dialogue between black women and feminism and with a critical analysis of the limits of feminism in relation to the question of race (hooks 1981). The work of theorists such as Gyatri Spivak and Chandra Talpade Mohanty also helped to bring questions about non-Western versions of feminist thought into academic discussion about this issue (see Parts Four and Five).

In the aftermath of these debates a growing number of studies have begun to explore the interrelationship between racism and sexism, racial inequality and gender inequality and the position of African–Caribbean, Asian and other migrant women in British society. This has helped to overcome the gender-blind approach of many studies of racial relations, though there are still many aspects of the position of black and ethnic minority women that have received little attention. Most attention has focused on: (a) the role of women in the migration process; (b) the employment and social position of black women; (c) family relations; and (d) the links between racial and gender equality. All these studies have contributed to a growing awareness of the complex sets of interrelationships that take place between racial, class and gender relations in specific socio-economic contexts (Anthias and Yuval-Davis 1992). They have also helped to shed light on often neglected but nevertheless crucial aspects of racialisation.

Debates between feminists about the boundaries of identity and the different positionings of black and white women have been an important undercurrent in recent times, and this is one of the central themes that is explored in a number of the extracts in Part Five. Perhaps one of the most controversial areas of debate has been the issue of whether feminists have over-concentrated on patriarchy, and neglected race and ethnicity as sources of women's oppression. This is certainly a theme that pervades many of the early black feminist critiques of the mainstream of feminist politics, and it has continued to be a key area of debate. It is certainly the case that many feminist texts from the 1960s and 1970s showed little or no awareness of the historical background and contemporary context of racial inequalities. Whatever the merits of the specific debates that have taken place over this issue, it is worth emphasising that contemporary feminism has had to take on board questions about race and ethnicity in a systematic manner. The mainstream of contemporary feminism has been forced in one way or another to come to terms with questions about race and racism. There is now a wealth of literature that has arisen out of the ongoing debates between white and black feminists over the past decade. What is more important, however, is that this dialogue has encouraged the development of grounded research on the position of black and minority women (Mohanty *et al*. 1991; Alexander and Mohanty 1997).

One interesting example of this is the growth of research on the position of migrant women in various societies. Studies of migration have tended in the past to make assumptions about migration that have either excluded or underplayed the position of women in the migration process. More recently an increasing amount of research has focused either directly or indirectly on the position of migrant women. A number of important studies have explored the impact of immigration and nationality legislation on black and ethnic minority women, their employment patterns, the impact of racism on their lives, and their struggles to improve their social and economic position.

Quite apart from the academic research that has taken up the question of race and gender, over the past decade we have seen a massive growth of writings by and about black and minority women. The works of novelists such as Toni Morrison have explored key aspects of the experience of black women in America through the form of the novel and have become another important contribution to current debates. A good example of the impact of Morrison's work is her novel *Beloved* whose narrative provides a powerful and chilling account of the experience of black Americans through and after slavery. As Morrison herself comments about the contemporary situation in America:

> . . . For both black and white American writers, in a wholly racialised society, there is no escape from racially inflected language, and the work writers do to unhobble the imagination from the demands of that language is complicated, interesting, and definitive.
>
> (Morrison 1992: 12–13)

In this context it is perhaps not surprising that literary texts, such as those of Morrison and Alice Walker among others, have come to occupy an important and vibrant role in contemporary debates about the historical interface between race and gender. This is perhaps because, more than traditional sociological studies, they have done much to give voice to the experience of black women and to highlight the lived realities of racial ideologies and practices.

Another important area in recent research has been the issue of the construction of black female sexuality in racial ideologies. There is a wealth of research that has shown that at various historical conjunctures sexuality has played an important role in the fantasies that make up the world of racism. This research has tended to have a historical focus, and to be concerned specifically with slavery and colonialism. It is also clear that aspects of contemporary popular culture and advertising involve the reproduction of images of black female sexuality and sensuality. The role that such images play in the articulation of racialised culture in the context of contemporary societies remains to be fully investigated (see the extract from Stoler in Part Four and Stoler 1995).

Perhaps the main achievement of the debates outlined above has been that they have helped to establish the complex historical linkages between racism and sexism and encouraged theoretical debate about the interrelationship between the two (Collins 1990; James and Busia 1993). Despite important contributions, however, questions about gender and sexism have remained a neglected aspect of the mainstream of studies of racial and ethnic relations. The main research centres in this field have been largely unaffected by the debates discussed above and they have done little or no substantive research with a clear gender dimension. Even where issues of race have been looked at there has been an implicit assumption that 'the three worlds of inequality' (race, class and gender) are somehow separate from each other. There is a long way to go before the gender dimension is fully integrated into the study of race and racism, but, as we shall see in Part Five and other parts of this Reader, it would be impossible to analyse important aspects of contemporary racism without serious consideration of the changing social relations which shape the position of minority women.

Race, culture and identity

A major dilemma we faced in putting together *Theories of Race and Racism* derives from the fact that we were attempting to provide an overview of a field that is constantly changing. Whilst it may have been possible two decades ago to provide a reliable guide to the sociology of race relations and see that as a relatively complete survey of key theoretical debates, this is no longer the case. In recent years it has become increasingly difficult to provide a reliable map of this field, particularly as it has become increasingly multidisciplinary and as it has spread out to include arenas that were largely neglected by previous generations of scholars. Thus, whilst the debates of the 1970s and 1980s continue to influence research agendas, a number of recent developments have led to a questioning of many of the certainties that dominated theorising in this field even a decade ago. Perhaps the most important influence in this new situation has been the decline of both mainstream and neo-Marxist approaches. In this context some have called for a radical revision of class analysis in order to incorporate political movements that mobilise around forms of identity other than class. Others have suggested a need for a move away from both narrow sociological and neo-Marxist theoretical models as a framework of analysis and have: (i) sought to develop a self-consciously multi-disciplinary approach to the study of race and racism and (ii) have taken on board some of the concerns of post-structuralism and postmodernism in relation to the analysis of changing forms of social and cultural identity.

One of the results of this shift is the growing concern with the status of cultural forms and a return to an analysis of the nature of ethnicity in metropolitan settings. The political naivety of the early work on ethnicity meant that for much of the 1980s the analysis of cultural processes and forms was rejected in favour of a focus on the politics of racism. The rejection of culture was tied up with the notion that one of the inherent dangers of focusing research on the culture of minority communities was the tendency to shift attention from racism to the characteristics of racialised minorities. However, the question of cultural production and the politics of identity are fast becoming an important area of contemporary debate. New perspectives are being developed which examine the ways in which cultural forms are being made and re-made producing complex social phenomena. These new syncretic cultures are being plotted within the global networks which have been formed by diasporic and transnational communities.

The process of reclaiming culture in critical debate has simultaneously involved a re-examination of how racism is conceptualised. As a number of the extracts that are included in Part Six make clear, a major influence in theoretical debates during the 1990s has been an engagement of theories about race and racism with wider controversies in the social sciences surrounding questions of culture and identity. One of the constant refrains in this discussion has been the need to avoid uniform and homogeneous conceptualisations of racism. Although not yet part of the agenda of mainstream research on race relations, a range of studies of racialised discourses in the mass media, literature, art and other cultural forms have begun to be produced. Reacting against what they see as the lack of an account of cultural forms of racial discourse, a growing number of scholars have sought to develop a more rounded picture of contemporary racial imagery by looking at the role of literature, the popular media and other cultural forms in representing changing images of race and ethnicity.

David Goldberg has pointed out that 'the presumption of a single monolithic racism is being displaced by a mapping of the multifarious historical formulations of *racisms*' (Goldberg 1993). In this context it is perhaps not surprising that a core concern of many recent texts in this field is to explore the interconnections between race and nationhood, patriotism and nationalism rather than analyse ideas about biological inferiority. One of the core ideas that is explored in a number of the extracts in Part Six is precisely this issue of the complex and varied nature of contemporary forms of racist discourses and political symbols.

Let us take the example of the changing terms of debate about race in Britain during recent times. The ascendancy of the political right in Britain during the 1980s prompted commentators to identify a 'new racism', or what Fanon (1967) referred to as 'cultural racism', within the political culture and in everyday life. This 'new racism' has been conceptualised as having its origins in the social and political crisis afflicting Britain. Its focus is the defence of the mythic 'British/ English way of life' in the face of challenges posed by the incursion of 'foreign influences'. In this environment it has become all too easy for new forms of racial discourse to achieve common currency in everyday debates about the role and position of minorities in British society. Similar trends towards the articula-tion of forms of cultural racism have been noted by commentators on the situation in a number of other societies in recent times, including France, Germany and the USA. We make this point because it seems to us that it highlights the need to situate racism and ideas about race as changing and historically situated. From this perspective the question of whether race is an ontologically valid concept or otherwise is in many ways not the most relevant question to ask, since it is perhaps more important to understand why certain racialised subjectivities become a feature of social relations at particular points in time and in particular geograph-ical spaces.

One of the most important features of the contemporary situation is that mani-festations of race are coded in a language that aims to circumvent accusations of racism (see contributions by Stuart Hall and David Goldberg in Part Two). In the case of contemporary racist discourses, for example, race is often coded in terms of 'difference' and 'culture'. However, the central feature of these processes is that the qualities of social groups are fixed, made natural, confined within a pseudo-biologically defined culturalism. What is clear from these writings is that a range of discourses on social differentiation may have a metonymic relationship to racism. As Goldberg shows clearly in his work on racist culture, the semantics of race are produced by a complex set of inter-discursive processes where the language of culture and nation invokes a hidden racial narrative. The defining feature of this process is the way in which it naturalises social formations in terms of a racial/cultural logic of belonging.

Another focus within the emerging literature on the cultural politics of racism has been the social construction of race and difference in literature and the cinema. This has been a neglected area of research but in recent years this has been remedied by the publication of a number of important studies of race, culture and identity. Originating largely from the United States, such studies have looked at a number of areas, including literature, the cinema and other popular cultural forms. They have sought to show that within contemporary societies our understandings of race, and the articulation of racist ideologies, cannot be reduced to economic, political or class relations. This type of approach is in fact more evident outside of sociology. The work of literary and cultural theorists in the United States and Britain has in recent years begun to explore seriously the question of race and racism, and has led to a flowering of studies which use the debates around post-structuralism and postmodernism as a way of approaching the complex forms of racialised identities in colonial and postcolonial societies.

Equally, it has also become clear that there is a need to shed the narrow confines of the race relations problematic and develop a more sophisticated analysis of the impact of various racisms on the white majority. A growing literature now exists on the politics of whiteness that is attempting to develop such a focus of enquiry. However, there are immediate difficulties with this endeavour, as Richard Dyer has shown in his discussion of whiteness in film and other cultural representations (see Dyer's paper in Part Six). Dyer contends that white ethnicity in the cinema is implicitly present but explicitly absent and as a result it has 'an everything and nothing quality'. In these representations whiteness is equated with normality and as such it is not in need of definition. Thus 'being normal' is colonised by the idea of 'being white'. From a different perspective, bell hooks has graphically discussed the terrorising effect that 'whiteness' has on the black imagination. Writing on her experience of growing up as a black woman in the American South she comments: 'whiteness in the black imagination is often a representation of terror' (hooks 1992: 342). Clearly there is a need for a research agenda which looks at the way white subjectivities are racialised, and how 'whiteness' is manifested in discourse, communication and culture.

This turn within critical writing has important implications. One of the fundamental criticisms of the sociology of race and ethnic relations is that it has too often focused on the victims rather than the perpetrators of racism. Prioritising whiteness as an area of critical endeavour has the potential to disrupt the sociological common sense that equates the discussion of racism with the empirical scrutiny of black communities. Toni Morrison in her analysis of whiteness in American novels comments:

> My project is an effort to avert the critical gaze from the racial object
> to the racial subject; from the described and imagined to the describers
> and imaginers; the serving to the served.
>
> (Morrison 1992: 90)

In the context of Britain, Stuart Hall, among others, has pointed out the urgency of deconstructing the meanings of whiteness, not just in order to counter racism but also in order to understand the complex realities faced by the African and Asian diaspora living in Britain (Hall 1993). There is already an emerging literature that is trying to provide a critical analysis of the complex meanings that are attached to ideas about whiteness in everyday cultural processes (Frankenberg 1993; Back 1996).

The analysis of whiteness is certainly an important theme in many current debates, though it is not always clear how far it has helped to develop a better analysis of contemporary expressions of racism. There are also a number of possible shortcomings in the recent turn towards whiteness. In the hurry to shift the critical gaze there is always a danger of suspending reflection on the analytical terms of this project. Like many of the debates on the ontological status of culture, there is a danger of reifying whiteness and reinforcing a unitary idea of race. In order to avoid this it is crucial to locate any discussion of whiteness in specific empirical and historical contexts. Equally, it is important to understand that whiteness is a political definition that has gained historical meaning in the context of white supremacy. Any discussion of whiteness must, therefore, incorporate an appreciation of how gendered processes are inextricably articulated within the semantics of race. In this sense, interrogating whiteness as a form of identity and a political discourse must (i) focus on de-colonising the definition of 'normal', and (ii) avoid the reification of whiteness as a social identity.

Whatever the merits of the recent turn towards an emphasis on culture and identity in the literature on race and racism, it is evident that questions of cultural production and change are an integral component of any contemporary conceptualisation of racism. Nevertheless, these theoretical debates need to be contextualised within a shifting political context. The certainties of the debates that have dominated much of the discussion on racism in the 1980s and 1990s have all but disappeared. What seems to characterise the contemporary period is, on the one hand, a complex spectrum of racisms and, on the other, the fragmentation of the definition of blackness as a political identity in favour of a resurgence of ethnicism and cultural differentiation. At the same time, and perhaps paradoxically, new cultures and ethnicities are emerging in the context of dialogue and producing a kaleidoscope of cultural syncretisms (Bhatt 1997).

Reformulating the agenda

As we have tried to show in this Introduction the study of race and racism has been rapidly transformed in recent times and this has in turn led to a reformulation of research agendas and the boundaries of scholarship in this field. In this period of change our main hope in putting together *Theories of Race and Racism* is that it can help to provide an overview of important debates about the status of race and racism and explore important theoretical and political dilemmas that are faced at the present time. We are aware that this process is not simply an academic process, since researchers in this field are almost inevitably forced to confront questions about politics. While some authors writing in the tradition of race and ethnic relations studies have been careful to separate the research process from political action, such a separation is in some ways impossible and even undesirable.

Perhaps the main lessons that we can learn from the rapid expansion of studies of race and racism in recent years are the following:

- first, that there is a need for greater theoretical clarity on key concepts;
- second, there is a need to broaden the research agenda to cover issues that have been neglected, such as culture and identity;
- third, there is a need for research agendas to address political and policy dilemmas in order to understand racism and how to counter it;
- fourth, there is a need to integrate the analysis of racism with a conceptualisation of related issues, such as gender and sexuality.

Precisely because the question of how to conceptualise racism is not purely an academic matter, it is important to develop analytic frameworks that explain the role of ideas about race in specific historical and political conjunctures. It is from this starting point that we can begin to understand the complex mechanisms through which contemporary racisms have evolved and adapted to new circumstances. A recurrent concern of the various extracts in Part Six is to outline some of the new areas of research that need further exploration.

In this context, unitary or simplistic definitions of racism become hard to sustain. However, it seems clear that contemporary racisms share some central features. They attempt to fix human social groups in terms of *natural* properties of belonging within particular political and geographical contexts. The assertion that racialised subjects do not belong within – say British society – is then associated with social and cultural characteristics designated to them within the logic of particular racisms. It follows from the above argument that racist discourses need to be rigorously contextualised. This means that racisms need to be situated within specific moments. The effect of a particular racist discourse needs to be placed in the conditions surrounding the moment of its enunciation.

In this context, the meanings of race and racism need to be located within particular fields of discourse and articulated to the social relations found within that context. It is then necessary to see what kinds of racialised identities are being formed within these contexts. Take, for example, the definition of the cate-gory 'black'. It is clear that it is a notion used somewhat differently in specific national situations, and that this has been influenced by particular historical and cultural processes. The contrasting usages of the category 'black' in America and Britain is a case in point. With regard to the ontological status of these classifi-cations we view them as political constructions of identity that need to be situated within specific social and discursive contexts. We in no way accept that these iden-tifications relate to 'natural communities', or that one notion is more politically legitimate than others. Rather they constitute moments where community and iden-tity is defined: manifestations of racial and ethnic closure. We are suggesting a position that builds into any analysis a rigorous scrutiny of racialised definitions, whether they are operated by the state or through political mobilisations that are occurring around racial and ethnic identities within minority communities. This approach seeks to decipher the meanings of racialised identities without attempting to prioritise one classification as more legitimate than another.

We are suggesting a model for conceptualising racisms that is:

- sensitive to local and contextual manifestations of racist discourse;
- able to connect local manifestations with wider or national public discourses;
- able to develop a sensitivity to the trans-local matrices of racist culture and ethnic absolutist movements.

Here we are particularly thinking of the ways in which racist cultures are being integrated across time and space through technological advances such as the Internet. In this way we are suggesting a model that situates racisms at both local, national and global levels. As yet, much theoretical work on racism has produced accounts of racism that derive contemporary forms of racism from public polit-ical discourse. This evidence is then used to generalise about broader trends within British society. We are suggesting that there is a need to move beyond the limits of this approach by situating racisms within particular settings before moving towards a more general account of their wider significance.

Theories of Race and Racism provides a guide through the complex debates about the ways in which ideas about race and racism need to be conceptualised in the present political environment. We are aware that this whole field of research is going through a rapid period of change and that it is not possible to cover all these transformations in one volume. It is clear that the coming period will pose serious questions with regard to the way racism is conceptualised, particularly in a context where new forms of racial and ethnic conflict have come to the fore in various parts of the globe. But precisely because of these uncertainties there is a need to go beyond the limited perspectives that have dominated academic discourses in recent years and meet the challenges we are likely to face in the century to come. We hope that in putting this Reader together we have provided some of the tools for moving beyond current preoccupations in order to analyse new trends and developments.

Using the Reader

One of our main hopes in putting this collection together was to make it accessible and usable. We have therefore included a number of features to help you get the most out of it. We have provided a general overview of the main thematic issues covered by the Reader in the course of the preceding Introduction and so it may be useful to go carefully through the arguments here before moving on to the specific Parts. In addition, at the beginning of each Part we have included an introduction that surveys the main arguments to be found in each contribution. The main point of these introductions is to provide a guide to the specific themes covered by the extracts in each Part and to clarify important points of debate. If you want to follow up other relevant important texts we have included separate lists for each part in the annotated Guide to Further Reading that comes at the end of the Reader. The suggestions contained there are not meant to be complete, but we have attempted to include texts that reflect a variety of conceptual perspectives and which are in themselves important contributions to their fields of study. Finally, at the end of each Part introduction we have included lists of Key Questions that can serve as a point of departure for thinking through the main themes that are covered in each Part.

References

Adorno. T. W. and Horkheimer, M. 1986. *Dialectic of Enlightenment*, London: Verso

Alexander, M. J. and Mohanty, C. T. (eds) 1997. *Feminist Genealogies, Colonial Legacies, Democratic Futures*, New York: Routledge

Anthias, F. and Yuval-Davis, N. 1992. *Racialized Boundaries*, London: Routledge

Appiah, K. A. 1992. *In My Father's House: Africa in the Philosophy of Culture*, London: Methuen

Back, L. 1996. *New Ethnicities and Urban Culture*, London: UCL Press

Banton, M. 1967. *Race Relations*, New York: Basic Books

—— 1991. 'The Race Relations Problematic', *British Journal of Sociology* 42, 1: 115–130

Bauman, Z. 1989. *Modernity and the Holocaust*, Oxford: Blackwell

Bhatt, C. 1997. *Liberation and Purity: Race, New Religious Movements and the Ethics of Postmodernity* London: UCL Press

Bulmer, M. and Solomos, J. (eds) 1999. *Ethnic and Racial Studies Today*, London: Routledge

Burleigh, M. and Wippermann, W. 1991. *The Racial State: Germany 1933–1945*, Cambridge: Cambridge University Press

Carby, H. V. 1987. *Reconstructing Womanhood*, New York: Oxford University Press

—— 1998. *Race Men*, Cambridge, MA: Harvard University Press

Centre for Contemporary Cultural Studies 1982. *The Empire Strikes Back: Race and Racism in '70s Britain*, London: Hutchinson

Collins, P. H. 1990. *Black Feminist Thought*, London: Unwin Hyman

Coombes A. 1994. *Reinventing Africa*, New Haven and London: Yale University Press

Davis, A. Y. 1982. *Women, Race and Class*, London: The Women's Press

Dirks, N. B. (ed.) 1992. *Colonialism and Culture*, Ann Arbor: University of Michigan Press

Du Bois, W. E. B. [1903] 1996. *The Souls of Black Folk*, New York: Penguin

Fanon, R. 1967. *Towards the African Revolution*, New York: Monthly Review Press

Frankenberg, R. 1993. *White Women, Race Matters: The Social Construction of Whiteness*, London: Routledge

Gilman, S. L. 1991. *The Jew's Body*, New York: Routledge

Gilman, S. L. and Katz, S. T. (eds) 1991. *Anti-Semitism in Times of Crisis*, New York: New York University Press

Gilroy, P. 1987. *There Ain't No Black in the Union Jack*, London: Hutchinson

—— 1990. 'One Nation Under a Groove: The Cultural Politics of 'Race' and Racism in Britain' in D. T. Goldberg (eds) *Anatomy of Racism*, Minneapolis: University of Minnesota Press

Goldberg, D. T. 1992. 'Polluting the Body Politic: Racist Discourse and Urban Location' in M. Cross and M. Keith (eds) *Racism, the City and the State*, (London: Routledge)

Goldberg, D. T. (ed.) 1990. *Anatomy of Racism*, Minneapolis: University of Minnesota Press

Hall, C. 1992. *White, Middle Class and Male: Explorations in Feminism and History*, Cambridge: Polity Press

Hall, S. 1980. 'Race Articulation and Societies Structured in Dominance' in UNESCO *Sociological Theories: Race and Colonialism*, Paris: UNESCO

—— 1990. 'Cultural Identity and Diaspora' in J. Rutherford (ed.) *Identity: Culture, Community, Difference*, London: Lawrence and Wishart

—— 1993. 'Culture, community, nation', *Cultural Studies* 7, 3: 349–63

hooks, b. 1981. *Ain't I A Woman: Black Women and Feminism*, Boston: South End Press

—— 1992. 'Representing Whiteness in the Black Imagination' in L. Grossberg, C. Nelson and P. Treichler (eds) *Cultural Studies*, London: Routledge

Hyam, R. 1990. *Empire and Sexuality: The British Experience*, Manchester: Manchester University Press

James, S. and Busia, A. (eds) 1993. *Theorizing Black Feminisms*, London: Routledge

Jenkins, R. (1986) 'Some Anthropological Models of Inter-Ethnic Relations' in J. Rex and D. Mason (eds) *Theories of Race and Ethnic Relations*, Cambridge: Cambridge University Press

—— (1997) *Rethinking Ethnicity: Arguments and Explorations*, London: Sage

Kohn, M. (1995) *The Race Gallery: The Return of Racial Science*, London: Jonathan Cape

Lorimer, D. A. (1978) *Colour, Class and the Victorians*, Leicester: Leicester University Press

MacKenzie, J. M. 1984. *Propaganda and Empire: The Manipulation of British Public Opinion 1880–1960*, Manchester: Manchester University Press

MacKenzie, J. M. (ed.) 1986. *Imperialism and Popular Culture*, Manchester: Manchester University Press

Mannoni, O. 1964. *Prospero and Caliban: The Psychology of Colonisation*, New York: Fredrick A. Praeger

Miles, R. 1982. Racism and Migrant Labour, London: George Allen and Unwin

—— 1984. 'Marxism Versus the "Sociology of Race Relations"?', Ethnic and Racial Studies 7, 2: 217–37

—— 1986. 'Labour Migration, Racism and Capital Accumulation in Western Europe', Capital and Class 28: 49–86

—— 1988. 'Racism, Marxism and British Politics', Economy and Society 17, 3: 428–60

—— 1989. Racism, London: Routledge

Miller, C. L. 1990. Theories of Africans, Chicago: University of Chicago Press

Mohanty, C. T., Russo, A., and Torres, L. (eds) 1991. Third World Women and the Politics of Feminism, Bloomington: Indiana University Press

Morrison, T. 1992. Playing in the Dark: Whiteness and the Literary Imagination, Cambridge MA: Harvard University Press

Mosse, G. L. 1966. The Crisis of German Ideology: Intellectual Origins of the Third Reich, London: Weidenfeld and Nicolson

—— 1985. Toward the Final Solution: A History of European Racism, Madison: University of Wisconsin Press

Mudimbe, V. Y. 1988. The Invention of Africa: Gnosis, Philosophy and the Order of Knowledge, Bloomington: Indiana University Press

—— 1994. The Idea of Africa, Bloomington: Indiana University Press

Parker, A., Russo, M., Sommer, D. and Yaeger, P. (eds) 1992. Nationalisms and Sexualities, New York: Routledge

Parry, B. 1998. Delusions and Discoveries: Studies on India in the British Imagination 1880–1930, London: Verso

Pieterse, J. M. 1992. White on Black: Images of Africa and Blacks in Western Popular Culture, New Haven and London: Yale University Press

Poliakov, L. 1974. The Aryan Myth, Brighton: Chatto Heinemann for Sussex University Press

Pratt, M. L. 1992. Imperial Eyes: Travel Writing and Transculturation, London: Routledge

Proctor, R. M. 1988. Racial Hygiene: Medicine Under the Nazis, Cambridge, MA: Harvard University Press

Rex, J. [1970] 1983. Race Relations in Sociological Theory, second edition, London: Routledge and Kegan Paul

—— 1979. 'Black Militancy and Class Conflict' in R. Miles and A. Phizacklea (eds) Racism and Political Action in Britain, London: Routledge and Kegan Paul

Rex, J. and Mason, D. (eds) 1986. Theories of Race and Ethnic Relations, Cambridge: Cambridge University Press

Rex, J. and Tomlinson, S. 1979. Colonial Immigrants in a British City, London: Routledge and Kegan Paul

Ross R. (ed.) 1982. Racism and Colonialism, The Hague: Martinus Nijhoff

Said, E. 1978. Orientalism, Harmondsworth: Penguin

Sharpe, J. 1993. Allegories of Empire: The Figure of Woman in the Colonial Text, Minneapolis: University of Minnesota Press

Solomos, J. and Back, L. 1996. Racism and Society, Basingstoke: Macmillan

Spivak, G. C. 1988. In Other Worlds: Essays in Cultural Politics, London: Routledge

Spurr, D. 1993. The Rhetoric of Empire, Durham NC and London: Duke University Press

Stoler, A. L. 1995. *Race and the Education of Desire: Foucault's History of Sexuality and the Colonial Order of Things*, Durham NC: Duke University Press

Wallace, M. [1979] 1990. *Black Macho and The Myth of the Superwoman*, London: Verso

Ware, V. 1992. *Beyond the Pale: White Women, Racism and History*, London: Verso

Weindling, P. 1989. *Health, Race and German Politics Between National Unification and Nazism 1870–1945*, Cambridge: Cambridge University Press

Williams, P. J. 1991. *The Alchemy of Race and Rights*, Cambridge, MA: Harvard University press

Wilson, W. J. 1973. *Power, Racism and Privilege*, New York: Macmillan

Wolf, E. 1999. *Envisioning Power: Ideologies of Dominance and Crisis*, Berkeley: University of California Press

Young, R. J. C. 1995. *Colonial Desire: Hybridity in Theory, Culture and Race*, London: Routledge

PART ONE

Origins and transformations

INTRODUCTION

THE EXTRACTS INCLUDED in this Part seek to explore in one way or another the origin of ideas about race and racism. While we do not aim to cover all possible aspects of this dimension, we have chosen to include contributions that reflect both the growing interest in the genealogy of racial thinking and the concern to place the question of racism within a historical framework. Given the fact that all six Parts of the Reader are closely interlinked, it is best to see Part One as essentially concerned with outlining the broad contours of ongoing debates about the origins and development of ideas about race. Indeed, a number of the themes that will be touched upon in this Part are ones that we shall return to, albeit from rather different angles, in other Parts of the Reader. As we have indicated in the Guide to Further Reading this is now one of the key areas of research and debate, and so if you want to follow up the issues that are touched upon here it may be as well for you to read some of the texts that we list there.

One of the areas that we have not been able to cover fully here is the issue of the impact of European expansion and exploration, particularly after 1492, and its impact on the construction of ideas about race and 'other' peoples. This is a subject that is imaginatively explored in Winthrop Jordan's classic reconstruction of the narratives of first contact that rapidly became evident in the case of English ideas about Africans. Jordan's reconstruction of these images and his attempt to place them in context, helps us to see the ways in which, from the earliest stages of European expansion into Africa and other parts of the globe, corporeal properties such as skin colour, hair and other phenotypical differences constructed an epidermal schema not only for anchoring difference but for placing different groups of humankind into distinct types. Jordan's account also usefully shows that the historical backdrop of European expansion and patterns of domination over the past few centuries is an important point of reference for an historically grounded study of racial ideas and the development of institutional forms of racism in different societies.

The dilemmas faced in analysing the history of ideas about race while avoiding the danger of presentism are explored sympathetically by Michael Banton. Banton's research into the history of the idea of race and the variety of ways it has been used to categorise humankind since the eighteenth century has played an important role in the development of the historical and sociological study of racial relations. In this particular piece he seeks to highlight important dilemmas that we face when we seek to analyse the development of ideas such as race, or indeed racism, over a long period of time without adequate recognition of the shifts in meaning that have emerged and taken shape over time. For Banton the most obvious consequence of presentism is that is means scholars have paid insufficient attention to the social, cultural and intellectual context within which ideas about race have emerged and spread. But he is also concerned to highlight the need to avoid the danger of reading directly from the present into the past.

The concern to place the changing meanings attached to race in context is also at the heart of Tzvetan Todorov's account of the development of ideas about race in French political and social thought in the eighteenth and nineteenth centuries. Although Todorov is writing from a perspective that is quite removed theoretically from that of Banton, he also shows an acute awareness of the importance of locating the development of ideas about race within the intellectual and social changes that have shaped societies such as France over the past three centuries or so. In particular, he is concerned with the question of how the values of the Enlightenment were distorted by racism and nationalism in such a way that led to the development of ideologies of racial superiority and hatred of 'Others'. From this perspective Todorov sees the nineteenth century as the highpoint of racial thinking, a period in which modern ideas which can be defined as racist took the form that we are familiar with today.

The next two extracts are by Oliver C. Cox and W. E. B. Du Bois, two of the first generation of black scholars to make an impact on academic debates in this field. Cox's contribution reflects one of the earliest attempts to place the question of racism, or racial prejudice, as he prefers to call it, centrally within a Marxist analytic framework. Cox's work was written from the perspective of historical sociology and he was particularly interested in the ways in which the origins of race prejudice could be seen to link quite closely with European expansion from the end of the fifteenth century onwards. For Cox the development of race prejudice was a social attitude propagated by exploiting classes for the purpose of stigmatising some group as inferior so that the exploitation of either the group itself, or its resources, or both, may be justified. It is from this angle that Cox sought to analyse both the Atlantic slave trade and the plantation slavery that came to characterise the Americas in the aftermath of European expansion. But he also used the same model to analyse other patterns of racial domination and exclusion in other parts of the globe historically and in contemporary times.

The extract from the work of W. E. B. Du Bois, which is the oldest of the extracts included in this Reader, is an example of the contribution of black thinkers such as Du Bois to a reconceptualisation of the role of race in shaping the experience of race in the United States of America. Written at the end of the nineteenth century, the Du Bois piece is particularly concerned with the position of the 'Negro race' in the context of American culture and society. What is interesting about this extract from Du Bois's work is the way it shows him attempting to engage in an evaluation of scientific ideas about race in order to question the way such ideas positioned American blacks, and other Africans, in the hierarchy of 'races'. Although this particular extract represents merely one facet of the rich diversity of Du Bois's scholarship it provides an interesting insight into the development of early black scholarship about race and racism, and the linkages with wider trends in research and debate. We have included a number of more contemporary black scholars in subsequent parts of this Reader and it may be helpful to compare their perspectives with those of Cox and Du Bois.

The final contribution in this part is from Gunnar Myrdal, and it is focused on the development of what he calls 'racial beliefs' in the United States. Myrdal's analysis was originally published in 1942 and he was concerned to explore the history of the 'Negro problem' in the United States. In this particular extract he seeks to look at the development of racial ideas and values about American blacks from the nineteenth century onwards. Myrdal's core concern was to explore the contradictions to be found in American society's treatment of black Americans in the context of the wider vision of a society based on equality of opportunity and justice. He was particularly concerned with how ideas of racial superiority became an established element of American culture and society. Much of Myrdal's study is taken up with detailed accounts of institutional processes of exclusion against American blacks and their role at different historical points. But he also showed an acute awareness of the role of racial ideologies in facilitating institutionalised behaviour. Indeed for Myrdal the 'chief hindrance to improving the Negro is the white man's firm belief in his inferiority'.

KEY QUESTIONS

- What role did the process of European expansion and exploration play in shaping images of Africans and of 'races'?
- Michael Banton argues that 'the historical study of racial thought and attitudes has often been flawed by an unreflecting presentism'. What are the implications of this argument for how we analyse the history of racial ideas?
- Examine Oliver C. Cox's argument that the origins of racism can be directly linked to the development of capitalism.
- In what ways does the work of W. E. B. Du Bois contribute to the analysis of the race question in the United States?
- Analyse Gunnar Myrdal's account of 'The American Dilemma' and how it may be resolved.

Chapter 1

Winthrop D. Jordan

FIRST IMPRESSIONS

[. . .]

ENGLISH VOYAGERS did not touch upon the shores of West Africa until after 1550, nearly a century after Prince Henry the Navigator had mounted the sustained Portuguese thrust southward for a water passage to the Orient. Usually Englishmen came to Africa to trade goods *with* the natives; the principal hazards of these ventures proved to be climate, disease, and the jealous opposition of the "Portingals" who had long since entrenched themselves in forts along the coast. The earliest English descriptions of West Africa were written by adventurous traders, men who had no special interest in converting the natives or, except for the famous Hawkins voyages, in otherwise laying hands on them. Extensive English participation in the slave trade did not develop until well into the seventeenth century. The first permanent English settlement on the African coast was at Kormantin in 1631, and the Royal African Company was not chartered for another forty years.[1] Initially, therefore, English contact with Africans did not take place primarily in a context which prejudged the Negro as a slave, at least not as a slave of Englishmen. Rather, Englishmen met Negroes merely as another sort of men.

Englishmen found the natives of Africa very different from themselves. Negroes looked different; their religion was un-Christian; their manner of living was anything but English; they seemed to be a particularly libidinous sort of people. All these clusters of perceptions were related to each other, though they may be spread apart for inspection, and they were related also to circumstances of contact in Africa, to previously accumulated traditions concerning that strange and distant continent, and to certain special qualities of English society on the eve of its expansion into the New World.

[. . .] The most arresting characteristic of the newly discovered African was his color. Travelers rarely failed to comment upon it; indeed when describing Negroes they frequently began with complexion and then moved on to dress (or rather lack of it) and manners. At Cape Verde, "These people are all blacke, and are called Negros, without any apparell, saving before their privities."[2] Robert Baker's narrative poem recounting his two voyages to the West African coast in 1562 and 1563 first introduced the natives with these engaging lines:

> And entering in [a river], we see
>   a number of blacke soules,
> Whose likelinesse seem'd men to be,
>   but all as blacke as coles.
> Their Captaine comes to me
>   as naked as my naile,
> Not having witte or honestie
>   to cover once his taile.[3]

Even more sympathetic observers seemed to find blackness a most salient quality in Negroes: "although the people were blacke and naked, yet they were civill."[4]

Englishmen actually described Negroes as *black* – an exaggerated term which in itself suggests that the Negros complexion had powerful impact upon their perceptions. Even the peoples of northern Africa seemed so dark that Englishmen tended to call them "black" and let further refinements go by the board. Blackness became so generally associated with Africa that every African seemed a black man. In Shakespeare's day, the Moors, including Othello, were commonly portrayed as pitchy black and the terms *Moor* and *Negro* used almost interchangeably.[5] With curious inconsistency, however, Englishmen recognized that Africans south of the Sahara were not at all the same people as the much more familiar Moors.[6] Sometimes they referred to Negroes as "black Moors" to distinguish them from the peoples of North Africa. During the seventeenth century the distinction became more firmly established and indeed writers came to stress the difference in color, partly because they delighted in correcting their predecessors and partly because Negroes were being taken up as slaves and Moors, increasingly, were not. In the more detailed and accurate reports about West Africa of the seventeenth century, moreover, Negroes in different regions were described as varying considerably in complexion. In England, however, the initial impression of Negroes was not appreciably modified: the firmest fact about the Negro was that he was "black."

The powerful impact which the Negro's color made upon Englishmen must have been partly owing to suddenness of contact. Though the Bible as well as the arts and literature of antiquity and the Middle Ages offered some slight introduction to the "Ethiope," England's immediate acquaintance with black-skinned peoples came with relative rapidity. While the virtual monopoly held by Venetian ships in England's foreign trade prior to the sixteenth century meant that people much darker than Englishmen were not entirely unfamiliar, really black men were virtually unknown except as vaguely referred to in the hazy literature about the sub-Sahara which had filtered down from antiquity. Native West Africans probably first appeared in London in 1554; in that year five "Negroes," as the legitimate trader William Towerson reported, were taken to England, "kept till they could speake the language," and then brought back again "to be a helpe to Englishmen" who were engaged in trade with Negroes on the coast. Hakluyt's later discussion of these Negroes, who he said "could wel agree with our meates and drinkes" though "the colde and moyst aire doth somewhat offend them," suggests that these "blacke Moores" were a novelty to Englishmen.[7] In this respect the English experience was markedly different from that of the Spanish and Portuguese who for centuries had been in close contact with North Africa and had actually been invaded and subjected by people both darker and more highly civilized than themselves. The impact of the Negro's color was the more powerful upon Englishmen, moreover, because England's principal contact with Africans came in West Africa and the Congo where men were not merely dark but almost literally black: one of the fairest-skinned nations suddenly came face to face with one of the darkest peoples on earth.

Viewed from one standpoint, Englishmen were merely participating in Europe's discovery that the strange men who stood revealed by European expansion overseas came in an astounding variety of colors. A Spanish chronicle translated into English in 1555 was filled with wonder at this diversity: "One of the marveylous thynges that god useth in the composition of man, is colour: whiche doubtlesse can not bee consydered withowte great admiration in beholding one to be white and an other blacke, beinge coloures utterley contrary. Sum lykewyse to be yelowe whiche is betwene blacke and white: and other of other colours as it were of dyvers liveres"[8] As this passage suggests, the juxtaposition of black and white was the most striking marvel of all. And for Englishmen this juxtaposition was more than a curiosity.

In England perhaps more than in southern Europe, the concept of blackness was loaded with intense meaning. Long before they found that some men were black, Englishmen found in the idea of blackness a way of expressing some of their most ingrained values. No other color except white conveyed so much emotional impact. As described by the *Oxford English Dictionary*, the meaning of *black* before the sixteenth century included, "Deeply stained with dirt; soiled, dirty, foul. . . . Having dark or deadly purposes, malignant; pertaining to or involving death, deadly; baneful, disastrous, sinister. . . . Foul, iniquitous, atrocious, horrible, wicked. . . . Indicating disgrace, censure, liability to punishment, etc." Black was an emotionally partisan color, the handmaid and symbol of baseness and evil, a sign of danger and repulsion.

Embedded in the concept of blackness was its direct opposite – whiteness. No other colors so clearly implied opposition, "beinge coloures utterlye contrary"; no others were so frequently used to denote polarization:

> Everye white will have its blacke,
> And everye sweete its sowre.[9]

White and black connoted purity and filthiness, virginity and sin, virtue and baseness, beauty and ugliness, beneficence and evil, God and the devil.[10]

Whiteness, moreover, carried a special significance for Elizabethan Englishmen: it was, particularly when complemented by red, the color of perfect human beauty, especially *female* beauty. This ideal was already centuries old in Elizabeth's time,[11] and their fair Queen was its very embodiment: her cheeks were "roses in a bed of lillies." (Elizabeth was naturally pale but like many ladies then and since she freshened her "lillies" at the cosmetic table.)[12]

[. . .] Black human beings were not only startling but extremely puzzling. The complexion of Negroes posed problems about its nature, especially its permanence and utility, its cause and origin, and its significance. Although these were rather separate questions, there was a pronounced tendency among Englishmen and other Europeans to formulate the problem in terms of causation alone, for if that nut could be cracked the other answers would be readily forthcoming; if the cause of human blackness could be explained, then its nature and significance would follow.

Not that the problem was completely novel. The ancient Greeks had touched upon it without ever really coming to grips with it. The story of Phaëton's driving the chariot sun wildly through the heavens apparently served as an explanation for the Ethiopian's blackness even before written records, and traces of this ancient fable were still drifting about during the seventeenth century.

> The Æthiopians then were white and fayre,
> Though by the worlds combustion since made black
> When wanton Phaëton overthrew the Sun.[13]

Less fancifully, Ptolemy had made the important suggestion that the Negro's blackness and woolly hair was caused by exposure to the hot sun and had pointed out that people in northern climates were white and those in temperate areas an intermediate color.[14] Aristotle, Antigonus, Pliny, and Plutarch, an impressive battery of authorities, had passed along the familiar story of a black baby born into a white family (telltale trace of some Ethiopian ancestor), but this was scarcely much help as to original cause. The idea that black babies might result from maternal impressions during conception or pregnancy found credence during the Middle Ages and took centuries to die out, if indeed it ever has entirely.[15] Before the fifteenth century, though, the question of the Negro's color can hardly be said to have drawn the attention of Englishmen or indeed of Europeans generally.

The opening of West Africa and the development of Negro slavery, which for the first time brought Englishmen frequently into firsthand contact with really black Negroes, made the question far more urgent and provided an irresistible playground for awakening scientific curiosity. The range of possible answers was rigidly restricted, however, by the virtually universal assumption, dictated by church and Scripture, that all mankind stemmed from a single source. Giordano Bruno's statement in 1591 that "no sound thinking person will refer the Ethiopians to the same protoplast as the Jewish one" was unorthodox at best. Indeed it is impossible fully to understand the various efforts at explaining the Negro's complexion without bearing in mind the strength of the tradition which in 1614 made the chronicler, the Reverend Samuel Purchas, proclaim vehemently: "the tawney Moore, blacke Negro, duskie Libyan, ash-coloured Indian, olive-coloured American, should with the whiter European become *one sheep-fold*, under *one great Sheepheard*, till *this mortalitie being swallowed up of Life*, wee may all *be one, as he and the father are one*

. . . without any more distinction of Colour, National, Language, Sex, Condition, all may bee *One* in him that is One, *and onely blessed for ever.*"[16]

In general, the most satisfactory answer to the problem was some sort of reference to the action of the sun, whether the sun was assumed to have scorched the skin, drawn the bile, or blackened the blood. People living on the Line had obviously been getting too much of it; after all, even Englishmen were darkened by a little exposure. How much more, then, with the Negroes who were "so scorched and vexed with the heat of the sunne, that in many places they curse it when it riseth."[17] The sun's heat was itself sometimes described as a curse – a not unnatural reaction on the part of those Englishmen who visited the West African coast where the weather was "of such putrifying qualitie, that it rotted the coates of their backs."[18] This association of the Negro's color with the sun became a commonplace in Elizabethan literature; as the Prince of Morocco apologized, "Mislike me not for my complexion,/ The shadow'd livery of the burnish'd sun,/ To whom I am a neighbour and near bred."[19]

Unfortunately this theory ran headlong into a stubborn fact of nature which simply could not be overridden: if the equatorial inhabitants of Africa were blackened by the sun, why not the people living on the same line in America? Logic required them to be the same color. As Ptolemy's formidably authoritative *Geographia* stated this logic, "Reason herself asserts that all animals, and all plants likewise, have a similarity under the same kind of climate or under similar weather conditions, that is, when under the same parallels, or when situated at the same distance from either pole."[20]

Yet by the middle of the sixteenth century it was becoming perfectly apparent that the Indians living in the hottest regions of the New World could by no stretch of the imagination be described as black. They were "olive" or "tawny," and moreover thay had long hair rather than the curious wool of Negroes; clearly they were a different sort of men. Peter Martyr, the official Spanish court chronicler whose accounts Richard Eden translated in 1555, made the point as early as 1516, a trifle over-enthusiastically to be sure: "in all the navigation, he [Columbus] never wente oute of the paralelles of Ethiope. . . . [Yet] the Ethiopians are all blacke, havinge theyr heare curld more lyke wulle then heare. But these people [in America] . . . are whyte, with longe heare, and of yellowe colour." Fortunately it did not take long to calm down this entrancing, overly Nordic presentation of the Indian. Toward the end of the century Richard Hakluyt picked up Eden's own account of a voyage of 1554 which had carefully noted that the Indians were "neither black, nor with curlde and short wooll on their heads, as they of Africke have, but of the colour of an Olive, with long and blacke heare on their heads."[21] Clearly the method of accounting for human complexion by latitude just did not work. The worst of it was that the formula did not seem altogether wrong, since it was apparent that in general men in hot climates tended to be darker than in cold ones. The tenacity of the old logic was manifest in many writers who clung to the latitudinal explanation and maintained stoutly that for one or many reasons the actual climate on the ground was more temperate in America than in Guinea and men accordingly less dark.[22]

Another difficulty with the climatic explanation of skin color arose as lengthening experience augmented knowledge about Negroes. If the heat of the sun caused the Negro's blackness, then his removal to cold northerly countries ought to result in his losing it; even if he did not himself surrender his peculiar color, surely his descendants must. By mid-seventeenth century it was becoming increasingly apparent that this expectation was ill founded: Negroes in Europe and northern America were simply not whitening up very noticeably. Still, the evidence on this matter was by no means entirely definite, and some observers felt that it was not yet all in hand. Though they conceded that lightening of black skin by mixture with Europeans should be ruled out of the experiment, these writers thought they detected a perceptible whitening of the unmixed African residing in colder climates, and they bolstered their case by emphasizing how long it was going to take to whiten up the African completely.[23]

[. . .] While distinctive appearance set Africans over into a novel category of men, their religious condition set them apart from Englishmen in a more familiar way. Englishmen and Christians everywhere were sufficiently acquainted with the concept of heathenism that they confronted its living representatives without puzzlement. Certainly the rather sudden discovery that the world was teeming with heathen people made for heightened vividness and urgency in a long-standing problem; but it was the fact that this problem was already well formulated long before contact with Africa which proved important in shaping English reaction to the Negro's defective religious condition.

In one sense heathenism was less a "problem" for Christians than an exercise in self-definition: the heathen condition defined by negation the proper Christian life. In another sense, the presence of heathenism in the world constituted an imperative to intensification of religious commitment. From its origin Christianity was a universalist, proselytizing religion, and the sacred and secular histories of Christianity made manifest the necessity of bringing non-Christians into the fold. For Englishmen, then, the heathenism of Negroes was at once a counter-image of their own religion and a summons to eradicate an important distinction between the two peoples.

The interaction of these two facets of the concept of heathenism made for a peculiar difficulty. On the one hand, to act upon the felt necessity of converting Negroes would have been to eradicate the point of distinction which Englishmen found most familiar and most readily comprehensible. Yet if they did not act upon this necessity, continued heathenism among Negroes would remain an unwelcome reminder to Englishmen that they were not meeting their obligations to their own faith – nor to the benighted Negroes. Englishmen resolved this implicit dilemma by doing nothing.

Considering the strength of the Christian tradition, it is almost startling that Englishmen failed to respond to the discovery of heathenism in Africa with at least the rudiments of a campaign for conversion. Although the impulse to spread Christianity seems to have been weaker in Englishmen than, say, in the Catholic Portuguese, it cannot be said that Englishmen were indifferent to the obligation imposed upon them by the overseas discoveries of the sixteenth century. While they were badly out of practice at the business of conversion (again in contrast to the Portuguese) and while they had never before been faced with the practical difficulties involved in Christianizing entire continents, they nonetheless were able to contemplate with equanimity and even eagerness the prospect of converting the heathen. Indeed they went so far as to conclude that converting the natives in America was sufficiently important to demand English settlement there. As it turned out, the well-publicized English program for converting Indians produced very meager results, but the avowed intentions certainly were genuine. It was in marked contrast, therefore, that Englishmen did not avow similiar intentions concerning Africans until the late eighteenth century. Fully as much as with skin color, though less consciously, Englishmen distinguished between the heathenisms of Indians and of Negroes.

The suggestive congruence of these twin distinctions between Negroes and Indians is not easy to account for. On the basis of the travelers' reports there was no reason for Englishmen to suppose Indians inherently superior to Negroes as candidates for conversion. While in the sixteenth and seventeenth centuries the Englishmen who had first-hand contact with Africans were not, unlike many of the Portuguese, engaged in missionary efforts, the same may be said of most English contact with Indians. On the other hand, America was not Africa. Englishmen contemplated settling in America, where voyagers had established the King's claim and where supposedly the climate was temperate; in contrast, Englishmen did not envision settlement in Africa, which had quickly gained notoriety as a graveyard for Europeans and where the Portuguese had been the first on the scene. Certainly these very different circumstances meant that Englishmen confronted Negroes and Indians in radically different social contexts and that Englishmen would find it far easier to contemplate converting Indians than Negroes. Yet it remains difficult to see why Negroes were not included, at least as a secondary target, by extension from the program actually directed at the Indians. The fact that English contact with Africans so frequently occurred in a context of slave dealing does not entirely explain the omission of Negroes, since in that same context the Portuguese and Spanish did sometimes attempt to minister to the souls of Negroes (somewhat perfunctorily, to be sure) and since Englishmen in America enslaved Indians when good occasion arose. Given these circumstances, it is hard to escape the conclusion that the distinction which Englishmen made as to conversion was at least in some small measure modeled after the difference they saw in skin color.

Although Englishmen failed to incorporate Negroes into the proselytizing effort which was enjoined by the Christian heritage, that heritage did much to shape the English reaction to Negroes as a people. Paradoxically, Christianity worked to make Englishmen think of Negroes as being both very much like themselves and very different. The emphasis on similarity derived directly from the emphatic Christian doctrine which affirmed that mankind was one. The Old Testament, most notably the book of Genesis, seemed absolutely firm on this point: all men derived from the same act of creation and had at first shared a common experience. So too the New Testament declared all nations to be of one blood. The strength of this universalist strain in Christianity was evident in the assurances offered by a number of English travelers in Africa that they had discovered rudiments of the Word among the most barbarous heathens. In 1623 Richard Jobson exclaimed that "they have a wonderous reference, to the leviticall law, as it is in our holy Bible related; the principalls whereof they are not ignorant in, for they do report concerning *Adam* and *Eve*, whom they call *Adama* and *Evahaha*, talking of *Noahs* flood, and of *Moses*, with many other things our sacred History makes mention of." Another commentator hinted at covert Calvinism in the jungle: "They keep their *Fetissoes* [Fetish] day, one day in seven, and that Tuesday (a Sabbath it seems is natural) more solemnly and strictly than the *Hollanders* do their Sunday."[24] To call the Sabbath "natural" among heathens was an invitation to the missionary to harvest the seed planted everywhere by God. Such a description also serves to demonstrate how powerfully the Christian tradition operated to make Englishmen and other Europeans consider the new peoples of the freshly opened world as being inherently similar to themselves.

At the same time, Christianity militated against the unity of man. Because Englishmen were Christians, heathenism in Negroes was a fundamental defect which set them distinctly apart. However much Englishmen disapproved of Popery and Mehometanism, they were accustomed to these perversions. Yet they were not accustomed to dealing face to face with people who appeared, so far as many travelers could tell, to have no religion at all.[25] Steeped in the legacy and trappings of their own religion, Englishmen were ill prepared to see any legitimacy in African religious practices. Judged by Christian cosmology, Negroes stood in a separate category of men.

[. . .] The condition of savagery – the failure to be civilized – set Negroes apart from Englishmen in an ill-defined but crucial fashion. Africans were *different* from Englishmen in so many ways: in their clothing, huts, farming, warfare, language, government, morals, and (not least important) in their table manners. Englishmen were fully aware that Negroes living at different parts of the coast were not all alike; it was not merely different reactions in the observers which led one to describe a town as "marveilous artificially builded with mudde walles . . . and kept very cleane as well in their streetes as in their houses" and another to relate how "they doe eate" each other "alive" in some places but dead in others "as we wolde befe or mutton."[26] No matter how great the actual and observed differences among Negroes, though, none of these black men seemed to live like Englishmen.

To judge from the comments of voyagers, Englishmen had an unquenchable thirst for the details of savage life. Partly their curiosity was a matter of scientific interest in the "natural productions" of the newly opened world overseas. To the public at large, the details of savage behavior appealed to an interest which was not radically different from the scientist's; an appetite for the "wonderful" seems to have been built into Western culture. It is scarcely surprising that civilized Englishmen should have taken an interest in reports about cosmetic mutilation, polygamy, infanticide, ritual murder and the like – of course *English* men did not really *do* any of these things themselves. Finally, reports about savages began arriving at a time when Englishmen very much needed to be able to translate their apprehensive interest in an uncontrollable world out of medieval, religious terms. The discovery of savages overseas enabled them to make this translation easily, to move from miracles to verifiable monstrosities, from heaven to earth.

As with skin color, English reporting of African customs constituted an exercise in self-inspection by means of comparison. The necessity of continuously measuring African practices with an English yardstick of course tended to emphasize the differences between the two groups, but it also made for heightened sensitivity to instances of similarity. Thus the Englishman's ethnocentrism tended to distort his perception of African culture in two opposite directions. While it led him to emphasize differences and to condemn deviations from the English norm, it led him also to seek out similarities (where perhaps none existed) and to applaud every instance of conformity to the appropriate standard. Though African clothing and personal etiquette were regarded as absurd, equivalents to European practices were at times detected in other aspects of African culture. Particularly, Englishmen were inclined to see the structures of African societies as analogous to their own, complete with kings, counselors, gentlemen, and the baser sort. Here especially they found Africans like themselves, partly because they knew no other way to describe a society and partly because there was actually good basis for such a view in the social organization of West African communities.[27]

Most English commentators seem to have felt that Negroes would behave better under improved circumstances; a minority thought the Africans naturally wicked, but even these observers often used "natural" only to mean "ingrained." (English accounts of West Africa did not emphasize ingrained stupidity in the natives; defect of "Reason" was seen as a function of savagery.)[28] Until well into the eighteenth century there was no debate as to whether the Negro's non-physical characteristics were inborn and unalterable; such a question was never posed with anything like sufficient clarity for men to debate it. There was no precise meaning in such statements about the Africans as, "Another (as it were) innate quality they have [is] to Steal any thing they lay hands of, especially from Foreigners . . . this vicious humor [runs] through the whole race of *Blacks*," or in another comment, that "it would be very surprizing if upon a scrutiny into their Lives we should find any of them whose perverse Nature would not break out sometimes; for they indeed seem to be born and bred Villains: All sorts of Baseness having got such sure-footing in them, that 'tis impossible to lye concealed."[29] These two vague suggestions concerning innate qualities in the Negro were among the most precise in all the English accounts of West Africa. It was sufficient to depict and describe. There might be disagreement as to the exact measure of tenacity with which the African clung to his present savage character, but this problem would yield to time and accurate description.

Despite the fascination and self-instruction Englishmen derived from expatiating upon the savage behavior of Africans, they never felt that savagery was as important a quality in Africans as it was in the American Indians. Two sets of circumstances made for this distinction in the minds of Englishmen. As was the case with heathenism, contrasting social contexts played an important role in shaping the English response to savagery in the two peoples. Inevitably, the savagery of the Indians assumed a special significance in the minds of those actively engaged in a program of bringing civilization into the American wilderness. The case with the African was different: the English errand into Africa was not a new or a perfect community but a business trip. No hope was entertained for civilizing the Negro's steaming continent, and Englishmen lacked compelling reason to develop a program for remodeling the African natives. The most compelling necessity was that of pressing forward the business of buying Negroes from other Negroes. It was not until the slave trade came to require justification, in the eighteenth century, that some Englishmen found special reason to lay emphasis on the Negro's savagery.

[. . .] If Negroes were likened to beasts, there was in Africa a beast which was likened to men. It was a strange and eventually tragic happenstance of nature that the Negro's homeland was the habitat of the animal which in appearance most resembles man. The animal called "oran-outang" by contemporaries (actually the chimpanzee) was native to those parts of western Africa where the early slave trade was heavily concentrated. Though Englishmen were acquainted (for the most part vicariously) with monkeys and baboons, they were unfamiliar with tailless apes who walked about like men.[30] Accordingly, it happened that Englishmen were introduced to the anthropoid apes and to Negroes at the same time and in the same place. The startlingly human appearance and movements of the "ape" – a generic term though often used as a synonym for the "orang-outang" – aroused some curious speculations.

In large measure these speculations derived from traditions which had been accumulating in Western culture since ancient times. Medieval bestiaries contained rosters of strange creatures who in one way or another seemed disturbingly to resemble men. There were the *simia* and the *cynocephali* and the *satyri* and the others, all variously described and related to one another, all jumbled in a characteristic amalgam of ancient reports and medieval morality. The confusion was not easily nor rapidly dispelled, and many of the traditions established by this literature were very much alive during the seventeenth century.

The section on apes in Edward Topsell's *Historie of Foure-Footed Beastes* (1607) serves to illustrate how certain seemingly trivial traditions and associations persisted in such form that they were bound to affect the way in which Englishmen would perceive the natives of Africa.[31] Topsell, who built principally upon the work of the great Swiss naturalist Konrad von Gesner (1516–65), was careful to distinguish tailless apes from monkeys. They were to be found in three regions: south of the Caucasus, India, and "*Lybia* and all that desart Woods betwixt *Egypt*, *Æthiopia* and *Libia*." When he came to describe the various kinds of "apes," however, Topsell was far less definite as to location than as to their general character: above all else, "apes" were venerous. In India the red apes were "so venerous that they will ravish their Women." Baboons were "as lustful and venerous as goats"; a baboon which had been "brought to the French king . . . above all loved the companie of women, and young maidens; his genitall member was greater than might match the quantity of his other parts." Pictures of two varieties of apes, a "Satyre" and an "Ægopithecus, graphically emphasized the "virile member."

In addition to stressing the "lustful disposition" of the ape kind, Topsell's compilation contained suggestions concerning the character of simian facial features. "Men that have low and flat nostrils," readers were told in the section on apes, "are Libidinous as Apes that attempt women, and having thicke lippes the upper hanging over the neather, they are deemed fooles, like the lips of asses and Apes." This rather explicit association was the persistent connection made between apes and devils. In a not altogether successful attempt to distinguish the "Satyre-apes" from the mythical creatures of that name, Topsell straightened everything out by explaining that it was "probable, that Devils take not any dænomination or shape from Satyres, but rather the Apes themselves from Devils whom they resemble, for there are many things common to the Satyre-apes and devilish Satyres." Association of apes and/or satyrs with devils was common in England: James I linked them in his *Daemonology* (1597).[32] The inner logic of this association derived from uneasiness concerning the ape's "indecent likenesse and imitation of man"; it revolved around evil and sexual sin; and, rather tenuously, it connected apes with blackness.

Given this tradition and the coincidence of contact, it was virtually inevitable that Englishmen should discern similarity between the man-like beasts and the beast-like men of Africa.[33] A few commentators went so far as to suggest that Negroes had sprung from the generation of ape-kind or that apes were themselves' the offspring of Negroes and some unknown African beast.[34] These contentions were squarely in line with the ancient tradition that Africa was a land "bringing dailie foorth newe monsters" because, as Aristotle himself had suggested, many different species came into proximity at the scarce watering places. Jean Bodin, the famous sixteenth-century French political theorist, summarized this wisdom of the ages with the categorical remark that "promiscuous coition of men and animals took place, wherefore the regions of Africa produce for us so many monsters."[35] Despite all these monsters out of Africa, the notion that Negroes stemmed from beasts in a literal sense did not receive wide credence; even the writers who advanced it did not suggest that the Negro himself was now a beast.

Far more common and persistent was the notion that there sometimes occurred "a beastly copulation or conjuncture" between apes and Negroes, and especially that apes were inclined wantonly to attack Negro women.[36] The very explicit idea that apes assaulted female human beings was not new; Negroes were merely being asked to demonstrate what Europeans had known for centuries. Englishmen seemed ready to credit the tales about bestial connections, and even as late as the 1730's a well-traveled, intelligent naval surgeon, John Atkins, was not at all certain that the stories were false: "At some Places the *Negroes* have been suspected of Bestiality with them [apes and monkeys], and by the Boldness and affection they are known under some Circumstances to express to our Females; the Ignorance and Stupidity on the other side, to guide or control Lust; but more from the near resemblances are sometimes met to the Human Species would tempt one to suspect the Fact." Atkins went on to voice the generally received opinion that if offspring were ever produced by such mixtures they would themselves be infertile: "Altho' by the way, this, like other *Hebridous* productions, could never go no farther; and as such a monstrous generation would be more casual and subject to Fatality, the Case must be uncommon and rare."[37]

[. . .] It was no accident that this affinity between Negroes and apes was so frequently regarded as sexual, for undertones of sexuality run throughout many English accounts of West Africa. To liken Africans – any human being – to beasts was to stress the animal within the man. Indeed the sexual connotations embodied in the terms *bestial* and *beastly* were considerably stronger in Elizabethan English than they are today, and when the Elizabethan traveler pinned these epithets upon the behavior of Negroes he was frequently as much registering a sense of sexual shock as describing swinish manners: "They are beastly in their living," young

Andrew Battell wrote, "for they have men in women's apparel, whom they keep among their wives."[38]

Lecherousness among the Negroes was at times merely another attribute which one would expect to find among heathen, savage, beast-like men. A passage in Samuel Purchas's collection makes evident how closely interrelated all these attributes were in the minds of Englishmen: "They have no knowledge of God; those that traffique and are conversant among strange Countrey people are civiller then the common sort of people, they are very greedie eaters, and no lesse drinkers, and very lecherous, and theevish, and much addicted to uncleanenesse: one man hath many wives as hee is able to keepe and maintaine."[39] Sexuality was what one expected of savages.

Clearly, however, the association of Africans with potent sexuality represented more than an incidental appendage to the concept of savagery. Long before first English contact with West Africa, the inhabitants of virtually the entire continent stood confirmed in European literature as lustful and venerous. About 1526 Leo Africanus (a Spanish Moroccan Moor converted to Christianity) supplied the most authoritative and influential description of the little-known lands of "Barbary," "Libya," "Numedia," and "Land of Negroes"; and Leo was as explicit as he was imaginative. In the English translation (ca. 1600) readers were informed concerning the "Negroes" that "there is no Nation under heaven more prone to Venery." Having reduced the "Numedians" to being "principally addicted unto treason, Treacherie, Murther, Theft and Robberie" and the inhabitants of Libya to living a "brutish kind of life" destitute of "any Religion, any Lawes, or any good form of living," Leo went on to disclose that "the Negroes likewise leade a beastly kind of life, being utterly destitute of the use of reason, of dexteritie of wit, and of all arts. Yea, they so behave themselves, as if they had continually lived in a Forrest among wild beasts. They have great swarmes of harlots among them; whereupon a man may easily conjecture their manner of living."[40] Nor was Leo Africanus the only scholar to elaborate upon the classical sources concerning Africa. In a highly eclectic work first published in 1566, Jean Bodin sifted the writings of ancient authorities and concluded that heat and lust went hand in hand and that "in Ethiopia . . . the race of men is very keen and lustful." Bodin announced in a thoroughly characteristic sentence, "Ptolemy reported that on account of southern sensuality Venus chiefly is worshiped in Africa and that the constellation of Scorpion, which pertains to the pudenda, dominates that continent."[41]

Depiction of the Negro as a lustful creature was not radically new, therefore, when Englishmen first met Negroes face to face. Seizing upon and reconfirming these long-standing and apparently common notions about Africa, Elizabethan travelers and literati spoke very explicitly of Negroes as being especially sexual. Othello's embraces were "the gross clasps of a lascivious Moor." Francis Bacon's New Atlantis (ca. 1624) referred to "an holy hermit" who "desired to see the Spirit of Fornication; and there appeared to him a little foul ugly Æthiop." Negro men, reported a seventeenth-century traveler, sported "large Propagators." In 1623 Richard Jobson, a sympathetic observer, reported that mandingo men were "furnisht with such members as are after a sort burthensome unto them"; it was the custom in that tribe not to have intercourse during pregnancy so as not to "destroy what is conceived." During this abstinence, Jobson explained, the man

"hath allowance of other women, for necessities sake," though this was not to be
considered "overstrange" since in the twenty-third chapter of Ezekiel two incon-
tinent sisters were "said to dote upon those people whose members were as the
members of asses." Jobson's explanation for the unusual size of these men was
incorporated neatly into the context of scriptural anthropology. "Undoubtedly,"
he wrote, "these people originally sprung from the race of *Canaan*, the sonne of
Ham, who discovered his father *Noahs* secrets, for which *Noah* awakening cursed
Canaan as our holy Scripture testifieth[;] the curse as by Scholemen hath been
disputed, extended to his ensuing race, in laying hold upon the same place, where
the originall cause began, whereof these people are witnesse."[43]

The neatness of Jobson's exegesis was unusual, but his initial observation was
not. Another commentator, the anonymous author of *The Golden Coast* (1665),
thought Negroes "very lustful and impudent, especially, when they come to hide
their nakedness, (for a *Negroes* hiding his Members, their extraordinary greatness)
is a token of their Lust, and therefore much troubled with the Pox."[44] By the eighteenth century a report on the sexual aggressiveness of Negro women was virtually
de rigueur for the African commentator. By then, of course, with many Englishmen
actively participating in the slave trade, there were pressures making for descriptions of "hot constitution'd ladies" possessed of a "temper hot and lascivious, making
no scruple to prostitute themselves to the *Europeans* for a very slender profit, so
great is their inclination to white men."[45] And surely it was the Negro women
who were responsible for lapses from propriety: "If they can come to the Place
the Man sleeps in, they lay themselves softly down by him, soon wake him, and
use all their little Arts to move the darling Passion."[46]

While the animus underlying these and similar remarks becomes sufficiently
obvious once Englishmen began active participation in the slave trade, it is less
easy to see why Englishmen should have fastened upon Negroes a pronounced
sexuality virtually upon first sight. Certainly the ancient notions distilled in the
alembics of Bodin and Leo Africanus must have helped pattern initial English perceptions. Yet it is scarcely possible that these notions were fully responsible for the
picture of Negro sexuality which developed so rapidly and in such explicit terms
in the sixteenth and early seventeenth centuries.

Another tradition was of possible relevance – the curse upon Ham's son
Canaan. According to the Scriptural account Ham's offense was that he had "looked
upon the nakedness of his father." To the post-Freudian ear this suggests castration. To early Jewish commentators it suggested not merely castration but other
sexual offenses as well. The Hebraic literature of *ca.* 200–600 A.D. which saw the
posterity of Ham and Canaan as smitten in the skin speculated as to whether Ham's
offense was (variously) castrating his father Noah (described in the Midrash Rabbah
as Noah's saying "You have prevented me from doing something in the dark"),
and (in the same source) as copulating "in the Ark," and (again) copulating "with
a dog . . . therefore Ham came forth black-skinned while the dog publicly exposes
its copulation." The depth and diffuse pervasiveness of these explosive associations
are dramatized in the mystic Zohar of the thirteenth century, where Ham, it was
said, "represents the refuse and dross of the gold, the stirring and rousing of the
unclean spirit of the ancient serpent."

What is especially striking in these commentaries is that for centuries they remained peculiar though not secret to Jewish scholars. Although some Christian writers in the early centuries of the church seem to have been aware of sexual connotations in Ham's offense, they appear never to have dilated upon them. With the onset of European expansion in the sixteenth century, some Christian commentators, or rather some commentators who were Christians, suddenly began speaking in the same mode which Jews had employed a thousand years and more before. Though the genealogy of Noah's descendants was always somewhat tangled, Ham always represented for the ancient Jews the southward peoples *including* the Canaanites, whom the Jews drove from the promised land and upon whom they fastened the millstone of sexual offenses which are repeatedly and so adamantly condemned and guarded against in the Pentateuch. More than two thousand years later a similar disquietude seems to have come over Europeans and Englishmen as they embarked upon a program of outward migration and displacement and exploitation of other peoples. The curse upon Ham's posterity took on for Christian Englishmen a potential immediacy and relevance which it could never have had if Englishmen had not as a people been undergoing an experience which they half sense was in some measure analogous to that of the ancient special people of God's word.[47]

[. . .] It was the case with English confrontation with Negroes, then, that a society in a state of rapid flux, undergoing important changes in religious values, and comprised of men who were energetically on the make and acutely and often uncomfortably self-conscious of being so, came upon a people less technologically advanced, markedly different in appearance and culture. From the first, Englishmen tended to set Negroes over against themselves, to stress what they conceived to be radically contrasting qualities of color, religion, and style of life, as well as animality and a peculiarly potent sexuality. What Englishmen did not at first fully realize was that Negroes were potentially subjects for a special kind of obedience and subordination which was to arise as adventurous Englishmen sought to possess for themselves and their children one of the most bountiful dominions of the earth. When they came to plant themselves in the new World, they were to find that they had not entirely left behind the spirit of avarice and insubordination. Nor does it appear, in light of attitudes which developed during their first two centuries in America, that they left behind all the impressions initially gathered of the *Negro* before he became pre-eminently the *slave*.

Notes and references

1   Kenneth G. Davies, *The Royal African Company* (London, 1957), 38–46; John W. Blake, trans. and ed., *Europeans in West Africa, 1450–1560; Documents to Illustrate the Nature and Scope of Portuguese Enterprise in West Africa, the Abortive Attempt of Castilians to Create an Empire There, and the Early English Voyages to Barbary and Guinea* (Works Issued by the Hakluyt Society, 2d Ser., 87 [1942]), II, 254–60.

2   "The voyage made by M. John Hawkins . . . to the coast of Guinea and the Indeas of Nova Hispania . . . 1564," in Richard Hakluyt, *The Principal Navigations,*

Voyages, Traffiques and Discoveries of the English Nation . . . 12 vols., 1598 ed. (Glasgow, 1903–05), X, 15. See Katherine Beverly Oakes, "Social Theory in the Early Literature of Voyage and Exploration in Africa" (unpubl. Ph.D. diss., University of California, Berkeley, 1944), 120–23.

3 "The First Voyage of Robert Baker to Guinie . . . 1562," in Richard Hakluyt, *The Principall Navigations, Voiages and Discoveries of the English Nation* . . . (London, 1589), 132. The entire poem was omitted in the 1598 edition.

4 "The Voyage of M. George Fenner . . . Written by Walter Wren" (1566), Hakluyt, *Principal Navigations*, VI, 270. All ensuing references are to this reprinted 1598 edition unless otherwise indicated.

5 Warner Grenelle Rice, "Turk, Moor and Persian in English Literature from 1550–1660, with Particular Reference to the drama" (unpubl. Ph.D. diss., Harvard University, 1926), 401–2n; Robert R. Cawley, *The Voyagers and Elizabethan Drama* (Boston, 1938), 31; Samuel C. Chew, *The Crescent and the Rose: Islam and England during the Renaissance* (N. Y., 1937), 521–24; Wylie Sypher, *Guinea's Captive Kings: British Anti-Slavery Literature of the XVIIIth Century* (Chapel Hill, 1942), 26.

6 An early instance is in "The Second Voyage to Guinea . . ." (1554), in Hakluyt, *Principal Navigations*, VI, 167–68. See the associations made by Leo Africanus, *The History and Description of Africa and of the Notable Things Therein Contained* . . ., trans. John Pory [*ca.* 1600], ed. Robert Brown, 3 vols. (London, 1896), I, 130.

7 Hakluyt, *Principal Navigations*, VI, 176, 200, 217–18. Just how little Europeans knew about Africa prior to the Portuguese explorations is evident in T. Simar, "La géographie de l'Afrique central dans l'antiquité et au moyen âge," *La Revue Congolaise*, 3 (1912), 1–23, 81–102, 145–69, 225–52, 288–310, 440–41.

8 Francisco López de Gómara, in Peter Martyr (D'Anghera), *The Decades of the Newe Worlde* . . . trans. Richard Eden (London, 1555), in Edward Arber, ed., *The First Three English Books on America* . . . (Birmingham, Eng., 1885), 338.

9 Thomas Percy, *Reliques of Ancient English Poetry* . . . , ed. Robert A. Willmott (London, 1857), 27 (Sir Cauline, pt. 2, stanza 1).

10 Numerous examples in Middle English, Shakespeare, the Bible, and Milton are given by P. J. Heather, "Colour Symbolism," *Folk Lore*, 59 (1948), 169–70, 175–78, 182–83; 60 (1949), 208–16, 266–76. See also Harold R. Isaacs, "Blackness and Whiteness," *Encounter*, 21 (1963), 8–21; Caroline F. E. Spurgeon, *Shakespeare's Imagery and What It Tells Us* (Boston, 1958), 64, 66–69, 158; Arrah B. Evarts, "Color Symbolism," *Psychoanalytic Review*, 6 (1919), 129–34; Don Cameron Allen, "Symbolic Color in the Literature of the English Renaissance," *Philological Quarterly*, 15 (1936), 81–92; and for a different perspective, Francis B. Gummere, "On the Symbolic use of the Colors Black and White in Germanic Tradition," *Haverford College Studies*, 1 (1889), 112–62.

11 Walter Clyde Curry, *The Middle English Ideal of Personal Beauty; As Found in the Metrical Romances, Chronicles, and Legends of the XIII, XIV, and XV Centuries* (Baltimore, 1916), 3, 80–98.

12 Elkin Calhoun Wilson, *England's Eliza* (Cambridge, Mass., 1939), 337; Charles Carroll Camden, *The Elizabethan Woman* (Houston, N. Y., and London, 1952), chap. 7; Cawley, *Voyagers and Elizabethan Drama*, 85; Elizabeth Jenkins, *Elizabeth the Great* (London, 1958), 62, 100, 159, 296; Gamaliel Bradford, *Elizabethan Women*, ed. Harold O. White (Boston, 1936), 82, 212; Violet A. Wilson *Queen*

Elizabeth's Maids of Honour and Ladies of the Privy Chamber (N. Y., n.d.), 4–5. Hugh Plat *Delightes for Ladies, Written Originally by Sir Hugh Plat, First Printed in 1602, London, England* ed. Violet and Hal W. Trovillion (Herrin, Ill., 1939), 87–94, 99, 102–3, contains advice on cosmetics.

13   R. Warwick Bond, ed., *The Poetical Works of William Basse (1602–1653)* (London, 1893), 279; Conway Zirkle, "The Early History of the Idea of the Inheritance of Acquired Characters and of Pangenesis," American Philosophical Society, *Transactions*, New Ser., 35 (1945–46), Pt. ii, 145. The original story of Phaëton is in Thomas Bulfinch, *Bulfinch's Mythology* (N. Y.: Modern Library, n.d.), 36–42; Edith Hamilton, *Mythology* (N. Y.: Mentor, 1953), 131–34.

14   [Claudius] Ptolemy, *Tetrabiblos*, trans. and ed. F. E. Robbins (Cambridge, Mass., and London, 1940), 121–25, 439.

15   Conway Zirkle, "The Knowledge of Heredity before 1900," L. C. Dunn, ed., *Genetics in the 20th Century: Essays on the Progress of Genetics during Its First 50 Years* (N. Y.: 1951), 42; Thorndike, "De Comlexionibus," *Isis*, 49 (1958), 400; Don Cameron Allen, *The Legend of Noah: Renaissance Rationalism in Art, Science and Letters* (Urbana, 1949), 119. For an interesting modification, Browne, "Of the Blackness of Negroes," Sayle, ed., *Works of Browne*, II, 375–76.

16   T[homas] Bendyshe, "The History of Anthroplogy," Anthropological Society of London, *memoirs*, 1 (1863–64), 355; Samuel Purchas, *Purchas his Pilgrimage. Or Relations of the World and the Religions Observed in All Ages and Places Discovered, from the Creation unto This Present*, 2d ed. (London, 1614), 656.

17   "Second Voyage to Guinea," Hakluyt, *Principal Navigations*, VI, 167; Cawley, *Voyagers and Elizabethan Drama*, 88–89, 159–60. A remarkably early suggestion that sun-blackened skin afforded protection against the sun "as if naturaliz'd" was made by John Ogilby, *Africa: Being an Accurate description of the Regions of Ægypt, Barbary, Lybia and Billedulgerid, the Land of Negroes, Guinee, Æthiopia, and the Abyssines . . . Collected and Translated from Most Authentick Authors, and Augmented with Later Observations* (London, 1670).

18   "The First Voyage to Guinea and Benin" (1553), Hakluyt, *Principal Navigations*, VI, 148.

19   *The Merchant of Venice*, II, i, 1–3; also Ben Jonson, "Masque of Blackness," Gifford, ed., *Works of Jonson*, VII, 12.

20   Edward L. Stevenson, trans. and ed., *Geography of Claudius Ptolemy* (N. Y., 1932), 31–32.

21   Martyr, *Decades of Newe Worlde*, trans. Eden, 88, 387–88; "Second Voyage to Guinea," Hakluyt, *Principal Navigations*, VI, 176.

22   Both Martyr and Hakluyt did so in the preceding passages; James Spedding, Robert L. Ellis, Douglas D. Heath, eds., *The Works of Francis Bacon . . .* 14 vols. (London, 1857–74), II, 473; John Selden's notes in *Works of Michael Drayton*, II, 675; John Ovington, *A Voyage to Suratt, in the Year 1869*, ed. H. G. Rawlinson (London, 1929), 285. For a more general statement of the influence of climate on complexion, Matthew Hale, *The Primitive Origination of Mankind, Considered and examined According to the Light of Nature* (London, 1677), 200–201.

23   A widely popular work, [Thomas Burnet], *The Theory of the Earth . . . the First Two Books . . .* , 2d ed. (London, 1691), 191, bk. II, chap. 2, announced that "after some generations they become altogether like the people of the Country where they are." Ovington, *Voyage to Suratt*, ed. Rawlinson, 285, was at pains to deny this "current Opinion."

24 Jobson, *Golden trade*, ed. Kingsley, 78 (probably there was good basis for Jobson's contention since the Negroes he referred to were Muslims); *The Golden Coast*, 80.

25 For example, Hakluyt, *Principal Navigations*, VI, 144.

26 Both seem to be eyewitness reports. "Voyage of Thomas Candish," Hakluyt, *Principal Navigations*, XI, 293; anonymous author on Hawkins' third voyage quoted in James A. Williamson, *Sir John Hawkins: The Time and the Man* (Oxford, 1927), 509. There is an interesting description of (almost certainly) the now well-known symbiotic relationship between Negroes and Pygmies in *The Golden Coast*, 66–67, "I have not found so much faith, nor faithfulness, no not in Israel."

27 An early instance is in Clements R. Markham, ed., *The Hawkins' Voyages during the Reigns of Henry VIII, Queen Elizabeth, and James I (Works Issued by the Hakluyt Soc.,* 1st Ser., 57 [1878]), 19.

28 For example, H[eylyn], *Microcosmus*, 379. But compare a later and precursively environmentalist argument that culturally dictated lack of mental and moral exercise had literally weakened the African brain: John Atkins, *The Navy Surgeon . . . and Physical Observations on the Coast of Guiney*, 2d ed. (London, 1742), 366 –67; also his *Voyage to Guinea*, 80–88.

29 Ogilby, *Africa*, 452; William Bosman, *A New and Accurate Description of the Coast of Guinea, Divided into the Gold, the Slave, and the Ivory Coasts . . .*, trans. from the Dutch (London, 1705), 117.

30 H. W. Janson, *Apes and Ape Lore in the Middle Ages and the Renaissance* (London, 1952), chap. 11; also Robert M. and Ada W. Yerkes, *The Great Apes: A Study of Anthropoid Life* (New Haven, 1929), 1–26; John C. Greene, *The Death of Adam: Evolution and Its Impact on Western Thought* (Ames, Iowa, 1959), chap. 6. I have oversimplified the confused state of terminology concerning simians; see M. F. Ashley Montague, *Edward Tyson, M.D., F.R.S., 1605–1708, and the Rise of Human and Comparative Anatomy in England; A Study in the History of Science* (Phila., 1943), 228, 244–49. By 1600 "baboons," "marmosets," "monkies," "apes" were common in literature; several (probably baboons) were on show in London. Yet a foreign visitor in 1598 did not list any sort of "apes" in the Tower menagerie, though there were lions there. W. Strunk, Jr., "The Elizabethan Showman's Ape," *Modern Language Notes*, 32 (1917), 215–21; Emma Phipson, *The Animal-Lore of Shakespeare's Time . . .* (London, 1883), 5.

31 Edward Topsell, *The Historie of Foure-Footed Beastes . . . Collected out of All the Volumes of Conradus Gesner, and All Other Writers to This Present Day* (London, 1607), 2–20.

32 G. B. Harrison, ed., *King James the First Daemonologie (1597) . . .* (London, 1924), 19.

33 Jobson, *Golden Trade*, ed. Kingsley, 186; Thomas Herbert, *A Relation of Some Yeares Travaile, Begunne Anno 1626. Into Afrique and the Greater Asia, Especially the Territories of the Persian Monarchie . . .* (London, 1634), 16–17; Herbert, *Some Years Travels* (1677), 16–17.

34 Herbert, *Some Years Travels*, 18; Zirkle, "Knowledge of Heredity," Dunn, ed., *Genetics in the 20th Century*, 39–40.

35 Quotation from Alexander B. Grosart, ed., *The Complete Works of Thomas Nashe*, 6 vols. (London and Aylesbury, 1883–85), I, 160: Aristotle, *Historia Animalium*, trans. D'Archy W. Thompson, in J. A. Smith and W. D. Ross, eds., *The Works of Aristotle*, IV (Oxford, 1910), 606b; Bodin, *Method of Easy Comprehension of History*, 105.

36   Quotation from Herbert, *Some Years Travels*, 18. Montague, *Edward Tyson*, 250–52; John Locke, *An Essay Concerning Human Understanding*, 2 vols. in 1 (London, 1721), II, 53 (Bk. III, chap. 6, sec. 23); Phillips, *Journal*, Churchill, comps., *Voyages*, VI, 211; William Smith, *A New Voyage to Guinea . . .* (London, 1744), 52; Zirkle, "Knowledge of Heredity," Dunn, ed., *Genetics in the 20th Century*, 39–40; Janson, *Apes and Ape Lore*, 267–76.

37   Atkins, *Voyage to Guinea*, 108; also his *Navy Surgeon*, 369.

38   Ernest George Ravenstine, ed., *The Strange Adventures of Andrew Battell of Leigh, in Angola and the Adjoining Regions. Reprinted from "Purchas His Pilgrimes" (ca. 1607)* (*Works Issued by the Hakluyt Soc.*, 2d Ser., 6 [London, 1901]), 18. The term *bestiality* was first used to denote sexual relations with animals early in the 17th century; it was thus used frequently only for about 150 years!

39   "A Description . . . of Guinea . . ." in Samuel Purchas, *Hakluytus Posthumus or Purchas His Pilgrimes, Contayning a History of the World in Sea Voyages and Lande Travells by Englishmen and Others*, 20 vols. (Glasgow, 1905–07), VI, 251.

40   Leo Africanus, *History and Description of Africa*, trans. Pory, ed. Brown, I, 180, 187. Leo continues concerning the Negroes, "except their conversation perhaps bee somewhat more tolerable, who dwell in the principall Townes and Cities: for it is like that they are somewhat more addicted to Civilitie." Leo's work was available to Englishmen in Latin from 1556.

41   Bodin, *Method for Easy Comprehension of History*, 103–6, 143.

42   Rice, *Turk, Moor, and Persian*, 401; *Othello*, I, i, 127; Spedding, Ellis, and Heath, eds., *Works of Francis Bacon*, III, 152; Ogilby, *Africa*, 451.

43   Jobson, *Golden Trade*, ed. Kingsley, 65–67.

44   *The Golden Coast*, 75–76.

45   Smith, *New Voyage to Guinea*, 146; Barbot, *Description of the Coasts*, Churchill, comps., *Voyages*, V, 34.

46   Smith, *New Voyage to Guinea*, 221–22, clearly based on Bosman, *New and Accurate Description*, 206–7.

47   I hope to discuss this complex matter more fully on another occasion and in the meantime cite only the sources directly quoted. Freedman and Simon, trans., *Midrash Rabbah*, I, 293; Sperling and Simon, trans., *Zohar*, I, 246.

Chapter 2

Michael Banton

THE IDIOM OF RACE
A critique of presentism

[. . .]

THE HISTORICAL STUDY of racial thought and attitudes has often
been flawed by an unreflecting presentism. Earlier writers are held up to scorn
without any adequate attempt to locate their understandings within the context of
the knowledge available to their generation. Modern writers all too easily neglect
the shifts in the meaning attributed to the word "race" (for a recent example of
serious study vulnerable to this criticism, see Horsman, 1976). This essay will
contend that as new modes of explanation of human variation have arisen, so the
word "race" has been used in new ways, but the old uses have often continued
side by side with the new ones. "Race" and associated words suggesting commonality of descent or character were developed into popular modes of thought and
expression in many European languages in the eighteenth century so that they
constituted an idiom in which people related themselves to others and developed
conceptions of their own attributes. In the nineteenth century this idiom was
extended through the identification of race with nation (and *Volk*), and the rise
of potent beliefs about national character. Where previously there had been an
emphasis upon supposed innate differences between persons distant in social rank,
the stress was shifted to differences between people of distinct nations. Political
circumstances helped mold these changes but they cannot be fully appreciated
without taking account of changes in scientific understanding.

Possibly the most notable feature of race as a concept is the way it has invei-
gled observers into assuming that the main issue is that of the nature of differences
between populations, and that they should concentrate upon what "race" *is*, as if
this would determine the one scientifically valid use for the word. Physical differences catch people's attention so readily that they are less quick to appreciate that

the validity of "race" as a concept depends upon its value as an aid in explanation. From this standpoint, the main issue is the use of the word "race," both in rational argument and in more popular connections, for people use beliefs about race, nationality, ethnicity and class as resources when they cultivate beliefs about group identities.

The failure to allow for changes in the sense in which the word race has been used has important consequences, for those who misunderstand the past of their society are likely to misunderstand the present, because people judge the present in the light of what they believe the past to have been. The past cannot be properly understood if changes in the significance of words are not allowed for. Historians and sociologists judge their predecessors, but will themselves be judged by a later generation because they are not standing outside history. Since the limitations of their knowledge will bemuse their successors, they should be charitable in assessing the limitations of their predecessors.

Race as descent

[. . .] Up to the eighteenth century at least, the dominant paradigm in Europe for explaining the differences between groups of people was provided by the Old Testament. It was the story of God's creating the world and, on the sixth day, of his making "Adam" (alternatively translated as "the man") in his own image. The Old Testament provided a series of genealogies by which it seemed possible to trace the peopling of the world and the relations which different groups bore to one another. Thus Augustine derided the idea that there might be men in unknown lands on the other side of the world because the suggestion that some of Adam's descendants might have sailed there was "excessively absurd." Many writers attempted to ascertain the date when the world was created by working back through these genealogies. Others attempted to explain the assumed inferiority of black people by reference to a curse supposedly placed by Noah on the descendants of Ham, decreeing that they should be servants of his sons Shem and Japheth; or by relating it to the dispersal of peoples after the fall of the tower of Babel. Implicit in such arguments is the assumption that differences are to be explained by tracing them back to particular events the consequences of which are then transmitted genealogically. This is also a view of the world in which God is likely to intervene to punish or reward particular individuals and in which men are therefore less motivated to develop and improve classificatory concepts like that of species. A species was seen simply as the product of an arbitrary action by the Creator.

Within a paradigm of explanation in terms of descent there were several possible ways of accounting for physical variation. First, it could be held that differences of color and such like were all part of God's design for the universe; perhaps, as in the hypothesis about the curse on Ham's descendants, they were the result of divine judgment; perhaps, though, they were a part of God's plan that had not yet been revealed or that man could not properly understand, and this led to a line of reasoning which may be called racial romanticism. Secondly, it could be held that physical differences were related in some way to climate and environment and were irrelevant to the important questions of man's obligations to do God's will. Thirdly, it was sometimes argued that since the differences between Europeans, Africans and Asians were repeated in successive generations they must have had separate ancestors. It was hazardous and perhaps unnecessary to challenge the story of Adam directly, so the doubters suggested that the Old Testament account was incomplete: Adam was the ancestor of the Europeans alone. The debate about whether mankind consisted of one or many stocks had to be cast in terms of the dominant paradigm and therefore it was phrased as a choice between monogenesis and polygenesis.

The use of "race" as a term in explanations of its kind is reflected in the first major definition of the word given in the *Oxford English Dictionary* (1910), viz. "I. A group of persons, animals, or plants, connected by common descent or origin." This is the principal sense in which the word is used in English in the sixteenth, seventeenth and eighteenth centuries, and it continues to be used, though rather less frequently, in this sense. But already in the sixteenth century the notion of likeness because of descent was generalized and "race" was used to denote instances of likeness without any claim of common descent, like Dunbar's reference in 1508 to "backbiters of sundry races" and Sidney's of 1580 to "the race of good men." As the Dictionary records, this use continued into the nineteenth century, as with Lamb's reference to "the two races of men", the men who borrow and the men who lend, but thereafter it was less frequent.

If there was a principle explaining the differences in the appearance of peoples, either theistic or atheistic, then it could have operated through either moral or physical causes. Moral causes would today be called cultural: they consisted of the ways in which men responded to their environment. Physical causes were inherited dispositions and capacities. Both monogenists and polygenists used the word "race" to designate the outwardly identifiable populations of their time, but the same word meant different things to them. The monogenists believed that men started off the same and had become different because of climate and their different response to environmental opportunities. The polygenists suspected that men must have been different to begin with and their understanding of race was later systematized as "type."

For an illustration of how people subscribing to these two schools of thought could use the same word in what superficially appears to be the same sense, but draws upon two different modes of explanation, it is appropriate to turn to an essay by the historian Macaulay on the capacities of Negroes. It was written in response to a report by a Major Moody, who contended that though blacks in the West Indies could work hard, their preference for leisure was such that they would not do so unless coerced. According to Macaulay's reading, Moody maintained that there was an instinctive and unconquerable aversion between the white and black races which stemmed from a physical cause. Against this, Macaulay contended that the blacks did not work harder because, unless they emigrated, they could not get an adequate return for their labor. The antagonism, he said, was caused by slavery and for the major to prove his case he needed to provide evidence of the alleged aversion in circumstances unaffected by slavery or the memory of it. Both men used the word "race" to designate blacks and whites: "the two races could not live together," wrote Moody, while his critic referred to the "policy which excludes strangers, of all races, from the interior of China and Japan". Where Moody stressed "the consequences arising from physical differences in form, colour, feature and smell," Macaulay referred to 'the Gypsey race, one of the most beautiful and intelligent on face of the earth . . . persecuted under a thousand pretexts . . . yet the remnant of a race still preserves its peculiar language and manners" (Macaulay, 1827: 137–38, 151–52). It should be noted that Macaulay, who elsewhere displayed his own variety of ethnocentrism, misrepresented his opponent's arguments (Williams, 1978), but yet it is still clear that for the one writer the history of a race was determined by its physical nature; for the other, its history was the story of how more varied circumstances caused it to become or remain distinctive.

Race as type

Classification by descent was more easily manageable so long as the number of species was fairly limited, but with the revival of observation and the exploration of new continents in early modern times, the number of known kinds of plants increased rapidly. It was time for someone to distinguish essential forms from accidental variations, and to define a stable unit on which botanical classification could be based. The problem was most pressing in botany, but in principle it applied to all biology. The man who did most to resolve it was the Swedish naturalist known to later generations as Linnaeus (1707–1778).

In Linnaeus' view, natural history consisted of describing the various productions of the earth, their appearance, their habits, their relations to each other, and their uses. Implicit in this conception of classification as the goal of science was the belief that nature had been constructed on a pattern discoverable, at least in part, by human reason. It was man's duty to study nature diligently so that he could come closer to God, could better understand his purpose, and could glorify Him in his works. At the heart of the conception of nature to which Linnaeus came was the idea of an *oeconomia*, a rationally ordered system of means and ends. The earth, with its delightful variety of climate and topography, was populated with an equally varied assemblage of living beings, each perfectly adapted to the region in which it lived. The economy of nature lay in the balance between its constituent elements. Linnaeus never tired of describing the mechanisms which maintained the adaptation of organism and environment and the equilibrium of species (Greene, 1959: 134–37). God had created not a series of individual species but a self-regulating system. He did not need to intervene in the day-to-day affairs of his creation.

The man who more than anyone else extended the method of Linnaeus to the study of the animal kingdom and – though only in outline – to that of man, was the French comparative anatomist Cuvier (1769–1832). The system which he hoped to discover by relating animal structure to conditions of existence was the "great catalogue in which all created beings have suitable names, may be recognized by distinctive characters, and [are] arranged in divisions and sub-divisions." Cuvier's method of classification rested heavily upon the conception of a type (defined by the *Oxford English Dictionary* as "a person or thing that represents the characteristic qualities of a class; a representative specimen"). If the right representative specimen was chosen, then the essential of the category could be understood. Cuvier divided man into three main subspecies (which he called races): Caucasian, Mongolian, and Ethiopian, which were further subdivided. He stated that they were all one species but they had been separated by some great natural catastrophe. He presented the three races as differing permanently in ability because of the biological differences between them that were as yet little understood. Thus the earlier physical cause interpretation of human variation was given a new foundation.

Cuvier's influence was immense, and during the course of the nineteenth century the notion of type was extended to the analysis of poetry, aesthetics, biography, personality, culture, social movements, and many kinds of differences other than those of interest to biologists. His teaching was one of the principal factors behind the emergence in the middle years of the nineteenth century of an international school of anthropological thought. It is important to note that the conception of type was independent of the Linnaean classificatory system. A zoological type could be a genus, a species, or a subspecies. Critics therefore protested that the notion of type was redundant since the Linnaean classifications would serve. As the usual criterion for a species was that its members could breed with one another, and since the races of man engaged so frequently in interbreeding, *Homo sapiens* must be one species. The typologists criticized the orthodox definition of species. Prominent among them were Charles Hamilton Smith, Samuel George Morton, Joseph Arthur de Gobineau, Robert Knox, Josiah Clark Nott, George Robins Gliddon, James Hunt, and Karl Vogt. They are often identified as proponents of "scientific racism" but their key concept was that of the permanence of types and their theory is better designated as "racial typology." Though there were variations from one writer to another and Vogt at least changed his opinions significantly, they more or less agreed in presenting man as a genus divided into types which in effect were species. They believed that each type was permanent and was suited to a particular zoological province of the earth's surface, but they recognized that the actual races of the contemporary world were all mixed. They accounted for this by arguing that hybrids were ultimately sterile so that though because of human foolishness, races might deviate from their type, nature kept the deviation within bounds. An alternative interpretation was advanced by Gobineau who believed that the mixing had gone much too far and had spoiled the stocks responsible for progress so that humanity was going into decline (see Banton 1977: 32–55).

The typological mode of explanation differed from the previous one in being agnostic about origins. The typologists rejected earlier beliefs that the earth was about six thousand years old. Whatever might have happened in earlier epochs, within the period for which there wasn't anatomical evidence types appeared to have been constant. One of the main attractions of typology was that it offered a theory of history purporting to explain the differential pattern of human progress. The record of history also contributed to the theory by revealing the special cultural attributes of types that went along with the physical differences. Since changes were the outcome of the essential characteristics of types in relation to particular environments, the theory attributed little significance to purely contingent events like the reported curse upon Ham's descendants. Though the typological theory could be reconciled with a belief in polygenesis it was really of a very different kind. For its appeal it relied on the one hand upon science rather than the Bible, and on the other, upon the growing European acceptance of an association between differences in physical appearance and ability to build a progressive civilization.

Some of these writers, like Smith, Nott, Gliddon, and Broca, made a clear distinction between "type" and "race." Gobineau, Knox and Hunt utilized the distinction but were less careful, and Knox indeed usually used "race" where on his own terms "type" would have been preferable. In the subsequent period a few writers did try to keep to the expression "type" but it is noticeable that in the very considerable literature about the nature of racial differences published in the United States after the Civil War there is a strong tendency to use the word "race" in the sense of "type." It is unfortunate that the major study on American writing in this period – apart from its strong inclination to presentism – regards race and type as synonymous. It does indeed quote a passage in which Nott refers to the "permanence of races, types, species, or permanent varieties, call them what you please" (Haller, 1971: 80) but when Nott, in *Types of Mankind* (1854: 95) wrote, "every race, at the present time, is more or less mixed," he was clearly referring to actual physically distinguishable populations and not to permanent types. Many of the passages in Haller's book (e.g., the reference in the American context to "both races," 1971: 208) refer to the latter usage and the interpretation of them is less clear than it would be were the distinction drawn. It would probably be worthwhile engaging in further more detailed research into the usage of the authors of the period in the light of Mayr's analysis (1972) of the multiple nature of the reorientation necessitated by Darwin's discovery of natural selection.

It could also be of interest to trace the ways in which the European idiom was carried to other continents. In South Africa before World War I, any reference to the races was likely to relate to the English-speaking and the Afrikaans-speaking sections of the white population. Equally, it was common to refer to the Zulu race, the Xhosa race, the Tswana race, differentiating groups within the African section of the population. Before World War II it seems to have been unusual to employ "race" to distinguish blacks from whites. Field Marshal Smuts wrote of the European type and the African type, identifying ethnic groups within these types as races (Graaff, 1973: 4). Most writers were less meticulous but it is interesting to note that the memorandum of Association marking the foundation in 1929 of the South African Institute of Race Relations sets out as the main objective the encouragement of "co-operation between the various sections and races of the population of South Africa" as if blacks and whites constituted sections that were divided into races (Horrell, 1976).

[. . .] It was noted in the previous section that the explanation of human differences by reference to descent was associated with a concern about the original creation and God's design for the world. One outcome of this was the conclusion that God had created men of different colors for a purpose, and that each color category had its part to play in his plan. The most striking illustration of this approach to race is found in the early nineteenth-century school of thought rather misleadingly called *natur-philosophie* (see Banton, 1977: 35–40). An echo of it can be heard in the New England writer Ralph Waldo Emerson who in 1844 was insisting that the civility of no race could be perfect so long as another race was degraded, for mankind was one. Yet within a decade Emerson had been attracted to Knox's explanations and was arguing that England's economic prowess was the result of "the rare coincidence of a good race and a good place" (Nicoloff, 1961: 124, 139). It is difficult to be certain but it looks as if here, in less than a decade, Emerson switched from a sense of race as descent to that of race as type. It is also relevant that he did so in a book that tried to analyze the character of the Englishman. In later years there was to be a minor literary industry producing volumes about national character, and it was rooted in the presuppositions of racial typology.

Race as subspecies

Darwin cut the ground from under the feet of the typologists by demonstrating that there were no permanent forms in nature. Each species was adapted to its environment by natural section, so that people of one racial type who migrated to a new habitat would there undergo change. The ups and downs of history could therefore not be explained in terms of the qualities of particular types. In the *Origin of Species* Darwin recognized "geographical races or sub-species" as local forms completely fixed and isolated, but concluded that since they did not differ from each other in important characteristics there was no certain way of deciding whether they should be considered species or varieties. He employed the word race primarily when referring to domestic races as the outcome of human breeding, and presented them as incipient species, for as his subtitle suggested, it was by natural selection that favored races became species (Darwin, 1859: 62–63, 73).

Darwin's revolution was so complex (Mayr, 1972) that it took decades even for the specialists to appreciate its implications. In the 1930s, more than seventy years after the publication of the *Origin of Species*, new lines of reasoning and research in biology led to the establishment of population genetics. Human variation was to be comprehended statistically in terms of the frequencies of given genes within the gene pool of the relevant population. This meant that for biologists, "population" was the successor concept to the discredited notion of racial type, and race could be legitimately used only as a synonym for subspecies, as explained above.

Yet the first adaptations of Darwinian thought to social affairs preserved much of the older mode of explanation, in part because the reorientation demanded of people was so great, and in part because of the particular circumstances of the late nineteenth century. That period saw unparalled technological advances which helped knit together the peoples of Europe in larger, more effective units, and to increase the gap between them and the peoples of most other regions. Social evolution was pictured therefore not as adaptation to changing environments but as the story of man's progress to superior modes of living. Sociologists represented it as a process in which men first lived in small bands, then successively as members of clans, tribes, peoples, states and empires. Groups designated as races were often thought to belong somewhere in such a scale; skin color and similar traits served as signs of membership in groups that had progressed in different measure, and therefore functioned as boundary markers. The conception of race as subspecies is not easily grasped by the man in the street, whereas that of race as type is much simpler and can easily be twisted to deal with conflicting evidence. The idea of race in the popular mind in the twentieth century has therefore usually been that of race as type. This conception was invalidated by Darwin's work, whereas that of race as descent was not. Although confusing, it is therefore still legitimate to use the word "race" in the earlier sense.

Race in current usage

The idea of race was important to Europeans in the late nineteenth century on account of its value in philosophies of history. It was widely believed that the success of the European powers sprang from the qualities inherent in the white race, or races, and that these promised continuing European supremacy. Probably there would be less support for such views in Europe and North America in the 1970s. The bulk of the population is more likely to believe that the ups and downs of nations in history are a reflection of technological skill and material resources, though this is not a question that has been thought worth detailed investigation. Probably more people would agree that the cultural characteristics of racial groups are an outcome of environment and opportunity than would consider them genetically determined. Those who believe that the universe was built by divine design and that everything in it has a place in that design might well echo the racial romanticism of an earlier era. One twentieth-century expression of this, though scarcely contemporary, is to be found in a history of the British and Foreign Bible Society (Canton, 1925), entitled *The Five Colours*. After the title page comes the verse:

> Not for one race nor one colour alone
> Was He flesh of your flesh and bone of your bone!
> Not for you only – for all men He died.
> 'Five were the colours', The Angel said,
> 'Yellow and black, white, brown and red;
> Five were the wounds from which he bled,
> On the Rock of Jerusalem crucified'.
> > "The Vision of Peter"

If race remains a word in popular usage, religious groups concerned for international harmony may well stress the complementarity of races and again employ metaphors of this kind.

In England in the years preceding and following World War II, the tendency was for less use to be made of the idiom of race. Sir Julian Huxley and A. C. Haddon, the senior anthropologist at Cambridge, set the tone in *We Europeans*, in which they declared that "the term race as applied to human groups should be dropped from the vocabulary of science" because it had "lost any sharpness of meaning" (1935: 107). Ideal types had to be distinguished from the existing mixed populations which might also be political and cultural units and were best called ethnic groups. The unity of race as a concept in either biological or social science was doubted by the leading authorities in both fields, while the extravagancies of Nazi rhetoric, coupled with the growing threats presented by their regime, helped to descredit it in popular usage. Earlier practices, such as that of identifying the French- and English-speaking sections of the Canadian population as "the two races" began to appear quaint. The same could be said of Sir Winston Churchill's rather archaic usage in his *History*, of which Book I was entitled "The Island Race." In 1957 he could still write about the early twentieth century, "meanwhile in Europe the mighty strength of the Teutonic race, hitherto baffled by division or cramped in lingering mediaeval systems, began to assert itself with volcanic energy" (1958: Preface). This echo of a previous century's parlance was a reminder of the change that had been occurring.

From the scientific standpoint it is unfortunate that just as the word "race" was being less used in any context where it might be thought to claim explanatory value, New Commonwealth immigration into England led to its greatly increased use in the press and in popular speech to designate the different population groups. An examination of the present use of the words "race," "races," and "racial" would probably show that they are employed chiefly to designate outwardly identifiable categories, and that people differ greatly in the degree to which they believe or assume that the labels explain anything. If questioned about why such groups should be called races, or what is the nature of race, many people will say that they are not sure but leave such matters to the experts. Since there are few situations in everyday life which require a precise use of "race" its employment in a diverse and loose fashion causes few problems.

Two situations calling for precise definition of ethnic or racial identification are provided by censuses and legislation. In the United States after World war II social scientists moved away from the use of race to designate social categories, preferring to write about minorities. The Federal government has been more slow to change: until recently they were using five "racial/ethnic categories," viz.:

1   *American Indian or Alaskan Native*: A person having origins in any of the original peoples of North America.
2   *Asian or Pacific Islander*: A person having origins in any of the original peoples of the Far East, Southeast Asia, or the Pacific Islands. This area includes, for example, China, Japan, Korea, the Philippine Islands, and Samoa.
3   *Black/Negro*: A person having origins in any of the black racial groups of Africa.
4   *Caucasian/White*: A person having origins in any of the original peoples of Europe, North Africa, the Middle East, or the Indian subcontinent.
5   *Hispanic*: A person of Mexican, Puerto Rican, Cuban, Central or South American, or other Spanish culture or origin, regardless of race.

[This list is quoted from the Federal Interagency Committee on Education Report, vol. 2(1), May 1975.]

The Association of Indians in America – i.e. of Indians from Asia – protested against their classification as whites. In May 1977 the President's Office issued a revision of Circular A–46. It modified category 1 by adding the qualification "and who maintains cultural identification through tribal affiliation or community recognition." To the first sentence of category 2 it added "the Indian subcontinent." Category 3 was redesignated "Black." The numbers of categories 4 and 5 were changed round; 5 is now designated simply "White," and the reference to the Indian subcontinent has been deleted. The circular further states that if separate race and ethnic categories are used, the minimum designations are:

(a)   Race:
  - American Indian or Alaskan Native
  - Asian or Pacific Islander
  - Black
  - White
(b)   Ethnicity
  - Hispanic origin
  - Not of Hispanic origin.

Thus "ethnicity" becomes a subdivision of the categories Black and White alone. The circular also lays down that when someone is "of mixed racial and/or ethnic origins" the category to be used is that which "most closely reflects the individual's recognition in his community." The designation "non-white" is no longer acceptable.

In Britain there is [currently] a controversy about categories to be used in the 1981 census. It is said that the procedure almost certain to be recommended by the Office of Population Censuses and Surveys contains the instruction: "*Race or ethnic group* (1) Please tick the appropriate box to show the race or ethnic group to which the person belongs or from which the person is descended. 1. White; 2. West Indian; 3. African; 4. Arab; 5. Turkish; 6. Chinese; 7. Indian; 8. Pakistani; 9. Bangladeshi, 10. Sri Lanka; 11. Other" (Mack, 1978).[1] It will be unfortunate if the word "race" is retained in this context by the American and British governments since this will add legitimacy to the lingering remains of the typological doctrine that were on their way to the lumber room of discarded science. The United States government's use of ethnicity as a subdivision of a racial category has little support in contemporary social science, but their practice of classifying individuals by their having origins in particular peoples seems far preferable to the British assumption that a person can belong to a race. It should also be noted that though the British Race Relations Act of 1976 penalizes discrimination on racial grounds, it does not define race, and that there is at present little case law that bears upon this question. The Act does, in Section 3 (i) define racial groups but only as "a group of persons defined by reference to colour, race, nationality or ethnic or national origins."

Consideration of these issues does, however, suggest that a fourth use of the word "race" is now being established. It is an administrative and political use which does not pretend to any explanatory significance but will doubtless be used to support old-style racial explanations. The political implications of the racial idiom have always been complex. It can be argued, for example, that a salient feature of the use some Englishmen made of it in the middle and later decades of the nineteenth century was to celebrate the positive qualities of their own stock and that the disparagement of the qualities of other stocks was to start with only an incidental consequence of their self-centeredness. (Sir Charles Dilke's *Greater Britain* of 1868 is an illustration of this.) Only as contact and conflict between Europeans and non-Europeans became closer did the political use of racial doctrines become important. In recent times peoples who have been the victims of such doctrines have been inclined to turn the tables by appealing for nonwhite solidarity against whites. In the United States some blacks prefer to identify themselves in racial terms because they believe that their experience of disadvantage has been so much more profound than that of white ethnic minorities. In the United Kingdom it seems as if people who stand to the left in political terms are the more inclined to identify New Commonwealth immigrant minorities in racial terms because they wish to challenge the typological preconceptions which seem still to be widespread in the white population. This appears to have been the major reason why the agency established under the 1976 Act has been called The Commission for Racial Equality whereas its predecessor was the Community Relations Commission. Therefore though it may seem desirable on strictly academic grounds to abandon the use of the word race, there are political pressures, from non-whites as well as whites, from radicals as well as conservatives, which are likely to keep it in current use and to shape the fourth stage in the career of this troublesome concept.

Other perspectives

If the meaning of the word race has changed in the way suggested, reflecting changes in popular understanding of the significance of phenotypical variation, then it is reasonable to expect that the character of the arguments which get classified as "racist" will have changed likewise. When race meant descent, then it may be expected that whites considered alliance with blacks as socially dishonorable. When race meant type, whites would have seen sexual union with blacks as producing stock physicaly inferior to whites but superior to blacks. When race meant subspecies, most members of the public would not have comprehended the work-ings of inheritance and selection, and since it takes time for scientific advances to reach the wider public it might be expected that the typological doctrine would have retained its appeal.[2] Now that race is coming to be defined by bureaucratic and political concerns it is not surprising that there is no agreement upon a clear definition of racism.

Historical evidence is not lacking to support this thesis at least in respect to the change between the first and second stages. In 1771 the Viceroy of Brazil ordered the degradation of an Amerindian chief who, "disregarding the signal honours which he had received from the Crown, had sunk so low as to marry a Negress, staining his blood with this alliance" (Boxer, 1963: 121). Such a state-ment recalls a judgment that in eighteenth-century Latin America the "almost pathological interest in genealogy" and honorable descent was characteristic of the age (Mörner, 1967: 59). It suggests that it is the social rather than the physical consequences of marriages between persons of contrasting status which are to be avoided, and can be placed alongside the French *memoire du roi* of 1777 that declared of the transplanted Africans in Saint Dominque:

Whatever distance they may be from their origin, they always keep the stain of slavery, and are declared incapable of all public functions. Even gentlemen who descend in any degree from a woman of color cannot enjoy the prerogatives of nobility. This law is harsh, but wise and necessary. In a country where there are fifteen slaves to one white, one cannot put too much distance between the two species . . .

(Hall, 1972: 183–84).

This is an explicitly political argument which utilizes a doctrine of descent – to which Europeans admitted exceptions when it suited them – in order to exclude a category of people from civil rights. It lacks the biological presupposition which a twentieth-century reader might expect.

Conclusion

[. . .] Physical differences between peoples have been observed throughout human history; all over the world people have developed words for delineating them. "Race" is a concept rooted in a particular culture and a particular period of history which brings with it suggestions about how these differences are to be explained. It lends itself to use in a variety of contexts and gets elaborated into a whole style or idiom of interpretation. In the earliest phase of its career "race" meant descent at a time when people understood little of the biology of descent. In the nineteenth century "race" became identified with a controversial scientific theory that was found to be erroneous and which, had science been a more logical and less human enterprise, should have been discarded after 1859. Instead, the old idea was salvaged and rebuilt on a foundation quite different from that of the pre-Darwinian era, while in the present it is being used for purely political purposes to identify communities without intending to imply that the chief differences between then stem from inheritance.

Some scholars overlook these differences in the meaning that has been given to the word; they interpret the racial attitudes of earlier centuries in terms of their own generation's understanding of biological variation and condemn anything which to a modern reader smacks of racial intolerance. This practice diminishes some of the differences between periods of history; it distracts attention from the forces for change which exist in the present and will extend into the future. Presentism tends to slow down the process whereby erroneous or unhelpful formulations are discarded, and it can be pernicious when analyses of past events are distorted by a desire to support a contemporary political strategy. Since all writers will be influenced in some degree by the circumstances of their own time, and most believe that it is possible to learn lessons from history, the problem is implicit in any account of another period, but it can still be kept under control. Since people's ideas about the special characteristics of their own time are influenced by their beliefs about previous periods they have a particular reason to be on their guard against presentism.

Notes

1   In March 1980 it was announced that the 1981 United Kingdom census would
     not contain any question on race or ethnic origin. See also White, 1979.
2   Although overlain by some other lines of thought, sophisticated writers for a
     time advanced social Darwinist theses that racial prejudice served an evolutionary
     function, while the slogan 'survival of the fittest' seemed to justify white aggres-
     siveness overseas.

References

Banton, Michael 1977. *The Idea of Race*, London: Tavistock.
Boxer, C. R. 1963. *Race Relations in the Portuguese Colonial Empire*, 1415–1825, Oxford:
     Clarendon Press.
Canton, William 1925. *The Five Colours*. London: The Bible House.
Churchill, Winston S. 1956–1958. *A History of the English-speaking Peoples*, London:
     Cassell.
Darwin, Charles 1959. *On the Origin of Species by Means of Selection; or, The Preservation
     of Favoured Races in the Struggle for Life*, (page references to New York: Mentor
     Books edition).
Graaff, J. F. de V. 1973. "Kosmos and Chaos: The racial attitudes of Jan Christian
     Smuts", unpublished MSc. Thesis, University of Bristol.
Greene, John C. 1959. *The Death of Adam*, New York: Mentor Books.
Hall, Gwendolyn Midlo 1972. "Saint Domingue," pp. 172–192 in David N. Cohen
     and Jack P. Greene (eds), *Neither Slave nor Free: The Freedmen of African Descent
     in the Slave Societies of the New World*, Baltimore: Johns Hopkins University press.
Haller, John S. 1971. *Outcasts from Evolution: Scientific Attitudes of Racial Inferiority
     1859–1900*, Urbana: University of Illinois Press.
Horrell, Muriel 1976. Personal communication.
Horsman, Reginald 1976. Origins of racial Anglo-Saxonism in Great Britain before
     1850", *Journal of the History of Ideas* 37: 387–410.
Huxley, Julian S. And Haddon, A. C. 1935. *We Europeans: A Survey of 'Racial' Problems*,
     London: Cape.
Macaulay, Thomas B. 1827. "The social and industrial capacities of Negroes", reprinted
     in *Race*, 1971, 13: 133–164.
Mack, Joanna 1978. "A question of race", *New Society* 43, 5 Jan: 8–9.
Mayr, Ernst 1972. "The nature of the Darwinian revolution" *Science*, 176: 981–989.
Mörner, Magnus 1967. *Race Mixture in the History of Latin America*, Boston: Little,
     Brown.
Nott, J. C. and Gliddon, Geo. R. 1854. *Types of Mankind: or, Ethnological Researches*,
     Philadelphia: Lippincott.
Nicoloff, Philip L. 1961. *Emerson on Race and History: an examination of "English Traits"*,
     New York: Columbia University Press.
White, R. M. 1979. "What's in a name? Problems in official and legal usages of 'race'",
     New Community, 7: 333–349.
Williams, David O. 1978. "Macaulay and the commission to Tortola", unpublished
     MSc. Thesis, University of Bristol.

Chapter 3

Tzvetan Todorov

translated by Catherine Porter

RACE AND RACISM

[. . .]

THE WORD "RACISM," in its usual sense, actually designates two very different things. On the one hand, it is a matter of *behavior*, usually a manifestation of hatred or contempt for individuals who have well-defined physical characteristics different from our own; on the other hand, it is a matter of *ideology*, a doctrine concerning human races. The two are not necessarily linked. The ordinary racist is not a theoretician; he is incapable of justifying his behavior with "scientific" arguments. Conversely, the ideologue of race is not necessarily a "racist," in the usual sense: his theoretical views may have no influence whatsoever on his acts, or his theory may not imply that certain races are intrinsically evil. In order to keep these two meanings separate, I shall adopt the distinction that sometimes obtains between "racism," a term designating behavior, and "racialism," a term reserved for doctrines. I must add that the form of racism that is rooted in racialism produces particularly catastrophic results: this is precisely the case of Nazism. Racism is an ancient form of behavior that is probably found worldwide; racialism is a movement of ideas born in Western Europe whose period of flowering extends from the mid-eighteenth century to the mid-twentieth.

Racialist doctrine, which will be our chief concern here, can be presented as a coherent set of propositions. They are all found in the "ideal type," or classical version of the doctrine, but some of them may be absent from a given marginal or "revisionist" version. These propositions may be reduced to five.

1   *The existence of races.* The first thesis obviously consists in affirming that there are such things as races, that is, human groupings whose members possess common physical characteristics; or rather (for the differences themselves are self-evident) it consists in affirming the relevance and the significance of that notion.

From this perspective, races are equated with animal species, and it is postulated that there is the same distance between two human races as between horses and donkeys: not enough to prevent reproduction, but enough to establish a boundary readily apparent to all. Racialists are not generally content to observe this state of affairs; they also want to see it maintained: they are thus opposed to racial mixing.

The adversaries of racialist theory have often attacked the doctrine on this point. First, they draw attention to the fact that human groups have intermingled from time immemorial; consequently, their physical characteristics cannot be as different as racialists claim. Next, these theorists add a two-pronged biological observation to their historical argument. In the first place, human beings indeed differ from one another in their physical characteristics; but in order for these variations to give rise to clearly delimited groups, the differences and the groups would have to coincide. However, this is not the case. We can produce a first map of the "races" if we measure genetic characteristics, a second if we analyze blood composition, a third if we use the skeletal system, a fourth if we look at the epidermis. In the second place, within each of the groups thus constituted, we find greater distances between one individual and another than between one group and another. For these reasons, contemporary biology, while it has not stopped studying variations among human beings across the planet, no longer uses the concept of race.

But this scientific argument is not really relevant to the argument against racialist doctrines: it is a way of responding with biological data to what is actually a question of social psychology. Scientists may or may not believe in "races," but their position has no influence on the perception of the man in the street, who can see perfectly well that the differences exist. From this individual's viewpoint, the only properties that count are the immediately visible ones: skin color, body hair, facial configuration. Furthermore, the fact that there are individuals or even whole populations that are the product of racial mixing does not invalidate the notion of race but actually confirms it. The person of mixed race is identified precisely because the observer is capable of recognizing typical representatives of each race.

2   *Continuity between physical type and character.* But races are not simply groups of individuals who look alike (if this had been the case, the stakes would have been trivial). The racialist postulates, in the second place, that physical and moral characteristics are interdependent; in other words, the segmentation of the world along racial lines has as its corollary an equally definitive segmentation along cultural lines. To be sure, a single race may possess more than one culture; but as soon as there is racial variation there is cultural change. The solidarity between race and culture is evoked to explain why the races tend to go to war with one another.

Not only do the two segmentations coexist, it is alleged, but most often a causal relation is posited between them: physical differences *determine* cultural differences. We can all observe these two series of variables, physical and mental, around us; each one can be explained independently, and the two explanations do not have to be related after the fact; or else the two series can be observed without requiring any explanation at all. Yet the racialist acts as if the two series were nothing but the causes and effects of a single series. This first assertion in turn implies the hereditary transmission of mental properties and the impossibility of modifying those properties by education. The quest for unity and order in the variety of lived experience clearly relates the racialist attitude to that of the scholar in general, who tries to introduce order into chaos and whose constructions affirm the kinship of things that remain separate in the phenomenal world. It must be added that up to now, no proof has been provided for the relation of determinism or even for the interdependence of race and culture. This does not mean, of course, that proof might not one day be found, or that the search for proof is in itself harmful. We must simply note that, for the time being, the hypothesis has turned out to be unproductive.

Here I should like to mention a recent proposal to maintain the causal relation while overturning it. This view no longer holds that physical characteristics determine mental ones; rather, it holds that culture acts on nature. If, within a given population, tall people are preferred to short people, or blonds are preferred to brunettes, the population as a whole will evolve toward the desired end: its value system will serve as a genetic filter. We can also imagine a population that would prefer physical strength to intelligence, or vice versa; once again, conditions will be favorable for an extension of the qualities valued. Such an inversion of perspective opens up new possibilities for the study of mind–body interactions.

3   *The action of the group on the individual.* The same determinist principle comes into play in another sense: the behavior of the individual depends, to a very large extent, on the racio-cultural (or "ethnic") group to which he or she belongs. This proposition is not always explicit, since it is self-evident: what is the use of distinguishing races and cultures, if one believes at the same time that individuals are morally nondetermined, that they act in function of their own will freely exercised, and not by virtue of their group membership – over which they have no control? Racialism is thus a doctrine of collective psychology, and it is inherently hostile to the individualist ideology.

4   *Unique hierarchy of values.* The racialist is not content to assert that races differ; he also believes that some are superior to others, which implies that he possesses a unitary hierarchy of values, an evaluative framework with respect to which he can make universal judgments. This is somewhat astonishing, for the racialist who has such a framework at his disposal is the same person who has rejected the unity of the human race. The scale of values in question is generally ethnocentric in origin: it is very rare that the ethnic group to which a racialist author belongs does not appear at the top of his own hierarchy. On the level of physical qualities, the judgment of preference usually takes the form of aesthetic appreciation: my race is beautiful, the others are more or less ugly. On the level of the mind, the judgment concerns both intellectual and moral qualities (people are stupid or intelligent, bestial or noble).

5   *Knowledge-based politics.* The four propositions listed so far take the form of descriptions of the world, factual observations. They lead to a conclusion that constitutes the fifth and last doctrinal proposition – namely, the need to embark upon a political course that brings the world into harmony with the description

provided. Having established the "facts," the racialist draws from them a moral judgment and a political ideal. Thus, the subordination of inferior races or even their elimination can be justified by accumulated knowledge on the subject of race. Here is where racialism rejoins racism: the theory is put into practice.

The refutation of this last inference is a task not for the scientist but rather for the philosopher. Science can refute propositions like the first three listed, but it may also turn out that what appears self-evident to biologists today may be considered an error tomorrow. Even if this were to happen, however, it would not justify behavior that could be properly condemned on other grounds. Geneticists are not particularly well qualified to combat racism. Subjecting politics to science, and thus subjecting what is right to what is, makes for bad philosophy, not bad science; the humanist ideal can be defended against the racist ideal not because it is more true (an ideal cannot be more or less true) but because it is ethically superior, based as it is on the universality of the human race.

The whole set of features described constitutes racialist doctrine; each of them taken alone can also be found independently of racialism. They are all necessary to racialism; the absence of any one of them produces a related but nevertheless distinct doctrine. We shall discover that the first proposition was rejected as early as the nineteenth century, leading to a "culturalism" that is in other respects very similar to racialism. In the twentieth century, the fourth proposition has also been frequently rejected, in situations where relativist neutrality has been favored over the obligation to judge (whereas this proposition was the only common feature of racialism and universalist humanism). There are also racialists who have no interest whatsoever in any possible political implications of their doctrines (this is the case with the most famous racialist of them all, Gobineau). Still, the conjunction of the five features must be considered the classical model of racialism. On the other hand, the supplementary elements of the doctrine mentioned here are optional – for example, the fear of racial mixing, or the belief that mental faculties are inherited, or the explanation of racial warfare.

Several common features indicate that racialism belongs to the spiritual family of scientism. Indeed, we have seen how the latter is characterized by its affirmation of an integral determinism (which includes the relation of the moral realm to the physical as well as the relation of the individual to the group). Scientism is also characterized by its demand that science formulate society's goals and indicate legitimate means for attaining them. One might call racialism the tip of the scientistic iceberg. Racialist theories are no longer in fashion today, but the scientistic doctrine continues to flourish. This is why I am inclined to conduct parallel analyses of racialist ideas as such and their general scientistic context.

[. . .] The most significant change in the notion of race in the late nineteenth century is its transposition from the physical to the cultural plane, under the influence of such authors as Renan, Taine, and Le Bon. [. . .] Let us now consider the notion of "historical" race shared by Taine and Le Bon.

Hippolyte Taine's place in the history of racialism is somewhat difficult to pin down. His influence is quite considerable, although his writings include only a few pages devoted to the issue of race. Moreover, there is a troubling discrepancy between his programmatic exposés and his own practice. Like Renan, his contemporary, Taine in fact swings back and forth between physical and cultural interpretations of the word "race," thus authorizing his disciples to find arguments in his writings in support of contradictory theses.

In his statements of principle, as we have seen, Taine aligns himself with an integral determinism (this is not the case with his practice). In his introduction to the *History of English Literature*, Taine's systematic presentation of the factors governing human behavior reduces them to three: race, surroundings, and epoch – that is, what man contributes in himself, what the external environment imposes on him, and finally the results of the interaction of these two factors. The "epoch" (*le moment*) is not actually the result of the era in which one lives, but rather the result of the phase of an internal evolution proper to each human group; in other words, it combines the two preceding factors, yet it becomes a determining factor in turn. "With the forces within and without, there is the work which they have already produced together, and this work itself contributes to produce that which follows". But just what does the contribution from "within" (called "race") consist of? What are its nature and its scope?

In "The Philosophy of Art in the Netherlands" ("Philosophy de l'art dans les Pays-Bas"), Taine attempts to draw a rigorous distinction between race and nation (or people), but he does so with the help of a metaphor that leaves room for a certain interpretive license. "I shall first show you the seed, that is to say the race, with its fundamental and indelible qualities, those that persist through all circumstances and in all climates; and next the plant, that is to say the people itself, with its original qualities expanded or contracted, in any case grafted on and transformed by its surroundings and its history" (*Philosophie de l'art*, in English *The Philosophy of Art*, II. But just what do these vegetable images yield when they are transposed onto the human species?

When he sets out to illustrate the influence of race, in the *History of English Literature*, Taine resorts to an example that seems to confirm the foregoing distinction. "A race, like the old Aryans, scattered from the Ganges as far as the Hebrides, settled in every clime, and every stage of civilization, transformed by thirty centuries of revolutions, nevertheless manifests in its languages, religions, literatures, philosophies, the community of blood and of intellect which to this day finds its offshoots together." Let us note here that while Taine may be talking about "blood" and "intellect," his list includes only intellectual products, languages and literatures, religions and philosophies; the common denominator of activities as numerous and varied as these can hardly be very powerful. In any event, race is presented here as a supranational entity.

However, the same text also includes statements that tend to identify race with nation. Races, according to Taine, "vary with various peoples." Why, then, are two terms needed instead of just one? He goes on to give examples of "regulating instincts and faculties implanted in a race" that involve the Germanic, Hellenic, and Latin races – or rather Spain, England, and France, which is to say nations and not races. In another passage, where he lists "the fundamental causes" that govern human behavior, Taine specifies that he means "nationality, climate, temperament"; here "nationality" appears again as a synonym for "race." At the same time, Taine says he intends to complete the task Montesquieu had set for himself: the description of "the special psychology of each special formation" – that is, the spirit of nations. And it must be said that in practice, physical characteristics play only a small part in Taine's analyses; thus, contrary to what his own distinctions imply, his races are nations, understood as "cultures."

We find the same ambiguity in the description of "race" itself. Race is what is innate; but is what is innate modifiable? Is it radically distinct from what is acquired? On the one hand, Taine implies that race is a stable entity. "There is one [fixed element], a character and spirit proper to the race, transmitted from generation to generation, remaining the same through cultural change, organizational shifts, and variation in products" (*Essais*, preface to the second edition, pp. xviii–xix). These are "the universal and permanent causes, present at every moment and in every case, everywhere and always acting, indestructible, and finally infallibly supreme" (*History of English Literature*). So much for the immutable side.

But at the same time, Taine makes precisely the opposite claim. The brief passages in the *History of English Literature* that describe the entity called "race" are oddly focused on the search for the *origin* of races – which is nothing other than an adaptation to the surroundings. The inside that was supposed to be opposed to the outside is only a slightly older outside. "As soon as an animal begins to exist, it has to reconcile itself with its surroundings; it breathes and renews itself, is differently affected according to the variations in air, food, temperature. Different climate and situation bring it various needs, and consequently a different course of activity; and thus, again, a different set of habits; and still again, a different set of aptitudes and instincts." It is no longer race and surroundings that are in opposition, but long and short time periods. "The race emigrates, like the Aryan, and the change of climate has altered in its case the whole economy, intelligence, and organization of society." Taine then falls back on another comparison in which he has given up the qualitative difference between seed and plant: the race is "a kind of lake, a deep reservoir wherein other springs have, for a multitude of centuries, discharged their several streams." Certain waters flow out of the lake, and others flow into it; but there is no difference in nature between them.

When he turns to the study of the "surroundings," Taine mentions the climate and geographical features, political circumstances, and social conditions as being among the most powerful environmental forces that act on men; taken together, "these prolonged situations, these surrounding circumstances" produce "the regulating instincts and faculties implanted in a race – in short, the mood of intelligence in which it thinks and acts at the present time." Thus, race no longer produces history, but rather history produces race (or the spirit of the nation). Moreoever, by modifying the institutions or forms of social life, one can transform race: such actions "are to nations what education, career, condition, abode are to individuals." The possibility of an educational project alluded to here is at the opposite pole from racialist thought, and it allows us to measure the full ambivalence of Taine's position (although properly speaking there is no contradiction, and Taine was probably conscious of the apparent inconsistency).

In his books (*Philosophy de l'art, Essais de critique*), Taine deals at length with "the spirit of nations." He uses the term "race," but he often leaves the impression that the word is only a substitute, sometimes synonymous with "nation," sometimes with "essential element" or "dominant faculty." Whatever the case, starting with Taine the word "race" comes into play with renewed vigor.

In the transformations that Renan and Taine, or even le Bon, bring to racialist doctrine, we can see a prefiguration of its contemporary outlines. The term 'race," having already outlived its usefulness, will be replaced by the much more appropriate term "culture"; declarations of superiority and inferiority, the residue of an attachment to the universalist framework, will be set aside in favor of a glorification of difference (a difference that is not valorized in itself). What will remain unchanged, on the other hand, is the rigidity of determinism (cultural rather than physical, now) and the discontinuity of humanity, compartmentalized into cultures that cannot and must not communicate with one another effectively. The period of classical racialism seems definitely behind us, in the wake of the widespread condemnation of Nazi Germany's policies toward Jews; thus, we can establish its chronological limits with a precision that is unusual in the history of ideas: from 1749 (Buffon) to 1945 (Hitler). Modern racialism, which is better known as "culturalism," originates in the writings of Renan, Taine, and Le Bon; it replaces physical race with linguistic, historical, or psychological race. It shares certain features with its ancestor, but not all; this has allowed it to abandon the compromising term "race" (and thus the first "proposition" of classical racialism). Nevertheless, it can continue to play the role formerly assumed by racialism. In our day, racist behaviors have clearly not disappeared, or even changed; but the discourse that legitimizes them is no longer the same; rather than appealing to racialism, it appeals to nationalist or culturalist doctrine, or to the "right to difference." [. . .]

Chapter 4

Oliver C. Cox

RACE RELATIONS
Its meaning, beginning, and progress

I N   A   D I S C U S S I O N   O F "the origin" of race relations it should be well to determine at the outset exactly what we are looking for. We shall proceed, therefore, by first eliminating certain concepts that are commonly confused with that of race relations. These are: ethnocentrism, intolerance, and "racism."

Ethnocentrism, as the sociologists conceive of it, is a social attitude which expresses a community of feeling in any group – the "we" feeling as over against the "others." This attitude seems to be a function of group solidarity, which is not necessarily a racial phenomenon. Neither is social intolerance [. . .] racial antagonism, for social intolerance is social despleasure or resentment against that group which refuses to conform to the established practices and beliefs of the society. Finally, the term "racism" as it has been recently employed in the literature seems to refer to a philosophy of racial antipathy. Studies on the origin of racism involve the study of the development of an ideology, an approach which usually results in the substitution of the history of a system of rationalization for that of a material social fact.[1] Indeed, it is likely to be an accumulation of an erratic pattern of verbalizations cut free from any on-going social system.

What then is the phenomenon, the beginnings of which we seek to determine? It is the phenomenon of the capitalist exploitation of peoples and its complementary social attitude. Again, one should miss the point entirely if one were to think of racial antagonism as having its genesis in some "social instinct" of antipathy between peoples. Such an approach ordinarily leads to no end of confusion.[2]

The beginning of racial antagonism

Probably a realization of no single fact is of such crucial significance for an understanding of racial antagonism as that the phenomenon had its rise only in modern times.[3] In a previous chapter on "the origin of caste" we have attempted to show that race conflict did not exist among the early Aryans in India, and we do not find it in other ancient civilizations. Our hypothesis is that racial exploitation and race prejudice developed among Europeans with the rise of capitalism and nationalism, and that because of the world-wide ramifications of capitalism, all racial antagonisms can be traced to the policies and attitudes of the leading capitalist people, the white people of Europe and North America.

[. . .] In the study of race relations it is of major importance to realize that their significant manifestations could not possibly have been known among the ancients. If we had to put our finger upon the year which marked the beginning of modern race relations we should select 1493–94. This is the time when total disregard for the human rights and physical power of the non-Christian peoples of the world, the colored peoples, was officially assumed by the first two great colonizing European nations. Pope Alexander VI's bill of demarcation issued under Spanish pressure on May 3, 1493, and its revision by the Treaty of Tordesillas (June 7, 1494), arrived at through diplomatic negotiations between Spain and Portugal, put all the heathen peoples and their resources – that is to say, especially the colored peoples of the world – at the disposal of Spain and Portugal.[4]

Sometimes, probably because of its very obviousness, it is not realized that the slave trade was simply a way of recruiting labor for the purpose of exploiting the great natural resources of America.[5] This trade did not develop because Indians and Negroes were red and black, or because their cranial capacity averaged a certain number of cubic centimeters; but simply because they were the best workers to be found for the heavy labor in the mines and plantations across the Atlantic.[6] If white workers were available in sufficient numbers they would have been substituted. As a matter of fact, part of the early demand for labor in the West Indies and on the mainland was filled by white servants, who were sometimes defined in exactly the same terms as those used to characterize the Africans. Although the recruitment of involuntary labor finally settled down to the African coasts, the earlier kidnapers did a brisk business in some of the most enlightened European cities. Moreover, in the process of exploiting the natural resources of the West Indies, the Spanish conquistadors literally consumed the native Indian population.

This, then, is the beginning of modern race relations. It was not an abstract, natural, immemorial feeling of mutual antipathy between groups, but rather a practical exploitative relationship with its socio-attitudinal facilitation – at that time only nascent race prejudice. Although this peculiar kind of exploitation was then in its incipience, it had already achieved its significant characteristics.[7] As it developed and took definite capitalistic form, we could follow the white man around the world and see him repeat the process among practically every people of color. Earl Grey was directly in point when he described, in 1880, the motives and purpose of the British in one racial situation:

> Throughout this part of the British Dominions the colored people are generally looked upon by the whites as an inferior race, whose interest ought to be systematically disregarded when they came into competition with their own, and who ought to be governed mainly with a view of the advantage of the superior race. And for this advantage two things

are considered to be especially necessary: first, that facilities should be afforded to the white colonists for obtaining possession of land heretofore occupied by the native tribes; and secondly, that the Kaffir population should be made to furnish as large and as cheap a supply of labor as possible.[8]

But the fact of crucial significance is that racial exploitation is merely one aspect of the problem of the proletarianization of labor, regardless of the color of the laborer. Hence racial antagonism is essentially political-class conflict. The capitalist exploiter, being opportunistic and practical, will utilize any convenience to keep his labor and other resources freely exploitable. He will devise and employ race prejudice when that becomes convenient.[9] As a matter of fact, the white proletariat of early capitalism had to endure burdens of exploitation quite similar to those which many colored peoples must bear today.

However, the capitalist spirit, the profit-making motive, among the sixteenth-century Spaniards and Portuguese, was constantly inhibited by the philosophy and purpose of the Roman Catholic Church. A social theory supporting the capitalist drive for the impersonal exploitation of the workers never completely emerged. Conversion to Christianity and slavery among the Indians stood at cross-purposes; therefore, the vital problem presented to the exploiters of labor was that of circumventing the assimilative effects of conversion to Christianity. In the West Indies the celebrated priest, Las Casas, was touched by the destructive consequences of the ruthless enslavement of the Indians, and he opposed it on religious grounds. But work had to be done, and if not voluntarily, then some ideology had to be found to justify involuntary servitude. "The Indians were represented as lazy, filthy pagans, of bestial morals, no better than dogs, and fit only for slavery, in which state alone there might be some hope of instructing and converting them to Christianity."[10]

The capitalist exploitation of the colored workers, it should be observed, consigns them to employments and treatment that is humanly degrading. In order to justify this treatment the exploiters must argue that the workers are inately degraded and degenerate, consequently they naturally merit their condition. It may be mentioned incidentally that the ruling-class conception of degradation will tend to be that of all persons in the society, even that of the exploited person himself; and the work done by degraded persons will tend to degrade superior persons who attempt to do it. [. . .]

The progress of racial antagonism

This, then, is the nature of racial antagonism; developing in Europe, it has been carried to all parts of the world. In almost fateful terms Kipling's celebrated poem written in 1899 describes a desperate conflict, "the white man's burden," a like obligation, incidentally, never assumed by any other race in all the history of the world:

Take up the White Man's burden –
Send forth the best ye breed –
Go bind your sons to exile

To serve your captives' need;
To wait in heavy harness,
On fluttered folk and wild –
Your new-caught, sullen peoples,
Half-devil and half-child.[11]

The Europeans have overthrown more or less completely the social system among every colored people with whom they have come into contact. The dynamism and efficiency of capitalistic culture concluded this. The stability of color and inertness of culture, together with effective control over firearms, subsequently made it possible for whites to achieve a more or less separate and dominant position even in the homeland of colored peoples. "The white man's conception of himself as the aristocrat of the earth came gradually through the discovery, as surprising to himself as to anyone else, that he had weapons and organization which made opposition to his ambition futile."[12]

It should be made clear that we do not mean to say that the white race is the only one *capable* of race prejudice. It is probable that without capitalism, a cultural chance occurrence among whites, the world might never have experienced race prejudice. Indeed, we should expect that under another form of economic organization, say socialism, the relationship between whites and peoples of color would be significantly modified.[13]

The depreciation of the white man's color as a social gift goes hand in hand with the westernization of the conquered peoples of color. The Hindus, for example, are the same color today as they were in 1750, but now the white man no longer appears to them to be the cultural magician of other days. His secret of domination has been exposed, and the Hindus are now able to distinguish between his white skin and that secret. Therefore, he is now left with only his nationalism and superior might, for should he pull a cultural rabbit out of his hat, some Hindu would promptly pull another, which might even overmatch the first. Krishnalal Shridharani puts it thus: "[The Saxon] has been accustomed to regarding himself as a supreme being for centuries. Now he faces a world which refuses to recognize him as such. With all his civilized values, he will have to go on the role of military tyrant."[14] There is no assumption, then, that race prejudice is a biological heritage of the white race.

But we should not lose sight of the fact that whites have pre-empted this attitude.[15] Since the belief in white superiority – that is to say, white nationalism – began to move over the world, no people of color has been able to develop race prejudice independent of whites. It may be, however, that the Japanese have now reached that stage of industrial development, nationalistic ambition, and military power sufficient to question their assignment to inferior racial rank; no other colored race has ever dared to do this.[16] Indeed, since 1905 the Japanese have known how it felt to overcome the white man and make him like it.

Furthermore, the Japanese are culturally ripe for a belief of their own in yellow superiority. But the problem now confronting them is not similar to that which lay before the Europeans when they began to take on the burden of exploiting the colored peoples of the world. The white opportunists had then come upon no race able to fathom their cultural superiority and power. Today, however, the

Japanese are not only blocked at every point by powerfully entrenched whites but also relatively limited in their possible area of dominance.

A still more crucial question is whether this world is large enough to accommodate more than one superior race. Barring the apparent illogic of the superlative, we should bear in mind that color prejudice is more than ethnocentrism; race prejudice must be actually backed up by a show of racial excellence, secured finally by military might.[17] No race can develop color prejudice merely by wishing to do so. It would be ridiculous for the Chinese to say that they are prejudiced against whites when Europeans segregate the Chinese even in China.[18] [. . .]

Notes

1   See Hannah Arendt; "Race-Thinking Before Racism," *The Review of Politics*, Vol. 6, January 1944, p. 36–73; and Frederick G. Detweiler, "The Rise of Modern Race Antagonisms," *The American Journal of Sociology*, vol. 37, March 1932, pp. 738–47.

2   Consider, for instance, the following definitive statement by professor Robert E. Park: "This [prejudice against the Japanese] is due to the existence in the human mind of a mechanism by which we inevitably and automatically classify every individual human being we meet. When a race bears an external mark by which every individual member of it can infallibly be identified, that race is by that fact set apart and segregated. Japanese, Chinese, and Negroes cannot move among us with the same freedom as members of other races because they bear marks which identify them as members of their race. This fact isolates them. . . . Isolation is at once a cause and an effect of race prejudice. It is a vicious circle – isolation, prejudice; prejudice, isolation." In Jesse F. Steiner, *The Japanese Invasion*, p. xvi.

Since, however, we may assume that all races "bear marks which identify them as members of their race," it must follow, according to Park, that a certain human capacity for classification makes it impossible for races to come together without racial antagonism and prejudice. We shall attempt to show that this instinct hypothesis is too simple.

3   Cf. Ina Corine Brown, *National Survey of the Higher Education of Negroes*, J. S. Office of Education, Misc. No. 6, Vol. I, pp. 4–8.

4   As early as 1455 Pope Nicholas V had granted the Portuguese exclusive right to their discoveries on the African coast, but the commercial purpose here was still very much involved with the crusading spirit.

5   In a discussion of the arguments over slavery during the Constitutional Convention, Charles A. Beard observes: "South Carolina was particularly determined, and gave northern representatives to understand that if they wished to secure their commercial privileges, they must make concessions to the slave trade. And they were met half way. Ellsworth said: 'As slaves multiply so fast in Virginia and Maryland that it is cheaper to raise than import them, whilst in the sickly rice swamps foreign supplies are necessary, if we go no farther than is urged, we shall be unjust towards South Carolina and Georgia. Let us not intermeddle. As population increases, poor laborers will be so plenty as to render slaves useless.'" *An Economic Interpretation of the Constitution*, p. 177. Quote from Max Farrand, *Records*, Vol. II, p.371.

6   In a discussion of the labor situation among the early Spanish colonists in America, Professor Bailey W. Diffie observes: "One Negro was reckoned as worth two, four, or even more Indians at work production." *Latin American Civilization*, p. 206.

7   Francis Augustus MacNutt describes the relationship in Hispaniola: "Columbus laid tribute upon the entire population of the island which required that each Indian above fourteen years of age who lived in the mining provinces was to pay a little bell filled with gold every three months; the natives of all other provinces were to pay one *arroba* of cotton. These amounts were so excessive that in 1496 it was found necessary to change the nature of the payments, and, instead of the gold and cotton required from the villages, labour was substituted, the Indians being required to lay out and work the plantations of the colonists in their vicinity." *Bartholomew De Las Casas*, p. 25.

8   Quoted by E. D. Morel, *The Black Man's Burden*, p. 30.

9   In our description of the uses of race prejudice in this essay we are likely to give the impression that race prejudice was always "manufactured" in full awareness by individuals or groups of entrepreneurs. This, however, is not quite the case. Race prejudice, from its inception, became part of the social heritage, and as such both exploiters and exploited for the most part are born heirs to it. It is possible that most of those who propagate and defend race prejudice are not conscious of its fundamental motivation. To paraphrase Adam Smith: They who teach and finance race prejudice are by no means such fools as the majority of those who believe and practice it.

10   Francis Augustus MacNutt, *Bartholomew De las Casas*, p. 83.

     It should be kept clearly in view that this colonial movement was not a transference of the feudal manorial economy to America. It was the beginning of an entirely different economic enterprise – the dawn of colonial capitalism, the moving out of "white" capital into the lands of colored peoples who had to be exploited unsentimentally and with any degree of ruthlessness in the interest of profits.

11   *Rudyard Kipling's Verse, 1885–1926*, p. 320.

12   Josef W. Hall (Upton Close), *The Revolt of Asia*, p. 4. In this early period there was a more or less conscious development of the exploitative system. In later years, however, the infants that were born into the developed society had, of course, to take it as they found it. The social system determined their behavior *naturally*; that is to say, the racial exploitation and racial antagonisms seemed natural and the *conscious* element frequently did not exist. In other words, the racial fate of the individual was determined before he was born.

13   See a popular discussion relative to this by Hewlett Johnson, *The Soviet Power*, Book V; Bernhard J. Stern, "Soviet Policy on national Minorities," *American Sociological Review*, June 1944, pp. 229–35, and particularly Joseph Stalin, *Marxism and the National Question*.

14   *Warning to the West*, p. 274.

15   Pearl S. Buck likes to repeat the fact that "we differ in one important regard from the peoples of Asia. Race has never been a cause for any division among those people. But race prejudice divides us deeply." "The Spirit Behind the Weapon," *Survey Graphic*, Vol. XXXI, No. 11, November 1942, p. 540.

     In a broad historical description of this process Leonard Woolf says: "In no other period of the world's history has there been such a vast revolution as the conquest of Asia and Africa by Europe. . . . Until very nearly the end of the nineteenth century, Europeans themselves regarded it with complacent pride as one of the chief blessings and glories of Western Civilization. The white race of Europe, they held, was physically, mentally, and morally superior to all other races; and God, with infinite wisdom and goodness, had created it and developed it so that it might be ready, during the reign of Queen Victoria in England, to take over and manage the affairs of all other people on earth and teach them to be, in so far as that was possible for natives and heathens, good Europeans and good Christians. Indeed, until the very end of the century, the natives and heathens themselves seemed to acquiesce in this view of the designs of providence and the blessings of being ruled by Europeans. It is true that in almost every case originally a considerable number of Africans and Asiatics had to be killed before the survivors were prepared to accept the domination or, as it was called, protection of the European State; but once the domination was established there were few revolts against European rule which could not be met with a punitive expedition." *Imperialism and Civilisation*, New York, 1928, pp.15–16.

16   And we should expect that all peoples of color will be gratified and inspired by this kind of accomplishment. It tends to restore their self-respect as nothing else can. "When the white man began his series of retreats before the yellow hordes," Krishnalal Shridharani writes, "it was soothing balm to the ancient wounds of Asia. More than any Japanese words the Japanese deeds made propaganda. The white man, the most hated creature in Asia, was put to flight at Hong Kong, in Malaya, in Burma, and above all at Singapore." *Warning to the West*, New York, 1942, p. 196.

Dr. Sun Yat-sen finds inspiration for all the colored peoples in Asia in the exploits of Japan. "Japan," he says, "is a good model for us, if we wish for prosperity of China. . . . Formerly it was thought that of all the people in the world only the whites were intelligent and gifted"; but today Japan has shown all this to be false and hope has returned to the peoples of Asia. *Le Triple Demisme*, French trans. By Pascal M. D'Elia, pp. 20–21.

One fairly widely read East Indian, P. S. Joshi, puts it in this way: "The whiteism steps an insane dance in all the continents of the world. There are in Asia only a handful of whites . . . . Still they have, by reason of their political might, introduced the colour bar in India, China, the Philippines and other countries. Had not Japan been triumphant over Russia, had not white prestige suffered a severe blow, the same colour bar would have spread . . . throughout the continent of Asia." *The Tyranny of Colour*, p. 4.

17   Raymond Kennedy emphasizes the point that in the belief of racial superiority the confidence in superior might is elemental. Thus he writes: "The European peoples were enabled, some four hundred years ago, to extend conquest over the entire 'native' world. The 'natives,' who were just as good, man for man, as the Europeans, lacked the superior material equipment of the latter, and were either slaughtered or subjugated. The possessors of guns came to believe that they were also possessors of superior racial endowments, and attributed their success not to material advantages, but to innate mental and physical superiority. They were white and the beaten peoples mostly black, brown, yellow, and red; consequently inferiority must be linked with color and race." *The Ageless Indies*, pp. 185–86. To the same effect see Leonard Woolf, op. cit, p. 12.

Lin Yutang puts the idea in his own way: "How did nineteenth century imperialism begin, and how did the white man go about conquering the world, and what made him think he was superior to other peoples? Because the white man had guns and the Asiatics had none. The matter was as simple as that." And he brings the argument up to date: "China will never . . . be accorded true equality until she is like Japan, twenty years from now, when she can build her own tanks and guns and battleships. When that time comes, there will be no need to argue about equality, such being the standards of the modern age." *Between Tears and Laughter*, pp. 21, 4.

18   In reporting on social conditions in China, Theodore H. White says: "No one can understand China today . . . who does not understand the hatred and bitterness of the intelligent Chinese for the foreign businessman who treated him like a coolie in his own land. In some cities this foreigner closed the public parks to Chinese; on some boats Chinese were not allowed to ride first-class." See "Life Looks at China," *Life*, May, 1, 1944, p. 100. See also Nathaniel Peffer, *The White Man's Dilemma*, Chap. IX.

Chapter 5

W. E. B. Du Bois

THE CONSERVATION OF RACES

THE AMERICAN NEGRO HAS ALWAYS felt an intense personal interest in discussions as to the origins and destinies of races: primarily because back of most discussion of race with which he is familiar, have lurked certain assumptions as to his natural abilities, as to his political, intellectual and moral status, which he felt were wrong. He has, consequently, been led to deprecate and minimize race distinctions, to believe intensely that out of one blood God created all nations, and to speak of human brotherhood as though it were the possibility of an already dawning to-morrow.

Nevertheless, in our calmer moments we must acknowledge that human beings are divided into races; that in this country the two most extreme types of the world's races have met, and the resulting problem as to the future relations of these types is not only of intense and living interest to us, but forms an epoch in the history of mankind.

It is necessary, therefore, in planning our movements, in guiding our future development, that at times we rise above the pressing, but smaller questions of separate schools and cars, wage discrimination and lynch law, to survey the whole question of race in human philosophy and to lay, on a basis of broad knowledge and careful insight, those large lines of policy and higher ideals which may form our guiding lines and boundaries in the practical difficulties of every day. For it is certain that all human striving must recognize the hard limits of natural law, and that any striving, no matter how intense and earnest, which is against the consti-tution of the world, is vain. The question, then, which we must seriously consider is this: What is the real meaning of Race; what has, in the past, been the law of race development, and what lessons has the past history of race development to teach the rising Negro people?

When we thus come to inquire into the essential difference of races we find it hard to come at once to any definite conclusion. Many criteria of race differences have in the past been proposed, as color, hair, cranial measurements and language. And manifestly, in each of these respects, human beings differ widely. They vary in color, for instance, from the marble-like pallor of the Scandinavian to the rich, dark brown of the Zulu, passing by the creamy Slav, the yellow Chinese, the light brown Sicilian and the brown Egyptian. Men vary, too, in the texture of hair from the obstinately straight hair of the Chinese to the obstinately tufted and frizzled hair of the Bushman. In measurement of heads, again, men vary; from the broad-headed Tartar to the medium-headed European and the narrow-headed Hottentot; or, again in language, from the highly-inflected roman tongue to the monosyllabic Chinese. All these physical characteristics are patent enough, and if they agreed with each other it would be very easy to classify mankind. Unfortunately for scientists, however, these criteria of race are most exasperatingly intermingled. Color does not agree with texture of hair, for many of the dark races have straight hair; nor does color agree with the breadth of the head, for the yellow Tartar has a broader head than the German; nor, again, has the science of language as yet succeeded in clearing up the relative authority of these various and contradictory criteria. The final word of science, so far, is that we have at least two, perhaps three, great families of human beings – the whites and Negroes, possibly the yellow race. That other races have arisen from the intermingling of the blood of these two. This broad division of the world's races which men like Huxley and Raetzel have introduced as more nearly true than the old five-race scheme of Blumenbach, is nothing more than an acknowledgement that, so far as purely physical characteristics are concerned, the differences between men do not explain all the differences of their history. It declares, as Darwin himself said, that great as is the physical unlikeness of the various races of men their likenesses are greater, and upon this rests the whole scientific doctrine of Human Brotherhood.

Although the wonderful developments of human history teach that the grosser physical differences of color, hair and bone go but a short way toward explaining the different roles which groups of men have played in Human Progress, yet there are differences – subtle, delicate and elusive, though they may be – which have silently but definitely separated men into groups. While these subtle forces have generally followed the natural cleavage of common blood, descent and physical peculiarities, they have at other times swept across and ignored these. At all times, however, they have divided human beings into races, which, while they perhaps transcend scientific definition, nevertheless, are clearly defined to the eye of the Historian and Sociologist.

If this be true, then the history of the world is the history, not of individuals, but of groups, not of nations, but of races, and he who ignores or seeks to override the race idea in human history ignores and overrides the central thought of all history. What, then, is a race? It is a vast family of human beings, generally of common blood and language, always of common history, traditions and impulses, who are both voluntarily and involuntarily striving together for the accomplishment of certain more or less vividly conceived ideals of life.

Turning to real history, there can be no doubt, first, as to the widespread, nay, universal, prevalence of the race idea, the race spirit, the race ideal, and as to its efficiency as the vastest and most ingenious invention for human progress. We, who have been reared and trained under the individualistic philosophy of the

Declaration of Independence and the laisser-faire [*sic*] philosophy of Adam Smith, are loath to see and loath to acknowledge this patent fact of human history. We see the Pharaohs, Caesars, Toussaints and Napoleons of history and forget the vast races of which they were but epitomized expressions. We are apt to think in our American impatience, that while it may have been true in the past that closed race groups made history, that here in conglomerate America *nous avons changer tout cela* – we have changed all that, and have no need of this ancient instrument of progress. This assumption of which the Negro people are especially fond, cannot be established by a careful consideration of history.

We find upon the world's stage today eight distinctly differentiated races, in the sense in which History tells us the word must be used. They are, the Slavs of eastern Europe, the Teutons of middle Europe, the English of Great Britain and America, the Romance nations of Southern and Western Europe, the Negroes of Africa and America, the Semitic people of Western Asia and Northern Africa, the Hindoos of Central Asia and the Mongolians of Eastern Asia. There are, of course, other minor race groups, as the American Indians, the Esquimaux and the South Sea Islanders; these larger races, too, are far from homogeneous; the Slav includes the Czech, the Magyar, the Pole and the Russian; the Teuton includes the German, the Scandinavian and the Dutch; the English include the Scotch, the Irish and the conglomerate American. Under Romance nations the widely-differing Frenchman, Italian, Sicilian and Spaniard are comprehended. The term Negro is, perhaps, the most indefinite of all, combining the Mulattoes and Zamboes of America and the Egyptians, Bantus and Bushmen of Africa. Among the Hindoos are traces of widely differing nations, while the great Chinese, Tartar, Corean and Japanese families fall under the one designation – Mongolian.

The question now is: What is the real distinction between these nations? Is it the physical differences of blood, color and cranial measurements? Certainly we must all acknowledge that physical differences play a great part, and that, with wide exceptions and qualifications, these eight great races of to-day follow the cleavage of physical race distinctions; the English and Teuton represent the white variety of mankind; the Mongolian, the yellow; the Negroes, the black. Between these are many crosses and mixtures, where Mongolian and Teuton have blended into the Slav, and other mixtures have produced the Romance nations and the Semites. But while race differences have followed mainly physical race lines, yet no mere physical distinctions would really define or explain the deeper differences – the cohesiveness and continuity of these groups. The deeper differences are spiritual, psychical, differences – undoubtedly based on the physical, but infinitely transcending them. The forces that bind together the Teuton nations are, then, first, their race identity and common blood; secondly, and more important, a common history, common laws and religion, similar habits of thought and a conscious striving together for certain ideals of life. The whole process which has brought about these race differentiations has been a growth, and the great characteristic of this growth has been the differentiation of spiritual and mental differences between great races of mankind and the integration of physical differences.

The age of nomadic tribes of closely related individuals represents the maximum of physical differences. They were practically vast families, and there were as many groups as families. As the families came together to form cities the physical differences lessened, purity of blood was replaced by the requirement of comicile, and all who lived within the city bound became gradually to be regarded as members of the group; *i.e.*, there was a slight and slow breaking down of physical barriers. This, however, was accompanied by an increase of the spiritual and social differences between cities. This city became husbandmen, this, merchant, another warriors, and so on. The *ideals of life* for which the different cities struggled were different. When at last cities began to coalesce into nations there was another breaking down of barriers which separated groups of men. The larger and broader differences of color, hair and physical proportions were not by any means ignored, but myriads of minor differences disappeared, and the sociological and historical races of men began to approximate the present division of races as indicated by physical researches. At the same time the spiritual and physical differences of race groups which constituted the nations became deep and decisive. The English nation stood for constitutional liberty and commercial freedom; the German nation for science and philosophy; the Romance nations stood for literature and art, and the other race groups are striving, each in its own way, to develop for civilization its particular message, its particular ideal, which shall help to guide the world nearer and nearer that perfection of human life for which we all long, that

"one far off Divine event."

This has been the function of race differences up to the present time. What shall be its function in the future? Manifestly some of the great races of today – particularly the Negro race – have not as yet given to civilization the full spiritual message which they are capable of giving. I will not say that the Negro race has yet given no message to the world, for it is still a mooted question among scientists as to just how far Egyptian civilization was Negro in its origin; if it was not wholly Negro, it was certainly very closely allied. Be that as it may, however, the fact still remains that the full, complete Negro message of the whole Negro race has not as yet been given to the world: that the messages and ideal of the yellow race have not been completed, and that the striving of the mighty Slavs has but begun. The question is, then: How shall this message be delivered; how shall these various ideals be realized? The answer is plain: By the development of these race groups, not as individuals, but as races. For the development of Japanese genius, Japanese literature and art, Japanese spirit, only Japanese, bound and welded together, Japanese inspired by one vast ideal, can work out in its fullness the wonderful message which Japan has for the nations of the earth. For the development of Negro genius, of Negro literature and art, of Negro spirit, only Negroes bound and welded together, Negroes inspired by one vast ideal, can work out in its fullness the great message we have for humanity. We cannot reverse history; we are subject to the same natural laws as other races and if the Negro is ever to be a factor in the world's history – if among the gaily-colored banners that deck the broad ramparts of civilization is to hang one uncompromising black, then it must be placed there by black hands, fashioned by black heads and hallowed by the travail of 200,000,000 black hearts beating in one glad song of jubilee.

For this reason, the advance guard of the Negro people – the 8,000,000 people of Negro blood in the United States of America – must soon come to realize that if they are to take their just place in the van of Pan-Negroism, then their destiny is *not* absorption by the white Americans. That if in America it is to be proven for the first time in the modern world that not only Negroes are capable of evolving individual men like Toussaint, the Saviour, but are a nation stored with wonderful possibilities of culture, then their destiny is not a servile imitation of Anglo-Saxon culture, but a stalwart originality which shall unswervingly follow Negro ideals.

It may, however, be objected here that the situation of our race in America renders this attitude impossible; that our sole hope of salvation lies in our being able to lose our race identity in the commingled blood of the nation; and that any other course would merely increase the friction of races which we call race prejudice, and against which we have so long and so earnestly fought.

Here, then, is the dilemma, and it is puzzling one, I admit. No Negro who has given earnest thought to the situation of his people in America has failed, at some time in life, to find himself at these cross-roads; has failed to ask himself at some time: What, after all, am I? Am I an American or am I a Negro? Can I be both? Or is it my duty to cease to be a Negro as soon as possible and be an American? If I strive as a Negro, am I not perpetuating the very cleft that threatens and separates Black and White America? Is not my only possible practical aim the subduction of all that is Negro in me to the American? Does my black blood place upon me any more obligation to assert my nationality than German, or Irish or Italian blood would?

It is such incessant self-questioning and the hesitation that arises from it, that is making the present period a time of vacillation and contradiction for the American Negro; combined race action is stifled, race responsibility is shirked, race enterprises languish, and the best blood, the best talent, the best energy of the Negro people cannot be marshalled to do the bidding of the race. They stand back to make room for every rascal and demagogue who chooses to cloak his selfish deviltry under the veil of race pride.

Is this right? Is it rational? Is it good policy? Have we in America a distinct mission as a race – a distinct sphere of action and an opportunity for race development, or is self-obliteration the highest end to which Negro blood dare aspire?

If we carefully consider what race prejudice really is, we find it, historically, to be nothing but the friction between different groups of people; it is the difference in aim, in feeling, in ideals of two different races; if, now, this difference exists touching territory, laws, language, or even religion, it is manifest that these people cannot live in the same territory without fatal collision; but if, on the other hand, there is substantial agreement in laws, language and religion; if there is a satisfactory adjustment of economic life, then there is no reason why, in the same country and on the same street, two or three great national ideals might not thrive and develop, that men of different races might not strive together for their race ideals as well, perhaps even better, than in isolation. Here, it seems to me, is the reading of the riddle that puzzles so many of us. We are Americans, not only by birth and by citizenship, but by our political ideals, our language, our religion. Farther than that, our Americanism does not go. At that point, we are Negroes, members of a vast historic race that from the very dawn of creation has slept, but half awakening in the dark forests of its African fatherland. We are the first fruits of this new nation, the harbinger of that black to-morrow which is yet destined to soften the whiteness of the Tuetonic to-day. We are that people whose subtle sense of song has given America its only American music, its only American fairy tales, its only touch of pathos and humor amid its mad money-getting plutocracy. As such, it is our duty to conserve our physical powers, our intellectual endowments, our spiritual ideals; as a race we must strive by race organization, by race solidarity, by race unity to the realization of that broader humanity which freely recognizes differences in men, but sternly deprecates inequality in their opportunities of development.

For the accomplishment of these ends we need race oganizations: Negro colleges, Negro newspapers, Negro business organizations, a Negro school of literature and art, and an intellectual clearing house, for all these products of the Negro mind, which we may call a Negro Academy. Not only is all this necessary for positive advance, it is absolutely imperative for negative defense. Let us not deceive ourselves at our situation in this country. Weighted with a heritage of moral iniquity from our past history, hard pressed in the economic world by foreign immigrants and native prejudice, hated here, despised there and pitied everywhere; our one haven of refuge is ourselves, and but one means of advance, our own belief in our great destiny, our own implicit trust in our ability and worth. There is no power under God's high heaven that can stop the advance of eight thousand thousand honest, earnest, inspired and united people. But – and here is the rub – they *must* be honest, fearlessly criticising their own faults, zealously correcting them; they must be *earnest*. No people that laughs at itself, and ridicules itself, and wishes to God it was anything but itself ever wrote its name in history; it *must* be inspired with the Divine faith of our black mothers, that out of the blood and dust of battle will march a victorious host, a mighty nation, a peculiar people, to speak to the nations of earth a Divine truth that shall make them free. And such a people must be united; not merely united for the organized theft of political spoils, not united to disgrace religion with whoremongers and ward-heelers; not united merely to protest and pass resolutions, but united to stop the ravages of consumption among the Negro people, united to keep black boys from loafing, gambling and crime; united to guard the purity of black women and to reduce that vast army of black prostitutes that is today marching to hell; and united in serious organizations, to determine by careful conference and thoughtful interchange of opinion the broad lines of policy and action for the American Negro.

This, is the reason for being which the American Negro Academy has. It aims at once to be the epitome and expression of the intellect of the black-blooded people of America, the exponent of the race ideals of one of the world's great races. As such, the Academy must, if successful, be

(a)   Representative in character.
(b)   Impartial in conduct.
(c)   Firm in leadership.

It must be representative in character; not in that it represents all interests or all factions, but in that it seeks to comprise something of the *best* thought, the most unselfish striving and the highest ideals. There are scattered in forgotten nooks and corners throughout the land, Negroes of some considerable training, of high minds, and high motives, who are unknown to their fellows, who exert far too little influence. These the Negro Academy should strive to bring into touch with each other and to give them a common mouthpiece.

The Academy should be impartial in conduct; while it aims to exalt the people it should aim to do so by truth – not by lies, by honesty – not by flattery. It should continually impress the fact upon the Negro people that they must not expect to have things done for them – they MUST DO FOR THEMSELVES; that they have on their hands a vast work of self-reformation to do, and that a little less complaint and whining, and a little more dogged work and manly striving would do us more credit and benefit than a thousand Force or Civil Rights bills.

Finally, the American Negro Academy must point out a practical path of advance to the Negro people; there lie before every Negro today hundreds of questions of policy and right which must be settled and which each one settles now, not in accordance with any rule, but by impulse or individual preference; for instance: What should be the attitude of Negroes toward the educational qualification for voters? What should be our attitude toward separate schools? How should we meet discriminations on railways and in hotels? Such questions need not so much specific answers for each part as a general expression of policy, and nobody should be better fitted to announce such a policy than a representative honest Negro Academy.

All this, however, must come in time after careful organization and long conference. The immediate work before us should be practical and have direct bearing upon the situation of the Negro. The historical work of collecting the laws of the United States and of the various States of the Union with regard to the Negro is a work of such magnitude and importance that no body but one like this could think of undertaking it. If we could accomplish that one task we would justify our existence.

In the field of Sociology an appalling work lies before us. First, we must unflinchingly and bravely face the truth, not with apologies, but with solemn earnestness. The Negro Academy ought to sound a note of warning that would echo in every black cabin in the land: *Unless we conquer our present vices they will conquer us*; we are diseased, we are developing criminal tendencies, and an alarmingly large percentage of our men and women are sexually impure. The Negro Academy should stand and proclaim this over the housetops, crying with Garrison: *I will not equivocate, I will not retreat a single inch, and I will be heard*. The Academy should seek to gather about it the talented, unselfish men, the pure and noble-minded women, to fight an army of devils that disgraces our manhood and our womanhood. There does not stand today upon God's earth a race more capable in muscle, in intellect, in morals, than the American Negro, if he will bend his energies in the right direction; if he will

> Burst his birth's invidious bar
> And grasp the skirts of happy chance,
> And breast the blows of circumstance,
> And grapple with his evil star.

In science and morals, I have indicated two fields of work for the Academy. Finally, in practical policy, I wish to suggest the following *Academy Creed*:

1   We believe that the Negro people, as a race, have a contribution to make to civilization and humanity, which no other race can make.

2   We believe it the duty of the Americans of Negro descent, as a body, to maintain their race identity until this mission of the Negro people is accomplished, and the ideal of human brotherhood has become a practical possibility.

3   We believe that, unless modern civilization is a failure, it is entirely feasible and practicable for two races in such essential political, economic and religious harmony as the white and colored people of America, to develop side by side in peace and mutual happiness, the peculiar contribution which each has to make to the culture of their common country.

4   As a means to this end we advocate, not such social equality between these races as would disregard human likes and dislikes, but such a social equilibrium as would, throughout all the complicated relations of life, give due and just consideration to culture, ability, and moral worth whether they be found under white or black skins

5   We believe that the first and greatest step toward the settlement of the present friction between the races – commonly called the Negro problem – lies in the correction of the immorality, crime and laziness among the Negroes themselves, which still remains as a heritage from slavery. We believe that only earnest and long continued efforts on our own part can cure these social ills.

6   We believe that the second great step toward a better adjustment of the relations between the races, should be a more impartial selection of ability in the economic and intellectual world, and a greater respect for personal liberty and worth, regardless of race. We believe that only earnest efforts on the part of the white people of this country will bring much needed reform in these matters.

7   On the basis of the foregoing declaration, and firmly believing in our high destiny, we, as American Negroes, are resolved to strive in every honorable way for the realization of the best and highest aims, for the development of strong manhood and pure womanhood, and for the rearing of a race ideal in America and Africa, to the glory of God and the uplifting of the Negro people.

Chapter 6

Gunnar Myrdal

RACIAL BELIEFS IN AMERICA

[. . .]

W
HEN THE NEGRO WAS FIRST ENSLAVED, his subjugation
was not justified in terms of his biological inferiority. Prior to the influences
of the Enlightenment, human servitude was taken as a much more unquestioned
element in the existing order of economic classes and social estates, since this way
of thinking was taken over from feudal and post-feudal Europe. The historical literature on this early period also records that the imported Negroes – and the captured
Indians – originally were kept in much the same status as the white indentured
servants.[1] When later the Negroes gradually were pushed down into chattel slavery
while the white servants were allowed to work off their bond, the need was
felt, in this Christian country, for some kind of justification above mere economic
expediency and the might of the strong. The arguments called forth by this need
were, however, for a time not biological in character, although they later easily
merged into the dogma of natural inequality. The arguments were broadly these;
that the Negro was a heathen and a barbarian, an outcast among the peoples of
the earth, a descendant of Noah's son Ham, cursed by God himself and doomed
to be a servant forever on account of an ancient sin.[2]

The ideas of the American Revolution added their influence to those of some
early Christian thinkers and preachers, particularly among the Quakers, in depre-
cating these arguments. And they gave an entirely new vision of society as it is
and as it ought to be. This vision was dominated by a radically equalitarian political morality and could not possibly include slavery as a social institution. The
philosophical ideas of man's natural rights merged with the Golden Rule of
Christianity, "Do unto others as you would have them do unto you."

How it actually looked in the minds of the enlightened slaveholders who played
a prominent role in the Revolution is well known, since they were under the urge

to intellectual clarity of their age, and in pamphlets, speeches, and letters frequently discussed the troubles of their conscience. Most of them saw clearly the inconsistency between American democracy and Negro slavery. To these men slavery was an "abominable crime," a "wicked cause," a "supreme misfortune," an "inherited evil," an "cancer in the body politic." Jefferson himself made several attacks on the institution of slavery, and some of them were politically nearly successful. Later in his life (1821) he wrote in his autobiography:

> . . . it was found that the public mind would not bear the proposition [of gradual emancipation], nor will it bear it even at this day. Yet the day is not far distant when it must bear it, or worse will follow. Nothing is more certainly written in the book of fate than that these people are to be free.[3]

It was among Washington's first wishes ". . . to see a plan adopted for the abolition of it [slavery]; but there is only one proper and effectual mode by which it can be accomplished and that is by legislative authority. . . ."[4]

Even in terms of economic usefulness slavery seemed for a time to be a decaying institution. Slave prices were falling. Public opinion also was definitely in motion. In the North where it was most unprofitable, slavery was abolished in state after state during this revolutionary era. Also Southern states took certain legislative steps against slave trade and relaxed their slave codes and their laws on manumission. It is probable that the majority of Americans considered Negro slavery to be doomed. But in the South the slaves represented an enormous investment to the slave owners, and the agricultural economy was largely founded on slave labor. When the Constitution was written, slavery had to be taken as an economic and political fact. It is, however, indicative of the moral situation in America at that time that the words "slave" and "slavery" were avoided. "Somehow," reflects Kelly Miller, "the fathers and fashioners of this basic document of liberty hoped that the reprobated institution would in time pass away when there should be no verbal survival as a memorial of its previous existence."[5]

In the first two decades of the nineteenth century, the Abolitionist movement was as strong in the South as in the North, if not stronger. A most fateful economic factor had, however, entered into the historical development, and it profoundly changed the complexion of the issue. Several inventions in the process of cotton manufacture, and principally Eli Whitney's invention of the cotton gin in 1794, transformed Southern agriculture. Increased cotton production and its profitability gave impetus to a southward and westward migration from the old liberal Upper South, and raised the prices of slaves which had previously been declining.[6]

In explaining the ensuing ideological reaction in the South we must not forget, however, that the revolutionary movement, typified by the Declaration of Independence, represented a considerable over-exertion of American liberalism generally, and that by the time of the writing of the Constitution a reaction was on its way. In Europe after the Napoleonic Wars a reaction set in, visible in all countries and in all fields of culture. The North released itself rather completely from the influences of the European reaction. The South, on the contrary, imbibed it and continued on an accentuated political and cultural reaction even when the

European movement had turned again toward liberalism. Around the 1830's, the pro-slavery sentiment in the South began to stiffen. During the three decades leading up to the Civil War, an elaborate ideology developed in defense of slavery. This Southern ideology was contrary to the democratic creed of the Old Virginia statesmen of the American Revolution.

The pro-slavery theory of the *ante-bellum* South is basic to certain ideas, attitudes, and policies prevalent in all fields of human relations even at the present time. The central theme in the Southern theory is the moral and political dictum that slavery did not violate the "higher law," that it was condoned by the Bible and by the "laws of nature," and that "free society," in contrast, was a violation of those laws.

More and more boldly as the conflict drew nearer, churchmen, writers, and statesmen of the South came out against the principle of equality as formulated in the Declaration of Independence. This principle came to be ridiculed as a set of empty generalities and meaningless abstractions. Common experience and everyday observation showed that it was wrong. Indeed, it was "exuberantly false, and arborescently fallacious":

> Is it not palpably nearer the truth to say that no man was ever born free and no two men were ever born equal, than to say that all men are born free and equal? . . . Man is born to subjection. . . . The proclivity of the natural man is to domineer or to be subservient.[7]

Here we should recall that Jefferson and his contemporaries, when they said that men were equal, had meant it primarily in the moral sense that they should have equal rights, the weaker not less than the stronger.[8] This was fundamentally what the South denied. So far as the Negroes were concerned, the South departed radically from the American Creed. Lincoln later made the matter plain when he observed that one section of the country thought slavery was *right* while the other held it to be *wrong*.

The militant Northern Abolitionists strongly pressed the view that human slavery was an offense against the fundamental moral law. Their spiritual ground was puritan Christianity and the revolutionary philosophy of human rights. They campaigned widely, but most Northerners – sensing the dynamite in the issue and not liking too well the few Negroes they had with them in the North – kept aloof. In the South the break from the unmodified American Creed continued and widened. Free discussion was effectively cut off at least after 1840. Around this central moral conflict a whole complex of economic and political conflicts between the North and the South grew up. The most bloody contest in history before the First World War became inevitable. De Tocqueville's forecast that the abolition of slavery would not mean the end of the Negro problem came true. It is with the American nation today, and it is not likely to be settled tomorrow.

It should be observed that in the pro-slavery thinking of the *ante-bellum* South, the Southerners stuck to the American Creed *as far as whites were concerned*; in fact, they argued that slavery was necessary in order to establish equality and liberty for the whites. In the precarious ideological situation – where the South wanted to defend a political and civic institution of inequality which showed increasingly great prospects for new land exploitation and commercial profit, but where they also wanted to retain the democratic creed of the nation – *the race doctrine of biological inequality between whites and Negroes offered the most convenient solution.*[9] The logic forcing the static and conservative ideology of the South to base itself partly on a belief in natural inequality is parallel but opposite to the tendency of the original philosophy of Enlightenment in Europe and the American Revolution to evolve a doctrine of natural equality in order to make room for progress and liberalism.[10]

[. . .] After the War and Emancipation, the race dogma was retained in the South as necessary to justify the caste system which succeeded slavery as the social organization of Negro–white relations. In fact, it is probable that racial prejudice increased in the South at least up to the end of reconstruction and probably until the beginning of the twentieth century.[11]

The North never had cleansed its own record in its dealing with the Negro even if it freed him and gave him permanent civil rights and the vote. In the North, however, race prejudice was never so deep and so widespread as in the South. During and after the Civil War it is probable that the North relaxed its prejudices even further. But Reconstruction was followed by the national compromise of the 1870s when the North allowed the South to have its own way with the Negroes in obvious contradiction to what a decade earlier had been declared to be the ideals of the victorious North and the polity of the nation. The North now also needed the race dogma to justify its course. As the North itself did not retreat from most of the Reconstruction legislation, and as the whole matter did not concern the average Northerner so much, the pressure on him was not hard, and the belief in racial inequality never became intense. But this period was, in this field, one of reaction in the North, too.

The fact that the same rationalizations are used to defend slavery and caste is one of the connecting links between the two social institutions. In the South the connection is psychologically direct. Even today the average white Southerner really uses the race dogma to defend not only the present caste situation but also *ante-bellum* slavery and, consequently, the righteousness of the Southern cause in the Civil War. This psychological unity of defense is one strong reason, among others, why the generally advanced assertion is correct that the slavery tradition is a tremendous impediment in the way of improvement of the Negro's lot. The caste system has inherited the defense ideology of slavery.

The partial exclusion of the Negro from American democracy, however, has in no way dethroned the American Creed. This faith actually became strengthened by the victorious War which saved the Union and stopped the Southerners from publicly denouncing the cherished national principles that all men are born equal and have inalienable civil rights. The question can be asked: What do the millions of white people in the South and in the North actually think when, year after year, on the national holidays dedicated to the service of the democratic ideals, they read, recite, and listen to the Declaration of Independence and the Constitution? Do they or do they not include Negroes among "all men"? The same question is raised when we observe how, in newspaper editorials and public speeches, unqualified and general statements are made asserting the principles and the fact of American democracy. Our tentative answer is this: In solemn moments, Americans try to forget about the Negroes as about other worries. If this is not possible they think in vague and irrational terms; in these terms the idea of the Negroes' biological inferiority is a nearly necessary rationalization.

The dogma of racial inequality may, in a sense, be regarded as a strange fruit of the Enlightenment. The fateful word *race* itself is actually not yet two hundred years old. The biological ideology had to be utilized as an intellectual explanation of, and a moral apology for, slavery in a society which went out emphatically to invoke as its highest principles the ideals of the inalienable rights of all men to freedom and equality of opportunity. It was born out of the conflict between an old harshly nonequalitarian institution – which was not, or perhaps in a short time could not be, erased – and the new shining faith in human liberty and democracy. Another accomplishment of early rationalistic Enlightenment had laid the theoretical basis for the racial defense of slavery; the recognition of *Homo sapiens* as only a species of the animal world and the emerging study of the human body and mind as biological phenomena. Until this philosophical basis was laid, racialism was not an intellectual possibility.

The influences from the American Creed thus had, and still have, a double-direction. On the one hand, the equalitarian Creed operates directly to suppress the dogma of the Negro's racial inferiority and to make people's thoughts more and more "independent of race, creed or color," as the American slogan runs. On the other hand, it indirectly calls forth the same dogma to justify a blatant exception to the Creed. The race dogma is nearly the only way out for a people so moralistically equalitarian, if it is not prepared to live up to its faith. A nation less fervently committed to democracy could, probably, live happily in a caste system with a somewhat less intensive belief in the biological inferiority of the subordinate group. *The need for race prejudice is, from this point of view, a need for defense on the part of the Americans against their own national creed, against their own most cherished ideals.* And race prejudice is, in this sense a function of equalitarianism. The former is a perversion of the latter.[12]

[. . .] This split in the American soul has been, and still is, reflected in scientific thought and in the literature on the Negro race and its characteristics. Thomas Jefferson, the author of the Declaration of Independence and the supreme exponent of early American liberalism, in his famous *Notes on Virginia* (1781–1782) deals with the Negro problem in a chapter on "The Administration of Justice and the Description of the Laws." He posits his ideas about race as an argument for emancipating the slaves, educating them, assisting them to settle in Africa:

> Deep-rooted prejudices entertained by the whites; ten thousand recollections, by the blacks, of the injuries they have sustained; new provocations; the real distinctions which nature has made; and many other circumstances, will divide us into parties, and produce convulsions, which will probably never end but in the extermination of the one or the other race.[13]

He goes on to enumerate the "real distinctions" between Negroes and whites and gives a fairly complete list of them as they were seen by liberal people of his time:

color, hair form, secretion, less physiological need of sleep but sleepiness in work, lack of reasoning power, lack of depth in emotion, poverty of imagination and so on. In all these respects he is inclined to believe that "it is not their condition, then, but nature, which has produced the distinction." But he is cautious in tone, has his attention upon the fact that popular opinions are prejudiced, and points to the possibility that further scientific studies may, or may not, verify his conjectures.[14]

This guarded treatment of the subject marks a high point in the early history of the literature on Negro racial characteristics. In critical sense and in the reservation for the results of further research, it was not surpassed by white writers until recent decades. As the Civil War drew nearer, intellectuals were increasingly mobilized to serve the Southern cause and to satisfy the Southern needs for rationalization. After Reconstruction their theories were taken over by the whole nation. Biology and ethnology were increasingly supplanting theology and history in providing justification for slavery and, later, caste. Even the friends of the Negroes assumed great racial differences, even if, out of charity, they avoided elaborating on them. The numerous enemies of the Negro left a whole crop of pseudo-scientific writings in the libraries, emphasizing racial differences. Robert W. Shufeldt's book, *America's Greatest Problem: the Negro*[15] which had considerable influence for a time – illustrating the inferiority argument by a picture of a Negro lad between two monkeys and filled with an imposing mass of presumed evidences for Negro inferiority – is a late example of this literature at its worst.[16]

Without much change this situation continued into the twentieth century. At this time the heavily prejudiced position of science on the race problem was, however, beginning to be undermined. Professor Franz Boas and a whole school of anthropologists had already come out against these arguments for racial differences based on the primitive people's lack of culture.[17] The outlines of a radically environmentalistic sociology were being drawn by W. G. Sumner, W. I. Thomas and C. H. Cooley. The early research on intelligence pronounced that there were considerable racial differences but it had already encountered some doubts as to validity.[18] Improved techniques in the fields of anatomy and anthropometry had begun to disprove earlier statements on Negro physical traits.[19]

The last two or three decades have seen a veritable revolution in scientific thought on the racial characteristics of the Negro. This revolution has actually a much wider scope: it embraces not only the whole race issue even outside the Negro problem, but the fundamental assumptions on the nature–nurture question. The social sciences in America, and particularly sociology, anthropology, and psychology,[20] have gone through a conspicuous development, increasingly giving the preponderance to environment instead of to heredity.

In order to retain a proper perspective on this scientific revolution, we have to recall that American social science is not many decades old. The biological sciences and medicine, firmly entrenched much earlier in American universities, had not, and have not yet, the same close ideological ties to the American Creed. They have been associated in America, as in the rest of the world, with conservative and even reactionary ideologies.[21] Under their long hegemony, there has been a tendency to assume biological causation without question, and to accept social explanations only under the duress of a siege of irresistible evidence. In political questions, this tendency favored a do-nothing policy. This tendency also, in the main, for a century and more, determined people's attitudes toward the racial traits of the Negro. In the years around the First World War, it exploded in a cascade of scientific and popular writings[22] with a strong racialistic bias, rationalizing the growing feeling in America against the "new" immigrants pouring into the country whose last frontier was now occupied and congregating in the big cities where they competed with American labor. In addition to the social friction they created, the idea that these newcomers represented an inferior stock provided much of the popular theory for the restrictive immigration legislation.[23]

The wave of racialism for a time swayed not only public opinion but also some psychologists who were measuring psychic traits, especially intelligence, and perhaps also some few representatives of related social sciences.[24] But the social sciences had now developed strength and were well on the way toward freeing themselves entirely from the old biologistic tendency. The social sciences received an impetus to their modern development by reacting against this biologistic onslaught. They fought for the theory of environmental causation. Their primary object of suspicion became more and more the old static entity, "human nature," and the belief that fundamental differences between economic, social, or racial groups were due to "nature."

From the vantage point of their present research front, the situation looks somewhat like this: a handful of social and biological scientists over the last fifty years have gradually forced informed people to give up some of the more blatant of our biological errors. But there must be still other countless errors of the same sort that no living man can yet detect, because of the fog within which our type of Western culture envelops us. Cultural influences have set up the assumptions about the mind, the body, and the universe with which we begin; pose the questions we ask; influence the facts we seek; determine the interpretation we give these facts; and direct our reaction to these interpretations and conclusions.

Social research has thus become militantly critical. It goes from discovery to discovery by challenging this basic assumption in various areas of life. It is constantly disproving inherent differences and explaining apparent ones in cultural and social terms. By inventing and applying ingenious specialized research methods, the popular race dogma is being victoriously pursued into every corner and effectively exposed as fallacious or at least unsubstantiated. So this research becomes truly revolutionary in the spirit of the cherished American tradition. A contrast is apparent not only in comparison with earlier strands of American social science but also with contemporary scientific trends in other countries. The democratic ones have, on the whole, followed a similar course, but America has been leading. It is interesting to observe how on this point the radical tendency in American social research of today dominates even the work and writings of scientists who feel and pronounce their own political inclination to be conservative.

What has happened is in line with the great traditions of the American Creed, the principles of which are themselves, actually, piecemeal becoming substantiated by research and elaborated into scientific theory. American social scientists might – in a natural effort to defend their objectivity – dislike this characterization, but to the outsider it is a simple and obvious fact that the social sciences in America at present have definitely a spirit in many respects reminiscent of eighteenth century

Enlightenment. The ordinary man's ideas have not, however, kept up to those of the scientist. Hardly anywhere else or in any other issue is there – in spite of intensive and laudable efforts to popularize the new results of research – such a wide gap between scientific thought and popular belief. At least potentially these ideas have, however, a much greater importance in America than could be assumed upon casual observation and for the reason that the ordinary American has a most honored place in his heart for equalitarianism.

This trend in social sciences to discount earlier notions of great differences in "nature" between the advantaged and the disadvantaged groups (rich–poor, men–women, whites–Negroes) runs parallel to another equally conspicuous trend in American political ideology since the First World War: an increased interest and belief in social reforms. The latter trend broke through in the course of the Great Depression following the crisis of 1920; and it materialized in the New Deal, whose principles, even if not methods, are now widely accepted. We have already stressed the strategic importance for political liberalism and radicalism of the modern social science point of view on the basic problem of nurture *versus* nature. The scientific trend in non-democratic countries during the same period – and specifically the sway of racialism over German universities and research centers under the Nazi regime – provides a contrast which vividly illustrates our thesis.

As always, we can, of course, assume that basically both the scientific trend and the political development in a civilization are functions of a larger synchronized development of social ideology. A suspicion is, then, natural that fundamentally the scientific trend in America is a rationalization of changed political valuations. This trend has, however, had its course during a remarkable improvement of observation and measurement techniques and has been determined by real efforts to criticize research methods and the manner in which scientific inferences are made from research data. It has, to a large extent, been running against expectation and, we may assume, wishes. This is the general reason why, in spite of the natural suspicion, we can feel confident that the scientific trend is, on the whole, a definite approach toward objective truth.

[. . .] Our characterization of the race dogma as a reaction against the equalitarian Creed of revolutionary America is a schematization too simple to be exact unless reservations are added. Undoubtedly the low regard for the Negro people before the eighteenth century contained intellectual elements which later could have been recognized as a racial theory in disguise. The division of mankind into whites, blacks, and yellows stretches back to ancient civilization. A loose idea that barbarism is something inherent in certain peoples is equally old. On the other hand, the masses of white Americans even today do not always, when they refer to the inferiority of the Negro race, think clearly in straight biological terms.

The race dogma developed gradually. The older Biblical and socio-political arguments in defense of slavery retained in the South much of their force long beyond the Civil War. Under the duress of the ideological need of justification for Negro slavery, they were even for a time becoming increasingly elaborated. Their decline during recent decades is probably a result of the secularization and urbanization of the American people, which in these respects, as in so many others,

represents a continuation of the main trend begun by the revolutionary ideological impulses of the eighteenth century. In this development, the biological
inferiority dogma threatens to become the lone surviving ideological support of
color caste in America.

In trying to understand how ordinary white people came to believe in the
Negro's biological inferiority, we must observe that there was a shift from theological to biological thinking after the eighteenth century. As soon as the idea was
spread that man belongs to the biological universe, the conclusion that the Negro
was *biologically* inferior was natural to the unsophisticated white man. It is obvious
to the ordinary unsophisticated white man, from his everyday experience, that the
Negro is inferior. *And inferior the Negro really is*; so he shows up even under scientific study. He is, on the average, poorer; his body is more often deformed; his
health is more precarious and his mortality rate higher; his intelligence performance, manners, and morals are lower. The *correct* observation that the Negro is
inferior was tied up to the *correct* belief that man belongs to the biological universe,
and, by twisting logic, the *incorrect* deduction was made that the inferiority is
biological in nature.

Race is a comparatively simple idea which easily becomes applied to certain
outward signs of "social visibility," such as physiognomy. Explanations in terms of
environment, on the contrary, tax knowledge and imagination heavily. It is difficult for the ordinary man to envisage clearly how such factors as malnutrition, bad
housing, and lack of schooling actually deform the body and the soul of people.
The ordinary white man cannot be expected to be aware of such subtle influences
as the denial of certain outlets for ambitions, social disparagement, cultural isolation, and the early conditioning of the Negro child's mind by the caste situation,
as factors molding the Negro's personality and behavior. The white man is, therefore, speaking in good faith when he says that he sincerely believes that the Negro
is racially inferior, not merely because he has an interest in this belief, but simply
because he has seen it. He "knows" it.

Tradition strengthens this honest faith. The factors of environment were, to
the ordinary white man, still less of a concrete reality one hundred years ago when
the racial dogma began to crystallize. Originally the imported Negro slaves had
hardly a trace of Western culture. The tremendous cultural difference between
whites and Negroes was maintained[25] and, perhaps, relatively increased by the
Negroes being kept, first, in slavery and, later, in a subordinate caste, while
American white culture changed apace. By both institutions the Negroes' acculturation was hampered and steered in certain directions. The Negroes, moreover,
showed obvious differences in physical appearance.

From the beginning these two concomitant differences – the physical and the
cultural – must have been associated in the minds of white people. "When color
differences coincide with differences in cultural levels, then color becomes symbolic
and each individual is automatically classified by the racial uniform he wears."[26]
Darker color, woolly hair, and other conspicuous physical Negro characteristics
became steadily associated with servile status, backward culture, low intelligence
performance and lack of morals. All unfavorable reactions to Negroes – which for
social if not for biological reasons, are relatively much more numerous than favorable reactions – became thus easily attributed to *every* Negro as a Negro, that is,

to the *race* and to the individual only secondarily as a member of the race. Whites categorize Negroes. As has been observed also in other racial contacts, visible characteristics have a power to overshadow all other characteristics and to create an illusion of a greater similarity between the individuals of the out-race and greater difference from the in-race than is actually warranted.[27]

This last factor is the more important as the unsophisticated mind is much more "theoretical" – in the popular meaning of being bent upon simple, abstract, clear-cut generalizations – than the scientifically trained mind.[28] This works in favor of the race dogma. To conceive that apparent differences in capacities and aptitudes could be cultural in origin means a deferment of judgment that is foreign to popular thinking. It requires difficult and complicated thinking about a multitude of mutually dependent variables, thinking which does not easily break into the lazy formalism of unintellectual people.

We should not be understood, however, to assume that the simpler concept of race is clear in the popular mind. From the beginning, as is apparent from the literature through the decades, environmental factors to some extent, have been taken into account. But they are discounted, and they are applied in a loose way – partly under the influence of vulgarized pre-Darwinian and Darwinian evolutionism – to the race rather than to the individual. The Negro race is said to be several hundreds of thousands of years behind the white man in "development." Culture is then assumed to be an accumulated mass of memories *in the race*, transmitted through the genes. A definite biological ceiling is usually provided: the mind of the Negro race cannot be improved beyond a given level. This odd theory is repeated through more than a century of literature: it is phrased as an excuse by the Negro's friends and as an accusation by his enemies. The present writer has met it everywhere in contemporary white America.

Closely related to this popular theory is the historical and cultural demonstration of Negro inferiority already referred to. It is constantly pointed out as a proof of his racial backwardness that in Africa the Negro was never able to achieve a culture of his own. Descriptions of hideous conditions in Africa have belonged to this popular theory from the beginning. Civilization is alleged to be the accomplishment of the white race; the Negro, particularly, is without a share in it.

Notes and references

1   See, for example: John H. Russell, *The Free Negro in Virginia, 1619–1865* (1913); J. C. Ballagh, *A History of Slavery in Virginia* (1902); John C. Hurd, *The Law of Freedom and Bondage in the United States* (1858–1862).

2   A weak variation of this popular theory – weak because it looked forward only to temporary subordination of backward peoples – was that in making the Negroes slaves, white men were educating and Christianizing them. This variation is known as the "white men's burden" doctrine and played an especially important role in nineteenth century exploitation. For some statements of this doctrine, see W. O. Brown, "Rationalization of Race Prejudice," *The International Journal of Ethics* (April, 1933), pp. 299–301.

3   H. A. Washington (editor), *The Writings of Thomas Jefferson* (1859), Vol. 1, p. 49.

4   Letter to Robert Morris, dated April 12, 1786. Jones Viles (editor), *Letters and Addresses of George Washington* (1908), p. 285.

5   "Government and the Negro," *Annals of the Academy of Political and Social Science* (November, 1928), p. 99.

6   This materialistic explanation is not a new idea. It was already seen clearly by some in the *ante-bellum* South. George Fitzhugh, for example, writes:

   "Our Southern patriots, at the time of the Revolution, finding Negroes expensive and useless, became warm anti-slavery men. We, their wiser sons, having learned to make cotton and sugar, find slavery very useful and profitable, and think it a most excellent institution. We of the South advocate slavery, no doubt, from just as selfish notices as induce the Yankees and English to deprecate it."

   "We have, however, almost all human and divine authority on our side of the argument. The Bible nowhere condemns, and throughout recognises slavery."
   (*Sociology for the South* [1854], p. 269)

7   Chancellor William Harper, "Memoir on Slavery," paper read before the Society for the Advancement of Learning of South Carolina, annual meeting at Columbia, South Carolina, 1837 (1838), pp. 6–8.

8   This stress on moral equality has not been lost throughout the ages. T. J. Woofter, Jr., a representative of modern Southern liberalism, writes:

   "It is desirable frankly to recognize the differences as they actually exist, but there is absolutely no ethical justification for the assumption that an advantaged group has an inherent right to exploit and oppress, and the prejudice based upon the assumptions is the most vicious enemy to human peace and cooperation."
   (*Basis of Racial Adjustment* [1925], p. 11)

   Vance, another Southern liberal, writes:

   "In a field where doubts abound, let us make one sweeping statement. If biological inferiority of the whole Negro group were a proved fact, it would, nevertheless, be to the benefit of both white and black to behave as though it did not exist. Only in this way can the Section be sure of securing, in the economic sphere, the best of which both races are capable." (Rupert B. Vance,
   Human Geography of the South [1932], p. 463)

9   "Prejudice of any sort, racial or otherwise, is regarded as derogatory to intellectual integrity, incompatible with good taste, and perhaps morally reprehensible. Hence the prejudiced in order to be secure in their illusions of rationality, impeccable taste, and moral correctness find rationalizations essential. The rationlization inoculates against insights as to the real nature of one's reactions. It secures the individual in his moral universe. It satisfies his impulse to rationality. The mind thus becomes an instrument, a hand-maiden, of the emotions, supplying good reasons for prejudiced reaction in the realm of racial, class, or sectarian contacts." (Brown, *op. cit.*, p. 294).

10   In this connection it is interesting to note, as an example of how political reaction fosters racialism, that in the *ante-bellum* South racial thinking also turned toward beliefs in biological differences between whites. The legend was spread that the white Southerners were a "master race" of Norman blood while New England was settled by descendants of the ancient British and Saxon serfs. The Northerners and Southerners, it was said, "are the same men who cut each other's throats in England, under the name of Roundheads and Cavaliers." The Southerners were a Nordic race with greater capacity to rule. (See James Truslow Adams, *America's*

Tragedy [1934], pp. 95 ff, 121, and 128 ff.) A late example of this ideology will be found in a chapter entitled "The Tropic Nordics," of H. J. Eckenrode, *Jefferson Davis, President of the South* (1923). The present writer has on several occasions in conversation with Southerners met vague reminiscences of this popular theory, usually related to the myth that the South, unlike the North, was settled mainly by English aristocrats. The more common theory of Southern racial superiority nowadays is, however, simply the assertion that the white Southerners belong predominantly to "the pure Anglo-Saxon race," as the South has received so few immigrants in recent decades when these were recruited from other European countries. In addition, one often meets the idea that "the poor whites" and generally the lower classes of whites are racially inferior, as they descend from indentured servants.

11   Guion G. Johnson, "History of Racial Ideologies,' unpublished manuscript written for this study (1940). Vol. 1, pp. 149, *passim*; Vol. 2, pp. 331, *passim*.

12   The same principle operates also outside the Negro problem. The American Creed, in its demand for equality, has strong support from the very composition of the new nation. As immigrants, or the descendants of immigrants with diverse national origins, Americans have an interest – outside of the Negro problem – in emphasizing the importance of environment and in discounting inheritance. In order to give a human and not only political meaning to the legend *e pluribus unum*, they feel the need to believe in the possibility of shaping a new homogeneous nation out of the disparate elements thrown into the melting pot. This interest plays on a high level of valuations where the individual identifies himself with the destiny of the nation. In daily life, however, the actual and obvious heterogeneity in origin, appearance, and culture of the American people acts as a constant stimulus toward prejudiced racial beliefs.

Thus – even outside the Negro problem – there is in America a considerable ambivalence in people's thoughts on race. On a lower valuation level, there appears to be in America an extreme belief in and preoccupation with all sorts of racial differences, while on a higher level a contrary ideology rules, equally extreme when compared with more homogeneous nations. The former side of the American personality is responsible for much friction and racial snobbishness in social life. The latter side finds its expression not only in empty speeches – what the Americans call "lip-service" – but also in national legislation and in actual social trends.

13   H. A. Washington (editor), *The Writings of Thomas Jefferson* (1854), Vol. 8, pp. 380–381.

14   *ibid*, pp. 380 ff.

15   1915.

16   Concerning this literature, see G. G. Johnson, *op. cit.*, Vol. 1, pp. 149, *passim*, Vol. 2, pp. 250–258 and 311–338.

17   Much of the earliest literature of this sort is summarized in W. I. Thomas (editor), *Sourcebook for Social Origins* (1909).

18   Cooley challenged Galton's hereditary explanation of racial genius in 1897. (Charles H. Cooley, "Genius, Fame and the Comparison of Races," *Annals of the American Academy of Political and Social Science* [May, 1897], pp. 317–358); see Chapter 6, Section 3.

19   Several scientists, for example, had criticized much of the early research on brain and skull differences. One of the most notorious of the exposés was that of

Robert B. Bean by Franklin P. Mall. Bean was a Southern student of Mall's in the latter's laboratory at Johns Hopkins. In an elaborate study of Negro skulls and brains, he attempted to show that the skulls were smaller than the skulls of white men, and that the brains were less convoluted and otherwise deficient. After Bean published his findings (Robert B. Bean, "Some Racial Peculiarities of the Negro Brain," *American Journal of Anatomy* [September, 1906], pp. 27–432), Mall repeated the measurements on many of the same specimens and found that Bean had completely distorted his measurements and conclusions. (Franklin P. Mall, "On Several Anatomical Characters of the Human brain, Said to Vary According to Race and Sex, With Especial Reference to the Weight of the Frontal Lobe," *American Journal of Anatomy* [February, 1909], pp. 1–32). Bean's sample, too, was grossly inadequate; it consisted of 103 Negroes and 49 whites in the Baltimore morgue who had been unclaimed at death.

20   The change toward environmentalism in American psychology has been most radical in child psychology, psychiatry and educational psychology, applied psychology, "social psychology," and other branches which are in close relation to social practice and social science. Undoubtedly the biologistic approach has still a stronghold in academic psychology proper. But even there a change is under way which can be registered by comparing the present situation with the one prevalent two or three decades ago. An indication is the almost complete abandonment of the "instinct" psychology.

21   This connection between biology and conservatism will have to be remembered when explaining why, with some outstanding exceptions, the medical profession has, on the whole, in all countries, taken a rather reactionary stand on questions of social and health reforms.

22   Perhaps the most influential of the popular racialistic writers were: Madison Grant, *The Passing of the Great Race* (1916); Lothrop Stoddard, *The Rising Tide of Color* (1920); Charles W. Gould, *America, A Family Matter* (1920).

23   The acts restricting immigration not only cut down the total number of immigrants admitted to the country, but also provided that those allowed entrance should be predominantly from Western and Northern Europe. The 1921 act permitted an immigration from each country equal to 3 per cent of the number of foreign-born from that country resident in the United States in 1910. The 1924 act reduced the quota to 2 per cent and set the determining date back to 1890. Immigration from the orient was completely prohibited, but that from independent countries in the Americas and from Canada was not restricted at all.

24   As examples we may cite the following: Carl C. Brigham, an outstanding psychologist who has since repudiated his book (*A Study of American Intelligence* [1923]); William McDougall, the father of many trends in psychology (*The Group Mind* [1920], and *Is America Safe for Democracy?* [1921]); Albert Bushnell Hart and H. H. Bancroft, the eminent historians (*The Southern South* [1920], and *Retrospection, Political and Personal* [1912]).

25   When we say that cultural differences were maintained, we do not refer one way or the other to the retention of African culture.

26   Reuter, *The Mulatto in the United States*, pp. 99–100.

27   Edward K. Strong, *The Second-Generation Japanese Problem* (1934), p. 100. The classic statement on the difference between categoric and sympathetic contacts is that of Nathaniel S. Shaler, *The Neighbor* (1904), pp. 207–227.

28   The tendencies of unsophisticated thinking to be "theoretical" are worthy of much more study than they have been given hitherto. They can be illustrated from all spheres of human life. To give an example outside our problem: The most human concept, *bona fide*, in jurisprudence is a late juristical development in all civilizations; originally legal systems are formalistic and behavioristic (they do not consider people's intentions); *bona fide* is even today only the trained lawyer's way of thinking and has, as yet, never and nowhere really been understood by the mass of laymen whose thinking of legal matters always seems formalistic to the lawyer. Similarly the simple "economic laws" are thought-forms adhered to by business people when they speculate in this strange field, while the economic theorists, instead, devote their labor to criticising, demolishing, and complicating economic theory. It is the common man, *and not the statistician who* "thinks in averages," or, rather, in pairs of *contrasting types*: good–bad, healthy–sick, man–woman, white–black. And the common man is likely to handle averages and types as if they applied to the individuals. He will confidently tell you something about "all Negroes," in the same breath as he observes an exception.

He is, further, likely to construct his types without a thought as to sampling difficulties. He has a tendency to forget about range and spread. He has, of course, a pragmatic understanding that things and happenings have their causes. Otherwise he would not be able to get on with his several pursuits in a rational way. But particularly when it comes to social questions, causation becomes to the untrained mind divested of complications. Social causation is to him mostly monistic, direct, apparent and simple. The very idea of causal interrelations within a mutually dependent system of a great many factors is usually entirely absent. In his thoughts on social causation he mingles his ideas about what is right and wrong. The unsophisticated mind is not questioning; it answers questions before they are stated.

Generally speaking, it is a fact that "to think in concrete terms" when reaching for generalizations is the endeavor of theoretical training and a mark of the highest intelligence, while "theoretical," abstract and formalistic thinking is the common man's philosophy.

PART TWO

Sociology, race and social theory

INTRODUCTION

THE MATERIAL INCLUDED IN PART ONE has hopefully helped to provide some of the background to contemporary theoretical debates about race and racism. We move on in this part to an exploration of attempts to locate the issue of race within the bounds of social theory. As we saw in the previous part from the extracts by Du Bois and Myrdal this is not completely a recent phenomenon as such, and attempts to theorise about racial relations have been made throughout the twentieth century. Indeed the first extract that we have chosen to include in here is from Robert Park, one of the founding figures of the Chicago School of sociology, whose writings from the 1920s and 1930s continue to exercise the interest of contemporary scholars. Park's work was centrally concerned with the development of race relations in the United States, and particularly in the context of the complex social and cultural relations that developed in the major urban conurbations. In the extract included in this volume he reflects on the meaning of the notion of 'race relations', and in doing so he attempts to provide an overview of the key elements of his theoretical perspective. Park's writings on race are difficult to summarise but a recurrent concern in his writings is with the subjective dimensions of racial consciousness that help to produce the conditions for the emergence of racial conflict.

From the classic account of Park we move on to the critique of the idea of race that was developed by the anthropologist Ruth Benedict. Benedict's text was originally published in 1943 but it continues to influence contemporary scholarship on the relationship between race and racism. Written at a time when there was much public concern about Nazi racial theories Benedict's text was concerned to challenge ideas of racial supremacy and to provide a basis for a rigorous analysis of the idea of race and its various meanings. Although in some ways her work is very much linked to the period in which it was written, its main arguments are still an important point for reflection, particularly at a time when new discourses of race are coming forth from a variety of sources.

The next extract in this Part, by John Rex, is taken from one of his early works and reflects his first sustained attempt to outline the broad theoretical contours of his analysis of race relations. Rex's work over the years has been concerned with the need to locate the study of race relations on a firm theoretical footing and in this piece he sets out the main elements of his conceptual model. Drawing to some extent on the work of Max Weber as well as Robert Park, among others, he attempts to develop a theoretical model for the analysis of different patterns of race relations that could potentially be applied to a variety of national situations. An important concern in Rex's work, and certainly the one that has exercised the most influence on subsequent generations of students and scholars, is the need to link the analysis of race relations to class as well as other social processes. Although Rex has been a vociferous critic of the more reductionist elements of neo-Marxist theories of race and racism, he has also consistently argued for the need to examine the interrelationships between race and class based forms of social consciousness.

In contrast to Rex, the extract from Robert Miles can be seen as a rejection of the whole idea of developing a sociology of race or race relations. In its place he seeks to develop an analytical model that is based on a broadly neo-Marxist theoretical framework, although one that is quite distinct from that of earlier Marxists, such as Oliver Cox (see Part One). Miles is particularly concerned to expose what he sees as the limitations of the whole 'race relations problematic' and to highlight the need to move beyond the category of race in social analysis. Over the past two decades Miles has been one of the most productive scholars in this field and has attempted to outline key elements of his theory both in more conceptual as well as more empirical work. But a recurrent theme in his work, which is reflected in this extract, is the attempt to reject the language and analytical models of 'race relations' in favour of an analytical model that seeks to analyse the processes that produce 'racialised groups' in specific social and historical conditions. Perhaps the most important theme in his work is the need to analyse racism as an ideology which is produced by specific economic and social processes, such as the defence of domination, subordination and privilege.

The extracts from Stuart Hall and David Goldberg are examples of the shifting terms of theoretical debates in this field in the past decade. Hall's piece is a particularly fine example of a growing body of work that seeks to explore the changing dimensions of how identities are formed and reformed in multicultural societies. An important point of departure for Hall, and other writers who have followed in his footsteps, is a recognition that an analysis of race and ethnic relations in contemporary societies needs to recognise the diversity of subject positions that have been formed over time. From this there follows an emphasis on the need to see racial identities as constantly crossed and recrossed by the categories of gender, class and ethnicity. In this regard Hall's argument has much in common with important undercurrents in recent feminist theorising about race and gender (see in particular the contributions in Part Five).

David Goldberg's piece is concerned particularly with the questions of how racial knowledge is produced and reproduced. Goldberg's work is inspired by the need to understand the historical, social and cultural conditions that produce racial knowledge and lead to the articulation of racist ideas and practices. An important aspect of Goldberg's innovative account of these issues is the argument that we need to locate the role of specific kinds of racism within particular time periods as well as geographical spaces. In this respect his arguments can be seen as tied up with a concern to understand how ideas about race, and the role of specific racial identities, help to structure political institutions, social relationships and cultural processes.

The final extract, from Howard Winant, returns us to the underlying question that holds all the contributions to this part together, namely the theoretical status of the concept of race. In an impressively wide-ranging overview of important themes in current debates, Winant is particularly concerned to draw out some of the main limitations of current theoretical debates, especially in a global environment that is going through processes of rapid social and cultural transformation. In doing so he reminds us that whatever the intricacies of conceptual debates the mundane realities of everyday politics may force us to confront new dimensions of race and racism in years to come.

KEY QUESTIONS

- How does Robert Park's concept of the 'race relations cycle' explain the development of race and ethnic relations in cities?
- John Rex's work seeks to outline a model for a 'distinct field of race relations studies'. What are the key elements of his model and how successful is it?
- Robert Miles argues that race constitutes a notion that may be a common term of reference within everyday discourse but is not useful analytically. Why does he argue this and what are the consequences of his analysis?
- Stuart Hall argues that in contemporary societies we are seeing the development of new ethnicities that cannot be grounded in a set of fixed trans-cultural or transcendental racial categories. How does this argument help us to understand the changing patterns of race and ethnic relations in today's world?
- David Goldberg argues that racial identities have become increasingly ambivalent and ambiguous, and that they need to be contextualised in terms of time and space. How would you utilise this argument to analyse the changing forms of racial identity in contemporary societies?
- How do recent theories of racism explain the changing expressions of racial ideologies and movements in contemporary societies?

Chapter 7

Robert E. Park

THE NATURE OF RACE RELATIONS

R ACE RELATIONS, AS THAT TERM is defined in use and wont in the United States, are the relations existing between peoples distinguished by marks of racial descent, particularly when these racial differences enter into the consciousness of the individuals and groups so distinguished, and by so doing determine in each case the individual's conception of himself as well as his status in the community. Thus anything that intensifies race consciousness; anything, particularly if it is a permanent physical trait, that increases an individual's visibility and by so doing makes more obvious his identity with a particular ethnic unit or genetic group, tends to create and maintain the conditions under which race relations, as here defined, may be said to exist. Race consciousness, therefore, is to be regarded as a phenomenon, like class or caste consciousness, that enforces social distances. Race relations, in this sense, are not so much the relations that exist between individuals of different races as between individuals conscious of these differences.

Thus one may say, without doing injustice to the sense in which the term is ordinarily used, that there are, to be sure, races in Brazil – there are, for example, Europeans and Africans – but not race relations because there is in that country no race consciousness, or almost none. One speaks of race relations when there is a race problem, and there is no race problem in Brazil, or if there is, it is very little if at all concerned with the peoples of African and European origin.[1]

On the other hand, when one speaks of race relations and the race problem in South Africa one does not think of the African and the European. The African does, to be sure, constitute a problem, but in South Africa, it is described as the "native problem." South Africa has, also, the problem of the Cape Coloured, a hybrid people of mixed Hottentot and European origin. The native, as the term is there used, is a Bantu, and of a quite different racial origin than the "native." South Africa has, likewise, the problem of the East Indian. Hindus were first imported into Natal about 1860 in the interest of the sugar industry in that province. However, when one speaks or writes in common parlance of the race problem in South Africa, it is to the relations existing between the English and the native Dutch or Africanders that this expression refers.

In this context and in this sense the expression race relations seems to describe merely the sentiments and attitudes which racial contacts invariably provoke and for which there is, apparently, no more substantial basis than an existing state of the public mind. For the purpose of this chapter, however, the term has been employed in a somewhat wider universe of discourse, in which it includes all the relations that ordinarily exist between members of different ethnic and genetic groups which are capable of provoking race conflict and race consciousness or of determining the relative status of the racial groups of which a community is composed.

Race relations, in this more inclusive sense, might comprise, therefore, all those situations in which some relatively stable equilibrium between competing races has been achieved and in which the resulting social order has become fixed in custom and tradition.

Under such circumstances the intensity of the race consciousness which a struggle for status inevitably arouses, where it did not altogether disappear, would be greatly diminished. The biracial organizations of certain social institutions that have come into existence in Southern states since emancipation exhibit the form which such racial accommodations sometimes take. Some of these, as in the case of the churches and the labor organizations, seem to have grown up quite spontaneously and have been accepted by both races as offering a satisfactory *modus vivendi*. In other instances, as in the case of the public school, the segregation which such dual or biracial organizations necessitate, in spite of certain advantages they offer, has been bitterly opposed even when they have later been reluctantly accepted by the colored people. They were opposed (1) because of the discrimination they inevitable involve and (2) because the separation of the races in the schools as elsewhere has seemed to imply the acceptance of an inferior civic and social status.

All this suggests that the term *race relations*, as here conceived, includes relations which are not now conscious or personal, though they have been; relations which are fixed in and enforced by the custom, convention, and the routine of an expected social order of which there may be at the moment no very lively consciousness.

Historically, the races of mankind at different times and places have lived together in a wide variety of ways. They have lived over long periods of time in a relationship not unlike that existing between the plant and animal species occupying the same territory, that is to say, a relationship of biotic interdependence, without interbreeding. Under these conditions the different races, like the different species, have been able to maintain their integrity as distinct races while living in a form of association that might be described as symbiotic rather than social. Examples of this sort of symbiosis among human creatures are the gypsies of Western Europe or the Wild Tribes of India, particularly the so-called "Criminal Tribes."

On the other hand, other racial stocks, notably those that have fused to create the existing peoples of Europe, have lived together in an intimacy so complete that the original racial differences that once distinguished them have almost wholly disappeared, or at best can now only be clearly determined by the formal investigations of anthropologists. This is the case, for example, of the Germanic and Slavic tribes which, politically united by the conquests of the Markgraf of Brandenburg and the Teutonic Knights, in the thirteenth century, eventually fused to produce the Prussian people.[2]

Evidence of this modern instance of racial amalgamation are the occasional "racial islands," particularly in East Prussia, where, because the process of fusion has not been completed, some remnants of the Slavic peoples and their cultures still persist. Perhaps the most notable example of this incomplete amalgamation and assimilation is the existence, a short distance from Berlin, of an ancient Wendish folk, which still preserves it language and culture, and still cherishes a kind of tribal identity. They are called the *Spree-wälder*, i.e., the people of the Spree Forest, where they exist in the midst of a German population, as a kind of racial and cultural enclave.

There are, however, numerous examples of such isolated racial islands nearer home. There are, for example, the interesting little communities of Negro, Indian, and white mixed bloods, of which there are a great number scattered about in out-of-the-way corners of the Southern and Eastern estates. Perhaps the most notable of these is the community of white and Negro half-castes, living near Natchitoches, Louisiana, described by Lyle Saxon in his recently published novel, *Children of Strangers*.[3]

All these various and divergent types of isolated, and more or less outcast racial and cultural groups, have recently been classed, for the purposes of comparison and study, as minority groups, although the term as originally used acquired its meaning in a European rather than American context. Among these such sectarian and religious groups as the Amish of Eastern Pennsylvania, or the Mormons of Utah, have sometimes been included.

The classic examples of such racial minorities, however, are the Jewish communities in Europe and the Near East, where Jews have maintained, in spite of their very intimate association with other peoples, their racial identity and their ancient tribal religion.

All these relations of cultural or racial minorities with a dominant people may be described, for our purposes, as types of race relationship, even though no evidences exist either of active race conflict, on the one hand, or of obvious racial diversity on the other.

[. . .] In the modern world, and particularly outside of Europe, wherever race relations – or what, in view of the steadily increasing race mixture, we have called race relations – have assumed a character that could be described as problematic, such problems have invariably arisen in response to the expansion of European peoples and European civilization.

In the period of four hundred years and more since Vasco da Gama rounded the Cape of Good Hope and Columbus landed at San Salvador, European discoveries and European enterprise have penetrated to the most remote regions of the earth. There is nowhere now, it seems – either in the jungles of the Malayan peninsula or the remote islands of New Guinea – a primitive people that has not, directly or indirectly, come under the influence of European peoples and European culture.[4]

The growth of European population is, among other evidences of European expansion, the one that is perhaps least obvious. However, the growth and decline of populations are basic to every other form of social or cultural change.

Between 1800 and 1930 the population of Europe increased from 180,000,000 to 480,000,000, and the number of individuals of European origin overseas amounts at the present to 160,000,000. During this period, and indirectly as a result of this emigration of European peoples, a corresponding movement of African and Asiatic peoples has been in progress. The number of people of African origin in the New World, that is, in North America, the West Indies, and South America, is at the present time, as near as can be estimated 37,000,000. Of this number something over 12,000,000 are in the United States and Canada; 8,148,000 are in Bermuda, Central America, and the West Indies; 14,200,000, including, according to the best estimates, 8,800,999 mulattoes, are in Brazil. The remainder, 2,400,000, are in South America.

Meanwhile oriental peoples, mainly Chinese and East Indians, in response to the demands for crude labor to do the rough work on Europe's advancing frontier, have been imported into almost every part of the world outside of Europe. There are settlements of both Hindus and Chinese in the West Indies, in Australia, South and East Africa, and the islands of the Pacific, particularly the Dutch East Indies, the Philippines, and the Hawaiian Islands. They are employed mainly, but not wholly, in plantation agriculture. They are imported to work in the gold mines. There are Chinese in Cuba, in Jamaica, and British Guiana. They were imported in the first instance to replace Negroes on the sugar plantations after emancipation. There are Japanese in Brazil as in the United States. They were brought to Brazil to work in the coffee plantations in São Paulo and to the United States to work in the fruit and vegetable gardens of the Pacific coast.

The number of Chinese, Indians, and Japanese who have gone abroad and are now living outside of their native states has been estimated at 16,084,371. There is in South Africa a Chinese community in the Transvaal and an Indian community in Natal. The Chinese were imported as laborers to work in the Rand gold mines; the Indians, to work on sugar plantations in Natal. In the West Indies, Indians and Chinese took the places, after emancipation in 1834, of Negroes on the plantations. Japanese, who are more recent emigrants, have gone mainly to Hawaii and Brazil.

There are, at the present time, between 16,000,000 and 17,000,000 people of Asiatic origin living in the diaspora, if I may use that term to designate not merely the condition but the place of dispersion of peoples.[5]

Of the Orientals in this diaspora, 10,000,000, it is estimated, are Chinese 2,125,000 are Indians, and 1,973,960 are Japanese. There are 1,900,000 Chinese in Siam; 1,800,000 in Malaya; 1,240,000 in the Dutch East Indies; 700,000 in Indo-China; 150,000 in Burma; 74,954 in the United States; 45,000 in Canada; and 4,090,046 in other parts of the world.

Of the 4,125,000 Indians abroad, 1,300,000 are in Burma; 628,000 in Malaya; 1,133,000 in Ceylon; 281,000 in the island of Mauritius; 278,000 are in South and East Africa; 133,277 are in the British island of Trinidad; 181,600 in British and Dutch Guiana; 76,000 are in the Fiji Islands; 6,101 in the United States and Canada, and 100,225 in other countries.

Of the 1,969,371 Japanese living outside Insular Japan, 1,351,383 are in Korea, the Island of Sakhalin, Manchuria, Formosa, or other parts of the world including China, which have become, or are in a process of incorporation in, the Japanese Empire. Of the remaining 617,988 Japanese abroad, 162,537 are in Brazil, and 297,651 are in the Unites States and Canada. Of the number of Japanese in the United States, 139,634 are in Hawaii.[6]

The Hawaiian Islands are occupied by what, from the point of race and cultural differences, is probably the most thoroughly scrambled community in the world. The census for the Hawaiian Islands, where, different from continental America, the population is classified by racial origin, recognizes twelve different racial categories, two of them hyphenated. They are: Hawaiian, Caucasian–Hawaiian, Asiatic–Hawaiian, Other Caucasian, Portuguese, Chinese, Japanese, Korean, Porto Rican, and Filipino. Among the laborers that have a various times been imported to perform the work on the plantations a considerable number were from Europe, among the Scandinavians, Germans, Galicians, Russians, Poles, Portuguese, and Spaniards.

Of the total population of 347,799 in Hawaii in 1930, 236,673 were Orientals, 562 were Negroes, and 46,311 were hybrids. Of this 46,311, or 47,560 according to another and different calculation, 5,404 were person who counted their ancestry in more than two races.[7] Commenting on the situation, one of these products of miscegenation, a very charming young lady, incidentally, remarked: "Mixed? Yes; I am a kind of league of nations in myself."

I have conceived the emigration of European peoples and the emigration of extra-European peoples – since most, if not all, of these movements have taken place in direct and indirect response to conditions in Europe – as integral parts of a single mass migration. So considered, this is, undoubtedly, the most extensive and momentous movement of populations in history. Its consequences, likewise, have been in proportion to its numbers. Everywhere that European peoples – including their commerce and culture – have penetrated they have invariably disturbed the existing population balance; undermined the local economic organization; imposed upon native societies, sometimes a direct form of control, more often political and judicial processes which were strange to them, but processes which have, at any rate, more or less completely superseded those of the native and local authorities. The invaders have frequently, but not always, inoculated the native peoples with new and devastating diseases. They have invariably infected them with the contagious ferment of new and subversive ideas.

All this disorganization and demoralization seems to have come about, however, in the modern world as it did in the ancient, as an incident of ineluctable historical and cultural processes; the processes by which the integration of peoples and cultures have always and everywhere taken place, though not always and everywhere at a pace so rapid or on so grand a scale.

It is obvious that race relations and all that they imply are generally, and on the whole, the products of migration and conquest. This was true of the ancient world and it is equally true of the modern. The interracial adjustments that follow such migration and conquest are more complex than is ordinarily understood. They involve racial competition, conflict, accommodation, and eventually assimilation, but all of these diverse processes are to be regarded as merely the efforts of a new social and cultural organism to achieve a new biotic and social equilibrium.

[. . .] What then, finally, is the precise nature of race relations that distinguish them, in all the variety of conditions in which they arise, from other fundamental forms of human relations? It is the essence of race relations that they are the relations of strangers; of peoples who are associated primarily for secular and practical purposes; for the exchange of goods and services. They are otherwise the relations of people of diverse races and cultures who have been thrown together by the fortunes of war, and who, for any reason, have not been sufficiently knit together by intermarriage and interbreeding to constitute a single ethnic community, with all that it implies.

Obviously that does not imply as much in the modern world as it did in the ancient; it does not imply as much in the Occident as it does in the orient, where society is still organized on the familial pattern. It possibly implies less in America, or parts of America where divorce is easy and people are not generally interested in genealogies, than it does in Europe.

Although people in America and the modern world are no longer bound and united as people once were by familial and tribal ties, we are, nevertheless, profoundly affected by sentiments of nationality, particularly where they have an ethnic and a cultural basis. Furthermore, national and cultural differences are often re-enforced by divergence of physical and racial traits. But racial differences would not maintain social distances to the extent they actually do if they were not symptoms of differences in custom, tradition, and religion, and of sentiments appropriate to them. Differences of race and custom mutually re-enforce one another, particularly when they are not broken up by intermarriage.[8]

Traditions and customs are ordinarily transmitted through the family and can be most effectively maintained by intermarrying, i.e., endogamous groups. Evidence of this is the fact that every religious society tends to assume the character of a caste or endogamous group in so far at least as it prohibits or discourages marriage outside of the church or the sect. The Catholic clergy are profoundly opposed to marriage outside of the church, and the Jews who are, perhaps, the most mixed of peoples, have only been able to preserve their tribal religion for three thousand years and more because by endogamy they converted a religious society into a racial minority.

It has become commonplace among students of anthropology that most of the traits which we attribute to the different historic races are, like language and a high-school education, acquired by each succeeding generation for itself, sometimes by painful experience and always by a more or less extended formal education. Nevertheless, it is likewise becoming more obvious to students of human nature and society that the things that one learns in the intimate association of the family are likely to be the more permanent and more profound in their effects upon one's character in determining the individual's conception of himself, his outlook on life, his relations to other people.

It is obvious that society, so far as it is founded on a familial or genetic basis is concerned – as a secular society based on commercial and political interest is not – with maintaining not merely a definite life program, but a manner, moral order, and style of life consistent with that conception.

All this implies that the family and religion, the home and the church, in spite of public schools and social welfare institutions of every sort, still have the major responsibility for directing the career of youth and transmitting that intimate personal and moral order in accordance with which individuals freely govern themselves. Where custom breaks down, order may still be maintained, not by custom but by the police.

The consequence of this is that where there are racial and cultural minorities, whether Jews, Negroes, Catholics or religious sects that do not intermarry, the conflicts ordinarily described as racial but which are mainly cultural, do everywhere tend to arise. They arise even in an equalitarian society, like our own where "all men are," in principle if not in fact, "born equal," and they arise perhaps more readily here than they do in a society based on caste, because in theory they should not arise.

The obvious source and origin of most, if not all of the cultural and racial conflicts which constitute our race problems, are, therefore, conflicts of the "we groups" and the "other groups," as Sumner calls them, groups which are, however, integral parts of a great cosmopolitan and a free society. They are the ineluctable conflicts between the "little world" of the family in its struggle to preserve its sacred heritage against the disintegrating consequences of contact with an impersonal "great world" of business and politics.

They are, in fact, individual instances of an irrepressible conflict between a society founded on kinship and a society founded on the market place; the conflict between the folk culture of the provinces and the civilization of the metropolis.

Looking at race relations in the long historical perspective, this modern world which seems destined to bring presently all the diverse and distant peoples of the earth together within the limits of a common culture and a common social order, strikes one as something not merely unique but milennial! Nevertheless, this new civilization is the product of essentially the same historical processes as those that preceded it. The same forces which brought about the diversity of races will inevitably bring about, in the long run, a diversity in the peoples in the modern world corresponding to that which we have seen in the old. It is likely, however, that these diversities will be based in the future less on inheritance and race and rather more on culture and occupation. That means that race conflicts in the modern world, which is already or presently will be a single great society, will be more and more in the future confused with, and eventually superseded by, the conflicts of classes.

Notes and references

1   See unpublished MS by Donald Pierson, *The Black Man in Brazil*.
2   "In 1226 the Polish Duke Conrad of Masovia invited the Teutonic Knights into his territory to combat the heathen Prussians. After a difficult struggle, the Order conquered the territory of the heathen Prussians, exterminated most of the native population, and invited German peasants and townspeople into the country as

settlers. In the fourteenth century the State ruled by the Knights was a power in northeastern Germany. It acquired Pommerellia and for a time the Neumark also, and through its connection with the Order of the Sword, of Livonia, extended its influence as far as Estonia. A string of flourishing cities sprang up along its coast" (*Encyclopaedia Britannica*, 14th ed., XVIII, 654).

3   Boston, 1937.

4   The situation seems to have brought about something approaching an anthropological crisis. Since there are now, or soon will be, no living examples of primitive peoples to investigate, anthropologists seem to have arrived at a crossroads with the following result: One school of thought is directing its attention more exclusively to antiquarian and prehistorical investigation, seeking to extend the limits of our knowledge of historical facts; another school is more particularly interested in the historical processes they observe going on about them in contemporary life – the processes of history in the making. But the processes of history, so far as they reveal the manner in which new societies and new civilizations have arisen on the ruins of their predecessors, are the processes by which new and more sophisticated types of personality have succeeded earlier and simpler types. Anthropology thus merges into sociology.

5   Diaspora is a Greek term for a nation or part of a nation separated from its own state or territory and dispersed among other nations but preserving its national culture. In a sense Magna Graecia constituted a Greek diaspora in the ancient Roman Empire, and a typical case of diaspora is presented by the Armenians, many of whom have voluntarily lived outside their small national territory for centuries. Generally, however, the term is used with reference to those parts of the Jewish people residing outside Palestine. It was used at first to describe the sections of Jewry scattered in the ancient Greco-Roman world and later to designate Jewish dispersion throughout the world in the twenty-five hundred years since the Babylonian captivity. Diaspora has its equivalents in the Hebrew words *galuth* (exile) and *golah* (the exiled), which, since the Babylonian captivity, have been used to describe the dispersion of Jewry. *Encyclopaedia of the Social Sciences*, V, 120–127.

6   Radhakamal Mukerjee, *Migrant Asia* (Rome, 1936), Appendix A. The figures for the Japanese in the United States and Brazil have been corrected in accordance with more recent figures.

7   Romanzo Adams, *Interracial marriage in Hawaii* (New York, 1937), pp. 12–20. See also Appendix C. pp. 334–345, for data relating to interracial marriages.

8   *Ibid*.

Chapter 8

Ruth Benedict

RACE: WHAT IT IS NOT

CHINESE HAVE A YELLOWISH SKIN and slanting eyes. Negroes have a dark skin and wide flat noses. Caucasians have a lighter skin and high thin noses. The colour and texture of the hair of these peoples differ as much as do their skin and noses. These are outward and visible signs by which we recognize race; they are racial characteristics. In briefest possible definition, race is a classification based on traits which are hereditary. Therefore when we talk about race we are talking about (1) hereditary and (2) traits transmitted by heredity which characterize all the members of a related group. The first necessity in discussing race is to outline what race is *not*. A great deal of the confusion about race comes from confusing hereditary traits with traits which are socially acquired.

In the first place, race and language are not the same. This should be obvious, for not all who speak Arab are Arabians and not all who speak English are of the White race. Nevertheless the confusion occurs constantly.

A man's hereditary features and the language he speaks depend upon two different sets of circumstances. His hereditary anatomy depends upon his remote ancestors, and his language depends upon the speech he heard when he was a child. From the point of view of human morphology these two are not even related, for whatever the inherited conformation of his oral cavity and vocal cords, a child learns to speak any language spoken about him, and children with the same oral conformation speak languages with the most different sounds. If not even a man's speech organs account for the language he speaks, still less do racial features like skin colour, cephalic index, eyes, and hair determine his mother tongue. The Negroes in America speak English or Spanish or Portuguese or French, depending upon the language of the country in which they live; and Negroes without White blood speak languages as readily as the light-brown. According to their associations they speak with the intonations of the poor White of the area or of the privileged minority. And this is not a situation which is new in the world. So the primitive Manchus who came from the Siberian tundras have for centuries spoken in China a pure Chinese, and the Arab language was spread after the ninth century over immense areas of northern Africa among peoples of Negroid blood.

When the people of one race speak the same language and that language is spoken only by that one race, as among some primitive tribes, this is not because the two are interdependent but because they both depend on a third circumstance. This circumstance under which both physical form and language take shape and become unique is isolation. In prehistoric times the world was sparsely populated, and in isolated regions both physical type and language might become different from those in any other part of the world. The process is so simple that it is the more remarkable that it did not happen oftener than it did. The principal reason why it did not was that isolation was so often broken. When two peoples became thoroughly intermingled by conquest or intermarriage, their descendants were racially one mixed type; but they spoke one or the other language.

There was also another factor which operated in history from the earliest times. Racial types maintain themselves over longer periods and over greater areas than language does; people of the same racial type commonly speak several languages which cannot be reduced to a common linguistic family. In the early history of mankind this must have been even truer than it is today, for widespread languages, like Bantu and Polynesian, were once restricted to small groups and have spread far and wide only in comparatively recent times; in parts of the world like the Caucasus and like aboriginal California the early condition still survives. Languages in these latter areas stop short at the margins of one valley, but the racial type is the same over great areas. From earliest times, therefore, language and race have had different histories and different distributions; in the modern world they are shuffled like suits in a pack of cards.

In spite, however, of the impossibility of arguing from race to language or from language to race, race and language are constantly confused. *Aryan*, the term now used in Germany for the preferred race, is the name of a group of languages which includes the Sanskrit of ancient India and languages of ancient Persia; and *Aryan* has also been commonly used as a term covering a much larger group of languages, the Indo-European, which includes not only Sanskrit and Old Persian but German, English, Latin, Greek, Armenian, and Slavic. In whichever sense *Aryan* is used, it is a language term and has no reference to a peculiar German racial heritage. Because of the ludicrous inapplicability of the first sense of the word *Aryan*, the Nazis, when they selected the term, were obviously thinking of it in the latter sense of *Indo-European*. But the people speaking Indo-European languages have no unity of racial type either in skin, in eye or hair colour, in cephalic index or in stature.

The foremost student of the Aryan languages in the last century, Max Müller, exposed the fallacy vigorously even in the 1880's – a fallacy which had already become current through the writings of Thomas Carlyle, the English historian J. R. Green, and the French racialist Count de Gobineau. "I have declared again and again," Max Müller writes, "that when I say Aryas (Aryans) I mean neither blood nor bones nor hair nor skull; I mean simply those who spoke an Aryan language. When I speak of them I commit myself to no anatomical characteristics. To me an ethnologist who speaks of Aryan race, Aryan blood, Aryan eyes and hair, is as great a sinner as a linguist who speaks of a dolichocephalic [narrow-headed] dictionary or a brachycephalic [broad-headed] grammar."[1] Nevertheless, as we shall see in discussing the history of racism in Europe, the list of sinners has increase rather than diminished since Max Müller's time.[2]

The fundamental reason why language cannot be equated with race is that language is learned behaviour, and race is a classification based on hereditary traits. Language is only one special instance of how learned behaviour varies in mankind without relation to physical type. It was not only the Chinese language that the Manchus learned in China; they took over Chinese architecture, the forms of Chinese family life, Chinese ethics, Chinese literature, Chinese food. It is not only the English language that American Negroes use; they become Baptists and Methodists and Pullman car porters. Instead of learning, as in Africa, the elaborate technicalities of "throwing the bones" for divination, they learn the technicalities of reading and writing; instead of the complexities of *mankala*, the intricate peg-game of Africa and the Near East, they learn to shoot craps. Their culture becomes American.

For culture is the sociological term for learned behaviour: behaviour which in man is not given at birth, which is not determined by his germ cells as is the behaviour of wasps or the social ants, but must be learned anew from grown people by each new generation. The degree to which human achievements are dependent on this kind of learned behaviour is man's great claim to superiority over all the rest of creation; he has been properly called "the culture-bearing animal." He does not grow wings or fins to cross the seas; he builds ships and airplanes, and the building and operating of these are culturally transmitted. He does not grow fangs and claws to kill his enemy; he invents gunpowder and Maxim guns. This non-biological transmission is a great advantage in that it allows for much greater adaptability to circumstances but it progressively lessens the importance of biologically transmitted behaviour.

This elementary truth is essential for the understanding of race. Race is biologically transmitted, and among the social insects and to a lesser degree among the carnivores their tastes in food, their ways of obtaining it, their aggressiveness or lack of aggressiveness in assuring their own survival are also biologically transmitted. That "the leopard cannot change his spots" means that the leopard, because he belongs to a certain species, will always be found stalking the jungle for his prey. But in man the great aggressors of yesterday become the mild peace-lovers of today. In the ninth century Scandinavians were the feared aggressive Vikings of the sea; in the present generation they are the peaceful non-aggressive exponents of co-operatives and the "middle way."

Even more commonly, at the present time the non-aggressors of yesterday become the aggressors; their race has not changed, but their behaviour has. Japan has a history of peace and non-aggression that cannot be matched in the Western World. During the first eleven centuries of her recorded history she was engaged in only one war abroad. Indeed this sole conflict ended in 1598, and from that time until 1853, when Japan opened her doors to intercourse with the world outside, the building of all ocean-going boats was forbidden by imperial decree to make certain that Japan would preserve her policy of isolationism. The ceremoniousness, the light-heartedness, the aesthetic appreciation of the Japanese were traits that passed current as their essential qualities. Since 1853 they have fought five times overseas and are well on their way to becoming one of the most aggressively warlike nations of the world. In the human race no centuries-long existence free from conflict as the lamb's guarantees that the next generation may not become the lion.

There is another aspect of this fact that race and culture are distinct. In world history, those who have helped to build the same culture are not necessarily in one race, and those of the same race have not all participated in one culture. In scientific language, culture is not a function of race.

The more we know about the fortunes and the vicissitudes of any civilization, the less it proves to be the peculiar offspring of an unmixed race. This is true even far back in prehistory, and an eminent archaeologist has said that the great social truth made clear by archaeology is that culture lives on and maintains itself though the race perish; either as conquerors or as peaceable settlers a new racial type carries on the old ways of life of the conquered or earlier occupants of the land. The archaeologist looking back over the long centuries sees, not the destruction of that civilization when one racial carrier was superseded, but the continuity of its history in the hands of one racial type after another. The growth of human civilization in the European Palaeolithic (Old Stone) Age has cultural, but not racial, continuity. The culture which neanderthal man possessed was after his disappearance carried forward by Cro-magnon man, given new embellishments by men of the later Old Stone Age, and elaborated by the races of the new Stone Age. Only the last two types are racially ancestral to modern man. This lack of racial continuity in the small corner of Europe during prehistory is better established for Europe than for other parts of the world because the archaeology of Europe is better known, but all that prehistoric research is uncovering in Africa, in Asia, and in Central America tells the same story.

This story has been repeated in Western civilization since the dawn of history, and the evidence of it constantly accumulates. A century ago the historian of Western civilization was content to begin with Greece, but today this is inadequate. Historical study has unrolled a longer history under our eyes. Greece was the inheritor of earlier Oriental civilizations and its early culture owed much to Egyptian influences. Essential cornerstones of our civilization are the inventions of other races. Perhaps we describe this civilization of ours as built on steel and gunpowder. But steel was invented either in India or in Turkestan, and gunpowder in China. Perhaps we prefer to identify our Western culture by its printing presses and literateness. But paper and printing were both borrowed from China. Our economic life with its great concentration of population is based on the cultivation of grains and of animals which are Neolithic inventions from Asia; corn and tobacco were first domesticated by the American Indian. Our control of nature is overwhelmingly dependent on mathematical calculations. But the so-called Arabic system of notation which is essential to all complicated mathematics was unknown in Europe in the Roman era; it was invented in Asia and introduced to our civilization by the Moors. Algebra was a method of calculation also borrowed by Europeans from Asiatic peoples.

Wherever we look, the truth is forced upon us that many different races have contributed to the growth of our culture, and that when we hold culture as the constant, race is a variable. The White race was once the borrower as today Japan is. The White race spent long centuries at the process and Japan as few decades, but by that token some literalists could argue the racial superiority of the Japanese over the White race.

When we look at the fact of cultural–racial separateness from the other side, this time holding race constant, we find that the culture of any one race is of many degrees of complexity. While certain groups of a given race forge ahead and set up great states or build great cities which are architectural triumphs or carry out great public works, other groups of the same race may remain primitive nomadic herdsmen. A race does not move forward as a whole. So some groups of Arabs built up great states under Sultans with regal splendour, the arts and sciences flourished, and they were in the vanguard of the civilization of their day. Other members of the same race were simple Bedouins following their herds from pasturage to pasturage. Similarly the primitive Amur River tribes of Siberia or the Yukaghir of the Siberian tundras are of the same race as the civilized Chinese. The Malay race also has its half-wild primitive tribes of the coastal Malay Peninsula and at the same time its centres of high civilization. Race is not a touchstone by which civilized people can be separated from uncivilized. Rude people of barbarian ancestry have shown themselves to be abundantly able to adopt the highest extant civilizations and to contribute to their development.

The Manchus were a rude and unnoted nomadic Tungu tribe, but first through contact with the Mongols, and later by their conquest of China in the mid-seventeenth century, they became the ruling dynasty of a country unsurpassed in riches and glory at that period. Wherever we look – to the Malays, the Manchus, the Mongols, the Arabs, or the Nordics – the same story repeats itself over and over.

The Nordics belong to this list, and no one need quarrel with the extravagant claims that have been made for their "manifest destiny" if these same claims are allowed also for all other rude peoples who have come to participate ably in the building of civilization. When, however, the Nordics are singled out as a peculiar instance and their participation in civilization credited to their racial type and not to be universal processes of history, it is easy to recognize the special pleading. It is closer to actual history to speak of them as Hooton does – as "the rawboned ruffians from the North,"[3] whose irruptions shattered the peace of early Europe – or to call attention, as Hankins[4] does, to the fact that they "destroyed civilizations more frequently than they created them." The point to note, however, is that they were a group with certain inherited features, and that though they were once rude, they later became exponents of a great civilization; their former rudeness in no way disqualified them from participating ably in its development.

History cannot be written as if it belonged to one race alone. Civilization has been gradually built, now out of the contributions of one race, now of another. When all civilization is ascribed to the "Nordics," the claim is the same one which any anthropolgist can hear any day from primitive tribes – only they tell the story of themselves. They too believe that all that is important in the world begins and ends with them; the creator gave to them exclusively in the beginning all that is good and at their downfall will destroy the world. We smile when such claims are made by a rude and tiny American Indian tribe or a naked Papuan of New

Guinea, but ridicule might just as well be turned against ourselves. After all, the world of these tribes extends but a little way beyond their borders and folk-tales serve them for history; their exaggerated claims are the result of ignorance. But when the same crude provincialism is put forward learnedly in our day, it is still a childish primitive error maintained in the face of all that historians have ascertained and in the face of modern knowledge of the whole extent of the globe.

Provincialism may rewrite history and play up only the achievements of the historian's own group, but it remains provincialism; it is not history. The lesson of history is that pre-eminence in cultural achievement has passed from one race to another, from one continent to another; it has embraced not whole "races" but certain fragments of an ethnic group which were for certain historical reasons favourably situated at the moment. Peace had been achieved for a certain period, or freedom from exploitation for certain groups. All those of the race who were within the range of these conditions profited by them, and the arts of life were advanced; individuals of whatever race rose to the opportunity and have often left their names enrolled in history. It has happened in Mesopotamia, in China, in India, in Egypt, in Greece, in Rome, and in England. Obviously no racial type has a monopoly of high culture.

It behooves us, therefore, to study race historically and biologically and anthropometrically without expecting race to account for all human achievements. Race is a scientific field of study. But human history is a vastly more complicated thing than a mere record of the distribution of anthropomorphic measurements, and cultural achievements are not mechanically transmitted and guaranteed by any racial inheritance.

Notes and references

1   *Biography of Words and the Home of the Aryans*, London, 1888, p. 120.
2   I have myself in this volume used *Slav*, which refers to languages, as a racial term. There is no word in popular usage which designates this group in biological terms.
3   Hooton, Earnest A., *Up from the Ape*, London, Allen & Unwin, 1931, p. 525.
4   Hankins, Frank H., *Racial Basis of Civilization*, New York, 1926, p. 350; London, Knopf, 1927.

Chapter 9

John Rex

RACE RELATIONS IN SOCIOLOGICAL THEORY

THE PROBLEM OF RACE AND RACISM challenges the conscience of the sociologist in the same way as the problem of nuclear weapons challenges that of the nuclear physicist. This is not to say that sociology can dictate to men and nations how they should behave toward one another any more than the nuclear physicist had some special competence to advise the American President whether or not he should drop the atom bomb on the Japanese. But it is to say that, in so far as whole populations have been systematically discriminated against, exploited and even exterminated, the sociologist might legitimately be asked to lay the causes of these events bare. The aim of this book is to provide a conceptual basis for doing this.

Conceptual discussion might well appear to some to involve fiddling while the gas ovens burn. Yet it is important to realise that sociology as a discipline has had some difficulty in coming to grips with this problem. The claim of the racists in the Europe of the nineteen-thirties was that race was a biological category, and that appeared to exclude sociological discussion. And, when the falseness of racist biology was systematically exposed, some sociologists were inclined to argue that the problem simply did not exist. Race was a category based upon some sort of false consciousness, and it was the duty of sociologists to reduce all statements about racial difference to statements about some other kind of socially differentiated structure, such as class. Only recently has the question been raised as to whether class really does have some kind of superior ontological status to race, and whether there is not a sense in which the 'race war' is not a more important central structural and dynamic principle in sociology than the class war.[1] A time has therefore arrived at which there is an urgent necessity for a reassessment of the rôle of the race concept in sociological theory.

It might perhaps be said that the fact that the concept of race and the problem of racism is primarily a problem for social science rather than for biology has been established in a quite uniquely authoritative way by a consensus of world experts. For, after the Second World War, UNESCO called together first a group of biologists and social scientists (in 1947) and then on two occasions groups of biologists (in 1951 and 1964), in order to give an authoritative opinion on the race question.[2] The biologists' final statement, made in 1964 and issued as the 'Moscow Declaration', represents the most up-to-date biological opinion on the subject. The full significance of this declaration can be assessed in the light of papers prepared for the Moscow conference and particularly from the introduction to these papers prepared by the Belgian biologist Jean Hiernaux, who has summarised the areas of agreement and disagreement among the experts.[3]

The biologists' conclusions are complex and technical and it would be quite beyond the scope of the present book to set them out in detail. Nonetheless it is important that we should indicate that they do not support certain popular conceptions as to the nature of race, which are systematically propagated by racist theorists, and which even today are widely accepted, even though they may not be so systematically rationalised as they were.

The popular conceptions to which we refer are as follows: first, that the differences in rights which exist between groups of men, within a nation, between nations and between groups which are internationally dispersed, rest upon differences of behaviour and of moral qualities which are genetically determined. Thus the maintenance of a particular political order in the world is represented as being 'scientifically' determined, rather than being based upon force, violence and usurpation. Many subsidiary propositions flow from these basic ones, but they are the essential intellectual core of the racist position.

The general position adopted by the biological experts in Moscow is that the concept of race, and more generally of genetic inheritance, which they feel justified in using, gives no support whatever to these popular conceptions. But this is best understood if we look briefly at what it was that the experts actually said under the headings of the use of the concepts of race and population, the rôle of heredity and environment in determining human characteristics, the actual nature of inter-group differences, the single or multiple origin of the human species, the degree of independence or association between different traits, the rôle of biological and cultural factors in evolution, the consequences of intergroup marriage, the survival value of proved differences between populations, and the possible inheritance of psychic characteristics.

The principal conclusions reached on these points appear to be as follows:[4]

1   Race is a taxonomic concept of limited usefulness as a means of classifying human beings, but probably less useful than the more general concept of populations. The former term is used to refer to 'groups of mankind showing well developed and primarily heritable physical differences from other groups'. The latter refers to a 'group whose members marry other members of the group more frequently than people outside the group' and hence have a relatively limited and distinctive range of genetic characteristics. In any case, however, whether we use the concept of race or population, the experts agree that human population groups constitute a continuum, and that the genetic diversity within groups is probably as great as that between groups.

2   It is agreed that observable human characteristics are, in nearly all cases, the result of biological and environmental factors. The sole difference which could be attributed to biological heredity alone was that relating to blood-groups and the populations which shared the same blood-group by no means coincided with 'races' in the popular usage of the term.

3   The various characteristics commonly grouped together as racial, and said to be transmitted en bloc, are, in fact, transmitted either independently or in varying degrees of association.

4   'All men living today belong to a single species and are derived from a common stock' even though opinions may differ as to how and when groups diverged from this common stock. Interbreeding between members of different groups is possible and productive and in 1964 as distinct from 1951 the experts saw a 'positive biological aspect of this process' (i.e. saw inter-breeding as possibly beneficial from an adaptive point of view) 'while at the same time repeating the denial, at all events in the light of present scientific knowledge, of any negative aspect for mankind in general'.

5   Taking into account the possibility of a looser usage of the term 'race' to refer to a national inbreeding population, it may not be desirable from a standpoint of combatting racism to deny that a particular national group may be referred to as a race, but rather to affirm that it is not justifiable to attribute cultural characteristics to the effect of genetic inheritance.

6   Human evolution has been affected to a unique degree as compared with the evolution of other species by migration and cultural evolution. The capacity to advance culturally is one shared by all members of *homo sapiens* and, once it exists, is of far greater significance for the evolution of the species than biological or genetic evolution.

Taken together these findings point clearly to one single conclusion. The concept of race as used by the biologists has no relevance to the political differences among men, and since the whole notion of race and racism as it appears in popular discussion is concerned with these political differences, the question which we have to face is what the characteristics are of those situations which men call racial.

If the possibility of racial differences being biologically based is excluded, two other possible bases, neither of them necessarily sociological, might in principle be considered. One is that there are psychological differences between members of different racial groups, the other that the term merely refers to culturally distinct groups. Neither of these possibilities, however, provides an adequate explanation of how it is that men come to be classified as racially different.

Many problems arise in the attempt to assess psychological differences between races. There are few tests if any which are so free of cultural content as to permit comparisons between subjects drawn from different cultural backgrounds, and it would certainly seem to be the case here, as it is more generally with biological characteristics, that differences between individuals within the same population are at least as great as those between groups. In any case, however, it is some-what difficult to see what could be meant by a purely psychological determina-tion of intergroup differences divorced from the notion of differences of genetic inheritance. If psychic character is thought of as the consequence of the socialisation process then we should have to say (a) that a variety of types emerges from the socialisation process amongst all groups and (b) that insofar as socialisation processes do vary between cultures and produce differing distributions of the various personality types, the psychological determination of intergroup differences would appear to be dependent upon cultural differences.

So far as the cultural causation of intergroup differences in appearance, behavioural characteristics, institutions, psychic character and so on is concerned, no one would deny it. There certainly are different nations and cultural minorities within nations to be observed in the world. The question is whether the problem of the differences between these groups is coincident with the differences between groups which are said to be racial. Our answer to this question is that, although these cultural differences, or as it is sometimes said, differences between ethnic groups, may sometimes become the basis of a race relations structure and of a race relations problem, this need by no means always be the case. Our task then would appear to lie in discovering which of these culturally differentiated groups come to be thought of as races, and also what other types of groups are so classified.

It would appear to be the case that there are two observable features of any situation in which a problem of race is said to exist. One is the obvious one that the groups are called races, with whatever deterministic overtones that term might appear to have. The other is that there seem to be a definite and restricted number of social structures in relation to which in popular conceptions the term racial is used and in which there would appear to be a need for some distinctive sociological term. At this point we have to look at the problem of race sociologically.

Clearly the problem of a sociology of race relations is a peculiar one as compared with most other special sociologies. It starts with the task of unmasking false biological or related theories. Having done this, the question is what it has to do next. A few writers have taken the view that beyond this all the sociologist has to do is to show the consequences of such theories being held, so that phenomena like those connected with anti-semitism in twentieth-century Europe would be seen or studied simply as the consequence of the preaching of racist ideas. This, however, would appear to involve cutting off the investigation of a causal chain more arbitrarily than is common in sociology. We should surely look not merely at the consequences of racist theory, but also at its causes and at its functions.

[. . .] The first American attempt at a theory of race relations and one which remains prominent even to the present day was W. Lloyd Warner's theory of colour-caste.[5] According to this theory American society includes both class and caste divisions. The white population may be classified as belonging to one of a number of strata (or, as Warner would prefer to say, classes), which are arrived at by placing individuals in terms of two methods, which Warner elaborated in his studies of Yankee City. One of these classified the individuals according to their score on an index of objective and quantifiable status characteristics. The other was based upon the subjective assessments which individuals made of one another's status. Having elaborated this picture of the American stratification system Warner then went on to consider its relationship to the absorption of ethnic minorities.

The Yankee City studies showed that most European minority groups moved up the stratification hierarchy over two or three generations, but that, so far as the negro population were concerned, however much they might achieve an improved position in terms of such objective status characteristics as income, they still found that there were barriers preventing their free association with whites at an equivalent level.

Warner suggested that the best way to conceptualise the relationship of the negroes to the stratification system was to begin by imagining that at the bottom of the stratification system there was a barrier far more impenetrable than those which divided the various strata or classes. When some of those beneath this barrier began to acquire characteristics which *prima facie* should have placed them higher up in the stratification system, the effect was not to breach the barrier but to tip it diagonally, so that there was the possibility of an individual negro becoming an upper-class negro, just as there was a possibility of a white becoming a poor white. There would, however, be less association between these two groups than there would between poor whites and middle-class whites or between upper class, middle-class and lower-class negroes.

Warner suggested that the barrier which thus split the stratification system into two was a caste barrier, at least in an incipient form, and he drew attention to similarities with the Hindu caste system, such as the taboos on intermarriage, eating together, and any other intimate form of association. Whether this fairly loose usage of the term caste is justified has been disputed, and probably the weight of opinion is against the introduction of the term caste to explain white–black relations in the United States. Nonetheless Warner's view that these relations cannot be explained in terms of normal stratification models survives, even if his notion of caste is rejected. Any adequate race relations theory must necessarily deal with this point.

O. C. Cox,[6] approaching the problem of the American negro from a sophisticated Marxist point of view, has sought to show that there are several crucial dissimilarities between intercaste and interracial relations as they occur in the United States, which make the use of the term caste in the latter case impermissible. He believes that a better theoretical construct for explaining race relations is that which may be derived from the Marxist theory of class conflict. Cox notes that the Hindu caste system is one in which there is a large measure of assent to the social inequalities and taboos on association amongst higher and lower castes, and that the central and characteristic feature of the system is the occupational specialisation of the castes. Neither of these two conditions prevails in the United States. The position of the negro worker in that society is that of the most exploited worker within a capitalist system of social relations of production. The absence of a race relations problem of the North American kind in Portuguese and Spanish Latin America is thus seen as explicable in terms of their being less advanced capitalist countries. So far from Catholic religion being a determining variable, its presence, like the absence of a race relations problem, is held to be dependent on the kind of economic system which exists.

Clearly the difficulty in sustaining Cox's theory is to show why it is that white workers are not in the same position as negro workers. The simplest Marxist way out of this is simply to attribute the subjectively felt divisions within the working class to a state of 'false consciousness' fostered in its own interest by the bour-geoisie. A non-Marxist alternative would involve the introduction of a secondary hypothesis at this point. Thus it could be said that the position of the negro was explicable in terms of his relation to the means of production, but that a prior distinction had been made as to who should fill inferior working class rôles, and that this distinction was based upon non-economic criteria. As we shall argue later, this modified Marxist position does have considerable value in understanding the race relations situation not merely of the United States, but, even more, that of the Union of South Africa.

[. . .] From this review of some of the basic sociological theories about the kinds of societies in which race relations situations and problems occur, we may now define our own approach to the problem of defining the sociological field of race relations. It includes the following three elements:

1   a situation of differentiation, inequality and pluralism as between groups;
2   the possibility of clearly distinguishing between such groups by their phys-ical appearance, their culture or occasionally merely by their ancestry;
3   the justification and explanation of this discrimination in terms of some kind of implicit or explicit theory, frequently but not always of a biological kind. [. . .]

Notes and references

1   See, for instance, R. Segal, *The Race War*, Cape, London, 1966; R. Debray, *Revolution in the Revolution*, Pelican, London, 1968; F. Fanon, *The Wretched of the Earth*, Macgibbon and Kee, London, 1965.
2   UNESCO, Paris, *Statements on Race and Race Prejudice*, 1950, 1951, 1964 and 1967.
3   Hiernaux, Introduction: 'The Moscow Expert Meeting', *International Social Science Journal*, Vol. XVII, No. 1, 1965, UNESCO, Paris.
4   *Ibid.*
5   W. Lloyd Warner, 'American Class and Caste', *American Journal of Sociology*, Vol. XLII, Sept. 1936, pp. 234–7.
6   O. C. Cox, *Caste, Class and Race*, Monthly Review Press, New York, 1959.

Chapter 10

Robert Miles

APROPOS THE IDEA OF
'RACE' . . . AGAIN

[. . .]

The idea of 'race' and the concept of racism

THE HISTORY OF THE CONSTRUCTION and reproduction of the idea of 'race' has been analysed exhaustively (e.g. Barzun 1938, Montagu 1964, Jordan 1968, 1974, Guillaumin 1972, Stepan 1982, Banton 1987). As a result, it is well understood that the idea of 'race' first appeared in the English language in the early seventeenth century and began to be used in European and North American scientific writing in the late eighteenth century in order to name and explain certain phenotypical differences between human beings. By the mid-nineteenth century, the dominant theory of 'race' asserted that the world's population is constituted by a number of distinct 'races', each of which has a biologically determined capacity for cultural development. Although the accumulation of scientific evidence during the early twentieth century (e.g. Barkan 1992) challenged this theory, it was the use of 'race' theory by the National Socialists in Germany that stimulated a more thorough critical appraisal of the idea of 'race' in Europe and North America and the creation of the concept of racism in the 1930s.

The concept of racism is therefore a recent creation in the English language (Miles 1989a: 42–3). It was first used as a title for a book written in the German language by Magnus Hirschfeld in 1933/4 which was translated and published in English in 1938. In *Racism*, Hirschfeld refuted nineteenth-century arguments which claimed the mantle of science to sustain the notion of the existence of a hierarchy of biologically distinct 'races'. But he did so without offering any formal definition of racism and without clarifying how racism is to be distinguished from the concept of xenophobia (1938: 227). During the same decade, a number of other books were published which sought to demonstrate that the idea of 'race' employed in Nazi ideology lacked any scientific foundation, some of which also used the concept of racism to label these ideologies (Huxley and Haddon 1935, Barzun 1938, Montagu 1974, Benedict 1983).

But on one matter, these writers were divided, that of whether or not 'races' nevertheless existed. On the one hand, Benedict (1983) legitimated nineteenth-century biological and anthropological classifications of the human population into three 'races'. On the other hand, Montagu (1974) argued that, in so far as there were biological differences between human beings, they did not correspond to these earlier classifications and he therefore recommended that the term 'race' be excised completely from scientific discourse.

Hence, the scientific and political critique of fascist ideologies that resulted in the creation of the concept of racism was not accompanied by a consistent rejection of either the idea of 'race' or the belief that the human population was divided into biologically distinct 'races'. Indeed, the dispute about whether or not the term 'race' should be used within science to refer to populations characterised by particular genetic profiles continues to this day (Miles 1982: 15–19). Thereby, the basis for the continued confusion of the two terms was created and has been maintained. All the while that it is thought that 'races' exist then there is the possibility, indeed even the necessity, to constitute a theory of how different 'races' interact with one another. In so far as the ideology of racism is identified as one determinant of these 'race relations', a theory of racism becomes entangled in a theory of 'race relations'. And in so far as Marxist writers have incorporated an idea of 'race' as an analytical, or even a descriptive, concept into their theorising about racism, they too have become similarly entangled.

A Marxist theory of 'race relations'?

One of the earliest Marxist texts to analyse 'race relations' was O.C. Cox's *Caste, Class and Race* (1970). It was first published in the United States in 1948. Despite the existence of another tradition of Marxist writing in the USA which claimed to theorise 'race', Cox's book was cited for a long time by Marxists and non-Marxists alike (e.g. Castles and Kosack 1972: 16, Rex 1983: 15–16), as *the* seminal Marxist statement, and the work of the Frankfurt school (which was produced during its exile from Germany: see Outlaw 1990: 69–72) was largely ignored.

Now, it is referred to rarely in the British and North American literature (see, for example, the passing reference in Omi and Winant 1986: 31), although recently one of the original British architects of the 'race relations' problematic has shown a renewed interest in it (Banton 1991). This silence results partly from the fact that there is no longer any widespread interest in Cox's central theme, namely a comparison between caste and 'race' relations. It is also because Cox denied Afro-Americans any autonomous political role, a view that is contrary to more recent political philosophies of 'black' resistance which advocate autonomous political organisation on the part of 'black' people. Finally, as we shall see, Cox rejected the use of racism as an analytical concept, a concept that has in the past three decades become central to Marxist analysis and to critical analysis more generally.

Nevertheless, at the time of its publication, *Caste, Class and Race* was a work of some originality and it remains a work of considerable scholarship. Cox set out to construct a Marxist theory of 'race relations' (1970: ix). He attempted this largely by means of an extended critique of extant writing on 'race relations' in the USA, most of which defined its object of analysis as 'race relations' in the southern States. His central argument was that 'race relations' were not similar, or equivalent, to 'caste relations', as most writers claimed at the time. As a result, a large part of *Caste, Class and Race* sought to establish the nature of caste in Indian society and then to demonstrate that 'race relations' in the USA did not exhibit the defining features of 'caste relations'. The decline in the significance of the caste thesis means that much of this argument has little relevance to contemporary concerns.

But Cox's alternative theorisation is of interest because of the way in which it incorporated the ideas of 'race' and 'race relations' and attributed them with analytical status within the framework of Marxism. As a result, Marxists could claim, *contra* 'bourgeois' theorists, that they too had a theory of 'race relations', a theory that was (at least as far as they were concerned) superior. But the ideas of 'race' and 'race relations' had no specifically Marxist content. Cox, in the manner of mainstream sociological thinking, noted and then passed by the uncertainties about the biological meaning of 'race', and defined 'race' as 'any group of people that is generally believed to be, and generally accepted as, a race in any given area of ethnic competition' (1970: 319). What distinguished a group as a 'race' was their real or imputed physical characteristics (1970: 402), and hence he defined 'race relations' as 'behaviour which develops among peoples who are aware of each other's actual or imputed physical differences' (1970: 320).

The process by which these significations were established and reproduced did not capture Cox's interest and, consequently, he accepted the existence of 'races' as distinctive, immutable collectivities. This verged on reification when he argued that it was impossible for human beings to establish 'new races' and that an individual becomes a member of a 'race' by birth in the course of inheriting certain inalienable physical characteristics (1970: 423). Thus, although he claimed that 'races' were social, and therefore human, constructions, once created they were attributed with the character of permanence: they became 'things in themselves', discrete social collectivities whose presence had to be related to other social collectivities. The problem then became one of locating 'races' within Marxist analysis, which attributes primacy to class and class relations.

In order to assess Cox's attempt to do this, another conceptual matter requires attention. In the light of the centrality of the concept of racism to much contemporary Marxist writing, it is intriguing that Cox explicitly rejected its use. He noted that the concept had been used, by Ruth Benedict, to refer to a 'philosophy of racial antipathy' (1970: 321, 480), and he repudiated this on the grounds that it tended to lead to the study of the origin and development of specific ideas. Although Cox did not use this terminology, he was in fact rejecting idealism. Cox sought alternatively to develop a materialist analysis that identified the class interests and exploitative practices which gave rise to what he preferred to describe as 'race prejudice', a notion that predated the creation of the concept of racism.

In the manner of the mechanistic and economistic Marxism that had not been challenged from within the Marxist tradition in the late 1940s, a now familiar argument resulted from this materialism. Cox proposed that, historically, 'race prejudice' was a recent phenomenon, and that its origin lay in the development of capitalism. He claimed that 'race relations' arose from the proletarianisation of labour power in the Caribbean, 'race prejudice' being the rationalisation developed by the bourgeoisie for its inhuman and degrading treatment of the work force. Thus, 'race prejudice' was defined as 'a social attitude propagated . . . by an exploiting class for the purpose of stigmatising some group as inferior so that the exploitation of either the group itself of its resources or both may be justified' (1970: 393). It therefore facilitated a process of labour exploitation, and hence arose after that system of exploitation had been established (1970: 532).

But exploitation and proletarianisation are, within the framework of Marxist theory, universal capitalist processes. Because 'race relations' are not deemed to have arisen from the process of proletarianisation within, for example, Europe, it follows that it is necessary to identify what distinguishes the exploitation and proletarianisation that give rise to 'race relations' in the Caribbean. 'Race relations', Cox argued, arose when the bourgeoisie successfully proletarianised 'a whole people' (i.e. a 'race'). This happened in the Caribbean and the USA but not in Europe, where only a section of 'white people' (i.e. part of the 'white race') were proletarianised (1970: 344). For Cox, this did not alter the *essential* identity of the two processes: in both instances, a group of people was subordinated to a bourgeoisie whose primary interest was the exploitation of the former's labour power. Hence, for Cox, 'racial antagonism' was in essence class conflict (or political-class conflict as he conceptualised class struggle) because the latter arose from the exploitation of labour power (1970: 333, 453, 536). It follows that 'race relations' and 'race prejudice' arose from the historically specific processes of colonialism and imperialism that accompanied the development of capitalism as a world economic system (1970: 483).

Cox theorised 'race relations' as, simultaneously, a specific form of group relations and a variant of class relations. Their specific character arose from the imputed existence of 'races' as collectives distinguished by real or alleged physical differences. Much of Cox's attention was focused upon 'races' distinguished by skin colour, and he referred to 'whites' and 'Negroes' as distinct 'races'. In this respect, his theoretical approach remained wholly within an emergent academic tradition which had incorporated common-sense understandings and definitions about 'race' into scientific analysis in the course of breaking with nineteenth-century biological and anthropological analysis. The work of Park, Warner, Dollard and Myrdal, about which Cox was so critical, was characterised by what was at the time a radical view that 'race relations' were social relations between collectivities which defined themselves as 'races', rather than biologically determined relations between biologically distinct and discrete 'races' (Banton 1987: 86–93, 99–110). These writers established 'race relations' as a particular sociological specialisation or field of study and Cox sustained and reinforced this paradigm by seeking and claiming to offer a Marxist theory of 'race relations'.

It is easy to criticise Cox's analysis for being functionalist and economistic (Miles 1980, 1982: 81–7, George 1984: 139–47). Here I identify an additional difficulty with Cox's analysis, the significance of which will be discussed further later in this chapter. We have seen that Cox argued that 'race prejudice' was a rationalisation of proletarianisation in the Caribbean. Cox did not elaborate on this interpretation, but it is not consistent with the Marxist conception of capitalism as a mode of production (although it is consistent with Wallerstein's (1979) 'world systems' analysis of capitalism).

If capitalism is understood as a mode of generalised commodity production in which the ownership and control of the means of production are held in the hands of the bourgeoisie, to which the working class is thereby forced to sell its labour power in return for a wage with which it can then purchase the means of subsistence in the form of commodities, the concept of proletarianisation refers to the social process by which a section of the population is transformed into sellers of labour power. Historically, this has entailed the divorce of a section of the population from the means of production in order that it should have no choice but to transform its labour power into a commodity which is exchanged within a labour market.

But this is not what happened during the colonisation of the Caribbean in the seventeenth century (Miles 1987: 73–93). In order to establish commodity production, those who gained control over much of the land (by a combination of force and the establishment of private property rights) brought first European and then African migrants to the region and created indentured and, subsequently, slave relations of production. Under these relations, the labourer did not commodify labour power but was forced to provide labour power to the person who either purchased by contract the right to utilise that labour power or purchased the individual as a chattel. There was no labour market where the buyers and sellers of labour power met to realise their material interests. Rather, labour power was exploited and a surplus realised by means of unfree relations of production. What distinguished the establishment of agricultural commodity production in the Caribbean, and in several other parts of the world, was the *absence* of proletarianisation.

It has been noted many times that Marx's theoretical and historical analysis of the development of the capitalist mode of production, by virtue of being confined to the example of England and more generally to Europe, is of little value to an analysis of the historical development of the forces and relations of production outside Europe (e.g. Robinson 1983). With certain exceptions, much of the theoretical and historical work intended to 'rescue' Marxist analysis from this lacuna was undertaken only after the 1960s. Consequently, when Cox was formulating his Marxist theory of 'race relations', he was doing so in a Eurocentric vacuum. Few attempts had been made within the Marxist tradition at that time to analyse systematically the activities of merchant and finance capital outside Europe.

Hence, we may regard his creation of a Marxist theory of 'race relations' as a refraction of the then contemporary silence within Marxist theory about the formation of unfree relations of production in the colonial context. In an attempt to comprehend and explain that context, Cox identified 'race relations' as the unique characteristic of the process of colonisation, a process which in all other respects had a universal, capitalistic character. Hence, Cox focused on the signification of phenotypical difference which was used subsequently by the colonising class to frame the expropriation of labour power, and so elevated the ideological notion of 'race' to the status of a theoretical concept within Marxist theory. [. . .]

The challenge of migration theory

The post-1945 migrations from the Caribbean and the Indian subcontinent brought to Britain men and women in search of a wage who were understood by state officials and large sections of the British population to be members of distinct 'races'. Rather than signify them as British subjects, which they were, they were designated as 'coloured' and 'colonial' people whose presence would change the 'racial character' of the British population (e.g. Carter *et al.* 1987: 335, also Joshi and Carter 1984). In the light of the fact that sections of the British ruling class commonly justified colonialism as an attempt to 'civilise inferior races' and sought special methods of administration and economic compulsion to achieve this (e.g. Lugard 1929), this is unsurprising. However, there was little political or academic interest in this migration until the hostile, and largely racist, reaction to the migration found a place on the domestic political agenda (Miles 1984b).

Up until 1958, 'race relations' were, in common-sense terms, a colonial 'problem': the racist attacks on British subjects of Caribbean origin in that year in England were interpreted by the state as evidence that the problem of 'race relations' had been transferred to the 'Mother Country'. When British academics began to take an interest in these domestic developments, they drew upon concepts, theories and political strategies derived from the United States and South Africa (Rich 1986a: 191–200), all of which had 'race relations' as the object of analysis. Most of these academics were anthropologists by training and liberal in political perspective (e.g. Banton 1967).

The first major challenge from within the Marxist tradition to this 'race relations' paradigm came with the work of Castles and Kosack published in the early 1970s (1972, 1973, cf. Bolaria and Li 1985). They demonstrated the parallels between determinants and consequences of migration to other nation states in north-west Europe. Thereby, they deflected the institutionalised comparison between British and the United States and South Africa (evident, for example, in the early writing of Banton (1967) and Rex (1970)), arguing that it was more useful to analyse comparatively the British experience of post-1945 migration in the context of the reconstruction of capitalism throughout Europe.

Castles and Kosack opened their seminal work by rejecting the dominant sociological paradigm of 'race relations'. They argued that all contemporary capitalist societies contain a distinct stratum of people who occupy the worst jobs and live in inferior housing, and that in many of these societies this stratum is composed of immigrants or the descendants of immigrants. This immigration was explained as a consequence of uneven capitalist development on a world scale and immigrant workers were identified as having a specific socio-economic function found in all capitalist societies, namely to fill undesirable jobs vacated by the indigenous working class in the course of the periodic reorganisation of production. This stratum of immigrant workers thereby came to constitute a 'lower stratum' of the working class, which was thereby fragmented. Hence, for Castles and Kosack, the analytical focus was not 'race' or 'race relations', but the interconnections between capital accumulation, migration and class formation (1973: 1–13).

But in proposing this paradigm shift, Castles and Kosack did not reject 'race' as an analytical concept. Rather, they subordinated it to a political economy of labour migration and class relations: that is, they retained the category of 'race' in order to deny its explanatory significance. When referring to the total number of eight million immigrants in western Europe, Castles and Kosack claimed that 'At the most two million of them can be considered as being racially distinct from the indigenous population' (1973: 2). In other words, because only a minority of the immigrants occupying this subordinate proletarian position were members of a 'race' distinct from that of the majority, neither 'race' nor racism could be the factor which determined occupation of this structural site in class relations (1973: 2). Rather, their social position was determined by the 'normal' working of the capitalist mode of production. The fact that Castles and Kosack used the idea of 'race' as a classificatory concept in this way without explanation or definition testifies to its unproblematic status amongst Marxist writers during the 1970s.

This political economy of migration paradigm has been embraced by Sivanandan (1982, 1990), who also criticised academic 'race relations' analysis and sought an alternative perspective on the British situation. Sivanandan reproduced several of the central themes in the work of Castles and Kosack (1973), and of Nikolinakos (1975). He referred specifically to the importance of a reserve army of labour (or an underclass) to sustain capitalist expansion and to divide the working class, and to the 'cheapness' of a migrant labour system wherein the costs of the production and reproduction of labour power are met within the social formation from which the migrant originates and to which he or she is returned (Sivanandan 1982: 105–6, 1990: 153–60, 189–91).

Sivanandan's initial focus was not so much upon western European capitalism in general as on British capitalism in particular. For example, he devoted considerable attention to the state immigration controls of the 1960s which transformed British subjects from the Commonwealth into aliens who could enter Britain only on a temporary basis with a work permit (Sivanandan, 1982: 108–11; 1983: 2–3). But his analysis of the British situation was effected by a set of general Marxist categories and via an analysis of capitalism as a world system, categories and a perspective which equally structure his more recent interest in Europe (1990: 153–60). Formally, there is little that is new in this aspect of Sivanandan's work. This is confirmed by his critique of the recent neo-Marxist analysis of Thatcherism which is signalled by the notion of 'New Times', a critique which reaffirms the importance of the fundamental struggle between capital and labour (1990: 19–59). What does distinguish Sivanandan's work, making his voice and contribution distinctive, is the central place that the idea of 'race' occupies in his analysis: for example, the journal that he edits is called *Race and Class*, a title that places the idea of 'race' on an analytical level equivalent to class.

Sivanandan's use of the idea of 'race' is usually subordinated to the concept of racism. Put another way, his focus on 'black struggle' highlights the resistance of some British citizens of Asian and Caribbean origin to the racism, particularly institutionalised racism, that structures their lives: in the course of analysing the nature and effects of racism, Sivanandan employs the idea of 'race'. For example,

Sivanandan claims that the migrant labour system 'prevents . . . the horizontal conflict of classes through the vertical integration of race – and, in the process, exploits both race and class at once' (1982: 104). Elsewhere, he refers to hierarchies of 'race' within the working class (1982: 113) and to the significance of learning about 'other races, about other people's cultures' (1983: 5). In these formulations 'race' is attributed with an independent reality, equivalent to class as well as to sex, as in the argument that 'racism is not . . . a white problem, but a problem of an exploitative white power structure; power is not something white people are born into, but that which they derive from their position in a complex race/sex/class hierarchy' (1985: 27). More recently, in an interview, he has commented concerning the journal that he edits: 'Yet *Race and Class* never subsumes race under class. It looks at race in terms of class, while at the same time bringing to an understanding of the class struggle the racial dimension' (1990: 14).

What Sivanandan means by his use of the idea of 'race' is rarely clearly stated: it usually functions to mark a symbolic site for the organisation of autonomous political resistance to capitalism, imperialism and racism, and, for this very reason, clarification of its meaning is unnecessary for him. But, in one of his less commonly cited papers in which he analyses South Africa as an exceptional capitalist formation, he does address (and reject) the argument that the use of the idea of 'race' implies a legitimation of racist classifications of the human species (1982: 161–71). He defends the common-sense definition of 'race' as a reference to a group of persons who share the same descent or origin, adding that group differences (presumably phenotypical differences) are 'an observable fact' (1982: 163). Thus, Sivanandan uses the idea of 'race' to refer to distinct, biologically defined groups of people. As a result, 'race' is as much a reality as class, both concepts referring to some quality that all people possess. Sivanandan observes, for example that 'Each man was locked into his class and his race, with the whites on top and the blacks below' (1982: 166), and that 'The settlers . . . were (and are) a slender minority, distinguished by race and colour' (1982: 168).

For Sivanandan, 'racial groups' therefore have a reality *sui generis*, a reality which parallels but also mediates class: hence, South Africa is exceptional only because 'race is class and class race – and the race struggle is the class struggle' (1982: 170). Yet, it is not the supposed reality of racial difference that matters theoretically or politically, but rather the use made of that difference by the 'race' (as mediated by class) that possesses the greatest amount of power. In other words, what matters most is the 'racist ideology that grades these differences in a hierarchy of power – in order to rationalise and justify exploitation' (1982: 163). For Sivanandan, the primary object of political struggle is the racism that legitimates capitalist exploitation and, hence, he observes that racism cannot be abolished by rejecting the idea of 'race' (1982: 162). However, it does not follow from this that the critique of the idea of 'race' is not an important moment in the struggle against racism.

The shift in Marxist theory away from the construction of a Marxist theory of 'race relations' towards an analysis of the expression and consequences of racism within the framework of a political economy of migration represented a major theoretical break. It permits an analysis of the expression and consequences of racism within the framework of the dynamic process of capital accumulation, and situates the analysis of racism at the centre of Marxist theory (e.g. Miles 1982, 1986). But, for the Marxist writers mentioned to this point (see also Wolpe 1980, 1986, Wallerstein 1988), this was accomplished in the absence of any critical evaluation of 'race' and 'race relations' as analytical concepts. Rather than sweep the theoretical shelf clean, these writers retained certain core ideas of the 'race relations' paradigm and repackaged them with the central Marxist concepts of class, capital accumulation, reserve army of labour, etc. For Castles and Kosack, and for Sivanandan, the idea of 'race' has been retained in a form which suggests that the human population is composed of a number of biological 'races'.

Marxist theories of political and ideological crisis

The development of a political economy of migration has been largely ignored by another strand of Marxist theory which has been concerned almost exclusively with the political and ideological crisis of British capitalism. This concern results from a preoccupation with the rejection of economism and an adoption of a field of analysis usually described as cultural studies. Given its concern with the social construction of meaning, one might expect that a cultural studies perspective, especially one that is allied with Marxism, would regard the critical evaluation of the idea of 'race' as a central and urgent task. Surprisingly, this has not been so.

The important work of Stuart Hall is central to this strand of Marxist theory. Hall's focus has been upon the role of the British state in reconstructing British society in the face of a series of political and ideological conflicts which have occurred in a conjuncture dominated by the declining profitability of British capital. Hall has devoted some attention to the role of the expression of racism in the resulting organic crisis of British capitalism and the rise of the authoritarian state (e.g. Hall *et al.* 1978, Hall 1978, 1980). While his observations have been theoretically grounded and influential, they are fragmented and have not been accompanied by a rigorous theoretical examination of the concepts employed.

Elsewhere, I have suggested that, in the absence of such theoretical work, Hall represents 'race' as an independent force in itself (Miles, 1982: 176–7). Here, I cite another example: in a much celebrated paper, Hall argues that 'At the economic level, it is clear that race must be given its distinctive and "relatively autonomous" effectivity, as a distinctive feature' (1980: 339). This reification of 'race' is reproduced in the equally well-known work of the 'Race and Politics Group' of the Centre for Contemporary Cultural Studies (CCCS), of which Hall was previously the Director. Hall's previously cited assertion was subsequently echoed approvingly in the work of the CCCS group (1982: 11, my emphasis):

> Although . . . we see race as a means through which other relations are secured or experienced, this does not mean that we view it as operating merely as a mechanism to express essentially non-racial contradictions and struggles in racial terms. These expressive aspects must be recognised, but *race must also be approached in its autonomous effectivity*.

In both these formulations, 'race' is represented as a determinant force, something which has real effects and consequences (although for the 'Race and Politics Group' these effects are absolutely rather than relatively autonomous). But what 'race' is, what the character of this 'feature' is, is never defined. We are left to search for the clues which identify the meaning that lies behind the silence.

Hall refers to 'different racial and ethnic groups' (1980: 339), suggesting that he employs 'race' to identify groups differentiated by biological characteristics (see also 1980: 342). If this is his meaning, it parallels Sivanandan's usage. But this does not help us comprehend the claim that 'race' is a reality which has relatively autonomous effects within social relations. Without additional clarification, the claim remains vacuous and each new, approving citation only reinforces its unintelligibility.

Similarly, the meaning attributed to the idea of 'race' in the work of the CCCS 'Race and Politics Group' (1982) is unclear and problematic (see Miles 1984a). One of the members of this group, Paul Gilroy, has subsequently responded to this critique, and to the broader argument upon which the critique was based (Miles 1982), as a prelude to an important analysis of the historical and contemporary expression of racisms, and their articulation with nationalism in Britain. Given that Gilroy states his agreement with my critique of 'race relations sociology' (1987: 40n), one expects him to reject the use of 'race' as an analytical concept in his more recent work. But this is not so. Moreover, the manner in which the idea of 'race' is theorised and celebrated in this recent text is characterised by a number of contradictions (Miles 1988).

Gilroy begins by claiming that the idea of 'race' has a descriptive value (1987: 149) *and* that it is an analytical concept (1987: 247): '"Race" must be retained as an analytical category not because it corresponds to any biological or epistemological absolutes, but because it refers investigation to the power that collective identities acquire by means of their roots in tradition.' But if there is a reason to attribute the idea of 'race' with analytical status, *that is if one represents it as a concept which can be employed to explain social processes*, it must refer to a real, identifiable phenomenon which can have (autonomous) effects on those processes. Yet, if this is so, it is not clear why ambiguity should be expressed about the concept by the (inconsistent) use of inverted commas around it. Is Gilroy wishing to signal that there is something essentially problematic about the use of the term (which is the justification for my consistent use of inverted commas)? Or is the occasional absence of inverted commas an indication of some real (but unexplained) difference in the usage and meaning of the term?

If 'race' is an analytical category that identifies a material object, what are its features? Gilroy offers several definitions. 'Race' is variously described as an effect of discourse (1987: 14), a political category that can accommodate different meanings (1987: 38, 39), and a relational concept (1987: 229). These descriptions are confusing. If 'race' is an effect of discourse, or a political category, or a relational concept, how is it distinguished from the other effects of discourse or other political categories or other relational concepts? These descriptions by themselves do not refer to any specifically identifiable phenomenon: they do not provide identifying criteria.

Elsewhere, 'race' is represented both as a thing in itself when Gilroy refers to the 'transformation of phenotypical variation into concrete systems of differentiation based on "race" and colour', as well as a social collectivity when he refers to 'racial groups' (1987: 18), when he defines 'race formation' as the 'manner in which "races" become organised in politics' (1987: 38), and when he claims that 'Races are political collectivities not ahistorical essences' (1987: 149). The former implicitly refers to what he subsequently identifies as an ahistorical essence because it has a biological character (although the distinction between 'race' and skin colour adds to the confusion), while the latter identifies a specific form of social collectivity – but we are not told how this differs from any other social collectivity (for example, classes). Hence, within Gilroy's text, 'races' are represented as really existing collectivities, although there is an ambiguity over whether these collectivities are biologically constituted or are the product of the articulation of racism and the expression of resistance by those thereby excluded and exploited. Ironically, his complaint that the Scarman Report fails to define what is meant by the reference to the Brixton riots as 'racial' (1987: 106) refracts precisely the same ambiguity in his own text.

This ambiguity is further expressed in the contradiction between the representation of 'race' as a particular type of social group and the argument that 'race' has never been anything other than an idea, a social representation of the Other as a distinct sort of human being. The latter is expressed in the claims that '"Race" has to be socially and politically constructed' (1987: 38) and that 'race' is only a device for the categorisation of human beings (1987: 218). These assertions parallel my own arguments (Miles 1982, 1984a) and hence I can agree with his claim that 'the attempt to make "race" always already a meaningful factor, in other words to racialise social and political phenomena, may be itself identified as part of the "race" problem' (Gilroy 1987: 116).

But Gilroy resists accepting the logical conclusion of this observation. The definition of a 'race' problem is synonymous with the racialisation of social relations, and this process of attributing meaning to real or invented somatic (and cultural) variation can only be analysed and deconstructed consistently by eliminating all conceptions of 'race' as a thing in itself, with the power to have effects. This does not require denying that the idea of 'race' is a constituent element of everyday common sense: the issue is whether or not such usage is transferred into the conceptual language that it used to comprehend and explain that common sense. I see no reason to do this. There are no 'races' and therefore no 'race relations'. There is only a belief that there are such things, a belief which is used by some social groups to construct an Other (and therefore the Self) in thought as a prelude to exclusion and domination, and by other social groups to define Self (and so to construct an Other) as a means of resisting that exclusion. Hence, if it is used at all, the idea of 'race' should be used only to refer descriptively to such uses of the idea of 'race'.

A comment is also required on Gilroy's apparent rejection of Marxism. Throughout 'There Ain't No Black in the Union Jack' (1987), he allies himself with those who argue that a Marxist analysis of capitalism based on the historical instance of nineteenth-century Europe is inappropriate in the late twentieth century. This argument takes a number of (not always consistent) forms, but usually includes the assertion that the number of people involved directly in industrial production in advanced 'capitalist' social formations is declining and that, as a result, the industrial proletariat can no longer be the leading and progressive political force that it was in the past.

Echoing writers such as Gorz and Touraine, Gilroy claims that the leading forces of resistance in the contemporary western world are social movements based around 'race', gender, demands for nuclear disarmament, etc., all of which are conceived as being disconnected from production relations. Consequently, 'if these struggles . . . are to be called class struggles, then class analysis must itself be thoroughly overhauled. I am not sure whether the labour involved in doing this makes it either a possible or a desirable task' (Gilroy 1987: 245). Class struggle, for Gilroy, has been transcended by 'the forms of white racism and black resistance' which he describes as 'the most volatile political forces in Britain today' (1987: 247).

If, in Gilroy's view, class theory cannot be overhauled, he has dispensed with a theory of class struggle in favour of what is sometimes called 'race' struggle. Here, Gilroy seems to identify with the 'Black radical tradition' as Robinson (1983) describes it, a tradition which rejects Marxism as an adequate theory of revolution for 'black people' (1983: 1–6) and which is terminating the 'experimentation with Western political inventories of change, specifically nationalism and class struggle' (1983: 451). This is confirmed by Gilroy's approval (1987: 38) of the work of Omi and Winant, which rejects class analysis on the grounds that it neglects 'the specificity of race as an autonomous field of social conflict' (Omi and Winant 1986: 52). [. . .]

'Race' as an ideological construction

Certain currents in the French materialist tradition offer a more reflexive and critical approach to the use of the idea of 'race' as an analytical concept, reaching conclusions which parallel my own (Miles 1982, 1984a, Miles and Phizacklea 1984: 1–19) and which are emergent within some critical, if not Marxist, writing in the USA (e.g. Fields 1982, 1990, Goldberg 1990b). The work of Colette Guillaumin is the most important in this context (e.g. 1972, 1980, 1988).

She has argued that use of the idea of 'race' necessarily suggests that certain social relationships are natural and therefore inevitable. Social relations described as 'racial' are represented as somatically determined and therefore outside historical, social determination. Consequently, the idea of 'race' is transformed into an active subject, a biological reality which determines historical processes. This amounts to a process of reification, as a result of which that which should be explained becomes an explanation of social relations. Guillaumin writes (1980: 39):

> Whatever the theoretical foundations underlying the various interpretations of 'racial' relations, the very use of such a distinction tends to imply the acceptance of some essential difference between type of social relation, some, somewhere, being specifically racial. Merely to adopt

the expression implies the belief that races are 'real' or concretely apprehensible, or at the best that the idea of race is uncritically accepted; moreover, it implies that races play a role in the social process not merely as an ideological form, but as an immediate factor acting as both determining cause and concrete means.

Guillaumin concludes (1980: 39, see also 1988: 26):

the fact that such relationships are thought of as racial by those concerned (and sometimes this is as true of the oppressed as of the oppressors) is a social fact, and it ought to be examined as carefully and sceptically as any other explanation offered by a society of its own mechanisms. Such explanations can only refer to a particular time and place.

The analytical task is therefore to explain why certain relationships are interpreted as determined by or expressive of 'race', rather than to accept without criticism and comment that they are and to freeze and legitimate that representation in the idea of 'race relations' as social relations between 'races'. Hence, any analytical use of the idea of 'race' disguises the fact that it is an idea created by human beings in certain historical and material conditions, and used to represent and structure the world in certain ways, under certain historical conditions and for certain political interests. The idea of 'race' is therefore *essentially* ideological (Guillaumin 1980: 59).

These arguments do not deny that there is considerable somatic variation between individual human beings. But the signification of phenotypical features in order to classify human beings into groups simultaneously designated as *natural* is not a universal feature of social relations. In Europe, it began in the eighteenth century: for the idea of naturalness is even more 'modern' than the idea of 'race' (Guillaumin 1988). Certain somatic features (some real and some imagined) were socially signified as natural marks of difference (e.g. skin colour), a difference that became known as a difference of 'race'. Moreover, these marks, conceived as natural, were then thought to explain the already existing social position of the collectivity thereby designated by the mark (cf. Fields 1990: 106). This social process of signification was (and remains) an important ideological moment in a process of domination. The idea of 'race' thereby came to express *nature*, something given and immutable, with the result that what was in fact the consequence of social relations became understood as *natural*: and so 'race' was thought of as a determinate force, requiring social relations of domination to be organised in a specific form, thereby obscuring their human construction. By utilising the idea of 'race' as an analytical concept, social scientists deny the historicity of this social process, freezing it with the idea that the naturalness of somatic difference ineluctably constitutes eternal human collectivities.

These arguments have been rarely addressed directly by Marxist writers, many of whom continue to defend the retention of 'race' as an analytical concept. Anthias (1990), for example, argues not only that 'race' should be retained as an analytical concept but also that its relationship to class should be specified. Anthias advocates retention of the idea of 'race' as an analytical concept to denote 'a particular way in which communal or collective differences come to be constructed and understood', one that refers to 'immutable fixed biologically or physiognomically based difference' (1990: 22). If this is all the meaning that the idea of 'race' embodies in being transformed into a concept, then this is precisely the meaning that is denoted by the concept of racialisation (Miles 1982: 120, 150, 1989: 74–7). In other words, the *social process* that Anthias refers to with the idea of 'race' is better denoted by the concept of racialisation.

But why does she ignore this concept in order to retain the idea of 'race' as an analytical concept? It is because she has chosen arbitrarily the class/'race' artic- ulation as the starting point for her analysis (1990: 19): having made such a choice, she is required to theorise the idea of 'race' into an analytical concept in order to sustain the paradigm which constitutes her point of departure. Thus, rather than *first* reflect critically on the historical evolution of the idea of 'race', and on the implications of its attributed meaning through time, in order to *second* reach a conclusion about the validity of transforming it into an analytical concept, Anthias precludes the very possibility of such an epistemological evaluation by electing without any critical reflection to employ the idea of 'race' as a concept positioned relative to class. As a result, while acknowledging the 'mythological representa- tions that surround it' (1990: 23) and while agreeing with me that the concept of racism should be separated from the idea of 'race' (1990: 22–4), she invests those very same mythological representations with an analytical status by treating the idea of 'race' as a scientific concept with an object in the real world. This is expressed in her various references to 'race formation', 'race processes', to the distinct ontological status of 'race', to 'race phenomena' and to 'racially organ- ised communities' (Anthias 1990: 20, 21, 35).

So, the case against the incorporation of the idea of 'race' into Marxist theory (and indeed into sociological theory) as an analytical concept can be summarised as follows (see also Miles 1982, cf. Goldberg 1990b). First, all theoretical work is an integral part of the social world. We live in a world in which the nineteenth- century biological conception of 'race', although discredited scientifically, remains an important presence in 'common sense': large numbers of people continue to believe, and to act as if they believe, that the world's population is divided into a number of discrete, biologically distinguishable groups, i.e. 'races' (cf. Fields 1990: 95–101). Although this conception (especially in its explicitly racist incar- nation) is rejected by most sociologists and Marxists, their conceptions and theories of 'race' and 'race relations', where they resonate in the wider structure of social relations, fail to challenge common sense. Indeed, by failing to explain consistently and explicitly their sociological conception of 'race' as a social construction, they implicitly (and often explicitly) endorse common sense (Rozat and Bartra 1980: 302, Smith 1989: 3, 11), and hence sustain an ideology which Barzun called a 'Modern Superstition' (1938) and which Montagu described as 'Man's [sic] Most Dangerous Myth' (1974).

A recent example of such an endorsement of the commonsense idea of 'race' is found in an argument which is intended to explicate 'the salience of race as a *social construct*': Smith (whose work, while not falling formally within the Marxist tradition, is nevertheless influenced by writing that is) suggests that the analysis of the salience of 'race' (1989: 3) 'should centre not on what race explains about

society, but rather on the questions of who, why and with what effect social significance is attached to racial attributes that are constructed in particular political and
socio-economic contexts'. Here, the reference to 'racial attributes' resonates with
all those 'mythological representations' of the nineteenth-century idea of 'race' as
a biological type of human being characterised by certain somatic attributes. While
there are all the usual sociological qualifiers (in the form of references to social
processes of signification and construction), Smith's reference to 'racial attributes'
as the *object* of the ascription of meaning implies that there is some biological
'reality' underlying the somatic features thereby signified: an attribute denotes the
existence of some other thing which, given the description 'racial', can only mean
that that thing is a 'race'. This is an example of the way in which the idea of 'race'
as a natural division lives on, is reconstituted and renewed, by a critical sociological analysis which seeks to deny such a 'reality' by reprocessing the idea of
'race' as an analytical concept.

This is also illustrated by a paper in a collection of essays intended to demonstrate recent advances in the critical analysis of racism (Goldberg 1990a). Christian
(1990) offers a radical analysis of Afro-American women's literature which priori-
tises as the conceptual framework 'the intersection of . . . race, class, and gender'
(1990: 135). The novel that is the central focus of her analysis is described as 'an
exploration of the ways in which race affects the relations among women', and its
author is considered to have demonstrated 'not only that race, class, and gender
intersect but that they are never pure, exclusive categories. None of these categories exist on their own. Rather there are men or women of one class or another,
of one race or another' (1990: 136, 143).

Thus, second, the reification of 'race' as an active subject, and 'race relations'
as a distinct variety of social relations, represents somatic differentiation as an
active determinant of social processes and structures. It follows that 'the ideological notion of "race" does not have the rigour of an objective scientific definition,
despite all later attempts to rationalise it' (Lecourt 1980: 282). Its use obscures
the active construction of the social world by those people who articulate racism
and by those who engage in exclusionary practices consistent with racism. Our
object of analysis, the active determinant of exclusion and disadvantage, is therefore not physical difference in itself, but the attribution of significance to certain
patterns of, or the imagined assertion of, difference and the use of that process of
signification to structure social relationships. The use of 'race' (and 'race relations') as analytical concepts disguises the social construction of difference,
presenting it as somehow inherent in the empirical reality of observable or imagined biological difference.

Third, the incorporation of ideological conceptions into Marxist and sociological theory has structured historical and empirical investigation in a manner
which leads to comparative analyses of limited theoretical and political (including
policy) relevance. By defining 'race' and 'race relations' as the subject of study,
comparative attention is directed to those other social formations where identical
social definitions prevail, usually South Africa and the USA. In other words,
comparative analysis is determined by certain common ideological features (i.e. by
phenomenal forms), rather than by a historical materialist analysis of the reproduction of the capitalist mode of production (i.e. by essential relations). Yet,

considered in terms of the historical dynamic of capitalist development, these two social formations (by virtue of their colonial origin and historical dependence on unfree labour) have little in common with post-1945 economic and political developments in Britain, despite sharing a common ideological definition of 'race' as a social problem (but see Small (1991) for an important alternative analysis).

Attention has thereby been distracted from the other social formations of north-west Europe where the interdependence of capital accumulation and labour migration has resulted, since 1945, in the permanent settlement of populations which are often culturally distinct from the indigenous populations. It is only in Britain that the political definition of this settlement as problematic has been defined as a matter of 'race': elsewhere it has been defined as a 'minority problem' or 'immigrant problem', for example. But these ideological variations are grounded in a common economic and political process, leaving one to pose the question 'Why?'. This question can only be investigated by first deconstructing 'race' as an analytical concept, for only then does investigation come to focus upon the political and ideological processes by which the idea of 'race' has been utilised to comprehend this process of migration and settlement.

Conclusion

In so far as Marxism asserts that all social relationships are socially constructed and reproduced in specific historical circumstances, and that those relationships are therefore in principle alterable by human agency, then it should not have space for an ideological notion that implies, and often explicitly asserts, the opposite. The task is therefore not to create a Marxist theory of 'race' which is more valid than conservative or liberal theories, but to deconstruct 'race', and to detach it from the concept of racism. By deconstructing the idea of 'race', the effects of the process of racialisation and of the expression of racism within the development of the capitalist world economic system are more clearly exposed (Miles 1982, 1987, 1989, Miles and Phizacklea 1984: 4–19) because the role of human signification and exclusionary practices is prioritised. And where racialisation and racism structure aspects of the reproduction of the capitalist mode of production or any other mode of production, then that mode appears in another of its historically specific forms.

This can be illustrated by returning to consider the argument that 'race relations' arose from the proletarianisation of labour in the Caribbean. I have already argued that there was no proletarianisation of labour in this region during the seventeenth and eighteenth centuries because slave rather than wage relations of production predominated after an initial period during which indentured labour was prevalent. In a context where unfree relations of production were widespread, the initial enslavement of Africans was not in itself remarkable. It was only after Africans were enslaved that African people were represented in negative terms as an Other and that certain of their phenotypical characteristics were signified as expressive of their being a different (and inferior) type of human being. This racialisation of a population that was confined to the provision of labour power under slave relations of production was intensified with the emergence of the idea of 'race' and its utilisation to dichotomise the owners of the means of production and the suppliers of labour power as being naturally different 'types' of human being.

Similar processes of racialisation and a similar expression of racism occurred elsewhere in the world (and not only outside Europe) in the eighteenth and nineteenth centuries as colonial settlement was followed by the expansion of commodity production. As in the case of the Caribbean, these instances were usually accompanied by the forced migration of a group of people who were destined to provide labour power under relations of direct politico-legal compulsion. I have argued elsewhere (1987: 186–95) that in all these instances of unfree relations of production, through a process of racialisation, racism became an ideological relation of production: that is to say, the ideology of racism constructed the Other as a specific and inferior category of being particularly suited to providing labour power within unfree relations of production. Racialisation and racism were thereby ideological forces which, in conjunction with economic and political relations of domination, located certain populations in specific class positions and therefore structured the exploitation of labour power in a particular ideological manner. [. . .]

References

Anthias, F. (1990) 'Race and class revisited – conceptualising race and racisms', *Sociological Review*, 38(1): 19–42.

Banton, M. (1967) *Race Relations*, London: Tavistock.

——(1987) *Racial Theories*, Cambridge: Cambridge University Press.

——(1991) 'The race relations problematic', *British Journal of Sociology*, 42(1): 115–30.

Barkan, E. (1992) *The Retreat of Scientific Racism: Changing Concepts of Race in Britain and the United States Between the World Wars*, Cambridge: Cambridge University Press.

Barzun, J. (1938) *Race: A Study in Modern Superstition*, London: Methuen.

Benedict, R. (1983) *Race and Racism*, London: Routledge and Kegan Paul.

Bolaria, B.S. and Li, P. (1985) *Racial Oppression in Canada*, Toronto: Garamond Press.

Carter, B., Harris, C. and Joshi, S. (1987) 'The 1951–55 Conservative government and the racialisation of black immigration', *Immigrants and Minorities*, 6: 335–47.

Castles, S. and Kosack, G. (1972) 'The function of labour immigration in western European capitalism', *New Left Review*, 73: 3–21.

——and Kosack, G. (1973) *Immigrant Workers and Class Structure in Western Europe*, London: Oxford University Press.

CCCS (Centre for Contemporary Cultural Studies) (1982) *The Empire Strikes Back: Race and Racism in 70s Britain*, London: Hutchinson.

Christian, B. (1990) 'What Celie knows that you should know', in D.T. Goldberg (ed.) *Anatomy of Racism*, Minneapolis: University of Minnesota Press.

Cox, O.C. (1970) *Caste, Class and Race*, New York: Monthly Review Press.

Fields, B.J. (1982) 'Ideology and race in American history', in J.M. Kousser and J.M. McPherson (eds) *Region, Race and Reconstruction: Essays in Honour of C. Vann Woodward*, New York: Oxford University Press.

——(1990) 'Slavery, race and ideology in the United States of America', *New Left Review*, 181: 95–118.

George, H. (1984) *American Race Relations Theory: A Review of Four Models*, Lanham: University Press of America.

Gilroy, P. (1987) *'There Ain't No Black in the Union Jack': The Cultural Politics of Race and Nation*, London: Hutchinson.

Goldberg, D.T. (ed.) (1990a) *Anatomy of Racism*, Minneapolis: University of Minnesota Press.

——(1990b) 'The social formation of racist discourse', in D.T. Goldberg (ed.) *Anatomy of Racism*, Minneapolis: University of Minnesota Press.

Guillaumin, C. (1972) *L'idéologie Raciste: Genèse et Langage Actuel*, Paris: Mouton.

——(1980) 'The idea of race and its elevation to autonomous scientific and legal status', in UNESCO, *Sociological Theories: Race and Colonialism*, Paris: UNESCO.

——(1988) 'Race and nature: the system of marks', *Feminist Issues*, 1988: 25–43.

Hall, S. (1978) 'Racism and reaction', in Commission for Racial Equality, *Five Views of Multi-Racial Britain*, London: Commission for Racial Equality.

——(1980) 'Race, articulation and societies structured in dominance', in UNESCO, *Sociological Theories: Race and Colonialism*, Paris: UNESCO.

——, Critcher, C., Jefferson, T., Clarke, J., and Roberts, B. (1978) *Policing the Crisis: Mugging, the State and Law and Order*, London: Macmillan.

Hirschfeld, M. (1938) *Racism*, London: Gollancz.

Jordan, W.D. (1968) *White Over Black: American Attitudes Toward the Negro, 1550–1812*, Chapel Hill: University of North Carolina Press.

——(1974) *The White Man's Burden: Historical Origins of Racism in the United States*, London: Oxford University Press.

Joshi, S. and Carter, B. (1984) 'The role of Labour in creating a racist Britain', *Race and Class*, 25: 53–70.

Lecourt, D. (1980) 'Marxism as a critique of sociological theories', in UNESCO, *Sociological Theories: Race and Colonialism*, Paris: UNESCO.

Lugard, F.D. (1929) *The Dual Mandate in British Tropical Africa*, Edinburgh: William Blackwood & Sons Ltd.

Miles, R. (1980) 'Class, race and ethnicity: a critique of Cox's theory', *Ethnic and Racial Studies*, 3(2): 169–87.

——(1982) *Racism and Migrant Labour: A Critical Text*, London: Routledge and Kegan Paul.

——(1984a) 'Marxism versus the "sociology of race relations"?', *Ethnic and Racial Studies*, 7(2): 217–37.

——(1984b) 'The riots of 1958: the ideological construction of "race relations" as a political issue in Britain', *Immigrants and Minorities*, 3(3): 252–75.

——(1986) 'Labour migration, racism and capital accumulation in western Europe', *Capital and Class*, 28: 49–86.

——(1987) *Capitalism and Unfree Labour: Anomaly or Necessity?*, London: Tavistock.

——(1988) 'Racism, Marxism and British politics', *Economy and Society*, 17(3): 428–60.

——(1989) *Racism*, London: Routledge.

——and Phizacklea, A. (1984) *White Man's Country: Racism in British Politics*, London: Pluto Press.

Montagu, A. (ed.) (1964) *The Concept of Race*, New York: Free Press.

——(1974) *Man's Most Dangerous Myth: The Fallacy of Race*, New York: Oxford University Press.

Nikolinakos, M. (1975) 'Notes towards a general theory of migration in late capitalism', *Race and Class*, 17(1): 5–18.

Omi, M. and Winant, H. (1986) *Racial Formation in the United States: From the 1960s to the 1980s*, New York: Routledge and Kegan Paul.

Outlaw, L. (1990) 'Toward a critical theory of "race"', in D.T. Goldberg (ed.) *Anatomy of Racism*, Minneapolis: University of Minnesota Press.

Rex, J. (1970) *Race Relations in Sociological Theory*, London: Weidenfeld and Nicolson.

——(1983) *Race Relations in Sociological Theory*, 2nd edition, London: Routledge and Kegan Paul.

Rich, P.B. (1986a) *Race and Empire in British Politics*, Cambridge: Cambridge University Press.

Robinson, C.J. (1983) *Black Marxism*, London: Zed Press.

Rozat, G. and Bartra, R. (1980) 'Racism and capitalism', in UNESCO, *Sociological Theories: Race and Colonialism*, Paris: UNESCO.

Sivanandan, A. (1982) *A Different Hunger: Writings on Black Resistance*, London: Pluto Press.

——(1983) 'Challenging racism: strategies for the '80s', *Race and Class*, 25(2): 1–12.

——(1985) 'RAT and the degradation of the black struggle', *Race and Class*, 26(4): 1–34.

——(1990) *Communities of Resistance: Writings on Black Struggles for Socialism*, London: Verso.

Small, S. (1991) 'Racialised relations in Liverpool: a contemporary anomaly', *New Community*, 17(4): 511–37.

Smith, S.J. (1989) *The Politics of 'Race' and Residence*, Cambridge: Polity Press.

Stepan, N. (1982) *The Idea of Race in Science: Great Britain, 1800–1945*, London: Macmillan.

Wallerstein, I. (1979) *The Capitalist World-Economy*, Cambridge: Cambridge University Press.

——(1988) 'Universalisme, racisme, sexisme: les tensions ideologiques du capitalisme', in E. Balibar and I. Wallerstein, *Race, Nation, Classe: Les Identités Ambiguës*, Paris: Editions La Découverte.

Wolpe, H. (1980) 'Capitalism and cheap labour-power in South Africa: from segregation to apartheid', in H. Wolpe (ed.), *The Articulation of Modes of Production: Essays from Economy and Society*, London: Routledge and Kegan Paul.

——(1986) 'Class concepts, class struggle and racism', in J. Rex and D. Mason (eds) *Theories of Race and Ethnic Relations*, Cambridge: Cambridge University Press.

Chapter 11

Stuart Hall

OLD AND NEW IDENTITIES, OLD AND NEW ETHNICITIES

[. . .]

WHAT I AM GOING TO DO first is to return to the question of identity and try to look at some of the ways in which we are beginning to reconceptualize that within contemporary theoretical discourses. I shall then go back from that theoretical consideration to the ground of a cultural politics. Theory is always a detour on the way to something more important.

I return to the question of identity because the question of identity has returned to us; at any rate, it has returned to us in British politics and British cultural politics today. It has not returned in the same old place; it is not the traditional conception of identity. It is not going back to the old identity politics of the 1960s social movements. But it is, nevertheless, a kind of return to some of the ground which we used to think in that way. I will make a comment at the very end about what is the nature of this theoretical–political work which seems to lose things on the one side and then recover them in a different way from another side, and then have to think them out all over again just as soon as they get rid of them. What is this never-ending theoretical work which is constantly losing and regaining concepts? I talk about identity here as a point at which, on the one hand, a whole set of new theoretical discourses intersect and where, on the other, a whole new set of cultural practices emerge. I want to begin by trying, very briefly, to map some of those points of intersection theoretically, and then to look at some of their political consequences.

The old logics of identity are ones with which we are extremely familiar, either philosophically, or psychologically. Philosophically, the old logic of identity which many people have critiqued in the form of the old Cartesian subject was often thought in terms of the origin of being itself, the ground of action. Identity is the ground of action. And we have in more recent times a psychological discourse of the self which is very similar: a notion of the continuous, self-sufficient, devel-opmental, unfolding, inner dialectic of selfhood. We are never quite there, but always on our way to it, and when we get there, we will at last know exactly who it is we are.

Now this logic of identity is very important in a whole range of political, theo-retical and conceptual discourses. I am interested in it also as a kind of existential reality because I think the logic of the language of identity is extremely important to our own self-conceptions. It contains the notion of the true self, some real self inside there, hiding inside the husks of all the false selves that we present to the rest of the world. It is a kind of guarantee of authenticity. Not until we get really inside and hear what the true self has to say do we know what we are "really saying."

There is something guaranteed about that logic or discourse of identity. It gives us a sense of depth, out there, and in here. It is spatially organized. Much of our discourse of the inside and the outside, of the self and other, of the indi-vidual and society, of the subject and the object, is grounded in that particular logic of identity. And it helps us, I would say, to sleep well at night.

Increasingly, I think one of the main functions of concepts is that they give us a good night's rest. Because what they tell us is that there is a kind of stable, only very slowly-changing ground inside the hectic upsets, discontinuities and ruptures of history. Around us history is constantly breaking in unpredictable ways but we, somehow, go on being the same.

That logic of identity is, for good or ill, finished. It's at an end for a whole range of reasons. It's at an end in the first instance because of some of the great de-centerings of modern thought. One could discuss this very elaborately – I could spend the rest of the time talking about it but I just wanted to slot the ideas into place very quickly by using some names as reference points.

It is not possible to hold to that logic of identity after Marx because although Marx does talk about man (he doesn't talk about women making history but perhaps they were slotted in, as the nineteenth century so often slotted women in under some other masculine title), about men and women making history but under conditions which are not of their own choosing. And having lodged either the indi-vidual or collective subject always within historical practices, we as individuals or as groups cannot be, and can never have been, the sole origin or authors of those practices. That is a profound historical decentering in terms of social practice.

If that was not strong enough, knocking us sideways as it were, Freud came knocking from underneath, like Hamlet's ghost, and said, "While you're being decentered from left to right like that, let me decenter you from below a bit, and remind you that this stable language of identity is also set from the psychic life about which you don't know very much, and can't know very much. And which you can't know very much by simply taking thought about it: the great continent of the unconscious which speaks most clearly when it's slipping rather than when it's saying what it means." This makes the self begin to seem a pretty fragile thing.

Now, buffeted on one side by Marx and upset from below by Freud, just as it opens its mouth to say, "Well, at least I speak so therefore I must *be* some-thing," Saussure and linguistics comes along and says "That's not true either, you know. Language was there before you. You can only say something by positioning yourself in the discourse. The tale tells the teller, the myth tells the myth-maker, etc. The enunciation is always from some subject who is positioned by and in discourse." That upsets that. Philosophically, one comes to the end of any kind of notion of a perfect transparent continuity between our language and something out there which can be called the real, or the truth, without any quotation marks.

These various upsets, these disturbances in the continuity of the notion of the subject, and the stability of identity, are indeed, what modernity is like. It is not, incidentally, modernity itself. That has an older, and longer history. But this is the beginning of modernity as trouble. Not modernity as enlightenment and progress, but modernity as a problem.

It is also upset by other enormous historical transformations which do not have, and cannot be given, a single name, but without which the story could not be told. In addition to the three or four that I have quoted, we could mention the relativisation of the Western narrative itself, the Western episteme, by the rise of other cultures to prominence, and fifthly, the displacement of the masculine gaze.

Now, the question of trying to come to terms with the notion of identity in the wake of those theoretical decenterings is an extremely problematic enterprise. But that is not all that has been disturbing the settled logic of identity. Because as I was saying earlier when I was talking about the relative decline, or erosion, the instability of the nation-state, of the self-sufficiency of national economies and consequently, of national identities as points of reference, there has simultaneously been a fragmentation and erosion of collective social identity.

I mean here the great collective social identities which we thought of as large-scale, all-encompassing, homogeneous, as unified collective identities, which could be spoken about almost as if they were singular actors in their own right but which, indeed, placed, positioned, stabilized, and allowed us to understand and read, almost as a code, the imperatives of the individual self: the great collective social identities of class, of race, of nation, of gender, and of the West.

These collective social identities were formed in, and stabilized by, the huge, long-range historical processes which have produced the modern world, just as the theories and conceptualizations that I just referred to very briefly are what constituted modernity as a form of self-reflection. They were staged and stabilized by industrialization, by capitalism, by urbanization, by the formation of the world market, by the social and the sexual division of labor, by the great punctuation of civil and social life into the public and the private; by the dominance of the nation-state, and by the identification between Westernization and the notion of modernity itself.

I spoke in my previous talk about the importance, to any sense of where we are placed in the world, of the national economy, the nation-state and of national cultural identities. Let me say a word here about the great class identities which have stabilized so much of our understanding of the immediate and not-so-immediate past.

[. . .] Identity means, or connotes, the process of identification, of saying that this here is the same as that, or we are the same together, in this respect. But something we have learnt from the whole discussion of identification, in feminism and psychoanalysis, is the degree to which that structure of identification is always constructed through ambivalence. Always constructed through splitting. Splitting between that which one is, and that which is the other. The attempt to expel the other to the other side of the universe is always compounded by the relationships of love and desire. This is a different language from the language of, as it were, the Others who are completely different from oneself.

This is the Other that belongs inside one. This is the Other that one can only know from the place from which one stands. This is the self as it is inscribed in the gaze of the Other. And this notion which breaks down the boundaries, between outside and inside, between those who belong and those who do not, between those whose histories have been written and those whose histories they have depended on but whose histories cannot be spoken. That the unspoken silence in between that which can be spoken is the only way to reach for the whole history. There is no other history except to take the absences and the silences along with what can be spoken. Everything that can be spoken is on the ground of the enormous voices that have not, or cannot yet be heard.

This doubleness of discourse, this necessity of the Other to the self, this inscription of identity in the look of the other finds its articulation profoundly in the ranges of a given text. And I want to cite one which I am sure you know but won't remember necessarily, though it is a wonderful, majestic moment in Fanon's *Black Skin, White Masks*, when he describes himself as a young Antillean, face to face with the white Parisian child and her mother. And the child pulls the hand of the mother and says, "Look, Mama, a black man." And he said, "For the first time, I knew who I was. For the first time, I felt as if I had been simultaneously exploded in the gaze, in the violent gaze of the other, and at the same time, recomposed as another."

The notion that identity in that sense could be told as two histories, one over here, one over there, never having spoken to one another, never having anything to do with one another, when translated from the psychoanalytic to the historical terrain, is simply not tenable any longer in an increasingly globalized world. It is just not tenable any longer.

People like me who came to England in the 1950s have been there for centuries; symbolically, we have been there for centuries. I was coming home. I am the sugar at the bottom of the English cup of tea. I am the sweet tooth, the sugar plantations that rotted generations of English children's teeth. There are thousands of others beside me that are, you know, the cup of tea itself. Because they don't grow it in Lancashire, you know. Not a single tea plantation exists within the United Kingdom. This is the symbolization of English identity – I mean, what does anybody in the world know about an English person except that they can't get through the day without a cup of tea?

Where does it come from? Ceylon – Sri Lanka, India. That is the outside history that is inside the history of the English. There is no English history without that other history. The notion that identity has to do with people that look the same, feel the same, call themselves the same, is nonsense. As a process, as a narrative, as a discourse, it is always told from the position of the Other.

What is more is that identity is always in part a narrative, always in part a kind of representation. It is always within representation. Identity is not something which is formed outside and then we tell stories about it. It is that which is narrated in one's own self. I will say something about that in terms of my own narration of identity in a moment – you know, that wonderful moment where Richard II says, "Come let us sit down and tell stories about the death of kings." Well, I am going to tell you a story and ask you to tell one about yourself.

We have the notion of identity as contradictory, as composed of more than one discourse, as composed always across the silences of the other, as written in and through ambivalence and desire. These are extremely important ways of trying to think an identity which is not a sealed or closed totality.

[. . .] Now I can turn to questions of politics. In this conception of an identity which has to be thought through difference, is there a general politics of the local to bring to bear against the great, over-riding, powerful, technologically-based, massively-invested unrolling of global processes which I was trying to describe in my previous talk which tend to mop up all differences, and occlude those differences? Which means, as it were, they are different – but it doesn't make any difference that they are different, they're just different.

No, there is no general politics. I have nothing in the kitbag. There is nothing I can pull out. But I have a little local politics to tell you about. It may be that all we have, in bringing the politics of the local to bear against the global, is a lot of little local politics. I do not know if that is true or not. But I would like to spend some time later talking about the cultural politics of the local, and of this new notion of identity. For it is in this new frame that identity has come back into cultural politics in Britain. The formation of the Black diasporas in the period of post-war migration in the fifties and sixties has transformed English social, economic and political life.

In the first generations, the majority of people had the same illusion that I did: that I was about to go back home. That may have been because everybody always asked me: when was I going back home? We did think that we were just going to get back on the boat; we were here for a temporary sojourn. By the seventies, it was perfectly clear that we were not there for a temporary sojourn. Some people were going to stay and then the politics of racism really emerged.

Now one of the main reactions against the politics of racism in Britain was what I would call "Identity Politics One," the first form of identity politics. It had to do with the constitution of some defensive collective identity against the practices of racist society. It had to do with the fact that people were being blocked out of and refused an identity and identification within the majority nation, having to find some other roots on which to stand. Because people have to find some ground, some place, some position on which to stand. Blocked out of any access to an English or British identity, people had to try to discover who they were. [. . .] It is the crucial moment of the rediscovery or the search for roots.

In the course of the search for roots, one discovered not only where one came from, one began to speak the language of that which is home in the genuine sense, that other crucial moment which is the recovery of lost histories. The histories that have never been told about ourselves that we could not learn in schools, that were not in any books, and that we had to recover.

This is an enormous act of what I want to call imaginary political re-identification, re-territorialization and re-identification, without which a counter-politics could not have been constructed. I do not know an example of any group or category of the people of the margins, of the locals, who have been able to mobilize themselves, socially, culturally, economically, politically in the last twenty or twenty-five years who have not gone through some such series of moments in order to resist their exclusion, their marginalization. That is how and where the margins begin to speak. The margins begin to contest, the locals begin to come to representation.

The identity which that whole, enormous political space produced in Britain, as it did elsewhere, was the category Black. I want to say something about this category which we all now so take for granted. I will tell you some stories about it.

I was brought up in a lower middle class family in Jamaica. I left there in the early fifties to go and study in England. Until I left, though I suppose 98 per cent of the Jamaican population is either Black or coloured in one way or another, I had never ever heard anybody either call themselves, or refer to anybody else as "Black." Never. I heard a thousand other words. My grandmother could differentiate about fifteen different shades between light brown and dark brown. When I left Jamaica, there was a beauty contest in which the different shades of women were graded according to different trees, so that there was a Miss Mahogany, Miss Walnut, etc.

People think of Jamaica as a simple society. In fact, it had the most complicated colour stratification system in the world. Talk about practical semioticians; anybody in my family could compute and calculate anybody's social status by grading the particular quality of their hair versus the particular quality of the family they came from and which street they lived in, including physiognomy, shading, etc. You could trade off one characteristic against another. Compared with that, the normal class stratification system is absolute child's play.

But the word "Black" was never uttered. Why? No Black people around? Lots of them, thousands and thousands of them. Black is not a question of pigmentation. The Black I'm talking about is a historical category, a political category, a cultural category. In our language, at certain historical moments, we have to use the signifier. We have to create an equivalence between how people look and what their histories are. Their histories are in the past, inscribed in their skins. But it is not because of their skins that they are Black in their heads.

I heard Black for the first time in the wake of the Civil Rights movement, in the wake of the de-colonization and nationalistic struggles. Black was created as a political category in a certain historical moment. It was created as a consequence of certain symbolic and ideological struggles. We said, "You have spent five, six, seven hundred years elaborating the symbolism through which Black is a negative factor. Now I don't want another term. I want that term, that negative one, that's the one I want. I want a piece of that action. I want to take it out of the way in which it has been articulated in religious discourse, in ethnographic discourse, in literary discourse, in visual discourse. I want to pluck it out of its articulation and rearticulate it in a new way."

In that very struggle is a change of consciousness, a change of self-recognition, a new process of identification, the emergence into visibility of a new subject. A subject that was always there, but emerging, historically.

You know that story, but I do not know if you know the degree to which that story is true of other parts of the Americas. It happened in Jamaica in the 1970s. In the 1970s, for the first time, Black people recognized themselves as Black. It was the most profound cultural revolution in the Caribbean, much greater than any political revolution they have ever had. That cultural revolution in Jamaica has never been matched by anything as far-reaching as the politics. The politics has never caught up with it.

You probably know the moment when the leaders of both major political parties in Jamaica tried to grab hold of Bob Marley's hand. They were trying to put their hands on Black; Marley stood for Black, and they were trying to get a piece of the action. If only he would look in their direction he would have legitimated them. It was not politics legitimating culture, it was culture legitimating politics.

Indeed, the truth is I call myself all kinds of other things. When I went to England, I wouldn't have called myself an immigrant either, which is what we were all known as. It was not until I went back home in the early 1960s that my mother who, as a good middle-class colored Jamaican woman, hated all Black people, (you know, that is the truth) said to me, "I hope they don't think you're an immigrant over there."

And I said, "Well, I just migrated. I've just emigrated." At that very moment, I thought, that's exactly what I am. I've just left home – for good.

I went back to England and I became what I'd been named. I had been hailed as an immigrant. I had discovered who I was. I started to tell myself the story of my migration.

Then Black erupted and people said, "Well, you're from the Caribbean, in the midst of this, identifying with what's going on, the Black population in England. You're Black."

At that very moment, my son, who was two and a half, was learning the colors. I said to him, transmitting the message at last, "You're Black." And he said, "No. I'm brown." And I said, "Wrong referent. Mistaken concreteness, philosophical mistake. I'm not talking about your paintbox, I'm talking about your head." That is something different. The question of learning, learning to be Black. Learning to come into an identification.

What that moment allows to happen are things which were not there before. It is not that what one then does was hiding away inside as my true self. There wasn't any bit of that true self in there before that identity was learnt. Is that, then, the stable one, is that where we are? Is that where people are?

I will tell you something now about what has happened to that Black identity as a matter of cultural politics in Britain. That notion was extremely important in the anti-racist struggles of the 1970s: the notion that people of diverse societies and cultures would all come to Britain in the fifties and sixties as part of that huge wave of migration from the Caribbean, East Africa, the Asian subcontinent, Pakistan, Bangladesh, from different parts of India, and all identified themselves politically as Black.

What they said was, "We may be different actual color skins but vis-a-vis the social system, vis-a-vis the political system of racism, there is more that unites us than what divides us." People begin to ask "Are you from Jamaica, are you from

Trinidad, are you from Barbados?" You can just see the process of divide and rule. "No. Just address me as I am. I know you can't tell the difference so just call me Black. Try using that. We all look the same, you know. Certainly can't tell the difference. Just call me Black. Black identity." Anti-racism in the seventies was only fought and only resisted in the community, in the localities, behind the slogan of a Black politics and the Black experience.

In that moment, the enemy was ethnicity. The enemy had to be what we called "multi-culturalism." Because multi-culturalism was precisely what I called previously "the exotic." The exotica of difference. Nobody would talk about racism but they were perfectly prepared to have "International Evenings," when we would all come and cook our native dishes, sing our own native songs and appear in our own native costume. It is true that some people, some ethnic minorities in Britain, do have indigenous, very beautiful indigenous forms of dress. I didn't. I had to rummage in the dressing-up box to find mine. I have been de-racinated for four hundred years. The last thing I am going to do is to dress up in some native Jamaican costume and appear in the spectacle of multi-culturalism.

Has the moment of the struggle organized around this constructed Black identity gone away? It certainly has not. So long as that society remains in its economic, political, cultural, and social relations in a racist way to the variety of Black and Third World peoples in its midst, and it continues to do so, that struggle remains.

Why then don't I just talk about a collective Black identity replacing the other identities? I can't do that either and I'll tell you why.

The truth is that in relation to certain things, the question of Black, in Britain, also has its silences. It had a certain way of silencing the very specific experiences of Asian people. Because though Asian people could identify, politically, in the struggle against racism, when they came to using their own culture as the resources of resistance, when they wanted to write out of their own experience and reflect on their own position, when they wanted to create, they naturally created within the histories of the languages, the cultural tradition, the positions of people who came from a variety of different historical backgrounds. And just as Black was the cutting edge of politics vis-a-vis one kind of enemy, it could also, if not understood properly, provide a kind of silencing in relation to another. These are the costs, as well as the strengths, of trying to think of the notion of Black as an essentialism.

What is more, there were not only Asian people of color, but also Black people who did not identify with that collective identity. So that one was aware of the fact that always, as one advanced to meet the enemy, with a solid front, the differences were raging behind. Just shut the doors, and conduct a raging argument to get the troops together, to actually hit the other side.

A third way in which Black was silencing was to silence some of the other dimensions that were positioning individuals and groups in exactly the same way. To operate exclusively through an unreconstructed conception of Black was to reconstitute the authority of Black masculinity over Black women, about which, as I am sure you know, there was also, for a long time, an unbreakable silence about which the most militant Black men would not speak.

To organize across the discourses of Blackness and masculinity, of race and gender, and forget the way in which, at the same moment, Blacks in the under class were being positioned in class terms, in similar work situations, exposed to the same deprivations of poor jobs and lack of promotion that certain members of the white working class suffered, was to leave out the critical dimension of positioning.

What then does one do with the powerful mobilizing identity of the Black experience and of the Black community? Blackness as a political identity in the light of the understanding of any identity is always complexly composed, always historically constructed. It is never in the same place but always positional. One always has to think about the negative consequences of the positionality. You cannot, as it were, reverse the discourses of any identity simply by turning them upside down. What is it like to live, by attempting to valorise and defeat the marginalization of the variety of Black subjects and to really begin to recover the lost histories of a variety of Black experiences, while at the same time recognizing the end of any essential Black subject?

[. . .] Third generation young Black men and women know they come from the Caribbean, know that they are Black, know that they are British. They want to speak from all three identities. They are not prepared to give up any one of them. They will contest the Thatcherite notion of Englishness, because they say this Englishness is Black. They will contest the notion of Blackness because they want to make a differentiation between people who are Black from one kind of society and people who are Black from another. Because they need to know that difference, that difference that makes a difference in how they write their poetry, make their films, how they paint. It makes a difference. It is inscribed in their creative work. They need it as a resource. They are all those identities together. They are making astonishing cultural work, the most important work in the visual arts. Some of the most important work in film and photography and nearly all the most important work in popular music is coming from this new recognition of identity that I am speaking about.

Very little of that work is visible elsewhere but some of you have seen, though you may not have recognized, the outer edge of it. Some of you, for example, may have seen a film made by Stephen Frears and Hanif Kureishi, called *My Beautiful Laundrette*. This was originally made as a television film for local distribution only, and shown once at the Edinburgh Festival where it received an enormous reception. If you have seen *My Beautiful Laundrette* you will know that it is the most transgressive text there is. Anybody who is Black, who tries to identify it, runs across the fact that the central characters of this narrative are two gay men. What is more, anyone who wants to separate the identities into their two clearly separate points will discover that one of these Black gay men is white and one of these Black gay men is brown. Both of them are struggling in Thatcher's Britain. One of them has an uncle who is a Pakistani landlord who is throwing Black people out of the window.

This is a text that nobody likes. Everybody hates it. You go to it looking for what are called "positive images" and there are none. There aren't any positive images like that with whom one can, in a simple way, identify. Because as well as the politics – and there is certainly a politics in that and in Kureishi's other film, but it is not a politics which invites easy identification – it has a politics which is grounded on the complexity of identification – it has a politics which is grounded on the complexity of identifications which are at work.

I will read you something which Hanif Kureishi said about the question of responding to his critics who said, "Why don't you tell us good stories about ourselves, as well as good/bad stories? Why are your stories mixed about ourselves?" He spoke about the difficult moral position of the writer from an oppressed or persecuted community and the relation of that writing to the rest of the society. He said it is a relatively new one in England but it will arise more and more as British writers with a colonial heritage and from a colonial or marginal past start to declare themselves.

"There is sometimes," he said, "too simple a demand for positive images. Positive images sometimes require cheering fictions – the writer as Public Relations Officer. And I'm glad to say that the more I looked at *My Beautiful Laundrette*, the less positive images I could see. If there is to be a serious attempt to understand present-day Britain with its mix of races and colours, its hysteria and despair, then writing about it has to be complex. It can't apologize, or idealize. It can't senti-mentalize. It can't attempt to represent any one group as having the total, exclusive, essential monopoly on virtue.

A jejune protest or parochial literature, be it black, gay or feminist, is in the long run no more politically effective than works which are merely public rela-tions. What we need now, in this position, at this time, is imaginative writing that gives us a sense of the shifts and the difficulties within our society as a whole.

If contemporary writing which emerges from oppressed groups ignores the central concerns and major conflicts of the larger society, and if these are willing simply to accept themselves as marginal or enclave literatures, they will automat-ically designate themselves as permanently minor, as a sub-genre. They must not allow themselves now to be rendered invisible and marginalized in this way by stepping outside of the maelstrom of contemporary history." [. . .]

Chapter 12

David Theo Goldberg

RACIAL KNOWLEDGE

[. . .]

WHAT I AM CALLING 'racial knowledge' is defined by a dual move-ment. It is dependent upon – it appropriates as its own mode of expression, its premises, and the limits of its determinations – those of established scientific fields of the day, especially anthropology, natural history, and biology. This scien-tific cloak of racial knowledge, its formal character and seeming universality, imparts authority and legitimation to it. Its authority is identical with, it parasiti-cally maps onto the formal authority of the scientific discipline it mirrors. At the same time, racial knowledge – racial science, to risk excess – is able to do this because it has been historically integral to the emergence of these authoritative scientific fields. Race has been a basic categorical object, in some cases a founding focus of scientific analysis in these various domains. This phenomenon has no doubt been facilitated by the definitive importance of difference in modernity's devel-opment of knowledge. As Foucault remarks:

> [A]ll knowledge, of whatever kind, proceeded to the ordering of its material by the establishment of differences and defined those differ-ences by the establishment of an order; this was true for mathematics, true also for *taxonomies* . . . and for the sciences of nature; and it was equally true for all those approximative, imperfect, and largely spon-taneous kinds of knowledge which are brought into play in the construction of the least fragment of discourse or in the daily process of exchange; and it was true finally for philosophical thought.[1]

Racial knowledge consists *ex hypothesi* in the making of difference; it is in a sense and paradoxically the assumption and paradigmatic establishment of difference.

An epistemology so basically driven by difference will 'naturally' find racialized thinking comfortable; it will uncritically (come to) assume racial knowledge as given.

Power is exercised epistemologically in the dual practices of naming and evaluating. In naming or refusing to name things in the order of thought, existence is recognized or refused, significance assigned or ignored, beings elevated or rendered invisible. Once defined, order has to be maintained, serviced, extended, operationalized. Naming the racial Other, for all intents and purposes, *is* the Other. There is, as Said makes clear in the case of the Oriental, no Other behind or beyond the invention of knowledge in the Other's name. These practices of naming and knowledge construction deny all autonomy to those so named and imagined, extending power, control, authority, and domination over them. To extend Said's analysis of the 'Oriental' to the case of race in general, social science of the Other establishes the limits of knowledge about the Other, for the Other is just what racialized social science knows. It knows what is best for the Other – existentially, politically, economically, culturally: In governing the Other, racialized social science will save them from themselves, from their own Nature. It will furnish the grounds of the Other's modification and modernization, establishing what will launch the Other from the long dark night of its prehistory into civilized time. The wiser, the more knowledgeable the governors are about subject races – at home or abroad, colonially or postcolonially – the less will their administrative rule or government require raw force. 'Good racial government' thus requires information about racial nature: about character and culture, history and traditions, that is, about the limits of the Other's possibilities. Information, thus, has two senses: detailed facts about racial nature; and the forming of racial character. Information is accordingly furnished both by academic research and through practical expertise, through reading and observation, in schools and universities, in courts and prisons.

Production of social knowledge about the racialized Other, then, establishes a library or archive of information, a set of guiding ideas and principles about Otherness: a mind, characteristic behavior or habits, and predictions of likely responses. The Other, as object of study, may be employed but only as informant, as representative translator of culture. The set of representations thus constructed and cataloged in turn confines those so defined within the constraints of the representational limits, restricting the possibilities available to those rendered racially other as it delimits their natures. The spaces of the Other – the colonies, plantations, reservations, puppet governments and client states, the villages and townships, or the prisons, ganglands, ghettoes, and crowded inner cities – become the laboratory in which these epistemological constructs may be tested. Even the literature, art, languages, and general cultural expression are appropriated as proper objects of 'scientific' evaluation. They are judged not as works among works of art in general, but the works or languages or expressions of the Other, representative of the cultural condition and mentality, of the state of Otherness – artifacts not art, primitive formulations not rationally ordered linguistic systems, savage or barbaric or uncivilized expressions not high culture. Learned societies linked to the colonial condition, even disciplines emerged for the sole purpose of studying various racial Others, or the racial Other as such, *its* metaphysical being. These societies have served to inform the colonial or urban administration on whose account they have flourished, but they have also been defined and confined by the relation: what they could experience or represent, who and under what conditions objects could be approached, engaged, studied. Knowledge, accordingly, is socially managed, regulated by the general concerns of social authority, and self-imposed by the specific interests and concerns of the disciplinary specialist.[2]

So the central role of scientific authority in constituting Otherness cements such constitution into an objective given, a natural law. The characterizations accompanying, promoting, or instrumental to such constitutional creation of Others become reified, objectified as unalterable, basic parts of people's natures. In this way, the various divisions of racialized personhood become set as naturally given, as universal and unavoidable. This epistemological manufacture of Otherness mirrors the abstraction typical if not inherent in philosophy's constitution of its discursive object, namely, pure concepts indicative of universal, objective truths. Here, in the philosophical setting and interrelations of personhood (of mind and body), of civil society, and of the State, it is not that the Other is necessarily denied or abnegated (though this has often been so). Rather, in the abstraction of ideas about persons, society, and politics, the philosophical abstraction becomes objectified, once objectified reified as natural, and so extended universally. Part, indeed, an idealized part, is substituted for the whole, and the specificity of the Other, or Otherness itself is silently denied. Those thus rendered Other are sacrificed to the idealization, excluded from the being of personhood, from social benefits, and from political (self-)representation.[3] Erased in the name of a universality that has no place for them, the subjects of real political economy are denied and silenced, ontologically and epistemologically and morally evicted. The universal claims of Western knowledge, then, colonial or postcolonial, turn necessarily upon the deafening suppression of its various racialized Others into silence.

This process of silencing furnishes the solution to what Bauman identifies as the 'technological challenge' faced by social knowledge in the face of the erratic, and so unpredictable behavior of an Other unruled, or insufficiently ruled, by Reason. Admitting the Other's subjectivity is at once to give up epistemological and political control; it is to admit scientific and administrative inefficiency. To retain control, the scientist as much as the administrator, the theoretical expert as much as the advisor and consultant has to control the variables, to manage the environment. The outcomes must be predictable, the more strictly so the better. Calculation is methodologically central, the more formalized the more acceptable. As Foucault remarks, 'Recourse to mathematics, in one form or another, has always been the simplest way of providing positive knowledge about man with a scientific style, form, and justification.' Racialized knowledge in the nineteenth and twentieth centuries has been no exception: witness phrenology, the measurement and weighing of skulls, IQ testing, and crime statistics.[4]

Implicit in these remarks is a hint of the relation between formally produced racialized knowledge, especially at the hands of social science, and the State. Etienne Balibar insists that the relationship to the Other at the heart of modern racism is necessarily mediated by State intervention.[5] One of the basic modes this intervention assumes is concern over production of racialized knowledge. State conceptual mediation is as old as the category of *race* itself. But state mediation

basically reinvents itself with each of the major conceptual developments in racialized thinking: with polygenism and the colonial encounter, with social Darwinism
and eugenics, with IQ testing, and, as we saw, with race relations analysis. We
should pursue the conceptual relations between racialized social science and the
State a little further.

Race, social science, and the State

Social science is important to the modern State both *functionally* and *ideologically*.
In the former sense, social science furnishes the State and its functionaries with
information, and it is often employed in formulating and assessing State policies
to satisfy social needs. Ideologically, the State often invokes expedient analyses and
the results of social science, whether by collaboration or appropriation, to legitimize State pursuits and to rationalize established relations of power and
domination. I do not mean to suggest that the functional and ideological exhaust
State support of social science, still less that these forms exhaust social science
itself. The State may support a research program because of its scientific value;
and much social science may have little formally to do with the State as such,
though work that studiously avoids *the social* barely deserves the name. More important, the State – or some particular state – may be the object of a *critical* social
science concerned with uncovering and attacking modes of repression. So State
Functional and State Ideological Social Science could both be objects of critical
analysis.

What I am calling State Functional Social Science can be conducted *in virtue
of* or *in service of* State ideology. Consider, for example, two related claims: 'People
[in South Africa] . . . do define themselves, in the first instance, as members of a
population group'; and 'The research . . . showed that population group/race/
nationality are first-order interpretations, categorizations or characteristics in terms
of which others are perceived'.[6] These assumptions are so deeply entrenched in
South African state ideology as to be unquestioned, and they are unquestioningly
endorsed by the research that reproduces them. The claims hold, if at all, only *in
virtue of* accepting the premises that ground the ideology; and in turn they give
foundation to the conclusion that possible 'solutions' to the South African dilemma
must be limited to producing 'constructive intergroup relations'.[7]

Consider, by contrast, the claim that white settlers arrived at the Cape of
Good Hope at the close of the seventeenth century coincidentally with African
tribes migrating from the north. Asserted by amateur colonial historians Theal and
Cory early in the twentieth century, common in most school history texts, and
until quite recently propounded by serious Afrikaner scholars, this claim was made
in service of state ideology.[8] (Perhaps it should be said that the claim *functions* as
ideology.) It was designed to substantiate the idea that whites originally laid equal
claim to the land with blacks and historically acquired control over (at least) 87
percent of South African territory by way of a 'just', and so justified war. The
deeper insinuation here, of course, is one of white superiority.

It seems obvious that State Ideological Social Science – the development and
use of (a) social theory to rationalize, legitimize, or conceal repressive or unjust

modes of social relation and expression – has functional value. That is, ideologically State Social Science need not merely define but may serve given state interests. It remains an open question, however, whether State Functional Social Science – social science prompted by State defined purposes and structures – signifies ideologically. One is tempted to say that the ideology expressed by a State committed technocratically to functional social science is a form of *instrumental* pragmatism. Here, knowledge is treated as strictly instrumental to predefined State purposes, never as sustaining critique. Untheorized pragmatisms either generate or (more usually) cover up underlying ideological rationalizations of events, relations, and structures.

The relevance of these distinctions to an understanding of racialized social science should become apparent as I proceed. Yet their application is seldom quite so straightforward. For example, during the 1980s, many South Africans were fond of citing data showing that the majority of that country's black population did not support the call to disinvest. It is difficult to establish, without knowing considerably more and in the context of political hegemony, whether the data and, more significantly, the studies that produced them were functional or ideological; whether the studies were performed in virtue or in service of (function as) state ideology, or simply from the desire to know; and whether the *use* of the data thus collected was purely pragmatic, or in virtue, or in service of state ideology.

The distinction between data and their use is one the positivist might appeal to in objecting that State Ideological Social Science is not social science at all; and I suspect that one who pursued this line of criticism would conclude likewise for functional social science in the way I have defined it. But this form of positivistic critique misses the deeper point that needs highlighting, namely, that social science – the study and analysis of human beings past, present, and future in their social relations – is affected in all kinds of ways by the *Weltanschauung* in terms of which it is conducted, that it is often conducted by and for the State, that it may be formative in constructing the 'imagined community' of racialized State- or nation-hood, and that once collected the data has to be interpreted before conclusions about social policy or action can be drawn. In short, there is nothing remotely resembling pure social data whose meaning and truth are incontestably self-evident.

Racialized knowledge production, and social science in particular, has been integral to State designs in both functional and ideological terms. It has often been noted that anthropology was handmaiden to colonialism. In furnishing information about those societies under the colonizing gun, anthropology both serviced the perceived needs of colonizing states and rationalized colonization as morally necessary for the sake of the colonized. Nevertheless, as Foucault reminds us, it should not be concluded that anthropology is nothing but a colonial discipline.[9] This was, understandably, the general sense of many suffering at the hands of anthropologizing colonialisms. This conclusion might be implied from the fact that with independence, especially in Africa, anthropology departments were replaced largely by sociology faculties at local universities. It should be remembered, though, that while Western governments may have withdrawn from former colonial territories, Western social scientists clearly did not. With the growing move to independence in those states marked as racially Other, political scientists were substituted for anthropologists in representing the functional and ideological interests of the West. Capitalism required new markets, and capital investment presupposed political stability. Western models of state formation were offered as necessary preconditions for the takeoff state[10] of modernizing economic development: Rational political organization – for example, the Westminster model for former British colonies – would rationalize efficient use of economic resources. Indigenous political organization reflected prehistory, objects for anthropological study not modernization. Once the battle for ongoing political allegiance had been more or less won by the lure of capital, economists almost automatically replaced political scientists as the prevailing postcolonial experts of choice. If imperialist direct rule was replaced under colonialism by indirect rule (a prototype of the sort of independence to follow), the outmoding of indirect rule by independence was accompanied by the institution of rule by other means – by economic control. The influence of economists, of direct representatives of Western capital, and of local technicians trained in the West furnished the skills necessary to rationalize control, in both senses of the term.[11] More or less radical social science, while undertaking to alter the thrust of epistemological colonization, has nevertheless done little to transform the terms of racialized knowledge production.

The terms used by social scientists to represent the racialized Other in the nineteenth and twentieth centuries reflected popular representations in dominant Western culture at the times in question. This truncated and all too partial reading of the history of social science in colonial and postcolonial control shows that the terms of popular representations of racialized Others were in many cases set by prevailing modes dominant in social science at the time. What follows is a critical reading of three conceptual schemata hegemonic in the production of contemporary racialized knowledge that now define and order popular conceptions of people racially conceived: the Primitive, the Third World, and the Underclass. These terms and the conceptual schemes they mark are the most prominent and general in silently ordering formal and popular knowledge of the Other in and through the study of cultural, political, and economic relations. [. . .]

The primitive

The word 'primitive' was first used in the late fifteenth century to refer to origins. In that sense, it assumed the connotations that were thought to accompany the image of an early, ancient, or first state, age, or period: old-fashioned, or rough, or rude. (It later acquired more neutral technical meanings in relation to the original words in a language, or members of the early Church.) The Enlightenment interest in human origins was, as we've seen, largely defined in physical terms. Original peoples or races were thought to have little or no social organization or cultural achievements worthy of mention, and the meaning of 'primitive' at the time seems to reflect this. It was in Darwin's wake that scholarly interest in the 'original' social and cultural condition of society really flourished, though even at this time the concept of *the Primitive* was not necessarily racialized. Many of the major theorists of 'primitive society' in the late nineteenth century initially approached the object of study as a set of legal issues, the standard for which was an analysis of Roman law. Included in the conception, accordingly, were Greek and Roman societies, those societies taken to be the primitive or early forerunners of modern Europe. The influence of this scholarly bent is reflected in the fact that art history initially included in the extension of the term 'primitive art' only pre-Renaissance Italian and Flemish painters. By the end of the century, the term had been broadened to include all ancient art; and by 1920, art's historical connotation had assumed the racialized reference it had long had beyond the boundaries of that discipline, referring strictly to art of non-Western cultures: Africa, Oceania, and South America.[12]

The idea of a *primitive society* invented, as Adam Kuper points out, by nineteenth-century legal anthropologists referred to some primeval origin to which society could be archaeologically traced. The idea reified the 'existence' of its referent through the crafting of a set of specialized instruments, ultimately those of applied mathematics, to get objectively at the 'real' nature of primitive society. Like *race*, then, the concept of *the Primitive* proved theoretically adaptable, appropriating novel theoretical developments as its own by being appropriable as a concept central and so seemingly necessary to theoretical advance. Almost as vacuous in connotation as *race*, *the Primitive* transformed in meaning as *race* did.[13] The Primitive assumed synonymy with the racial Other, a technical nomenclature for a popular category. Popular and scientific discourse merged, mutually influencing the terms of discursive formalization and expression. Indeed, the set of meanings that attaches to contemporary usage of 'the Primitive' and 'primitive societies', and by extension to 'Primitivism' is a legacy of this past century of scholarly and popular coproduction. Its transformative capacity makes it particularly suited as a basic trope, a primary element of racist expression.

Formally, primitive societies were theorized in binary differentiation from a civilized order: nomadic rather than settled; sexually promiscuous, polygamous, and communal in family and property relations rather than monogamous, nuclear, and committed to private property; illogical in mentality and practicing magic rather than rational and scientific. In popular terms, nonwhite primitives have come to be conceived as childlike, intuitive, and spontaneous; they require the iron fist of 'European' governance and paternalistic guidance to control inherent physical violence and sexual drives.[14] If, Platonistically, there is conceived to be a primitive lurking deep in the soul of the civilized, it is ruled by Reason, contained and controlled by civility and the institutions of civil society. For the Civilized have a history, but the Primitive have none: their histories are frozen.[15]

It is a remarkable conceit, this, to think of 'a people' having no history, no past, no movement from one time to another, frozen stiff like a wax figure in Madame Tussaud's or the Museum of Man. Remarkable in its arrogance, in its abnegation of those seemingly so unlike themselves that *they* can assume away humanity, banish it to the shadows of their assumptions about what human beings are or are not; remarkable in its lack of self-conscious skepticism about their own limits and excesses, their own warts and odors and blemishes, of what they can or cannot do or know, of their own productive capacities and incapacities, developments and destructions. Remarkable, too, in its denial of the invented relationships between Self and Other in modernity and now postmodernity that have been necessary in making possible the standard of living achieved by the 'civilized', 'developed', 'progressive', 'historical' beings. If the Primitive has no history at all, it is only because the theoretical standard-bearers of Civilization have managed first to construct a Primitive Subject and then to obliterate *his* history.

I do not mean to deny the importance of the anthropological critique of the primitivist discourse throughout much of this century. Two related points need stressing about the counterdiscourses. First, if Kuper is correct, although primitivist ideas no longer dominate anthropological theory, they continue to stamp initiation into the discipline and to be circulated at the fringes. Indeed, they continue to structure popular ideas about the racial and distant Other, as in the Blair brothers' popular 'Adventure' public television series, or National Geographic features, or coffee table books.[16] Second, this popular discourse of the Primitive has partially been sustained by the fact that the anthropological critique of the discourse is *internal*, so much so that it reproduces (even if it transforms) key concepts: primitive society, the primitive or savage mind, totemism, and animism. Contemporary sophisticates often know all too fashionably the critical references but are largely ignorant of their content. This partial, superficial knowing promotes reproduction of the categories under critique rather than internalizing the point of the critique itself.

There is an important sense in which this latter criticism also applies to scholarly production about the Primitive that borrows from, but is strictly beyond, anthropological confines. Two examples, quite different in various ways, will illustrate the point. The first is Marianna Torgovnick's widely cited book, *Gone Primitive*, to which I have already referred in passing. The second is the controversial Museum of Modern Art exhibition on 'Primitivism', and its accompanying two-volume catalog. While Torgovnick discusses the MOMA exhibition in considerable detail, I will analyze each in turn.

Torgovnick is concerned with the way modernists and postmodernists construct notions of the Primitive and import them into contemporary culture. She studies the various ways in which the discourse of primitivism signifies, both in racialized terms and in ways that have little if anything to do with racialized conceptions. In spite of her self-conscious resolve to distance herself from the discourse, it silently takes hold of her. On one hand, Torgovnick insists that in constructing a notion of the Primitive 'we become primitive'. One would think she would accordingly take more seriously Kuper's warning that there never was anything like a 'primitive society', that there is no coherent way of specifying what it is, that the history of the discourse is 'a history of an illusion'.[17] On the other hand, Torgovnick repeatedly, if tentatively, reaffirms the existence of primitive cultures that differ from 'our' modern or postmodern ones.[18] A critique of primitivist discourse that so readily reiterates the discursive terms at issue tends to reproduce the terms it is committed to resisting.

In an interesting and revealing discussion of the Tarzan phenomenon as primitivizing texts, Torgovnick offers a good example of the penetration of social scientific categories of racial Otherness into, and their distribution by, popular culture. Edgar Rice Burroughs, Tarzan's American author, conducted nonprofessional research on plant and animal life in Africa, and he was no doubt familiar with popular anthropological knowledge in the first half of the twentieth century. So, as Torgovnick points out, the reticence and ultimate denial of miscegenation

that Burroughs constructs of Tarzan's sexual relations with female apes is reflective of and reinforces prevailing dispositions in the United States toward interracial
intercourse. But it is one deeply reflective, at the same time, both of the poly-
genic presuppositions lingering from nineteenth-century anthropology in popular
literature and of eugenic dispositions socially influential in the United States well
into the 1920s.[19]

Torgovnick's understated commitment to the categories of primitivist discourse
is reflected in her appreciation of Burroughs having Tarzan join the Waziri of West
Africa in '*their* dance and fashioning within *their* societal norms'. There is an unstated
assumption throughout that the reader is one with the postmodernist 'we', that
the Primitive is in no position to read such a text. The 'we' here, of which Tarzan
represents a recent predecessor, is identical with the anthropological 'we'. Indeed,
Tarzan may be read as the figure of an anthropologist. He enters the 'primitive'
world of Africa 'to learn what hierarchies exist in the human world and by
suppressing his doubts about their inevitability and basis'.[20] This is the anthropological drive, and the implication of this 'realist' ethnography – seemingly neutral
in its objectivity but masking the imperialist imperative – is the affirmation of
'Western hierarchies', of superiority and subjection.[21]

Thus, *Gone Primitive* becomes an example of the production of social knowledge reproducing certain sorts of established presuppositions about relations
between racialized natures. Torgovnick approves of what she takes to be the central
thematic of the Tarzan series: leaving nature as it is, being true to nature, living
in 'harmony with nature, without troubling relations of hierarchy and otherness'.[22]
It is as though this utopian naturalism escapes racist expression, which may yet be
advanced through the assumption of natural difference. It also leaves resistance to
racisms unproblematically coming to terms with nature, with what Torgovnick
leaves (and one is left to assume she takes) as natural difference, with the
differences of racialized natures – analogized in keeping with a long history of
racist expression in terms of apes! 'Going primitive' in Torgovnick's reading, then,
is ultimately to 'go home' to a space of comfort and balance, to a space that is
supposed to save us from 'our estrangement from ourselves and our culture'.[23]
While this domesticated construal at least centralizes the inventedness of the
Primitive, it uncritically recreates the notion of the West's power over its creation,
its appropriation as its own, as 'home' precisely, a place of comfort, a 'return
to origins'. If this is a place to which it belongs, to which it has privileged access
– or which belongs to it – the Western self must surely be justified in its
appropriation. What is missing from the text is an account of the expense of the
appropriation, the real life and death expense, for those so constructed as primitive. [. . .]

The Third World

[. . .] The theory of three worlds was first proposed in 1952 by a French demog-
rapher, Alfred Sauvy, writing in the newspaper *L'Observateur*. Sauvy provocatively
suggested that the notion of the 'Third World' was a product of developing
superpower antagonisms expressing themselves in terms of the cold war. The

notion came to reflect superpower anxiety about escalating postcolonial conflict, the fear of expanding rival spheres of interest over vast territories, numbers of people, and resources. It also expressed alarm among the newly decolonized or decolonizing at revitalized control by the iron fist of superpower domination. In this sense, as Pletsch argues, the concept of a *Third World* is nothing more than the by-product of aggression between the First and Second worlds.

This threefold division has been accompanied by, indeed, it has been defined in terms of sets of accompanying characterizations.[24] For social scientists and political theorists who have been seminal in constructing the model, the First World is strictly modern, scientifically and technologically ordered, ruled by utilitarian decision procedures. Governed by the laws of economic nature, of rational self-interest, it is unconstrained and self-regulating, the embodiment of the liberal, autonomous Kantian state. Of all societies, it is (as Pletsch says) the most natural, that which all others should seek to emulate, for it is guided by the invisible hand of universal Reason. The First World is thus efficient, democratic, and free.

The Second World, the space of (once) communist domination, is conceived as modernized and technologically developed, and so partially rational. But it is stricken unnaturally by ideology and by a socialist elite who must rely upon repression to maintain its privileges. This ideological veil and repressive reliance prevents the Second World from being completely efficient, and unless it emulates the First World, it is destined sooner or later to stagnate. (The recent economic and political devolution of the Second World is being taken in many ways as triumphant vindication of the naturalism of the First, and so as confirmation of the model.)

The Third World is also defined in economic and political terms. The accompanying geographical, environmental, and psychological characterizations are more or less expressly linked to racialized premises. Pletsch suggests that, but possibly for 'left' and 'right', the three-world division is 'the most primitive' scheme of political classification in social science. The rootedness of racialized discourse in modernity and the centrality of 'black' and 'white' within this discourse suggests that these racial designations are classificatory 'primitives' as basic perhaps as 'left' and 'right'.[25] It is in virtue of this racializing of the Third World that the First and Second worlds also silently assume racial character. The Third World is located baking beneath the tropical sun in contrast to the moderate climate of the Northern Hemisphere so conducive to intellectual productivity. It is the world of tradition and irrationality, underdeveloped and overpopulated, disordered and chaotic. It is also non-European and nonwhite.

There has been considerable debate about how the world should be divided in three. Different configurations will result when one employs only economic or only political criteria, or some mix. The divisions will differ again from one interpretation of economic criteria to another, from level of production or development or technology, say, to capacity of the rich countries to exploit the poor. The climatic–geographic consideration, historically associated with race, has led a country like Greenland, for example, to be considered part of the First World, while others like Korea or Singapore or Taiwan, Kuwait or Saudi Arabia, at least until recently, to 'belong' to the Third World, and still others like some Southern European countries to hover politically, and economically, and ideologically between the two. States with populations considered racially polarized, like Israel or South Africa, are ambiguous: Under one interpretation of the criteria they turn out to 'belong' to the First World; under the other, to *be* Third. I am not interested here, at least not primarily, in pursuing the theoretical politics of representing the three worlds. Rather, my concern is to indicate how in its conception and articulation this tripartite division is racialized; how it perpetuates, conceptually and actually, racialized relations – relations of domination, subjugation, and exclusion.

From the outset, the concept of *the Third World* captured the popular, political, and scientific imaginations. Journalists took to the term like vultures to a slain carcass. It came to dominate the way social science conceived of the world, of the basic differences between states, of what Pletsch calls the division of labor within the social sciences. The three-world scheme ordered the focal object of each discipline: Mainstream economics, sociology, and political science respectively concentrated on wealth, status, and power, especially in capitalist societies. Communist studies and international relations focused on the Second World. Area studies, development economics, and anthropology analyzed the 'underdeveloped' and 'traditional societies' of the Third World.[26] The study of Western civilization, the classics or the Great Books is regarded as foundational, as the base and structure for knowledge, value, morality, and good citizenship. By contrast, area studies, and in particular specialization in geographical and cultural fields concerning Otherness are standardly taken to have little if any intrinsic value. They are, if anything, deemed only instrumentally valuable. They are not pursued as knowledge *of* the field for its own sake, for the value inherent in it. At best, they are thought to furnish knowledge *about* the Other, the better to deal with *him*. This amounts to 'knowing *how*', not 'knowing *that*', to use a well-known epistemological distinction. The instrumental knowledge promoted concerns how to civilize, how to approach and relate to the Other.

More significantly, perhaps, the terms 'First World' and 'Second World' are rarely used. States so conceived are usually called capitalist or (formerly) communist, the West or the East, and their populations are termed European, (North) American and, generically, Westerners or East Europeans. 'The West' is similarly a sliding sign. Initially designating countries west of the iron curtain, its scope came to include those countries and their inhabitants that are capitalist in their mode of production, politically free with democratic institutions, culturally modernized, and largely white. Thus, the designation usually includes Australasia, which is almost as far east as one can go without being west, but excludes Japan (surely a First World state if there are any) and does so implicitly on racialized grounds, as in the title of a recent book by a British official with the European Community, *Japan Versus the West*. Indeed, 'the West' has included South Africa insofar as that country has been considered white or non-African. (Under *apartheid*, Japanese have been considered, for obvious reasons, 'honorary whites'.) The grandson of H. F. Verwoerd, for example, expressed a common sentiment among whites in South Africa when he once explained to me that he had 'gone over to Africa' (he meant Zambia). This is reiterated in a plaque at the Afrikaans Language Monument near Cape Town (which ironically is located on a hill across from the prison, in the valley below, from which Nelson Mandela was finally released): 'Afrikaans', the plaque reads, 'is the language that links western Europe and Africa;

. . . it forms a bridge between the enlightened West and magical Africa.' Implicit in these claims is a deep-seated presupposition that South Africa is a European country (in racial, cultural, political, and economic commitments), not an African one. Within a historical context of political economy, power, and dominant culture, this characterization strikes me as highly suggestive.[27]

By contrast, 'Third World' is the generic term of choice in referring not only to those states that are taken to be underdeveloped but to populations considered traditional in their productive and cultural ways. Sometimes, 'the Third World' carries no racialized connotation: Argentina, for example, is often regarded as a Third World country (though not one that immediately comes to mind when using the term generically), and its population is not usually considered to be racially Other. Yet here, too, racial characterization can take over: Argentinean players in the 1990 World Cup were repeatedly described by British football commentators, in a reinvocation of themes of the Falkland campaign, as 'naturally violent', displaying the sort of behaviour to be expected of 'the Latin temperament'. Equally, the 'exotic' players of the 'Cinderella team' from the Cameroon – some players sported dreadlocks and wore 'traditional' jewelry – were characterized as 'exciting', but 'wild' and 'undisciplined'.[28]

The racial connotations carried by the ascription, 'the Third World', are captured most clearly in their usage by those in the United States and Europe who warn that blacks, the *Gastarbeiter* immigrants, and asylum seekers are turning their respective societies economically and culturally into Third World countries. In the political and cultural theater of the United States, Kirk Varnedoe is not that far from David Duke or Patrick Buchanan, or indeed from George Bush, in claiming that 'Third World nations have intensified their concern for the integrity of their own tribal arts'. As a range of conservative political figures portray an undifferentiated blackness or Otherness for political effect and reduce it to an unspecified Third World, so Varnedoe reifies an undifferentiated Third World and reduces it to the level of the Primitive. In a recent *New York Sunday Times* article on the declining fortunes of Detroit, Ze'ev Chafets draws a similar analogy between what he describes as the tragic decline of that city under black rule and the inevitable decline of independent African nations.[29] In a similar vein, the racialized situation of guest workers in Europe, not that different from Mexican migrants in California, is increasingly obviated against the reconstructed measuring stick of a European identity. Their strictly economic status as guest workers transforms into a supra-national, superracial one against the backdrop of a European identity. Europe, after all, was central to the initial manufacture of racialized identities and racist exclusions. It is an irony too great to be bypassed that the unification of a European 'we', racially exclusionary in reinvented fashion, occurs exactly half a millennium after voyages of discovery that prompted the initial manufacture of racial Otherness. Whereas European racism might initially be described as exclusion at a distance, it is now what Balibar terms 'internal exclusion', and it takes place at the world level.[30] Migrant labour, then, is nothing else than racialized exploitation, an off-the-books form of what Worsley calls 'cost-free aid from the Third World to the First'.[31] The analogy with South Africa is accordingly worth pursuing [. . .]. Insofar as South Africa is considered a black country, it is 'naturally' designated Third World. In a recent visit to South Africa, I found whites widely bemoaning their observation that 'the new South Africa' is fast becoming 'a Third World country'. It follows that the notorious migrant labor system *apartheid* merely formalized must be a form of relatively free service to those identified as (ex-)European. [. . .]

The underclass

The notion of *the Underclass* has been present in social science literature for some considerable time. Myrdal used the term in passing in *The American Dilemma* and returns to it more firmly nearly twenty years later. Myrdal's use was strictly economic, designating the persistently unemployed and underemployed, those marginalized or completely excluded from the postindustrial economy.[32] With structural transformations in the capitalist economy that began to be obviated towards the close of the 1970s, the connotation of the term in social science shifted from degrees of unemployment to deep-seated, chronic poverty. This shift signaled a series of conceptual chains forged as much by the popular media as by social scientists. The Underclass population came to be characterized in behavioral terms, as a set of pathological social attitudes, actions, and activities. The outward, visible sign of these pathologies was race. Thus, the notion was relinked to the nineteenth-century conceptions of the 'undeserving poor', the 'rabble', and the 'lumpenproletariat'.[33] Accordingly, 'the Underclass' has come to signify not just the unemployed but the permanently unemployed and unemployable. It has come to include, particularly in the popular but also in the academic and political imaginations, those poor considered unmotivated to work – especially, women on welfare, vicious street criminals, drug pushers and addicts, hustlers and urban gangs, winos and the mentally deranged homeless. If these conditions are permanent, then they are necessary, and necessarily unchangeable, and so it would seem there is no responsibility for doing anything about them save improving the criminal justice response.

The conditions of the Underclass are accordingly reduced to individual pathologies and the poverty of culture that generates the social disease of deviance. '"Underclass" describes a state of mind and a way of life. It is at least as much a cultural as an economic condition.'[34] The claim that the Underclass consists of pathological individuals is 'established' by way of comparison with the 'deserving poor', those adult, law-abiding, two-parent families that, despite steady male employment, are unable to make ends meet.[35] The supposed fact that the underclass condition is produced by the poverty of culture is 'explained' in terms of the absence of moral virtues disabling individuals from 'deferring gratification, planning ahead, and making sacrifices for future benefit'.[36] So the social conditions of the undeserving poor can be blamed upon their own character.

The interpenetrating lists of individual pathologies and cultural poverty that have been taken by social scientists and journalists alike to make up the Underclass condition carry patently racialized connotations. Though technically and historically the Underclass is purported to be 'interracially' constituted (poverty is supposed to know no color), it is obvious that blacks are for the most part being thus chronically identified. If there is a single identifying criterion of Underclass membership, it is *idleness*. And as J. M. Coetzee makes clear in relation to the history of white South African writing, idleness has long expressed a central idea of racialized representation.[37] In group terms, blacks in the United States, Britain, and now South Africa are often aggregated into Underclass characterization by the term's conceptual extension: by police, on the street, in the media, at school. And they are so referenced whether they technically meet the sliding criteria or not.

Inner city culture conjures up the very real political economy of racialized space that the concept of the *Underclass* is assumed to be theorizing. The individual pathologies and wanting culture of the Underclass are seen to be expressed against the blighted backdrop of the urban ghetto. Causal responsibility for the set of Underclass conditions nevertheless is largely traced not to urban location – this is thought to be a mere manifestation, a symptom – but to the pathological population, to its culture. It is this causal inversion that William Julius Wilson undertakes to rectify in his important work on the Underclass.

Wilson has been careful to evade the poverty of culture thesis. He conceptualizes the Underclass as the set of individuals lacking training and skills, those experiencing long-term unemployment, and those not part of the labor force. Wilson seeks to explain the social position of the Underclass primarily in terms of the 'mismatch' hypothesis.[38] Inner city residents in the past two decades have been caught by structural changes in the U.S. economy that have left them without the technological skills necessary for the financial service jobs their spatial position would otherwise give them access to. This dislocation has two main effects: The 'concentration effect' results in a large number of single parent families, the unemployed, and criminals ghettoized into a relatively small and intense urban area with diminishing social services. The 'isolation effect' leaves these people cut off from the ameliorating influence of a middle class, black and white, who have fled for the suburbs.

Though Wilson dismisses the poverty of culture position, he has not found the case for individual pathologies quite so objectionable. Included in his underclass membership are street criminals, welfare mothers, and other social deviants. His notion of *the Underclass* is thus identified against a paradigm of a healthy body politic from which the Underclass population by definition diverges.[39] Although Wilson stresses that the Underclass includes many nonblacks, he is equally clear that his work focuses on the much larger black segment of the Underclass. These considerations prompt two implications for Wilson's analysis. The first is that he racializes the concept almost in spite of himself. The weight of Wilson's scientific stature behind the use of the concept authorizes even its more dubious, racially obvious policy and popular usages, no matter Wilson's own guarded qualifications. The second implication is at the explanatory level. Wilson predicates his structural economic analysis of the state of the Underclass on the idea of isolated, albeit spatially concentrated individuals. It is this methodological assumption that leaves Wilson holding on to the descriptive schemata of individual pathology. And it is in part this assumption that leads him to downplay the place of racism in his explanatory account of the black Underclass, as well as to de-emphasize race-specific programs as viable solutions.

Wilson finds it important, particularly in his more recent work, to recognize the effects on the black Underclass of racism, past and present. Nevertheless, his overriding emphasis throughout has been to stress the relatively greater weight of class considerations in the explanation of Underclass conditions. Class *structure* is specified in terms of individuals' 'attachment to the labor force'; in terms, that is, of *individual* job opportunities or access to job network and information systems.[40] Contrast this, for example, with Marx's notion of 'the proletariat', which is conceived as the *group* whose members own nothing but their labor power. This individualist methodological presupposition – perhaps it is even ontological – forces Wilson to underplay the influence of group effects. Similarly, Wilson thinks nonracialized programs aimed universally at alleviating poverty have far better political prospects in the racially tense political arena of the United States than race-based programs, which he takes to be racially polarizing. However, it is well-known that universally cast legislation and class- rather than race-specific antipoverty programs end up benefiting the white poor far more than the black.[41] One explanation for this is the ongoing perception among enforcers and administrators, linked to the prevailing image of the Underclass, that the former are deserving poor, the latter undeserving. Wilson has undertaken to integrate structural factors in the plight of the Underclass with individual and cultural ones. This is a commendable undertaking, but it is Wilson's peculiar mix that proves troubling. Thus, while he acknowledges racialized experiences and racism, they are almost completely untheorized in the explanatory schema and openly criticized in relation to policy considerations.

Wilson's analysis has been widely influential, even upon critics of his work. One of his deeper influences is related to this individualizing that is at the heart of his conceptual and explanatory account. In a set of interesting critical remarks on Wilson's work, Jennifer Hochschild praises Wilson's courage for insisting on the disturbing shift in the social values of the inner city black poor. As evidence of this shift, Hochschild quotes from unpublished work of the urban sociologist Elijah Anderson. Anderson notes the 'general sense of alienation, lack of opportunity, and demoralization of certain aspects of the black community'. Nevertheless, Anderson seems to be noting something more subtly complex than Hochschild is implying, namely, that the shift in values among the urban black poor is structurally related, a frustrated response to the perception of perpetuated, racially defined limits the black poor find themselves facing. The frustration has become especially acute in light of the failed promises the civil rights era seemed to hold out.[42] Anderson's structurally defined observation is at odds with Hochschild's ambivalent individualism, an individualism that becomes highlighted in Hochschild's analysis of possible courses of action. Here, she locates responsibility for responding to the plights and problems of the racialized poor primarily with those closest to the problems: the individuals directly in touch with those whose values are seen to need transforming. These include parents, schoolteachers, social workers, police, potential employers, and local politicians. True, Hochschild proceeds from here to structural considerations and state obligations, but the latter are secondary, an afterthought, though a recognizably necessary one. Hochschild individualizes the issues by locating the nexus of both the problem of poverty and of the starting point for transforming its complex of individual and structural considerations with the poverty of culture. She works out from this localized individual space of responsibility, expanding the universe of obligation outward from the 'problematic individual' ultimately to the political.[43] This presupposes that the problems lie foremost with deviant individual expression and only vaguely with policies, prejudice, economic structure and political self-interest, the failure of moral imagination and application, and the poverty of political discourse.

Experience might have taught us that where technologies of conceptualization create distance between what is needed and those with the responsibility and means to respond to the needs, little is likely to be done. The virtue of Wilson's work is its recognition of the complex interaction all the way up and down, so to speak, between individual responsibilities (local *and* distant) and transformed structures. *The Underclass*, I want to insist, is one conceptual technology that stands in the way of fully satisfying that recognition. Naming the Underclass makes the Underclass, nominates it into existence, and constitutes its members at once as Other.

Wilson's understanding of the force of race and the effects of racisms in the account of contemporary poverty in a deeply racialized social order like the United States rests upon his underestimating the perpetual disadvantages blacks continue to suffer, irrespective of their class position. Employment opportunities for whites are considerably greater than for blacks across the class spectrum. Geographically defined unemployment rates for blacks are often double that for whites. The rates of unemployment for both male and female blacks with one or more years of college are greater than those for whites who failed to complete high school. Unlike the experience of inadequately educated immigrants, many educated blacks have to settle for relatively poor jobs, while uneducated blacks have to live with no legitimate work at all. As Fainstein concludes in his subtle and convincing analysis of Wilson's 'mismatch' analysis, racism pervades the U.S. economy. It is

> built into the routine decisions of employers: the way they organize the division of labor, how they allocate men, women, blacks, and whites among jobs; what they decide to pay different kinds of workers, and the implicit criteria they utilize in hiring and promotion. Combined with virulent racism in housing markets, which keeps blacks concentrated in residential ghettoes in central cities and increasingly in suburban jurisdictions, outright discrimination along with more subtle forms of channeling in labor markets goes a long way toward explaining black economic disadvantage.[44]

Managing inflation through unemployment, for example, is a tax on the poor and, in the context of deeply racialized employment differentiation, upon blacks in particular.[45] This further disadvantages the truly disadvantaged, and it benefits those relatively well-off in ways analogous to the largely free aid Third World migrant labor finds itself 'forced' into furnishing the First World.

So, in general, the notion of *the Underclass* explicitly erases the exclusionary experiences of racisms from social science analysis while silently enthroning the demeaning impact of race-based insinuations and considerations. It distinguishes the especially impoverished from the ordinary poor while aggregating together those whose conditions of experience in various ways – in terms of race, gender, and class – may be quite different. It thus promotes a single policy solution for perhaps very different difficulties and social problems people find themselves facing.[46]

In a society whose advantages and opportunities are racially ordered, a concept like *the Underclass* will almost inevitably assume racial connotation. No matter the protestations of social scientists of Wilson's standing, race will likely be tied to pathological considerations of an *under*class. As others have noted, in analyses where there is an underclass, there too implicitly must be supposed to be an overclass. However, we find both in social science and popular accounts no mention of this.

The justification Wilson offers for using the concept turns on its identification of the structurally marginal position of some people in the labor force and the linking of this economic marginality to spatial location. He rightly criticizes Hochschild's substitute, 'the estranged poor', for failing to reflect the relationship between people's experience in the labor market and their neighborhood environment.[47] If Wilson's notion of *the Underclass* passes for the most part silently over the racial characterization of this relationship, Hochschild's term seems to erase it altogether. I would like to suggest *the racially marginalized* as an alternative. It explicitly captures the class dimension of economic marginality; it references the ghetto as the spatial location of the racially marginalized (Wilson admits that the white poor seldom live in ghetto areas); it differentiates those who are racialized but nonmarginal from those who deeply experience the material effects of exclusion, namely, the racial poor; and in foregrounding the processes of marginalization, it refuses moralistic judgments as first causes of the marginal condition. Accordingly, it directs analysis properly away from individualized character traits, or their lack, to what Hughes identifies as the 'isolated deprivation of the (impacted) ghetto'. The concept of *the racially marginalized* thus clearly captures the intersection of race and class that multiplies the depth of structural dislocation.[48] It also bridges the imaginary conceptual divide between those ghettoized in the racialized locations of urban sites, the 'urban jungles' throughout 'the West' and those marginalized in 'the Third World', between those situated as the 'Underclass' and those whose (supposed lack of) history is reduced to 'the Primitive'.[49]

There is a further dimension to the power of social science in effecting the 'objects' of its studies, one that is especially pertinent in the case of the racially marginalized. Debates in social science concerning important policy-related questions take place over a specified time span – a decade, say. During this time, the exchange becomes more precise – in the conceptual apparatus used, in hypothesis specification, testing, data accumulation, and analysis. Wilson's 'mismatch' hypothesis is a case in point. In the meantime, *en passant*, policy decisions are implemented on the basis of one or another of the contesting positions in the unresolved debate, a debate that may never see satisfactory resolution. The policies are necessarily partial (in both senses), just as the debate is incomplete. Researchers proceed to new issues, driven by perceived social needs, or their own interests, or available funding. Monies for research on the black super poor, or for that matter on black racial attitudes[50] have been notoriously difficult to come by, especially after the Moynihan and Kerner reports were issued in the late 1960s. Of course, there are real lives that are affected by the policies. So all too often the resolution of the issues under debate, insofar as there is resolution at all, is embodied in the lives of those trapped between the threads of tattered policies.

Blauner and Wellman emphasize the political and economic power major research universities represent to poor black populations whose neighborhoods are often adjacent to and controlled by the university trustees. University researchers are seen by communities to stand in positions of control, power, and exploitation, with little or no benefits accruing to the 'objects' of the research.[51] I have argued that racialized power is primarily conceived through conceptual orders like the Primitive, the Third World, and the Underclass. These are constitutive metaphors of racialized experience, the power of which consists in their ability to order and order anew racialized exclusions. In terms of social science, power is here expressed, managed, and extended in and through representing racial Others – to themselves and to the world.

As with 'black', it may be possible for those objectified by these categories to appropriate them, assuming the categories in assertive self-ascription. This appropriation is what I earlier called 'standing inside the terms', making them one's own, giving new meaning to and thereby redirecting them as forms of political engagement and critique. Of the three notions, 'the Third World' has come closest to this, perhaps because it is less deeply positioned in the history and rhetoric of racialized discourse than the other two. Nevertheless, it has to take extraordinary effort on the part of all, or nearly all, so characterized to redirect the original connotations the three terms carry. For a term like 'primitive' this would prove exceptionally difficult. Where it is still used, its referential scope proves to be partial and vague, temporally vacant and spatially diffuse. Those so referenced are rarely in a position of power, politically and technologically, to take on the category as a form of self-reference, even should they choose to. In the case of 'the Underclass', the lack of representational power seems equally obvious. Indeed, it might be added that to the extent that people so referenced assume some semblance of representational authority, they cease under the imposed criteria to be 'underclass' or 'primitive'.

As we have seen, it is not necessary that members of any group get racialized, though some groups – blacks and American Indians especially – are more likely than others to be. Nor once racialized does it necessarily follow that all members will be treated in racial terms or that any one member be so treated all or even much of the time. Once a group is racialized, and especially where the racial creation of the group runs deep into the history of its formation, however, the more likely will it be that the group and its members are made to carry its racialized nature with them.

Thus, not only is it the case, as Bauman observes, that the great effort exerted by the social sciences in studying race and racism has done little to alter the self-conception of the social sciences,[52] it is perhaps more emphatically the case that the social sciences have done much to create, authorize, legitimate, and extend both the figures of racial Otherness and the exclusions of the various racisms. The ways in which the production of social knowledge in the name of science continues more or less silently, more or less explicitly, to do so will be obviated by analyzing two contemporary texts produced in and representative of differing though not unrelated racialized contexts. The first reads race strictly as Africa; the second undertakes to normalize racial comprehension in/of South Africa by reinventing it in terms of 'Western' social science.

A dying racism?

Terence Ranger has long been concerned with representing Africa to and in the West. Where earlier social scientists engaged in what Mudimbe properly calls inventing Africa,[53] Ranger is committed to reinventing it. In the text I want to focus on here, his definitive statement on 'race relations', Ranger re-presents the civilizing mission of liberal good works in terms of charity beginning not at but from the home. Like earlier social science about the Other, then, it could be said that Ranger pursues Torgovnick's primitivizing search for (a) home in modernity's space-time of 'transcendental homelessness'. And as before, the invention of this idealized home can only be sustained by the destructive denial of the Other's actual home.

The auspicious occasion of Ranger's remarks is his inaugural lecture in 1987 as (Cecil John) Rhodes Professor of Race Relations at Oxford University. Ranger might thus be permitted some largesse, but the form the lecture assumes is the metaphor of a reimagined imperialism. In the address, 'Rhodes, Oxford, and the Study of Race Relations', Ranger engages in a range of metaphorical transmutations: metaphorical in the literary construction of his lecture; metaphorical in standing for the epistemological reproduction of the rule over Africa (which by implication cannot epistemologically rule itself, for it requires Oxford once again to know it, to be represented to itself); and metaphorical again for the place of racialized representation in Britain, in the terms of Ranger's, of Rhodes's Oxford.

Ranger's lecture transposes the Rhodes Chair of Race Relations into a Central African Kingdom; the Oxford pro-vice-chancellor, the highest-ranking university representative present, into a tribal elder; Ranger himself into an ascending king, a ruler over the domain of African Studies, not just at Oxford but universally; thus, Race Relations (itself a severe circumscription of a domain and a reification of its terms of representation as givens) into a certain sort of African Studies; race into what *others* are; and finally, Cecil John Rhodes, of all people, into a 'tutelary deity', a 'patron divinity' of Africa, of Race Relations as African Studies.[54]

The rhetorical medium of Ranger's transmutations is the description of the figure of Rhodes as deity of African Studies. Ranger admits the Janus-faced nature of the figure: At once appealing and fraternal, paternalistic and condescending to local Africans, Rhodes approached African leaders as equals and as servants. Expressing a desire to live as peaceful neighbor or landlord, Rhodes was consumed with the drive for and expression of personal, political, and economic power. This figure of contradictory power Ranger contrasts with an antidotive figure, a 'companion deity' with whom Ranger more easily identifies, a figure representing 'abnegation and powerlessness'. This is the figure of Arthur Shearly Cripps – British, white, a missionary (though 'radical'), and above all 'a quintessential Oxford man'. Yet, concludes Ranger with just a hint of melancholy, Cripps's humanism – his 'pastoralism and medievalism', traveling on foot in his missionary Africa 'like *his* African *flock*' – is inadequate to salvage Africa for Oxford; it is unable 'to conceptualize Africa'.[55]

The moral of Ranger's narrative for Oxford – the University, that is – is neither to save nor ruthlessly to modernize (Rhodes's) Africa. 'Oxford must settle for a relationship of equality (if it is not in itself absurd to speak of equality between a university and a continent).'[56] It is self-evidently absurd to speak in this way. But Ranger, recall, is speaking not anymore of a university but of the Oxfordian Kingdom, not of Africa but of African Studies, not of Africans but of Race Relations, over all of which he is assuming titular control. In moving to the concluding moments of his inauguration, to the assumption of his throne, Ranger reveals the state-to-be of the study of race relations at Oxford: an African Studies Centre not in the mold of any white divinity of the past – a Rhodes or Cripps or Smuts – but with the view to the need for understanding Africa 'as much as Africa needs to understand us'.[57]

It is unclear in whose name the 'us' is being spoken here – Oxford, Britain, Europe, or the West. Postmodern irony and self-consciousness are not beyond the assertion of postcolonial power. What is clear is that Ranger refers by 'race' only to Africans, to the traditional Other; and clearer yet what his intentions are in representing Africa: to bring Africans to Oxford so as to be able 'to render [them] accurately – to speak of, sometimes even *for* Africans in Oxford'.[58] The power of representation remains fit for the king. In his construction of race and ethnicity in the name of Rhodes, not a word about race in contemporary Britain, about the 'empire striking back' or the 'lack of black in the Union Jack'; no mention of the vast study of race relations and the critical debate about racial construction and exclusion. Not a word, that is, about the state of British race analysis impossible to ignore beyond the shadows of Oxford's ivied bastions. No reference to race in the city of Oxford, of the testy relation between racialized town dwellers and the wearers of the university gown. Nothing about the fact that there are more African students attending Oxford than there are black British students, nor about the almost total lack of black faculty representation.

Ranger is at one with Oxford's past, the appropriate wearer of Rhodes's crown: Race is Africa! The World Bank would do no better than to respond to Ranger's explicit appeal, to buy its knowledge of Africa – of an undifferentiated Africa if the language of this document is anything to go by, and despite all its qualifications – to fund his Centre. Ranger's Kingdom is a market, a place to trade, to bring Africans once more to sell – this time their intellectual energy and their knowledge[59] (though sometimes, too, the Other must understand, knowledge will have to be given them, they will have to be re-presented). Once more, African labor, this time intellectual, becomes foreign aid for the glorification of the great white man's rule. [. . .]

Notes

1   Foucault (1970), p. 346.
2   I have adapted loosely and liberally from Said's stimulating analysis of Orientalism. Said (1979a), pp. 31–49. Cf. Wolf (1981), p. 388; Mudimbe (1988), pp. 1–43; and on art, Nettleton and Hammond-Tooke, eds. (1989).
3   This expresses philosophically what anthropological ethnography has long prac-ticed: 'given the dominant rhetoric of anthropological discourse, the Other's ethnographic presence goes together with his theoretical absence. In ethnography, as we know it, the Other is displayed, and therefore contained, as an object of

representation; the Other's voice, demands, teachings are usually absent from our theorizing.' Fabian (1990), p. 771.

4   Foucault (1970), p. 351; more generally, see Bauman (1989), pp. 179–80. And on the epistemological politics of the social sciences in historical context, see Mafeje (1976).

5   Balibar (1991), p. 15.

6   Human Sciences Research Council (HSRC of South Africa) (1985), p. 6. This may seem an extreme case. But substituting various other states for South Africa in the quotations – the United States, Israel, Britain, to name only the more obvious – will hardly change their significance. In the case of the United States, there may be more self-consciousness and skepticism about the designations, a greater personal and institutional wrestling with the identifications than may have once been the case in South Africa, though even in this respect the latter may now be in the process of emulating the former. I have learned, not without cost and whether one intends it or not, that claims about South Africa, however generally stated, are dated: This is written in June 1991.

7   HSRC (1985), p. 157. It should be pointed out that leading South African ideologues are no longer committed to this claim, which is not the same as saying that they are no longer committed to some more or less formal racialized dispensation. I will be analyzing this document in greater detail later in the chapter.

8   A booklet published by the South African state in 1969, *Progress through Separate Development*, makes just this claim. However, the South African Museum, a state-sponsored national institution, for example, now acknowledges the arrival of blacks in South Africa two thousand years ago.

9   For evidence of the collaboration between anthropological study and colonial administration: 'It has been said that modern anthropology is destined to be of great assistance to colonial governments in providing the knowledge of the social structure of native groups upon which a sound and harmonious Native Administration, as envisaged in indirect Rule, should be built. Let me say that I for one firmly believe in the possibility of such cooperation between anthropologists and administrators.' S. F. Nadel, *A Black Byzantium* (1942), quoted in Frank (1979), p. 206. Cf. Foucault (1988), p. 162. Anthropologists have become much more self-conscious about the processes of what Johannes Fabian calls 'othering'. They no longer assume 'the givenness of the Other as the object of their discipline'. Fabian (1990), p. 755. In the first draft, I used 'peoples' in referring to the colonized. Alena Goldberg reminded me most forcefully that this, too, was to invoke, perhaps euphemistically, a category of the sort I am engaged in critiquing.

10   Theorization of 'development' in terms of stages can be traced to the Enlightenment. The four-stage theory of human development proposed by the Russian Semyon Efimovich Desnitsky, a student of Adam Smith's, is typical: The earliest mode of human development consists of 'peoples' living by hunting-gathering. The second stage consists of 'peoples' engaged in the pastoral lives of shepherds. The third stage is agricultural. And the fourth consists of 'peoples' living by commerce. ('Peoples' is the term used by Desnitsky in the eighteenth century.) See Meek (1976), p. 5. W. W. Rostow's five-stage theory of economic development has been the major influence in mainstream developmental economics in the past three decades.

11   See Mafeje (1976); and Mudimbe (1988), p. 44. The contemporary experience

of South Africa in relation to the World Bank and the IMF is revealing. With the lifting of sanctions, the South African government is voluntarily subjecting itself to the 'advice' of these funding bodies without expecting further loans in the short term. Thus, they are using the economic expertise now being exported in the name of the G7 to rationalize greater privatization of nationalized industries, reduction in the tax rates, and introduction of an increasingly regressive tax structure in the form of a comprehensive value added tax, reduced government social service expenditures, and diminished welfare commitments.

12   Cf. Kuper (1988), pp. 1–4; Torgovnick (1990), pp. 18–19; Rubin (1984), p. 2.

13   Kuper thinks that *transformations* in the significations of theoretical concepts have played a major role in science, at least as significant as the role advocated by Kuhn's 'paradigms'. Kuper (1988), pp. 10–14.

14   On the formal qualities of the Primitive, see Kuper (1988), p. 5; on the popular conception, see Torgovnick (1990), pp. 8, 99, 192. Torgovnick points out that the concept was also used to rationalize control of 'lower classes, minorities, and women . . . the primitives at home' (p. 192). This rationalization was sustained by the economy of conceptual identification in the late nineteenth century between racial Others, mainly blacks and Jews, women, and the working class. Torgovnick also points out that primitive society became the 'testing ground' for early twentieth-century psychoanalytic hypotheses about human sexuality (p. 7). She is only partially correct in ascribing this to the anthropological constitution of the Other and its corollary assumption that the Primitive was the Other in us, the precivilized form through which, in the form of our ancestry, we passed. The rush of sex theorists into the field of anthropological study also had to do with prevailing Victorianism in sexual matters, the veil of taboos prohibiting frank, open, unbiased study of sex in civilized society. If Victorianism proved to be the push, the lure of the Savage was the invitation behind the veil of taboos, the pull of an object pristine and pure, unself-conscious, and so perhaps a view into the unconscious.

15   Levi-Strauss, perhaps a little gingerly, refers to these (non)histories as 'cold'. Wolf (1981), p. 385.

16   Kuper (1988), pp. 13–14. Compare Leni Riefenstahl's popular photographic collection of African bodies with Lawrence and Lorne Blair's *Ring of Fire*, an account of their journeys through Indonesia. For more on the latter, see Torgovnick (1990), pp. 177–82.

17   Torgovnick (1990), p. 38; Kuper (1988), pp. 7–9.

18   Three brief quotes should suffice: '[The Asmat of New Guinea] is a good example of how rare an untouched example of a primitive culture really is'. 'The tropes and categories through which we view primitive societies establish relations of power between them and us.' And '[these are] some of our greatest thinking and thinkers about the primitive'. Torgovnick (1990), p. 280 n. 3, pp. 11 and 190.

19   Torgovnick (1990), ch. 2. Torgovnick (p. 186) badly misrepresents the history of racial theorizing in claiming that post-Darwinist views on race were a return to the monogenist conception that predated polygenism, and that monogenism 'became the antiracist position' while polygenism 'became the assumption of the racist position'. That Gould, in another context, calls this a common misreading of the debate does not mitigate her mistake. Gould (1991), p. 13.

20   Torgovnick (1990), pp. 69–70. My emphases.

21   On realism as the dominant mode of ethnographical writing, see Fabian (1990).
22   Torgovnick (1990), p. 71. Similarly, she approves largely of the 1980s film *Greystoke: The Story of Tarzan*, failing to question why this film at that time.
23   Ibid., p. 185.
24   My characterization of the three worlds has been informed by Pletsch (1981), pp. 569–74; and Worsley (1984), ch. 1, and p. 308. See also Tipps (1973), esp. pp. 204, 208.
25   Pletsch (1981), p. 565.
26   Ibid., p. 581.
27   Gorra suggests that the characterization can be generalized in the colonial context to Africa as (being) Europe's, as belonging to Europe. Gorra (1991), p. 87. This spatial appropriation of Africa is accompanied, as Patricia Williams so forcefully argues, by an eviction of the cultural legacy of Africa from the denial of black contributors to the canon of 'Western civilization'. P. J. Williams (1991), pp. 113–14.
28   As I was composing this, an article appeared in *The New York Sunday Times*, June 23, 1991, on the expressed commitment of the Congress Party in India (newly returned to power after Rajiv Ghandi's assassination) to a 'free market' economy. The article referred to the encouragement of this newfound capitalism as expressed by 'a senior *Western* diplomat'. Whose interests, one wonders, does this diplomat represent? The cementing of 'the West' in the aftermath of the Gulf War seems at once and paradoxically impenetrable and transparent. By contrast, adding a 'Fourth World' to distinguish between different sorts of non-Western states simply reiterates the restrictions of the three-world system.
29   See Ridgeway (1990), p. 21; Varnedoe (1984a), p. 679. Chafets (1990), pp. 20–6.
30   Balibar (1991a), p. 14; cf. Balibar (1990), pp. 283–94. Two points attest to this growing phenomenon: In Germany, those initially deemed *Gastarbeiter* were later referred to as 'foreign workers' and now just as 'the foreigners'. There is no immigration law, only *Auslandergesetz*, or 'foreigner's law', dating back to 1965 and evocative of 1938 Nazi legislation, which it appears to emulate. Non-alien residents of European Community countries have the right of entry, employment, and self-employment. Rathzel (1990), pp. 32 ff.
31   Worsley (1984), pp. 238, 236.
32   Myrdal (1962).
33   Gans (1990), p. 271; Jencks (1988), p. 23; Innis and Feagin (1989), p. 14.
34   Magnet (1989), p. 130.
35   Jencks (1988), p. 23; Reed (1988). An article in the *Chronicle of Higher Education* in 1988 described the 'social pathologies' as including 'teenage pregnancies, out of wedlock births, single parent families, poor educational achievement, chronic unemployment, welfare dependency, drug abuse, and crime'. Coughlin (1988).
36   This is Boxill's critical characterization of the 'poverty of culture' thesis. Boxill (1991), p. 588.
37   For an explicit expression of the Underclass in terms of idleness, see Jencks (1988), p. 24. Cf. Coetzee (1989), pp. 12–35. Another indication of the racialized character of the Underclass is revealed in its popular use to characterize animal pecking orders. Gans reports finding a new story referring to 'underclass Mexican iguanas'. Gans (1990), p. 272.
38   Wilson (1987), p. 126. In a more recent paper, Wilson seeks to develop a

'broader theoretical . . . framework that integrates social structural and cultural arguments'. Wilson (1991b), p. 1.

39   Reed (1988), p. 168.

40   Wilson (1991a), p. 600.

41   Where they help blacks in any measure at all, these programs tend to assist the black middle class more than the black poor, for the former are in a better position to take advantage of them because of better knowledge, greater institutional access, and more available resources.

42   Hochschild (1991), p. 564. Contrast E. Anderson (1990), pp. 72, 112–13.

43   Hochschild (1991), pp. 575 ff.

44   Fainstein (1986), p. 440. See also pp. 418, 439. Duster notes that when inner city businesses relocate to areas where employment of black youth is less likely, the proportion of blacks in the community may be one of the decisive considerations. Duster (1988), p. 3. Jencks also addresses this point. Jencks (1988). Even in respect to welfare treatment, whites on welfare fare better than those who are not white. See Torres (1988), p. 1058.

45   Hochschild (1991), p. 563.

46   On this latter point, see Gans (1990), p. 274.

47   Wilson (1991a), pp. 600–602. Cf. Hochschild (1991), p. 561. In his presidential address to the American Sociological Association, Wilson pertinently substitutes for his use of 'the Underclass' the term 'the ghetto poor'. And he does this commendably 'to focus our attention less on controversy and more on research and theoretical issues'. He nevertheless emphasizes that he 'hop[es] that I would not lose any of the theoretical meaning that this concept [the Underclass] has had in my writing'. Wilson (1991b), p. 11.

48   Hughes (1989), pp. 191–2.

49   Defending the Bush administration's new 'violence initiative' to 'identify early in their lives people who may be prone to violent or antisocial behaviour', the senior health official in the Health Department, Dr. Frederick Goodwin, argued that 'male monkeys, especially in the wild . . . roughly half of them survive to adulthood. The other half die by violence. That is the natural way of it for males, to knock each other off . . . the same hyperaggressive monkeys who kill each other are also hypersexual, so they copulate more. . . . Maybe it isn't just the careless use of the word when people call certain areas of certain cities jungles, that we may have gone back to what might be more natural, without all of the social controls that we have imposed on ourselves as a civilization over thousands of years in our own evolution.' *The New York Times*, February 28, 1992, p. A:7. Torgovnick also insists on using the term the 'urban jungle' in her analysis of contemporary primitivism discussed above. Theodore Lowi rightly asks why we now need concepts like 'culture of poverty' and 'underclass' in relation to black ghettos but not formerly in relation to Jewish or Irish ones. Lowi (1988), p. 855. On 'the West', see Young (1990), Derrida (1992).

50   Surveys of racial attitudes of whites in the United States date at least to the 1950s. The first major social science survey of the racial attitudes of blacks nationwide in over twenty years only recently appeared. Sigelman and Welch (1991). The same is largely true in South Africa. Blauner and Wellman discuss some of the political issues involved in conducting attitude research among the black poor. Blauner and Wellman (1973), pp. 310–30. The title of

Ladner's well-known volume, *The Death of White Sociology*, strikes one with the hindsight of nearly two decades and in spite of some dramatic changes, as overly optimistic.

51   Blauner and Wellman (1973), p. 315.
52   Bauman (1989), p. 85.
53   See, for example, the book *Becoming More Civilized* by self-described liberal social psychologist Leonard Doob. Published in 1960, Doob's study is concerned with the psychological effects of Africans as they 'become more civilized'. 'Civilization is intended as a description of the differences between the values of people who 'unwittingly live next to one another in the bush and those who wittingly live on top of one another in modern apartment houses'. Though Doob does not intend the term to designate or justify inferiority or superiority, the comparison of the irrational necessity of bush life with the free choice of modernity reproduces a presumption long considered to be well-established. See Doob (1960), pp. ix–x.
54   Ranger (1989), pp. 1–3.
55   Ibid., pp. 1–13, 18. My emphasis. Religious animism is converted into referential animalism – again!
56   Ibid., p. 19.
57   Ibid., p. 21.
58   Ibid., p. 22. My emphasis.
59.   Ibid., p. 24.

References

Anderson, E. (1990) *Streetwise: Race, Class, and Change in an Urban Community* (Chicago: University of Chicago Press).

Balibar, E. (1991) '*Es Gibt Keinen Staat in Europa*: Racism and Politics in Europe Today', *New Left Review* 187 (May-June): 5–19.

Balibar, E. (1990) 'Paradoxes of Universality'. In D. T. Goldberg, ed., *Anatomy of Racism* (Minneapolis: University of Minnesota Press).

Bauman, Z. (1989) *Modernity and the Holocaust* (Oxford: Polity Press).

Blauner, R. and Wellman, D. (1973) 'Toward the Decolonization of Social Research'. In J. Ladner, ed., *The Death of White Sociology* (New York: Random House).

Boxill, B. (1991) 'Wilson on the Truly Disadvantaged', *Ethics* 101 (April): 579–92.

Chafets, Z. (1990) 'The Tragedy of Detroit', *New York Sunday Times Magazine* (July 29): 20–6, 38, 42, 50–1.

Coetzee, J. M. (1989) *White Writing* (New Haven: Yale University Press).

Coughlin, E. K. (1988) 'Worsening Plight of the Underclass Catches Attention', *The Chronicle of Higher Education* (March): A5.

Derrida, J. (1992) *The Other Heading* (Bloomington: Indiana University Press).

Doob, L. (1960) *Becoming More Civilized* (New Haven: Yale University Press).

Duster, T. (1988) 'Social Implications of the "New" Black Underclass', *The Black Scholar* (May/June): 2–9.

Fabian, J. (1990) 'Presence and Representation: The Other and Anthropological Writing', *Critical Inquiry* 16 (Summer): 753–72.

Fainstein, N. (1986) 'The Underclass/Mismatch Hypothesis as an Explanation for Black Economic Deprivation', *Politics and Society* 15, 4: 403–51.

Foucault, M. (1988) 'The Political Technologies of Individuals'. In L. H. Martin, H. Gutman, and P. Hutton, eds., *Technologies of the Self*, (Minneapolis: University of Minnesota Press).

Foucault, M. (1970) *The Order of Things* (New York: Random House).

Frank, A. G. (1979) 'Anthropology = Ideology, Applied Anthropology = Politics'. In G. Huizer and B. Mannheim, eds., *The Politics of Anthropology* (The Hague: Mouton).

Gans, H. (1990) 'Reconstructing the Underclass: The Term's Dangers as a Planning Concept', *APA Journal* 271 (Summer): 271–77.

Gorra, M. (1991) 'Tact and Tarzan', *Transition* 52: 80–91.

Gould, S. J. (1991) 'The Birth of the Two-Sex World', *New York Review of Books* XXXVIII, 11 (June 13): 11–13.

Hochschild, J. (1991) 'The Politics of the Estranged Poor', *Ethics* 101 (April): 560–78.

Hughes, M. A. (1989) 'Misspeaking Truth to Power: A Geographical Perspective on the "Underclass" Fallacy', *Economic Geography* 65, 3 (July): 187–207.

Human Sciences Research Council (HSRC) (1985) *The South African Society: Realities and Future Prospects* (New York: Greenwood Press).

Innis, L. and Feagin, J. (1989) 'The Black "Underclass" Ideology in Race Relations Analysis', *Social Justice* 16, 4 (Winter): 13–34.

Jencks, C. (1988) 'Deadly Neighborhoods', *The New Republic* (June 13): 23–32.

Kuper, A. (1988) *The Invention of Primitive Society* (London: Routledge).

Lowi, T. (1988) 'The Theory of the Underclass: A Review of Wilson's *The Truly Disadvantaged*', *Policy Studies Review* 7, 4 (Summer): 852–8.

Mafeje, A. (1976) 'The Problem of Anthropology in Historical Perspective: An Inquiry into the Growth of the Social Sciences', *Canadian Journal of African Studies* X, 2: 307–33.

Magnet, M. (1989) 'America's Underclass: What to Do?', *Fortune* 115 (May 11): 130.

Meek, R. L. (1976) *Social Science and the Noble Savage* (Cambridge: Cambridge University Press).

Mudimbe, V. (1988) *The Invention of Africa* (Bloomington, IN: Indiana University Press).

Myrdal, G. (1962) *The Challenge to Affluence* (New York: Vintage Books).

Nettleton, A. and Hammond-Tooke, D., eds (1989) *African Art in Southern Africa: From Tradition to Township* (Johannesburg: Ad. Donker).

Pletsch, C. (1981) 'The Three Worlds, or the Division of Labor in the Social Sciences, circa 1950–75', *Comparative Studies in Society and History* 23, 4 (October): 565–90.

Ranger, T. (1989) *Rhodes, Oxford, and the Study of Race Relations* (Oxford: Clarendon Press).

Rathzel, N. (1990) 'Germany: One Race, One Nation?', *Race and Class* 32, 3: 31–48.

Reed, A. (1988) 'The Liberal Technocrat', *The New Republic* (Feb. 6): 167–70.

Ridgeway, J. (1990) 'Here He Comes, Mr. America', *The Village Voice* (October 9): 21.

Rubin, W., ed. (1984) *"Primitivism" in 20th Century Art: Affinity of the Tribal and the Modern* Vols I and II (New York: Museum of Modern Art).

Said, E. W. (1979a), 'Knowing the Oriental'. In E. W. Said, *Orientalism* (New York: Vintage Books).

Sigelman, L. and Welch, S. (1991) *Black Americans' Views of Racial Inequality: The Dream Deferred* (Cambridge: Cambridge University Press).

Tipps, D. (1973) 'Modernization Theory and the Comparative Study of Societies: A Critical Perspective', *Comparative Studies in Society and History* 15, 2: 119–226.

Torgovnick, M. (1990) *Gone Primitive: Savage Intellects, Modern Lives* (Chicago: University of Chicago Press).

Torres, G. (1988) 'Local Knowledge, Local Color: Critical Legal Studies and the Law of Race Relations', *San Diego Law Review* 25 (December): 1043–107.

Varnedoe, K. (1984a) 'Contemporary Explorations'. In W. Rubin, ed., *"Primitivism" in 20th Century Art: Affinity of the Tribal and the Modern* Vol. II (New York: Museum of Modern Art).

Williams, P. J. (1991) *The Alchemy of Race and Rights: Diary of a Law Professor* (Cambridge: Harvard University Press).

Wilson, W. J. (1991a) 'The Truly Disadvantaged Revisited: A Response to Hochschild and Boxill', *Ethics* 101 (April): 593–609.

Wilson, W. J. (1991b) 'Studying Inner City Social Dislocations: The Challenge of Public Agenda Research', *American Sociological Review* 56 (February): 1–14.

Wilson, W. J. (1987) *The Truly Disadvantaged: The Inner City, the Underclass, and Public Policy* (Chicago: Chicago University Press).

Wolf, E. (1981) *Europe and the People Without History* (Berkeley: University of California Press).

Worsley, P. (1984) *The Three Worlds* (London: Weidenfeld and Nicolson).

Young, R. (1990) *White Mythologies: Writing History and the West* (London: Routledge).

Chapter 13

Howard Winant

THE THEORETICAL STATUS
OF THE CONCEPT OF RACE

RACE USED TO BE A RELATIVELY intelligible concept; only recently have we seriously challenged its theoretical coherence. Today there are deep questions about what we actually mean by the term. But before (roughly) World War II, before the rise of nazism, before the end of the great European empires, and particularly before the decolonization of Africa, before the urbanization of the U.S. black population and the rise of the modern civil rights movement, race was still largely seen in Europe and North America (and elsewhere as well) as an essence, a natural phenomenon, whose meaning was fixed, as constant as a southern star.

In the earlier years of this century, only a handful of pioneers, people like W. E. B. Du Bois and Franz Boas, conceived of race in a more social and historical way. Other doubters included avant-garde racial theorists emerging from the intellectual ferment of the Harlem renaissance; black nationalists and pan-Africanists who sought to apply the rhetoric of national self-determination expressed at Versailles to the mother continent, and who returned from the battlefields of France to the wave of antiblack race riots that swept the United States in 1919; a few Marxists (whose perspectives had their own limitations); and to some extent the Chicago school of sociology led by Robert Ezra Park. But even these intellectuals and activists made incomplete breaks with essentialist notions of race, whether biologistic or otherwise deterministic.

That was then; this is now. Today the theory of race has been utterly transformed. The socially constructed status of the concept of race, which I have labeled the *racial formation* process, is widely recognized (Omi and Winant 1986), so much so that it is now often *conservatives* who argue that race is an illusion. The main task facing racial theory today, in fact, is no longer to critique the seemingly "natural" or "commonsense" concept of race – although that effort has not by any means been entirely completed. Rather, the central task is to focus attention on the *continuing significance and changing meaning of race*. It is to argue against the recent discovery of the illusory nature of race; against the supposed contemporary transcendence of race; against the widely reported death of the concept of race; and against the replacement of the category of race by other, supposedly more objective, categories like ethnicity, nationality, or class. All these initiatives are mistaken at best, and intellectually dishonest at worst.

In order to substantiate these assertions, we must first ask, what is race? Is it merely an illusion? An ideological construct utilized to manipulate, divide, and deceive? This position has been taken by many theorists, and activists as well, including many who have heroically served the cause of racial and social justice in the United States. Or is race something real, material, objective? This view too has its adherents, including both racial reactionaries and racial radicals.

In my view both of these approaches miss the boat. The concept of race is not an ideological construct, nor does it reflect an objective condition. Here I first reflect critically on these two opposed viewpoints on the contemporary theory of race. Then I offer an alternative perspective based on the approach of racial formation.

Race as an ideological construct

The assertion that race is an ideological construct – understood in the sense of a "false consciousness" that explains other "material" relationships in distorted fashion – seems highly problematic. This is the position taken by the prominent historian Barbara Fields in a well-known article, "Slavery, Race and Ideology in the United States of America."[1] Although Fields inveighs against various uses of the race concept, she directs her critical barbs most forcefully against historians who "invoke race as a historical explanation" (101).

According to Fields, the concept of race arose to meet an ideological need: its original effectiveness lay in its ability to reconcile freedom and slavery. The idea of race provided "the means of explaining slavery to people whose terrain was a republic founded on radical doctrines of liberty and natural rights" (114). But, Fields says, to argue that race – once framed as a category in thought, an ideological explanation for certain distinct types of social inequality – "takes on a life of its own" in social relationships is to transform (or "reify") an illusion into a reality. Such a position could be sustained "only if *race* is defined as innate and natural prejudice of color":

> Since race is not genetically programmed, racial prejudice cannot be genetically programmed either, but must arise historically. . . . The preferred solution is to suppose that, having arisen historically, race then ceases to be a historical phenomenon and becomes instead an external motor of history; according to the fatuous but widely re-peated formula, it "takes on a life of its own." In other words, once historically acquired, race becomes hereditary. The shopworn metaphor thus offers camouflage for a latter-day version of Lamarckism. (101; emphasis original)

Thus, race is either an illusion that does ideological work or an objective biological fact. Since it is certainly not the latter, it must be the former. No intermediate possibility – consider, for example, the Durkheimian notion of a "social fact" – is considered.

Some of this account – for example, the extended discussion of the origins of North American race thinking – can be accepted without major objection.[2] Furthermore, Fields effectively demonstrates the absurdity of many commonly held ideas about race. But her position is so extreme that at best it can only account for the *origins* of race thinking, and then only in one social context. To examine how race thinking evolved from these origins, how it responded to changing socio-cultural circumstances, is ruled out. Why and how did race thinking survive after emancipation? Fields cannot answer, because the very perpetuation of the concept of race is ruled out by her theoretical approach. As a relatively orthodox Marxist, Fields could argue that changing "material conditions" continued to give rise to changes in racial "ideology," except that even the limited autonomy this would attach to the concept of race would exceed her standards. Race cannot take on a life of its own; it is a pure ideology, an illusion.

Fields simply skips from emancipation to the present, where she disparages opponents of "racism" for unwittingly perpetuating an illusory concept of race. In denunciatory terms, Fields concludes by arguing for abolition of the concept:

> Nothing handed down from the past could keep race alive if we did not constantly reinvent and re-ritualize it to fit our own terrain. If race lives on today, it can do so only because we continue to create and re-create it in our social life, continue to verify it, and thus continue to need a social vocabulary that will allow us to make sense, not of what our ancestors did then, but of what we choose to do now. (118)

Fields is unclear about how "we" should jettison the ideological construct of race, and one can well understand why. By her own logic, racial ideologies cannot be abolished by acts of will. One can only marvel at the ease with which she distinguishes the bad old slavery days of the past from the present, when "we" anachronistically cling, as if for no reason, to the illusion that race retains any meaning. We foolishly throw up our hands and acquiesce in race thinking, rather than . . . doing what? Denying the racially demarcated divisions in society? Training ourselves to be "color-blind"?[3]

I venture to say that only a historian (however eminent) could have written such an article. Why? Because at the least a sociologist would know W. I. Thomas's famous dictum that if people "define situations as real, they are real in their consequences" (Thomas and Thomas 1928: 572). Nor is Fields alone in claiming that racial ideology persists because people insist on thinking racially. Her position is espoused by many, on both the left and the right of racial debates.[4]

In any case, the view that race is a kind of false consciousness is held not only by intellectuals, based on both well-intentioned and ulterior motivations; it also has a commonsense character. One hears in casual discussion, for example, or in introductory social science classes, variations on the following statement: "I don't care if a person is black, white, or purple, I treat them exactly the same; a person's just a person to me . . ." Furthermore, some of the integrationist aspirations of racial minority movements, especially civil rights movement, invoke this sort of idea. Consider the famous line from the "I Have a Dream" speech, the line that made Shelby Steele's career: "that someday my four little children will be judged, not by the color of their skin, but by the content of their character."

The core criticisms of this "race as ideology" approach are two: first, it fails to recognize the salience a social construct can develop over half a millennium or more of diffusion, or should I say enforcement, as a fundamental principle of social organization and identity formation. The longevity of the race concept and the enormous number of effects race thinking (and race acting) has produced guarantee that race will remain a feature of social reality across the globe, and a fortiori in the United States, despite its lack of intrinsic or scientific merit (in the biological sense). Second, and related, this approach fails to recognize that at the level of experience, of everyday life, race is a relatively impermeable part of our identities. U.S. society is so thoroughly racialized that to be without racial identity is to be in danger of having no identity. To be raceless is akin to being genderless. Indeed, when one cannot identify another's race, a microsociological crisis of interpretation results, something perhaps best interpreted in ethnomethodological or Goffmanian terms. To complain about such a situation may be understandable, but it does not advance understanding.

Race as an objective condition

On the other side of the coin, it is clearly problematic to assign objectivity to the race concept. Such theoretical practice puts us in quite heterogeneous, and sometimes unsavory, company. Of course, the biologistic racial theories of the past do this: here I am thinking of such precursors of fascism as Gobineau and Chamberlain (Mosse 1978), of the eugenicists such as Lothrop Stoddard and Madison Grant, and of the "founding fathers" of scientific racism such as Agassiz, Broca, Terman, and Yerkes (Kevles 1985; Chase 1977). Indeed, an extensive legacy of this sort of thinking extends right up to the present. Stephen Jay Gould (1981) makes devastating critiques of such views.

But much liberal and even radical social science, though firmly committed to a social as opposed to a biological interpretation of race, nevertheless also slips into a kind of objectivism about racial identity and racial meaning. This is true because race is afforded an easy and unproblematic coherence all too frequently. Thus, to select only prominent examples, Daniel Moynihan, William Julius Wilson, Milton Gordon, and many other mainstream thinkers theorize race in terms that downplay its flexibility and historically contingent character. Even these major thinkers, whose explicit rejection of biologistic forms of racial theory would be unquestioned, fall prey to a kind of creeping objectivism of race. For in their analyses a modal explanatory approach emerges as follows: sociopolitical circumstances change over historical time, racially defined groups adapt or fail to adapt to these changes, achieving mobility or remaining mired in poverty, and so on. In this logic there is no reconceptualization of group identities, of the constantly shifting parameters through which race is thought about, group interests are assigned, statuses are ascribed, agency is attained, and roles are performed.

Contemporary racial theory, then, is often "objectivistic" about its fundamental category. Although abstractly acknowledged to be a sociohistorical construct, race *in practice* is often treated as an objective fact: one simply *is* one's race; in the contemporary United States, if we discard euphemisms, we have five color-based racial categories: black, white, brown, yellow, and red.

This is problematic, indeed ridiculous, in numerous ways. Nobody really belongs in these boxes; they are patently absurd reductions of human variation. But even accepting the nebulous "rules" of racial classification – "hypodescent," and so forth[5] – many people do not fit anywhere: into what categories should we place Turks, for example? People of mixed race? South Asians? Objectivist treatments, lacking a critique of the *constructed* character of racial meanings, also clash with experimental dimensions of the issue. If one does not "act" black, or white, or whatever, that is just deviance from the norm. There is in these approaches an insufficient appreciation of the *performative* aspect of race, as postmodernists might call it.[6]

To summarize the critique of this "race as objective condition" approach, then, it fails on three counts: First, it cannot grasp the processual and relational character of racial identity and racial meaning. Second, it denies the historicity and social comprehensiveness of the race concept. And third, it cannot account for the way actors, both individual and collective, have to manage incoherent and conflictual racial meanings and identities in everyday life. It has no concept, in short, of what Omi and I have labeled *racial formation*.

Toward a critical theory of the concept of race

The foregoing clearly sets forth the agenda that any adequate theorization of the race concept must fulfill. Such an approach must be theoretically constructed so as to steer between the Scylla of "race as illusion" and the Charybdis of "racial objectivism." Such a critical theory can be consistently developed, I suggest, drawing upon the racial formation approach. Such a theoretical formulation, too, must be explicitly historicist: it must recognize the importance of historical context and contingency in the framing of racial categories and the social construction of racially defined experiences.

What would be the minimum conditions for the development of a critical, processual theory of race? I suggest three conditions for such a theory:

 – It must apply to contemporary *political* relationships.
 – It must apply in an increasingly *global* context.
 – It must apply across *historical time*.

Let us address each of these points very briefly.

Contemporary Political Relationships. The meaning and salience of race is forever being reconstituted in the present. Today such new relationships emerge chiefly at the point where some *counterhegemonic* or *postcolonial* power is attained. At that point the meanings and the political articulations of race proliferate.

Examples include the appearance of competing racial *projects*, by which I mean efforts to institutionalize racial meanings and identities in particular social structures: notably those of individual, family, community, and state. As egalitarian movements contend with racial "backlash" over sustained periods of time, as binary logics of racial antagonism (white/black, *ladino/indio*, settler/native, etc.) become more complex and decentered, political deployment of the concept of race comes to signal qualitatively new types of political domination, as well as new types of opposition.

Consider the U.S. example. In terms of domination, it is now possible to perpetuate racial domination without making any explicit reference to race at all. Subtextual or "coded" racial signifiers, or the mere denial of the continuing significance of race, may suffice. Similarly, in terms of opposition, it is now possible to resist racial domination in entirely new ways, particularly by limiting the reach and penetration of the political system into everyday life, by generating new identities, new collectivities, new (imagined) communities that are relatively less permeable to the hegemonic system.[7] Much of the rationale for Islamic currents among blacks in the United States, for the upsurge in black anti-Semitism, and to some extent for the Afrocentric phenomenon, can be found here. Thus the old choices – integration versus separatism, assimilation versus nationalism – are no longer the only options.

In the "underdeveloped" world, proliferation of so-called postcolonial phenomena also have significant racial dimensions, as the entire Fanonian tradition (merely to select one important theoretical current) makes clear. Crucial debates have now been occurring for a decade or more on the question of postcolonial subjectivity and identity, the insufficiency of the simple dualism of "Europe and its others," the subversive and parodic dimensions of political culture at and beyond the edges of the old imperial boundaries, and so forth.[8]

The Global Context of Race. The geography of race is becoming more complex. Once more easily seen in terms of imperial reach, in terms of colonization, conquest, and migration, racial space is becoming *globalized* and thus accessible to a new kind of comparative analysis. This only becomes possible now, at a historical moment when the distinction "developed/underdeveloped" has been definitively overcome. Obviously, by this I do not mean that now there are no disparities between North and South, rich and poor. Rather, I mean that the movement of capital and labor has internationalized all nations, all regions. Today we have reached the point where the empire strikes back,[9] as former (neo)colonial subjects, now redefined as "immigrants," challenge the majoritarian status of the formerly metropolitan group (the whites, the Europeans, the "Americans" or "French," etc.). Meanwhile, phenomena such as the rise of "diasporic" models of blackness, the creation of "panethnic"[10] communities of Latinos and Asians (in such countries as the United Kingdom and the United States), and the breakdown of borders in both Europe and North America all seem to be internationalizing and racializing previously national polities, cultures, and identities. To take just one example, popular culture now internationalizes racial awareness almost instantaneously, as reggae, rap, samba, and various African pop styles leap from continent to continent.

Because of these transformations, a global comparison of hegemonic social/ political orders based on race becomes possible. I think that in a highly specified form, that is, not as mere reactions or simple negations of "Western" cultural/ theoretical dominance, such notions as diasporic consciousness or racially informed standpoint epistemologies deserve more serious attention as efforts to express the contemporary globalization of racial space.[11] Furthermore, to understand such phenomena as the construction of new racial identities or in terms of the pan-ethnicity dynamic is to recognize that the territorial reach of racial hegemony is now global.

The dissolution of the transparent racial identity of the formerly dominant group, that is to say, the advancing racialization of whites in Europe and the United States, must also be recognized as proceeding from the increasingly globalized dimensions of race. As previous assumptions erode, white identity loses its transparency, the easy elision with "racelessness" that accompanies racial domination. "Whiteness" becomes a matter of anxiety and concern.

The Emergence of Racial Time. Some final notes are in order in respect to the question of the epochal nature of racial time. Classical social theory had an Enlightenment-based view of time, a perspective that understood the emergence of modernity in terms of the rise of capitalism and the bourgeoisie. This view was by no means limited to Marxism. Weberian disenchantment and the rise of the Durkheimian division of labor also partake of this temporal substrate. Only rarely does the racial dimension of historical temporality appear in this body of thought, as, for example, in Marx's excoriation of the brutalities of "primitive accumulation":

> The discovery of gold and silver in America, the extirpation, enslavement, and entombment in mines of the aboriginal population, the beginning of the conquest and looting of the East Indies, the turning of Africa into a warren for the commercial hunting of blackskins, signalized the rosy dawn of the era of capitalist production. These idyllic proceedings are the chief momenta of primitive accumulation. On their heels treads the commercial war of the European nations with the globe for a theater. It begins with the revolt of the Netherlands from Spain, assumes giant dimensions in England's Anti-Jacobin War, and is still going on in the opium wars with China, etc. (1967: 751)

Yet even Marx frequently legitimated such processes as the inevitable and ultimately beneficial birth pangs of classlessness – by way of the ceaselessly revolutionary bourgeoisie.

Today such teleological accounts seem hopelessly outmoded. Historical time could well be interpreted in terms of something like a racial *longue durée*: for has there not been an immense historical rupture represented by the rise of Europe, the onset of African enslavement, the *conquista*, and the subjugation of much of Asia? I take the point of much poststructural scholarship on these matters to be quite precisely an effort to explain "Western" or colonial time as a huge project demarcating human "difference," or more globally as Todorov, say, would argue, of framing partial collective identities in terms of externalized "others" (Todorov 1985). Just as, for example, the writers of the *Annales* school sought to locate the deep logic of historical time in the means by which material life was produced –

diet, shoes, and so on[12] – so we might usefully think of a racial *longue durée* in which the slow inscription of phenotypical signification took place upon the human body, in and through conquest and enslavement, to be sure, but also as an enormous act of expression, of narration.

In short, just as the noise of the big bang still resonates through the universe, so the overdetermined construction of world "civilization" as a product of the rise of Europe and the subjugation of the rest of us still defines the race concept. Such speculative notes, of course, can be no more than provocations. Nor can I conclude this effort to reframe the agenda of racial theory with a neat summation. There was a long period – centuries – in which race was seen as a natural condition, an essence. This was succeeded although not entirely superseded by a shorter but potent way of thinking about race as subordinate to supposedly more concrete, "material" relationships; during that period, down to now, race was understood as an illusion, an excrescence. Perhaps now we are approaching the end of that racial epoch too.

To our dismay, we may have to give up our familiar ways of thinking about race once more. If so, there may also be some occasion for delight. For it may be possible to glimpse yet another view of race, in which the concept operates neither as a signifier of comprehensive identity nor of fundamental difference, both of which are patently absurd, but rather as a marker of the infinity of variations we humans hold as a common heritage and hope for the future.

Notes

1   Page references will be given in the text.
2   Minor objections would have to do with Fields's functionalist view of ideology, and her claim that the race concept only "came into existence" (101) when it was needed by whites in North American colonies beginning in the late seventeenth century. The concept of race, of course, has a longer history than that.
3   Fields's admirer David Roediger also criticizes her on this point: "At times she nicely balances the ideological creation of racial attitudes with their manifest and ongoing importance and their (albeit ideological) *reality*. . . . But elsewhere, race disappears into the 'reality' of class" (Roediger 1991, 7–8; emphasis original).
4   Another important thinker who has at least flirted with the idea of race as illusion is Kwame Anthony Appiah. See Appiah 1986.
5   This concept is developed in Harris 1964.
6   "The question of identification is never the affirmation of a pregiven identity, never a self-fulfilling prophecy – it is always the production of an image of identity and the transformation of the subject in assuming that image" (Homi K. Bhabha, "Interrogating Identity," p. 188).
7   The work of Paul Gilroy (1991) on the significance of black music in Afro-diasporic communities is particularly revealing on this point.
8   There is a vast literature by now on these matters. The founding statement is undoubtedly Edward Said's *Orientalism* (1978); also useful is Bhabha 1990a.
9   I borrow this phrase not from George Lucas but from the book of that title edited at the Centre for Contemporary Cultural Studies, 1982.

10   David Lopez and Yen Espiritu define panethnicity as "the development of bridging organizations and solidarities among subgroups of ethnic collectivities that are often seen as homogeneous by outsiders." Such a development, they claim, is a crucial feature of ethnic change – "supplanting both assimilation and ethnic particularism as the direction of change for racial/ethnic minorities." While panethnic formation is facilitated by an ensemble of cultural factors (e.g., common language and religion) and structural factors (e.g., class, generation, and geographical concentration), Lopez and Espiritu conclude that a specific concept of race is fundamental to the construction of panethnicity (Lopez and Espiritu 1990: 198).

11   Similar points are made in Mudimbe 1988, Rabinow 1986, and Harding 1987.

12   For example, the magisterial work of Fernand Braudel 1981.

References

Appiah, Kwame Anthony, "The Uncompleted Argument: Du Bois and the Illusion of Race," in Henry Louis Gates, ed., *"Race," Writing, and Difference* (Chicago: University of Chicago Press, 1986).

Bhabha, Homi K., "DissemiNation: Time, Narrative, and the Margins of the Modern Nation," in idem, ed., *Nation and Narration* (London: Routledge, 1990a).

——, "Interrogating Identity: The Postcolonial Prerogative," in David Theo Goldberg, ed., *Anatomy of Racism* (Minneapolis: University of Minnesota Press, 1990b).

Braudel, Fernand, *The Structures of Everyday Life: The Limits of the Possible*, vol. I of Braudel, *Civilization and Capitalism, 15th–18th Century*, trans. Sian Reynolds (New York: Harper & Row, 1981).

Centre for Contemporary Cultural Studies, *The Empire Strikes Back: Race and Racism in 70s Britain* (London: Hutchinson, 1982).

Chase, Allan, *The Legacy of Malthus: The Social Costs of the New Scientific Racism* (New York: Knopf, 1977).

Fields, Barbara Jeanne, "Slavery, Race and Ideology in the United States of America," *New Left Review* 181 (May/June 1990).

Gilroy, Paul, *"There Ain't No Black in the Union Jack": The Cultural Politics of Race and Nation* (Chicago: University of Chicago Press, 1991).

Gould, Stephen J., *The Mismeasure of Man* (New York: Norton, 1981).

Harding, Sandra, *The Science Question in Feminism* (Ithaca, N.Y.: Cornell University Press, 1987).

Harris, Marvin, *Patterns of Race in the Americas* (New York: Walker, 1964).

Kevles, Daniel J., *In the Name of Eugenics: Genetics and the Uses of Human Heredity* (New York: Knopf, 1985).

Lopez, David, and Yen Espiritu, "Panethnicity in the United States: A Theoretical Framework," *Ethnic and Racial Studies* 13 (1990).

Marx, Karl, *Capital*, vol. I (New York: International Publishers, 1967).

Mosse, George, *Toward the Final Solution: A History of European Racism* (New York: Howard Fertig, 1978).

Mudimbe, V. Y., *The Invention of Africa: Gnosis, Philosophy, and the Order of Knowledge* (Bloomington: Indiana University Press, 1988).

Omi, Michael, and Howard Winant, *Racial Formation in the United States: From the 1960s to the 1980s* (New York: Routledge, 1986).

Rabinow, Paul, "Representations Are Social Facts: Modernity and Post-Modernity in Anthropology," in James Clifford and George E. Marcus, eds., *Writing Culture: The Poetics and Politics of Ethnography* (Berkeley: University of California Press, 1986).

Roediger, David R., *The Wages of Whiteness: Race and the Making of the American Working Class* (New York: Verso, 1991).

Said, Edward, *Orientalism* (New York: Pantheon, 1978).

Thomas, W. I., and Dorothy Swaine Thomas, *The Child in America* (New York: Knopf, 1928).

Todorov, Tsvetan, *The Conquest of America: The Question of the Other*, trans. Richard Howard (New York: Harper & Row, 1985).

PART THREE

Racism and anti-semitism

INTRODUCTION

ONE OF THE REGRETTABLE FEATURES of much contemporary theorising about race and racism has been the tendency to leave the question of anti-semitism to one side, treating it almost as a separate issue. This is in spite of the fact that one of the most consistent themes that runs through racist thinking and the values articulated by racist and fascist movements throughout this century has been anti-semitism. The extracts we have been able to include in this Part are, of course, merely examples of a much wider body of work that has been produced over the years (see Guide to Further Reading). But in including these extracts we hope that we have at least given an indication of the kinds of questions that we need to think about in exploring the relationship between racism and anti-semitism.

The first extract from George Mosse sets out to provide a brief overview of the ways in which myths and counter myths about 'the Jew' emerged and evolved. Drawing on a variety of historical sources, Mosse attempts to situate what he sees as the main elements of myths about Jews and the way these myths evolved and changed over time. In addition he is concerned to show how the evolving racial mythologies about Jews helped to construct them as a kind of 'race apart'. To take the particular example of the image of the 'wandering Jew' Mosse attempts to show that such myths helped to construct Jews as the 'eternal foreigner' who would be unable to become a part of the 'people'. Interestingly enough Mosse's argument also shows that at least some Jews were influenced by racial thought and to some extent sought to develop 'counter-myths' about race and Jewish identity in order to question anti-semitism.

The next extract by Theodor Adorno and Max Horkheimer was originally written in 1944. Both Adorno and Horkheimer were leading members of the Frankfurt School of critical theory and they were in exile in the United States at the time. Given their experience as exiles from Nazi Germany it is perhaps not surprising that they saw the main arguments of their work on anti-semitism as an attempt to understand 'the actual reversion of enlightened civilisation to barbarism'. More specifically, however, Adorno and Horkheimer's analysis is preoccupied by the need to make sense of how anti-semitism in Nazi Germany led to the 'policy of extermination', the idea that 'Jews must be wiped from the face of the earth'. This is of course a question on which much has been written, both in the period immediately after the Second World War and in more recent times. But this extract helps to pose the need for an explanation of the relationship between anti-semitism and the Holocaust.

Perhaps the most influential recent attempt to provide a theoretical frame-work for the analysis of anti-semitism is to be found in the work of the sociologist Zygmunt Bauman. Bauman is particularly concerned with the question of the reasons why the Holocaust could happen in the context of modernity. The broad outline of his argument links up with some of the analytical arguments to be found in the work of Adorno and Horkheimer as well as the historical accounts of Mosse. A recurrent theme in his analysis is the way he attempts to show that the exter-mination and genocide of the Jews by the Nazi racial state was not the product of irrationality, but very much an integral part of the 'rational world of modern civilisation'. From this basic premise he attempts to show how it was precisely the development of technology, large impersonal state bureaucracies and modern science that provided the necessary conditions for the institutionalisation of a policy of extermination against Jews.

The next two extracts focus on the question of the role of images and stereo-types in the construction of 'the Jew'. The first extract is from Sander Gilman, one of the most prolific and controversial figures in this field, and is concerned particularly with the changing terms of debate about the body in discourses about Jews. Using recent debates in America about the construction of Jews as white, Gilman sets out to show the tenuous and historically contingent nature of this ascription of 'whiteness'. Writing in his usual powerful narrative style Gilman uses the imagery of 'the Jewish nose' as a way of exploring the changing representa-tions of the skin colour of Jews from the nineteenth century onwards. His account links up with the broader discussion of whiteness that has become such an impor-tant theme in debates about race and racism in recent years (see contributions by Ruth Frankenberg in Part Five and by Richard Dyer in Part Six.

Gilman's analysis also links up with the concerns of the final extract in this part by Matthew Jacobson. This extract is symptomatic of a renewed interest by historians and others in the meanings attached to whiteness in America, particu-larly in relation to immigrant groups such as the Irish, Jews and Italians among others. Drawing on research about the construction of Jewishness in American culture from the nineteenth century onwards Jacobson's account is specifically concerned with the ways in which Jews have been constructed as both white and Other. He also argues forcefully that images based on 'racial Jewishness' were not simply the product of anti-semitism, since Jewish writers and commentators were also constructing their own versions of what 'Jewishness' meant. In this sense Jacobson's analysis can be taken as a case study of the importance of historical and cultural processes in shaping the meanings that are attached to racial categories.

KEY QUESTIONS

- Theodor Adorno and Max Horkheimer argue that 'the fascists do not view the Jews as a minority but an opposing race'. What does this argument tell us about the nature of Nazi anti-semitism?
- Critically review George Mosse's analysis of the relationship between anti-semitism and racism.
- Zygmunt Bauman has argued 'modern civilisation was not the Holocaust's sufficient condition; it was, however, most certainly its necessary condition'. Review the implications of this argument for the analysis of the Holocaust.
- Analyse Sander Gilman's account of the role of changing images of 'the Jew' in racial discourses.
- 'The history of racial Jewishness is not merely the history of anti-semitism' (Matthew Jacobson). What do you understand by this argument?
- Should the analysis of anti-semitism be seen as separate from the question of racism?
- Some commentators have talked of the existence of 'anti-semitism without Jews'. Discuss the implications of this argument.

Chapter 14

George L. Mosse

THE JEWS: MYTH AND COUNTER-MYTH

T HE MYSTERY OF RACE TRANSFORMED the Jew into an evil
principle. This was nothing new for the Jew; after all, anti-Christ had been
a familiar figure during the Middle Ages. But in the last decades of the nineteenth
century and the first half of the twentieth, the traditional legends which had swirled
about the Jews in the past were revived as foils for racial mysticism and as instruments of political mobilization. Accusations of ritual murder, the curse of Ahasverus
the wandering Jew, and fantasies about the universal Jewish world conspiracy had
never vanished from the European consciousness even during the Enlightenment.
Now they were to be revitalized and given renewed force.

The accusation of ritual murder – the so-called blood libel – had medieval
roots in the legend that Jews murdered Christian children and drank their blood
during the feast of Passover. As part of their religious ceremonial, the Jews allegedly
performed a "ritual murder," typical of the perverse nature of their religion and
the evil it represented. Moreover, this Jewish use of blood blasphemed the sacrifice of Christ on the Cross, for Easter and Passover coincided. The blood libel
provided the basis for an accusation of atavism, because in contrast to civilized
people, Jews supposedly practiced human sacrifice. The so-called Jewish conspiracy
against the Gentile world was also built into this myth from the beginning, for no
Jew, so it was thought, would inform on any other Jew, while talkative Gentiles
were bribed with gold to remain silent about this ritual of human sacrifice.

The myth of the use and misuse of the sacred substance of blood served to
separate out the Jews from the Christians. Blood libel had always surfaced in
periods of stress. At the end of the nineteenth century, the times seemed out of
joint and ritual murder accusations once more swept through eastern Europe.
Between 1890 and 1914, there were no less than twelve trials of Jews for ritual
murder; the last murder charge was leveled as late as 1930, in the Rutho-Carpathian
Mountains by the prosecutor of the Czechoslovak government.[1]

The blood libel remained alive chiefly in the underdeveloped countries of eastern Europe and the Russian Empire. Within the Russian Empire the government shrewdly exploited the belief in order to provoke pogroms, and every lost Christian child was a menace to the local Jewish community, one of whose members might be accused of murder. Western and central Europe had also made use of this legend, but in these regions the accusations receded in time, especially among urban segments of the population where secularism had made large inroads. In rural regions the myth continued, encouraged in particular by the Catholic Church, which had trouble ending its long association with the accusation of ritual murder. Local priests still proclaimed its truth at times during the nineteenth and even into the twentieth century, and medieval saints like Simon of Trent, who were worshipped into our own day, kept the legend of martyred children supposedly brutally murdered by the Jews before the eyes of the pious.[2]

[. . .] If the blood libel encouraged Christians to look upon the Jew as harbinger of evil, the legend of the wandering Jew exemplified the curse laid upon that race by Christ himself. The figure of Ahasverus appears in legend as a Jew who sped Christ along to his crucifixion and refused him comfort or shelter. As a result, Ahasverus is doomed to a life of wandering, without a home, despised as rootless and disinherited. The wandering Jew, who can neither live nor die, also heralds terror and desolation.[3] This medieval tale of the "wicked Jew" (as Ahasverus was often called) did not fade in the nineteenth century but instead became symbolic of the cursed fate of the Jewish people. The restless age and the restless Jew both became symbols of a desolate modernity.

Ahasverus in legend is also associated with conspiracies against the righteous. In France, he symbolized the conspiracy of Jews and Masons against the nation. However, at times the wandering Jew could become a hero and the conspiracy be laid on other shoulders. Eugène Sue's *The Wandering Jew* (*Le Juif Errant*, 1844–45), the most famous Ahasverus story of the century, turns him into a hero who foils a Jesuit conspiracy. Then again, during the First World War the English satirized Emperor William II as Ahasverus who had driven Christ from his door and was now wandering through Europe in the vain search of peace.[4] Nevertheless, for the most part the ancient legend retained its original form, and remained symbolic of the curse which the Jewish people brought upon themselves and all they touched. These legends, whether the blood libel or that of the wandering Jew, offered explanation and coherence in a world of industrialization, instability, and bewildering social change, just as they had earlier been used as explanation for famines, sickness, and all manner of natural catastrophes.

The legend of the wandering Jew re-enforced the view of the Jew as the eternal foreigner, who would never learn to speak the national language properly or strike roots in the soil. This myth, in turn, was linked to the supposed oriental origin of the Jew as described in the Bible. The Jew was assumed to be fixed for all time as a desert nomad wandering through the Sinai. The Viennese Orientalist Adolf Wahrmund popularized this image in his *Law of the Nomads and Contemporary Jewish Domination* (*Das Gesetz des Nomadenthums und die heutige Judenherrschaft*, 1887). The Jews had been nomads in the past, and were still nomads today, claimed Wahrmund. This explained their shiftlessness in commerce, and their rootless, cosmopolitan way of thought, as opposed to the rooted Aryan peasantry.

Wahrmund carried on the tradition of proving Aryan peasant origins through linguistics. Both as nomads and Asians, the Jews were indeed Ahasverus, not because of the curse of Christ, but because they were still a desert people.[5] Thus, an anti-Jewish image rooted in religion was secularized and given new credence by means of a pseudo-scientific environmentalism.

Such legends catered to the love of the romantic and the unusual. The nineteenth century, which popularized Frankenstein and human vampires, was fascinated by horror stories that had a real people as their foil. The novel *Biarritz*, written in 1868 by Hermann Goedsche (under the pen name Sir John Redcliffe), was not only typical of this love of the unusual, but also significant as one of the chief sources of the notorious forged *Protocols of the Elders of Zion*.

The setting of *Biarritz* is the Jewish cemetery of Prague. Significantly, other more famous writers, such as Wilhelm Raabe, used the identical setting to tell stories of Jewish mysteries and secret deeds. The Jewish cemetery in Prague was a romantic site; moreover, it was accessible, for Prague, although part of the Austrian Empire, was considered a German city. It was easy to travel there and to see for oneself the sights of the ghetto, while the other ghettos of eastern Europe were in regions with "obscure" languages and difficult to reach. The tourist from Germany or Austria, for example, would feel at home staying in the large German section of Prague and visiting the picturesque sights. The clash of different cultures, which was exemplified by the ghettos still existing in eastern Europe, could be symbolized through the Jewish cemetery in Prague with its mysterious graves and caftaned figures – at least as seen by the tourist from the West. Goedsche summed up this symbolism when he wrote that Prague was the only German city where Jews still lived in isolation.[6]

In this way, Goedsche set the scene for a meeting of the thirteen Jewish elders in the cemetery. He named them the "cabalistic Sanhedrin," referring to the many legends associated with the Jewish Cabalah and thus giving a wider historical dimension to the assembly at the cemetery. For Goedsche, the mystery of the Cabalah consisted in "the power of gold."[7] Thus through the Cabalah he cemented the traditional association of the Jews with base materialism. One of the elders is Ahasverus, the wandering Jew; his presence among the thirteen clearly shows how Goedsche exploited old anti-Semitic traditions.[8]

The elders meet as the representatives of the chosen people, who show "the tenacity of a snake, the cunning of a fox, the look of a falcon, the memory of a dog, the diligence of an ant, and the sociability of a beaver."[9] The association of Jews with animal imagery should not surprise us; it was noted earlier when discussing the rise of the stereotype in the eighteenth century. The blacks suffered an identical fate when they were constantly compared to monkeys. Likening the so-called inferior races to animals put them low on the chain of being and, by analogy, robbed them of their humanity.

In the eerie setting of the cemetery, the elders conspire to take over the world. They plot to concentrate all capital into their hands; to secure possession of all land, railroads, mines, houses; to occupy government posts; to seize the press and direct all public opinion. This bizarre plan was later to be borrowed from *Biarritz* and, as a "Rabbi's speech," circulated all over the Russian and Austrian Empires.

The myth of the sinister Jewish conspiracy was not confined to eastern Europe. Only a year after *Biarritz* appeared, Gougenot de Mousseaux in a polemic against the Jews of France depicted them as devotees of a secret mystery-religion presided over by the devil himself.[10] Thus, the rapidly growing belief in occult forces during the last decades of the nineteenth century intersected with a revitalized medieval demonology. Indeed, Mousseaux declared that the devil was the King of the Jews, and his version of the Jewish plot would become part of the more famous *Protocols*, just as *Biarritz* also fed into this forgery.

The Protocols of the Elders of Zion became both the climax and the synthesis of these conspiracy theories. They were forged in France in the midst of the Dreyfus Affair, with the assistance of the Russian secret police, probably between 1894 and 1899. The French right wanted a document in order to link Dreyfus to the supposed conspiracy of his race, and the Russian secret police needed it to justify czarist anti-Jewish policy. This time the "learned elders of Zion," again meeting in the Jewish cemetery of Prague, reflected every aspect of the modern world which the reactionaries in France and Russia, but also in the rest of Europe, feared so much.

The weapons that the elders were to use to achieve world domination ranged from the use of the French Revolution's slogan, "Liberty, Equality, Fraternity," to the spreading of liberalism and socialism. The people of the world would be deprived of all faith in God and their strength undermined by encouraging public criticism of authority. At the same time, a financial crisis would be provoked and gold in the hands of the Jews would be manipulated in order to drive up prices. Eventually, "there should be in all states in the world, besides ourselves, only the masses of the proletariat, a few millionaires devoted to our interests and our own police and soldiers."[11] Blind obedience would then be demanded to the King of Jews, the ruler of the universe. In short, the conspiracy myth fed into the uncertainties and fears of the nineteenth century, bridging the gap between ancient anti-Semitic legend and the modern Jews in a world of dramatic change.

What if the Gentiles discovered this plot and began to attack the Jews? In this case the elders would use a truly horrible weapon, for soon all the national capitals of the world would be undermined by a network of underground railways. If there should be danger to the Jews, these tunnels would be used to blow up the cities and kill their inhabitants. Such a nightmare bears traces of the fear of a new technology, but also of the stories of horror and fantasy so popular at the time. Furthermore, the elders would destroy the Gentiles by inoculating them with diseases.

Opposition to inoculation was to become a part of racist thought. In 1935 the *Weltkampf*, a Nazi anti-Jewish journal, stated that inoculation had been invented by the Jews in order to subvert the Aryan blood, citing the *Protocols* as its evidence.[12] Racism is basic to the nightmare of the *Protocols*, for the Jews were considered an evil race, coherent and well organized. The mystery of race had found one of its most popular supposed proofs in the conspiracy of the elders of Zion.

Conspiracy theories might have been less popular and effective had it not been for certain past and present Jewish organizations which to some Gentiles seemed to serve a sinister purpose. In Russia it was charged that the Jewish communal organizations, which had been dissolved by Czar Nicholas I in 1844, were still alive and active as a secret Jewish government linked to foreign interests.[13] An element of spurious reality was lent to these conspiracy charges with the founding of the "Alliance Israélite Universelle" in 1860 by French Jews. The Alliance was intended to aid Jews in nations where they were deprived of civic rights, and to support schools for North African Jews. These worthy purposes were, of course, ignored and the Alliance seen as the exposed tip of an iceberg of conspiracy.

Aside from the reality of the Alliance, anti-Semites and racists pointed to the Masons as another existing secret conspiracy directed by Jews — the *Protocols* had linked Jewish and Masonic conspiracies. The fight against Masons in turn called the Catholic Church into action. The Anti-Masonic World Congress of 1897 was supported by Pope Leo XIII, and was placed under the protection of the Virgin Mary. During the Congress, the Jews were specifically linked to the anti-Catholic Masonic conspiracy, and the Union Antimaçonnique which was founded at that time received support from Drumont and other French racists.[14] An anti-Masonic movement also existed in Germany, and eventually, under the Nazis, an anti-Masonic museum was established, but this particular myth was strongest in Catholic France.

Powerful though the groups might have been that at times supported such theories and pointed to the Alliance or Masons as proof, they were still a minority (except, perhaps, among the Catholic clergy). Such myths and legends about the Jews were used in order to mobilize those who wanted to protect both traditional Christianity and traditional society. But much of the future importance of these anti-Jewish myths consisted in their association with a secular nationalism which lacked the traditional Christian inhibitions against embracing racism. Certainly, as we shall see, the line between Christian anti-Semitism and racism was thin; but the national mystique could without question accept these myths as inherent in the Jewish race. There was no need for secular nationalism to confront the problem of how Jews could be changed into Christians through baptism if their race was inherently evil, nor was it necessary as a part of the drama of Christian salvation to disentangle the Jews of the Old Testament from their inferior racial status. All racists did better to ignore Christianity whenever possible.

In this regard, a journalist like Wilhelm Marr in Germany was typical. His *Jewry's Victory over Teutonism* (*Der Sieg des Judentums über das Germanentum*, 1879) rejected the Christian accusations against the Jews as unworthy of the enlightened, but then repeated all the myths about rootless and conspiratorial Jews. For Marr the Jews were stronger than the Germans, for they were winning the racial battle for survival. He suggested a counteroffensive, spearheaded by anti-Semitic Russia.

The one-time member of the German diet, Hermann Ahlwardt, became more famous than Marr with the publication of his *The Desperate Struggle Between Aryan and Jew* (*Der Verzweiflungskampf der arischen Völker mit dem Judentum*, 1890). Two years later, this primary school principal wrote a book in a similar vein entitled *New Revelations: Jewish Rifles* (*Neue Enthüllungen Judenflinten*, 1892), in which he once more sounded the alarm against the Jewish threat. Here, he contended that the Jewish armament firm of Löwe was selling defective rifles to the German army as part of a universal world Jewish conspiracy to destroy the Reich. And for all the absurdity of the allegation, the government initiated an inquiry into the charges.[15]

As yet, the attempts to act as if the Jewish conspiracy were true remained on the fringes of European thought and, apart from Russia, unsuccessful in immediate terms. They were forerunners of the concerted war against the Jews which began only after the trauma of the First World War, in 1918, and of men like Hitler who not only believed in the *Protocols* but eventually had the means to act as if they were true. The anti-Masonic and anti-Jewish lodge founded by Jules Guérin in Paris during the 1890's was seen as ludicrous.[16] And the first international congress of the tiny rival anti-Semitic groups (mainly from Germany, Austria, and Hungary) meeting in Dresden in 1882 seemed scarcely more important, though it conceived itself as a rallying point against the Jewish world conspiracy. Its purpose was to consolidate the anti-Jewish struggle, but the congress could not overcome tensions between Christian anti-Semites like Adolf Stoecker and the racists, who were prone to violence and who denied that a baptized Jew differed from the rest of his race. The second meeting of this congress in 1883 bore the title "Alliance Antijuive Universelle" and clearly pointed to the Alliance Israélite as symbolic of the enemy.[17]

The legends about the Jews, as part of racial mysticism, penetrated beyond the relatively small groups who were obsessed with the Jewish conspiracy and had little time for other concerns. More important, however, such legends became a mechanism through which rightist movements sought to change society. The imaginary threat posed by the Jews could be used to rally people behind such interest groups as agriculture unions and conservative parties in their battle with liberals and Socialists. But Catholic and Protestant movements could also appeal to traditional legends about the Jews in order to fight atheism more effectively. Above all, those who wanted to reinvigorate the national mystique by emphasizing equality among the people used the Jews as a foil. Here, typically enough, an agitator like Wilhelm Marr, who was a democrat believing in universal suffrage and freedom of thought, accused the Jews of being liberals – a people without roots, who sought to substitute the slavery of finance capital for that of oppression by kings.[18] Such National Socialists, as they were called long before Adolf Hitler usurped the term, will occupy us later. Moreover, racism was firmly allied to nationalism through the mystery of race and even to science through Darwinism. Within these frameworks, the legends about the Jews which we have mentioned were kept alive, now as part of the race war that seemed imminent.

Even "The Universal Races Congress" of 1911, held in London and intended to reflect humanistic and Christian values, assumed that "pure" races could be said to exist, though such opponents of racism as John Dewey, Annie Besant, and the American black leader W. E. B. DuBois attended.[19] This Congress was one more sign of the abiding and deep interest in race.

Were the Jews themselves exempt from the influence of racial thought which seemed so widely spread throughout European society? Did the Jews themselves counter the myth of the Jew as an evil principle with a myth of the Jew as a pure and noble race? Many, indeed most Jews who were highly assimilated in central or western Europe regarded themselves as full members of the nations in which they lived – not as separate people but rather as one of the tribes, like the Saxons, Bavarians, or Alsatians, which made up the larger nation. The First World War enhanced such tendencies, and after 1918 Jewish veterans associated in many

European nations provided the principal support for such attempted national integration. However, those Jews who regarded themselves as a separate people must be our special concern. Did Jewish nationalism follow European nationalism in making an alliance with racism?

The racial ideas of Gobineau had been introduced to the readers of the Zionist *Die Welt* in 1902, not merely to sing the praises of racial purity, but mainly to counter the accusation that Jews were degenerate people. Gobineau had admired the Jews precisely because they had not given in to modern degeneracy, and now his theories could be used to best advantage in order to prove that "Jewry has maintained its . . . toughness, thanks to the purity of its blood." Miscegenation must be avoided at all costs. The Jewish and Aryan races could not interpenetrate, they could only live side by side in mutual understanding.[20] The influences of racism were clearly accepted here, even if the concept of the blood was not defined in terms of "blood and soil," but rather as the vehicle of the drives and peculiarities of the soul. Yet, this annexation of Gobineau (and of Houston Stewart Chamberlain, as we shall see later) proved the exception rather than the rule among Jews. If some Jews were attracted to racism, it was the science of race which seemed to have more appeal to them.

Jews, for example, contributed to the German *Journal for Racial and Social Biology*. But like most of the contributors to that journal, a belief in the reality of race did not mean that any one race was necessarily superior to another. For example, Elias Auerbach, one of the pioneers of Zionist settlement in Palestine, wrote in 1907 that while the Jewish race had been a mixture in the dim past, it was now pure because it had kept itself separate through centuries. He concluded his article with a quote from Gobineau to the effect that a Volk will never die while it can maintain its purity and uniqueness of composition.[21] Yet Auerbach advocated a binational Jewish–Arab Palestine, and opposed any domination of one people by another. It was possible to believe in pure races and still not be a racist; indeed, this was a trait shared by most Jews who believed in a Jewish race, and by many Gentiles as well.

Auerbach did not stand alone in his belief in race. The German writer J. M. Judt in *Jews as Race* (*Die Juden als Rasse*, 1903) was more specific, for he wrote that, as a race, Jews share common physical and physiognomic traits.[22] Even earlier, in 1881, Richard Andree, a German who was not a Jew but the founder of the discipline of ethnography and demography as applied to the Jews, had asserted that they represented a definite racial type kept intact through thousands of years. But for Andree, Jews and Aryans had a common root: both were Caucasians. Both were also the bearers of modern culture, in contrast to blacks who had remained in their primitive state.[23] Andree, like Judt, attempted to base his arguments on anthropology as well as physiognomy.

But it was the Austrian physician, anthropologist, and Zionist Ignaz Zollschan (1877–1948) who became the most famous theoretician of the Jews as a race. His major work, *The Racial Problem with Special Attention to the Theoretical Foundation of the Jewish Race* (*Das Rassenproblem unter Besonderer Berücksichtigung der Theoretischen Grundlagen der Jüdischen Rassenfrage*, 1910), held that race is transmitted by the human cell and thus not subject to outside influence. In this large work Zollschan praised Houston Stewart Chamberlain's racial ideals, such as the nobility that racial purity confers on a group and the necessity of developing the race to ever greater heights of heroism. Zollschan thought that Chamberlain was right about race, but wrong about the Jews. He felt that the evolution of culture could not be due to one race alone (such as the Aryans), but must be created by a series of pure races, including the Jews. The undesirable, materialistic aspect of the contemporary Jewish race would vanish when it found nationhood and escaped the ghetto.[24] Zollschan's ideal, as he restated it in 1914, was for a nation of pure blood, untainted by diseases of excess or immorality, with a highly developed sense of family, and deep-rooted, virtuous habits.[25] The linkage of racial mysticism and middle-class morality could hardly be demonstrated with greater clarity.

Zollschan broke with Zionism after the First World War, believing quite erroneously that the postwar world would see the decline of anti-Semitism and the end of ideas of national sovereignty.[26] At the same time, he also began to reject his earlier belief in races – a process which culminated in his *Racism Against Civilization* (published in London in 1942). By this time, the lengthening shadow of the Nazis in Europe made it difficult for any Jew to uphold ideas of race, even if he had done so earlier.

However, before the Nazis, and especially before the First World War, the debate among Jews as to whether or not Jews were a race had been a lively one, especially in the German *Journal of Jewish Demography and Statistics*. The guiding spirit behind this journal was the social Darwinist Arthur Ruppin. Ruppin was in charge of Jewish settlement in Palestine from 1908 until his death in 1942. Like Auerbach he believed, however ambivalently, in the existence of races. Yet during his many decades in Palestine he was a committed binationalist. At first Ruppin thought race to be an instinct which could not be changed, though typically enough his *Darwinism and Social Science* (*Darwinismus und Sozialwissenschaft*, 1903) advocated eugenics, and not a doctrine of racial superiority. Beauty and strength depended on factors of inheritance, not on environment, and in this connection Ruppin did talk about racial types. When he contemplated *The Jewish Fate and Future* (*Jüdisches Schicksal und die Zukunft*) in 1940, however, he condemned the confusion of "people" with "race," and referred to Virchow's findings among the German schoolchildren which denied the existence of pure races.

Jewish acceptance of the notion of race was ambivalent at best; being the foil of racism did not necessarily mean imitating the enemy. What about those orthodox religious Jews who believed in the reality of the concept of the chosen people? For the majority of such Jews, chosenness meant giving a living example of how life should be lived, and did not entail any claims to domination. Moreover, all peoples could be considered righteous, even Gentiles, provided they observed the seven Noahic laws instead of the 613 commandments binding on pious Jews. Thus belief in monotheism, and obedience to commandments against stealing, murder, false judgment, and adultery, as well as abstinence from eating live limbs of animals, would qualify anyone as chosen. No racism was inherent in this orthodoxy.

To be sure, the Hasidic rabbinical dynasties believed that qualities of leadership were at times transmitted by the blood; but this was not held to consistently, and in any case was no more racist than traditional notions of royal descent. But for all the denial of racism in theory, the borderline to racism was at times as furtively crossed by such orthodox Jews as by believing Christians, who were also supposed to reject it. The true believer in the nineteenth and twentieth centuries always retained some secular elements of superiority and domination within his belief.[27]

Again, Zionism was not in fact racist in its orientation, in spite of the occasional ideas of Zollschan or even Auerbach, both of whom were not really important in the movement. Yet, Theodor Herzl himself once wrote that whether Jews remained in their host nations or emigrated, the race must first be improved wherever it was found. It was necessary to make it work-loving, warrior-like, and virtuous.[28] Herzl often reflected his Viennese environment, whether in his vague and general use of the word "race" or in his condemnation of "kikes" who refused to follow his lead. Nevertheless, he stated that "No nation has uniformity of race."[29]

Much more typical were those influential young Zionists who at the beginning of this century believed in a national mystique without at the same time believing in race. Whenever the Zionist movement attempted to be scientific, they proclaimed in 1913, it got mired in skull measurement and all sorts of "racial nonsense."[30] Judaism, instead, was an inner cultural unity, the revelation of belief in the substance of Jewish nationality. World history, as the young Zionist Robert Weltsch put it in 1913, is not made by zoologists but by ideas. He compared Jewish nationality to Bergson's *élan vital*. The mystery of the Volk was accepted, but the racism which was often part of these mysteries in Gentile society was rejected.[31]

Even during the 1930's, when Max Brod asserted that race was basic to Jewish separateness, he meant this as an exhortation to eugenics; but for Brod, as for Martin Buber, the Jewish Volk became only a stepping stone to human unity and equality reflecting the oneness of God. Jewish nationalism did not embrace racism at a time when other nationalisms in Europe were becoming ever more racist themselves.

Those who did not believe in the existence of any Jewish race – and they were the overwhelming majority among the Jews – referred to the Jewish physician Maurice Fishberg's influential *Racial Characteristics of Jews* (*Die Rassenmerkmale der Juden*, 1913). Fishberg, a famed doctor and anthropologist living in New York, held that Jews have no such characteristics, and attacked Elias Auerbach for believing in a Jewish race. As proof for his contention, Fishberg cited the existence of those blond Jews who could be found all over Europe, tall Jews with long heads, Greek noses, and blue eyes. This "Aryan type among Jews," as he called it, must be the result of miscegenation with the Nordic and the Slavic races.[32] But another, even more influential and non-Jewish voice was raised to contend that Jews were no race or even a separate people. Felix von Luschan, an Austrian professor at the University of Berlin, had already replied to Auerbach that there was no Jewish race, but only a Jewish religious community, and that Zionism seemed opposed to all culture by forcing Jews back into the Orient where barbarism ruled. This highly respected Gentile anthropologist asserted that Jews, like everyone else, were a racial mixture. Indeed, for von Luschan there was only one race, *Homo sapiens*. No inferior races existed, only people with different cultures from our own; and the characteristics which divided men had their origin in climatic, social, and other environmental factors. Men like Chamberlain, he wrote, were not scientists but poets.[33]

Many Zionists who used words like "blood" or "race" actually agreed with von Luschan. Despite the scientific predilections of the nineteenth century, the use of terms like "blood," "race," "people," and "nation" was often imprecise and inter-changeable. Blood and race were sometimes shorthand for the transmission of spiritual factors and had nothing to do with appearance or racial purity. The "new man" of whom both racists and Zionists dreamed was opposed to rationalism, but for the Zionists he represented a "humanitarian nationalism" that was both volun-taristic and pluralistic.[34]

Ideas about the mystery of race remained strongest in central Europe, though the legends about Jews found a home in France as well as in the more primitive Balkan regions. Rootless and conspiratorial, the Jew became a myth. As revealed by Ahasverus or by the *Protocols of the Elders of Zion*, he was the adversary, all the more effective in that medieval myths were applied to modern times. The fears and superstitions of a bygone age had sunk deeply into the European conscious-ness, and could be used to mobilize people against the frustrations of the present. Still, European civilization was, after all, a Christian civilization, in spite of the increasing inroads of secularism. If racism had presented itself as a science and as a national belief, what was to be the attitude of the Christian churches toward race?

Notes and references

1   *The Jews of Czechoslovakia*, The Society for the History of Czechoslovak Jews (Philadelphia – New York, 1968), 152.

2   See, for example, Jeannine Verdes-Leroux, *Scandale Financier et Antisémitique: Le Krach de l'Union Générale* (Paris, 1969), 223.

3   George K. Anderson, *The Legend of the Wandering Jew* (Providence, 1965), 21, 22.

4   *Raemaeker's Cartoons* (n.d., n.p.), Part 3, p. 69.

5   Josef Müller, *Die Entwicklung des Rassenantisemitismus in den Letzten Jahrzehnten des 19. Jahrhunderts* (Berlin, 1940), 25, 67; Müller analyzes the *Antisemitische Correspondenz* from, roughly, 1887 until 1892.

6   Quoted in Herman Bernstein, *The History of a Lie* (New York, 1921), 23.

7   *Ibid.*, 32.

8   *Ibid.*

9   *Ibid.*, 33.

10   Norman Cohn, *Warrant for Genocide* (New York, 1966), 43. I have followed this classic work in my discussion of the *Protocols*.

11   *Protocols of the Learned Elders of Zion* (Union, N.J., n.d.), 25. This is a modern version of the English edition of 1922.

12   *Ibid.*, 33; *Arbeiterzeitung* (Vienna), December 3, 1933 (Wiener Library Clipping Collection, Tel Aviv).

13   H. Lutostanski, *The Talmud and the Jew* (n.p., 1876), *passim*.

14   *Actes du Premier Congrès Antimaçonnique Internationale*, September 24 to 30, 1894, at Trente (Fournay, 1897), 119, 124.

15   Paul W. Massing, *Rehearsal for Destruction* (New York, 1967), 94.

16   The Paris police called it "anti-Jewish confetti," Archives de la Préfecture de Police, Paris, B. a/1341.

17 *Schmeitzner's Internationale Monatsschrift*, II (January 1883), *passim*; *ibid*., II (May 1883), *passim*. Schmeitzner was the secretary of the congress.

18 Mosche Zimmermann, "Gabriel Riesser und Wilhelm Marr im Meinungsstreit," *Zeitschrift des Vereins für Hamburgische Geschichte*, vol. 61 (1975), 59–84.

19 Michael D. Biddiss, "The Universal Races Congress of 1911," *Race*, XIII (July 1971), 43.

20 Max Jungmann, "Ist das Jüdische Volk degeneriert?", *Die Welt*, 6. Jahrg., Nr. 24 (June 13, 1902).

21 Elias Auerbach, "Die Jüdische Rassenfrage," *Archiv für Rassenund Gesellschafts Biologie*, IV (1907), 333.

22 J. M. Judt, *Die Juden als Rasse: Eine Analyse aus dem Gebiet der Anthropologie* (Berlin, 1903), 213. This was published by the Jewish publishing house, Jüdischer Verlag.

23 Richard Andree, *Zur Volkskunde der Juden* (Bielefeld and Leipzig, 1881), 3, 10, 25.

24 Ignaz Zollschan, *Das Rassenproblem unter Besonderer Berücksichtigung der Theoretischen Grundlagen der Jüdischen Rassenfrage* (Vienna and Leipzig, 1910), 8, 235, 260ff., 427.

25 Ignaz Zollschan, *The Jewish Question* (New York, 1914), 14.

26 Adolf Böhm, *Die Zionistische Bewegung*, II (Tel Aviv, 1937), 84.

27 No study of this problem exists. I am grateful to Miss Deborah Herschmann and Mr. Warren Green for the information upon which this discussion of orthodox Jewry is based. See also the reliance on Noahic law as a code of morals for non-Jews in Germany in Sidney M. Bolkosky, *The Distorted Image: German Jewish Perceptions of Germans and Germany, 1918–1935* (New York, 1975), 80.

28 Theodor Herzl quoted in *Die Welt*, XVIII (July 3, 1914).

29 Amos Elon, *Herzl* (New York, 1975), 171, 251.

30 Moses Calvary in *Die Welt*, XVII (November 7, 1913), 540.

31 Robert Weltsch in *Die Welt*, XVII (March 21, 1913), 366.

32 Maurice Fishberg, *Die Rassenmerkmale der Juden* (Munich, 1913), 49, 51; see also Maurice Fishberg, "Zur Frage der Herkunft des blonden Elementes in Judentum," *Zeitschrift für Demographie und Statistik der Juden* (1907).

33 Felix von Luschan, *Völker, Rassen, Sprachen* (Berlin, 1922), 25, 169.

34 Gustav Krojanker, *Zum Problem des Neuen Deutschen Nationalismus* (Berlin, 1932), 17, 19.

Chapter 15

Theodor W. Adorno and Max Horkheimer

ELEMENTS OF ANTI-SEMITISM
The limits of Enlightenment

[. . .]

FOR SOME PEOPLE TODAY anti-Semitism involves the destiny of mankind; for others it is a mere pretext. The Fascists do not view the Jews as a minority but as an opposing race, the embodiment of the negative principle. They must be exterminated to secure happiness for the world. At the other extreme we have the theory that the Jews have no national or racial characteristics and simply form a group through their religious opinions and tradition. It is claimed that only the Jews of Eastern Europe have Jewish characteristics, and then only if they have not been fully assimilated. Neither doctrine is wholly true or wholly false.

The first is true to the extent that Fascism has made it true. The Jews today are the group which calls down upon itself, both in theory and in practice, the will to destroy born of a false social order. They are branded as absolute evil by those who are absolutely evil, and are now in fact the chosen race. Whereas there is no longer any need for economic domination, the Jews are marked out as the absolute object of domination pure and simple. No one tells the workers, who are the ultimate target, straight to their face – for very good reasons; and the Negroes are to be kept where they belong: but the Jews must be wiped from the face of the earth, and the call to destroy them like vermin finds an echo in the heart of every budding fascist throughout the world. The portrait of the Jews that the nationalists offer to the world is in fact their own self-portrait. They long for total possession and unlimited power, at any price. They transfer their guilt for this to the Jews, whom as masters they despise and crucify, repeating *ad infinitum* a sacrifice which they cannot believe to be effective.

The other, liberal, theory is true as an idea. It contains the image of a society in which irrational anger no longer exists and seeks for outlets. But since the liberal theory assumes that unity among men is already in principle established, it serves as an apologia for existing circumstances. The attempt to avert the extreme threat by a minorities policy and a democratic strategy is ambiguous, like the defensive stance of the last liberal citizens. Their impotence attracts the enemy of impotence. The existence and way of life of the Jews throw into question the generality with which they do not conform. The inflexible adherence to their own order of life has brought the Jews into an uncertain relationship with the dominant order. They expected to be protected without themselves being in command. Their relationship with the ruling nations was one of greed and fear. But the arrivistes who crossed the gulf separating them from the dominant mode of life lost that cold, stoic character which society still makes a necessity. The dialectical link between enlightenment and domination, and the dual relationship of progress to cruelty and liberation which the Jews sensed in the great philosophers of the Enlightenment and the democratic, national movements are reflected in the very essence of those assimilated. The enlightened self-control with which the assimilated Jews managed to forget the painful memories of domination by others (a second circumcision, so to speak) led them straight from their own, long-suffering community into the modern bourgeoisie, which was moving inexorably toward reversion to cold repression and reorganization as a pure "race." But race is not a naturally special characteristic, as the folk mystics would have it. It is a reduction to the natural, to sheer force, to that stubborn particularity which in the status quo constitutes the generality. Today race has become the self-assertion of the bourgeois individual integrated within a barbaric collective. The harmony of society which the liberal Jews believed in turned against them in the form of the harmony of a national community. They thought that anti-Semitism would distort that order which in reality cannot exist without distorting men. The persecution of the Jews, like any other form of persecution, is inseparable from that system of order. However successfully it may at times be concealed, force is the essential nature of this order – and we are witnessing its naked truth today.

[. . .] Modern society, in which primitive religious feelings and new forms of religion as well as the heritage of revolution are sold on the open market, in which the Fascist leaders bargain over the land and life of nations behind locked doors while the habituated public sit by their radio sets and work out the cost; a society in which the word which it unmasks is thereby legitimized as a component part of a political racket: this society, in which politics is not only a business but business the whole of politics, is gripped by a holy anger over the retarded commercial attitudes of the Jews and classifies them as materialists, and hucksters who must give way to the new race of men who have elevated business into an absolute.

Bourgeois anti-Semitism has a specific economic reason: the concealment of domination in production. In earlier ages the rulers were directly repressive and not only left all the work to the lower classes but declared work to be a disgrace, as it always was under domination; and in a mercantile age, the industrial boss is an absolute monarch. Production attracts its own courtiers. The new rulers simply took off the bright garb of the nobility and donned civilian clothing. They declared that work was not degrading, so as to control the others more rationally. They claimed to be creative workers, but in reality they were still the grasping overlords of former times. The manufacturer took risks and acted like a banker or commercial wizard. He calculated, arranged, bought and sold. On the market he competed for the profit corresponding to his own capital. He seized all he could, not only on the market but at the very source: as a representative of his class he made sure that his workers did not sell him short with their labor. The workers had to supply the maximum amount of goods. Like Shylock, the bosses demand their pound of flesh. They owned the machines and materials, and therefore compelled others to produce for them. They called themselves producers, but secretly everyone knew the truth. The productive work of the capitalist, whether he justifies his profit by means of gross returns as under liberalism, or by his director's salary as today, is an ideology cloaking the real nature of the labor contract and the grasping character of the economic system.

And so people shout: Stop thief! – but point at the Jews. They are the scapegoats not only for individual maneuvers and machinations but in a broader sense, inasmuch as the economic injustice of the whole class is attributed to them. The manufacturer keeps an eye on his debtors, the workers, in the factory and makes sure that they have performed well before he pays them their money. They realize the true position when they stop to think what they can buy with this money. The smallest magnate can dispose of a quantity of services and goods which were available to no ruler in the past; but the workers receive a bare minimum. It is not enough actually to experience how few goods they can buy on the market; the salesmen continue to advertise the merits of things which they cannot afford. The relationship between wage and prices shows what is kept from the workers. With their wages they accept the principle of settlement of all their demands. The merchant presents them with the bill which they have signed away to the manufacturer. The merchant is the bailiff of the whole system and takes the hatred of others upon himself. The responsibility of the circulation sector for exploitation is a socially necessary pretence.

The Jews were not the sole owners of the circulation sector. But they had been active in it for so long that they mirrored in their own ways the hatred they had always borne. Unlike their Aryan colleagues, they were still largely denied access to the origins of surplus value. It was a long time before, with difficulty, they were allowed to own the means of production. Admittedly, in the history of Europe and even under the German emperors, baptized Jews were allowed high positions in industry and in the administration. But they had to justify themselves with twice the usual devotion, diligence, and stubborn self-denial. They were only allowed to retain their positions if by their behavior they tacitly accepted or confirmed the verdict pronounced on other Jews: that was the purpose of baptism. No matter how many great achievements the Jews were responsible for, they could not be absorbed into the European nations; they were not allowed to put down roots and so they were dismissed as rootless. At best the Jews were protected and dependent on emperors, princes or the absolute state. But the rulers themselves all had an economic advantage over the remainder of the population. To the extent that they could use the Jews as intermediaries, they protected them against the masses who had to pay the price of progress. The Jews were the colonizers for progress. From the time when, in their capacity as merchants, they helped to spread Roman civilization throughout Gentile Europe, they were the representatives – in harmony with their patriarchal religion – of municipal, bourgeois and, finally, industrial conditions. They carried capitalist ways of life to various countries and drew upon themselves the hatred of all who had to suffer under capitalism. For the sake of the economic progress which is now proving their downfall, the Jews were always a thorn in the side of the craftsmen and peasants who were declassed by capitalism. They are now experiencing to their own cost the exclusive, particularist character of capitalism. Those who always wanted to be first have been left far behind. Even the Jewish president of an American entertainment trust lives hopelessly on the defensive in his cocoon of cash. The kaftan was a relic of ancient middle-class costume. Today it indicates that its wearer has been cast onto the periphery of a society which, though completely enlightened, still wishes to lay the ghosts of its distant past. Those who proclaimed individualism, abstract justice, and the notion of the person are now degraded to the condition of a species. Those who are never allowed to enjoy freely the civil rights which should allow them human dignity are referred to, without distinction, as "the Jew." Even in the nineteenth century the Jews remained dependent on an alliance with the central power. General justice protected by the state was the pledge of their security, and the law of exception a specter held out before them. The Jews remained objects, at the mercy of others, even when they insisted on their rights. Commerce was not their vocation but their fate. The Jews constituted the trauma of the knights of industry who had to pretend to be creative, while the claptrap of anti-Semitism announced a fact for which they secretly despised themselves; their anti-Semitism is self-hatred, the bad conscience of the parasite.

[. . .] The howling voice of Fascist orators and camp commandants shows the other side of the same social condition. The yell is as cold as business. They both expropriate the sounds of natural complaint and make them elements of their technique. Their bellow has the same significance for the pogrom as the noise generator in the German flying bomb: the terrible cry which announces terror is simply turned on. The cry of pain of the victim who first called violence by its name, the mere word to designate the victim (Frenchman, Negro, or Jew), generates despair in the persecuted who must react violently. The victims are the false counterparts of the dread mimesis. They reproduce the insatiability of the power which they fear. Everything must be used and all must obey. The mere existence of the other is a provocation. Every "other" person who "doesn't know his place" must be forced back within his proper confines – those of unrestricted terror. Anyone who seeks refuge must be prevented from finding it; those who express ideas which all long for, peace, a home, freedom – the nomads and players – have always been refused a homeland. Whatever a man fears, that he suffers. Even the last resting place is emptied of peace. The destruction of cemeteries is not a mere excess of anti-Semitism – it is anti-Semitism in its essence. The outlawed naturally arouse the desire to outlaw others. Violence is even inflamed by the marks which violence has left on them. Anything which just wants to vegetate must be rooted out. In the chaotic net regulated escape reactions of the lower animals, in the convolutions of the sudden swarm, and the convulsive gestures of the martyred, we see the mimetic impulse which can never be completely destroyed. In the death struggle of the creature, at the opposite pole from freedom, freedom still shines out irresistibly as the thwarted destiny of matter. It is opposed by the idiosyncracy which claims anti-Semitism as its motive.

The mental energy harnessed by political anti-Semitism is this rationalized idosyncracy. All the pretexts over which the Führer and his followers reach agreement, imply surrender to the mimetic attraction without any open infringement of the reality principle – honorably, so to speak. They cannot stand the Jews, yet imitate them.

There is no anti-Semite who does not basically want to imitate his mental image of a Jew, which is composed of mimetic cyphers: the argumentative movement of a hand, the musical voice painting a vivid picture of things and feelings irrespective of the real content of what is said, and the nose – the physiognomic *principium individuationis*, symbol of the specific character of an individual, described between the lines of his countenance. The multifarious nuances of the sense of smell embody the archetypal longing for the lower forms of existence, for direct unification with circumambient nature, with the earth and mud. Of all the senses, that of smell – which is attracted without objectifying – bears clearest witness to the urge to lose oneself in and become the "other." As perception and the perceived – both are united – smell is more expressive than the other senses. When we see we remain what we are; but when we smell we are taken over by otherness. Hence the sense of smell is considered a disgrace in civilization, the sign of lower social strata, lesser races and base animals. The civilized individual may only indulge in such pleasure if the prohibition is suspended by rationalization in the service of real or apparent practical ends. The prohibited impulse may be tolerated if there is no doubt that the final aim is its elimination – this is the case with jokes or fun, the miserable parody of fulfillment. As a despised and despising characteristic, the mimetic function is enjoyed craftily. Anyone who seeks out "bad" smells, in order to destroy them, may imitate sniffing to his heart's content, taking unrationalized pleasure in the experience. The civilized man "disinfects" the forbidden impulse by his unconditional identification with the authority which has prohibited it; in this way the action is made acceptable. If he goes beyond the permitted bounds, laughter ensues. This is the schema of the anti-Semitic reaction. Anti-Semites gather together to celebrate the moment when authority permits what is usually forbidden, and become a collective only in that common purpose. There rantings are organized laughter. The more terrible their accusations and threats and the greater their anger, the more compelling their scorn. Anger, scorn, and embittered imitation are actually the same thing. The purpose of the Fascist formula, the ritual discipline, the uniforms, and the whole apparatus, which is at first sight irrational, is to allow mimetic behavior. The carefully thought out symbols (which are proper to every counterrevolutionary movement), the skulls and disguises, the barbaric drum beats, the monotonous repetition of words and gestures, are simply the organized imitation of magic practices, the mimesis of mimesis. The leader with his contorted face and the charisma of approaching hysteria take command. The leader acts as a representative; he portrays what is forbidden to everyone else in actual life. Hitler can gesticulate like a clown, Mussolini strike false notes like a provincial tenor, Goebbels talk endlessly like a Jewish agent whom he wants murdered, and Coughlin preach love like the savior whose crucifixion he portrays – all for the sake of still more bloodshed. Fascism is also totalitarian in that it seeks to make the rebellion of suppressed nature against domination directly useful to domination.

This machinery needs the Jews. Their artificially heightened prominence acts on the legitimate son of the gentile civilization like a magnetic field. The gentile sees equality, humanity, in his difference from the Jew, but this induces a feeling of antagonism and alien being. And so impulses which are normally taboo and conflict with the requirements of the prevailing form of labor are transformed into conforming idiosyncrasies. The economic position of the Jews, the last defrauded frauds of liberalistic ideology, affords them no secure protection. Since they are so eminently fitted to generate these mental induction currents, they serve such functions involuntarily. They share the fate of the rebellious nature as which Fascism uses them: they are employed blindly yet perspicaciously. It matters little whether the Jews as individuals really do still have those mimetic features which awaken the dread malady, or whether such features are suppressed. Once the wielders of economic power have overcome their fear of the Fascist administrators, the Jews automatically stand out as the disturbing factor in the harmony of the national society. They are abandoned by domination when its progressive alienation from nature makes it revert to mere nature. The Jews as a whole are accused of partic-ipating in forbidden magic and bloody ritual. Disguised as accusation, the subconscious desire of the aboriginal inhabitants to return to the mimetic practice of sacrifice finds conscious fulfillment. When all the horror of prehistory which has been overlaid with civilization is rehabilitated as rational interest by projection onto the Jews, there is no restriction. The horror can be carried out in practice, and its practical implementation goes beyond the evil content of the projection. The fantasies of Jewish crimes, infanticide and sadistic excess, poisoning of the nation, and international conspiracy, accurately define the anti-Semitic dream, but remain far behind its actualization. Once things have reached this stage, the mere word "Jew" appears as the bloody grimace reflected in the swastika flag with its combination of death's head and shattered cross. The mere fact that a person is called a Jew is an invitation forcibly to make him over into a physical semblance of that image of death and distortion. [. . .]

Chapter 16

Zygmunt Bauman

MODERNITY, RACISM, EXTERMINATION

[. . .]

THERE IS AN APPARENT PARADOX in the history of racism, and Nazi racism in particular.

In the by far most spectacular and the best known case in this history, racism was instrumental in the mobilization of anti-modernist sentiments and anxieties, and was apparently effective primarily because of this connection. Adolf Stöcker, Dietrich Eckart, Alfred Rosenberg, Gregor Strasser, Joseph Goebbels, and virtually any other prophet, theorist and ideologue of National Socialism used the phantom of the Jewish race as a lynch-pin binding the fears of the past and prospective victims of modernization, which they articulated, and the ideal *volkisch* society of the future which they proposed to create in order to forestall further advances of modernity. In their appeals to the deep-seated horror of the social upheaval that modernity augured, they identified modernity as the rule of economic and monetary values, and charged Jewish racial characteristics with responsibility for such a relentless assault on the *volkisch* mode of life and standards of human worth. Elimination of the Jews was hence presented as a synonym of the rejection of modern order. This fact suggests an essentially pre-modern character of racism; its natural affinity, so to speak, with anti-modern emotions and its selective fitness as a vehicle for such emotions.

On the other hand, however, as a conception of the world, and even more importantly as an effective instrument of political practice, racism is unthinkable without the advancement of modern science, modern technology and modern forms of state power. As such, racism is strictly a modern product. Modernity made racism possible. It also created a demand for racism; an era that declared achievement to be the only measure of human worth needed a theory of ascription to redeem boundary-drawing and boundary-guarding concerns under new conditions which made boundary-crossing easier than ever before. Racism, in short, is a thoroughly modern weapon used in the conduct of pre-modern, or at least not exclusively modern, struggles.

From heterophobia to racism

Most commonly (though wrongly), racism is understood as a variety of inter-group resentment or prejudice. Sometimes racism is set apart from other sentiments or beliefs of the wider class by its emotional intensity; at other times, it is set apart by reference to hereditary, biological and extra-cultural attributes which, unlike the non-racist variants of group animosity, it normally contains. In some cases writers about racism point out the scientific pretensions that other, non-racist yet similarly negative stereotypes of foreign groups, do not usually possess. Whatever the feature chosen, however, the habit of analysing and interpreting racism in the framework of a larger category of prejudice is seldom breached.

As racism gains in saliency among contemporary forms of intergroup resentment, and alone among them manifests a pronounced affinity with the scientific spirit of the age, a reverse interpretive tendency becomes ever more prominent; a tendency to extend the notion of racism so as to embrace all varieties of resentment. All kinds of group prejudice are then interpreted as so many expressions of innate, natural racist predispositions. One can probably afford not to be too excited by such an exchange of places and view it, philosophically, as just a question of the definitions, which can, after all, be chosen or rejected at will. On a closer scrutiny, however, complacency appears ill-advised. Indeed, if all intergroup dislike and animosity are forms of racism, and if the tendency to keep strangers at a distance and resent their proximity has been amply documented by historical and ethnological research as a well-nigh universal and perpetual attribute of human groupings, then there is nothing essentially and radically novel about the racism that has acquired such a prominence in our time; just a rehearsal of the old scenario, though admittedly staged with somewhat updated dialogues. In particular, the intimate link of racism with other aspects of modern life is either denied outright or left out of focus.

In his recent impressively erudite study of prejudice,[1] Pierre-André Taguieff writes synonimically of racism and heterophobia (resentment of the different). Both appear, he avers, 'on three levels', or in three forms distinguished by the rising level of sophistication. The 'primary racism' is in his view universal. It is a natural reaction to the presence of an unknown stranger, to any form of human life that is foreign and puzzling. Invariably, the first response to strangeness is antipathy, which more often than not leads to aggressiveness. Universality goes hand-in-hand with spontaneity. The primary racism needs no inspiring or fomenting; nor does it need a theory to legitimize the elemental hatred – though it can be, on occasion, deliberately beefed up and deployed as an instrument of political mobilization.[2] At such a time it can be lifted to another level of complexity and turn into a 'secondary' or (rationalized) racism. This transformation happens when a theory is supplied (and internalized) that provides logical foundations for resentment. The repelling Other is represented as ill-willed or 'objectively' harmful –

in either case threatening to the well-being of the resenting group. For instance, the resented category can be depicted as conspiring with the forces of evil in the form construed by the resenting group's religion, or it can be portrayed as an unscrupulous economic rival; the choice of the semantic field in which 'harmfulness' of the resented Other is theorized is presumably dictated by the current focus of social relevance, conflicts and divisions. Xenophobia, or more particularly ethnocentrism (both coming into their own in the age of rampant nationalism, when one of the most closely defended lines of division is argued in terms of shared history, tradition and culture), is a most common contemporary case of 'secondary racism'. Finally, the 'tertiary', or mystifactory, racism, which presupposes the two 'lower' levels, is distinguished by the deployment of a quasi-biological argument.

In the form in which it has been constructed and interpreted by Taguieff, the tri-partite classification seems logically flawed; if the secondary racism is already characterized by the theorizing of primary resentment, there seems to be no good reason for setting aside just one of the many possible ideologies that can (and are) used for this purpose as a distinctive feature of a 'higher-level' racism. The third-level racism looks much like a unit in the second-level set. Perhaps Taguieff could defend his classification against this charge were he, instead of separating biological theories because of the supposedly 'mystifactory' nature (one can argue without end about the degree of mystification in all the rest of the second-level racist theories), pointing to the tendency of biological argument to emphasize the irreversibility and incurability of the damaging 'otherness' of the Other. One could indeed point out that – in our age of artificiality of the social order, of the putative omnipotence of education and, more generally, of social engineering – biology in general, and heredity in particular, stand in public consciousness for the area still off-limits for cultural manipulation; something we do not know yet how to tinker with and to mould and reshape according to our will. Taguieff, however, insists that the modern biological–scientific form of racism does not appear 'different in nature, operation and function, from traditional discourses of disqualifying exclusion',[3] and focuses instead on the degree of 'deliric paranoia' or extreme 'speculativess' as on distinctive features of the 'tertiary racism'.

I suggest, on the contrary, that *it is precisely the nature, function and the mode of operation of racism that sharply differ from heterophobia* – that diffuse (and sentimental rather than practical) unease, discomfort, or anxiety that people normally experience whenever they are confronted with such 'human ingredients' of their situation as they do not fully understand, cannot communicate with easily and cannot expect to behave in a routine, familiar way. Heterophobia seems to be a focused manifestation of a still wider phenomenon of anxiety aroused by the feeling that one has no control over the situation, and that thus one can neither influence its development, nor foresee the consequences of one's action. Heterophobia may appear as either a realistic or an irrealistic objectification of such anxiety – but it is likely that the anxiety in question always seeks an object on which to anchor, and that consequently heterophobia is a fairly common phenomenon at all times and more common still in an age of modernity, when occasions for the 'no control' experience become more frequent, and their interpretation in terms of the obtrusive interference by an alien human group becomes more plausible.

I suggest as well that, so described, *heterophobia ought to be analytically distin-guished from contestant enmity*, a more specific antagonism generated by the human practices of identity-seeking and boundary-drawing. In the latter case, sentiments of antipathy and resentment seem more like emotional appendages to the activity of separation; separation itself demands an activity, an effort, a sustained action. The alien of the first case, however, is not merely a too-close-for-comfort, yet clearly separate category of people easy to spot and keep at a required distance, but a collection of people whose 'collectiveness' is not obvious or generally recog-nized; its collectiveness may be even contested and is often concealed or denied by the members of the alien category. The alien in this case threatens to pene-trate the native group and fuse with it – if preventive measures are not set out and vigilantly observed. The alien, therefore, threatens the unity and the identity of the alien group, not so much by confounding its control over a territory or its freedom to act in the familiar way, but by blurring the boundary of the territory itself and effacing the difference between the familiar (right) and the alien (wrong) way of life. This is the 'enemy in our midst' case – one that triggers a vehement boundary-drawing bustle, which in its turn generates a thick fall-out of antagon-ism and hatred to those found or suspected guilty of double loyalty and sitting astride the barricade.

Racism differs from both heterophobia and contestant enmity. The difference lies neither in the intensity of sentiments nor in the type of argument used to rationalize it. *Racism stands apart by a practice of which it is a part and which it rational-izes: a practice that combines strategies of architecture and gardening with that of medicine – in the service of the construction of an artificial social order, through cutting out the elements of the present reality that neither fit the visualized perfect reality, nor can be changed so that they do.* In a world that boasts the unprecedented ability to improve human conditions by reorganizing human affairs on a rational basis, racism mani-fests the conviction that a certain category of human beings cannot be incorporated into the rational order, whatever the effort. In a world notable for the continuous rolling back of the limits to scientific, technological and cultural manipulation, racism proclaims that certain blemishes of a certain category of people cannot be removed or rectified – that they remain beyond the boundaries of reforming practices, and will do so for ever. In a world proclaiming the formidable capacity of training and cultural conversion, racism sets apart a certain category of people that cannot be reached (and thus cannot be effectively cultivated) by argument or any other training tools, and hence must remain perpetually alien. To summa-rize: in the modern world distinguished by its ambition to self-control and self-administration racism declares a certain category of people endemically and hopelessly resistant to control and immune to all efforts at amelioration. To use the medical metaphor; one can train and shape 'healthy' parts of the body, but not cancerous growth. The latter can be 'improved' only by being destroyed.

The consequence is that *racism is inevitably associated with the strategy of estrange-ment*. If conditions allow, racism demands that the offending category ought to be removed beyond the territory occupied by the group it offends. If such condi-tions are absent, racism requires that the offending category is physically exterminated. Expulsion and destruction are two mutually exchangeable methods of estrangement.

Of the Jews, Alfred Rosenberg wrote: 'Zunz calls Judaism the whim of [the Jewish] soul. Now the Jew cannot break loose from this "whim" even if he is baptized ten times over, and the necessary result of this influence will always be the same: lifelessness, anti-Christianity and materialism.'[4] What is true about religious influence applies to all the other cultural interventions. Jews are beyond repair. Only a physical distance, or a break of communication, or fencing them off, or annihilation, may render them harmless.

Racism as a form of social engineering

Racism comes into its own only in the context of a design of the perfect society and intention to implement the design through planned and consistent effort. In the case of the Holocaust, the design was the thousand-year *Reich* – the kingdom of the liberated German Spirit. It was that kingdom which had no room for anything but the German Spirit. It had no room for the Jews, as the Jews could not be spiritually converted and embrace the *Geist* of the German *Volk*. This spiritual inability was articulated as the attribute of heredity or blood – substances which at that time at least embodied the other side of culture, the territory that culture could not dream of cultivating, a wilderness that would be never turned into the object of gardening. (The prospects of genetic engineering were not as yet seriously entertained.)

The Nazi revolution was an exercise in social engineering on a grandiose scale. 'Racial stock' was the key link in the chain of engineering measures. In the collection of official plaidoyers of Nazi policy, published in English on Ribbentrop's initiative for the purposes of international propaganda and for this reason expressed in a carefully tempered and cautious language, Dr Arthur Gütt, the Head of the National Hygiene Department in the Ministry of Interior, described as the major task of the Nazi rule 'an active policy consistently aiming at the preservation of racial health', and explained the strategy such policy had necessarily to involve: 'If we facilitate the propagation of healthy stock by systematic selection and by elimination of the unhealthy elements, we shall be able to improve the physical standards not, perhaps, of the present generation, but of those who will succeed us.' Gütt had no doubt that the selection-cum-elimination such a policy envisaged 'go along the lines universally adopted in conformity with the researches of Koch, Lister, Pasteur, and other celebrated scientists'[5] and thus constituted a logical extension – indeed, a culmination – of the advancement of modern science.

Dr Walter Gross, the Head of the Bureau for Enlightenment on Population Policy and Racial Welfare, spelled out the practicalities of the racial policy: reversing the current trend of 'declining birth-rate among the fitter inhabitants and unrestrained propagation among the hereditary unfit, the mentally deficient, imbeciles and hereditary criminals, etc.'[6] As he writes for an international audience unlikely to applaud the determination of the Nazis, unencumbered as they were by things so irrational as public opinion or political pluralism, to see the accomplishment of modern science and technology to their logical end, Gross does not venture beyond the necessity to sterilize the hereditary unfit.

The reality of racial policy was, however, much more gruesome. Contrary to Gütt's suggestion, the Nazi leaders saw no reason to restrict their concerns to 'those who will succeed us'. As the resources allowed, they set about to improve the *present* generation. The royal road to this goal led through the forceful removal of *unwertes Leben*. Every vehicle would do to secure progress along this road. Depending on circumstances, references were made to 'elimination', 'ridding', 'evacuation', or 'reduction' (read 'extermination'). Following Hitler's command of 1 September 1939, centres had been created in Brandenburg, Hadamar, Sonnenstein and Eichberg, which hid under a double lie: they called themselves, in hushed conversations between the initiated, 'euthanasia institutes', while for the wider consumption they used still more deceitful and misleading names of a Charitable Foundation for 'Institutional Care' or the 'the Transport of the Sick' – or even the bland 'T4' code (from 4 Tiergartenstrasse, Berlin, where the co-ordinating office of the whole killing operation was located).[7] When the command had to be rescinded on 28 August 1941 as the result of an outcry raised by a number of prominent luminaries of the Church, the principle of 'actively managing the population trends' was in no way abandoned. Its focus, together with the gassing technologies that the euthanasia campaign had helped to develop, was merely shifted to a different target: the Jews. And to different places, like Sobibór or Chelmno.

Unwertes Leben remained the target all along. For the Nazi designers of the perfect society, the project they pursued and were determined to implement through social engineering split human life into worthy and unworthy; the first to be lovingly cultivated and given *Lebensraum*, the other to be 'distanced', or – if the distancing proved unfeasible – exterminated. Those simply alien were not the objects of strictly racial policy: to them, old and tested strategies traditionally associated with contestant enmity could be applied: the aliens ought to be kept beyond closely guarded borders. Those bodily and mentally handicapped made a more difficult case and called for a new, original policy: they could not be evicted or fenced off as they did not rightfully belong to any of the 'other races', but they were unworthy to enter the thousand-year *Reich* either. The Jews offered an essentially similar case. They were not a race like the others; they were an anti-race, a race to undermine and poison all other races, to sap not just the identity of any race in particular, but the racial order itself. (Remember the Jews as the 'non-national nation', the incurable enemy of the nation-based order as such.) With approval and relish, Rosenberg quoted Weiniger's self-deprecatory verdict on the Jews as 'an invisible cohesive web of slime fungus (plasmodium), existing since time immemorial and spread over the entire earth'.[8] Thus the separation of the Jews could only be a half-measure, a station on the road to the ultimate goal. The matter could not possibly end with the cleansing of Germany of the Jews. Even residing far from the German borders, the Jews would continue to erode and disintegrate the natural logic of the universe. Having ordered his troops to fight for the supremacy of the *German* race, Hitler believed that the war he kindled was waged in the name of *all races*, a service rendered to racially organized humankind.

In this conception of social engineering as a scientifically founded work aimed at the institution of a new, and better, order (a work which necessarily entails the containment, or preferably elimination, of any disruptive factors), racism was indeed resonant with the world-view and practice of modernity. And this, at least, in two vital respects.

First, with the Enlightenment came the enthronement of the new deity, that of Nature, together with the legitimation of science as its only orthodox cult, and of scientists as its prophets and priests. Everything, in principle, had been opened to objective inquiry; everything could, in principle, be known – reliably and truly. Truth, goodness and beauty, that which is and that which ought to be, had all become legitimate objects of systematic, precise observation. In turn, they could legitimize themselves only through objective knowledge which would result from such observation. In George L. Mosse's summary of his most convincingly documented history of racism, 'it is impossible to separate the inquiries of the Enlightenment philosophies into nature from their examination of morality and human character . . . [From] the outset . . . natural science and the moral and aesthetic ideals of the ancient joined hands.' In the form in which it was moulded by the Enlightenment, scientific activity was marked by an 'attempt to determine man's exact place in nature through observation, measurements, and comparisons between groups of men and animals' and 'belief in the unity of body and mind'. The latter 'was supposed to express itself in a tangible, physical way, which could be measured and observed'.[9] Phrenology (the art of reading the character from the measurements of the skull) and physiognomy (the art of reading the character from facial features) captured most fully the confidence, strategy and ambition of the new scientific age. Human temperament, character, intelligence, aesthetic talents, even political inclinations, were seen as determined by Nature; in what way exactly, one could find out through diligent observation and comparison of the visible, material 'substratum' of even the most elusive or concealed spiritual attributes. Material sources of sensual impressions were so many clues to Nature's secrets; signs to be read, records written down in a code which science must crack.

What was left to racism was merely to postulate a systematic, and genetically reproduced distribution of such material attributes of human organism as bore responsibility for characterological, moral, aesthetic or political traits. Even this job, however, had already been done for them by respectable and justly respected pioneers of science, seldom if ever listed among the luminaries of racism. Observing *sine ira et studio* the reality as they found it, they could hardly miss the tangible, material, indubitably 'objective' superiority that the West enjoyed over the rest of the inhabited world. Thus the father of scientific taxonomy, Linnaeus, recorded the division between the residents of Europe and inhabitants of Africa with the same scrupulous precision as that which he applied while describing the difference between crustacea and fishes. He could not, and he did not, describe the white race otherwise than 'as inventive, full of ingenuity, orderly, and governed by laws . . . By contrast the Negroes were endowed with all the negative qualities which made them a counterfoil for the superior race: they were regarded as lazy, devious, and unable to govern themselves.'[10] The father of 'scientific racism', Gobineau, did not have to exercise much inventiveness to describe the black race as of little intelligence, yet of overdeveloped sensuality and hence a crude, terrifying power (just as the mob on the loose), and the white race as in love with freedom, honour and everything spiritual.[11]

In 1938, Walter Frank described the persecution of Jews as the saga of 'German scholarship in a struggle against World Jewry'. From the very first day of the Nazi rule, scientific institutes, run by distinguished university professors of biology, history and political science, had been set up to investigate 'the Jewish question' according to the 'international standards of advanced science'. Reichinstitut für Geschichte des neuen Deutschlands, Institut zum Studium der Judenfrage, Institut zur Erforschung des jüdischen Einflusses auf das deutsche kirchliche Leben, and the notorious Rosenberg's Institut zur Enforschung der Judenfrage were just a few of the many scientific centres that tackled theoretical and practical issues of 'Jewish policy' as an application of scholarly methodology, and never were they short of qualified staff with academically certified credentials. According to a typical rationale of their activity, the

> whole cultural life for decades has been more or less under the influence of biological thinking, as it was begun particularly around the middle of the last century, by the teachings of Darwin, Mendel and Galton and afterwards has been advanced by the studies of Plötz, Schallmayer, Correns, de Vries, Tschermak, Baur, Rüdin, Fischer, Lenz and others . . . It was recognized that the natural laws discovered for plants and animals ought also be valid for man . . .[12]

Second – from the Enlightenment on, the modern world was distinguished by its activist, engineering attitude toward nature and toward itself. Science was not to be conducted for its own sake; it was seen as, first and foremost, an instrument of awesome power allowing its holder to improve on reality, to re-shape it according to human plans and designs, and to assist it in its drive to self-perfection. Gardening and medicine supplied the archetypes of constructive stance, while normality, health, or sanitation offered the archmetaphors for human tasks and strategies in the management of human affairs. Human existence and cohabitation became objects of planning and administration; like garden vegetation or a living organism they could not be left to their own devices, lest should they be infested by weeds or overwhelmed by cancerous tissues. Gardening and medicine are functionally distinct forms of the same activity of *separating and setting apart useful elements destined to live and thrive, from harmful and morbid ones, which ought to be exterminated.* [. . .]

From repellence to extermination

'Christian theology never advocated extermination of the Jews', writes George L. Mosse, 'but rather their exclusion from society as living witnesses to deicide. The pogroms were secondary to isolating Jews in ghettos.'[13] 'A crime', Hannah Arendt asserts, 'is met with punishment; a vice can only be exterminated.'[14]

Only in its modern, 'scientific', racist form, the age-long repellence of the Jews has been articulated as an exercise in sanitation; only with the modern reincarnation of Jew-hatred have the Jews been charged with an ineradicable vice, with an immanent flaw which cannot be separated from its carriers. Before that, the Jews were sinners; like all sinners, they were bound to suffer for their sins, in an earthly or other-worldly purgatory – to repent and, possibly, to earn redemption. Their suffering was to be seen so that the consequences of sin and the need for repentance are seen. No such benefit can possibly be derived from watching vice, even if complete with its punishment. (If in doubt, consult Mary Whitehouse.) Cancer, vermin or weed cannot repent. They have not sinned, they just lived according to their nature. There is nothing to punish them for. By the nature of their evil, they have to be exterminated. Alone with himself, in his diary, Joseph Goebbels spelled this out with the same clarity we previously noted in the abstract historiosophy of Rosenberg: 'There is no hope of leading the Jews back into the fold of civilized humanity by exceptional punishments. They will forever remain Jews, just as we are forever members of the Aryan race.'[15] Unlike the 'philosopher' Rosenberg, Goebbels was, however, a minister in a government wielding an awesome and unchallenged power; a government, moreover, which – thanks to the achievements of modern civilization – could conceive of the possibility of life without cancer, vermin or weeds, and had at its disposal material resources to make such a possibility into a reality.

It is difficult, perhaps impossible, to arrive at the idea of extermination of a whole people without race imagery; that is, without a vision of endemic and fatal defect which is in principle incurable and, in addition, is capable of self-propagation unless checked. It is also difficult, and probably impossible, to arrive at such an idea without the entrenched practice of medicine (both of medicine proper, aimed at the individual human body, and of its numerous allegorical applications), with its model of health and normality, strategy of separation and technique of surgery. It is particularly difficult, and well-nigh impossible, to conceive of such an idea separately from the engineering approach to society, the belief in artificiality of social order, institution of expertise and the practice of scientific management of human setting and interaction. For these reasons, *the exterminatory version of anti-Semitism ought to be seen as a thoroughly modern phenomenon*; that is, something which could occur only in an advanced state of modernity.

These were not, however, the only links between exterminatory designs and the developments rightly associated with modern civilization. Racism, even when coupled with the technological predisposition of the modern mind, would hardly suffice to accomplish the feat of the Holocaust. To do that, it would have had to be capable of securing the passage from theory to practice – and this would probably mean energizing, by sheer mobilizing power of ideas, enough human agents to cope with the scale of the task, and sustaining their dedication to the job for as long as the task would require. By ideological training, propaganda or brainwashing, racism would have to imbue masses of non-Jews with the hatred and repugnance of Jews so intense as to trigger a violent action against the Jews whenever and wherever they are met.

According to the widely shared opinion of the historians, this did not happen. In spite of the enormous resources devoted by the Nazi regime to racist propaganda, the concentrated effort of Nazi education, and the real threat of terror against resistance to racist practices, the popular acceptance of the racist programme (and particularly of its ultimate logical consequences) stopped well short of the level an emotion-led extermination would require. As if further proof was needed, this fact demonstrates once again *the absence of continuity or natural progression between heterophobia or contestant enmity and racism*. Those Nazi leaders who hoped to capitalize on the diffuse resentment of the Jews to obtain popular support for the racist policy of extermination were soon forced to realize their mistake.

Yet even if (an unlikely case, indeed) the racist creed was more successful, and volunteers for lynching and throat-cutting were many times more numerous, mob violence should strike us as a remarkably inefficient, blatantly pre-modern form of social engineering or of the thoroughly modern project of racial hygiene. Indeed, as Sabini and Silver have convincingly put it, the most successful – widespread and materially effective – episode of mass anti-Jewish violence in Germany, the infamous *Kristallnacht*, was

> a pogrom, an instrument of terror . . . typical of the long-standing
> tradition of European anti-Semitism not the new Nazi order, not the
> systematic extermination of European Jewry. Mob violence is a prim-
> itive, ineffective technique of extermination. It is an effective method
> of territorizing a population, keeping people in their place, perhaps
> even of forcing some to abandon their religious or political convictions,
> but these were never Hitler's aims with regard to the Jews: he meant
> to destroy them.[16]

There was not enough 'mob' to be violent; the sight of murder and destruction put off as many as it inspired, while the overwhelming majority preferred to close their eyes and plug their ears, but first of all to gag their mouths. Mass destruction was accompanied not by the uproar of emotions, but the dead silence of unconcern. It was not public rejoicing, but public indifference which 'became a reinforcing strand in the noose inexorably tightening around hundreds of thousands of necks.'[17] *Racism is a policy first, ideology second. Like all politics, it needs organization, managers and experts.* Like all policies, it requires for its implementation a division of labour and an effective isolation of the task from the disorganizing effect of improvization and spontaneity. It demands that the specialists are left undisturbed and free to proceed with their task.

Not that indifference itself was indifferent; it surely was not, as far as the success of the Final Solution was concerned. It was the paralysis of that public which failed to turn into a mob, a paralysis achieved by the fascination and fear emanating from the display of power, which permitted the deadly logic of problem-solving to take its course unhampered. In Lawrence Stoke's words, 'The failure when the regime first set insecurely in power to protest its inhumane measures made prevention of their logical culmination all but impossible, however unwanted and disapproved this undoubtedly was.'[18] The spread and the depth of hetero-phobia was apparently sufficient for the German public not to protest against violence, even if the majority did not like it and remained immune to racist indoc-trination. Of the latter fact the Nazis found numerous occasions to convince themselves. In her impeccably balanced account of German attitudes Sarah Gordon quotes an official Nazi report which vividly expressed Nazi disappointment with public responses to the *Kristallnacht*:

> One knows that anti-Semitism in Germany today is essentially confined
> to the party and its organizations, and that there is a certain group in

the population who have not the slightest understanding for anti-Semitism and in whom every possibility of empathy is lacking.

In the days after *Kristallnacht* these people ran immediately to Jewish businesses . . .

This is to a great extent because we are, to be sure, an anti-Semitic people, an anti-Semitic state, but nevertheless in all manifestations of life in the state and people anti-Semitism is as good as unexpressed . . . There are still groups of *Spiessern* among the German people who talk about the poor Jews and who have no understanding for the anti-Semitic attitudes of the German people and who interceded for Jews at every opportunity. It should not be that only the leadership and party are anti-Semitic.[19]

Dislike of violence – particularly of such violence as could be seen and was meant to be seen – coincided, however, with a much more sympathetic attitude towards administrative measures taken against Jews. A great number of Germans welcomed an energetic and vociferously advertised action aimed at the segregation, separation, and disempowering of the Jews – those traditional expressions and instruments of heterophobia or contestant enmity. In addition, many Germans welcomed the measures portrayed as the punishment of the Jew (as long as one could pretend that the punished was indeed the conceptual Jew) as an imaginary (yet plausible) solution to quite real (if subconscious) anxieties and fears of displacement and insecurity. Whatever the reasons of their satisfaction, they seemed to be radically different from those implied by the Streicher-style exhortations to violence as an all-too-realistic way of repaying imaginary economic or sexual crimes. From the point of view of those who designed and commanded the mass murder of the Jews, Jews were to die not because they were resented (or at least not primarily for this reason); *they were seen as deserving death (and resented for that reason) because they stood between this one imperfect and tension-ridden reality and the hoped-for world of tranquil happiness.* [. . .] the disappearance of the Jews was instrumental in bringing about the world of perfection. The absence of Jews was precisely the difference between that world and the imperfect world here and now.

Examining neutral and critical sources in addition to official reports, Gordon has documented a widespread and growing approval of 'ordinary Germans' for the exclusion of Jews from positions of power, wealth and influence.[20] The gradual disappearance of Jews from public life was either applauded or studiously overlooked. Unwillingness of the public to partake personally of the persecution of the Jews was, in short, combined with the readiness to go along with, or at least not to interfere with, the action of the State. 'If most Germans were not fanatical or "paranoid" anti-Semites, they were "mild", "latent", or passive anti-Semites, for whom the Jews had become a "depersonalized", abstract, and alien entity beyond human empathy and the "Jewish Question" a legitimate subject of state policy deserving solution.'[21]

These considerations demonstrate once more the paramount importance of the other, operational rather than ideological, link between the exterminatory form of antisemitism and modernity. The *idea* of extermination, discontinuous with the traditional heterophobia and dependent for that reason on the two implacably modern phenomena of racist theory and the medical-therapeutic syndrome, provided the first link. But the modern idea needed also suitably modern means of implementation. It found such means in modern bureaucracy.

The only adequate solution to problems posited by the racist world-view is a total and uncompromising isolation of the pathogenic and infectious race – the source of disease and contamination – through its complete spatial separation or physical destruction. By its nature, this is a daunting task, unthinkable unless in conjunction with the availability of huge resources, means of their mobilization and planned distribution, skills of splitting the overall task into a great number of partial and specialized functions and skills to co-ordinate their performance. In short, the task is inconceivable without modern bureaucracy. To be effective, modern exterminatory antisemitism had to be married to modern bureaucracy. And in Germany it was. In his famous Wandsee briefing, Heydrich spoke of the 'approval' or 'authorization' of the RSHA Jewish policy by the *Führer*.[22] Faced with the *problems* arising from the idea and the purpose this idea determined (Hitler himself preferred to speak of 'prophecy' rather than of a purpose or a task), the bureaucratic organization called *Reichsicherheithauptamt* set about designing proper practical *solutions*. It went about it the way all bureaucracies do: counting costs and measuring them against available resources, and then trying to determine the optimal combination. Heydrich underlined the need to accumulate practical experience, stressed the graduality of the process, and the provisional character of each step, confined by as-yet-limited practical know-how; RSHA was actively to seek the best solution. The *Führer* expressed his romantic vision of the world cleansed of the terminally diseased race. The rest was the matter of a not at all romantic, coolly rational bureaucratic process.

The murderous compound was made of a typically modern ambition of social design and engineering, mixed with the typically modern concentration of power, resources and managerial skills. In Gordon's terse and unforgettable phrase, 'when the millions of Jewish and other victims pondered their own imminent deaths and wondered "why must I die, since I have done nothing to deserve it?" probably the simplest answer would have been that power was totally concentrated in one man, and that man happened to hate their "race".'[23] The man's hatred and the concentrated power did not have to meet. (Indeed, no satisfactory theory has been offered to date which proves that antisemitism is functionally indispensable for a totalitarian regime; or, *vice versa*, that the presence of antisemitism in its modern, racialist, form, inevitably results in such a regime. Klaus von Beyme has found in his recent study that, for instance, Spanish falangists took particular pride in the absence of a single antisemitic remark in all the writings of Antonio Primo de Rivera, while even such a 'classical' Fascist as Franco's brother-in-law Serrano Suñer declared racism in general as a heresy for a good Catholic. French neo-Fascist Maurice Bardech stated that the persecution of the Jews was Hitler's greatest error and remained *hors du contrat fasciste*.[24]) But they did. And they may meet again.

Looking ahead

The story of modern antisemitism – in both its heterophobic and in its modern, racist, forms – is unfinished, as is the history of modernity in general and the modern state in particular. Modernization processes seem to move in our days away from Europe. Though some sort of boundary-defining device seemed to be necessary in the passage modern, 'garden-type' culture, as well as during the most traumatic dislocations in societies undergoing the modernizing change, the selection of Jews for the role of such a device was in all probability dictated by the particular vicissitudes of European history. The connection between Judeophobia and European modernity was historical – and, one may say, historically unique. On the other hand, we know only too well that cultural stimuli travel relatively freely, if also unaccompanied by structural conditions closely related to them in their place of origin. Stereotype of the Jew as an order-disturbing force, as an incongruous cluster of oppositions that saps all identities and threatens all efforts at self-determination, has been long ago sedimented in the highly authoritative European culture and is available for export and import transaction, like everything else in that culture which is widely recognized as superior and trustworthy. This stereotype, like so many other culturally framed concepts and items before, can be adopted as a vehicle in the solution of local problems even if historical experience of which it was born has been locally missing; even if (or perhaps particularly if) societies which adopt it have had no previous first-hand knowledge of the Jews.

It has been recently noted that antisemitism survived the populations it had been ostensibly targeted against. In countries where the Jews have all but disappeared, antisemitism (as sentiment, of course, married now to practices related primarily to other targets than the Jews) continues unabated. Even more remarkable is the dissociation between the acceptance of anti-Jewish sentiments and any other national, religious or racial prejudices, with which it was thought to be closely correlated. Neither are the antisemitic feelings related today to group or individual idiosyncracies, and particularly to anxiety-generating unresolved problems, acute uncertainty etc. Bernd Martin, who explored the Austrian case of 'antisemitism without Jews' has coined the term *cultural sedimentation* to account for a relatively new phenomenon: certain (usually morbid or otherwise unprepossessing or shameful) human features or behavioural patterns have come to be defined in popular consciousness as Jewish. In the absence of practical tests of such conjunction, the negative cultural definition and the antipathy to the features to which it refers feed and reinforce each other.[25]

To many other cases of contemporary antisemitism, however, the explanation in terms of 'cultural sedimentation' does not fit. In our global village, news travels fast and wide, and culture has long become a game without frontiers. *Rather than a product of cultural sedimentation, contemporary antisemitism seems to be subject to the processes of cultural diffusion*, today much more intense than at any time in the past. Like other objects of such diffusion, antisemitism, while retaining affinity with its original form, is on the way transformed – sharpened or enriched – to adapt to the problems and needs of its new home. Of such problems and needs there is no shortage in the times of 'uneven development' of modernity with its attendant tensions and traumas. Judeophobic stereotype offers a ready-made intelligibility to the otherwise puzzling and frightening dislocations and previously unexperienced forms of suffering. For instance, in Japan it has become in recent years increasingly popular as a universal key to the understanding of unanticipated obstacles in the path of economic expansion; the activity of world Jewry is proposed as the explanation of events so diverse as the over-valuation of the yen and the alleged threat of fall-out in the case of another Czernobyl-style nuclear mishap followed by another Soviet cover-up.[26]

One variety of antisemitic stereotype that travels easily is described in length by Norman Cohn as the image of the Jews as an international conspiracy set on ruining all local powers, decomposing all local cultures and traditions, and uniting the world under Jewish domination. This is, to be sure, the most vituperative and potentially lethal form of antisemitism; it was under the auspices of this stereotype that extermination of the Jews was attempted by the Nazis. It seems that in the contemporary world the multi-faceted imagery of Jewry, once drawing inspiration from multiple dimensions of 'Jewish incongruity', tends to be tapered down to just one fairly straightforward attribute: that *of a supra-national elite, of invisible power behind all visible powers, of a hidden manager of allegedly spontaneous and uncontrollable, but usually unfortunate and baffling turns of fate.*

The now dominant form of antisemitism is a product of theory, not of elementary experience; it is supported by the process of teaching and learning, not by intellectually unprocessed responses to the context of daily interaction. At the beginning of this century by far the most widespread variant of antisemitism in the affluent countries of Western Europe was one aimed at impoverished and strikingly alien masses of Jewish immigrants; it arose from the unmediated experience of the native lower classes, which were alone in touch with the strange and bizarre foreigners and which responded to their disconcerting and destabilizing presence with mistrust and suspicion. Their feelings were seldom shared by the elites, who had no direct experience of interaction with Yiddish-speaking newcomers and for whom the immigrants were not essentially distinct from the rest of the unruly, culturally depressed and potentially dangerous lower classes. As long as it remained unprocessed by a theory which only middle-class or upper-class intellectuals could offer, the elemental heterophobia of the masses stayed (to paraphrase the famous adage of Lenin) at the level of 'trade-union consciousness'; it could hardly be lifted from there as long as reference was made only to the low-level experience of intercourse with the Jewish poor. It could be generalized into a platform for mass unrest simply by adding up individual anxieties and presenting private troubles as shared problems (as it has been in the case of Mosley's British Movement, aimed above all against London's East End, or the present-day British National Front, aimed at the likes of Leicester and Notting Hill, and the French, targeted at Marseilles). It could advance as far as the demand to 'send the aliens back where they came from'. Yet there was no road leading from such heterophobia or even boundary-drawing anxiety of the masses, in a way a 'private affair' of the lower classes, to sophisticated antisemitic theories of universal ambitions, like this of a deadly race or the 'world conspiracy'. To capture popular imagination, such theories must refer to facts normally inaccessible and unknown to the masses and certainly not located within the realm of their daily and unmediated experience.

Our previous analysis has brought us, however, to the conclusion that the true role of the sophisticated, theoretical forms of antisemitism lay not so much in its capacity to foment the antagonist practices of the masses, as in its unique link with the social-engineering designs and ambitions of the modern state (or, more precisely, the extreme and radical variants of such ambitions). On the evidence of the present trends towards withdrawal of the Western state from direct management of many areas of previously controlled social life, and towards a pluralism-generating, market-led structure of social life, it seems unlikely that a racist form of antisemitism may be again used by a Western state as an instrument of a large-scale social-engineering project. For a *foreseeable* future, to be more precise; the post-modern, consumer-oriented and market-centred condition of most Western societies seems to be founded on a brittle basis of an exceptional economic superiority, which for the time being secures an inordinately large share of world resources but which is not bound to last forever. One can assume that situations calling for a direct take-over of social management by the state may well happen in some not too distant future – and then the well-entrenched and well-tested racist perspective may again come handy. In the meantime, the non-racist, less dramatic versions of Judeophobia may be on numerous less radical occasions deployed as means of political propaganda and mobilization.

With the Jews moving today massively towards the upper-middle classes, and hence out of reach of the direct experience of the masses, group antagonisms arising from freshly fomented concerns with boundary-drawing and boundary-maintenance tend to focus today in most Western countries on immigrant workers. There are political forces eager to capitalize on such concerns. They often use a language developed by modern racism to argue in favour of segregation and phys-ical separation: a slogan successfully used by the Nazis on their road to power as a means of gaining the support of the combative enmity of the masses for their own racist intentions. In all countries that attracted in the time of post-war economic reconstruction large numbers of immigrant workers, the popular press and the populistically-inclined politicians supply innumerable examples of the new uses to which racist language is currently put. Gérard Fuchs, as well as Pierre Jouve and Ali Magoudi,[27] have recently published large collections and convincing analyses of these uses. One can read of *Le Figaro* magazine of 26 October 1985 dedicated to the question 'Will we still be French in thirty years?' or of prime minister Jacques Chirac speaking in one breath of his government's determination to fight with great firmness for the strengthening of personal security and of the identity of the French national community. The British reader, to be sure, has no need to look to French authors in the search for quasi-racist, segregationist language in the service of the mobilization of popular heterophobia and boundary fears.

However abominable they are, and however spacious is the reservoir of poten-tial violence they contain, heterophobia and boundary-contest anxieties do not result – directly or indirectly – in genocide. *Confusing heterophobia with racism and the Holocaust-like organized crime is misleading and also potentially harmful, as it diverts scrutiny from the genuine causes of the disaster, which are rooted in some aspects of modern mentality and modern social organization*, rather than in timeless reactions to the strangers or even in less universal, yet fairly ubiquitous identity conflicts. In the initiation and perpetuation of the Holocaust, traditional heterophobia played but an auxiliary role. The truly indispensable factors lay elsewhere, and bore at the utmost a merely historical relation to more familiar forms of group resentment. The *possibility* of the Holocaust was rooted in certain universal features of modern civilization: its *implementation* on the other hand, was connected with a specific and not at all universal relationship between state and society. [. . .]

Notes and references

1   Cf. Pierre-André Taguieffe, *La force du préjugé: essai sur le racism et ses doubles* (Parish: La Decouverte, 1988).

2   Taguieff, *La force du préjugé*, pp. 69–70. Albert Memmi, *Le racisme* (Paris: Gallimard, 1982) maintains that 'racism, not anti-racism, is truly universal' (p. 157), and explains the mystery of its alleged universality by reference to another mystery: the instinctive fear invariably inspired by all difference. One does not understand the *different*, which by the same token turns into the *unknown* and the unknown is a source of terror. In Memmi's view, the horror of the unknown 'stems from the history of our species, in the course of which the unknown was the source of danger' (p. 208). It is suggested therefore that the putative universality of racism is a product of species learning. Having thus acquired a pre-cultural foundation, it is essentially immune to the impact of individual training.

3   Taguieff, *La force du préjugé*, p. 91.

4   Alfred Rosenberg, *Selected Writings* (London: Jonathan Cape, 1970), p. 196.

5   Arthur Gütt, 'Population Policy', in *Germany Speaks* (London: Thornton Butterworth, 1938), pp. 35–52.

6   Walter Gross, 'National Socialist Racial Thought', in *Germany Speaks*, p. 68.

7   Cf. Gerald Fleming, *Hitler and the Final Solution* (Oxford: Oxford University Press, 1986), pp. 23–5.

8   Alfred Rosenberg (ed.), Dietrich Eckart: Ein Vermächtnis (Munich, Frz. Eher, 1928). Quoted after George L. Mosse, *Nazi Culture: A Documentary History* (New York: Schocken Books, 1981), p. 77.

9   George. L. Mosse, *Toward a Final Solution: A History of European Racism* (London, J. M. Dent & Son, 1978), p. 2.

10   Mosse, *Toward the Final Solution*, p. 20.

11   Cf. Mosse, *Toward the Final Solution*, p. 53.

12   Max Wienreich, *Hitler's Professors: The Part of Scholarship in Germany's Crimes against the Jewish People* (New York: Yiddish Scientific Institute, 1946), pp. 56, 33.

13   Mosse, *Toward the Final Solution*, p. 134.

14   Hannah Arendt, *Origins of Totalitarianism* (London: Allen & Unwin, 1962), p. 87.

15   Diary of Joseph Goebbels, in *Survivors, Victims, and Perpetrators: Essays on the Nazi Holocaust*, ed. Joel E. Dinsdale (Washington: Hemisphere Publishing Company, 1980), p. 311.

16   John R. Sabini & Maury Silver, 'Destroying the Innocent with a Clear Conscience: A Sociopsychology of the Holocaust', in *Survivors, Victims, and the Perpetrators*, p. 329.

17   Richard Grünberger, *A Social History of the Third Reich* (London: Weidenfeld & Nicholson, 1971), p. 460.

18 Lawrence Stokes, 'The German People and the Destruction of the European Jewry', *Central European History*, no. 2 (1973), pp. 167–91.

19 Quoted after Sarah Gordon, *Hitler, Germans, and the 'Jewish Question'* (Princeton: Princeton University Press, 1984), pp. 159–60.

20 Cf. Gordon, *Hitler, Germans, and the 'Jewish Question'*, p. 171.

21 Christopher R. Browning, *Fateful Months* (New York: Holmes & Meier, 1985), p. 106.

22 *Le dossier Eichmann et la solution finale de la question juive* (Paris: Centre de documentation juive contemporaine, 1960), pp. 52–3.

23 Gordon, *Hitler, Germans, and the 'Jewish Question'*, p. 316.

24 Klaus von Beyme, *Right-Wing Extremism in Western Europe* (London: Frank Cass, 1988), p. 5. In a recent study Michael Balfour surveyed conditions and motives which prompted various strata of German Weimar society to offer enthusiastic, mild or lukewarm support to the Nazi thrust for power, or at least refrain from active resistance. Many reasons are listed, general as well as specific to a given section of the population. The direct appeal of Nazi antisemitism figures prominently, however, in only one case (of the educated part of the *obere Mittelstand*, who felt threatened by the 'disproportionate competition' of the Jews), and even in this case merely as one of many factors found attractive, or at least worth trying, in the Nazi programme of the social revolution. Cf. *Withstanding Hitler in Germany 1933–45* (London: Routledge, 1988), pp. 10–28.

25 Cf. Bernd Martin, 'Antisemitism before and after Holocaust', in *Jews, Antisemitism and Culture in Vienna*, ed. Ivor Oxaal (London: Michael Pollak and Gerhard Botz, 1987).

26 *Jewish Chronicle*, 15 July 1988, p. 2.

27 Cf. Gérard Fuchs, *Ils resteront: le défi de l'immigration* (Paris: Syros, 1987); Pierre Jouve & Ali Magoudi, *Les dits et les non-dits de Jean-Marie Le Pen: enquéte et psychanalyse* (Paris: La Decouverte, 1988).

Chapter 17

Sander L. Gilman

ARE JEWS WHITE?
Or, The History of the Nose Job

[. . .]

THE PERSONAL COLUMNS IN the *Washingtonian*, the local city magazine in Washington, D.C., are filled with announcements of individuals "in search of" mates ("in search of" is the rubric under which these advertisements are grouped). These advertisements are peppered with various codes so well known that they are never really explained: "DWM [Divorced White Male] just recently arrived from Boston seeks a non-smoking, financially secure 40+ who loves to laugh" . . . or "SJF [Jewish Single Female], Kathleen Turner type, with a zest for life in search of S/DJM . . . for a passionate relationship." Recently, I was struck by a notice which began "DW(J)F [Divorced White (Jewish) Female] – young, 41, Ph.D., professional, no kids . . . seeks S/D/WWM, exceptional mind, heart & soul . . ."[1] What fascinated me were the brackets: advertisements for "Jews" or for "African Americans" or for "Whites" made it clear that individuals were interested in choosing their sexual partners from certain designated groups within American society. But the brackets implied that here was a woman who was both "White" and "Jewish." Given the racial politics of post-civil rights America, where do the Jews fit in? It made me ask the question, which the woman who placed the personals advertisement clearly was addressing: are Jews white? and what does "white" mean in this context? Or, to present this question in a slightly less polemical manner, how has the question of racial identity shaped Jewish identity in the Diaspora? I am not addressing what the religious, ethnic, or cultural definition of the Jew is – either from within or without Judaism or the Jewish community – but how the category of race present within Western, scientific, and popular culture, has shaped Jewish self-perception.

My question is not merely an "academic" one – rather I am interested in how the representation of the Jewish body is shaped and, in turn, shapes the sense of Jewish identity. My point of departure is the view of Mary Douglas:

> The human body is always treated as an image of society and . . . there
> can be no natural way of considering the body that does not involve
> at the same time a social dimension. Interest in its apertures depends
> on the preoccupation with social exits and entrances, escape routes and
> invasions. If there is no concern to preserve social boundaries, I would
> not expect to find concern with bodily boundaries.[2]

Where and how a society defines the body reflects how those in society define themselves. This is especially true in terms of the "scientific" or pseudo-scientific categories such as race which have had such an extraordinary importance in shaping how we all understand ourselves and each other. From the conclusion of the nineteenth century, the idea of "race" has been given a positive as well as a negative quality. We belong to a race and our biology defines us, is as true a statement for many groups, as is the opposite: you belong to a race and your biology limits you. Race is a constructed category of social organization as much as it is a reflection of some aspects of biological reality. Racial identity has been a powerful force in shaping how we, at the close of the twentieth century, understand ourselves – often in spite of ourselves. Beginning in the eighteenth century and continuing to the present, there has been an important cultural response to the idea of race, one which has stressed the uniqueness of the individual over the uniformity of the group. As Theodosius Dobzhansky noted in 1967: "Every person has a genotype and a life history different from any other person, be that person a member of his family, clan, race, or mankind. Beyond the universal rights of all human beings (which may be a typological notion!), a person ought to be evaluated on his own merits."[3] Dobzhansky and many scientists of the 1960s dismissed "race" as a category of scientific evaluation, arguing that whenever it had been included over the course of history, horrible abuses had resulted.[4] At the same time, within Western, specifically American culture of the 1960s, there was also a transvaluation of the concept of "race." "Black" was "beautiful," and "roots" were to be celebrated, not denied. The view was that seeing oneself as being a part of a "race" was a strengthening factor. We at the close of the twentieth century have, however, not suddenly become callous to the negative potential of the concept of "race." Given its abuse in the Shoah[5] as well as in neo-colonial policies throughout the world,[6] it is clear that a great deal of sensitivity must be used in employing the very idea of "race." In reversing the idea of "race," we have not eliminated its negative implications, we have only masked them. For it is also clear that the meanings associated with "race" impacts on those included within these constructed categories. It forms them and shapes them. And this can be a seemingly positive or a clearly negative response. There is no question that there are "real," i.e., shared genetic distinctions within and between groups. But the rhetoric of what this shared distinction comes to mean for the general culture and for the "group" so defined becomes central to any understanding of the implications of race.

Where I would like to begin is with that advertisement in the *Washingtonian* and with the question which the bracketed (J) posed: are Jews white? To begin to answer that question we must trace the debate about the skin color of the Jews, for skin colour remains one of the most salient markers for the construction of race in the West over time. The general consensus of the ethnological literature of the late nineteenth century was that the Jews were "black" or, at least, "swarthy." This view had a long history in European science. As early as 1691 François-Maximilien Misson, whose ideas influenced Bufon's *Natural History*, argued against the notion that Jews were black:

> 'Tis also a vulgar error that the Jews are all black; for this is only true of the Portuguese Jews, who marrying always among one another, beget Children like themselves, and consequently the Swarthiness of their Complexion is entail'd upon their whole Race, even in the Northern Regions. But the Jews who are originally of Germany, those, for example, I have seen at Prague, are not blacker than the rest of their Countrymen.[7]

But this was a minority position. For the eighteenth- and nineteenth-century scientist the "blackness" of the Jew was not only a mark of racial inferiority, but also an indicator of the diseased nature of the Jew. The "liberal" Bavarian writer Johan Pezzl, who travelled to Vienna in the 1780s, described the typical Viennese Jew of his time:

> There are about five hundred Jews in Vienna. Their sole and eternal occupation is to counterfeit, salvage, trade in coins, and cheat Christians, Turks, heathens, indeed themselves. . . . This is only the beggarly filth from Canaan which can only be exceeded in filth, uncleanliness, stench, disgust, poverty, dishonesty, pushiness and other things by the trash of the twelve tribes from Galicia. Excluding the Indian fakirs, there is no category of supposed human beings which comes closer to the Orang-Utan than does a Polish Jew. . . . Covered from foot to head in filth, dirt and rags, covered in a type of black sack . . . their necks exposed, the color of a Black, their faces covered up to the eyes with a beard, which would have given the High Priest in the Temple chills, the hair turned and knotted as if they all suffered from the "plica polonica."[8]

The image of the Viennese Jew is that of the Eastern Jew, suffering from the diseases of the East, such as the *Judenkratze*, the fabled skin and hair disease also attributed to the Poles under the designation of the "plica polonica."[9] The Jews' disease is written on the skin. It is the appearance, the skin color, the external manifestation of the Jew which marks the Jew as different. There is no question for a non-Jewish visitor to Vienna upon first seeing the Jew that the Jew suffers from Jewishness. The internal, moral state of the Jew, the Jew's very psychology, is reflected in the diseased exterior of the Jew. As mentioned earlier, "plica polonica" is a real dermatologic syndrome. It results from living in filth and poverty. But it was also associated with the unhygienic nature of the Jew and, by the mid-nineteenth century, with the Jew's special relationship to the most frightening disease of the period, syphilis.[10] For the non-Jew seeing the Jew it mirrored popular assumptions about the Jew's inherent, essential nature. Pezzl's contemporary,

Joseph Rohrer, stressed the "disgusting skin diseases" of the Jew as a sign of the group's general infirmity.[11] And the essential Jew for Pezzl is the Galician Jew, the Jew from the Eastern reaches of the Hapsburg Empire.[12] (This late eighteenth-century view of the meaning of the Jew's skin color was not only held by non-Jews. The Enlightenment Jewish physician Elcan Isaac Wolf saw this "black yellow" skin color as a pathognomonic sign of the diseased Jew.[13]) Following the humoral theory of the times, James Cowles Pritchard (1808) commented on the Jews' "choleric and melancholic temperaments, so that they have in general a shade of complexion somewhat darker than that of the English people . . ."[14] Nineteenth-century anthropology as early as the work of Claudius Buchana commented on the "inferiority" of the "black" Jews of India.[15] By the mid-century, being black, being Jewish, being diseased, and being "ugly" come to be inexorably linked. All races, according to the ethnology of the day, were described in terms of aesthetics, as either "ugly" or "beautiful."[16] African blacks, especially the Hottentot, as I have shown elsewhere, became the epitome of the "ugly" race.[17] And being ugly, as I have also argued, was not merely a matter of aesthetics but was a clear sign of pathology, of disease. Being black was not beautiful. Indeed, the blackness of the African, like the blackness of the Jew, was believed to mark a pathological change in the skin, the result of congenital syphilis. (And, as we shall see, syphilis was given the responsibility for the form of the nose.) One bore the signs of one's diseased status on one's anatomy, and by extension, in one's psyche. And all of these signs pointed to the Jews being a member of the "ugly" races of mankind, rather than the "beautiful" races. In being denied any association with the beautiful and the erotic, the Jew's body was denigrated.[18]

Within the racial science of the nineteenth century, being "black" came to signify that the Jews had crossed racial boundaries. The boundaries of race were one of the most powerful social and political divisions evolved in the science of the period. That the Jews, rather than being considered the purest race, are because of their endogenous marriages, an impure race, and therefore, a potentially diseased one. That this impurity is written on their physiognomy. According to Houston Stewart Chamberlain, the Jews are a "mongrel" (rather than a healthy "mixed") race, who interbred with Africans during the period of the Alexandrian exile.[19] They are "a mongrel race which always retains this mongrel character." Jews had "hybridized" with blacks in Alexandrian exile. They are, in an ironic review of Chamberlain's work by Nathan Birnbaum, the Viennese-Jewish activist who coined the word "Zionist," a "bastard" race, the origin of which was caused by their incestuousness, their sexual selectivity.[20]

Jews bear the sign of the black, "the African character of the Jew, his muzzle-shaped mouth and face removing him from certain other races . . .," as Robert Knox noted at mid century.[21] The physiognomy of the Jew which is like that of the black ". . . the contour is convex; the eyes long and fine, the outer angles running towards the temples; the brow and nose apt to form a single convex line; the nose comparatively narrow at the base, the eyes consequently approaching each other; lips very full, mouth projecting, chin small, and the whole physiognomy, when swarthy, as it often is, has an African look."[22] It is, therefore, not only the color of the skin which enables the scientist to see the Jew as black, but also the associated anatomical signs, such as the shape of the nose. The Jews were quite literally seen as black. Adam Gurowski, a Polish noble, "took every light-colored mulatto for a Jew" when he first arrived in the United States in the 1850s.[23]

[. . .] Jews look different, they have a different appearance, and this appearance has pathognomonic significance. Skin color marked the Jew as both different and diseased. For the Jewish scientist, such as Sigmund Freud, these "minor differences in people who are otherwise alike . . . form the basis of feelings of strangeness and hostility between them."[24] This is what Freud clinically labeled as the "narcissism of minor differences." But are these differences "minor" either from the perspective of those labeling or those labeled? In reducing this sense of the basis of difference between "people who are otherwise alike," Freud was not only drawing on the Enlightenment claim of the universality of human rights, but also on the Christian underpinnings of these claims. For this "narcissism" fights "successfully against feelings of fellowship and overpower[s] the commandment that all men should love one another." It is the Christian claim to universal brotherly love that Freud was employing in arguing that the differences between himself, his body, and the body of the Aryan, are trivial. Freud comprehended the special place that the Jew played in the demonic universe of the Aryan psyche. But he marginalized this role as to the question of the Jew's function "as an agent of economic discharge . . . in the world of the Aryan ideal" rather than as one of the central aspects in the science of his time.[25] What Freud was masking was that Jews are not merely the fantasy capitalists of the paranoid delusions of the anti-Semites, they also mirror within their own sense of selves the image of their own difference.

By the close of the nineteenth century, the "reality" of the physical difference of the Jew as a central marker of race had come more and more into question. Antithetical theories, such as those of Friedrich Ratzel, began to argue that skin color was a reflex of geography, and could and did shift when a people moved from one part of the globe to another. Building on earlier work by the President of Princeton University at the close of the eighteenth century, Samuel Stanhope Smith (1787), the Jews came to be seen as the adaptive people par excellence. "In Britain and Germany they are fair, brown in France and in Turkey, swarthy in Portugal and Spain, olive in Syria and Chaldea, tawny or copper-coloured in Arabia and Egypt."[26] William Lawrence commented in 1823 that "their colour is everywhere modified by the situation they occupy."[27] The questionability of skin color as the marker of Jewish difference joined with other qualities which made the Jew visible.

By the latter half of the nineteenth century, Western European Jews had become indistinguishable from other Western Europeans in matters of language, dress, occupation, location of their dwellings and the cut of their hair. Indeed, if Rudolf Virchow's extensive study of over 10,000 German schoolchildren published in 1886 was accurate, they were also indistinguishable in terms of skin, hair, and eye color from the greater masses of those who lived in Germany.[28] Virchow's statistics sought to show that wherever a greater percentage of the overall population had lighter skin or bluer eyes or blonder hair there was a greater percentage of Jews also had lighter skin or bluer eyes or blonder hair. But although Virchow attempted to provide a rationale for the sense of Jewish acculturation, he still assumed that Jews were a separate and distinct racial category. George Mosse has commented, "the separateness of Jewish schoolchildren, approved by Virchow, says something about the course of Jewish emancipation in Germany. However, rationalized, the survey must have made Jewish schoolchildren conscious of their minority status and their supposedly different origins."[29] Nonetheless, even though they were labeled as different, Jews came to parallel the scale of types found else-where in European society.

A parallel shift in the perception of the Jewish body can be found during the twentieth century in the United States. It is not merely that second- and third-generation descendants of Eastern European Jewish immigrants do not "look" like their grandparents; but they "look" American. The writer and director Philip Dunne commented on the process of physical acculturation of Jews in Southern California during the twentieth century:

> You could even see the physical change in the family in the second generation – not resembling the first generation at all. Of course, this is true all across the country, but it is particularly noticeable in people who come out of very poor families. . . . One dear friend and colleague of mine was a product of a Lower East Side slum. He was desperately poor. And he grew up a rickety, tiny man who had obviously suffered as a child. At school, he told me, the goyim would scream at him. Growing up in California, his two sons were tall, tanned, and blond. Both excelled academically and in athletics. One became a military officer, the other a physicist. They were California kids. Not only American but Californian.[30]

But the more Jews in Germany and Austria at the fin de siècle looked like their non-Jewish contemporaries, the more they sensed themselves as different and were so considered. As the Anglo-Jewish social scientist Joseph Jacobs noted, "it is some quality which stamps their features as distinctly Jewish. This is confirmed by the interesting fact that Jews who mix much with the outer world seem to lose their Jewish quality. This was the case with Karl Marx . . ."[31] And yet, as we know, it was precisely those Jews who were the most assimilated, who were passing, who feared that their visibility as Jews could come to the fore. It was they who most feared being seen as bearing that disease, Jewishness, which Heinrich Heine, said the Jews brought from Egypt.

In the 1920s, Jacob Wassermann chronicled the ambivalence of the German Jews towards their own bodies, their own difference. Wassermann articulates this difference within the terms of the biology of race. He writes that: "I have known many Jews who have languished with longing for the fair-haired and blue-eyed individual. They knelt before him, burned incense before him, believed his every word; every blink of his eye was heroic; and when he spoke of his native soil, when he beat his Aryan breast, they broke into a hysterical shriek of triumph."[32] Their response, Wassermann argues, is to feel disgust for their own body, which even when it is identical in *all* respects to the body of the Aryan remains different: "I was once greatly diverted by a young Viennese Jew, elegant, full of suppressed ambition, rather melancholy, something of an artist, and something of a charlatan. Providence itself had given him fair hair and blue eyes; but lo, he had no confidence in his fair hair and blue eyes: in his heart of hearts he felt that they were spurious."[33] The Jew's experience of his or her own body was so deeply impacted by anti-Semitic rhetoric that even when that body met the expectations for perfection in the community in which the Jew lived, the Jew experienced his or her body as flawed, diseased.[34] If only one could change those aspects of the body which marked one as Jewish!

But nothing, not acculturation, not baptism, could wipe away the taint of race. No matter how they changed, they still remained diseased Jews. And this was marked on their physiognomy. Moses Hess, the German–Jewish revolutionary and political theorist commented, in his *Rome and Jerusalem* (1862) that "even baptism will not redeem the German Jew from the nightmare of German Jew-hatred. The Germans hate less the religion of the Jews than their race, less their peculiar beliefs than their peculiar noses. . . . Jewish noses cannot be reformed, nor black, curly, Jewish hair be turned through baptism or combing into smooth hair. The Jewish race is a primal one, which had reproduced itself in its integrity despite climactic influences. . . . The Jewish type is indestructible:"[35] The theme of the Jew's immutability was directly tied to arguments about the permanence of the negative features of the Jewish race.

On one count, Hess seemed to be wrong – the external appearance of the Jew did seem to be shifting. His skin seemed to be getting whiter, at least in his own estimation, though it could never get white enough. Jews, at least in Western Europe, no longer suffered from the disgusting skin diseases of poverty which had once marked their skin. But on another count, Hess was right. The Jew's nose could not be "reformed." Interrelated with the meaning of skin was the meaning of the Jew's physiognomy, especially the Jew's nose. And it was also associated with the Jew's nature. George Jabet, writing as Eden Warwick, in his *Notes on Noses* (1848) characterized the "Jewish, or Hawknose," as "very convex, and preserves its convexity like a bow, throughout the whole length from the eyes to the tip. It is thin and sharp." Shape also carried here a specific meaning: "It indicates considerable Shrewdness in worldly matters; a deep insight into character, and facility of turning that insight to profitable account."[36] Physicians, drawing on such analogies, speculated that the difference of the Jew's language, the very mirror of his psyche, was the result of the form of the his nose. Thus Bernhard Blechmann's rationale for the *Mauscheln* of the Jews, their inability to speak with other than a Jewish intonation, is that the "muscles, which are used for speaking and laughing are used inherently different from those of Christians and that this use can be traced . . . to the great difference in their nose and chin."[37] The nose becomes one of the central loci of difference in seeing the Jew. [. . .]

Notes and references

1   *Washingtonian* 26, 4 (January 1991), p. 196.
2   Mary Douglas, *Natural Symbols* (New York: Pantheon Books, 1970), p. 70.
3   Theodosius Dobzhansky, "On Types, Genotypes, and the Genetic Diversity in Populations," in J.N. Spuhler, ed., *Genetic Diversity and Human Behavior* (Chicago: Aldine, 1967), p. 12.

4 See for example, Peter A. Bochnik, *Die mächtigen Diener: Die Medizin und die Entwicklung von Frauenfeindlichkeit und Antisemitismus in der europäischen Geschichte* (Reinbek bei Hamburg: Rowohlt, 1985).

5 Robert Jay Lifton, *The Nazi Doctors: Medical Killing and the Psychology of Genocide* (New York: Basic Books, 1986).

6 See Oliver Ransford, *"Bid the Sickness Cease": Disease in the History of Black Africa* (London: John Murray, 1983).

7 François-Maximilien Misson, *A New Voyage to Italy*, 2 vols. (London: R. Bonwicke, 1714), 2: 139.

8 Johan Pezzl, *Skizze von Wien: Ein Kultur- und Sittenbild aus der josephinischen Zeit*, ed. Gustav Gugitz and Anton Scholssar (Graz: Leykam-Verlag, 1923), pp. 107–8.

9 On the meaning of this disease in the medical literature of the period see the following dissertations on the topic: Michael Scheiba, *Dissertatio inauguralis medica, sistens quaedam plicae pathologica: Germ. Juden-Zopff, Polon. Koltun: quam . . . in Academia Albertina pro gradu doctoris . . . subjiciet defensurus Michael Scheiba . . .* (Regiomonti: Litteris Reusnerianis, 1739) and Hieronymus Ludolf, *Dissertatio inauguralis medica de plica, vom Juden-Zopff . . .* (Erfordiae: Typis Groschianis, 1724)

10 Harry Friedenwald, *The Jews and Medicine: Essays*. 2 vols. (Baltimore: The Johns Hopkins University Press, 1944), 2: 531.

11 Joseph Rohrer, *Versuch über die jüdischen Bewohner der östereichischen Monarchie* (Vienna: n.p., 1804), p. 26. The debate about the special tendency of the Jews for skin disease, especially "plica polonica," goes on well into the twentieth century. See Richard Weinberg, "Zur Pathologie der Juden," *Zeitschrift für Demographie und Statistik der Juden* 1 (1905): 10–11.

12 Wolfgang Häusler, *Das galizische Judentum in der Habsburgermonarchie im Lichte der zeitgenössischen Publizistik und Reiseliteratur von 1772–1848* (Vienna: Verlag für Geschichte und Politik, 1979). On the status of the debates about the pathology of the Jews in the East after 1919 see *Voprosy biologii i patologii evreev* (Leningrad: State Publishing House, 1926).

13 Elcan Isaac Wolf, *Von den Krankheiten der Juden* (Mannheim: C.F. Schwan, 1777), p. 12.

14 James Cowles Pritchard, *Researches into the Physical History of Man* (Chicago: The University of Chicago Press, 1973), p. 186.

15 Claudius Buchanan, *Christian Researches in Asia, with Notices of the Translation of the Scriptures into the Oriental Languages* Boston: Samuel T. Armstrong, 1811), p. 169. On the background to these questions see George W. Stocking, Jr., *Victorian Anthropology* (New York: The Free Press, 1987).

16 Léon Poliakov, *The Aryan Myth: A History of Racist and Nationalist Ideas in Europe*, trans. Edmund Howard (New York: Basic Books, 1974), pp. 155–82.

17 Sander L. Gilman, *On Blackness without Blacks: Essays on the Image of the Black in Germany*, Yale Afro-American Studies (Boston: G. K. Hall, 1982).

18 See Cheryl Herr, "The Erotics of Irishness," *Critical Inquiry* 17 (1990): 1–34.

19 Houston Stewart Chamberlain, *Foundations of the Nineteenth Century*, trans. John Lees, 2 vols. (London: John Lane/The Bodley Head, 1913), 1: 389.

20 Nathan Birnbaum, "Über Houston Stewart Chamberlain," in his *Ausgewählte Schriften zur jüdischen Frage* (Czernowitz: Verlag der Buchhandlung Dr. Birnbaum & Dr. Kohut, 1910), 2: 201.

21 Robert Knox, *The Races of Men: A Fragment* (Philadelphia: Lea and Blanchard, 1850), p. 134.

22 Knox, *Races of Men*, p. 133.

23 Adam G. De Gurowski, *America and Europe* (New York: D. Appleton, 1857), p. 177.

24 Sigmund Freud, *Standard Edition of the Complete Psychological Works of Sigmund Freud*, ed. and trans, J. Strachey, A. Freud, A. Strachey, and A. Tyson, 24 vols. (London: Hogarth, 1955–74), 11: 199; 18: 101; 21: 114.

25 ibid. 21: 120.

26 Samuel Stanhope Smith, *An Essay on the Causes of the Variety of Complexion and Figure in the Human Species* (Cambridge: MASS: The Belknap Press, 1965), p. 42.

27 William Lawrence, *Lectures on Physiology, Zoology, and the Natural History of Man* (London: James Smith, 1823), p. 468.

28 Rudolf Virchow, "Gesamtbericht über die Farbe der Haut, der Haare und der Augen der Schulkinder in Deutschland," *Archiv für Anthropologie* 16 (1886): 275–475.

29 George L. Mosse, *Toward the Final Solution: A History of European Racism* (New York: Howard Fertig, 1975), pp. 90–91.

30 Cited from an interview by Neal Gabler, *An Empire of Their Own: How the Jews Invented Hollywood* (New York: Crown, 1988), pp. 242–42.

31 "Types," *The Jewish Encyclopedia*. 12 vols (New York: Funk and Wagnalls, 1906), 12: 295.

32 Wassermann, *My Life*, p. 156

33 Wassermann, *My Life*, p. 156.

34 On the cultural background for this concept see Jacob Katz, *Out of the Ghetto: The Social Background of Jewish Emancipation 1770–1870* (Cambridge, MASS: Harvard University Press, 1973) and Rainer Erb and Werner Bergmann, *Die Nachtseite der Judenemanzipation: Der Widerstand gegen die Integration der Juden in Deutschland 1780–1860* (Berlin: Metropol. 1989).

35 Moses Hess, *Rom und Jerusalem*. 2nd ed. (Leipzig: M. W. Kaufmann, 1899), Brief IV. Cited in the translation from Paul Lawrence Rose, *Revolutionary Antisemitism in Germany from Kant to Wagner* (Princeton: Princeton University Press, 1990), p. 323.

36 Eden Warwick, *Notes on Noses* (1848: London: Richard Bentley, 1864), p. 11. On the general question of the representation of the physiognomy of the Jew in mid-nineteenth-century culture see Mary Cowling, *The Artist as Anthropologist: The Representation of Type and Character in Victorian Art* (Cambridge: Cambridge University Press, 1989), pp. 118–19, 332–33.

37 Bernhard Blechmann, *Ein Beitrag zur Anthropologie der Juden* (Dorpat: Wilhelm Just, 1882), p. 11.

Chapter 18

Matthew F. Jacobson

LOOKING JEWISH, SEEING JEWS

W HEN JOHANN BLUMENBACH sat down to delineate *The Natural Varieties of Man* in 1775, he lighted upon the "racial face" of the Jews as the most powerful example of "the unadulterated countenance of nations." The principle of stable racial types was illustrated "above all [by] the nation of the Jews, who, under every climate, remain the same as far as the fundamental configuration of face goes, remarkable for a racial character almost universal, which can be distinguished at the first glance even by those little skilled in physiognomy."[1]

The racial character of Jewishness in the New World ebbed and flowed over time. The saga of Jewishness-as-difference in North America properly begins as early as 1654, when Peter Stuyvesant wrote to the Amsterdam Chamber of the Dutch West India Company that Christian settlers in New Amsterdam had "deemed it useful to require [Jews] in a friendly way to depart." Stuyvesant went on to pray "that the deceitful race — such hateful enemies and blasphemers of the name of Christ — be not allowed further to infect and trouble this new colony."[2] In the early republic Jewishness was most often taken up as a matter not of racial difference marked by physicality, but of religious difference marked by a stubborn and benighted failure to see Truth. Jews were "un-Christian," as in the laws limiting the right of office-holding in Maryland; they were "infidels" in more heated rhetoric. Then, like other non-Anglo-Saxon immigrants who entered under the terms of the 1790 naturalization law, Jews were increasingly seen as a racial group (in their case as Orientals, Semites, or Hebrews) in the mid to late nineteenth century — particularly as the demographics of immigration tilted away from German and other West European Jews, and toward the Yiddish-speaking Jews of Eastern Europe. Finally, again like other non-Anglo-Saxon immigrants, Jews gradually became Caucasians over the course of the twentieth century.

Thus anti-Semitism and the racial odyssey of Jews in the United States are neither wholly divisible from nor wholly dependent upon the history of whiteness and its vicissitudes in American political culture. When Henry James writes, "There were thousands of little chairs and almost as many little Jews; and there was music in the open rotunda, over which Jews wagged their big noses," it is useful to know that he is drawing upon a long European tradition of anti-Jewish imagery buttressed by arrangements of institutional power and political custom. It is also useful to know, however, that James's sensibilities could be as easily unsettled by a gang of Italian "ditchers" or a variety of other immigrant arrivals. After a visit to "the terrible little Ellis Island" in 1906, James ventured that the sight would bring "a new chill in [the] heart" of any long-standing American, as if he had "seen a ghost in his supposedly safe old house." American natives, he wrote, had been reduced to a state of "*unsettled possession*" of their own country; and it was not the Jew alone, but the "inconceivable alien" in general, who had him so worried.[3]

Yet as with Irish immigrants, who came ashore already carrying the cultural and political baggage of Saxon oppression, the Jews' version of becoming Caucasian cannot be understood apart from their particular history of special sorrows in the ghettos of Eastern Europe, apart from the deep history of anti-Semitism in Western culture, apart from anti-Semitic stereotypes that date back well before the European arrival on North American shores, or apart, finally and most obviously, from the historic cataclysm of the Holocaust.

[. . .] Like Irishness, Italianness, Greekness, and other probationary white-nesses, visible Jewishness in American culture between the mid-nineteenth and mid-twentieth centuries represented a complex process of social value *become* perception: social and political meanings attached to Jewishness generate a kind of physiognomical surveillance that renders Jewishness itself discernible as a partic-ular pattern of physical traits (skin color, nose shape, hair color and texture, and the like – what Blumenbach called "the fundamental configuration of face." The visible markers may then be interpreted as outer signs of an essential, immutable, inner moral–intellectual character; and that character, in its turn – attested to by physical "difference" – is summoned up to explain the social value attached to Jewishness in the first place. The circuit is ineluctable. Race is social value become perception; Jewishness seen is social value naturalized and so enforced.

This is not to say that people all "really" look alike; rather, it is to argue that those physical differences which register in the consciousness as "*difference*" are keyed to particular social and historical circumstances. (We might all agree that Daniel Patrick Moynihan "looks Irish," for instance; but unlike our predecessors, we at the turn of the twenty-first century are not likely to note his Irishness first thing.) Thus a writer defending the "better" Jews (what a later generation would tellingly call "white Jews") in the *North American Review* in 1891 could collapse the distinction between behavior and physicality, arguing that "among cultured Jews the racial features are generally less strongly defined." (When Jews are of the "better" type, that is, the observing eye need not scout their Jewishness.)[4] That same year, meanwhile, in *The Witch of Prague*, the novelist Marion Crawford could thoroughly fuse physicality and inner character in his portrait of Jewish evil. In the Jewish quarter one encountered

> throngs of gowned men, crooked, bearded, filthy, vulture-eyed . . .
> hook-nosed and loose-lipped, grasping fat purses, in lean fingers, shaking

greasy curls that straggled out under caps of greasy fur, glancing to the
left and right with quick, gleaming looks that pierced the gloom like
fitful flashes of lightening . . . a writhing mass of humanity, intoxicated
by the smell of gold, mad for its possession, half hysteric with fear of
losing it, timid, yet dangerous, poisoned to the core by the sweet sting
of money, terrible in intelligence, vile in heart, contemptible in body,
irresistible in the unity of their greed – the Jews of Prague.[5]

Not, indeed, have conceptions of a racial Jewishness necessarily been confined to negative depictions. The point is a critical one. [. . .] Yiddish writers like
Abraham Cahan and Morris Winchevsky were as quick as their non-Jewish contemporaries to assign a distinctly racial integrity to Jewishness and Jews. Racial
perceptions of Jewishness are not simply a subject for the annals of anti-Semitism,
in other words; nor does racial ascription necessarily denote a negative assessment
of a given group in every case. Among the secularized Jews of the *haskala*, or
Jewish enlightenment, responses to "the Jewish Question" (such as Zionism, or
bundist Yiddish socialism) rested solidly upon *racial* notions of a unified Jewish
"peoplehood." In the sciences, too, it was not only the virulent Madison Grants
and the Lothrop Stoddards, but Jewish scientists like Maurice Fishberg and Joseph
Jacobs, who advanced the scholarly idea of Jewish racial purity.[6] (Nor, for that
matter, were Jewish versions of Jewish racial difference in every instance *positive*,
either: as the *American Hebrew* remarked in response to the immigrant waves from
further east in Europe [1894], the acculturated German Jew "is closer to the christian sentiment around him than to the Judaism of these miserable darkened
Hebrews.")[7]

Thus the history of racial Jewishness is not merely the history of anti-Semitism;
it encompasses the ways in which both Jews and non-Jews have construed
Jewishness – and the ways in which they have *seen* it – over time. It encompasses
not only arguments, like Madison Grant's, that "the mixture of a European and a
Jew is a Jew," or the view of Jews as "mud people" – the progenitors of all
nonwhites – which circulates in far right theology in the 1990s.[8] It also comprises
the race pride of a Morris Winchevsky or a Leon Kobrin, and the social forces
under whose influence such conceptions of peoplehood have largely given way. By
1950 Ludwig Lewisohn could assert that "no sane man regards Jewish characteristics as 'racial.'"[9] And yet as late as the 1970s Raphael Patai would still be trying
to dispel "the myth of the Jewish race"; and later still Philip Roth would be wincing
at the "nasty superstitions" attached to racial Jewishness.

A few remarks on the strategy of the present inquiry are in order. The definition of "Jewishness" under investigation here is quite narrow. Surely religion
and culture can figure prominently in the ascription of Jewishness by Jews
or non-Jews, anti-Semites or philo-Semites. This discussion does not seek to
exhaust Jewishness in all of its dimensions or in its full range of possibilities; rather,
it investigates strictly ethnoracial conceptions and perceptions of Jewishness
(answers to the question, is Jewishness a parcel of biological, heritable traits?).
Such conceptions, and the inevitable debates over them, have been central to
some Jews themselves as they pondered their common destiny irrespective of
religious devotion, and to non-Jews wrestling with questions of immigration, inter-

group relations, and the smooth functioning of the polity. I begin by sketching the emergence of a visible, physical – biological – Jewishness in common American understanding during the period preceding the mid-twentieth century. This history loosely parallels the chronology laid out for whiteness in general [. . .], although in the case of Jews World War II will present a sharper turning point than 1924 in the final transformation toward Caucasian whiteness. The investigation ends, then, with a close reading of Arthur Miller's *Focus* (1945), a sustained inquiry into the properties of Jewishness rendered at precisely that post-Nazi moment – like *Gentleman's Agreement* – when "racial" Jewishness was still alive, yet a newly intolerable, conception.

"Are Jews white?" asks Sander Gilman. The question gets at the fundamental instability of Jewishness as racial difference, but so does its wording fundamentally misstate the contours of whiteness in American political culture.[10] From 1790 onward Jews were indeed "white" by the most significant measures of that appellation: they could enter the country and become naturalized citizens. Given the shades of meaning attaching to various racial classifications, given the nuances involved as whiteness slips off toward Semitic or Hebrew and back again toward Caucasian, the question is not *are* they white, nor even how white are they, but how have they been both white and Other? What have been the historical terms of their probationary whiteness? [. . .]

The idea of a unique Jewish physicality or Jewish "blood" was not new to nineteenth-century America. As James Shapiro has recently argued, theology heavily influenced early modern conceptions of both racial and national difference in Europe, and so the alien Jew figures prominently in European discussion as early as the sixteenth century. In 1590 Andrew Willet argued that "Jews have never been grafted onto the stock of other people." In 1604 the Spaniard Prudencio de Sandoval combined a proto-racialist argument of hereditary Jewish evil with a kind of racialism-by-association with the other Other, the Negro: "Who can deny that in the descendants of the Jews there persists and endures the evil inclination of their ancient ingratitude and lack of understanding, just as in Negroes [there persists] the inseparability of their blackness?" Such ideas evidently crossed the Atlantic early on in the settlement of the New World, assuming even more directly racialist overtones in Increase Mather's comments on the "blood" of nations and the purity of the Jews in 1669:

> The providence of God hath suffered other nations to have their blood mixed very much, as you know it is with our own nation: there is a mixture of British, Roman, Saxon, Danish, [and] Norman blood. But as for the body of the Jewish nation, it is far otherwise. Let an English family live in Spain for five or six hundred years successively, and they will become Spaniards. But though a Jewish family live in Spain a thousand years, they do not degenerate into Spaniards (for the most part).[11]

Until the second half of the nineteenth century, however, it was generally not their "blood" but their religion that marked the Jews as a people apart. The Jew was the perpetual "Historical Outsider," in Frederic Jaher's phrase, whose perceived difference derived above all from "Christian hostility." The Jew's difference was primarily cast in terms of the "infidel" or the "blasphemer" (one Jacob Lambrozo was indicted in Maryland for denouncing Jesus as a "necromancer," for example), and discussion was occasionally infused with a dose of long-standing European rumor (such as the twelfth-century "blood libel" that Jews needed Christian blood for certain holiday fêtes) or stereotypes of Jews as well-poisoners and usurers. Although the popular view of Jews was "amply negative" in the colonies, by Jaher's account, it was far better there than in Europe; and their status was characterized by a general state of toleration disrupted only by occasional anti-Semitic outbursts, as when the New York Assembly disfranchised them in 1737, or when Savannah freeholders resisted the expansion of a Jewish cemetery in 1770.[12]

These religiously grounded ideas about the Jewish alien could occasionally take on a racialist cast in the new nation, just as they had in early modern Europe. In a rabid denunciation of the Jacobin propensities of the Democratic Society in 1795, for instance, one Federalist publisher asserted that the democrats would be "easily known by their physiognomy"; they seem to be "of the tribe of Shylock: they have that leering underlook and malicious grin."[13] But generally Jews remained "free [though unchristian] white persons" in the early republic, and the overt depictions of the Jew as a racial Other rose sharply only in the second half of the nineteenth century, particularly in the decades after what John Higham has called "a mild flurry of ideological anti-Semitism" during the Civil War. Now it was not only that Jews could be known in their greed (or their Jacobinism or their infidelism or their treachery) by their physiognomy, but that their physiognomy itself was significant – denoting, as it did, their essential unassimilability to the republic. Only now did the "Israelitish nose" stand for something in and of itself – not greed, or usury, or infidelism, or well-poisoning, but simply "difference." Only now was the dark Jew equated with "mongrelization," that catch-all term for "unfitness" in American political culture.[14] Thus a century after Johann Blumenbach introduced as scientific fact the remarkable stability of the Jews when it came to "the funda- mental configuration of face," the New York *Sun* offered this vernacular explanation of "why the Jews are kept apart" (1893):

> Other races of men lose their identity by migration and by inter- marrying with different peoples, with the result that their peculiar characteristics and physiognomies are lost in the mess. The Jewish face and character remain the same as they were in the days of PHARAOH. Everybody can distinguish the Jewish features in the most ancient carv- ings and representations, for they are the same as those seen at this day. Usually a Jew is recognizable as such by sight. In whatever country he is, his race is always conspicuous . . . After a few generations other immigrants to this country lose their race identity and become Americans only. Generally the Jews retain theirs undiminished, so that it is observable by all men.[15]

Others, as we have seen, strongly contested the blithe assertion that "other im- migrants to this country lose their race identity," but the *Sun* was nonetheless expressing a point of impressive consensus on the unassimilability of the Jews.

This intensifying perception of a distinctly racial Jewishness coincided with two entangling developments between the 1850s and the early twentieth century: the rise of the racial sciences, and the rise of what John Higham has called "discriminatory" (as opposed to "ideological") anti-Semitism.[16] Popular accounts of the racial Otherness of Jews, that is, at once framed, and were framed by, a scientific discourse of race on the one hand, and a set of social practices (including hiring and admissions patterns, and the barring of Jews from certain Saratoga resorts) on the other. This coincidence of scientific racialism, discriminatory practice, and the popular expression of racial Jewishness attests to the centrality of race as an organizer of American social life. It also attests to the similarity between the Jewish odyssey from white to Hebrew and, say, the Irish odyssey from white to Celt. Despite its capacity to absorb and adapt unique, long-standing anti-Semitic notions of Jewish greed and the like, the racial ideology encompassing Jewishness in the United States in the latter half of the nineteenth century did set Jews on a social trajectory similar to that traveled by many other probationary "white persons." The full texture of anti-Semitism in this country thus combined strains of an international phenomenon of Jew-hatred with the mutability of American whiteness.[17]

The rise of races and phenotypes in scientific discourse, as described earlier, was a creature of the age of European expansionism and exploration. Non-European races were "discovered" and became "known" through the technologies of conquest; then scientific accounts of these races, in their turn, justified and explained colonial domination and slavery. But Jews received a fair amount of attention even in this context, in part because of the mutual accommodations of scientific and religious understandings of genesis (or Genesis) and "difference," and in part because, as somewhat anomalous Europeans, Jews put stress upon the ideas of consanguinity and race which undergirded emergent European nationalisms. Just as the alien Jew raised questions as to who could or could not be truly "English" in Shakespeare's England, so romantic nationalisms of the nineteenth century had to come to terms with the anomalous Jew in an effort to theorize and police the "imagined community" of the nation. As one scholar puts it, science itself was "often either motivated by or soon annexed to political causes."[18] Just as the plunder of exploration and slavery formed the context within which Africans became "known" to Western science, so Jewish emancipation, debates over citizenship, and the emergence of modern nationalism formed the context within which science comprehended "the Jewish race." Were "Jewish traits" properly attributed to social isolation, environment, or immutable character? Could Jews be compatriots of non-Jews? Could they be redeemed as Europeans?

Thus from the outset scientific writings on Jews in Europe tended to focus upon questions of assimilation, most often emphasizing the race's stubborn immutability – which is to say, its unassimilability. As Gobineau wrote in his essay *Sur l'Inégalité des Races Humaines*, the "Jewish type" has remained much the same over the centuries; "the modifications it has undergone . . . have never been enough, in any country or latitude, to change the general character of the race. The warlike Rechabites of the Arabian desert, the peaceful Portuguese, French, German and Polish Jews – they all look alike . . . The Semitic face looks exactly the same as it appears on the Egyptian paintings of three or four thousand years ago."[19] The Jews may be incorporated, but they will forever be Jews. In *Races of Man* (1950),

Robert Knox similarly noted Jews' essential physicality, leaving little doubt as to the further question of racial merit:

> Brow marked with furrows or prominent points of bone, or with both; high cheek-bones; a sloping and disproportioned chin; and elongated, projecting mouth, which at the angles threatens every moment to reach the temples; a large, massive, club-shaped, hooked nose, three or four times larger than suits the face – these are features which stamp the African character of the Jew, his muzzle-shaped mouth and face removing him from certain other races . . . Thus it is that the Jewish face never can [be], and never is, perfectly beautiful.[20]

The presumed immutability of the Jews became a staple of American science by mid-century as well, even though slavery and the question of Negro citizenship still dominated racial discussion. In *Types of Mankind* (1855) Josiah Nott remarked that the "well-marked Israelitish features are never beheld out of that race"; "The complexion may be bleached or tanned . . . but the Jewish features stand unalterably through all climates." In *Natural History of the Human Races* (1869) John Jeffries, too, argued that "the Jews have preserved their family type unimpaired; and though they number over five million souls, each individual retains the full impress of his primitive typical ancestors".[21] And of course we have already seen where these "observations" on Jewish racial integrity tended in the age of eugenics.

In this connection the British scholar Joseph Jacobs deserves special attention. A Jew himself, Jacobs was, as he announced in the preface to *Studies in Jewish Statistics* (1891), "inclined to support the long-standing belief in the substantial purity of the Jewish race."[22] For Jacobs, according to the historian John Efron, Jewish race science represented "a new form of Jewish self-defense" and his own work a new genre of political resistance, "the scientific apologia." But if aimed toward the redemption, rather than the renunciation, of racial Jewishness, Jacobs's work rests upon the same logic of "difference" as the most virulent of his anti-Semitic contemporaries. Indeed, it is in Jacobs's work perhaps above all that we glimpse the depth of "difference" associated with Jewish racial identity in this period. "Even more in Jewesses than in Jews," he wrote, "we can see that cast of face in which the racial so dominates the individual that whereas of other coun-tenances we say, 'That is a kind, a sad, a cruel, or a tender face,' of this our first thought is, 'That is a Jewish face.' . . . Even the negroes of Surinam, when they see a European and a Jew approaching, do not say, 'Here are two whites,' but, 'Here is a white and a Jew.'"[23]

Just as earlier scientific approaches to the righteousness of slavery (the work of Josiah Nott and John Van Evrie, for instance) had seized upon the degeneracy of the "mulatto" as proof of the unbridgeable divide separating black from white, so Jacobs went into great detail on the "infertility of mixed marriages" between Jews and non-Jews, on the basis of statistics kept in Prussia and Bavaria between 1875 and 1881. The variance in fecundity, according to Jacobs, was an average of 4.41 children for Jewish–Jewish marriages to 1.65 for Jewish–Gentile marriages in Prussia; and 4.7 to 1.1 in Bavaria. He also charted various physical

characteristics of Jews and non-Jews in different regions, including the color of
eyes, hair, and skin. (Only 65.4 percent of Austrian Jews had "white" skin, he
found, as compared with more than 80 percent of the Gentiles.)[24]

Like conceptions of Anglo-Saxon, Celtic, or Teutonic racial character, scientific observations on the Hebrew passed from the rarified discourse of ethnological
journals into the American vernacular and the American visual lexicon of race as
well. Racial depiction did not necessarily entail a negative judgment; racially
accented declarations of *philo*-Semitism were common enough. William Cullen
Bryant lamented that Edwin Booth's rendering of Shylock, for instance, failed to
do justice to "the grandeurs of the Jewish race." He later sang of "the wonderful
working of the soul of the Hebrew."[25] James Russell Lowell, in an ambivalent
twist, couched highly sympathetic remarks on Jewishness in a language of physicality and character, but also drew upon the common, anti-Semitic imagery of his
day. "All share in government of the world was denied for centuries to perhaps
the ablest, certainly the most tenacious, race that ever lived in it," he wrote compas-
sionately in "Democracy" (1884), " . . . a race in which ability seems as natural
and hereditary as the curve of their noses . . . We drove them into a corner, but
they had their revenge . . . They made their corner the counter and banking house
of the world, and thence they rule it and us with the ignoble scepter of finance."[26]
Lowell's respect for "perhaps the ablest" race is the basis for an indictment of
Christian political conduct, and particularly its lamentable exclusions. Even if blame
lies at the doorstep of Christians, however, the Jewish "revenge" Lowell envisions
taps the popular currents of nineteenth-century anti-Semitism.

[. . .] In *The Ambivalent Image*, her study of Jews in American cultural imagery,
Louise Mayo has amassed an invaluable compendium of racial figures of Jewishness
across time. Although Mayo's project did not entail theorizing the relationship
between racial Jewishness and the American social order, her work supports the
trajectory of Anglo-Saxondom and its Others sketched out above. Racial depictions of Jews would become most urgent, of course, as immigration figures climbed
in the decades following Russia's May Laws of 1881. Nonetheless, as Mayo has so
nicely laid bare in her cultural excavations, Hebrews appeared as a counterpoint
to Anglo-Saxons in American cultural representation long before actual Hebrews
began to disembark in huge numbers at Castle Garden and Ellis Island toward the
end of the century. This seems part of the reflex toward an Anglo-supremacist
exclusivity beginning in the 1840s. Thus in the cosmos of American popular literature, for instance, George Lippard could remark in *Quaker City* (1844), "Jew was
written on his face as though he had fallen asleep for three thousand years at the
building of the Temple"; in Peter Hamilton Meyers's *The Miser's Heir* (1854) a
certain character's "features . . . proclaim him a Jew"; and in J. Richter Jones's
Quaker Soldier (1866), a Jew is characterized by the "hereditary habits of his race."[27]
By the early twentieth century a Jewish group could organize a grassroots boycott
of certain New York theaters, protesting their "scurrilous and debasing imperson-
ations of the Hebrew type." Judge Hugo Pam, the leader of the boycott, argued
that the theater was fostering "race prejudice" because so many theater goers "get
their impressions of the race from the stage Jew." (Significantly, this group took
its cue from Irish activists, who, Pam said, had succeeded in eliminating "stage
lampoons of the Celtic race" from popular theater.)[28]

Racial depictions of Jewishness circulated not only in cultural productions themselves, but also in cultural commentary, as when *Harper's Weekly* reported that the audience of the Yiddish theater was "remarkably strange in appearance to an Anglo-Saxon," or when *Bookman* reviewed Abraham Cahan's *Yekl* as a penetrating look at the Yidish immigrant's "racial weakness." William Dean Howells, too, discussed Cahan's novella in racial terms, identifying Cahan as a "Hebrew" and his ghetto sketches as "so foreign to our race and civilization." [29]

Wherever "difference" was cast as race, certainly, the weight of the culture in general tended most often toward negative depiction. Nativist discussion of immigration restriction in the 1890s and the eugenics movement of the earlier twentieth century, of course, states Jewish difference most boldly. Sounding the familiar chord of race and republicanism, Henry Cabot Lodge warned that Jews "lack the nobler abilities which enable a people to rule and administer and to display that social efficiency in war, peace, and government without which all else is vain." The *Illustrated American* was blunter still, crying in 1894 that "the inroad of the hungry Semitic barbarian is a positive calamity." In a piece on immigration and anarchism, the *New York Times*, too, lamented the arrival of "unwashed, ignorant, unkempt, childish semi-savages," and remarked upon the "hatchet-faced, sallow, rat-eyed young men of the Russian Jewish colony." In response to Franz Boas's innovative argument that in fact no biological chasm did separate new immigrants from America's "old stock," Lothrop Stoddard dismissed his views as "the desperate attempt of a Jew to pass himself off as 'white.'" [30]

Franz Boas's argument notwithstanding, increasingly in the years after the Russian May Laws and the pogroms of 1881, Jews, too, embraced race as a basis for unity. This was particularly true among some Zionists and freethinkers for whom religion had ceased meaningfully to explain their ties to the "folk." The "Jewish Question" as it was posed during the period of pogroms in the East and the Dreyfus Affair in the West generated new secular and political notions of Jewish peoplehood in response. It was in this period, for instance, that Joseph Jacobs began his forays into Jewish race science in Europe. And, as John Efron has amply documented, the *racial* individuality of the Jews as a people was of particular interest within the budding Zionist movement. Aron Sandler's *Anthropologie und Zionismus* (1904), for instance, mobilized the scientific language of a distinct racial genius in order to press the necessity of a Jewish territory where that genius could properly take root and develop. [31]

Indeed, a much longer tradition entwined Jewish nationalism with Jewish racialism. The proto-Zionist Moses Hess, in *Rome and Jerusalem* (1862), had flatly announced that "Jewish noses cannot be reformed, nor black, curly, Jewish hair be turned through baptism or combing into smooth hair. The Jewish race is a primal one, which had reproduced itself in its integrity despite climatic influences . . . The Jewish type is indestructible." [32] The American proto-Zionist Emma Lazarus, too, wrote in *Epistle to the Hebrews* (1887) that Judaism was emphatically *both* a race and a religion. She rhapsodized over the Jews' "fusion of Oriental genius with Occidental enterprise and energy," "the fire of our Oriental blood," and "the deeper lights and shadows of [Jews'] Oriental temperament." She lamented that Jews in America tended to be condemned "as a race" for failings of a single individual. At once demonstrating her own commitment to racialism, yet marking the extent to which race was a contested concept, she lamented the Jews' lack of unanimity on their own racial status: "A race whose members are recognized at a glance, whatever be their color, complexion, costume or language, yet who dispute the cardinal fact as to whether they are a race, cannot easily be brought into unanimity upon more doubtful propositions," she sighed.[33]

In the 1890s and early 1900s immigrant writers in the United States like Abraham Cahan, Leon Kobrin, Abraham Liessen [Abraham Wald], and Bernard Gorin also lighted upon race both as a way of understanding their own secular Jewishness and as a way of couching their (socialist) appeals to the Yiddish masses. And even as late as the 1920s and 1930s a literature of Jewish assimilation toyed with race in its exploration of Jewish destiny in the New World.[34] What of today and of America?" asked Ludwig Lewisohn. "Were the Jews Germans? Are they Americans? . . . I am not talking about citizenship and passports or external loyalties. What are the inner facts?"[35]

The Island Within (1928), an immigrant saga tracing several generations of a German–Jewish family from Germany in the mid-nineteenth century to the United States in the early twentieth, is Lewisohn's exploration of precisely these "inner facts." "How was it," the novel's young hero, Arthur, wants to know, "that, before they went to school, always and always, as far back as the awakening of consciousness, the children knew that they were Jews? . . . There was in the house no visible symbol of religion and of race." What does Jewishness consist in? What is its basis, especially in the crucible of a transnational history in which questions of national belonging are so vexed?

Arthur vows to understand. Along the way in this ethnoracial *Bildungsroman*, he takes up anthropology and studies the "variableness of racial types" (but later discovers, to his distaste, that his professor rather undemocratically believes in "fixed qualitative racial differences," and so he searches elsewhere). A neighbor, Mrs. Goldman, provides a simple formula: "Jews always have been Jews and they always will be." The tautology actually foreshadows Arthur's own resolution at the end of the novel.[36]

Throughout the quest, race is central both to Arthur's crisis and to its resolution; for him it becomes a measure of his own alienation. He first registers the degree of his assimilation when he discovers that his own father "looks Jewish" to him: "His father's profile under the hat, pale and unwontedly sorrowful, looked immemorially Jewish . . . Arthur realized instantly that this perception of his was itself an un-Jewish one and showed how he had grown up to view his very parents slightly from without and how, indeed, in all thoughts and discussions, he treated the Jews as objects of his discourse." Some two hundred pages later, after a good deal of soul-searching and after many tortured conversations on the subject of Jewishness, Arthur discovers and reclaims his own "island within" – his own immutable, unshakable Jewishness. "You didn't know you were going to resurrect the Jew in you?" asks his Gentile wife, Elizabeth. He responds, "You're quite right . . . But really I didn't even have to resurrect the Jew. I just put away a pretense." Thus eternal Jewishness (what a generation of Yiddish speakers had called *dos pintele yid*, "the quintessence of the Jew"), if racially ambiguous, does have distinctly racial connotations. "It's kind of an argument, isn't it, against mixed marriages?" asks Elizabeth. "I'm afraid it is."[37]

In *I Am a Woman – and a Jew* (1926), Leah Morton [Elizabeth Stern], too, recounted her marriage to a non-Jew, her foray into the world of social work, her secularization, and her eventual re-embrace of Jewishness (if not exactly of Judaism), all in the terms of her relationship to the "race." The authenticity of this narrative has recently been questioned; but it is nonetheless significant that this public embrace of her Jewish identity – however real or imagined – is cast in the thoroughly racial terms of the period's public discourse of Jewishness as difference.[38] Of New York's Bohemia, she wrote, "They were frankly Jewish. They had Jewish names, Jewish faces and the psychology of the Jew." Upon her first taste of public life in the settlement house movement, Leah came to realize that "here, in this office, I was not a girl representing a race. I was not a Jewish maiden responsible to a race, as at home." This fairly conveys Morton's own version of that Jewish immutability so stressed by writers from Knox and Gobineau to Jacobs and Cahan. "Was there a Jewish 'race'?" she asks. "Scientists were taking sides, saying, yes, or no, as they decided. What did it matter to us who were Jews? There was a Jewish people, something that belonged to us," in Moreton's estimation, finally comes through when she discovers and embraces "all that we, who are Jews, 'part Jews' or 'all Jews' share." This is Morton's version of the "island within": "We Jews are alike. We have the same insensities, the sensitiveness, poetry, bitterness, sorrow, the same humor, the same memories. The memories are not those we can bring forth from our minds: they are centuries old and are written in our features, in the cells of our brain."[39]

This, then, was the vision of difference that the blackface of an Al Jolson or an Eddie Cantor sought to efface. *The Jazz Singer* marks the beginning of the drift by which American Jews became racial Caucasians and illustrates Frantz Fanon's contention that, when it comes to race-hatred or race-acceptance, "one has only not to be a nigger."[40] As with all racial transformations, the next leg of the Jews' odyssey – the cultural trek from Hebrew to Caucasian – would be a gradual affair, glacial rather than catastrophic. A new paradigm was in ascendance in the 1920s and after; perhaps nothing demonstrates so well the power of that paradigm in redefining Jews as the odd, archaic ring that so much of the material in the foregoing pages now has. Whether it is Leah Morton writing proudly of the features and the brain cells of the eternal Jew, or Lothrop Stoddard commenting upon the slim prospects of Franz Boas's passing himself off as "white," these commentators from the mid-nineteenth century to the early twentieth were clearly speaking from a racial consciousness not our own. [. . .]

Jews did not disappear from racial view overnight in the mid-1920s, nor had racial Jewishness vanished completely even by the 1940s. An *Atlantic Monthly* piece entitled "The Jewish Problem in America" (1941) could still assert that the Jew had become European "only in residence; by nature he did not become an Occidental; he could not possibly have done so." Comparing Jews to another problematic "Oriental" group, Armenians, this writer went on to wonder "whether [differences] can be faded out by association, *miscegenation*, or other means of composition."[41] When Nazi policy began to make news in the 1930s and early 1940s, too, headlines in journals like the *Baltimore Sun* and the *Detroit Free Press* revealed the extent to which Americans and Germans shared a common lexicon of racial

Jewishness: American papers unself-consciously reported upon the Nazis' "steps to solve [the] race problem," "laws restricting [the] rights of Hebrews," and the "persecution of members of the Jewish race." Hearst papers remarked upon the "extermination of an ancient and cultured race," while the Allentown (Pennsylvania) *Chronicle and News* commented upon Jews' inability to assimilate with "any other race."[42]

World War II and the revelations of the horrors of Nazi Germany were in fact part of what catapulted American Hebrews into the community of Caucasians in the mid-twentieth century.[. . .] The feverish and self-conscious revision of "the Jewish race" was at the very heart of the scientific project to rethink the "race concept" in general – the racial devastation in Germany, that is, was largely responsible for the mid-century ascendance of "ethnicity."

Changes wrought in the U.S. social order by the war itself and by the early Cold War, too, helped to speed the alchemy by which Hebrews became Caucasian. From A. Phillip Randolph's threatened march on Washington, to African–Americans' campaign for Double Victory, to the major parties' civil rights planks in 1944 and the rise of the Dixiecrats in 1948, the steady but certain ascendance of Jim Crow as *the* pressing political issue of the day brought the ineluctable logic of the South's white–black binary into play with new force in national life. Postwar prosperity and postindustrial shifts in the economy, too, tended to disperse Jews geographically, either to outlying suburbs or toward sunbelt cities like Los Angeles and Miami – in either case, to places where whiteness itself eclipsed Jewishness in racial salience. As scholars like Deborah Dash Moore and Karen Brodkin Sacks have written, Jews became simply "white or Anglo" in the regional racial schemes of the sunbelt; and racially tilted policies like the GI Bill of Rights and the Federal Housing Authority's "whites only" approach to suburban housing loans re-created Jews in their new regime of racial homogenization. Nikhil Singh has rightly called the postwar suburban boom a case of "state sponsored apartheid;" its hardening of race along exclusive and unforgiving lines of color held tremendous portent for Jews and other white races.[43] And finally, ironically, if racialism had historically been an important component of Zionism, the establishment of a Jewish state ultimately had the opposite effect of whitening the Jews in cultural representations of all sorts: America's client state in the Middle East became, of ideological necessity and by the imperatives of American nationalism, a *white* client state. This revision was popularized not only in mainstream journalism, but in Technicolor extravaganzas on Middle Eastern history like *The Ten Commandments* and *Exodus*.[44] [. . .]

Notes and references

1   Johann Fredrich Blumenbach, *On the Natural Varieties of Mankind* [1775, 1795] (New York: Bergman, 1969), p. 234.
2   In Morris U. Schapps,. ed., *A Documentary History of Jews in the United States, 1654–1875* (New York: Schoken, 1950, 1971), pp. 1–2.
3   Henry James, "Glasses," *Atlantic Monthly*, Feb. 1896, p. 145; William Boelhower, *Through a Glass Darkly: Ethnic Semiosis in American Literature* (New York: Oxford,

1987), pp. 17–40, 21; Henry James, *The American Scene* [1906] (n.l.: Library of America, 1993), pp. 425–427. See also Karen Brodkin Sacks, "How Did Jews Become White Folks?" in Steven Gregory and Roger Sanjek, eds, *Race* (New Brunswick: Rutgers University Press, 1994), pp. 79–85.

4   *North American Review*, 152 (1891), p. 128. On "white Jews" see Louis Binstock, "Fire-Words," *Common Ground*, Winter 1947, pp. 83–84, and Laura Z. Hobson, *Gentleman's Agreement* (New York: Simon and Schuster, 1947), pp. 154–155.

5   F. Marion Crawford, *The Witch of Prague* (1891) (London: Sphere Books, 1974), p. 186.

6   Matthew Frye Jacobson, *Special Sorrows: The Diasporic Imagination of Irish, Polish, and Jewish Immigrants in the United States* (Cambridge: Harvard University Press, 1995), pp. 102–105, and " 'The Quintessence of the Jew': Polemics of Nationalism and Peoplehood in Turn-of-the-Century Yiddish Fiction," in Werner Sollors and Marc Schell, eds, *Multilingual America* (New York: New York University Press, forthcoming); John Efron, *Defenders of the Race: Jewish Doctors and Race Science in Fin-de-Siècle Europe* (New Haven: Yale University Press, 1994).

7   Hasia Diner, *In the Almost Promsied Land: American Jews and Blacks, 1915–1935* [1977] (Baltimore: Johns Hopkins University Press, 1995), pp. 8–9.

8   Madison Grant, *The Passing of the Great Race: or, The Racial Basis of European History* (New York: Scribners, 1916), pp. 15–16: James William Gibson, *Warrior Dreams: Violence and Manhood in Post-Vietnam America* (New York: Hill and Wang, 1994), p. 72.

9   Ludwig Lewisohn, *The American Jew: Character and Destiny* (New York: Farrar, Straus and Co., 1950), p. 23.

10   Sander Gillman, *The Jew's Body* (New York: Routledge, 1991), chapter 7; Sacks, "How Did Jews Become White Folks?"

11   James Shapiro, *Shakespeare and the Jews* (New York: Columbia University Press, 1996), pp. 36, 168, 169, 170; see pp. 167–193 on early modern English conceptions of nationality and the Jewish alien.

12   Frederic Cople Jaber, *A Scapegoat in the New Wilderness: The Origins and Rise of Anti-Semitism in America* (Cambridge: Harvard University Press, 1994), pp. 17, 82, 87–88, 106, 112. For Jaher's view of the Christian roots of the Jew as "Historical Outsider," see pp. 17–81 passim.

13   Jaher, *Scapegoat*, p. 133.

14   Ibid., pp. 222, 232; on the worsening image, see pp. 170–241; on the proto-racialism of older stereotypes, see pp. 192–194. John Higham, *Send These to Me: Immigrants in Urban America* [1975] (Baltimore: Johns Hopkins University Press, 1984), p. 123. Jeffrey Melnick notes an interesting swing in American discourse between the Jew as "mongrel" and the Jew as racially "pure" – both are bad. *A Right to Sing the Blues* (Cambridge: Harvard University Press, forthcoming).

15   *New York Sun,* April 24, 1893, p. 6.

16   Higham, *Send These to Me*, pp. 117–152. On Jews and the racial sciences see Robert Singerman, "The Jew as Racial Alien: The Genetic Component of American Anti-Semitism," in David Gerber, ed., *Anti-Semitism in American History* (Urbana: University of Illinois Press, 1987), pp. 103–128, and below.

17   John Higham, "Ideological Anti-Semitism in the Gilded Age," and "The Rise of Social Discrimination," in *Send These to Me*, pp. 95–116, 117–152. On "status panic" and American anti-Semitism, see p. 141.

18   Efron, *Defenders*, p. 63.

19   Michael Bediss, ed., Arthur Comte de Gobineau, *Selected Political Writings* (New York: Harper and Row, 1970), p. 102: William Stanton, *The Leopard's Spots: Scientific Attitudes towards Race in America, 1815–59* (Chicago: University of Chicago Press, 1960), pp. 147–148: George Stocking, ed., *Bones, Bodies, Behavior: Essays on Biological Anthropology* (Madison: University of Winconsin Press, 1988); Thomas Gossett, *Race: The History of an Idea in America* (New York: Schocken, 1963).

20   Quoted in Efron, *Defenders*, p. 51.

21   Josiah Nott, *Types of Mankind* (Philadelphia: Lippincott, 1855), pp. 117, 118; John P. Jeffries, *Natural History of the Human Races* (New York: Edward O. Jenkins, 1869), p. 123.

22   Joseph Jacobs, *Studies in Jewish Statistics, Social, Vital, and Anthropometric* (London: D. Nutt, 1891), p. xxx.

23   Ibid., p. xxviii; Efron, *Defenders*, pp. 58–90, 59.

24   Jacobs, *Jewish Statistics*, pp. v, xiv; Efron, *Defenders*, pp. 79–80; Maurice Fishberg, *The Jews: A Study of Race and Environment* (n.l.: Walter Scott, 1911); Sander Gilman, *The Case of Sigmund Freud: Medicine and Identity at the Fin de Siècle* (Baltimore: Johns Hopkins University Press, 1993), pp. 11–68; Sander Gilman, *Freud, Race, and Gender* (Princeton: Princeton University Press, 1993), pp. 12–48.

25   Quoted in Louise Mayo, *The Ambivalent Image: Nineteenth-Century America's Perception of the Jew* (Rutherford: Fairleigh Dickinson University Press, 1988), p. 77.

26   James Russell Lowell, "Democracy" [1884], in *Essays, Poems, and Letters* (New York: Odyssey Press, 1948), p. 153.

27   Mayo, *Ambivalent Image*, pp. 44, 53, 54.

28   New York *Times*, April 25, 1913, p. 3.

29   Mayo, *Ambivalent Image*, pp. 75–76, 154; Howells quoted in Bernard Richards, "Abraham Cahan Cast in a New Role," in Cahan, *Yekl, the Imported Bridegroom, and Other Stories* (New York: Dover, 1970), p. vii.

30   Mayo, *Ambivalent Image*, pp. 58, 156, 172; Stoddard quoted in Michael Rogin, *Blackface, White Noise: Jewish Immigrants in the Hollywood Melting Pot* (Berkeley: University of California Press, 1996), p. 89. The Dillingham Commission was uncharacteristically sanguine regarding Jews' prospects for assimilation in 1911, asserting that "the Jews of to-day are more truly European than Asiatic or Semitic." Nonetheless, the report did note that "Israelites" were "preserving their own individuality to a marked degree." *Reports of the Immigration Commission: Dictionary of Races and peoples* (Washington D.C.: Government Printing Office, 1911), pp. 73, 74.

31   Efron, *Defenders*, pp. 123–174.

32   Quoted in Gilman, *The Jew's Body*, p. 179.

33   Emma Lazarus, *An Epistle to the Hebrews* [1887] (New York: Jewish Historical Society, 1987), pp. 9, 20, 21, 78, 80.

34   Jacobson, *Special Sorrows*, pp. 97–111; Melnick, *A Right to Sing the Blues*.

35   Ludwig Lewisohn, *The Island Within* (New York: Modern Library, 1928), p. 43.

36   Ibid., pp. 103–104, 146, 154–155, 168.

37   Ibid., pp. 148, 346.

38   Laura Browder, "*I Am a Woman – And a Jew:* Ethnic Imposter Autobiography and the Creation of Immigrant Identity," paper delivered at the ASA annual conference, Kansas City, November 1, 1996.

39 Leah Morton [Elizabeth Stern], *I Am a Woman — And A Jew* [1926] (New York: Markus Wiener, 1986), pp. 347, 62, 193, 360. The text also contains racialized references to Irish and Polish immigrants and to Nordic natives, pp. 175, 245, 299.

40 Frantz Fanon, *Black Skin, White Masks* [1952] (New York: Grove Wiedenfeld, 1967), p. 115.

41 Albert Nock, "The Jewish Problem in America" *Atlantic Monthly*, July 1941, p. 69 (emphasis added). In rebuttal, see Marie Syrkin, "How Not to Solve the 'Jewish Problem,'" *Common Ground*, Autumn 1941, p. 77.

42 Deborah Lipstadt, *Beyond Belief: The American Press and the Coming of the Holocaust, 1933–1945* (New York: Free Press, 1986), pp. 59–60, 88, 93, 157. See also Elazar Barkan, *The Retreat of Scientific Racism: Changing Concepts of Race in Britain and the United States between the World Wars* (Cambridge: Cambridge University Press, 1992), chapter 6; Stefan Kuhl, *The Nazi Connection: Eugenics, American Racism, and German National Socialism* (New York: Oxford, 1994).

43 Deborah Dash Moore, *To The Golden Cities: Pursuing the American Jewish Dream in Miami and L.A.* (New York: Free Press, 1994), p. 55; Sacks, "How Did Jews Become White Folks?" pp. 86–98; Rogin, *Blackface, White Noise*, p. 265; Nikhil Pal Singh, "'Race' and Nation in the American Century: A Genealogy of Color and Democracy" (Ph.D. diss., Yale University, 1995), Douglass Massey and Nancy Denton, *American Apartheid: Segregation and the Making of the Underclass* (Cambridge: Harvard University Press, 1993), pp. 51–54.

44 Moore, *Golden Cities*, pp. 227–261; Alan Nadel, *Containment Culture: American Narratives, Postmodernism, and the Atomic Age* (Durham: Duke University press, 1995), pp. 90–116. On the racial dynamics of American involvement in the Middle East, see also Soheir A. Morsy, "Beyond the Honorary 'White' Classification of Egyptians: Societal Identity in Historical Context," in Gregory and Senjak, *Race*, pp. 175–198.

PART FOUR

Colonialism, race and the other

INTRODUCTION

THE ROLE OF COLONIALISM and its associated institutions in shaping contemporary ideas about race and racism has been an underlying concern in some of the more historical literature in this field. For example the connection between scientific racism and imperialism and colonialism has been explored is some detail by a number of scholars. But in recent years the growth of interest in postcolonial theory, particularly in the fields of literary theory and cultural studies, has brought about a new interest in the role that race played in structuring social relationships in colonial societies. The various extracts in this part are all in one way or another concerned with various aspects of this question. The first extract is from the work of Frantz Fanon, which has exerted an influence on theoretical debates about race and colonialism for over four decades now. Indeed 'The Fact of Blackness' is one of the most referenced texts in this area and has been interpreted in a variety of ways. An underlying theme in Fanon's work is that colonialism represented a relationship of domination and subordination, the oppression of one racialised group by another and the production of racialised meanings about both the 'coloniser' and the 'colonised'. Fanon is particularly concerned with the ways in which colonial institutions and the ideologies associated with them constructed ideas about race through representations of 'blackness', the 'negro', the 'native' and other notions. Perhaps more importantly he is also concerned with the ways in which the colonised 'Others' saw themselves and their position within colonial societies and the struggle against colonialism.

A number of the other extracts in this part engage in one way or another with Fanon's work, although they often have a more specific focus on particular expressions of colonial discourse. The next two extracts by Lola Young and Anne

McClintock are a case in point. Both are concerned with cultural mechanisms for the expression of colonial ideas and values. Young's concern is with the question of representations of race, gender and sexuality in the cinema, and she bases much of her argument on a detailed analysis of particular films. But from a broad conceptual angle she is also concerned with questions that were at the heart of Fanon's account of the colonial situation. What is particularly interesting about Young's account, however, is that she seeks to use the analysis of 'imperial culture' as represented in films as a way of framing the changing ideas about race as well as gender and sexuality.

The extract from Anne McClintock's work explores some of the same territory as Young, though her focus in this extract is on the narratives of Henry Rider Haggard, a British colonial administrator and writer. McClintock's focus on a nuanced textual analysis of Haggard's writings reflects the influence of literary theory in this field and the attempt to utilise an analysis of texts to uncover the workings of colonial and postcolonial discourses. Whatever the merits of the shift towards textual analysis that has become evident in recent years, part of the strength of McClintock's account is precisely the result of the attention to the representations of race, gender and sexuality that underpin the work of writers such as Haggard. Taking Haggard's classic *King Solomon's Mines* as her main point of reference she attempts to show how key themes in his work linked up to wider fears about race and degeneration in both Britain and the colonies.

The next extract from Chandra Talpade Mohanty is closely linked to arguments that have been going on within feminist scholarship for the past two decades, and it should thus be read in conjunction with the extracts in Part Five as well as the other extracts in this part. Mohanty's critical account of Western feminist discourses focuses particularly on what she sees as the lacunae of feminist theorising in relation to questions about race and colonialism. At a broader level she suggests that there is a need to broaden the boundaries of feminist scholarship in order to allow for a fuller understanding of the important differences that exist in the ways women in the West are positioned as compared to women in other parts of the globe. Underlying Mohanty's argument is a concern to explore the continuities and discontinuities between the experiences of different groups of women, and to highlight the relevance of class in shaping other patterns of inequality.

The contributions of both Young and McClintock have already touched upon the issue of the question of sexuality in the colonial situation. The extract by Ann Stoler takes this argument a step further by exploring in some detail the interrelationship between 'sexual affronts' and 'racial frontiers' in colonial South East Asia. Stoler's analysis is particularly focused on the interweaving of sexual desire for the 'Other' with the fear of 'race mixing' and its consequences that characterised colonial situations. Drawing on her research in relation to the Dutch East Indies she highlights the ways in which both sexual and racial boundaries were used to construct images of both 'Europeans' and the colonial 'Others'. But she also insists on the need to look closely at the ways in which the colonial administrations needed to set up complex institutional mechanisms to police these boundaries.

The final voice in this part is that of Homi Bhabha, whose work has done much to popularise the study of race within the emerging field of postcolonial studies. Bhabha's work is deeply influenced, somewhat idiosyncratically, by the work of both Fanon and by the conceptual framework of Michel Foucault. His work has become an important influence on the development of postcolonial theory. In this particular extract Bhabha focuses on the relationship between race, time and modernity. Starting his account with a discussion of Fanon's work he moves on to discuss the ways in which questions of race and identity have been reconfigured by wider processes of social and cultural change which are dislocating the central structures and processes of modern societies and undermining the frameworks which gave individuals stable anchorage in the social world. This in turn links up with a recurrent theme in this reader as a whole, namely the question of how modern societies deal with 'difference'.

KEY QUESTIONS

- How can Frantz Fanon's essay on 'The Fact of Blackness' be used to analyse the development of racism in colonial societies?
- In what ways were racial ideas and institutions an integral element of the colonial situation?
- What are the implications of Chandra Talpade Mohanty's critical analysis of Western feminist discourses for an analysis of racism?
- Explore the implications of Ann Stoler's argument that colonialism involved the construction of both racial and sexual boundaries.
- Examine Homi Bhabha's argument that postcolonial writing involves a critical dialogue within and beyond the limits of modernity.
- Discuss the ways in which Anne McClintock's essay on 'The White Family of Man' illustrates the interface between race, gender and sexuality in structuring colonialism.

Chapter 19

Frantz Fanon

THE FACT OF BLACKNESS

Translated by Charles Lam Markmann

"**D**IRTY NIGGER!**"** Or simply, "Look, a Negro!"
     I came into the world imbued with the will to find a meaning in things, my spirit filled with the desire to attain to the source of the world, and then I found that I was an object in the midst of other objects.

Sealed into that crushing objecthood, I turned beseechingly to others. Their attention was a liberation, running over my body suddenly abraded into nonbeing, endowing me once more with an agility that I had thought lost, and by taking me out of the world, restoring me to it. But just as I reached the other side, I stumbled, and the movements, the attitudes, the glances of the other fixed me there, in the sense in which a chemical solution is fixed by a dye. I was indignant; I demanded an explanation. Nothing happened. I burst apart. Now the fragments have been put together again by another self.

As long as the black man is among his own, he will have no occasion, except in minor internal conflicts, to experience his being through others. There is of course the moment of "being for others," of which Hegel speaks, but every ontology is made unattainable in a colonized and civilized society. It would seem that this fact has not been given sufficient attention by those who have discussed the question. In the *Weltanschauung* of a colonized people there is an impurity, a flaw that outlaws any ontological explanation. Someone may object that this is the case with every individual, but such an objection merely conceals a basic problem. Ontology — once it is finally admitted as leaving existence by the wayside — does not permit us to understand the being of the black man. For not only must the black man be black; he must be black in relation to the white man. Some critics will take it on themselves to remind us that this proposition has a converse. I say that this is false. The black man has no ontological resistance in the eyes of the white man. Overnight the Negro has been given two frames of reference within which he has had to place himself. His metaphysics, or, less pretentiously, his customs and the sources on which they were based, were wiped out because they were in conflict with a civilization that he did not know and that imposed itself on him.

The black man among his own in the twentieth century does not know at what moment his inferiority comes into being through the other. Of course I have talked about the black problem with friends, or, more rarely, with American Negroes. Together we protested, we asserted the equality of all men in the world. In the Antilles there was also that little gulf that exists among the almost-white, the mulatto, and the nigger. But I was satisfied with an intellectual understanding of these differences. It was not really dramatic. And then . . .

And then the occasion arose when I had to meet the white man's eyes. An unfamiliar weight burdened me. The real world challenged my claims. In the white world the man of color encounters difficulties in the development of his bodily schema. Consciousness of the body is solely a negating activity. It is a third-person consciousness. The body is surrounded by an atmosphere of certain uncertainty. I know that if I want to smoke, I shall have to reach out my right arm and take the pack of cigarettes lying at the other end of the table. The matches, however, are in the drawer on the left, and I shall have to lean back slightly. And all these movements are made not out of habit but out of implicit knowledge. A slow composition of my *self* as a body in the middle of a spatial and temporal world – such seems to be the schema. It does not impose itself on me; it is, rather, a definitive structuring of the self and of the world – definitive because it creates a real dialectic between my body and the world.

For several years certain laboratories have been trying to produce a serum for "denegrification"; with all the earnestness in the world, laboratories have sterilized their test tubes, checked their scales, and embarked on researches that might make it possible for the miserable Negro to whiten himself and thus to throw off the burden of that corporeal malediction. Below the corporeal scheme I had sketched a historico-racial schema. The elements that I used had been provided for me not by "residual sensations and perceptions primarily of a tactile, vestibular, kinesthetic, and visual character,"[1] but by the other, the white man, who had woven me out of a thousand details, anecdotes, stories. I thought that what I had in hand was to construct a physiological self, to balance space, to localize sensations, and here I was called on for more.

"Look, a Negro!" It was an external stimulus that flicked over me as I passed by. I made a tight smile.

"Look, a Negro!" It was true. It amused me.

"Look, a Negro!" The circle was drawing a bit tighter. I made no secret of my amusement.

"Mama, see the Negro! I'm frightened!" Frightened! Frightened!" Now they were beginning to be afraid of me. I made up my mind to laugh myself to tears, but laughter had become impossible.

I could no longer laugh, because I already knew that there were legends, stories, history, and above all *historicity*, which I had learned about from Jaspers. Then, assailed at various points, the corporeal schema crumbled, its place taken by a racial epidermal schema. In the train it was no longer a question of being aware of my body in the third person but in a triple person. In the train I was given not one but two, three places. I had already stopped being amused. It was not that I was finding febrile coordinates in the world. I existed triply: I occupied space. I moved toward the other . . . and the evanescent other, hostile but not opaque, transparent, not there, disappeared. Nausea. . . .

I was responsible at the same time for my body, for my race, for my ancestors. I discovered my blackness, my ethnic characteristics; and I was battered down by tom-toms, cannibalism, intellectual deficiency, fetichism, racial defects, slaveships, and above all else, above all: "Sho' good eatin'."

On that day, completely dislocated, unable to be abroad with the other, the white man, who unmercifully imprisoned me, I took myself far off from my own presence, far indeed, and made myself an object. What else could it be for me but an amputation, an excision, a hemorrhage that spattered my whole body with black blood? But I did not want this revision, this thematization. All I wanted was to be a man among other men. I wanted to come lithe and young into a world that was ours and to help to build it together.

But I rejected all immunization of the emotions. I wanted to be a man, nothing but a man. Some identified me with ancestors of mine who had been enslaved or lynched: I decided to accept this. It was on the universal level of the intellect that I understood this inner kinship – I was the grandson of slaves in exactly the same way in which President Lebrun was the grandson of tax-paying, hard-working peasants. In the main, the panic soon vanished.

In America, Negroes are segregated. In South America, Negroes are whipped in the streets, and Negro strikers are cut down by machine-guns. In West Africa, the Negro is an animal. And there beside me, my neighbor in the university, who was born in Algeria, told me: "As long as the Arab is treated like a man, no solution is possible."

"Understand, my dear boy, color prejudice is something I find utterly foreign. . . . But of course, come in, sir, there is no color prejudice among us. . . . Quite, the Negro is a man like ourselves. . . . It is not because he is black that he is less intelligent than we are. . . . I had a Senegalese buddy in the army who was really clever. . . ."

Where am I to be classified? Or if you prefer, tucked away?

"A Martinican, a native of 'our' old colonies."

Where shall I hide?

"Look at the nigger! . . . Mama, a Negro! . . . Hell, he's getting mad. . . . Take no notice, sir, he does not know that you are as civilized as we. . . ."

My body was given back to me sprawled out, distorted, recolored, clad in mourning in that white winter day. The Negro is an animal, the Negro is bad, the Negro is mean, the Negro is ugly; look, a nigger, it's cold, the nigger is shivering, the nigger is shivering because he is cold, the little boy is trembling because he is afraid of the nigger, the nigger is shivering with cold, that cold that goes through your bones, the handsome little boy is trembling because he thinks that the nigger is quivering with rage, the little white boy throws himself into his mother's arms: Mama, the nigger's going to eat me up.

All round me the white man, above the sky tears at its navel, the earth rasps under my feet, and there is a white song, a white song. All this whiteness that burns me. . . .

I,sit down at the fire and I become aware of my uniform. I had not seen it. It is indeed ugly. I stop there, for who can tell me what beauty is?

Where shall I find shelter from now on? I felt an easily identifiable flood mounting out of the countless facets of my being. I was about to be angry. The fire was long since out, and once more the nigger was trembling.

"Look how handsome that Negro is! . . ."

"Kiss the handsome Negro's ass, madame!"

Shame flooded her face. At last I was set free from my rumination. At the same time I accomplished two things: I identified my enemies and I made a scene. A grand slam. Now one would be able to laugh.

The field of battle having been marked out, I entered the lists.

What? While I was forgetting, forgiving, and wanting only to love, my message was flung back in my fact like a slap. The white world, the only honorable one, barred me from all participation. A man was expected to behave like a man. I was expected to behave like a black man — or at least like a nigger. I shouted a greeting to the world and the world slashed away my joy. I was told to stay within bounds, to go back where I belonged.

They would see, then! I had warned them, anyway. Slavery? It was no longer even mentioned, that unpleasant memory. My supposed inferiority? A hoax that it was better to laugh at. I forgot it all, but only on condition that the world not protect itself against me any longer. I had incisors to test. I was sure they were strong. And besides . . .

What! When it was I who had every reason to hate, to despise, I was rejected? When I should have been begged, implored, I was denied the slightest recognition? I resolved, since it was impossible for me to get away from an *inborn complex* to assert myself as a BLACK MAN. Since the other hesitated to recognize me, there remained only one solution: to make myself known.

In *Anti-Semite and Jew* (p. 95), Sartre says: "They [the Jews] have allowed themselves to be poisoned by the stereotype that others have of them, and they live in fear that their acts will correspond to this stereotype. . . . We may say that their conduct is perpetually overdetermined from the inside."

All the same, the Jew can be unknown in his Jewishness. He is not wholly what he is. One hopes, one waits. His actions, his behavior are the final determinant. He is a white man, and, apart from some rather debatable characteristics, he can sometimes go unnoticed. He belongs to the race of those who since the beginning of time have never known cannibalism. What an idea, to eat one's father! Simple enough, one has only not to be a nigger. Granted, the Jews are harassed — what am I thinking of? They are hunted down, exterminated, cremated. But these are little family quarrels. The Jew is disliked from the moment he is tracked down. But in my case everything takes on a *new* guise. I am given no chance. I am overdetermined from without. I am the slave not of the "idea" that others have of me but of my own appearance.

I move slowly in the world, accustomed now to seek no longer for upheaval. I progress by crawling. And already I am being dissected under white eyes, the only real eyes. I am *fixed*. Having adjusted their microtomes, they objectively cut away slices of my reality. I am laid bare. I feel, I see in those white faces that it is not a new man who has come in, but a new kind of man, a new genus. Why it's a Negro!

I slip into corners, and my long antennae pick up the catch-phrases strewn over the surface of things – nigger underwear smells of nigger – nigger teeth are white – nigger feet are big – the nigger's barrel chest – I slip into corners, I remain silent, I strive for anonymity, for invisibility. Look, I will accept the lot, as long as no one notices me!

"Oh, I want you to meet my black friend. . . . Aimé Césaire, a black man and a university graduate. . . . Marian Anderson, the finest of Negro singers. . . . Dr. Cobb, who invented white blood, is a Negro. . . . Here, say hello to my friend from Martinique (be careful, he's extremely sensitive). . . ."

Shame, Shame and self-contempt. Nausea. When people like me, they tell me it is in spite of my color. When they dislike me, they point out that it is not because of my color. Either way, I am locked into the infernal circle.

I turn away from these inspectors of the Ark before the Flood and I attach myself to my brothers, Negroes like myself. To my horror, they too reject me. They are almost white. And besides they are about to marry white women. They will have children faintly tinged with brown. Who knows, perhaps little by little. . . .

I had been dreaming.

"I want you to understand, sir, I am one of the best friends the Negro has in Lyon."

The evidence was there, unalterable. My blackness was there, dark and unarguable. And it tormented me, pursued me, disturbed me, angered me.

Negroes are savages, brutes, illiterates. But in my own case I knew that these statements were false. There was a myth of the Negro that had to be destroyed at all costs. The time had long since passed when a Negro priest was an occasion for wonder. We had physicians, professors, statesmen. Yes, but something out of the ordinary still clung to such cases. "We have a Senegalese history teacher. He is quite bright. . . . Our doctor is colored. He is very gentle."

It was always the Negro teacher, the Negro doctor; brittle as I was becoming, I shivered at the slightest pretext. I knew, for instance, that if the physician made a mistake it would be the end of him and of all those who came after him. What could one expect, after all, from a Negro physician? As long as everything went well, he was praised to the skies, but look out, no nonsense, under any conditions! The black physician can never be sure how close he is to disgrace. I tell you, I was walled in: No exception was made for my refined manners, or my knowledge of literature, or my understanding of the quantum theory.

I requested, I demanded explanations. Gently, in the tone that one uses with a child, they introduced me to the existence of a certain view that was held by certain people, but, I was always told, "We must hope that it will very soon disappear." What was it? Color prejudice.

It [colour prejudice] is nothing more than the unreasoning hatred of
one race for another, the contempt of the stronger and richer peoples

for those whom they consider inferior to themselves, and the bitter resentment of those who are kept in subjection and are so frequently insulted. As colour is the most obvious outward manifestation of race it has been made the criterion by which men are judged, irrespective of their social or educational attainments. The light-skinned races have come to despise all those of a darker colour, and the dark-skinned peoples will no longer accept without protest the inferior position to which they have been relegated.[2]

I had read it rightly. It was hate; I was hated, despised, detested, not by the neighbor across the street or my cousin on my mother's side, but by an entire race. I was up against something unreasoned. The psychoanalysts say that nothing is more traumatizing for the young child than his encounters with what is rational. I would personally say that for a man whose only weapon is reason there is nothing more neurotic than contact with unreason.

I felt knife blades open within me. I resolved to defend myself. As a good tactician, I intended to rationalize the world and to show the white man that he was mistaken.

In the Jew, Jean-Paul Sartre says, there is

> a sort of impassioned imperialism of reason: for he wishes not only to convince others that he is right; his goal is to persuade them that there is an absolute and unconditioned value to rationalism. He feels himself to be a missionary of the universal; against the universality of the Catholic religion, from which he is excluded, he asserts the "catholicity" of the rational, an instrument by which to attain to the truth and establish a spiritual bond among men.[3]

And, the author adds, though there may be Jews who have made intuition the basic category of their philosophy, their intuition

> has no resemblance to the Pascalian subtlety of spirit, and it is this latter – based on a thousand imperceptible perceptions – which to the Jew seems his worst enemy. As for Bergson, his philosophy offers the curious appearance of an anti-intellectualist doctrine constructed entirely by the most rational and most critical of intelligences. It is through argument that he establishes the existence of pure duration, of philosophic intuition; and that very intuition which discovers duration or life, is itself universal, since anyone may practice it, and it leads towards the universal, since its objects can be named and conceived.[4]

With enthusiasm I set to cataloguing and probing my surroundings. As times changed, one had seen the Catholic religion at first justify and then condemn slavery and prejudices. But by referring everything to the idea of the dignity of man, one had ripped prejudice to shreds. After much reluctance, the scientists had conceded that the Negro was a human being; *in vivo* and *in vitro* the Negro had been proved analogous to the white man: the same morphology, the same histology. Reason was confident of victory on every level. I put all the parts back together. But I had to change my tune.

That victory played cat and mouse; it made a fool of me. As the other put it, when I was present, it was not; when it was there, I was no longer. In the abstract there was agreement: The Negro is a human being. That is to say, amended the less firmly convinced, that like us he has his heart on the left side. But on certain points the white man remained intractable. Under no conditions did he wish any intimacy between the races, for it is a truism that "crossings between widely different races can lower the physical and mental level. . . . Until we have a more definite knowledge of the effect of race-crossings we shall certainly do best to avoid crossings between widely different races."[5]

For my own part, I would certainly know how to react. And in one sense, if I were asked for a definition of myself, I would say that I am one who waits; I investigate my surroundings, I interpret everything in terms of what I discover, I become sensitive.

In the first chapter of the history that the others have compiled for me, the foundation of cannibalism has been made eminently plain in order that I may not lose sight of it. My chromosomes were supposed to have a few thicker or thinner genes representing cannibalism. In addition to the *sex-linked*, the scholars had now discovered the *racial-linked*.[6] What a shameful science!

But I understand this "psychological mechanism." For it is a matter of common knowledge that the mechanism is only psychological. Two centuries ago I was lost to humanity, I was a slave forever. And then came men who said that it all had gone on far too long. My tenaciousness did the rest; I was saved from the civilizing deluge. I have gone forward.

Too late. Everything is anticipated, thought out, demonstrated, made the most of. My trembling hands take hold of nothing; the vein has been mined out. Too late! But once again I want to understand.

Since the time when someone first mourned the fact that he had arrived too late and everything had been said, a nostalgia for the past has seemed to persist. Is this that lost original paradise of which Otto Rank speaks? How many such men, apparently rooted to the womb of the world, have devoted their lives to studying the Delphic oracles or exhausted themselves in attempts to plot the wanderings of Ulysses! The pan-spiritualists seek to prove the existence of a soul in animals by using this argument: A dog lies down on the grave of his master and starves to death there. We had to wait for Janet to demonstrate that the aforesaid dog, in contrast to man, simply lacked the capacity to liquidate the past. We speak of the glory of Greece, Artaud says; but, he adds, if modern man can no longer understand the *Choephoroi* of Aeschylus, it is Aeschylus who is to blame. It is tradition to which the anti-Semites turn in order to ground the validity of their "point of view." It is tradition, it is that long historical past, it is that blood relation between Pascal and Descartes, that is invoked when the Jew is told, "There is no possibility of your finding a place in society." Not long ago, one of those good Frenchmen said in a train where I was sitting: "Just let the real French virtues keep going and the race is safe. Now more than ever, national union must be made a reality. Let's have an end of internal strife! Let's face up to the foreigners (here he turned toward my corner) no matter who they are."

It must be said in his defense that he stank of cheap wine; if he had been capable of it, he would have told me that my emancipated-slave blood could not possibly be stirred by the name of Villon or Taine.

An outrage!

The Jew and I: Since I was not satisfied to be racialized, by a lucky turn of fate I was humanized. I joined the Jew, my brother in misery.

An outrage!

At first thought it may seem strange that the anti-Semite's outlook should be related to that of the Negro-phobe. It was my philosophy professor, a native of the Antilles, who recalled the fact to me one day: "Whenever you hear anyone abuse the Jews, pay attention, because he is talking about you." And I found that he was universally right – by which I meant that I was answerable in my body and in my heart for what was done to my brother. Later I realized that he meant, quite simply, an anti-Semite is inevitably anti-Negro.

[. . .] From time to time one would like to stop. To state reality is a wearing task. But, when one has taken it into one's head to try to express existence, one runs the risk of finding only the nonexistent. What is certain is that, at the very moment when I was trying to grasp my own being, Sartre, who remained The Other, gave me a name and thus shattered my last illusion. While I was saying to him:

> "My negritude is neither a tower nor a cathedral,
> it thrusts into the red flesh of the sun,
> it thrusts into the burning flesh of the sky,
> it hollows through the dense dismay of its own pillar of patience . . ."

while I was shouting that, in the paroxysm of my being and my fury, he was reminding me that my blackness was only a minor term. In all truth, in all truth I tell you, my shoulders slipped out of the framework of the world, my feet could no longer feel the touch of the ground. Without a Negro past, without a Negro future, it was impossible for me to live my Negrohood. Not yet white, no longer wholly black, I was damned. Jean-Paul Sartre had forgotten that the Negro suffers in his body quite differently from the white man.[7] Between the white man and me the connection was irrevocably one of transcendence.[8]

But the constancy of my love had been forgotten. I defined myself as an absolute intensity of beginning. So I took up my negritude, and with tears in my eyes I put its machinery together again. What had been broken to pieces was rebuilt, reconstructed by the intuitive lianas of my hands.

My cry grew more violent: I am a Negro, I am a Negro, I am a Negro. . . .

And there was my poor brother – living out his neurosis to the extreme and finding himself paralyzed:

THE NEGRO: I can't, ma'am.
LIZZIE: Why not?
THE NEGRO: I can't shoot white folks.
LIZZIE: Really! That would bother them, wouldn't it?
THE NEGRO: They're white folks, ma'am.

LIZZIE: So what? Maybe they got a right to bleed you like a pig just because they're white?

THE NEGRO: But they're white folks.

A feeling of inferiority? No, a feeling of nonexistence. Sin is Negro as virtue is white. All those white men in a group, guns in their hands, cannot be wrong. I am guilty. I do not know of what, but I know that I am no good.

THE NEGRO: That's how it goes, ma'am. That's how it always goes with white folks.

LIZZIE: You too? You feel guilty?

THE NEGRO: Yes, ma'am.[9]

It is Bigger Thomas – he is afraid, he is terribly afraid. He is afraid, but of what is he afraid? Of himself. No one knows yet who he is, but he knows that fear will fill the world when the world finds out. And when the world knows, the world always expects something of the Negro. He is afraid lest the world know, he is afraid of the fear that the world would feel if the world knew. Like that old woman on her knees who begged me to tie her to her bed:

"I just know, Doctor: Any minute that thing will take hold of me."

"What thing?"

"The wanting to kill myself. Tie me down, I'm afraid."

In the end, Bigger Thomas acts. To put an end to his tension, he acts, he responds to the world's anticipation.[10]

So it is with the character in *If He Hollers Let Him Go* – who does precisely what he did not want to do. That big blonde who was always in his way, weak, sensual, offered, open, fearing (desiring) rape, became his mistress in the end.

The Negro is a toy in the white man's hands; so, in order to shatter the hellish cycle, he explodes. I cannot go to a film without seeing myself. I wait for me. In the interval, just before the film starts, I wait for me. The people in the theater are watching me, examining me, waiting for me. A Negro groom is going to appear. My heart makes my head swim.

The crippled veteran of the Pacific war says to my brother, "Resign yourself to your color the way I got used to my stump; we're both victims."[12]

Nevertheless with all my strength I refuse to accept that amputation. I feel in myself a soul as immense as the world, truly a soul as deep as the deepest of rivers, my chest has the power to expand without limit. I am a master and I am advised to adopt the humility of the cripple. Yesterday, awakening to the world, I saw the sky turn upon itself utterly and wholly. I wanted to rise, but the disemboweled silence fell back upon me, its wings paralyzed. Without responsibility, straddling Nothingness and Infinity, I began to weep.

Notes

1   Jean Lhermitte, *L'Image de notre corps* (Paris, Nouvelle Revue critique, 1939), p. 17.
2   Sir Alan Burns, *Colour Prejudice* (London, Allen and Unwin, 1948), p. 16.
3   *Anti-Semite and Jew* (New York, Grove Press, 1960), pp. 112–13.
4   Ibid., p. 115.
5   Jon Alfred Mjoen, "Harmonic and Disharmonic Race-crossings," The Second International Congress of Eugenics (1921), *Eugenics in Race and State*, vol. II, p. 60, quoted in Sir Alan Burns, *op. cit.*, p. 120.
6   In English in the original. (Translator's note.)
7   Though Sartre's speculations on the existence of The Other may be correct (to the extent, we must remember, to which *Being and Nothingness* describes an alienated consciousness), their application to a black consciousness proves fallacious. That is because the white man is not only The Other but also the master, whether real or imaginary.
8   In the sense in which the word is used by Jean Wahl in *Existence humaine et transcendance*) (Neuchâtel, La Baconnière, 1944).
9   Jean-Paul Sartre, *The Respectful Prostitute*, in *Three Plays* (New York, Knopf, 1949), pp. 189, 191. Originally, *La Putain respectueuse* (Paris, Gallimard, 1947). See also *Home of the Brave,* a film by Mark Robson.
10   Richard Wright, *Native Son* (New York, Harper, 1940).
11   By Chester Himes (Garden City, Doubleday, 1945).
12   *Home of the Brave.*

Chapter 20

Lola Young

IMPERIAL CULTURE
The primitive, the savage and white civilization[1]

[. . .]

IN THIS CHAPTER I WILL examine how racialized discourses manifested themselves in texts, in terms of ideologies of superiority and inferiority
and where they connected with beliefs about femininity and masculinity, and sexuality. Critical analyses of orientalist, colonialist and primitivist discourses will be
considered in terms of their applicability to imperialist texts. I will analyse specific
representations of Otherness in some literary instances of the late nineteenth
century, suggesting how these images were subsequently consolidated and constituted in the cinema.

This chapter marks the beginning of the analysis of specific films which are
of interest because of the ways in which they engage with racial and sexual issues. I
am not concerned here with films that have an aggressive imperialist vision since in
many respects these tend to be less interesting in terms of tensions and contradictions within the text. The British archetype of this kind of jingoistic, compulsively
xenophobic film is probably *Sanders of the River* (1935). Films such as *The Song of
Freedom* (1936) and *Men of Two Worlds* (1946) are more engrossing as they slide
between an aggressive objectification of black African subjects, marking them as an
ignorant, 'primitive' undifferentiated mass, and an acknowledgement that specific
individuals can be redeemed by being properly schooled in the moral and cultural
values of western Europe. Another point of interest is that both *The Song of Freedom*
and *Men of Two Worlds* show the black protagonists living and working in England at
some stage and it is possible to see their interaction with white English people in
terms of class as well as 'race'. In *Sanders of the River* (1935), *Rhodes of Africa* (1936)
and other similar dramas, all the 'natives' are safely contained in Africa and the
virtues of colonialism unequivocally extolled. Another reason for including *The Song
of Freedom* and for devoting a chapter to imperialism and British cinema is that

doing so provides a context for the discussions in later chapters about the kinds of representations against which black film-makers in particular have reacted. [. . .]

Analysing colonial discourse

There have been a number of critiques of the discourses of Orientalism, primitivism and colonialism which have been helpful in identifying the role of ideology and discourse in the constitution of the colonized Other. A persistent critic of the way in which 'knowledge' and western European supremacist ideologies have constructed the Other and informed European culture, has been Edward Said (Said, 1985 and 1993). Although specifically referring to the way in which the notion of the Orient is a product of the western European imperial imagination, Said's theses in *Orientalism* can be usefully extended to a discussion of the way in which other cultures have been figured, although it is also necessary to bear in mind the specificities of the particular examples being discussed (Said, 1985). Said analyses Orientalism as an attempt to contain and control the Otherness of the Orient.

Said refers to a discourse of Orientalism, a set of terms, ideas and ways of constructing and thinking about the subject. Orientalism may be seen as preparing the way for colonialism discursively, ideologically and rhetorically. Both Orientalism and colonialism denied subject peoples'. human agency and resistance and constructed explanatory models to account for the alterity of those subjects.

Similarly, much literary production during the late nineteenth century is replete with examples of 'knowledge' about the character of Africans based on white supremacist attitudes towards 'race'. In particular the notion of atavism – the belief that the 'primitive' people of Africa constituted an earlier stage of human development – often recurs: all the references to primeval swamps, to primitive rituals, the colonial subjects' perceived deficiency of language, intellect and culture attest to this belief. The texts are saturated with metaphors of 'darkness' infused with the presupposition of the positive associations of whiteness, light and so on, and negative attributes of blackness, dirtiness, ignorance, evil and so on.[2] The cultural (Christian) mission was, then, to introduce 'civilization' to the 'primitive' Other. Similar tropes are evident in the films of the 1930s such as *Sanders of the River* (1935), *The Song of Freedom* (1936), *King Solomon's Mines* (1937), *The Drum* (1938) and *The Four Feathers* (1939), and indeed, later in *Men of Two Worlds* (1947) and *Simba* (1955).

Marianna Torgovnick uses the idea of primitivism to identify and explicate a primitivist discourse in which the judgements of white Europeans about the intelligence, rationality and sexual practices of those deemed Other, are not acknowledged to be ideologically formed but are taken as categorical statements about the 'primitive' world (Torgovnick, 1990: 8).[3] Such convictions are abundant in the literature and cinema of imperialism. The necessity for Europeans of defining the primitive, Torgovnick argues, may be considered as an attempt to define the qualities and boundaries of white identity; an exploration of the self without problematizing the normalization of whiteness and its equation with civilization.

In specific instances, such as in the case of women, and in the case of the masses – frequently characterized as a teeming, primeval horde – some white people are attributed the qualities of 'primitiveness' thus becoming an internal Other. There are a number of instances when white women are positioned in ways analogous to the way in which black people – and working class people – are positioned albeit with variations in the woman's relative hierarchical status, and depending on her class and the degree of her heterosexual attraction. Torgovnick acknowledges this when she observes:

> gender issues always inhabit Western versions of the primitive. Sooner or later those familiar tropes for primitives become the tropes conventionally used for women. Global politics, the dance of colonizer and colonized, becomes sexual politics, the dance of male and female.
>
> (Torgovnick, 1990: 17)

Torgovnick's analysis conceptualizes these two issues – of primitivist discourse and patriarchal discourse – as parallel, linear developments and this does not allow for an analysis of the intersections and discontinuities. I argue that these discourses sometimes converge, and sometimes overlap in the cinematic examples which follow. Furthermore, in Torgovnick's examples there is little sense of the historical role of scientific and historiographical discourses in providing the 'objective proof' for the development of ideas about the relative statuses of black/white and male/female which I argue is crucial to an understanding of the potency and persistence of ideologies of racial and gender difference, and sexuality.[4]

As has been discussed [. . .], both Homi Bhabha and Edward Said in their accounts of colonialist and Orientalist discourses see the construction of stereotypes as crucial to the imperialist hegemonic project. Elaborating on Said's critique of the European 'archive' of knowledge, Bhabha asserts that colonial discourse is:

> a form of knowledge and identification that vacillates between what is always 'in place', already known, and something that must be anxiously repeated . . . as if the essential duplicity of the Asiatic or the bestial sexual licence of the African that needs no proof, can never really, in discourse, be proved.
>
> (Bhabha, 1983: 18)

The necessity for vacillation is occasioned because the discourse attempts to fix and stabilise that which is not static. The desire for scientism, exemplified in the valorization of systematic categorization based on empiricism, inevitably produces some instances which refuse to be contained by the conceptual boundaries established. In these cases either the lines of demarcation have to be re-ordered or the exceptions denied, and this is why stereotypes are protean rather than stable.

Although a good deal of what is expressed with regard to racial differences is contradictory there is 'a rigorous subconscious logic' which:

> defines the relations between the covert and overt policies and between the material and discursive practices of colonialism. The ideological functions of colonialist fiction . . . must be understood . . . in terms of the exigencies of domestic – that is, European and colonialist –

politics and culture; and the function of racial difference, of the fixation on and fetishization of native savagery and evil, must be mapped
in terms of these exigencies and ideological imperatives.

(JanMohamed, 1985: 62–63)

For this fetishization and demonization to cohere and 'make sense', there had to
be in place a systematic oppositional differentiation in *all* spheres, made between
colonizer and colonized: that such a dichotomous relationship existed was not often
challenged by the middle of the nineteenth century, even amongst those who had
opposed slavery. Once such notions enter the popular domain and hence discourse
and ideology, then they are, to all intents and purposes 'reality', since

The work of ideology is to present the position of the subject as fixed
and unchangeable, an element in a given system of differences which
is human nature and the world of human experience, and to show
possible action as an endless repetition of "normal", familiar action.

(Belsey 1980: 90)

The conventional practices of colonial/imperial cinematic realist representations
attributed fixed, inferior characteristics to black people, basing such characterizations on an archive of 'knowledge' about the African character, and, arguably, the
cumulative effect of such images was to limit informed public debate and to justify
policies regarding colonial rule. It is important to remember that the beginnings
of cinema coincided with the peak of colonial expansion towards the end of the
nineteenth and the first decades of the twentieth centuries. Imperialist growth and
policies had to be sustained and the emergent mass medium of the cinema offered
the opportunity to promote and consolidate colonial policy overseas. It should also
be noted, as Ella Shohat points out, that:

Western cinema not only inherited and disseminated colonial discourse,
but also created a system of domination through monopolistic control
of film distribution and exhibition in much of Asia, Africa, and Latin
America.

(Shohat 1991:45)

Masculine, feminine

During the peak period of colonial expansion, a number of fictional works emerged
that were fantasized depictions of Africa and its people which served as an exotic
background against which white men could act out and test the prescribed masculine qualities such as courage, tenacity and self-control. These narratives are
characterized by their vision of a robust, bourgeois, homosocial masculinity.

Newspapers, popular entertainment, postcards and comics in the first
decade of the twentieth century constantly reinforced the idea of war as glamorous, character-building and fascinating: an activity which occurred in far-off
exotic places, away from what was seen as the stifling confinement of domesticity.
These images and fantasies were inextricably linked to conceptualizations of

masculinity, and the idea of what constitutes masculinity was a key site for confrontations springing from racial conflict, since in racially stratified societies, the notion of masculinity is not only determined by its being in opposition to femininity but by its racial specificity.

Ideas about masculinity, as is the case with other socially constructed categories, are in a continual state of flux and specific to historical time and place, although this is not always recognized to be the case. Particular ideas about what constitutes 'manliness' in terms of physical and athletic prowess became dominant in the late nineteenth century through public concern about British men's physical weakness at a time of expanding imperial conquests and the demand for the defence of existing colonies (Bristow, 1991; Roper and Tosh, 1991: 19).

There was also a crisis of masculinity which arose because of the success of the bourgeois vision of domestic life. Crucial to this lifestyle was the man's duty to provide moral and religious support, and the adoption of an ideology of hard work and thrift. In the bourgeois household, the home was the domain of the economically dependent wife whilst the rough world of industrial capitalism and work was the province of the male. The home was thus associated with the feminine since that was where the woman could exercise what power she did have. The bourgeois feminine world was that of domesticity, physical weakness, emotional displays, and masculinity was the antithesis of these characteristics.

White women – both middle and working class – and black people are again both implicated here as both were characterized as being dependent on others, and as being defined only through their oppositional relationship to white middle class men.[5] Although during the nineteenth century black and working class women were expected to carry out arduous physical labour, white middle class women were assigned a position of physical delicacy and fragility and were placed on a pedestal of sexual unattainability. The idealization of white female sexual purity and the valorization of 'masculine' attributes such as courage, autonomous action and independence served to privilege the celebration of essentialized characteristics of masculinity and femininity. Whilst it is the case that white middle class women were used and abused, they also colluded in shoring up the structures of supremacy and domination, supporting both class and racial stratification [. . .]

The desire to look on and control the female body had limited acceptability in regard to white women: with the institutionalization of black people's inferior status, no such inhibitions existed in regard to the bodies of African women. [. . .] During the late eighteenth and nineteenth centuries the black female body was subjected to rigorous scientific examination and her naked body placed on public display, the vast majority of such investigatory work being carried out, of course, by white male doctors and scientists. However, even into the twentieth century, the story was different when it came to white women who wished to exercise their privileged racial status through the right to look as is made clear in the following passage from a popular magazine, *Titbits,* 21 July, 1917:

> Some years ago we used to have large bodies of natives sent from Africa
> on military service or in some travelling show, and it was a revelation

of horror and disgust to behold the manner in which English women
would flock to see these men, whilst to watch them fawning upon these
black creatures and fondling them and embracing them, as I have seen
dozens of times, was a scandal and a disgrace to English womanhood.
How then is it possible to maintain as the one stern creed in the policy
of the Empire the eternal supremacy of white over black?

(quoted in Henriques, 1974:141)

Here the links between bestiality and sexuality, the gendering of the criteria by
which sexual impropriety is judged, femininity, and the putative effects of transgressive sexual relations on the imperial project and white supremacy are decisively
articulated. [. . .]

Black femininity

[. . .] An analysis of representations of black femininity in the genre of colonial
and imperial literary adventures and their cinematic successors needs to take
account of the African women's metaphoric status which has arisen from the intersection of these discourses on gender, 'race' and sexuality.[6] The literary texts are
of note, not just because of the recurring metaphors and themes, but because
several important films of the 1930s such as *King Solomon's Mines* (1937), *The Four
Feathers* (1939) and *Sanders of the River* (1935) were based on these novels.

   In imperial literature regarding the terrain, there is much talk of 'penetration', 'conquering the interior' and so on. Africa is characterized as feminine with
all the contradictory connotations of passivity, uncontrollability, desire and danger
and indicating the extent to which colonial metaphors are gendered. An indicator
of the elision of African landscapes and the (forbidden) desire for (black) feminity
is embedded in Freud's use of the term, 'dark continent'.

> The seduction and conquest of the African woman became a metaphor
> for the conquest of Africa itself. A powerful erotic symbolism linked
> a woman's femininity so strongly to the attraction of the land that they
> became one single idea, and to both were attributed the same irre-
> sistible, deadly charm.
>
> (Nicholas Monti, quoted in Doane, 1991: 213)

The feminization of the landscape points to a fascination with, and desire for,
African women which cannot be made explicit or elaborated due to its transgressive nature: thus the desire may only be articulated through displacement. A prime
example of this figurative displacement occurs in H. Rider Haggard's novel *King
Solomon's Mines* (1885). From the perspective of the imperial 'I/eye' of his hero,
Alan Quatermain, Haggard gives a detailed description of the African landscape
which likens the mountainous panorama to a woman's breasts:

> . . . I attempt to describe that extraordinary grandeur and beauty of
> that sight, language seems to fail me. I am impotent even at its memory.

> Before us rose two enormous mountains . . . These mountains . . . are shaped after the fashion of a woman's breasts, and at times the mists and shadows beneath them take the form of a recumbent woman veiled mysteriously in sleep. Their bases swell gently from the plain, looking at that distance perfectly round and smooth; and on top of each is a vast hillock covered with snow, exactly corresponding to the nipple on the female breast.
>
> (Haggard, 1979: 56–57)

Significantly, Quatermain, white hero and narrator of the novel, on recalling the beauty of the sight of that landscape admits to being cast back into the pre-symbolic realm without language, rendered speechless and impotent 'even at its memory' (Bristow, 1991: 127). The loss of the accoutrements of civilization and culture is figured through sexual impotence: these fears are the continual fears of the oppressor. Those African 'breasts' recall the dependency of infant on mother and as a consequence, the anger experienced at being separated from her, the primary love-object, and it is the enforced recognition of difference which produces 'impotence'.

That the sight of these 'breasts', the female's visible signifiers of sexual difference and maternity. should generate such powerlessness and be effected through Africa is indicative of the anxieties being displaced onto the land and onto black women. If white men's fear of white women is based on the 'uncontrollable' sexual arousal instigated by them, then since African women have been frequently described as hypersexual and are phenotypically marked as inherently and immutably different, the anxieties instigated by sexual difference are exacerbated. In the case of both females and males, the contention that blacks are oversexed is historically linked to and 'proven' by alleged anatomical excesses in one form or another. Whether or not there was or is any empirical evidence to support or deny such beliefs is irrelevant: it is the fact that such notions were, and still are, considered meaningful, are still perpetuated either directly or indirectly, and are still the subject of many ribald jokes, that is the significant issue.

At the same time as functioning as a contrast through which the white European male could conceive of himself as fearless, active, independent, in control, virile and so on, the African woman also represented a double negation of that heroic self, being not-male, not-white. Freud's epistemology, as Shohat argues: 'assumes the (white) male as the bearer of knowledge, who can penetrate woman and text, while she, as a remote region, will let herself be explored until truth is uncovered' (Shohat, 1991: 58). The question is, the truth about whom? Through the sexualization of the feminized African landscape, lying passively on its (her) back displaying naked splendour and availability (for penetration and conquest), the white male unconscious can indulge itself in fantasizing about his assault on, his merging with the forbidden object of fascination and desire. But there is fear embedded in that desire, hence the necessity for denial.

Although black women were seen as 'not-male', neither were they seen as women in the same sense that white women were. Since slavery, African females had been seen as at once women – inasmuch as they were sexualized, reproductive and subordinate — and not-women, that is not pure, not feminine, not fragile but strong and sexually knowing and available. Thus an implicit contrast was established between white (middle class) and black women and this generated the complex set of relations under colonialism [. . .]

This in itself posed a number of problems for white men in their actual and fictional imperial adventures. Given the firmly established ideas about the inferiority of black people, it was unacceptable for white men on their travels across Africa to admit openly to engaging in interracial sexual activity. Referring to Edgar Wallace's eponymous hero, from the novel, *Sanders of the River,* Jeffrey Richards notes:

> Not surprisingly he [Sanders] is unshakeably opposed to miscegenation. When a succession of young officers become enamoured of the beautiful M'Lino he sends them home declaring: 'Monkey tricks of that sort are good enough for the Belgian Congo and for Togoland but they aren't good enough for this little strip of wilderness.'
> (Richards, 1973: 31)

Again, there is the linking of simian imagery with black people and sexual activity, and the often repeated assertion that the colonialism practised by other European powers was immoral and brutal as opposed to Britain's 'benign', paternalistic version.[7]

The European, as JanMohamed argues, has a choice when confronted with what she or he imagines as an unfathomable, alien Otherness. Hypothetically, she or he:

> has the option of responding to the Other in terms of identity or difference. If he assumes that he and the Other are essentially identical, then he would tend to ignore the significant divergences and to judge the Other according to his own cultural values. If, on the other hand, he assumes the Other is irremediably different, then he would have little incentive to adopt the viewpoint of that alterity: he would again turn to the security of his own perspective. Genuine and thorough comprehension of Otherness is possible only if the self can somehow negate or at least severely bracket the values, assumptions, and ideology of his culture.
> (JanMohamed, 1985: 64–65)

First though, white people have to recognize the 'values, assumptions and ideology' and to acknowledge the extent to which Otherness is a construction arising from those assumptions and beliefs. JanMohamed's argument is here locked into its own binarism, as he posits two alternatives and imputes a stability and cohesion in colonial and primitivist discourses which is illusory as has been argued by Homi Bhabha. Neither is it clear just what constitutes a significant difference or how singular a cultural perspective might be. Nonetheless, such an analysis recognizes the contradictions inherent in the colonialists' hazardous psychic positioning. Violation of the Other, whether literally, metaphorically, or representationally, must of necessity also be an act of cultural masochism since the Other is necessarily a part of the self constructed in and through difference.

> This establishment of the other *as* other is promoted by the initial drive to establish self-identity by identifying *with* the other. Negating others, *denigrating* them, becomes in part, thus, also self-negation and self-effacement.
>
> (Goldberg, 1993: 60)

This assertion regarding self-effacement should not be understood as a relinquishing of power, rather it comes as a result of possessing and naturalizing relations of power.

As the embodiment of an 'archive' of fantasies, 'primitives', 'orientals' and colonized black people have been expected to behave in particular ways and obliged to occupy particular positions in films. The power to define the Other – a power derived from economic and political dominance – is clearly demonstrated in the construction of the colonial subject represented in the literature and cinema of Empire: African men were at once feared and admired, being the objects of feelings of repulsion and veneration. White masculine cultural superiority is signified through the comparisons of weaponry (the 'savage' with the spear versus the gentleman with the revolver being a contest of phallic symbols), intelligence and courage. In these texts white masculinity is constantly revered, femininity excluded and derided and racism is naturalized.

The ambivalence that was structured into the consciousness of so many fictional adventurer heroes in Africa during that period finds expression in the recognition of the Africans' 'beauty' and the incongruity of their 'evil'. Rarely are Africans portrayed as individuated human beings. The primitive, homogeneous mass is emblematic of the Manichean confrontation between Self and Other; a scene often re-enacted in the cinema and literature of Empire.[8]

The testing of white masculinity was explicitly represented through combat with the savage Other: more covertly (though there are exceptions to which I will refer later) white masculinity was concerned with establishing white male virility within a heterosexual context, and the feminine metaphors used to describe Africa, including the controlling trope of the 'dark continent' itself indicate the repression of the feminine. Part of the explanation for the repression of the sexual element lies with the fact that:

> the whole genre bears the distinct imprint of the public school. The virtues and characteristics of the Imperial archetype are the virtues and characteristics bred into him by his public school. The male camaraderie and the subordinate role of women reflects the all-male environment of the public schools.
>
> (Richards, 1973: 220)

It would seem that the flight from the feminine and the domestic must be absolute: and with white women absent, homosexuality unspeakable and interracial heterosexual relations unthinkable, what is the white male hero to do in terms of sexual expression but circumscribe the field of sexual activity and sublimate sexual thoughts?

The cinema of empire

During the late 1920s, Britain's Colonial Office decided to exploit the propaganda qualities of film as it set out to explore how best to capitalize on cinema's potential for disseminating imperial ideology. By the 1920s North American cinema was already dominant. There was concern that some of the images of white people could be interpreted as deriding European or British culture and that steps should be taken to counter this. For example, the films of Charlie Chaplin were immensely popular but much of his work involved the humiliation of respectable male figures, men of authority and propriety such as clergymen and policemen, and eventually such texts were censored for screenings in the colonies (Smyth 1983: 129–143). In the USA during the 1920s the Hays Office codes ensured sexual propriety by establishing a code of conduct for film-makers which severely limited, in particular, the sexual content of films. The North American Production Code of the Motion Picture Producers and Directors of America, Inc. (1930–1934) made its policy on the representation of interracial sex explicit: 'Miscegenation (sex relation between the white and black races) is forbidden' (quoted in Shohat, 1991: 66). Also subject to censorship were any representations of white women behaving seductively (Smyth, 1983). In Kenya and Rhodesia (now Zimbabwe) where there were substantial white populations, viewing was racially segregated and censorship practised until at least the late 1940s according to whether the black population or white people were the intended audience.[9]

Although there were significant numbers of black people in Britain during the early part of the twentieth century, in the 1930s Otherness was almost always located 'out there' geographically, in adventure films such as *King Solomon's Mines* (1937), *The Drum* (1938) and *The Four Feathers* (1939). Africa was still conceptualized as belonging to prehistory, its peoples supposedly uncivilized.

In colonialist adventure films and literature, it is often the case that Africa's primeval existence is figured through the lush vegetative landscape, and edenic vistas. The strange animals and the strange people are seen as one entity, one powerful evocation of an exoticism impossible to find within the confines of Europe. However, although the primitive and the exotic were depicted as being in a location far removed from Britain, the texts in the imperial adventure genre served to confirm white European notions of cultural superiority and are thus, essentially parochial and introspective, telling us about how whiteness imagined itself rather than about these Other cultures.

An illustration of this 'speaking of self' in the guise of discussing the Other occurred when European men encountered tribal kinship structures based on polyandry and polygyny: they viewed these familial practices as expressions of an allegedly excessive black sexuality which was to be both tamed and exploited.

That such polygamous practices exemplified a supposed black male sexual potency which was both feared and envied is still evidenced in *Sanders of the River*

(1935), where 'Sandy the strong, Sandy the wise' (Leslie Banks) dissuades ten young 'African' women who all wish to marry Bosambo (Paul Robeson in a revealing animal print loincloth) by proclaiming that Bosambo is already married to five older women, stronger than any of them. In fact Bosambo is not married to anyone but Sanders' role at this point is to actively control the potential reproduction of his favourite 'native' – an ex-convict – by introducing him to the concept of a monogamous heterosexual relationship. [. . .]

Different worlds

It would be misleading to suggest that Britain's hegemonic colonial practices met with or maintained uniform success or to assume that all black African opposition was located in Africa. Although the black population of Britain was still relatively small during the 1930s, there were a number of politically active people who saw the issue of black equality in this country as inextricable from questions of colonial policy. This activity led to the establishment of a number of organizations opposed to colonialism and racism. Pan-African sentiment grew whilst white people's participation in these political struggles was increasingly felt to be unacceptable: building on the connections between people of the African diaspora was considered to be the most effective way of organizing campaigns against oppression. Barbara Bush has noted that:

> In their efforts to improve race relations white liberals worked from a middle-class perspective, and thus to them "racial equality" usually implied equality for cultured, Europeanized blacks such as Paul Robeson and Harold Moody.
>
> (Bush, 1981: 47)

Paul Robeson is a complex figure in terms of what he signified for both black and white audiences, and he did what he could to challenge supremacist ideologies in the film industry and wider society. He had the advantages of being both articulate and clever, and conforming to the conventional role of black male as performer and sporting personality, and – in the British context – of being from the USA.[11] African–American actors have often been preferred over British-based black people in a number of British films, a practice which still goes on today and which signals a degree of exoticism attributed to the black Other from 'elsewhere' which accrues in a limited way to the black Other within.[12]

Paul Robeson starred in *The Song of Freedom* (1936) with Elizabeth Welch, another African–American singer who lived in Britain. The film's opening sequence, beginning as it does with a mass of running, clamouring, African 'natives' – whose threatening, uncivilized demeanour is diminished by the angle of the shot which sees them running away from the camera – immediately draws the audience into the perspective of the explorer seeking to discover the Otherness of Africa. The legend, 'AFRICA' appears as the scene dissolves into a classic mountain/sea/landscape shot of a tropical island. Again, a caption appears in order to anchor the meaning of the visuals: 'The island of Casanga, off the west coast – in the year

1700 AD. The island had not yet attracted the attention of the slave traders on the mainland' we are told but 'its people suffered as fierce an oppression under their hereditary Queen Zinga – tyrant, despot, mistress of cruelty.' This last phrase may be indicative of a disaffection with female heads of state and matrilinearity and is significant if only because so few of the films set in Africa feature autonomous women. However to claim Queen Zinga as a powerful woman is to ignore the derisory treatment her character is given and the sadistic overtones of her 'mistress of cruelty' label.

Queen Zinga is played as a woman with a face fixed in a grimace, matted hair and an oiled body indicating a perpetual sweatiness. Zinga – wearing animal pelts, shells and beads – is flanked by further representations of primitiveness: tribal iconography consisting of archetypal primitive 'African' statues and two men whose bodies merge with the statues. In the face of the violent irrational matriarch, the men are reduced to ciphers. Zinga's men are passive male bodies, echoing the stance of the statues through both their physical positions and the way that they hold their shields. The interplay here between sexual and racial difference is marked. There is an appeal to white patriarchy: note that women who rule are insane megalomaniacs and to wield power is unnatural for them. Power strips women of their femininity – Zinga's gender is initially ambiguous – and men under matriarchy lack dignity, losing their ability to act autonomously.

This early sequence introduces us to a mad, cruel primitive African woman who is the opposite of most cinematic images of white femininity. In relation to her physical appearance and demeanour, the white male audience is interpellated as superior through their rationality, their intellect and the physical attraction of 'their' women. The primitivization of Zinga does not invite white women to identify with her or to be identified with her.

The process of cinematic identification of viewing subjects with characters and situations in the film is, however, a complex one and it should be acknowledged that identity may be characterized as fragmented with only an illusory coherence (Ellis, 1988: 43). It is not possible to assert that black people always or exclusively identify with black characters, although one can posit that black audiences viewing this type of film may experience a range of feelings which might vary according to context.

Fanon felt that, through representation:

> The Negro is a toy in the white man's hands . . . I cannot go to a film without seeing myself. I wait for me. In the interval, just before the film starts, I wait for me. The people in the theater are watching me, examining me, waiting for me.
>
> (Fanon, 1986: 140)

He then painfully reconstructs the sense of embarrassment and internalized self hatred which may entrap the black viewer of such texts: a viewer fixed by the gaze of the film-maker and white members of the audience. Fanon is explicit about the different effects that films such as *Tarzan* may have on black people, depending on the viewing context:

> In the Antilles, the young Negro identifies himself *de facto* with Tarzan
> against the Negroes. This is much more difficult for him in a European
> theater, for the rest of the audience, which is white, automatically iden-
> tifies him with the savages on the screen.
>
> (Fanon, 1986: 152–153)

Paul Robeson is close to the 'noble savage' archetype in *The Song of Freedom*. His popularity as a singer is extensively brought into play in the film. His ability to sing is naturalized, reiterating the notion that all black people are able to sing spontaneously, without training: this 'natural' ability is then used as a crucial marker for his racially defined and differentiated subjectivity. John Zinga/Paul Robeson is both a 'natural' singer and a natural worker – he is, in this narrative, after all, of royal descent and thus not so feckless and unreliable as the average black male. Perhaps this royal lineage is intended to account for his resilience, as, in spite of being conceived during the Middle Passage, into slavery – which according to the film was not an unpleasant experience – Zinga manages to make his way to England.

Zinga's naturalness is contrasted with the white upper class people who disembark from the ship in the docks where he is employed: they are remote from the world of physical labour which is going on around them. One of these passengers is an opera director, Gabriel Donozetti; his status as a foreign Other, albeit 'white' is established through his feminization: that is to say that arm and hand movements associated with 'feminine' gestures are deployed to signify both his exoticism and his distance from the experience of manual labour. Donozetti is a purveyor of opera, the exemplary cultural form of the privileged classes.

Part of what is interesting about this film is the fact that John Zinga's class allegiance is to the dockers with whom he works. The narrative posits a somewhat utopian vision of racial harmony in England where racism is clearly not an issue but where divisions based on social class are immutable and natural. 'Race' does, however, intrude on this cosy scenario on an unconscious level. For example, Zinga's nobility and royal lineage serve to make him only on a par with white workers, rather than according him the privileges of upper middle class English society. His entrée into the upper echelons of English society is made possible by his voice rather than by his birth and is strictly limited.

African–American film historian Donald Bogle describes John and Ruth Zinga as living 'a rather arch domestic life . . . who together are almost too wholesome and bourgeois to be true' (Bogle, 1988: 197). In her gingham dress the character of Ruth certainly looks as though she is designed to fit in with the minimum of visual disruption but their social status is rather that of the respectable, socially aspirant working class rather than the middle class.

John Zinga yearns to travel to Africa, even though he has no idea of his ancestry and it is posited that such a yearning is inbred. Richard Dyer suggests that this aspect of Robeson's characterization which surfaces in his other films too, may be an unconscious expression of the problematic relationship between African–Americans and Africa.[13] I think it has as much to do with white people's (sometimes unconscious) desire to see Africans returned to their 'natural' habitat; that is, Africa. The fact of black people being out of place here is emphasized by their isolation and the focus on their discomfiture in white English society.

Bogle's short commentary on *The Song of Freedom* is not able to be developed due to the encyclopedic nature of his book: it is beyond the scope of his work to attempt to account for some of the more interesting and contradictory aspects of the text. For example in the first domestic scene we see, John Zinga looks longingly at a poster depicting an 'African' landscape. This poster is in a pivotal location above the fireplace and the association here between home–hearth–heart is made clear as it becomes the focus of the audience's gaze, of Ruth's gaze and, of course, of Zinga's gaze. The caption on the poster encourages the reader to 'Go where there's sunshine! Christmas and New Year tours to South Africa': standing in front of this image is the ubiquitous archetypal African statue. The juxtaposition of these divergent representations of Africanness potentially establish a tension between the Zingas' English working-class lifestyle and what are held to be their cultural and racial origins. Ruth mildly castigates John for his desire to be in Africa by interrupting his fantasies with 'you're happy here: the people are kind' to which John responds with 'oh they're grand people . . . somewhere down there are *our* people Ruth and I've got a feeling they're grand people too. The people we belong to. Funny . . . that [white] fellow didn't want to go . . . natural – he's leaving his people to go out among strangers: he'll be out of place – lonely maybe. However hard I try, I always feel the same here.' Thus John Zinga makes explicit the 'unnaturalness' of black people in England whilst pointing to the reluctance of the white traveller as confirmation of the notion that people should remain with 'their own people'. It does not appear to matter how friendly or decent the host society is, these attempts at crossing the racial divide are bound to fail. Why Zinga should aspire to travel to South Africa is not established. It seems that the poster might be appropriate in a white working class home where South Africa would represent an opportunity to improve their social standing, and perhaps it is there in order to indicate the extent of Zinga's assimilation. It may perhaps also indicate that South Africa was considered an appropriate political system under which black people should work: clearly delineated statuses for black and white, systematic and inflexible ordering and categorization and supporting legislation were already in place by the 1930s. [. . .]

People from different worlds

Men of Two Worlds does not have the presence of a star persona such as Paul Robeson but ten years after *The Song of Freedom*, it is still foregrounding similar issues and themes. Interestingly, the title *Men of Two Worlds* resonates with more recent descriptions of young black people in Britain as being 'trapped between two cultures' [. . .]

This time the black male protagonist is named Kisenga – which sounds similar to Casanga, the island in *The Song of Freedom* – and he is a concert pianist rather than an opera singer but still firmly located within the realms of high rather than the emergent popular culture. Kisenga's music is a hybrid of traditional 'African' and classical European music, signifying that Kisenga is Europeanized but retains, as he puts it, 'the thousand years of Africa in his blood.' He decides to go to Africa to help 'his' people plagued by the tsetse fly which causes sleeping sickness.

Again the ignorance and primitivism of the 'African native' is embodied in the figure of the manipulative witch doctor who will not allow his fellow villagers to take the medicine prescribed by Doctor Munroe (Phyllis Calvert), the white female doctor. As is the case in *The Song of Freedom*, the principal evil of the witch doctor's rule is seen as his rejection of European values and his abhorrence of white people's presence in Africa.

A rationale for refusing to move away from the infestation is not attributed to this 'primitive' tribal community: they merely act, they do not think. This reinforces white European assumptions about rational motivation being absent amongst 'primitive' people. In contrast to the childlike Africans, the archetypal figure of the District Commissioner, Randall (Eric Portman), is the voice of Europe masculine reason, trying to get the Litu – Kisenga's people – to move to a place which is not infested with tsetse flies. When the community, influenced by the 'witch doctor' reject European medicine it is seen as evidence of their irrationality and they thus forfeit any claim to be thought of as autonomous human beings. This is a similar justification for domination to that proposed during the eighteenth and nineteenth centuries.

Another point to note is how, just as in the earlier imperial literature described above, 'natives' are depicted as a primeval, undifferentiated horde. This colonialist tendency is identified by Albert Memmi as a strategy of depersonalization named by him as 'the mark of the plural.' Memmi, talking in general terms, notes: 'The colonized is never characterized in an individual manner; he is only to drown in an anonymous collectivity ("They are this." "They are all the same.")' (Memmi, 1990: 151). In *Sanders of the River* (1935), *The Song of Freedom* (1936), *Men of Two Worlds* (1947) and *Simba* (1955), only the quiescent or Europeanized Africans are allowed the privilege of individual subjectivity and the limits of this autonomy are strictly defined.

Men of Two Worlds has the characteristics of a film which was a tired attempt to revitalize and sustain the myth of benevolent British paternal colonial rule when it was already clear that the British Empire had little life left in it. However, there is a point of interest to which I would draw attention: Phyllis Calvert's performance as the doctor. Her disgust at the sight and proximity of the black people in the film is almost palpable. Her whole body seems to be infused with a nervous tension that manifests itself in the way she speaks, moves and relates to the other actors. She refuses to engage in eye contact with Kisenga and on occasion acts as though he does not exist, talking and looking through or past him. She barely acknowledges his presence and ensures that their bodies are never close enough to make contact even when they pass each other in narrow spaces. The extent to which Calvert's demeanour is intended to be a trait of her character is not clear. It could be that this hypertense performance is attributable to the repression of sexuality which informs the film and the taboos regarding interracial relationships between black men and white women which were even more marked then than they are today.

Made in 1955 *Simba*, represents yet another reworking of these themes of the black African male who is educated and has taken on in some clearly signalled sense western European culture. Here though, British fear regarding the increasingly vociferous demands for autonomy, and colonial subjects' rebellion against the experience of subordination is manifested in what Dyer calls 'the rigid binarism, with white standing for modernity, reason, order, stability, and black standing for backwardness, irrationality, chaos and violence' (Dyer, 1988: 49). The role of the bad Other is displaced from the witch doctor and intensified in relation to the Mau-Mau in *Simba*. This text is a late entry into the colonial adventure canon, coming as it did towards the end of British colonial rule in Africa. It does not engage with the black presence in England and may be seen as representing the terror of the imminent end of Empire and the assumption of white supremacy.

Conclusion

It was necessary to conceptualize and depict the colonial Other as an infantile, sexually licentious savage in order to justify continued economic exploitation, surveillance and the ruthless wielding of power. Bhabha sees the attribution of such qualities as perverse contradictions:

> The black is both savage (cannibal) and yet the most obedient and digni-
> fied of servants (the bearer of food); he is the embodiment of rampant
> sexuality and yet innocent as a child; he is mystical, primitive, simple-
> minded and yet the most worldly and accomplished liar, and
> manipulator of social forces. In each case what is being dramatised is
> a separation – *between* races, cultures, histories, within *histories* – a sepa-
> ration between *before* and *after* that repeats obsessively the mythical
> moment of disjunction.
>
> (Bhabha, 1983: 34)

Attributing cannibalism to savage Others serves at once as justification for taming those savages, as a confirmation of white European supremacy and as a screen onto which to project guilty repression of the knowledge that it is the white oppressor who behaves in a cannibalistic manner. The act of cannibalism also functions as a useful metaphor for colonial exploitation [. . .] There is also in evidence in these anxious repetitions of colonial tropes, the fear of being re-absorbed into the dark, articulated as a fear of the dark or being swallowed, or ingested by the Other. In order to exercise 'mastery' over that 'darkness', to pre-empt the retaliation that they guiltily fear will be enacted against them, acts of violation are perpetrated, such as rapine penetration, and genocide.

   The notion of British colonialism as a global civilizing mission is explicit in *Sanders of the River* (1935), *The Song of Freedom* (1936), and *Men of Two Worlds* (1946), and reflects the narcissism embedded in colonial and neo-colonial fantasies. The central character of the white male is represented as whole, unified and coherent, a perception constantly in danger of disruption through the mirror-image of the black Other. Embedded in the psyche is the 'knowledge' that differ-ence – specifically racial and sexual difference – subverts and disrupts the notion of cohesion and order and this anxiety needs to be constantly mollified. These films served as comforting narratives for a nation which, used to assuming spiritual, cultural and political superiority, was traumatised by the Indian 'mutiny' and the subsequent fear of further destabilizing uprisings and acts of resistance. Through cinema – and literature – the old self-assurance could be re-asserted with the likes of 'Sandy the strong, Sandy the wise' able to rule over devoted black subjects, in spite of being vastly outnumbered.

Five years before *Simba* was made, Basil Dearden's *Pool of London* was released. This film indicates a significant break with the colonial adventure genre since no direct link is made between the black male character and Africa. Although he works on a ship which necessitates him spending long periods away from London, his presence is not specifically marked as unnatural or out of place. However, attempts to date a white woman are thwarted in order to avoid any controversy.

Significant numbers of black settlers from Africa, South Asia and the Caribbean came to Britain after the Second World War and it is to these groups that film-makers who wished to explore racial difference turned in the latter part of the 1950s. Exoticism and Otherness no longer had to be sought 'out there' – indeed, could not now be with the imminent demise of this phase of colonialism – since the Other was actually 'here'. This marks the moment where the *numbers* of black people became imbued with more significance than they had been before. Although represented as living in Britain, in *The Song of Freedom* (1936), *The Proud Valley* (1939) and *Men of Two Worlds* (1946), black people posed little threat because one way or another they did not settle in or reproduce in Britain. The numbers of black people involved outside of well-established communities in Cardiff, Bristol and Liverpool were perceived as insignificant. The narratives dealt with such problems as did arise by removing the source – in these three examples the African men – through death or repatriation. Vast numbers of Africans in Africa were not so problematic since one efficient District Commissioner could control them all with the assistance of a compliant 'native' chief.

The term 'racial problem' – previously associated with the racial traumas of South Africa and the USA – took on a whole new dimension in the 1950s when black people started to settle across Britain and themes relating to sexuality which had previously been studiously avoided became issues demanding attention.

Notes

1   Raymond Williams notes the ambiguities and uncertainties which have accrued to the term 'imperialism'. In the late nineteenth century, imperialism was usually defined as 'primarily a political system in which colonies are governed from an imperial centre' (Williams, 1988: 159). However, imperialism also has a set of meanings where the emphasis is on the economic rather than the political, thus the term connotes 'an economic system of external investment and the pene-tration and control of markets and sources of raw materials' (ibid.: 159–160). In the context of this book, the emphasis is on the former meaning, rather than the latter.

   There are several variations on this genre of film and literature: of particular note is the representation of the Indian sub-continent and its peoples. This is, however, outside the scope of this book.

2   However, these texts should not be thought of as ideologically homogeneous tracts as there is often evidence of contradictory feelings about the Empire and

the demands it made, particularly on young men: see Joseph Conrad's *Heart of Darkness* (1989) for example which is, broadly speaking, anti-imperialist but suffused with imperial rhetoric. In his concluding chapter, Joseph Bristow (1991) discusses some of the ambivalences in writing of the late nineteenth century. For debates conducted amongst Victorians, see Christine Bolt (1971); for an informative account of Conrad's stance on imperialism as evidenced in his writings, see Benita Parry (1983); for an introduction to, and references for the role of the Pan-African movement in the 1920s and 1930, see Peter Fryer (1984), and Walter Rodney (1988); a leading Pan-Africanist who came to Britain whose work is relevant here is George Padmore, (1936).

3   Torgovnick's use of 'we' and 'they' is problematic since it serves to reinforce the Euro-American dominant cultural status in determining who is 'us' and who is 'them'. Torgovnick attempts to justify it thus:

> The 'we' as I use it in this section basically denotes the 'we' that imag-ines a primitive 'them', a cultural 'we' . . . I use the we strategically, to prevent myself and my reader from backing away, too easily, from the systems of us/them thinking that structure all discourse about the civilized and the primitive . . . But at times . . . that 'we' is intended to produce a sense of discomfort or misfit. The 'we' is necessary to expose a shared illusion: the illusion of a representative primitive 'them' as opposed to a monolithic unified, powerful 'us'.
>
> (Torgovnick, 1990: 6)

Unfortunately, the effect of using that 'we' is to consolidate white European dominance as the extent to which her desire to make 'us' feel uncomfortable will be experienced as helpful by those who have always felt excluded from the academic 'we' is questionable.

4   For a cogent analysis of the metaphoric status of this comparison between black people and women, see Nancy Leys Stepan (1990: 38–57).

5   For more on the formation and consolidation of ideas about masculinity and dependency in the Victorian era, see Catherine Hall (1992).

6   A substantial body of critical work which engages with gender and racial rela-tions, the realm of the psyche and the material aspects of British colonialist and imperialist cinema has not been established, However, much productive analyt-ical work has been carried out on nineteenth century literature. For more detailed analysis in this subject area, see Brian Street (1975); Benita Parry (1983); Patrick Brantlinger (1988); Joseph Bristow (1991). For work on cultural forms other than literature, see John Mackenzie (1984), and for an exploration of the links between white English public school life, masculinity and the literature and films of Empire, see Jeffrey Richards (1973).

7   Both the association of animal imagery with black women and the inferior model of colonization offered by the Belgians are evident in Joseph Conrad's *Heart of Darkness* (1989: 80).

8   These ideas about the massed 'native' Other were also the mainstay of the Western genre of North American cinema where the confrontation would be between Native American and Euro-American.

9   For examples of some of the films affected by censorship in Kenya and Northern Rhodesia in the 1940s, see Rosaleen Smyth (1983: 346, note 28).

10   Harold Moody was founder of the League of Coloured People in 1931.
11   For an examination of Paul Robeson's cross-over appeal, see Richard Dyer
       (1986).
12   For example, in the casting of African–American Denzil Washington as a former
       black soldier from London in *For Queen and Country* (1988) and similarly, Forrest
       Whittaker in *The Crying Game* (1992).
13   See Dyer (1986). Interestingly, in a biography of Robeson, it is claimed that he
       felt that *The Song of Freedom* was the 'first true one he has done about that conti-
       nent [Africa]' (Foner, 1978: 31).

References

Belsey, C. (1980) *Critical Practice*, London: Methuen.

Bhabha, H. K. (1983) 'The Other Question . . .' in *Screen*, volume 24, number 6,
       November/December: 18–36.

Bogle, D. (1988) *Blacks in American Films and Television: An Illustrated Encyclopedia*, New
       York: Simon and Schuster Inc.

Bolt, C. (1971) *Victorian Attitudes to Race*, London: Routledge and Kegan Paul.

Brantlinger, P. (1988) *Rule of Darkness: British Literature and Imperialism*, Ithaca: Cornell
       University.

Bristow, J. (1991) *Empire Boys: Adventures in a Man's World*, London: HarperCollins
       Academic.

Bush, B. (1981) 'Blacks in Britain: the 1930s' in *History Today*, September.

Conrad, J. (1989) *Heart of Darkness*, London: Penguin, (originally published in 1902).

Doane, M. A. (1991) *Femmes Fatales: Feminism, Film Theory, Psychoanalysis*, New York:
       Routledge.

Dyer, R. (1988) 'White' in *Screen: The Last 'Special Issue' on Race?'* volume 29, number
       4, Autumn: 44–65.

Ellis, J. (1988) *Visible Fictions: Cinema, Television, Video*, London: Routledge.

Fanon, F. (1986) *Black Skin, White Masks*, (translated by Charles Lam Markmann),
       London: Pluto Press, (originally published in 1952).

Foner, P. S. (1978) *Paul Robeson Speaks: Writings, Speeches, Interviews: 1918–1974*,
       London: Quartet.

Fryer, P. (1984) *Staying Power: The History of Black People in Britain*, London: Pluto
       Press.

Goldberg, D. T. (1993) *Racist Culture: Philosophy and the Politics of Meaning*, Cambridge,
       Massachusetts and Oxford, UK: Blackwell.

Haggard, H. R. (1979) *King Solomon's Mines*, London: Octopus Books, (originally
       published in 1885).

Hall, C. (1992) *White, Male and Middle Class: Explorations in Feminism and History*,
       Cambridge: Polity Press.

Henriques, F. (1974) *Children of Caliban: Miscegenation*, London: Secker and Warburg.

JanMohamed, A. R. (1985) 'The Economy of Manichean Allegory: The Function of
       Racial Difference in Colonialist Literature' in *Critical Enquiry*, number 12,
       Autumn: 59–87.

MacKenzie, J. (1984) *Propaganda and Empire: The Manipulation of Public Opinion*,
       1880–1960. Manchester: Manchester University Press.

Memmi, A. (1990) *The Colonizer and the Colonized*, (translated by Howard Greenfield),
       London: Earthscan Publications, (originally published in 1957).

Padmore, George (1936) *Africa: How Britain Rules Africa*, London: Wishart Books.

Parry, B. (1983) *Conrad and Imperialism: Ideological Boundaries and Visionary Frontiers*, London: Macmillan.

Richards, J. (1973) *Visions of Yesterday*, London: Routledge and Kegan Paul Ltd.

Rodney, W. (1988) *How Europe Underdeveloped Africa*, London: Bogle L'Ouverture Publications.

Roper, M. and Tosh, J. (eds) (1991) *Manful Assertions: Masculinities in Britain Since 1800*, London: Routledge.

Said, E. W. (1985) *Orientalism*, Harmondsworth: Penguin.

Said, E. W. (1993) *Culture and Imperialism*, London: Chatto and Windus.

Shohat, E. (1991) 'Gender and the Culture of Empire: Toward a Feminist Ethnography of the Cinema' in *Quarterly Review of Film and Video*, volume 13: 45–84.

Smyth, R. (1983) 'Movies and Mandarins: the Official Film and British Colonial Africa' in J. Curran, and V. Porter (eds) *British Cinema History*, London: Weidenfeld and Nicholson: 129–43.

Stepan, N.L. (1990) 'Race and Gender: the Role of Analogy in Science' in D. T. Goldberg (ed.) *Anatomy of Racism*, Minneapolis: University of Minnesota Press.

Torgovnick, M. (1990) *Gone Primitive: Savage Intellects, Modern Lives*, Chicago and London: University of Chicago Press.

Williams, R. (1988) *Keywords: A Vocabulary of Culture and Society*, London: Fontana.

Chapter 21

Anne McClintock

THE WHITE FAMILY OF MAN
Colonial discourse and the reinvention
of patriarchy

U NTIL THE 1860S SOUTH AFRICA was, from the imperial point
of view, a far-flung outpost of scant allure. In 1867, however, an Afrikaner
child chanced upon the first South African diamond. The discovery of the diamond
fields at once drew "this most stagnant of colonial regions" into the eddies of
modern imperial capitalism and "a land that had seen boat-load after boat-load of
emigrants for New Zealand and Australia pass it unheeding by now saw men
tumbling on to its wharves and hurrying up country to the mines."[1]

Among these new arrivals was Henry Rider Haggard, an obscure youth of
nineteen, who, after a few years of unremarkable service in the colonial administration, returned to Britain to become the most spectacularly successful novelist
of his time.[2] In 1885, a few months after the carving up of Africa among the "lords
of humankind" at Berlin, Haggard published *King Solomon's Mines*, instantly and
easily outselling all his contemporaries.[3] *She* appeared soon after, in 1887, to a
riotous fanfare of applause. Almost overnight, this obscure youth had become an
author of unparalleled commercial success and renown.[4]

King Solomon's Mines was intimately concerned with events in South Africa
following the discovery of diamonds and then gold: specifically, the reordering of
women's sexuality and work in the African homestead and the diversion of black
male labor into the mines. The story illuminates not only relations between the
imperial metropolis and the colonies but also the refashioning of gender relations
in South Africa, as a nascent capitalism penetrated the region and disrupted already
contested power relations within the homesteads. Despite recent recognition
that some of the crucial conflicts in the nineteenth century took place over the
African homestead economy, for the most part the story of women's work and
women's resistance has been shunted to the sidings of history. Because women
were the chief farmers, they were the primary producers of life, labor and food
in the precolonial era. Their work was thus the single most valuable resource in

the country, apart from the land itself. Yet we know very little about how pre-colonial societies were able to subordinate women's work and as little about the changes wrought on these societies by colonial conquest and the penetration of merchant and mining capital.

Haggard's *King Solomon's Mines* offers an unusual glimpse into some of the fundamental dynamics of that contest. The novel was in large part an attempt to negotiate contradictions in the colonial effort to discipline female sexuality and labor, both in the European metropolis and in the colonies. The conflicts between male and female generative power and between domesticity and imperialism, were not only the obsessive themes of Haggard's work but also a dominant preoccupation of his time. Much of the fascination of Haggard's writing for male Victorians was that he played out his phantasms of patriarchal power in the arena of empire, and thus evoked the unbidden relation between male middle- and upper-middle-class power in the metropolis and control of black female labor in the colonies. In this way, *King Solomon's Mines* becomes more than a Victorian curiosity; instead it brings to light some of the fundamental contradictions of the imperial project as well as African attempts to resist it. [. . .]

The regeneration of the family of man: an imperial narrative

Although Haggard was mediocre and disinherited in Britain, once he stepped onto South African soil, he rose immediately into the most exclusive white elite of the country. His appointment to the colonial administration was nothing more glamorous than housekeeper to the largely male family of white bureaucrats in Pietermaritzburg, Natal. But as general factotum to Sir Henry Bulwer, tasked with handling the "champagne and sherry policy" of Natal's brass-band and cavalry administration, his prestige and self-esteem were enormously enhanced.[5] Standing discreetly at the elbow of the paramount white authority in Natal, he was a far cry from the hapless dolt at Scoones. Indeed, a local newspaper announced the new arrival in Cape Town of a "Mr. Waggart."

Haggard's regenerative arrival in South Africa is illuminating in this respect, for the turnabout in his career rehearses a critical moment in late male Victorian culture: the transition, that Said identifies, from filiation to affiliation. Haggard's redemption in the colonial service vividly rehearses this transition from failed filiation within the feudal family manor – essentially a failure of class reproduction – to affiliation with the colonial bureaucracy. Through affiliation with the colonial administration, he was quite explicitly compensated for his loss of place in the landed, patriarchal family and was, moreover, provided with a surrogate father in the form of Theophilus Shepstone, Natal's Administrator of Native Affairs. Haggard was in this respect representative of a specific moment in imperial culture, in which the nearly anachronistic authority of the vanishing feudal family, invested in its sanctioned rituals of rank and subordination, was displaced onto the colonies and reinvented within the new order of the colonial administration.

This displacement gives rise to a paradox. One witnesses in the colonies a strange shadow-effect of the state of the family in Britain. George Orwell once acidly described the British ruling class as "a family with the wrong members in control." Drawing on the by now well-established figure of organic degeneration, he had a vision of Britain ruled over by a decrepit family of "irresponsible uncles and bedridden aunts." Yet, as Williams notes, what Orwell regretted was not so much the existence of a ruling family but rather its decay of ability. The image of the family as the model of social order has so powerful a hold over Orwell's imagination that he could not yet dispense with it in favor of a notion such as class, and he could express his unease only in terms of biological decay. At the same time, for Orwell, a family ruled by irresponsible uncles and bedridden aunts was a pathological family, for the father was nowhere to be seen. It did not seem noteworthy, either to Orwell or to Williams, that the image also admits no mother.

Here an important relation makes itself felt. Orwell saw the social group from which he came, the great service families, "pushed down in importance by the growth of the centralized bureaucracy and by the monopoly trading companies."[7] The failure of the idea of filiation within the great landed and service families stemmed in part from the growth of the imperial bureaucracy, which not only usurped the social function of the service families, displacing administrative power beyond the network of the family but also seriously undermined the image of the patriarchal paterfamilias as ultimate originary power. Yet if the growth of the bureaucracy unseated the patriarch as the image of centralized and individual male power, one witnesses in the colonies the reinvention of the tradition of fatherhood, displaced onto the colonial bureaucracy as a surrogate, restored authority. In other words, the figure of the paterfamilias was most vigorously embraced in the colonies at just that moment when it was withering in the European metropolis. The colony became the last opportunity for restoring the political authority of fatherhood, and it is therefore not surprising that one finds its most intense expressions in the colonial administration, the very place that threatened it. Nor is it surprising that the reinvention of the patriarch in the colonies took on a pathological form.

Patriarchal regeneration: *King Solomon's Mines*

Allan Quartermain – gentleman, hunter, trader, fighter and miner (named, not accidentally, after a father surrogate who had befriended Haggard as a youth) – began to write "the strangest story" that he knows for prophylactic reasons, as an act of biological hygiene. A confounded lion having mauled his leg, he is laid up in Durban in some pain and is unable to get about. Writing the book will relieve some of the frustration of his impotence – it will return him to health and manhood. Further, he will send it to his son, who is studying to be a doctor at a London hospital and is therefore obliged to spend a good deal of his time cutting up dead bodies. Quartermain intends his imperial adventure to breathe "a little life into things" for his boy, Harry, who will as a result be better fitted to pursue the technology of sanitation, the task of national hygiene, the restoration of the race. The book will thus be a threefold narrative of imperial recuperation, embracing three realms and moving from one to the other in a certain privileged order: from the physical body of the white patriarch restored in the colonies to the familial bond with the son/doctor in Britain to the national body politic. At the same time, the narrative reveals that the attempted regeneration of late Victorian Britain depended on the reordering of labor in the colonies; in this case, the attempted reconstruction of the Zulu nation through control of female reproductive and labor power.

The task of paterfamilial restoration that motivates the narration of the journey to King Solomon's Mines finds its analog in the motivation for the fictional journey itself. Quartermain, Captain Good and Sir Henry Curtis set out for King Solomon's Mines primarily to find Sir Henry's younger brother, Neville. Left without a profession or a penny when his father died intestate, Neville quarreled with Sir Henry and set off for South Africa in search of a fortune – a small mimicry of the flight of many of the distressed gentry to the colonies. At the end of the novel Neville is found in the wilderness, clad in ragged skins, his beard grown wild, his leg crushed in an accident – a living incarnation of the degeneration and wounded manhood thought to imperil the white race when abandoned too long in the racial "wilderness." Thus at both the level of the telling of the story and of the story told, the narrative is initiated through a double crisis of male succession and is completed with the regeneration of ruptured family bonds, promising therewith the continuity, however tenuous, of the landed patriarch.

Yet as it happens, Haggard's family romance of fathers, sons and brothers regenerating each other through the imperial adventure is premised on the reordering of another family: the succession of the Kukuana royal family. This reordering requires the death of the "witch-mother" Gagool. Only with her death is female control over generation aborted and the "legitimate" king restored, presided over by the regenerated white "fathers," who will carry away the diamonds to restore the landed gentry in Britain.

[. . .] In *King Solomon's Mines* we find two theories of human racial development. Both are intimately dependent on each other and both are elaborated within the metaphor of the family. On one hand, the narrative presents the historical decline from white ("Egyptian") fatherhood to a primordial black degeneracy incarnated in the black mother. On the other hand, the narrative presents the story of the familial progress of humanity from degenerate native "child" to adult white father. Haggard shared the popular notion that civilization as embodied by colonials was hazardous to the African, who, "by intellect and by nature . . . is some five centuries behind. . . . Civilization, it would seem, when applied to black races, produces effects diametrically opposite to those we are accustomed to in white nations: it debases before it can elevate." Most crucially, the dynamic principle that animates the hierarchy of racial and gender degeneration, transforming a static depiction of debasement into a narrative of historical progress, is the principle of imperial conquest.

Feminizing the "Empty Lands"

The journey to King Solomon's mines is a genesis of racial and sexual order. The journey to origins, as Pierre Macherey points out is "not a way of showing the absolute or beginning but a way of determining the genesis of order, of succession." [8] Donna Haraway has observed that the colonial safari was a kind of traveling minisociety, an icon of the whole enterprise of imperialism fully expressive of its racial and sexual division of labor.[9] It is therefore fitting that Quartermain's party consists of three white gentlemen; a Zulu "gentleman" ("*kesbla*" [sic] or "ringed man"), who nevertheless lags in development some five hundred years behind the whites; three Zulu "boys," still in a state of native "childhood" in relation to the whites; and the racially degenerate "Hottentot," Ventvogel. Thus we set out with the Family of Man in place, fully expressive of fixed divisions of class and race, with the female entirely repressed – a fitting racial hierarchy with which to reinvent the genesis of the species.

True to the trope of anachronistic space, the journey into the interior is, like almost all colonial journeys, figured as a journey forward in space but backward in time. As the men progress, they enter the dangerous zones of racial degeneration. Entering the fever lands and the place of the tsetse fly, the men leave their sick animals and proceed on foot. On the edge of the burning desert that stretches between them and Solomon's blue mountains, they cross into the borderlands of pathology. Stepping into the desert, they step into the zone of prehistory. Their journey across the untenanted plain traces an evolutionary regression from adult virility into a primordial landscape of sun and thirst inhospitable to all except insect life. True to the narrative of recapitulation that underlies the journey, the men slowly slough off their manhood. The sun sucks their blood from them; they stagger like infants unable to walk and escape death only by digging a womb-hole in the earth in which they bury themselves.

Notably, Ventvogel here enters his proper racial element. "Being a Hottentot," and therefore untouched by the sun, his "wild-bred" instincts awaken and he sniffs the air "like an old Impala ram." Uttering guttural exclamations, he runs about and smells out the "pan bad water" (39). Again in keeping with the narrative of recapitulation, adult racial degeneration to the primitive state of the "Hottentot" is accompanied by sexual degeneration to the "female" condition, and both states are attended by linguistic degeneration to an infantile state of preverbal impotence. As we know from the map, the "pan bad water" represents the corrupted female head. At this point, just over the perilous threshold of race, the place of prehistory merges with the place of the female. The landscape becomes suddenly feminized – the sky blushes like a girl, the moon waxes wan and at the very moment that Ventvogel smells the bad water, the men lay eyes for the first time on Sheba's Breasts.

Here, the prescribed narrative of racial, sexual and linguistic degeneracy confirms itself. At the sight of the mountains "shaped exactly like a woman's breasts," their snowy peaks "exactly corresponding to the nipple on the female breast," Quartermain plunges into the condition of reduced manhood and linguistic degeneration characteristic of the "Hottentot" female state. He "cannot describe" what he saw: "Language seems to fail me. . . . To describe the grandeur of the whole view is beyond my powers" (38, 39). This crisis of representation is a ritualistic moment in the colonial narrative whereby the colonized land rises up in all its unrepresentability, threatening to unman the intruder: "I am impotent even before its memory." Yet this is a subterfuge, a pretense of the same order as writing "cannibals" on the colonial map, for Quartermain contains the eruptive power of the black female by inscribing her into the narrative of racial degeneracy.

As the men leave the plains of prehistory and scale Sheba's Breasts, Ventvogel's racial debility begins to tell. "Like most Hottentots" he cannot take the cold and freezes to death in the cave on Sheba's nipple, proving himself unfit to accompany the other men on their journey to the restoration of the paternal origin. At the same time, his death discloses a prior historical failing. In the cave where Ventvogel dies, they find, in fetal position, the frozen skeletal remains of the Portuguese trader, Jose da Silvestre. These remains are a memento of the racial and class unfitness of the first wave of colonial intruders in these parts and thereby a historical affirmation of the superior evolutionary fitness of the English gentry over the Portuguese trader. To inscribe this liminal moment of succession into history. Quartermain takes up da Silvestre's "rude pen," the "cleft-bone" signifying mastery and possession: "It is before me as I write – sometimes I sign my name with it" (45).

Standing aloft on Sheba's Breasts, the men re-enter history. Monarchs of all they survey, their proprietary act of seeing inscribes itself on the land.[10] Leaving Ventvogel and the tongueless zone of prehistory, they re-enter language. Nevertheless, this moment is not a moment of origin but rather the beginning of a historical return and regression, for the journey has already been made. As Macherey has observed, the colonial journey "cannot be an exploration in the strict sense of the word but only discovery, retrieval of a knowledge already complete."[11] The landscape before them is not originary – it cannot find its principle of order within itself. "The landscape lay before us like a map," written over with European history. The mountain peaks are "Alplike", Solomon's Road looks at first like "a sort of Roman road," then like Saint Gothard's in Switzerland. The landscape is not, properly speaking, African, because it is already the subject of conquest. One of the tunnels through which the men pass is carved in ancient statuary, one "exceedingly beautiful" representing a whole battle-scene with a convoy of captives being marched off in the distance. Thus, "the journey . . . is disclosed as having ineluctably happened before. . . . To explore is to follow, that is to say, to cover once again, under new conditions, a road already actually travelled. . . . The conquest is only possible because it has already been accomplished."[12]

Macherey's observations are important because if the narrative of origins is, more properly speaking, the genesis of an order and a hierarchy and if the order the white men intend to impose is that of colonization and the primary stages of the primitive stages of the primitive accumulation of capital, then their conquest finds its legitimacy only by virtue of the fact that the conquest had already taken place at a previous moment in history. King Solomon, whom Haggard regarded as white, had already proved his titular right to the treasure of the mines, had already carved his road over the land. All that had to be accomplished to succeed to the treasure was a demonstration of *family* resemblance. A poetics of blood inheritance had to be written whereby the white gentlemen could succeed as rightful heirs to the riches. [. . .]

Inventing traditions: white fathers and black kings

Natal, where Haggard found himself in 1875, was one of the most unpromising of British colonies. Lacking any vital raw materials for export and lying hundreds of miles from the markets of Cape Town, it was poor, isolated and vulnerable. During the early years of the nineteenth century, the area had seen much turbulence and distress as local chiefdoms rivaled each other for land and power under the pressure of narrowing environmental resources. Between 1816 and 1828, the Zulu leader Shaka had fashioned from the upheavals a formidable military kingdom that drew into its orbit many smaller clans, destroying or scattering the rest in a great chain effect of disruption (the *mfecane*). The small bands of fierce Boer nomads, pushed into this cleared buffer zone in the 1830s. The British, however, had been granted land on the coast by Shaka and bristled at the prospect of Port Natal falling into the hostile hands of the Voortrekkers. They hastily summoned troops from the Cape and snatched Natal from the Boers in 1843. Nevertheless, the British were reluctant to lose the Boers themselves, for they needed denser settlement to counter the potentially overwhelming presence of the Zulus in Zululand which hemmed them in to the north (the principle source, with Zimbabwe, of Haggard's Kukuanaland). The British offered the Boers huge farms over the heads of the indigenous Africans, but many Boers preferred to trek inland once more, becoming absentee owners or selling their land to speculators. Huge areas of land in Natal were left fallow and untended, yet closed to settlement. This was the paradox that plagued Natal's white farmers: a shortage of land in a vast country of thousands of acres and a shortage of labor in a land with a population of thousands of Africans.

After the discovery of diamonds in 1867 and gold in 1884 the paradox deepened as black labor left for the mineral fields and better wages of the interior. Haggard, in 1882, in his first published writing, *Cetywayo and His White Neighbours*, called this paradox "the unsolved riddle of the future, the Native Question."[13] It is this riddle that *King Solomon's Mines* attempts to resolve, revealing in the process that the problems of land and labor are rooted in the fundamental question of who was to control the women's labor – an issue fought out at a number of levels: between black women and men within the Zulu homestead, among black men and between white colonists and black men.

Many elements of the Zulu family drama are present in *King Solomon's Mines*. In 1856 a crisis had broken out over the rightful heir of the Zulu king, Mpande, a struggle that prefigured the crisis of male succession reenacted in the novel. As in Haggard's tale, the blood rivalry between Mpande's sons, Cetshwayo and Mbulazi, climaxed in a battle in 1856: an eyewitness account of the actual battle provided Haggard with many of the details he used for the battle scene in the novel. Haggard's depiction of the degenerate usurper king, Twala, is resonant of racist images of Cetshwayo as a gorilla-like monster in the popular illustrated papers. In both the novel and its historical counterpart, moreover, white men interfere in the crisis of male inheritance and arrogate to themselves the powers of white *patria potestas*. This gives them the authority to inaugurate what they believe will be a subservient black monarch, on terms favorable to the colonial state.

In the historical case, Cetshwayo emerged as victor and Shepstone visited the Zulu court to confer official blessings on him in 1861. However, instead of the adulatory welcome he confidently expected, Shepstone, like Haggard's heroes, only narrowly avoided death. Nevertheless, the parties were reconciled and in September 1873 Shepstone proceeded to enact a pompous ceremony of monarchical recognition that he alone took seriously. Cetshwayo was proclaimed king with a great deal of pomp and ritual invented by Shepstone for the occasion. Shepstone saw himself grandly "standing in the place of Cetshwayo's father and so representing the nation" and enunciated four articles that he regarded as necessary for putting an end to "the continual slaughter that darkens the history of Natal." These articles are strikingly similar to the articles of control Haggard's heroes would demand in *King Solomon's Mines*.

Shepstone clearly felt he had been instituted as nominal founding father of the Zulu nation, and he and Haggard made a good deal of rhetorical fuss of his new status as father of the Zulus. The coronation was not simply Shepstone's whimsy, however, but was a symptomatic replica of the invented traditions of monarchical inauguration that colonials were enacting all over British Africa. In what Terence Ranger has called "the invented tradition of the 'Imperial Monarchy' " the colonists — lacking, as they did, a single body of legitimating ritual — offered Africans a fantastic mummery of tinsel and velvet royalty that bore scant resemblance to the political reality of the British monarchy.[14] In Britain the monarch had shrunk to a ceremonial figurehead. The centers of political power lay elsewhere, on the desks of industrial magnates, in the corridors of parliament, in the shipyards and mills. In the African colonies, however, the figure of the king rose to its feet and walked abroad again. The anachronistic ideology of the imperial monarchy became a widespread administrative cult, full of invention and pretense, of which Shepstone's coronation of Cetshwayo (like Haggard's coronation of Umbopa) were symptomatic.

Ranger calls "the 'theology' of an omniscient, omnipotent and omnipresent monarchy . . . almost the sole ingredient of imperial ideology as it was represented to the Africans."[15] He thereby neglects, however, what was arguably the most authoritative and influential of all invented rituals in the colonies: the patriarch, or landed paterfamilias. Most significant in political impact, moreover, was the newly invented hierarchy between the white "father" and the black king.

In colonial documents, for example, Shepstone is referred to with ritualistic insistence as the "father-figure" of Natal. Sir Henry Bulwer called him "one of the Colonies' earliest fathers – the very Nestor of the Colony."[16] Shepstone was generally referred to by black people (no doubt obliging his fantasy) as "Somtsewu," which, as Jeff Guy says, "notwithstanding much speculation on its meaning along the lines of 'mighty hunter' . . . is a word of Sesotho origin meaning 'Father of Whiteness'."[17] Haggard, like Shepstone himself, understood the name to carry the entirely unfounded implication that the Zulus regarded Shepstone as the originary potentate of the black people themselves: Shepstone is "par excellence their great white chief and 'father'." In a message to Lobengula, chief of the Ndebele, Shepstone announced portentously: "The Lieutenant Governor of Natal is looked upon as the Father of all."[18]

Shepstone took the title of father and everything that sprang from it in terms of political authority very seriously indeed, not only as a title but as a political and administrative practice that had serious consequences for the history of South

Africa. One example from many can suffice. In the 1850s he and Bishop Colenso of Natal, before their famous squabble, hatched a megalomaniacal plot to solve the "native question" by founding a Black Kingdom (like Kukuanaland) south of Natal, over which they would rule autocratically as founding patriarchs – each embodying, respectively, the absolute powers of "Father of the Church" and "Father of the state." In a letter to members of the Church of England, Colenso claimed he was called "Sokuleleka" ("Father of Raising Up") and "Sobantu" ("Father of the People"). Not to be outdone, Shepstone would be "Father of Whiteness." Both men thus arrogated to themselves, as Haggard's heroes do, all powers of male generation and succession. Their roles would be nothing less than the generators of civilization and the regenerators of the ancient Family of Man.

Shepstone manipulated the invented traditions of fathers and kings, mimicking allegiance to certain customs of Zulu chieftainship, while retaining for himself the superior status of father – the same solution to conflicting patriarchies that Haggard's tale rehearses. Thus Shepstone drew on an ideology of divine father-hood, as preordained and natural, the founding source of all authority. The black king, on the other hand, was his symbolic reproduction, mortal, invested with authority only by virtue of his mimicry of the originary power of the father.

For these reasons, I suggest, the reinvention of fathers and kings in South Africa can be seen as a central attempt to mediate a number of contradictions: between the imperial bureaucracy and the declining landed gentry in Britain; between the colonial ruling patriarchy and the indigenous patriarchies of precapi-talist polities; and last but most significantly, between women and men of all races. Here we come across the final and most important dynamic underlying both Haggard's tale and the emergent economy of the colonial state.

The invention of idleness

Shepstone's policy was based on an intimate sense of the precarious balance of power in Natal and Zululand. He knew that the frail colony could ill afford to antagonize the Zulus and that it lacked the military muscle and the finances to forcibly drive black men off their lands and into wage labor. As the missionary Henry Callaway asked ruefully, "How are 8,000 widely scattered whites to compel 200,000 coloureds to labor, against their will?"[19] Out of this riddle rose the exceptionally vituperative discourse on the degenerate "idleness" of the blacks. Of all the stigmata of degeneration invented by the settlers to mark themselves from the Africans, the most tirelessly invoked was idleness: the same stigma of racial unworth that Haggard saw as marking the Kukuana's degeneration and loss of title to the diamonds.

It is scarcely possible to read any travel account, settler memoir or ethno-graphic document without coming across a chorus of complaints about the sloth, idleness, indolence or torpor of the natives, who, the colonists claimed, preferred scheming and fighting, lazing and wanton lasciviousness to industry. Typical is Captain Ludlow's remark on visiting the Umvoti Mission Station: "The father of the family leant on his hoe in his mielie garden, lazily smoking his pipe. . . . It is amusing to watch one of them pretending to work."[20] Haggard saw the racial hatred of whites rooted in this stubborn abstraction of African labor: "The average white man . . . detests the Kaffir and looks on him as a lazy good-for-nothing, who ought to work for him and will not work for him."[21]

The idea of idleness was neither descriptively accurate of the laboring black farmers nor new. The settlers brought with them to South Africa the remnants of a three-hundred-year-old British discourse that associated poverty with sloth. Beginning in the sixteenth century in Britain, an intricate discourse on idleness had emerged, not only to draw distinctions between laboring classes but also to sanction and enforce social discipline, to legitimize land plunder and to alter habits of labor. After 1575, the unemployed or unruly poor, for example, were no longer banished beyond the city walls but were dragooned into "houses of correction" where they were treated as a resource to meet the needs of the growing manufactories. Walling up discontent and fettering the desperate during the crises of unemployment, the houses of confinement, often attached to manufactures and providing them with labor, also taught new habits and forms of industry. It appears that many of the inmates of the houses of correction were women, suggesting that the houses were threshold institutions, mediating the gradual transfer of productive labor from the family to the factory.

The discourse on idleness is, more properly speaking, a discourse on work – used to distinguish between desirable and undesirable labor. Pressure to work was, more accurately, pressure to alter traditional habits of work. During the land revolution and the war on the cottages of the eighteenth century, Official Board of Agriculture reports of the time praised the land enclosures for robbing the lower orders of economic independence, thereby forcing laborers to work every day of the year. At the same time, the discourse on idleness is also a register of labor resistance, a resistance then lambasted as torpor and sloth.

Colonists borrowed and patched from British discourses and couched their complaints in the same images of degeneracy, massing animal menace and irrationality familiar to European descriptions of the dangerous urban underclasses. The missionary Aldin Grout wrote to James Kitchenham: "They see our tools and our work but seldom ask a question about these or express a wish to do the other." Lady Barker opined: "It is a new and revolutionary idea to a Kaffir that he should do any work at all." James Bryce agreed: "The male Kaffir is a lazy fellow who likes talking and sleeping better than continuous physical exertion and the difficulty of inducing him to work is the chief difficulty that European mine-owners in South Africa complain of."

But the African pastoralists differed markedly from the uprooted and immiserated British proletariat with which the settlers were familiar. The Africans still enjoyed a measure of self-sufficiency and were, on the whole, better farmers than the white interlopers.[22] As Slater notes, "many whites in fact came to depend upon African agricultural produce for their very subsistence."[23] Settler fortunes were constantly imperiled by the self-sufficiency of the black farmers. Complaints about black sloth were as often complaints about different habits of labor. If black people entered into wage relations for whites, it was often reluctantly or briefly, to earn money, buy guns or cattle, then to return home. Thus the discourse on idleness was not a monolithic discourse imposed on a hapless people. Rather it was a realm of contestation, marked with the stubborn refusal of Africans to alter their customs of work as well as by conflicts within the white communities.

Most importantly, I suggest, the assault on African work habits was at its root an assault on polygyny and the women farmers: the fundamental dynamic underlying both *King Solomon's Mines* and the native policy of Natal. The question, bitterly contested for decades, was who was to benefit from women's labor.

Marriage maidens and mines

One need not look far to see that the root of the problem of black labor lay in women's role in production. When Froude visited Natal, he noted grimly: "The government won't make the Kaffirs work." Then at once he came upon the cause of the problem. Male "indolence," he saw, was rooted regrettably but inevitably in the "detestable systems of polygamy and female slavery."

> My host talks much and rather bitterly on the Nigger question. If the Kafir would work, he would treble his profits. . . . It is an intricate problem. Here in Natal are nearly 400,000 natives. . . . They are allowed as much land as they want for their locations. They are polygamists and treat their women as slaves, while they themselves are idle or worse.[24]

Missionaries and colonists voiced their repugnance for polygyny in moral tones, placing it firmly within the discourse of racial degeneration. The practice of polygyny was seen to mark African men, as Haggard had marked King Twala, as wallowing in the depths of sexual abandon: the "African sin." Yet colonial documents readily reveal that the assault on polygyny was an assault on African habits of labor that withheld from the resentful farmers the work of black men and women. The excess labor that a black man controlled through his wives was seen as a direct and deadly threat to the profits of the settlers. As Governor Pine complained: "How can an Englishman with one pair of hands compete with a native with five to twenty slave wives?"[25] Likewise, Haggard's knowledge of women's productive power animates his fear of Gagool in *King Solomon's Mines*.

Black women in Natal become the ground over which white men fought black men for control of their land and labor. As Guy has shown, precapitalist societies in southern Africa depended on the control of *labor power*, rather than the control of *products*. The fundamental unit of Zulu society was the homestead (*umuzi, imizi*), in which a single male (*ummumzana*) held authority over his wife or wives, their children, livestock, gardens and grazing lands. Each homestead was more or less independent, with women growing food on land held in trust for the chief of the clan. Each wife worked her own fields, living with her children in a separate house that took its name from her. A strict gendered division of labor prevailed, as women did most of the agricultural and domestic work – hoeing, planting, gathering and tending the crops, building and tending the houses, making implements and clothes, taking care of the daily cooking and the houses, as well as the bearing and raising of the children. The men broke the ground in the first stages, made some of the implements and tended the cattle. In short, the homestead was based on the systematic exploitation of women's labor and the transformation of that labor into male social and political power.

The symbolic means for transforming woman's work into male power was the *ukulobolo,* or marriage exchange. A new homestead was formed when a man was given permission to leave the royal barracks, or his father's homestead and marry a wife from a different clan. The marriage was formalized by the transfer of *lobolo* from the new husband to the wife's father, usually in the form of cattle. Colonialists berated this system as base and commercial: but it was, rather, a ceremonial exchange that guaranteed the transfer of a woman's labor and sexuality. If she did not produce children or the work expected, the cattle could be reduced in number, or returned and the marriage dissolved. At the same time, the cattle could be retained if the new husband was seen to ill-treat his wife. Nevertheless, the society was not egalitarian and most of the homesteads had only one or two wives. Power in the form of cattle and wives was gathered in the upper reaches of the chiefly lineages, and chiefs distributed power back down the social hierarchy by control-ling the distribution of cattle and wives to their sons and loyal supporters. *Labolo* was thus a symbolic, rather than a commercial, exchange whereby women's labor power was embodied in movable herds of cattle and exchanged among men across time and space.

At the same time, it is of the greatest significance that women's work freed men to fight in the Zulu army. The relation between women's labour and the Zulu fighting force is crucial. Women in the family homesteads provided a surplus of food for themselves and for the men in the barracks. The unequal distribution of women allowed male power to be hierarchically ranked within an arena of male competition for the basic resource of labor power. Thus whoever controlled the regulation of marriage controlled the power base of the economy. The dominant class was men over the marriageable age, the subordinate class women and children. Guy calls this "a fundamental cleavage so deep it can usefully be called one of class," but the fundamental division was gender, for a male child could leave the subordinate class at a certain age when he entered into marriage with a woman, that is, into a gendered division of labor in which he exploited his wife's labor power.

In *Cetywayo,* Haggard devoted a good deal of space to polygyny, which he recognized as lying at the heart of Zulu power. In a metaphor that nicely expressed the relation between matrimonial and military power, he advised: "Deprive them of their troops of servants in the shape of wives and thus force them to betake themselves to honest labor like the rest of mankind."[26] Tampering with the circu-lation of women was thus tantamount to severing the jugular vein of male Zulu power.

Indeed, this approach was precisely Shepstone's policy. In the face of the bitter ire of the farmer-settlers, Shepstone doggedly pursued a policy of segregation, administration and compromise. In the reserves, wretchedly apportioned as they were, blacks were allowed to retain access to land under "customary law" (as were the Kukuanas in Haggard's tale). The communal household was to be retained, since black resistance to changes in polygyny proved too tenacious. But the family would be gradually modified by diverting the profits of female labor out of the homestead into the colonial treasury in the form of hut and marriage taxes.

Knowing that an outright ban on polygyny was impractical, both Shepstone and Haggard favored a hut tax. The hut tax was, in fact, a tax on wives and thus the surest means of driving African men into wage labor. By legislating control of the rates of the hut taxes over the years, the Shepstone administration tried to take control of the traffic in women's work out of black men's hands, while driving these men into work on the white farms and mines. This put an administrative fetter on polygyny even as it turned the women's labor power into a sizable source of revenue for the dwindling treasury. The tax on women's labor would in fact become the principle source of revenue for the state. Significantly, what this fact reveals is that there was no objection to exploiting marriage and women's work as a commercial transaction as long as white men and not black men benefited from it. At the same time, to administer this gradual process of cultural attrition, ductile chiefs would be appointed to supervise and implement the process.

However, in 1876 the situation abruptly changed. The discovery of diamonds marked a new imperial initiative in southern Africa as Lord Carnarvon, British Secretary of State for the Colonies, hatched a scheme to confederate South Africa. Shepstone was given the responsibility of annexing the Transvaal and it was Haggard himself who raised the British flag over a reluctant Boer republic in 1876. The annexation shattered the uneasy balance between the Boers, Natal and the Zulus and set in train a series of events that led inexorably to the invasion of Zululand. Both Shepstone and Haggard deplored the invasion on the practical grounds that it was untimely and doomed to disaster. They remained convinced that the surest way to control the labor and land of South Africa was by segregation, indirect rule through selected chiefs, and the regulated diversion of labor from the reserves into the state economy.

Indeed, Haggard's fanatical tale is faithful to Shepstone's political blueprint for Zululand – Kukuanaland would remain territorially separate but in effect a "black colony" of Natal, while a compliant black leader who accepted the racial patrimony of the whites would be installed. True to Shepstone's segregationist policy, white men would not be allowed to settle there. At the same time, true to Haggard's own class loyalties – though not to the outcome of history – the booty from the mines would be placed in the hands of the landed gentry, not in the hands of the mining capitalists. Finally, the labor of black women is hidden from history, rendered as invisible as Gagool crushed beneath the rock.

In this way, *King Solomon's Mines* figures the reinvention of white imperial patriarchy through a legitimizing racial and gender politics. It asserts a white patriarch in control of a subservient black king, who grants white racial superiority and entitlement to the diamonds. It reorganizes production and reproduction within the black family by usurping the chief's control of the lives and labor of women. At the same time, it violently negates the African women's sexual and labor power.

Indeed, the Victorian obsession with treasure troves and treasure maps is a vivid example of commodity fetishism – the disavowal of the origins of money in labor. Finding treasure implies that gold and diamonds are there simply to be discovered, thereby denying the work of digging them out of the earth and thus the contested right to ownership. In the treasure fetish, money is seen to breed itself – just as in Haggard's tale the men give birth to themselves in the mine-womb.

Thus the narrative of phallic regeneracy is assured by the control of women in the arena of empire. The plundering of the land and the minerals is given

legitimacy through the erasure of the mother and the reinvention of white patriarchy within the organic embrace of the regenerated Family of Man. It is only
fitting, therefore that Haggard was himself enabled (by the fantastically approving
British reception of his tale of phallic and racial regeneration) to buy the landed
estate from which he had been disinherited.

Notes and references

1   C. W. De Kiewet, *A History of South Africa: Social and Economic* (London: Oxford
     University Press, 1941), p. 119.
2   Haggard was in South Africa from 1875 to 1881. In 1876 he personally raised
     the British flag over a disgruntled Transvaal.
3   Henry Rider Haggard, *King Solomon's Mines* (London: Signet, 1965). All further
     references to this edition are cited in the text by page number.
4   *King Solomon's Mines* was reprinted four times in the first three months, sold
     31,000 copies in the first year and has never been out of print since its publi-
     cation. *She*, too, was an instant bestseller and has been translated into over
     twenty languages and made into numerous films and plays as well as an opera.
     It too has not been out of print in Britain in the last century. Ella Shohat discusses
     film versions of both novels in "Gender and the Culture of Empire: Toward a
     Feminist Ethnography of the Cinema," *Quarterly Review of Film and Video*, 13, 1–3
     (Spring 1991): 45–84.
5   Henry Rider Haggard, *Days of My Life* (London: Longmans Green and Co., 1926),
     p. 36.
6   George Orwell, in S. Orwell and I. Angus eds, *The Collected Essays, Journalism
     and Letters of George Orwell*, vol. 11 (London: Secker and Warburg, 1968),
     p. 67.
7   Raymond Williams, *George Orwell: A Collection of Critical Essays* (Engelwood Cliffs:
     Prentice Hall, 1975), p. 20.
8   Pierre Macherey, *A Theory of Literary Production* (London: Routledge & Kegan
     Paul, 1978), p. 265.
9   Donna Haraway, *Private Visions: Gender, Race and Nature in the World of Modern
     Science* (London: Routledge, 1989), p. 52.
10   See Mary Louise Pratt's fine analysis of this trope in *Imperial Eyes: Travel Writing
     and Transculturation* (New York: Routledge, 1992).
11   Macherey, *A Theory of Literary Production*, p. 183.
12   Macherey, *A Theory of Literary Production*, p. 183.
13   Haggard, *Cetywayo and His White Neighbours* (London: Trubner and Co., 1882),
     p. 281. See also Jeff Guy, *The Destruction of the Zulu Kingdom* (Johannesburg:
     Ravan Press, 1982); and H. Slater, "The Changing Pattern of Economic Relations
     in Rural Natal, 1838–1914," in Shula Marks and A. Atmore, eds, *Economy and
     Society in Pre-Industrial South Africa* (London: Longmans, 1980).
14   Terence Ranger, "The Invention of Tradition in Colonial Africa," in Eric
     Hobsbawm and Terence Ranger, eds., *The Invention of Tradition* (Cambridge:
     Cambridge University Press, 1983). See also David Cannadine, "The Context,
     Performance and Meaning of Ritual: The British Monarchy and the 'Invention
     of Tradition,' 1820–1977," in Hobsbawm and Ranger. For an excellent explo-

ration of the invention of Zulu tradition, see Shula Marks, *The Ambiguities of Dependence: Class, Nationalism and the State in Twentieth Century Natal* (Johannesburg: Ravan Press, 1986).

15   Ranger, *The Invention of Tradition*, p. 212.
16   Quoted by Ruth E. Gordon, *Shepstone: The Role of the Family in the History of South Africa, 1820–1890* (Cape Town: Balkema, 1968), p. 309.
17   Guy, *The Destruction of the Zulu Kingdom*, p. 51 (n).
18   Haggard, *Days of My Life*, p. 9.
19   Henry Callaway, *A Memoir*, ed. M. S. Benham (London: 1896), p. 88.
20   W. R. Ludlow, *Zululand and Cetywayo* (London: Simpkin, Marshal, 1882), p. 18.
21   Haggard, *Cetywayo*, p. 57.
22   Patrick Harries, "Plantations, Passes and Proletarians: Labor and the Colonial State in Nineteenth Century Natal," *Journal of Southern African Studies* 13, 2, 375.
23   H. Slater, *The Changing Patterns*, p. 156.
24   Froude, *Short Studies*, p. 370–71.
25   Quoted in H. J. Simons. *African Women: Their Legal Status in South Africa* (Evanston: Northwestern University Press, 1968), p. 21.
26   Haggard, *Cetywayo*, p. 52.

Chapter 22

Chandra Talpade Mohanty

UNDER WESTERN EYES
Feminist scholarship and colonial discourses[1]

ANY DISCUSSION OF THE INTELLECTUAL and political construction of "third world feminisms" must address itself to two simultaneous projects: the internal critique of hegemonic "Western" feminisms, and the formulation of autonomous, geographically, historically, and culturally grounded feminist concerns and strategies. The first project is one of deconstructing and dismantling; the second, one of building and constructing. While these projects appear to be contradictory, the one working negatively and the other positively, unless these two tasks are addressed simultaneously "third world" feminisms run the risk of marginalization or ghettoization from both mainstream (right and left) and Western feminist discourses.

It is to the first project that I address myself. What I wish to analyze is specifically the production of the "third world woman" as a singular monolithic subject in some recent (Western) feminist texts. The definition of colonization I wish to invoke here is a predominantly *discursive* one, focusing on a certain mode of appropriation and codification of "scholarship" and "knowledge" about women in the third world by particular analytic categories employed in specific writings on the subject which take as their referent feminist interests as they have been articulated in the U.S. and Western Europe. If one of the tasks of formulating and understanding the locus of "third world feminisms" is delineating the way in which it resists and *works against* what I am referring to as "Western feminist discourse," an analysis of the discursive construction of "third world women" in Western feminism is an important first step.

Clearly Western feminist discourse and political practice is neither singular nor homogeneous in its goals, interests, or analyses. However, it is possible to trace a coherence of *effects* resulting from the implicit assumption of "the West" (in all its complexities and contradictions) as the primary referent in theory and praxis. My reference to "Western feminism" is by no means intended to imply that it is a monolith. Rather, I am attempting to draw attention to the similar effects of various textual strategies used by writers which codify Others as non-Western and hence themselves as (implicitly) Western. It is in this sense that I use the term *Western feminist*. Similar arguments can be made in terms of middle-class urban African or Asian scholars producing scholarship on or about their rural or working-class sisters which assumes their own middle-class cultures as the norm, and codifies working-class histories and cultures as Other. Thus, while this essay focuses specifically on what I refer to as "Western feminist" discourse on women in the third world, the critiques I offer also pertain to third world scholars writing about their own cultures, which employ identical analytic strategies.

It ought to be of some political significance, at least, that the term *colonization* has come to denote a variety of phenomena in recent feminist and left writings in general. From its analytic value as a category of exploitative economic exchange in both traditional and contemporary Marxisms (cf. particularly contemporary theorists such as Baran 1962, Amin 1977, and, Gunder-Frank 1967) to its use by feminist women of color in the U.S. to describe the appropriation of their experiences and struggles by hegemonic white women's movements (cf. especially Moraga and Anzaldúa 1983, Smith 1983, Joseph and Lewis 1981, and Moraga 1984), colonization has been used to characterize everything from the most evident economic and political hierarchies to the production of a particular cultural discourse about what is called the "third world."[2] However sophisticated or problematical its use as an explanatory construct, colonization almost invariably implies a relation of structural domination, and a suppression — often violent — of the heterogeneity of the subject(s) in question.

My concern about such writings derives from my own implication and investment in contemporary debates in feminist theory, and the urgent political necessity (especially in the age of Reagan/Bush) of forming strategic coalitions across class, race, and national boundaries. The analytic principles discussed below serve to distort Western feminist political practices, and limit the possibility of coalitions among (usually white) Western feminists and working-class feminists and feminists of color around the world. These limitations are evident in the construction of the (implicitly consensual) priority of issues around which apparently *all* women are expected to organize. The necessary and integral connection between feminist scholarship and feminist political practice and organizing determines the significance and status of Western feminist writings on women. In the third world, for feminist scholarship, like most other kinds of scholarship, is not the mere production of knowledge about a certain subject. It is a directly political and discursive *practice* in that it is purposeful and ideological. It is best seen as a mode of intervention into particular hegemonic discourses (for example, traditional anthropology, sociology, literary criticism, etc.); it is a political praxis which counters and resists the totalizing imperative of age-old "legitimate" and "scientific" bodies of knowledge. Thus, feminist scholarly practices (whether reading, writing, critical, or textual) are inscribed in relations of power — relations which they counter, resist, or even perhaps implicitly support. There can, of course, be no apolitical scholarship.

The relationship between "Woman" — a cultural and ideological composite Other constructed through diverse representational discourses (scientific, literary, juridical, linguistic, cinematic, etc.) — and "women" — real, material subjects of their collective histories – is one of the central questions the practice of feminist scholarship seeks to address. This connection between women as historical subjects and the re-presentation of Woman produced by hegemonic discourses is not a relation of direct identity, or a relation of correspondence or simple implication.[3] It is an arbitrary relation set up by particular cultures. I would like to suggest that the feminist writings I analyze here discursively colonize the material and historical heterogeneities of the lives of women in the third world, thereby producing/re-presenting a composite, singular "third world woman" – an image which appears arbitrarily constructed, but nevertheless carries with it the authorizing signature of Western humanist discourse [4]

I argue that assumptions of privilege and ethnocentric universality, on the one hand, and inadequate self-consciousness about the effect of Western scholarship on the "third world" in the context of a world system dominated by the West, on the other, characterize a sizable extent of Western feminist work on women in the third world. An analysis of "sexual difference" in the form of a cross-culturally singular, monolithic notion of patriarchy or male dominance leads to the construction of a similarly reductive and homogeneous notion of what I call the "third world difference" – that stable, ahistorical something that apparently oppresses most if not all the women in these countries. And it is in the production of this "third world difference" that Western feminisms appropriate and "colonize" the constitutive complexities which characterize the lives of women in these countries. It is in this process of discursive homogenization and systematization of the oppression of women in the third world that power is exercised in much of recent Western feminist discourse, and this power needs to be defined and named.

[. . .] My critique is directed at three basic analytic principles which are present in (Western) feminist discourse on women in the third world. Since I focus primarily on the Zed Press Women in the Third World series, my comments on Western feminist discourse are circumscribed by my analysis of the texts in this series.[5] This is a way of focusing my critique. However, even though I am dealing with feminists who identify themselves as culturally or geographically from the "West," as mentioned earlier, what I say about these presuppositions or implicit principles holds for anyone who uses these methods, whether third world women in the West, or third world women in the third world writing on these issues and publishing in the West. Thus, I am not making a culturalist argument about ethnocentrism; rather, I am trying to uncover how ethnocentric universalism is produced in certain analyses. As a matter of fact, my argument holds for any discourse that sets up its own authorial subjects as the implicit referent, i.e., the yardstick by which to encode and represent cultural Others. It is in this move that power is exercised in discourse.

The first analytic presupposition I focus on is involved in the strategic location of the category "women" vis-à-vis the context of analysis. The assumption of women as an already constituted, coherent group with identical interests and desires, regardless of class, ethnic or racial location, or contradictions, implies a notion of gender or sexual difference or even patriarchy which can be applied universally and cross-culturally. (The context of analysis can be anything from kinship structures and the organization of labor to media representations.) The second analytical presupposition is evident on the methodological level, in the uncritical way "proof" of universality and cross-cultural validity are provided. The third is a more specifically political presupposition underlying the methodologies and the analytic strategies, i.e., the model of power and struggle they imply and suggest. I argue that as a result of the two modes – or rather, frames – of analysis described above, a homogeneous notion of the oppression of women as a group is assumed, which, in turn, produces the image of an "average third world woman." This average third world woman leads an essentially truncated life based on her feminine gender (read: sexually constrained) and her being "third world" (read: ignorant, poor, uneducated, tradition-bound, domestic, family-oriented, victimized, etc.). This, I suggest, is in contrast to the (implicit) self-representation of Western women as educated, as modern, as having control over their own bodies and sexualities, and the freedom to make their own decisions [. . .]

"Women" as a category of analysis, or: we are all sisters in struggle

By women as a category of analysis, I am referring to the crucial assumption that all of us of the same gender, across classes and cultures, are somehow socially constituted as a homogeneous group identified prior to the process of analysis. This is an assumption which characterizes much feminist discourse. The homogeneity of women as a group is produced not on the basis of biological essentials but rather on the basis of secondary sociological and anthropological universals. Thus, for instance, in any given piece of feminist analysis, women are characterized as a singular group on the basis of a shared oppression. What binds women together is a sociological notion of the "sameness" of their oppression. It is at this point that an elision takes place between "women" as a discursively constructed group and "women" as material subjects of their own history[6] Thus, the discursively consensual homogeneity of "women" as a group is mistaken for the historically specific material reality of groups of women. This results in an assumption of women as an always already constituted group, one which has been labeled "powerless," "exploited," "sexually harassed," etc., by feminist scientific, economic, legal, and sociological discourses. (Notice that this is quite similar to sexist discourse labeling women weak, emotional, having math anxiety, etc.) This focus is not on uncovering the material and ideological specificities that constitute a particular group of women as "powerless" in a particular context. It is, rather, on finding a variety of cases of "powerless" groups of women to prove the general point that women as a group are powerless.

In this section I focus on five specific ways in which "women" as a category of analysis is used in Western feminist discourse on women in the third world. Each of these examples illustrates the construction of "third world women" as a homogeneous "powerless" group often located as implicit *victims* of particular socioeconomic systems. I have chosen to deal with a variety of writers – from Fran Hosken, who writes primarily about female genital mutilation, to writers from the Women in International Development school, who write about the effect of development policies on third world women for both Western and third world audiences. The similarity of assumptions about "third world women" in all these texts forms the basis of my discussion. This is not to equate all the texts that I analyze, nor is it to equalize their strengths and weaknesses. The authors I deal with write with varying degrees of care and complexity; however, the *effect* of their representation of third world women is a coherent one. In these texts women are defined as victims of male violence (Fran Hosken); victims of the colonial process (Maria Cutrufelli); victims of the Arab familial system (Juliette Minces); victims of the economic development process (Beverley Lindsay and the [liberal] WID School); and finally, victims of *the* Islamic code (Patricia Jeffery). This mode of defining women primarily in terms of their *object status* (the way in which they are affected or not affected by certain institutions and systems) is what characterizes this particular form of the use of "women" as a category of analysis. In the context of Western women writing/studying women in the third world, such objectification (however benevolently motivated) needs to be both named and challenged. As Valerie Amos and Pratibha Parmar argue quite eloquently, "Feminist theories which examine our cultural practices as 'feudal residues' or label us 'traditional,' also portray us as politically immature women who need to be versed and schooled in the ethos of Western feminism. They need to be continually challenged . . ." (1984, 7).

Women as victims of male violence

Fran Hosken, in writing about the relationship between human rights and female genital mutilation in Africa and the Middle East, bases her whole discussion/ condemnation of genital mutilation on one privileged premise: that the goal of this practice is "to mutilate the sexual pleasure and satisfaction of woman" (1981, 11). This, in turn, leads her to claim the woman's sexuality is controlled, as is her reproductive potential. According to Hosken, "male sexual politics" in Africa and around the world "share the same political goal: to assure female dependence and subservience by any and all means" (14). Physical violence against women (rape, sexual assault, excision, infibulation, etc.) is thus carried out "with an astonishing consensus among men in the world" (14). Here, women are defined consistently as the *victims* of male control – the "sexually oppressed."[7] Although it is true that the potential of male violence against women circumscribes and elucidates their social position to a certain extent, defining women as archetypal victims freezes them into "objects-who-defend-themselves," men into "subjects-who-perpetrate violence," and (every) society into powerless (read: women) and powerful (read: men) groups of people. Male violence must be theorized and interpreted within specific societies, in order both to understand it better and to effectively organize to change it.[8] Sisterhood cannot be assumed on the basis of gender; it must be forged in concrete historical and political practice and analysis.

Women as universal dependents

Beverly Lindsay's conclusion to the book *Comparative Perspectives of Third World Women: The Impact of Race, Sex and Class* (1983, 298, 306) states: "dependency relationships, based upon race, sex and class, are being perpetuated through social, educational, and economic institutions. These are the linkages among Third World Women." Here, as in other places, Lindsay implies that third world women constitute an identifiable group purely on the basis of shared dependencies. If shared dependencies were all that was needed to bind us together as a group, third world women would always be seen as an apolitical group with no subject status. Instead, if anything, it is the *common context* of political struggle against class, race, gender, and imperialist hierarchies that may constitute third world women as a strategic group at this historical juncture. Lindsay also states that linguistic and cultural differences exist between Vietnamese and black American women, but "both groups are victims of race, sex, and class." Again black and Vietnamese women are characterized by their victim status.

Similarly, examine statements such as "My analysis will start by stating that all African women are politically and economically dependent" (Cutrufelli 1983, 13), "Nevertheless, either overtly or covertly, prostitution is still the main if not the only source of work for African women" (Cutrufelli 1983, 33). *All* African women are dependent. Prostitution is the only work option for African women as a *group*. Both statements are illustrative of generalizations sprinkled liberally through a recent Zed Press publication, *Women of Africa: Roots of Oppression,* by Maria Rosa Cutrufelli, who is described on the cover as an Italian writer, sociologist, Marxist, and feminist. In the 1980s, is it possible to imagine writing a book entitled *Women of Europe: Roots of Oppression?* I am not objecting to the use of universal groupings for descriptive purposes. Women from the continent of Africa can be descriptively characterized as "women of Africa." It is when "women of Africa" becomes a homogeneous sociological grouping characterized by common dependencies or powerlessness (or even strengths) that problems arise – we say too little and too much at the same time.

This is because descriptive gender differences are transformed into the division between men and women. Women are constituted as a group via dependency relationships vis-à-vis men, who are implicitly held responsible for these relationships. When "women of Africa" as a group (versus "men of Africa" as a group?) are seen as a group precisely because they are generally dependent and oppressed, the analysis of specific historical differences becomes impossible, because reality is always apparently structured by divisions – two mutually exclusive and jointly exhaustive groups, the victims and the oppressors. Here the sociological is substituted for the biological, in order, however, to create the same – a unity of women. Thus, it is not the descriptive potential of gender difference but the privileged positioning and explanatory potential of gender difference as the *origin* of oppression that I question. In using "women of Africa" (as an already constituted group of oppressed peoples) as a category of analysis, Cutrufelli denies any historical specificity to the location of women as subordinate, powerful, marginal, central, or otherwise, vis-à-vis particular social and power networks. Women are taken as a unified "powerless" group prior to the analysis in question Thus, it is then merely a matter of specifying the context *after the fact*. "Women" are now placed in the context of the family, or in the workplace, or within religious networks, almost as if these systems existed outside the relations of women with other women, and women with men.

The problem with this analytic strategy, let me repeat, is that it assumes men and women are already constituted as sexual–political subjects prior to their entry into the arena of social relations. Only if we subscribe to this assumption is it possible to undertake analysis which looks at the "effects" kinship structures, colonialism, organization of labor, etc., on women, who are defined in advance as a group. The crucial point that is forgotten is that women are produced through these very relations as well as being implicated in forming these relations. As Michelle Rosaldo argues, "woman's place in human social life is not in any direct sense a product of the things she does (or even less, a function of what, biologically, she is) but the meaning her activities acquire through concrete social interactions" (1980, 400). That women mother in a variety of societies is not as significant as the value attached to mothering in these societies. The distinction between the act of mothering and the status attached to it is a very important one – one that needs to be stated and analyzed contextually.

Married women as victims of the colonial process

In Lévi-Strauss's theory of kinship structure as a system of the exchange of women, what is significant is that exchange itself is not constitutive of the subordination of women; women are not subordinate because of the *fact* of exchange, but because of the *modes* of exchange instituted, and the values attached to these modes. However, in discussing the marriage ritual of the Bemba, a Zambian matrilocal, matrilineal people, Cutrufelli in *Women of Africa* focuses on the fact of the marital exchange of women before and after Western colonization, rather than the value attached to this exchange in this particular context. This leads to her definition of Bemba women as a coherent group affected in a particular way by colonization. Here again, Bemba women are constituted rather unilaterally as victims of the effects of Western colonization.

Cutrufelli cites the marriage ritual of the Bemba as a multistage event "whereby a young man becomes incorporated into his wife's family group as he takes up residence with them and gives his services in return for food and maintenance" (43). This ritual extends over many years, and the sexual relationship varies according to the degree of the girl's physical maturity. It is only after she undergoes an initiation ceremony at puberty that intercourse is sanctioned, and the man acquires legal rights over her. This initiation ceremony is the more important act of the consecration of women's reproductive power, so that the abduction of an uninitiated girl is of no consequence, while heavy penalty is levied for the seduction of an initiated girl. Cutrufelli asserts that the effect of European colonization has changed the whole marriage system. Now the young man is entitled to take his wife away from her people in return for money. The implication is that Bemba women have now lost the protection of tribal laws. However, while it is possible to see how the structure of the traditional marriage contract (versus the postcolonial marriage contract) offered women a certain amount of control over their marital relations, only an analysis of the political significance of the actual practice which privileges an initiated girl over an uninitiated one, indicating a shift in female power relations as a result of this ceremony, can provide an accurate account of whether Bemba women were indeed protected by tribal laws *at all times.*

However, it is not possible to talk about Bemba women as a homogeneous group within the traditional marriage structure. Bemba women *before* the initiation are constituted within a different set of social relations compared to Bemba women *after* the initiation. To treat them as a unified group characterized by the fact of their "exchange" between male kin is to deny the sociohistorical and cultural specificities of their existence, and the differential *value* attached to their exchange before and after their Initiation. It is to treat the initiation ceremony as a ritual with no political implications or effects. It is also to assume that in merely describing the *structure* of the marriage contract, the situation of women is exposed. Women as a group are positioned within a given structure, but there is no attempt made to trace the effect of the marriage practice in constituting women within an obviously changing network of power relations. Thus, women are assumed to be sexual–political subjects prior to entry into kinship structures.

Women and familial systems

Elizabeth Cowie (1978), in another context, points out the implications of this sort of analysis when she emphasizes the specifically political nature of kinship structures which must be analyzed as ideological practices which designate men and women as father, husband, wife, mother, sister, etc. Thus, Cowie suggests, women as women are not *located* within the family. Rather, it is *in* the family, as an effect of kinship structures, that women as women are *constructed,* defined within and by the group. Thus, for instance, when Juliette Minces (1980) cites *the* patriarchal family as the basis for "an almost identical vision of women" that Arab and Muslim societies have, she falls into this very trap (see especially p. 23). Not only is it problematical to speak of a vision of women shared by Arab and Muslim societies (i.e., over twenty different countries) without addressing the particular historical, material, and ideological power structures that construct such images, but to speak of the patriarchal family or the tribal kinship structure as the origin of the socioeconomic status of women is to again assume that women are sexual–political subjects prior to their entry into the family. So while on the one hand women attain value or status within the family, the assumption of a singular patriarchal kinship system (common to all Arab and Muslim societies) is what apparently structures women as an oppressed group in these societies! This singular, coherent kinship system presumably influences another separate and given entity, "women." Thus, all women, regardless of class and cultural differences, are affected by this system. Not only are *all* Arab and Muslim women seen to constitute a homogeneous oppressed group, but there is no discussion of the specific *practices* within the family which constitute women as mothers, wives, sisters, etc. Arabs and Muslims, it appears, don't change at all. Their patriarchal family is carried over from the times of the prophet Mohammed. They exist, as it were, outside history.

Women and religious ideologies

A further example of the use of "women" as a category of analysis is found in cross-cultural analyses which subscribe to a certain economic reductionism in describing the relationship between the economy and factors such as politics and ideology. Here, in reducing the level of comparison to the economic relations between "developed and developing" countries, any specificity to the question of women is denied. Mina Modares (1981), in a careful analysis of women and Shi'ism in Iran, focuses on this very problem when she criticizes feminist writings which treat Islam as an ideology separate from and outside social relations and practices, rather than a discourse which includes rules for economic, social, and power relations within society. Patricia Jeffery's (1979) otherwise informative work on Pirzada women in purdah considers Islamic ideology a partial explanation for the status of women in that it provides a justification for the purdah. Here, Islamic ideology is reduced to a set of ideas whose internalization by Pirzada women contributes to the stability of the system. However, the primary explanation for purdah is located in the control that Pirzada men have over economic resources, and the personal security purdah gives to Pirzada women.

By taking a specific version of Islam as *the* Islam, Jeffery attributes a singularity and coherence to it. Modares notes " 'Islamic Theology' then becomes imposed on a separate and given entity called 'women.' A further unification is reached: Women (meaning *all women*), regardless of their differing positions within societies, come to be affected or not affected by Islam. These conceptions provide the right ingredients for an unproblematic possibility of a cross-cultural study of women" (63). [. . .]

Women and the development process

The best examples of universalization on the basis of economic reductionism can be found in the liberal "Women in Development" literature. Proponents of this school seek to examine the effect of development on third world women, sometimes from self-designated feminist perspectives. At the very least, there is an evident interest in and commitment to improving the lives of women in "developing" countries. Scholars such as Irene Tinker and Michelle Bo Bramsen (1972), Ester Boserup (1970), and Perdita Huston (1979) have all written about the effect of development policies on women in the third world.[9] All three women assume "development" is synonymous with "economic development" or "economic progress." As in the case of Minces's patriarchal family, Hosken's male sexual control, and Cutrufelli's Western colonization, development here becomes the all-time equalizer. Women are affected positively or negatively by economic development policies, and this is the basis for cross-cultural comparison.

For instance, Perdita Huston (1979) states that the purpose of her study is to describe the effect of the development process on the "family unit and its individual members" in Egypt, Kenya, Sudan, Tunisia, Sri Lanka, and Mexico. She states that the "problems" and "needs" expressed by rural and urban women in these countries all center around education and training, work and wages, access to health and other services, political participation, and legal rights. Huston relates all these "needs" to the lack of sensitive development policies which exclude women as a group or category. For her, the solution is simple: implement improved development policies which emphasize training for women fieldworkers, use women trainees, and women rural development officers, encourage women's cooperatives, etc. Here again, women are assumed to be a coherent group or category prior to their entry into "the development process." Huston assumes that all third world women have similar problems and needs. Thus, they must have similar interests and goals. However, the interests of urban, middle-class, educated Egyptian housewives, to take only one instance, could surely not be seen as being the same as those of their uneducated, poor maids. Development policies do not affect both groups of women in the same way. Practices which characterize women's status and roles vary according to class. Women are constituted as women through the complex interaction between class, culture, religion, and other ideological institutions and frameworks. They are not "women" – a coherent group – solely on the basis of a particular economic system or policy. Such reductive cross-cultural comparisons result in the colonization of the specifics of daily existence and the complexities of political interests which women of different social classes and cultures represent and mobilize.

Thus, it is revealing that for Perdita Huston, women in the third world countries she writes about have "needs" and "problems," but few if any have "choices" or the freedom to act. This is an interesting representation of women in the third world, one which is significant in suggesting a latent self-presentation of Western women which bears looking at. She writes, "What surprised and moved me most as I listened to women in such very different cultural settings was the striking commonality – whether they were educated or illiterate, urban or rural – of their most basic values: the importance they assign to family, dignity, and service to others" (1979, 115). Would Huston consider such values unusual for women in the West?

What is problematical about this kind of use of "women" as a group, as a stable category of analysis, is that it assumes an ahistorical, universal unity between women based on a generalized notion of their subordination. Instead of analytically *demonstrating* the production of women as socioeconomic political groups within particular local contexts, this analytical move limits the definition of the female subject to gender identity, completely bypassing social class and ethnic identities. What characterizes women as a group is their gender (sociologically, not necessarily biologically, defined) over and above everything else, indicating a monolithic notion of sexual difference. Because women are thus constituted as a coherent group, sexual difference becomes coterminous with female subordination, and power is automatically defined, in binary terms: people who have it (read: men), and people who do not (read: women). Men exploit, women are exploited. Such simplistic formulations are historically reductive; they are also ineffectual in designing strategies to combat oppressions. All they do is reinforce binary divisions between men and women.

What would an analysis which did not do this look like? Maria Mies's work illustrates the strength of Western feminist work on women in the third world which does not fall into the traps discussed above. Mies's study of the lace makers of Narsapur, India (1982), attempts to carefully analyze a substantial household industry in which "housewives" produce lace doilies for consumption in the world market. Through a detailed analysis of the structure of the lace industry, production and reproduction relations, the sexual division of labor, profits and exploitation, and the overall consequences of defining women as "non-working housewives" and their work as "leisure-time activity," Mies demonstrates the levels of exploitation in this industry and the impact of this production system on the work and living conditions of the women involved in it. In addition, she is able to analyze the "ideology of the housewife," the notion of a woman sitting in the house, as providing the necessary subjective and sociocultural element for the creation and maintenance of a production system that contributes to the increasing pauperization of women, and keeps them totally atomized and disorganized as workers. Mies's analysis shows the effect of a certain historically and culturally specific mode of patriarchal organization, an organization constructed on the basis of the definition of the lace makers as "non-working housewives" at familial, local, regional, statewide, and international levels. The intricacies and the effects of particular power networks not only are emphasized, but they form the basis of Mies's analysis of how this particular group of women is situated at the center of a hegemonic, exploitative world market. [. . .]

Methodological universalisms, or: women's oppression is a global phenomenon

Western feminist writings on women in the third world subscribe to a variety of methodologies to demonstrate the universal cross-cultural operation of male dominance and female exploitation. I summarize and critique three such methods below, moving from the simplest to the most complex.

First, proof of universalism is provided through the use of an arithmetic method. The argument goes like this: the greater the number of women who wear the veil, the more universal is the sexual segregation and control of women (Deardon 1975, 4–5). Similarly, a large number of different, fragmented examples from a variety of countries also apparently add up to a universal fact. For instance, Muslim women in Saudi Arabia, Iran, Pakistan, India, and Egypt all wear some sort of a veil. Hence, this indicates that the sexual control of women is a universal fact in those countries in which the women are veiled (Deardon 1975, 7, 10). Fran Hosken writes, "Rape, forced prostitution, polygamy, genital mutilation, pornography, the beating of girls and women, purdah (segregation of women) are all violations of basic human rights" (1981, 15). By equating purdah with rape, domestic violence, and forced prostitution, Hosken asserts its "sexual control" function as the primary explanation for purdah, whatever the context. Institutions of purdah are thus denied any cultural and historical specificity, and contradictions and potentially subversive aspects are totally ruled out.

In both these examples, the problem is not in asserting that the practice of wearing a veil is widespread. This assertion can be made on the basis of numbers. It is a descriptive generalization. However, it is the analytic leap from the practice of veiling to an assertion of its general significance in controlling women that must be questioned. While there may be a physical similarity in the veils worn by women in Saudi Arabia and Iran, the specific meaning attached to this practice varies according to the cultural and ideological context. In addition, the symbolic space occupied by the practice of purdah may be similar in certain contexts, but this does not automatically indicate that the practices themselves have identical significance in the social realm. For example, as is well known, Iranian middle-class women veiled themselves during the 1979 revolution to indicate solidarity with their veiled working-class sisters, while in contemporary Iran, mandatory Islamic laws dictate that all Iranian women wear veils. While in both these instances, similar reasons might be offered for the veil (opposition to the Shah and Western cultural colonization in the first case, and the true Islamicization of Iran in the second), the concrete *meanings* attached to Iranian women wearing the veil are clearly different in both historical contexts. In the first case, wearing the veil is both an oppositional and a revolutionary gesture on the part of Iranian middle-class women; in the second case, it is a coercive, institutional mandate (see Tabari 1980 for detailed discussion). It is on the basis of such context-specific differenti-ated analysis that effective political strategies can be generated. To assume that the mere practice of veiling women in a number of Muslim countries indicates the universal oppression of women through sexual segregation not only is analytically reductive, but also proves quite useless when it comes to the elaboration of oppositional political strategy.

Second, concepts such as reproduction, the sexual division of labor, the family, marriage, household, patriarchy, etc., are often used without their specification in local cultural and historical contexts. Feminists use these concepts in providing explanations for women's subordination, apparently assuming their universal applicability. For instance, how is it possible to refer to "the" sexual division of labor when the *content* of this division changes radically from one environment to the next, and from one historical juncture to another? At its most abstract level, it is the fact of the differential assignation of tasks according to sex that is signif-icant; however, this is quite different from the *meaning* or *value* that the content of this sexual division of labor assumes in different contexts. In most cases the assigning of tasks on the basis of sex has an ideological origin. There is no ques-tion that a claim such as "women are concentrated in service-oriented occupations in a large number of countries around the world" is descriptively valid. Descriptively, then, perhaps the existence of a similar sexual division of labor (where women work in service occupations such as nursing, social work, etc., and men in other kinds of occupations) in a variety of different countries can be asserted. However, the concept of the "sexual division of labor" is more than just a descrip-tive category. It indicates the differential *value* placed on "men's work" versus "women's work."

Often the mere existence of a sexual division of labor is taken to be proof of the oppression of women in various societies. This results from a confusion between and collapsing together of the descriptive and explanatory potential of the concept of the sexual division of labor. Superficially similar situations may have radically different, historically specific explanations, and cannot be treated as identical. For instance, the rise of female-headed households in middle-class America might be construed as a sign of great independence and feminist progress, whereby women are considered to have *chosen* to be single parents, there are increasing numbers of lesbian mothers, etc. However, the recent increase in female-headed households in Latin America,[10] where women might be seen to have more decision-making power, is concentrated among the poorest strata, where life choices are the most constrained economically. A similar argument can be made for the rise of female-headed families among black and Chicana women in the U.S. The positive correlation between this and the level of poverty among women of color and white working-class women in the U.S. has now even acquired a name: the feminization of poverty. Thus, while it is possible to state that there is a rise in female-headed households in the U.S. and in Latin America, this rise cannot be discussed as a universal indicator of women's independence, nor can it be discussed as a universal indicator of women's impoverishment. The *meaning* of and *explanation* for the rise obviously vary according to the sociohistorical context.

[. . .] To summarize: I have discussed three methodological moves identifiable in feminist (and other academic) cross-cultural work which seeks to uncover a universality in women's subordinate position in society. The next and final section pulls together the previous sections, attempting to outline the political effects of the analytical strategies in the context of Western feminist writing on women in the third world. These arguments are not against generalization as much as they are for careful, historically specific generalizations responsive to complex realities. Nor do these arguments deny the necessity of forming strategic political identities and affinities. Thus, while Indian women of different religions, castes, and classes might forge a political unity on the basis of organizing against police brutality toward women (see Kishwar and Vanita 1984), an *analysis* of police brutality must be contextual. Strategic coalitions which construct oppositional political identities for themselves are based on generalization and provisional unities, but the analysis of these group identities cannot be based on universalistic, ahistorical categories.

This last section returns to an earlier point about the inherently political nature of feminist scholarship, and attempts to clarify my point about the possibility of detecting a colonialist move in the case of a hegemonic first–third world connection in scholarship. The nine texts in the Zed Press Women in the Third World series that I have discussed[11] focused on the following common areas in examining women's "status" within various societies: religion, family/kinship structures, the legal system, the sexual division of labor, education, and finally, political resistance. A large number of Western feminist writings on women in the third world focus on these themes. Of course the Zed texts have varying emphases. For instance, two of the studies, *Women in Palestine* (Bendt and Downing 1982) and *Indian Women in Struggle* (Omvedt 1980), focus explicitly on female militance and political involvement, while *Women in Arab Society* (Minces 1980) deals with Arab women's legal, religious, and familial status. In addition, each text evidences a variety of methodologies and degrees of care in making generalizations. Interestingly enough, however, almost all the texts assume "women" as a category of analysis in the manner designated above.

Clearly this is an analytical strategy which is neither limited to these Zed Press publications nor symptomatic of Zed Press publications in general. However, each of the particular texts in question assumes "women" have a coherent group identity within the different cultures discussed, prior to their entry into social rela-tions. Thus, Omvedt can talk about "Indian women" while referring to a particular group of women in the State of Maharashtra, Cutrufelli about "women of Africa," and Minces about "Arab women" as if these groups of women have some sort of obvious cultural coherence, distinct from men in these societies. The "status" or "position" of women is assumed to be self-evident, because women as an already constituted group are *placed* within religious, economic, familial, and legal struc-tures. However, this focus whereby women are seen as a coherent group across contexts, regardless of class or ethnicity, structures the world in ultimately binary, dichotomous terms, where women are always seen in opposition to men, patriarchy is always necessarily male dominance, and the religious, legal, economic, and familial systems are implicitly assumed to be constructed by men. Thus, both men and women are always apparently constituted whole populations, and relations of dominance and exploitation are also posited in terms of whole people – wholes coming into exploitative relations. It is only when men and women are seen as different categories or groups possessing different *already constituted* categories of experience, cognition, and interests as *groups* that such a simplistic dichotomy is possible.

What does this imply about the structure and functioning of power relations? The setting up of the commonality of third world women's struggles across classes and cultures against a general notion of oppression (primarily the group in power – i.e., men) necessitates the assumption of what Michel Foucault (1980, 135–45) calls the "juridico-discursive" model of power, the principal features of which are "a negative relation" (limit and lack), an "insistence on the rule" (which forms a binary system), a "cycle of prohibition," the "logic of censorship," and a "unifor-mity" of the apparatus functioning at different levels. Feminist discourse on the third world which assumes a homogeneous category – or group – called women necessarily operates through the setting up of originary power divisions. Power relations are structured in terms of a unilateral and undifferentiated source of power and a cumulative reaction to power. Opposition is a generalized phenom-enon created as a response to power – which, in turn, is possessed by certain groups of people.

The major problem with such a definition of power is that it locks all evolu-tionary struggles into binary structures – possessing power versus being powerless. Women are powerless, unified groups. If the struggle for a just society is seen in terms of the move from powerless to powerful for women as a *group*, and this is the implication in feminist discourse which structures sexual difference in terms of the division between the sexes, then the new society would be structurally identical to the existing organization of power relations, constituting itself as a simple *inversion* of what exists. If relations of domination and exploitation are defined in terms of binary divisions – groups which dominate and groups which are dominated – surely the implication is that the accession to power of women as a group is sufficient to dismantle the existing organization of relations? But women as a group are not in some sense essentially superior or infallible. The crux of the problem lies in that initial assumption of women as a homogeneous group or category ("the oppressed"), a familiar assumption in Western radical and liberal feminisms.[12]

What happens when this assumption of "women as an oppressed group" is situated in the context of Western feminist writing about third world women? It is here that I locate the colonialist move. By contrasting the representation of women in the third world with what I referred to earlier as Western feminisms' self-presentation in the same context, we see how Western feminists alone become the true "subjects" of this counterhistory. Third world women, on the other hand, never rise above the debilitating generality of their "object" status.

While radical and liberal feminist assumptions of women as a sex class might elucidate (however inadequately) the autonomy of particular women's struggles in the West, the application of the notion of women as a homogeneous category to women in the third world colonizes and appropriates the pluralities of the simultaneous location of different groups of women in social class and ethnic frameworks; in doing so it ultimately robs them of their historical and political *agency*. Similarly, many Zed Press authors who ground themselves in the basic analytic strategies of traditional Marxism also implicitly create a "unity" of women by substituting "women's activity" for "labor" as the primary theoretical determinant of women's situation. Here again, women are constituted as a coherent group not on the basis of "natural" qualities or needs but on the basis of the sociological "unity" of their role in domestic production and wage labor (see Haraway 1985, esp. p. 76). In other words, Western feminist discourse, by assuming women as a coherent, already constituted group which is placed in kinship, legal, and other structures, defines third world women as subjects *outside* social relations, instead of looking at the way women are constituted *through* these very structures.

Legal, economic, religious and familial structures are treated as phenomena to be judged by Western standards. It is here that ethnocentric universality comes into play. When these structures are defined as "underdeveloped" or "developing" and women are placed within them, an implicit image of the "average third world woman" is produced. This is the transformation of the (implicitly Western) "oppressed woman" into the "oppressed third world woman." While the category of "oppressed woman" is generated through an exclusive focus on gender difference "the oppressed third world woman" category has an additional attribute – the "third world difference!" The "third world difference" includes a paternalistic attitude toward women in the third world.[13] Since discussions of the various themes I identified earlier (kinship, education, religion, etc.) are conducted in the context of the relative "underdevelopment" of the third world (which is nothing less than unjustifiably confusing development with the separate path taken by the West in its development, as well as ignoring the directionality of the first–third world power relationship), third world women as a group or category are automatically and necessarily defined as religious (read "not progressive"), family-oriented (read "traditional"), legal minors (read "they-are-still-not-conscious-of-their-rights"), illiterate (read "ignorant"), domestic (read "backward"), and sometimes revolutionary (read "their-country-is-in-a-state-of-war; they-must-fight!") This is how the "third world difference" is produced.

When the category of "sexually oppressed women" is located within particular systems in the third world which are defined on a scale which is normed through Eurocentric assumptions, not only are third world women defined in a particular way prior to their entry into social relations, but since no connections are made between first and third world power shifts, the assumption is reinforced that the third world just has not evolved to the extent that the West has. This mode of feminist analysis, by homogenizing and systematizing the experiences of different groups of women in these countries, erases all marginal and resistant modes and experiences.[14] It is significant that none of the texts I reviewed in the Zed Press focuses on lesbian politics or the politics of ethnic and religious marginal organizations in third world women's groups. Resistance can thus be defined only as cumulatively reactive, not as something inherent in the operation of power. If power, as Michel Foucault has argued recently, can really be understood only in the context of resistance,[15] this misconceptualization is both analytically and strategically problematical. It limits theoretical analysis as well as reinforces Western cultural imperialism. For in the context of a first/third world balance of power, feminist analyses which perpetrate and sustain the hegemony of the idea of the superiority of the West produce a corresponding set of universal images of the "third world woman," images such as the veiled woman, the powerful mother, the chaste virgin, the obedient wife, etc. These images exist in universal, ahistorical splendor, setting in motion a colonialist discourse which exercises a very specific power in defining, coding, and maintaining existing first/third world connections.

To conclude, then, let me suggest some disconcerting similarities between the typically authorizing signature of such Western feminist writings on women in the third world, and the authorizing signature of the project of humanism in general – humanism as a Western ideological and political project which involves the necessary recuperation of the "East" and "Woman" as Others. Many contemporary thinkers, including Foucault (1978, 1980), Derrida (1974), Kristeva (1980), Deleuze and Guattari (1977), and Said (1978), have written at length about the underlying anthropomorphism and ethnocentrism which constitute a hegemonic humanistic problematic that repeatedly confirms and legitimates (Western) Man's centrality. Feminist theorists such as Luce Irigaray,(1981), Sarah Kofman (see Berg 1982), and Helene Cixous (1981) have also written about the recuperation and absence of woman/women within Western humanism. The focus of the work of all these thinkers can be stated simply as an uncovering of the political *interests* that underlie the binary logic of humanistic discourse and ideology whereby, as a valuable recent essay puts it, "the first (majority) term (Identity, Universality, Culture, Disinterestedness, Truth, Sanity, Justice, etc.), which is, in fact, secondary and derivitive (a construction), is privileged over and colonizes the second (minority) term (difference, temporality, anarchy, error, interestedness, insanity, deviance, etc.), which is in fact, primary and originative" (Spanos 1984). In other words, it is only insofar as "Woman/Women" and "the East" are defined as *Others*, or as peripheral, that (Western) Man/Humanism can represent him/itself as the center. It is not the center that determines the periphery, but the periphery that, in its boundedness determines the center. Just as feminists such as Cristeva and Cixous deconstruct the latent anthropomorphism in Western discourse, I have suggested a parallel strategy in this essay in uncovering a latent ethnocentrism in particular feminist writings on women in the third world.[16]

As discussed earlier, a comparison between Western feminist self-presentation and Western feminist re-presentation of women in the third world yields significant results. Universal images of "the third world woman" (the veiled woman, chaste virgin, etc.), images constructed from adding the "third world difference" to "sexual difference," are predicated upon (and hence obviously bring into sharper focus) assumptions about Western women as secular, liberated, and having control over their own lives. This is not to suggest that Western women *are* secular, liberated, and in control of their own lives. I am referring to a *discursive* self-presentation, not necessarily to material reality. If this were a material reality, there would be no need for political movements in the West. Similarly, only from the vantage point of the West is it possible to define the "third world" as underdeveloped and economically dependent. Without the overdetermined discourse that creates the *third* world, there would be no (singular and privileged) first world. Without the "third world woman," the particular self-presentation of Western women mentioned above would be problematical. I am suggesting, then, that the one enables and sustains the other. This is not to say that the signature of Western feminist writings on the third world has the same authority as the project of Western humanism. However, in the context of the hegemony of the Western scholarly establishment in the production and dissemination of texts, and in the context of the legitimating imperative of humanistic and scientific discourse, the definition of "the third world woman" as a monolith might well tie into the larger economic and ideological praxis of "disinterested" scientific inquiry and pluralism which are the surface manifestations of a latent economic and cultural colonization of the "non-Western" world. It is time to move beyond the Marx who found it possible to say: They cannot represent themselves; they must be represented.

Notes

This essay would not have been possible without S. P. Mohanty's challenging and careful reading. I would also like to thank Biddy Martin for our numerous discussions about feminist theory and politics. They both helped me think through some of the arguments herein.

1   This is an updated and modified version of an essay published in *Boundary 2* 12, no. 3/13, no. 1 (Spring/Fall 1984), and reprinted in *Feminist Review*, no. 30 (Autumn 1988).

2   Terms such as *third* and *first world* are very problematical both in suggesting over-simplified similarities between and among countries labeled thus, and in implicitly reinforcing existing economic, cultural, and ideological hierarchies which are conjured up in using such terminology. I use the term "*third world*" with full awareness of its problems, only because this is the terminology available to us at the moment. The use of quotation marks is meant to suggest a continuous questioning of the designation. Even when I do not use quotation marks, I mean to use the term critically.

3   I am indebted to Teresa de Lauretis for this particular formulation of the project of feminist theorizing. See especially her introduction in de Lauretis, *Alice Doesn't: Feminism, Semiotics, Cinema* (Bloomington: Indiana University Press, 1984) see also Sylvia Wynter, "The Politics of Domination," unpublished manuscript.

4   This argument is similar to Homi Bhabha's definition of colonial discourse as strategically creating a space for a subject people through the production of knowledges and the exercise of power. The full quote reads: "[colonial discourse is] an apparatus of power . . . an apparatus that turns on the recognition and disavowal of racial/cultural/historical differences. Its predominant strategic function is the creation of a space for a subject people through the production of knowledges in terms of which surveillance is exercised and a complex form of pleasure/unpleasure is incited. It (i.e. colonial discourse) seeks authorization for its strategies by the production of knowledges by coloniser and colonised which are stereotypical but antithetically evaluated" (1983, 23).

5   The Zed Press Women in the Third World series is unique in its conception. I choose to focus on it because it is the only contemporary series I have found which assumes that "women in the third world" are a legitimate and separate subject of study and research. Since 1985, when this essay was first written, numerous new titles have appeared in the Women in the Third World series. Thus, I suspect that Zed has come to occupy a rather privileged position in the dissemination and construction of discourses by and about third world women. A number of the books in this series are excellent, especially those which deal directly with women's resistance struggles. In addition, Zed Press consistently publishes progressive feminist, antiracist, and antiimperialist texts. However, a number of the texts written by feminist sociologists, anthropologists, and journalists are symptomatic of the kind of Western feminist work on women in the third world that concerns me. Thus, an analysis of a few of these particular works in this series can serve as a representative point of entry into the discourse I am attempting to locate and define. My focus on these texts is therefore an attempt at an internal critique: I simply expect and demand more from this series. Needless to say, progressive publishing houses also carry their own authorizing signatures.

6   Elsewhere I have discussed this particular point in detail in a critique of Robin Morgan's construction of "women's herstory" in her introduction to *Sisterhood Is Global: The International Women's Movement Anthology* (New York: Anchor Press/Doubleday, 1984). See my "Feminist Encounters: Locating the Politics of Experience," *Copyright* 1, "Fin de Siècle 2000," 30–44, especially 35–37.

7   Another example of this kind of analysis is Mary Daly's (1978) *Gyn/Ecology*. Daly's assumption in this text, that women as a group are sexually victimized, leads to her very problematic comparison between the attitudes toward women witches and healers in the West, Chinese footbinding, and the genital mutilation of women in Africa. According to Daly, women in Europe, China, and Africa constitute a homogeneous group as victims of male power. Not only does this label (sexual victims) eradicate the specific historical and material realities and contradictions which lead to and perpetuate practices such as witch hunting and genital mutilation, but it also obliterates the differences, complexities, and heterogeneities of the lives of, for example, women of different classes, religions, and nations in Africa. As Audre Lorde (1983) pointed out, women in Africa share a long tradition of healers and goddesses that perhaps binds them together more appropriately than their victim status. However, both Daly and Lorde fall prey to universalistic assumptions about "African women" (both negative and positive). What matters is the complex, historical range of power differences, commonalities, and resistances that exist among women in Africa which construct African women as "subjects" of their own politics.

8   See Eldhom, Harris, and Young (1977) for a good discussion of the necessity to theorize male violence within specific societal frameworks, rather than assume it as a universal fact.

9   These views can also be found in differing degrees in collections such as Wellesley Editorial Committee, ed., *Women and National Development: The Complexities of Change* (Chicago: University of Chicago Press, 1977), and *Signs*, Special Issue, "Development and the Sexual Division of Labor," 7, no. 2 (Winter 1981). For an excellent introduction of WID issues, see ISIS, *Women in Development: A Resource Guide for Organization and Action* (Philadelphia: New Society Publishers, 1984). For a politically focused discussion of feminism and development and the stakes for poor third world women, see Gita Sen and Caren Grown, *Development Crises and Alternative Visions: Third World Women's Perspectives* (New York: Monthly Review Press, 1987).

10   Olivia Harris, "Latin American Women – An Overview," in Harris, ed *Latin American Women* (London: Minority Rights Group Report no. 57, 1983), 4–7. Other MRG Reports include Ann Deardon (1975) and Rounaq Jahan (1980).

11   List of Zed Press publications: Patricia Jeffery, *Frogs in a Well: Indian Women in Purdah* (1979); Latin American and Caribbean Women's Collective, *Slaves of Slaves: The Challenge of Latin American Women* (1980); Gail Omvedt, *We Shall Smash This Prison: Indian Women in Struggle* (1980); Juliette Minces, *The House of Obedience: Women in Arab Society* (1980); Bobby Siu, *Women of China: Imperialism and Women's Resistance, 1900–1949* (1981); Ingela Bendt and James Downing, *We Shall Return: Women in Palestine* (1982); Maria Rosa Cutrufelli, *Women of Africa: Roots of Oppression* (1983); Maria Mies, *The Lace Makers of Narsapur: Indian Housewives Produce for the World Market* (1982); Miranda Davis, ed., *Third World/Second Sex: Women's Struggles and National Liberation* (1983).

12.   For succinct discussions of Western radical and liberal feminisms, see Hester Eisenstein. *Contemporary Feminist Thought* (Boston: G. K. Hall & Co., 1983), and Zillah Eisenstein, *The Radical Future of Liberal Feminism* (New York: Longman, 1981).

13   Amos and Parmar (1984) describe the cultural stereotypes present in Euro-American feminist thought: "The image is of the passive Asian woman subject to oppressive practices within the Asian family with an emphasis on wanting to 'help' Asian women liberate themselves from their role. Or there is the strong, dominant Afro-Caribbean woman, who despite her 'strength' is exploited by the 'sexism' which is seen as being a strong feature in relationships between Afro-Caribbean men and women" (9). These images illustrate the extent to which *paternalism* is an essential element of feminist thinking which incorporates the above stereotypes, a paternalism which can lead to the definition of priorities for women of color by Euro-American feminists.

14   I discuss the question of theorizing experience in my "Feminist Encounters" (1987) and in an essay coauthored with Biddy Martin, "Feminist Politics: What's Home Got to Do with It?" in Teresa de Lauretis, ed., *Feminist Studies/Critical Studies* (Bloomington: Indiana University Press, 1986), 191–212.

15   This is one of M. Foucault's (1978, 1980) central points in his reconceptualization of the strategies and workings of power networks.

16   For an argument which demands a *new* conception of humanism in work on third world women, see Marnia Lazreg (1988). While Lazreg's position might appear to be diametrically opposed to mine, I see it as a provocative and potentially

positive extension of some of the implications that follow from my arguments. In criticizing the feminist rejection of humanism in the name of "essential Man," Lazreg points to what she calls an "essentialism of difference" within these very feminist projects. She asks: "To what extent can Western feminism dispense with an ethics of responsibility then writing about different women? The point is neither to subsume other women under one's own experience nor to uphold a separate truth for them. Rather, it is to allow them to *be* while recognizing that what they are is just as meaningful, valid, and comprehensible as what we are. . . . Indeed, when feminists essentially deny other women the humanity they claim for themselves, they dispense with any ethical constraint. They engage in the act of splitting the social universe into us and them, subject and objects" (99–100).

This essay by Lazreg and an essay by S. P. Mohanty (1989) entitled "Us and Them: On the Philosophical Bases of Political Criticism" suggest positive directions for self-conscious cross-cultural analyses, analyses which move beyond the deconstructive to a fundamentally productive mode in designating overlapping areas for cross-cultural comparison. The latter essay calls not for a "humanism" but for a reconsideration of the question of the "human" in a posthumanist context. It argues that (1) there is no necessary "incompatibility between the deconstruction of Western humanism" and such "a positive elaboration" of the human, and moreover that (2) such an elaboration is essential if contemporary political–critical discourse is to avoid the incoherences and weaknesses of a relativist position.

References

Amin, Samir. 1977. *Imperialism and Unequal Development.* New York: Monthly Review Press.

Amos, Valerie, and Pratibha Parmar. 1984 "Challenging Imperial Feminism." *Feminist Review* 17:3–19.

Baran, Paul A. 1962. *The Political Economy of Growth.* New York: Monthly Review Press.

Berg, Elizabeth. 1982, "The Third Woman." *Diacritics* (Summer):11–20.

Bhabha, Homi. 1983. "The Other Question – The Stereotype and Colonial Discourse." *Screen* 24. no. 6:23.

Boserup, Ester. 1970. *Women's Role in Economic Development.* New York: St. Martin's Press; London: Allen and Unwin.

Cixous, Helene. 1981. "The Laugh of the Medusa." In Marks and De Courtivron (1981).

Cowie, Elizabeth. 1978. "Woman as Sign." *m/f* 1:49–63.

Cutrufelli, Maria Rosa. 1983. *Women of Africa: Roots of Oppression.* London: Zed Press.

Daly, Mary. 1978. *Gyn/Ecology: The Metaethics of Radical Feminism.* Boston: Beacon Press.

Deardon, Ann, ed. 1975. *Arab Women.* London: Minority Rights Group Report no. 27.

de Lauretis, Teresa. 1984. *Alice Doesn't: Feminism, Semiotics, Cinema.* Bloomington: Indiana University Press.

—— 1986. *Feminist Studies/Critical Studies.* Bloomington: Indiana University Press.

Deleuze. Giles, and Felix Guattari. 1977. *Anti-Oedipus: Capitalism and Schizophrenia.* New York: Viking.

Derrida, Jacques. 1974. *Of Grammatology.* Baltimore. Johns Hopkins University Press.

Eisenstein, Hester. 1983. *Contemporary Feminist Thought.* Boston: G. K. Hall and Co.

Eisenstein, Zillab. 1981. *The Radical Future of Liberal Feminism.* New York: Longman.

Eidhom, Felicity, Olivia Harris, and Kate Young. 1977. "Conceptualising Women." *Critique of Anthropology "Women's Issue",* no. 3.

Foucault, Michel. 1978. *History of Sexuality: Volume One.* New York: Random House.

—— 1980. *Power/Knowledge.* New York: Pantheon.

Gunder-Frank, Audre. 1967. *Capitalism and Underdevelopment in Latin America.* New York: Monthly Review Press.

Haraway, Donna. 1985. "A Manifesto for Cyborgs: Science, Technology and Socialist Feminism in the 1980s." *Socialist Review* 80 (March/April):65–108.

Harris, Olivia. 1983a. "Latin American Women – An Overview." In Harris (1983b).

—— 1983b. *Latin American Women.* London: Minority Rights Group Report no. 57.

Hosken Fran. 1981. "Female Genital Mutilation and Human Rights." *Feminist Issues* 1, no. 3.

Huston, Perdita. 1979. *Third World Women Speak Out.* New York: Praeger.

Irigaray, Luce. 1981. "'This Sex Which Is Not One" and "When the Goods Get Together." In Marks and De Courtivron (1981).

Jahan. Rounaq, ed. 1980. *Women in Asia.* London: Minority Rights Group Report no. 45.

Jeffery, Patricia. 1979. *Frogs in a Well: Indian Women in Purdah.* London: Zed Press.

Joseph, Gloria, and Jill Lewis. 1981. *Common Differences: Conflicts in Black and White Feminist Perspectives.* Boston: Beacon Press.

Kishwar, Madhu, and Ruth Vanita. 1984. *In Search of Answers: Indian Women's Voices from Manushi.* London: Zed Press.

Kristeva, Julia. 1980. *Desire in Language.* New York: Columbia University Press.

Lazreg, Marnia. 1988. "Feminism and Difference: The Perils of Writing as a Woman on Women in Algeria." *Feminist Issues* 14, no. 1 (Spring):81–107.

Lindsay, Beverley, ed. 1983. *Comparative Perspectives of Third World Women: The Impact of Race, Sex and Class.* New York: Praeger.

Lorde, Audre. 1983. "An Open Letter to Mary Daly." In Moraga and Anzaldua (1983), 94–97.

Mies Maria. 1982. *The Lace Makers of Narsapur: Indian Housewives Produce for the World Market.* London: Zed Press.

Minces Juliette. 1980. *The House of Obedience: Women in Arab Society.* London: Zed Press.

Modares, Mina. 1981. "Women and Shi'ism in Iran." *m/f* 5 and 6:61–82.

Mohanty, Chandra Talpade. 1987. "Feminist Encounters: Locating the Politics of Experience." *Copyright* 1, "Fin de Siecle 2000," 30–44.

Mohanty, Chandra Talpade, and Biddy Martin. 1986. "Feminist Politics: What's Home Got to Do with It?" In de Lauretis (1986).

Mohanty, S. P. 1989. "Us and Them: On the Philosophical Bases of Political Criticism." *Yale Journal of Criticism* 2 (March):1–31.

Moraga, Cherríe. 1984. *Loving in the War Years.* Boston: South End Press.

Moraga, Cherríe, and Gloria Anzaldúa, eds. 1983. *This Bridge Called My Back: Writings by Radical Women of Color.* New York: Kitchen Table Press.

Morgan, Robin, ed. 1984. *Sisterhood Is Global: The International Women's Movement*

Anthology. New York: Anchor Press/Doubleday; Harmondsworth: Penguin.

Rosaldo, M. A. 1980. "The Use and Abuse of Anthropology: Reflections on Feminism and Cross-Cultural Understanding." *Signs* 53:389–417.

Said, Edward. 1978. *Orientalism*. New York: Random House.

Sen, Gita, and Caren Grown. 1987. *Development Crises and Alternative Visions: Third World Women's Perspectives*. New York: Monthly Review Press.

Smith, Barbara, ed. 1983. *Home Girls: A Black Feminist Anthology*. New York: Kitchen Table Press.

Spanos, William V. 1984. "Boundary 2 and the Polity of Interest: Humanism, the 'Center Elsewhere' and Power." *Boundary* 2 12, no. 3/13, no. 1 (Spring/Fall).

Tabari, Azar. 1980. "The Enigma of the Veiled Iranian Women." *Feminist Review* 5:19–32.

Tinker, Irene, and Michelle Bo Bramsen, eds. 1972. *Women and World Development*. Washington, D.C.: Overseas Development Council.

Chapter 23

Ann L. Stoler

SEXUAL AFFRONTS AND RACIAL FRONTIERS
European identities and the cultural politics of exclusion in colonial Southeast Asia

T HIS ESSAY IS CONCERNED WITH the construction of colonial categories and national identities and with those people who ambiguously straddled, crossed, and threatened these imperial divides. It begins with a story about *métissage* (interracial unions) and the sorts of progeny to which it gave rise (referred to as *métis,* mixed bloods) in French Indochina at the turn of the century. It is a story with multiple versions about people whose cultural sensibilities, physical being, and political sentiments called into question the distinctions of difference which maintained the neat boundaries of colonial rule. Its plot and resolution defy the treatment of European nationalist impulses and colonial racist policies as discrete projects, since here it was in the conflation of racial category, sexual morality, cultural competence and national identity that the case was contested and politically charged. In a broader sense, it allows me to address one of the tensions of empire which this essay only begins to sketch: the relationship between the discourses of inclusion, humanitarianism, and equality which informed liberal policy at the turn of the century in colonial Southeast Asia and the exclusionary, discriminatory practices which were reactive to, coexistent with, and perhaps inherent in liberalism itself.[1]

Nowhere is this relationship between inclusionary impulses and exclusionary practices more evident than in how métissage was legally handled, culturally inscribed, and politically treated in the contrasting colonial cultures of French Indochina and the Netherlands Indies. French Indochina was a colony of commerce occupied by the military in the 1860s and settled by *colons* in the 1870s with a métis population which numbered no more than several hundred by the turn of the century.[2] The Netherlands Indies by contrast, had been settled since the early 1600s with those of mixed descent or born in the Indies numbering in the tens of thousands in 1900. They made up nearly three-quarters of those legally designated as European. Their *Indische* mestizo culture shaped the contours of colonial

society for its first two hundred years.[3] Although conventional historiography
defines sharp contrasts between French, British, and Dutch colonial racial policy
and the particular national metropolitan agendas from which they derived, what
is more striking is that similar discourses were mapped onto such vastly different
social and political landscapes.[4]

In both the Indies and Indochina, with their distinct demographics and internal
rhythms, métissage was a focal point of political, legal, and social debate. Conceived
as a dangerous source of subversion, it was seen as a threat to white prestige, an
embodiment of European degeneration and moral decay.[5] This is not to suggest
that the so-called mixed-blood problem was of the same intensity in both places
nor resolved in precisely the same ways. However, the issues which resonated in
these different colonies reveal a patterned set of transgressions that have not been
sufficiently explored. I would suggest that both situations were so charged, in part
because such mixing called into question the very criteria by which Europeanness
could be identified, citizenship should be accorded, and nationality assigned.
Métissage represented not the dangers of foreign enemies at national borders, but
the more pressing affront for European nation-states, what the German philosopher, Fichte, so aptly defined as the, essence of the nation, its "interior frontiers."[6]

The concept of an interior frontier is compelling precisely because of its
contradictory connotations. As Etienne Balibar has noted, a frontier locates both
a site of enclosure and contact, of observed passage and exchange. When coupled
with the word interior, frontier carries the sense of internal distinctions within a
territory (or empire); at the level of the individual, frontier marks the moral
predicates by which a subject retains his or her national identity despite location
outside the national frontier and despite heterogeneity within the nation-state. As
Fichte deployed it, an interior frontier entails two dilemmas: the purity of the
community is prone to penetration on its interior and exterior borders, and
the essence of the community is an intangible "moral attitude," "a multiplicity of
invisible ties."[7]

Viewing late nineteenth-century representations of a national essence in these
terms, we can trace how métissage emerges as a powerful trope for internal contamination and challenge conceived morally, politically, and sexually.[8] The changing
density and intensity of métissage's discursive field outlines the fault lines of colonial authority: In linking domestic arrangements to the public order, family to the
state, sex to subversion, and psychological essence to racial type, métissage might
be read as a metonym for the biopolitics of the empire at large.

In both Indochina and the Netherlands Indies, the rejection of métis as a distinct
legal category only intensified how the politics of cultural difference were played
out in other domains.[9] In both colonies, the *métis-indo* problem produced a discourse
in which facile theories of racial hierarchy were rejected, while confirming the
practical predicates of European superiority at the same time. The early Vietnamese
and Indonesian nationalist movements created new sources of colonial vulnerability, and some of the debates over the nature and definition of Dutch and French
national identity must be seen in that light. The resurgence of European nationalist rhetoric may partly have been a response to nationalist resistance in the
colonies, but it cannot be accounted for in these terms alone.[10] For French
Indochina, discourses about the dangers of métissage were sustained in periods of

quiescence and cannot be viewed as rhetorics of reaction *tout court*. This is not to suggest that there was no correspondence between them.[11] But anticolonial challenges in Indo-china, contrary to the discourse which characterized the métis as a potential subversive vanguard, were never predominantly led nor peopled by them. And in the Indies, where persons of mixed descent made up a potentially powerful constituency, the bids they made for economic, social, and political reform were more often made in contradistinction to the demands of the native population, not in alliance with them.

Although the content of the métis problem was partially in response to popular threats to colonial rule, the particular form that the securing of European privilege took was not shaped in the colonies alone. The focus on moral unity, cultural genealogy, and language joined the imagining of European colonial communities and metropolitan national entities in fundamental ways. Both visions embraced a moral rearmament, centering on the domestic domain and the family as sites in which state authority could be secured or irreparably undermined.[12]

[. . .] I explore that question here by working off of a seemingly disparate set of texts and contexts: a criminal court proceeding in Haiphong in 1898; the Hanoi campaign against child abandonment in the early 1900s; the protracted debate on mixed marriage legislation in the Indies between 1887 and 1898; and finally, the confused and failed efforts of the Indo-European movement itself in the Indies to articulate its opposition to "pure-blood" Dutch by calling upon race, place, and cultural genealogy to make its demands.

In each of these texts, class, gender, and cultural markers deny and designate exclusionary practices at the same time. We cannot determine which of these categories is privileged at any given moment by sorting out the fixed primacy of race over gender or gender over class. On the contrary, I trace an unstable and uneven set of discourses in which different institutional authorities claimed primacy for one over another in relationship to how other authorities attempted to designate how political boundaries were to be protected and assigned. For mid-Victorian England, Mary Poovey argues that discourses about gender identity were gradually displaced in the 1850s by the issue of national identity.[13] However, the contestations over métissage suggest nothing linear about these developments. Rather, class distinctions, gender prescriptions, cultural knowledge, and racial membership were simultaneously invoked and strategically filled with different meanings for varied projects.

Patriarchal principles were not always applied to shore up government priorities. Colonial authorities with competing agendas agreed on two premises: Children had to be taught both their place and race, and the family was the crucial site in which future subjects and loyal citizens were to be made. These concerns framed the fact that the domestic life of individuals was increasingly subject to public scrutiny by a wide range of private and government organizations that charged themselves with the task of policing the moral borderlands of the European community and the psychological sensibilities of its marginal, as well as supposedly full-fledged, members.

At the heart of this tension between inclusionary rhetorics and exclusionary practices was a search for essences that joined formulations of national and racial identity – what Benedict Anderson has contrasted as the contrary dreams of

"historical destinies" and "eternal contaminations."[14] Racism is commonly understood as a visual ideology in which somatic features are thought to provide the
crucial criteria of membership. But racism is not really a visual ideology at all;
physiological attributes only signal the non-visual and more salient distinctions of
exclusion on which racism rests. Racism is not to biology as nationalism is to
culture. Cultural attributions in both provide the observable conduits, the indices
of psychological propensities and moral susceptibilities seen to shape which individuals are suitable for inclusion in the national community and whether those of
ambiguous racial membership are to be classified as subjects or citizens within it.
If we are to trace the epidemiologies of racist and nationalist thinking, then it is
the cultural logics that underwrite the relationship between fixed, visual representations and invisible protean essences to which we must attend. This convergence
between national and racial thinking achieves particular clarity when we turn to
the legal and social debates in the colonies that linked observable cultural styles
of parenting and domestic arrangement to the hidden psychological requirements
for access to French and Dutch citizenship in this period.

Cultural competence, national identity, and métissage

In 1898 in the French Indochinese city of Haiphong, the nineteen-year-old son of
a French minor naval employee, Sieur Icard, was charged with assaulting without
provocation a German naval mechanic, striking his temple with a whip, and
attempting to crush his eye. The boy was sentenced by the tribunal court to six
months in prison.[15] Spurred by the father's efforts to make an appeal for an attenuated prison term, some higher officials subsequently questioned whether the
penalty was unduly severe. Clemency was not accorded by the Governor-General,
and the boy, referred to by the court as "Nguyen van Thinh dit Lucien" (called
Lucien) was sentenced to bear out his full term. The case might have been less
easily dismissed if it were not for the fact that the son was métis, the child of a
man who was a French citizen and a woman who was a colonial subject, his concubine and Vietnamese.

The granting of a pardon rested on two assessments: whether the boy's cultural
identity and his display of French cultural competence supported his claim to French
citizenship rights. Because the Governor-General's letters listed the boy as Nguyen
van Thinh dit Lucien, they thereby invoked not only the double naming of the
son, privileging first Nguyen van Thinh over Lucien, but suggested the dubious
nature of his cultural affinities, giving the impression that his real name was Nguyen
van Thinh, although he answered to the name Lucien. The father, Sieur Icard,
attempted to affirm the Frenchness of his son by referring to him as Lucien and
eliminated reference to Nguyen. But the angry president of Haiphong's tribunal
court used only the boy's Vietnamese name, dropping Lucien altogether and put
the very kinship between the father and son in question by naming Icard as the
"alleged" father.

Icard's plea for pardon, which invoked his own patriotic sentiments as well
as those of his son, was carefully conceived. Icard protested that the court had
wrongly treated the boy as a *"vulgaire annamite"* (a common Annamite) and not as

the legally recognized son of a French citizen. Icard held that his son had been provoked and only then struck the German in retaliation. But more important, Lucien had been raised in a French patriotic milieu, in a household in which Germans were held in "contempt and disdain." He pointed out that their home was full of drawings of the 1870 (Franco-Prussian) War and that like any impressionable [French] boy of his age, Lucien and his imagination were excited by these images.

The tribunal's refusal to accept the appeal confronted and countered Icard's claims. At issue was whether Nguyen van Thinh dit Lucien could really be considered culturally and politically French and whether he was inculcated with the patriotic feelings and nationalist sentiments which might have prompted such a loyal response. The tribunal argued that Icard was away sailing too much of the time to impart such a love of *patrie* to his son and that Icard's "hate of Germans must have been of very recent origin since he had spent so much time sailing with foreigners."[16] The non-French inclinations of the boy were firmly established with the court's observation that Lucien was illiterate and knew but a few French words. Icard's argument was thus further undermined since Icard himself "spoke no annamite" and therefore shared no common language with his offspring.

Although these counter-arguments may have been sufficient to convince the Governor-General not to grant leniency, another unclarified but damning reason was invoked to deny the son's case and the father's appeal: namely, the "immoral relations which could have existed between the detainee and the one who declared himself his father.[17] Or as put by Villeminot, the city attorney in Haiphong charged with further investigating Icard's appeal, the boy deserved no leniency because "his morality was always detestable" and the police reports permitted one "to entertain the most serious suspicions concerning the nature of the relations which Nguyen van Thinh maintained with his alleged father."[18]

Whether these were coded allegations of homosexuality or referred to a possibly illegal recognition of the boy by Icard (pretending to be his father) is unclear. Icard's case came up at a time when acts of "fraudulent recognition" of native children were said to be swelling the French citizenry with a bastard population of native poor.[19] Perversion and immorality and patriotism and nationalist sentiments were clearly considered mutually exclusive categories. As in nineteenth-century Germany, adherence to middle-class European sexual morality was one implicit requisite for full-fledged citizenship in the European nation-state.[20]

But with all these allusions to suspect and duplicitous behavior perhaps what was more unsettling in this case was another unspeakable element in this story: Namely, that Icard felt such a powerful sentiment between himself and his son and that he not only recognized his Eurasian son but went so far as to plead the case of a boy who had virtually none of the exterior qualities (skin tone, language, or cultural literacy), and therefore could have none of the interior attributes of being French at all. What the court seemed to have condemned was a relationship in which Icard could have shown such dedication and love for a child who was illiterate, ignorant of the French language, and who spent most of his time in a cultural milieu that was much less French than Vietnamese. Under such circumstances, Icard's concern for Lucien was inappropriate and improper; his fatherly efforts to excuse his son's misdeeds were neither lauded by the lower courts nor the Governor-General. On the contrary, paternal love and responsibility were not to be disseminated arbitrarily as Icard had obviously done by recognizing his progeny but allowing him to grow up Indochinese. In denying the father's plea, the court passed sentence both on Icard and his son: Both were guilty of transgressing the boundaries of race, culture, sex, and patrie. If Icard (whose misspellings and profession belied his lower-class origins) was not able to bring his son up in a proper French milieu, then he should have abandoned him all together.

What was perhaps most duplicitous in the relationship was that the boy could both be Nguyen van Thinh in cultural sensibilities and Lucien to his father, or, from a slightly different perspective, that Lucien's physical and cultural non-French affinities did not stand in the way of the father's love. Like the relationship with the boy's mother, which was easily attributed to carnal lust, Icard's choice to stand up for his son was reduced to a motive of base desires, sexual or otherwise. Neither father nor son had demonstrated a proper commitment to and identification with those invisible moral bonds by which racist pedigrees and colonial divides were marked and maintained.

Cultural neglect, native mothers, and the racial politics of abandonment

The story invokes the multiple tensions of colonial cultures in Southeast Asia and would be of interest for that alone. But it is all the more startling because it so boldly contradicts the dominant formulation of the "métis question" at the turn of the century as a problem of "abandonment," of children culturally on the loose, sexually abused, economically impoverished, morally neglected, and politically dangerous. European feminists took up the protection of abandoned mixed-blood children as their cause, condemning the irresponsibility and double standards of European men, but so too did colonial officials who argued that these concubinary relations were producing a new underclass of European paupers, of rootless children who could not be counted among the proper European citizenry, whose sartorial trappings merely masked their cultural incompetence, who did not know what it meant to be Dutch or French. The consequences of mixed unions were thus collapsed into a singular moral trajectory, which, without state intervention, would lead to a future generation of Eurasian paupers and prostitutes, an affront to European prestige and a contribution to national decay.

If we look more closely at what was identified as abandonment, the cultural and historical peculiarities of this definition become more apparent. In his comprehensive history of child abandonment in western Europe, John Boswell commonly uses "abandonment" to refer to "the *voluntary* relinquishing of control over children by their natural parents or guardians" and to children who were exposed at the doors of churches or in other public spaces and less frequently for those intentionally exposed to death.[21] Boswell argues that ancient and contemporary commentators have conflated abandonment with infanticide far more than the evidence suggests. Nevertheless, perceptions and policies on abandonment were integrally tied to issues of child mortality. Jacques Donzelot argues that in nineteenth-century France abandonment often led to high rates of child mortality and that the intensified policing of families was morally justified for those reasons among others.[22] This does not suggest that abandonment always led to death nor that this was always its intent. The point is that in the colonial context, in contrast, discussions of abandonment rarely raise a similar concern for infanticide or even obliquely address this eventuality.

The abandonment of métis children invoked, in the colonial context, not a biological but a social death – a severing from European society, a banishment of "innocents" from the European cultural milieu in which they could potentially thrive and where some reformers contended they rightfully belonged.[23] Those officials who wrote about métis children argued that exposure in the colonial context was to the native milieu, not the natural elements, and to the immoral influence of native women whose debased characters inclined them to succumb to such illicit unions in the first place. Moreover, abandonment, as we shall see, was not necessarily voluntary, nor did both parents, despite the implication in Boswell's definition, participate in it. The statutes of the Society for the Protection and Education of Young French Métis of Cochinchine and Cambodia defined the issue of abandonment in the following way:

> Left to themselves, having no other guide than their instincts and their passions, these unfortunates will always give free rein to their bad inclinations; the boys will increase the ranks of vagabonds, the girls those of prostitution.
>
> Left to their mothers and lost in the milieu of Annamites, they will not become less depraved. It must not be forgotten that in most cases, the indigenous woman who consents to live with a European is a veritable prostitute and that she will never reform. When, after several years of free union with Frenchmen, the latter disappear or abandon her, she fatally returns to the vice from which she came and she nearly always sets an example of debauchery, sloth, and immorality for her children. She takes care of them with the sole purpose of later profiting from their labor and especially from their vices.
>
> For her métis son, she seeks out a scholarship in a school with the certainty that when her child obtains a minor administrative post, she will profit from it. But, in many cases, the child, ill-advised and ill-directed, does not work and when he leaves school, abandons himself to idleness and then to vagabondage; he procures his means of existence by extortion and theft.
>
> Abandoned métisse girls are no better off; from the cradle, their mothers adorn them with bracelets and necklaces and maintain in them a love of luxury innate in the Annamites. Arriving at the age of puberty, deprived of any skills which would help them survive, and pushed into a life by their mothers that they have a natural tendency to imitate, they will take to prostitution in its diverse forms to procure the means necessary to keep themselves in luxury.[24]

Here, abandonment has specific race, cultural, and gender coordinates. Most frequently, it referred to the abandonment of métis children by European fathers and their abandonment of the children's native mothers with whom these men lived outside of marriage. The gaze of the colonial state was not directed at children abandoned by native men but only at the progeny of mixed unions. Most significantly, the child, considered abandoned whether he or she remained in the care of the mother, was most frequently classified that way precisely because the child was left to a native mother and to the cultural surroundings in which she lived. But the term abandonment was also used freely in another context to condemn those socially *déclassé* European men who chose to reside with their mixed-blood children in the supposedly immoral and degraded native milieu. In designating cultural rather than physical neglect, abandonment connoted at least two things: that a proper French father would never allow his offspring prolonged contact nor identification with such a milieu and that the native mother of lower class origins would only choose to keep her own children for mercenary purposes.

If abandonment of métis offspring by European men was considered morally reprehensible, the depraved motives of colonized women who refused to give up their children to the superior environment of state institutions were considered worse. Thus the president of The Hanoi Society for the Protection of Métis Youths in 1904 noted that "numerous mothers refuse to confer their children to us . . . under the *pretext* of not wanting to be apart from them, despite the fact that they may periodically visit them at school." [25] But if maternal love obscured more mercenary quests to exploit their young for profits and pleasure, as was often claimed, why did so many women not only refuse to hand over their children but reject any form of financial assistance for them? Cases of such refusal were not uncommon. In 1903 the Haiphong court admonished a métisse mother who was herself "raised with all the exterior signs of a European education" for withdrawing her daughter from a government school "for motives which could not be but base given the mother's character." [26] Resistance also came from the children themselves: in 1904, the seventeen-year-old métisse daughter of an Annamite woman cohabited with the French employer of her mother's Annamite lover, declaring that she *volontairement* accepted and preferred her own situation over what the Society for the Protection of Métis Youths could offer. [27] Numerous reports are cited of métisse girls forced into prostitution by *concubin*, that is, by native men who were the subsequent lovers of the girls' native mothers. These cases expressed another sexual and cultural transgression that metropolitan social reformers and colonial authorities both feared: namely, a "traffic in *filles françaises*" for the Chinese and Annamite market, not for Europeans. [28]

The portrait of abandonment and charitable rescue is seriously flawed, for it misses the fact that the channeling of abandoned métis children into special state institutions was part of a larger (but failed) imperial vision. These children were to be molded into very special colonial citizens; in one scenario, they were to be the bulwark of a future white settler population, acclimatized to the tropics but loyal to the state. [29] As proposed by the French Feminist caucus at the National Colonial Exposition of 1931, métisse young women could:

> marry with Frenchmen, would accept living in the bush where young women from the metropole would be hesitant to follow their husbands,

> . . . [and would form] the foundation of a bourgeoisie, attached at one
> and the same time to their native land and to the France of Europe.[30]

This perspective on mixed marriages was more optimistic than some, but echoes the commonly held view that if métisse girls were rescued in time, they could be effectively educated to become *bonnes menagères* (good housekeepers) of a settled Indochina, wives or domestics in the service of France. Similar proposals, as we shall see, were entertained in the Indies in the same period and there too met with little success. However, in both contexts, the vision of fortifying the colonial project with a mixed-blood yeomanry was informed by a fundamental concern: What could be done with this mixed population, whose ambiguous positioning and identifications could make them either dangerous adversaries or effective partisans of the colonial state?

Fraudulent recognitions and other dangers of métissage

The question of what to do with the métis population prompted a number of different responses, but each hinged on whether métis should be classified as a distinct legal category subject to special education or so thoroughly assimilated into French culture that they would pose no threat. In French Indochina, the model treatment of métis in the Netherlands Indies was invoked at every turn. In 1901, Joseph Chailley-Bert, director of the *Union Colonial Française*, was sent on a government mission to Java to report on the status of métis in the Indies and on the efficacy of Dutch policy towards them. Chailley-Bert came away from Batavia immensely impressed and convinced that segregation was not the answer. He was overwhelmed by the sheer numbers of persons of mixed descent who occupied high station in the Indies, with wealth and cultivation rivaling those of many "full-blooded" Europeans. He argued that the Dutch policy not to segregate those of mixed descent nor distinguish between illegitimate and legitimate children was the only humane and politically safe course to pursue. He urged the government to adopt several Dutch practices: that abandoned métis youth be assigned European status until proof of filiation was made, that private organizations in each legal grouping (i.e., European and native) be charged with poor relief rather than the government; and that European standing not be confined to those with the proper "dosage of blood" alone. In the Indies he noted that such a ruling would be impossible because the entire society was in large part métis and such a distinction would allow a distance between the aryan without mix and the asiatic hybrids."[31]

Monsieur A. July, writing from Hanoi in 1905, similarly applauded "the remarkably successful results" of the Indies government policy rejecting the legal designation of métis as a caste apart. He argued that France's abolition of slavery and call for universal suffrage had made a tabula rasa of racial prejudice; however, he was less sanguine that France's political system could permit a similar scale of naturalization as that practiced by the Dutch, since not all young métis could be recognized as *citoyen français* for reasons he thought better not to discuss. Firmin Jacques Montagne, a head conductor in the Department of Roads and Bridges also urged that French Indochina follow the Indies path, where the Dutch had not only "safeguarded their prestige, but also profited from a force that if badly directed, could turn against Dutch domination."[32] Based on the account of a friend who administered a plantation on Java he urged that métis boys in Indochina, as in the Indies, should be educated in special institutions to prepare them to be soldiers and later for modest employment in commerce or on the estates.

These appeals to Dutch wisdom are so curious because they reflected neither the treatment of the poor Indo-European population in the Indies, nor what administrative quandaries were actually facing Dutch officials there. In the very year of Chailley-Bert's visit to Batavia, the Indies government began a massive investigation of the recent proliferation of European pauperism and its causes. Between 1901 and 1903 several thousands of pages of government reports outlined the precarious economic conditions and political dangers of a population legally classified as European but riddled with impoverished widows, beggars, vagrants, and abandoned children who were mostly Indo-Europeans.[33] The pauperism commission identified an "alarming increase" of poor Europeans born in the Indies or of mixed parentage, who could neither compete for civil service positions with the influx of "full-blooded" Dutch educated in Europe nor with the growing number of better-educated Indonesians now qualified for the same jobs.[34]

The Dutch did investigate Indo-European adult life and labor, but the focus of the commissions' concern was on children and their upbringing in the parental home (*opvoeding in de ouderlijkewoning*).[35] Among the more than 70,000 legally classified Europeans in the Indies in 1900, nearly 70 percent knew little Dutch or none at all. Perhaps the more disturbing finding was that many of them were living on the borderlands of respectable bourgeois European society in styles that indicated not a failed version of European culture but an outright rejection of it.[36]

The causes of the situation were found in the continued prevalence of concubinage, not only among subaltern European military barred from legal marriage but also among civil servants and European estate supervisors for whom marriage to European women was either formally prohibited or made an economically untenable option. Although government and private company policies significantly relaxed the restrictions imposed on the entry of women from Europe after the turn of the century, non-conjugal mixed unions, along with the gendered and racist assumptions on which they were based, were not about to disappear by government fiat. In Indochina, French officials had to issue repeated warnings against concubinage from 1893 to 1911 (just when the societies for protection of métis youth were most active), suggesting the formation of another generation that threatened not to know where they belonged.[37] The pauperism commission condemned the general moral environment of the Indies, targeting concubinage as the source of a transient "rough and dangerous pauper element" that lived off the native population when they could, disgracing European prestige and creating a financial burden for the state.[38]

But Indo-European pauperism in the Indies could not be accounted for by concubinage alone. The pauperism commission's enquiry revealed a highly stratified educational system in which European youths educated in the Indies were categorically barred from high-level administrative posts and in which middling Indo-Europeans were offered only a rudimentary training in Dutch, a basic requisite for any white collar job.[39] European public (free) schools in the Indies, like those in Indochina, were largely schools for the poor (*armenscholen*) attended by and really only designed for a lower-class of indigent and mixed-blood Europeans.[40]

A concrete set of reforms did form a response, to some extent, to concubinage and educational inequities, but European pauperism was located in a more unsettling problem: It was seen to have deeper and more tenacious roots in the surreptitious penetration of inlanders into the legal category of European.[41] Because the European legal standing exempted men both from labor service and from the harsher penal code applied to those of native status, officials argued that an underclass of European soldiers and civilians was allegedly engaged in a profitable racket of falsely recognizing native children who were not their own for an attractive fee. Thus, the state commission argued, European impoverishment was far more limited than the statistics indicated: The European civil registers were inflated by lowlife mercenaries and, as in Indochina, by *des sans-travail* (the unemployed), who might register as many as thirty to forty children who did not have proper rights to Dutch or French citizenship at all.[42]

The issue of fraudulent recognition, like concubinage, hinged on the fear that children were being raised in cultural fashions that blurred the distinctions between ruler and ruled and on the fear that uneducated native young men were acquiring access to Dutch and French nationality by channels, such as false filiation, that circumvented state control. Such practices were allegedly contingent on a nefarious class of European men who were willing to facilitate the efforts of native mothers who sought such arrangements. Whether there were as many fraudulent recognitions of métis children in Indochina, or *kunstmatig gefabriceerde Europeanen* (artificially fabricated Europeans) in the Indies as authorities claimed is really not the point. The repeated reference to fictitious, fraudulent, and fabricated Europeans expressed an underlying preoccupation of colonial authorities, shared by many in the European community at large, that illicit incursions into the Dutch and French citizenry extended beyond those cases labelled fraudulent recognition by name. We should remember that Nguyen van Thinh dit Lucien's condemnation was never explicitly argued on the basis of his suspect parentage, but on the more general contention that his behavior had to be understood as that of an *indigene* in disguise, not as a citizen of France. Annamite women who had lived in concubinage were accused of clothing their métisse daughters in European attire, while ensuring them that their souls and sentiments remained deeply native.[43]

Colonial officials wrestled with the belief that the Europeanness of métis children could never be assured, despite a rhetoric affirming that education and upbringing were transformative processes. Authorities spoke of abandoned métisse daughters as *les filles françaises* when arguing for their redemption, but when supporting segregated education, these same authorities recast these youths as physically marked and morally marred with "the faults and mediocre qualities of their [native] mothers" as "the fruits of a regrettable weakness."[44] Thus, abandoned métis children not only represented the sexual excesses and indiscretions of European men but the dangers of a subaltern class, degenerate (*verwilderen*) and lacking paternal discipline (*gemis aan vaderlijke tucht*), a world in which mothers took charge.[45] To what extent the concern over neglected métis children was not only about the negative influence of the native milieu but about the threat of single-mother families as in Europe and America in the same period is difficult to discern.[46]

The absence of patriarchal authority in households of widows and native women who had exited from concubinary domestic arrangements was clearly seen as a threat to the proper moral upbringing of children and sanctioned the intervention of the state. Métis children undermined the inherent principles upon which national identity thrived – those *liens invisibles* (invisible bonds) that all men shared and that so clearly and comfortably marked off *pur-sang* French and Dutch from those of the generic colonized.

The option of making métis a legal category was actively debated in international colonial fora through the 1930s but was rejected on explicitly political grounds. French jurists persuasively argued that such a legal segregation would infest the colonies with a destructive virus, with a "class of *déraciné, déclassé,*" "our most dangerous enemies," "insurgents, irreconcilable enemies of our domination."[47] The legal rejection of difference in no way diminished the concern about them. On the contrary, it produced an intensified discourse in which racial thinking remained the bedrock on which cultural markers of difference were honed and more carefully defined.

This was nowhere clearer than in the legal discussion about whether and by what criteria children of unknown parents should be assigned French or native nationality.[48] Under a 1928 *décret,* all persons born in Indochina (that is, on French soil) of unknown parents of which one was presumed to be French could obtain recognition *of "la qualité de français."*[49] Presumed Frenchness rested on two sorts of certainty: the evaluation of the child's "physical features or race" by a "medico-legal expert" and a "moral certainty" derived from the fact that the child "has a French name, lived in a European milieu and was considered by all as being of French descent."[50] Thus, French citizenship was not open to all métis but restricted by a "scientific" and moral judgment that the child was decidedly non-indigene.[51] As we have seen in the case of Nguyen van Thinh dit Lucien, however, the name Lucien, the acknowledged paternity by Icard, and the patriotic ambience of the household were only sufficient for the child to be legally classified as French, not for him to be treated as French by a court of law. Inclusionary laws left ample room for an implementation based on exclusionary principles and practices.

The moral outrage and crusade against abandonment attended to another underlying dilemma for those who ruled. Métis youth not only had to be protected from the "demoralisation of the special milieu" in which they were raised but, as important, educated in a way that would not produce unreasonable expectations nor encourage them to harbor desires for privilege above their station simply because French or Dutch blood flowed in their veins. The aim of the Hanoi society for the protection of métis youth was "to inculcate them with our sense of honor and integrity, while only suggesting to them modest tastes and humble aspirations."[52] Similarly, in the Indies, Indo-European pauperism was commonly attributed to the "false sense of pride" of Indos who refused to do manual labor or take on menial jobs, who did not know that "real Dutchmen" in the Netherlands worked with their hands. The assault was double-edged. It blamed those impoverished for their condition but also suggested more subtly that if they were really Dutch in spirit and drive, such problems of pauperism would not have arisen. [. . .]

Jus sol, jus sanguinis, **and nationality**

> In the civilized world, no one may be without a relationship to the state.[53]

J. A. Nederburgh, one of the principal architects of Indies colonial law in 1898, engaged the question of national identity and membership more directly than many of his contemporaries. He argued that in destroying racial purity, colonialism had made obsolete the criteria of *jus soli* (place of birth) and *jus sanguinis* (blood descent) for determining nationality. Colonial *vermenging* (mixing or blending), he contended, had produced a new category of "wavering classes," large groups of people whose place of birth and mixed genealogies called into question the earlier criteria by which rights to metropolitan citizenship and designations of colonial subject had once been assigned. Taking the nation to be those who shared "morals, culture, and perceptions, feelings that unite us without one being able to say what they are," Nederburgh concluded that one could not differentiate who had these sensibilities by knowing birthplace and kinship alone. He pointed to those of "pure European blood" who

> for years remained almost entirely in native surroundings [*omgeving*] and became so entirely nativized [*verlandschen*] that they no longer felt at ease among their own kind [*rasgenooten*] and found it difficult to defend themselves against *Indische* morals and points of view.[54]

He concluded that surroundings had an "overwhelming influence," with "the power to almost entirely neutralise the effects of descent and blood."[55] Although Nederburgh's claim may seem to suggest a firm dismissal of racial supremacy, we should note that he was among the most staunchly conservative legalists of his time, a firm defender of the superiority of Western logic and law.[56] By Nederburgh's cultural account, Europeans, especially children "who because of their age are most susceptible and often the most exposed" to native influence in school and native servants at home, who remained too long in the Indies "could only remain *echte-Europeesch* (truly European) in thought and deed with much exertion."[57] While Nederburgh insisted that he was not "against *Indische* influence per se," he recommended that the state allocate funds to bring up European children in Holland.[58] Some eight years later, at the height of the Ethical Policy, another prominent member of the colonial elite made a similar but more radical recommendation to close all schools of higher education in Batavia and to replace them with state-subsidized education in Holland to improve the quality of the colored (*kleuringen*) in the civil servant ranks.[59] Both proposals derived from the same assumption: that it was "impossible for persons raised and educated in the Indies to be bearers [*dragers*] of Western culture and civilization."[60]

Attention to upbringing, surroundings, and milieu did not disengage personal potential from the physiological fixities of race. Distinctions made on the basis of *opvoeding* (upbringing) merely recoded race in the quotidian circumstances that enabled acquisition of certain cultural competencies and not others. The focus on milieu naturalized cultural difference, sexual essence, and moral fiber of

Europeanness in new kinds of ways. I have discussed elsewhere how the shift in the colonies to white endogamy and away from concubinage at the turn of the century, an intensified surveillance of native servants, and a sharper delineation of the social space in which European children could be brought up and where and with whom they might play marked out not only the cultural borders of the European community but indicated how much political security was seen to reside in the choices of residence, language, and cultural style that individuals made. Personal prescriptions for inclusion as citizens of the Dutch state were as stringent and intimate as those that defined the exclusion of its subjects.[61] The wide gap between prescription and practice suggests why the prescriptions were so insistently reiterated, updated, and reapplied. Among those classified as European, there was little agreement on these prescriptions, which were contested, if not openly defied.

In 1884, legal access to European equivalent status in the Indies required a "complete suitability [*geschiktheid*] for European society," defined as a belief in Christianity, fluency in spoken and written Dutch, and training in European morals and ideas.[62] In the absence of an upbringing in Europe, district authorities were charged with evaluating whether the concerned party was "brought up in European surroundings as a European."[63] But European equivalence was not granted simply on the display of a competence and comfort in European norms. It required that the candidate "no longer feel at home" (*niet meer thuis voelt*) in native society and has already "distanced" himself from his native being *(Inlander-zijn)*. In short the candidate could neither identify nor retain inappropriate senses of belonging or longings for the milieu from which she or he came.[64] The mental states of potential citizens were at issue, not their material assets alone. Who were to be the arbitrators? Suitability to which European society and to which Europeans? The questions are disingenuous because the coding is clear: cultural competence, family form, and a middle-class morality became the salient new criteria for marking subjects, nationals, citizens, and different kinds of citizens in the nation-state. As European legal status and its equivalent became accessible to an ever broader population, the cultural criteria of privilege were more carefully defined. European women who subscribed to the social prescription of white endogamy were made the custodians of a new morality – not, as we shall see, those "fictive" European women who rejected those norms.

Colonial practice contradicted the moral designations for European national and racial identity in blatant ways: which European morality was to be iconized? That embraced by those European men who cohabited with native women, became nativized, and supported their offspring? Or the morality of European men who retained their cultural trappings as they lived with native women who bore métis children, then departed for Europe unencumbered when their contracts were done? Or was it the morality of colonial officials who barred the filing of paternity suits against European men by native women or the morality of those who argued for it on the grounds that it would hinder fraudulent acknowledgments and easy recognitions by lower-class European men? What can we make of the ruling on European equivalence for non-native residents that stipulated that candidates must be from regions or states that subscribed to a monogamous family law?[65] How did this speak to the thousands of Indisch Dutch men for whom concubinage was the most frequently chosen option? And finally, if national identity was, as often stated, "an indescribable set of invisible bonds," what did it mean when a European woman upon marriage to a native man was legally reclassified to follow his nationality? As we shall see, these invisible bonds, in which women only had a conjugal share by proxy to their husbands, were those enjoyed by some but not all men. The paradox is that native women married to European men were charged with the upbringing of children, with the formative making of Dutch citizens, and with culturally encoding the markers of race. Colonial cultures created problematic contexts in which patriarchal principles and criteria for citizenship seemed to be at fundamental odds. At a time when European feminists were turning to motherhood as a claim to citizenship, this notion of "mothers of citizens" meant something different in colonial politics, where definitions of proper motherhood served to clarify the blurred boundaries of nation and race.[66]

The mixed-marriage law of 1898

The mixed-marriage law of 1898 and the legal arguments which surrounded it are of special interest on several counts. Nowhere in the Dutch colonial record is the relationship between gender prescription, class membership, and racial category so contentiously debated and so clearly defined; nowhere is the danger of certain kinds of mixing so directly linked to national image while references to race are denied.[67] This is a liberal discourse ostensibly about the protection of native (men's) rights and later viewed as the paragon of ethical intent to equalize and synchronize colonial and metropolitan law. But, as Willem Wertheim noted nearly forty years ago, it did far more to buttress racial distinctions than to break them down.[68]

Legal attention to mixed marriages was not new in the Indies but had never been formalized as it was to be now.[69] Mixed marriages had been regulated by government decree and church decretals soon after the East Indies Company established a settlement in Batavia in the early seventeenth century. The decree of 1617 forbidding marriages between Christian and non-Christian remained intact for over 200 years. With the new Civil Code of 1848, the religious criteria were replaced with the ruling that marriage partners of European and native standing would both be subject to European law.

The legislation on mixed marriages prior to 1898 was designed to address one kind of union but not others. The 1848 ruling allowed European men already living in concubinage with non-Christian native women to legalize those unions and the children borne from them. Although the civil law of 1848 was derived from the Napoleonic civil code, a dominant principle of it had been curiously ignored: that upon marriage a woman's legal status was made that of her husband. As Dutch jurists were to argue a half-century later because mixed marriages had then been overwhelmingly between European men and native women, the latter's legal incorporation could be easily assumed. This, however, was no longer the case in the 1880s when Indies colonial officials noted two troubling phenomena: First, more women classified as European were choosing to marry non-European men; and second, concubinage continued to remain the domestic arrangement of choice over legal marriage.[70] Legal specialists argued that concubinage was a primary cause of Indo-European impoverishment and had to be discouraged. However, the mixed-marriage rulings as they stood, were so complicated and costly that people continued to choose cohabitation over legal marriage. Perhaps more disturbing still, some European, Indo-European, and native women opted to retain their own legal standing (thereby protecting their own material assets and those they could bestow on their children), thus rejecting marriage altogether.[71]

Colonial lawyers were thus faced with a conundrum: How could they implement a ruling that would facilitate certain kinds of mixed marriages (over concubinage) and condemn others. Two basic premises were accepted on all sides: that the family was the bulwark of state authority and that the unity of the family could only be assured by its unity in law.[72] Thus, legitimate children could not be subject to one law and their father to another, nor could women hold native status while their husbands retained that of a European.[73] Given this agreement there were two possible solutions: either the "superior European standing" of either spouse would determine the legal status (and nationality) of the other; or, alternatively, the patriarchal principle – that is, a woman follows the legal status of her husband (regardless of his origin) – would be applied. Principles of cultural and male supremacy seem to be opposed. Let us look at why they were not.

Those who argued that a European woman should retain her European standing in a mixed marriage did so on the grounds, among others, that European prestige would be seriously compromised. The liberal lawyer, J. H. Abendanon, cogently argued that European women would be placed in a "highly unfavorable and insecure position"; by being subject to adat, she risked becoming no more than a concubine if her native husband took a second wife, as polygamy under Islamic law was not justification for divorce. Others pointed out that she would be subject to the penal code applied to those of native status. Should she commit a crime, she would be treated to "humiliating physical and psychological punishment," for which her "physical constitution" was unsuited. Her relegation to native status would thus cause an "outrageous scandal" in the European community at large.[74]

The argument above rested on one central but contested assumption: that all women classified as European deserved the protection and privilege of European law. However, those who made the countercase that the patriarchal principle be applied regardless of origin, argued that the quality of women with European standing was not the same. Although the state commission noted that mixed marriages between European women and native men were relatively few, it underlined their marked and "steady increase among certain classes of the inhabitants".[75] Such mixed marriages, all but unthinkable in 1848 but now on the rise among Indo-European and even full-blooded European women with native men, were attributed to the increasing impoverishment and declining welfare of these women on the one hand and of the "intellectual and social development" among certain classes of native men on the other.[76] The latter issue, however, was rarely addressed because the gender hierarchy of the argument was contingent on assuming that women who made such conjugal choices were neither well-bred nor deserving of European standing.

One lawyer, Taco Henny, argued that the category, European, was a legal fiction not indicative of those who actually participated in the cultural and moral life of the European community and that the majority of women who made such choices were "outwardly and inwardly indistinguishable from natives." Because these women tended to be of lower-class origin or mixed racial descent, he held that they were already native in culture and inclination and needed no protection from that cultural milieu in which they rightly belonged. Similarly, their subjection to the native penal code was no reason for scandal because it was appropriate to their actual station. They were already so far removed from Dutch society proper that it would cause no alarm.

If Taco Henny's argument was not convincing enough, Pastor van Santen made the case in even bolder terms:

> The European woman who wants to enter into such a marriage has already sunk so deep socially and morally that it does not result in ruin, either in her own eyes or those of society. It merely serves to consolidate her situation.[77]

Such arguments rested on an interior distinction between echte Dutch women and those in whom "very little European blood actually flowed in their veins" within the category of those classified as European. Pastor van Santen's claim that this latter group had already fallen from cultural and racial grace had its "proof" in yet another observation: "that if she was still European in thought and feeling, she would never take a step that was so clearly humiliating and debasing in the eyes of actual (werkelijk) European women."[78] This reasoning (which won in the end) marshaled the patriarchal tenets of the civil code to exclude women of a certain class and cultural milieu from Dutch citizenship rights without directly invoking race in the legal argument.

But this gendered principle did more work still and could be justified on wider grounds. First, such legislation defined a "true" European woman in accepted cultural terms: first, by her spousal choice, and, second, by her maternal sentiments. She was to demonstrate that she put her children's interests first by guarding their European standing, which would be lost to her future progeny if she married a non-European under the new law. As such, it strongly dissuaded "true" European women from choosing to marry native men. This was its implicit and, according to some advocates, its explicit intent. In addition, it spoke on the behalf of well-to-do native men, arguing that they would otherwise lose their access to agricultural land and other privileges passed from fathers to sons under adat law.[79] Finally, the new legislation claimed to discourage concubinage, as native men could thus retain their customary rights and would not be tempted to live with Indo-European and "full-blooded" European women outside of marriage. But perhaps most important, this appeal to patriarchy prevented the infiltration of increasing numbers of native men into the Dutch citizenry, particularly those of the middling classes, who were considered to have little to lose and much to gain by acquiring a Dutch nationality. Those who supported "uplifting" native men to European status through marriage would in effect encourage marriages of convenience at the expense of both European women who were drawn to such unions and those who prided themselves on the cultural distinctions that defined them as European."[80] Here again, as in the fraudulent recognitions of métis children, at issue was the undesirability of an increase in "the number of persons who would only be European in name."[81]

In the end, the mixed-marriage ruling and the debates surrounding it were more an index than a cause of profound changes in thinking about sexual practice, national identity, and colonial morality. Mixed marriages increased between native women and European men between 1900 and 1920. This was evident in the declining number of acknowledgments of children born out of wedlock and in an increased number of single European men who now married their *huishoudster* (housekeeper or sexual companion or both).[82] Condemnation of concubinage came simultaneously from several sources. The Pauperism Commission had provided new evidence that concubinage was producing an underclass of Indos that had to be curbed. By treating prostitution and the huishoudster system in the colonies as similar phenomena, the *Nederlandschen Vrouwenbond* (Dutch Women's Association) conflated the distinct options such arrangements afforded women and rallied against both.[83] The *Sarekat Islam,* one of the strongest native nationalist organizations, also campaigned against concubinage on religious grounds that may have discouraged some native women from such unions.[84] Still, in 1920 half the métis children of a European father and native mother were born outside of marriage. After 1925 the number of mixed marriages fell off again as the number of Dutch-born women coming to the Indies increased fourfold.

Hailed as exemplary liberal legislation, the mixed-marriage ruling was applied selectively on the basis of class, gender, and race. By reinvoking the Napoleonic civil code, European men were assured that their "invisible bonds" of nationality remained intact regardless of their legal partner. European women, on the other hand, were summarily (but temporarily) disenfranchised from their national community on the basis of conjugal choice alone.[85] Those mixed marriages which derived from earlier cohabitations between European men and native women were not the unions most in question, and jurists of different persuasions stated as much throughout the debate. These marriages were considered unproblematic on the assumption that a native woman would be grateful for, and proud of, her elevated European status and content with legal dependence on a European man. Were native women easily granted European legal standing and Dutch citizenship because there was no danger that they could or would fully exercise their rights? The point is never discussed because racial and gender privileges were in line.

But what about the next generation of métis? Although the new ruling effectively blocked the naturalization of native adult men through marriage, it granted a new generation of métis children a European standing by affixing their nationality to their father's. Would this generation be so assuredly cut from their mother's roots as well? The persistent vigilance with which concern for omgeving, upbringing, class, and education were discussed in the 1920s and 1930s suggests that there were resounding doubts. The Netherlands Indies Eugenics Society designed studies to test whether children of Europeans born in the Indies might display different "racial markers" than their parents.[86] Eugenicist logic consolidated discussions about national identity and cultural difference in a discourse of "fitness" that specified the interior frontiers of the nation, reaffirming yet again that upbringing and parenting were critical in deciding who would be marked as a fictive compatriot or true citizen.

Although the race criterion was finally removed from the Indies constitution in 1918 under native nationalist pressure, debates over the psychological, physical, and moral make-up of Indo-Europeans intensified in the 1920s and 1930s more than they had before. A 1936 doctoral dissertation at the University of Amsterdam could still "explain the lack of energy" of Indo-Europeans by the influence of a sapping and warm, dank climate; by the bad influence of the "energy-less Javanese race" on Indo-Europeans; and by the fact that "halfbloods" were not descended from the "average European" and the "average Javanese."[87] In the 1920s, the European-born Dutch population was visibly closing its ranks, creating new cultural boundaries while shoring up its old ones. Racial hate (rassenhaat) and representation were watchwords of the times. A renewed disdain for Indos permeated a discourse that heightened in the Depression as the nationalist movement grew stronger and as unemployed "full-blooded" Europeans found "roaming around" in native villages blurred with the ranks of the Indo poor. How the colonial state distinguished these two groups from one another and from "natives" on issues of unemployment insurance and poor relief underscored how crucial these interior frontiers were to the strategies of the emerging welfare state.[88]

Indo-Europeans and the quest for a fatherland

The slippage between race and culture, as well the intensified discussions of racial membership and national identity, were not invoked by the echte-Europeesche population alone. We have seen that the moral geography of the colonies had a metonymic quality: Despite the huge numbers of Europeans of mixed parentage and substantial economic means, the term Indo was usually reserved for that segment who were verindische (indianized) and poor. Less clear are the cultural, political, and racial criteria by which those of mixed descent identified themselves. The contradictory and changing criteria used by the various segments of the Indo-European movement at the turn of the century highlight how contentious and politically contingent these deliberations were.

It is not accidental that the term Indo-European is difficult to define. In the Indies it applied to those of mengbloeden (mixed blood) of European and native origin, to Europeans born in the Indies of Dutch nationality and not of native origin, and to those pur-sang Europeans born elsewhere who referred to the Indies as a "second fatherland."[89] The semantics of mixing thus related to blood, place, and belonging to different degrees and at different times. Soeria Soemirat, one of the earliest publications of the Indo-European constituency in the late 1890s, included among its members all Indies-born Europeans and took as its central goal the uplifting of the (Indo)-European poor. The Indisch Bond formed in 1898, was led by an Indies-born European constituency that spoke for the Indo poor but whose numbers were rarely represented in their ranks. At the heart of both organizations was the push for an Indisch vaderland, contesting both the popular terms of Indonesian nationalism and the exclusionary practices of the Dutch-born (totok) society.[90]

The Indo-European movement never developed as a nationalist movement. As "socially thin" as Benedict Anderson suggests its creole counterpart was in the Americas, it could neither enlist a popular constituency nor dissociate from its strong identification with the European-born Dutch elite. The Indisch movement often made its bids for political and economic power by invoking Eurasian racial superiority to inlanders while concurrently denying racial criteria for judging their status vis-à-vis European-born Dutch. The subsequent effort in 1912 to form an *Indische Partij* with the motto "Indies for the Indiers") was stridently antigovernment, with a platform that addressed native as well as poor Indo welfare. Despite an inclusionary rhetoric, its native and poor Indo constituency were categorically marginalized and could find no common political ground. By 1919, when native nationalist mobilization was gaining strength, the need for a specifically *Indo-Bond* took on new urgency and meaning. As its founder argued, it would be a "*class-verbond* (class-based association) to support the interests of the larger Indo-group."[92] This organization, eventually called the Indo-Europeesch Verbond (IEV), with more than 10,000 members in 1924, continued to plead the cause of the Indo poor while remaining unequivocally loyal to the Dutch colonial state. This truncated version of a much more complicated story, nevertheless, illustrates the unsettling point that the poor Indo constituency never achieved a political voice. However large their numbers, they were silently rejected from the early Indonesian nationalist movement and could only make their demands based on claims to a cultural and racial alliance with those Dutch who ruled.[93] [. . .]

Rootlessness and cultural racism

With rootedness at the center stage of nationalist discourse, the notion of rootlessness captured a range of dangers about métissage.[94] Abandoned métis youths were generically viewed as vagrants in Indochina, as child delinquents in the Indies, as de facto stateless subversives without a patrie.[95] In times of economic crisis "free-roaming European bastards" were rounded up for charity and goodwill in efforts to avert a racial disgrace. Liberal colonial projects spent decades creating a barrage of institutions to incorporate, inculcate, and insulate abandoned métis youths. But the image of rootlessness was not only applied to those who were abandoned.

In 1938, government officials in Hanoi conducted a colony-wide enquiry to monitor the physical and political movements of métis. The Resident of Tonkin recommended a comprehensive state-sponsored social rehabilitation program to give métis youths the means to function as real *citoyens* on the argument that with "French blood prevailing in their veins," they already "manifested an instinctive attachment to France."[96] But many French in Indochina must have been more equivocal about their instinctive patriotic attachments. The fear that métis might revert to their natural inclinations persisted, as did a continuing discourse on their susceptibility to the native milieu, where they might relapse to the immoral and subversive states of their mothers.

Fears of métissage were not confined to colonial locales. We need only read the 1942 treatise, *Les Métis*, of René Martial who combined his appointment on the faculty of medicine in Paris with eugenic research on the *anthro-biologie des races*. For him, métis were categorically persons of physical and mental deformity. He saw métis descent as a frequent cause both of birth defects in individuals and of the contaminated body politic of France. As he put it,

> Instability, the dominant characteristic of métis, . . . is contagious, it stands in opposition to the spirit of order and method, it generates indeterminable and futile discussion and paralyzes action. It is this state of mind that makes democracies fail that live with this chimera of racial equality, one of the most dangerous errors of our times, defended with piety by pseudo-French who have found in it a convenient means to insinuate themselves everywhere.[97]

That Martial's spirit continues to thrive in contemporary France in the rhetoric of Le Pen is not coincidental. The discourses on métissage in the early twentieth century and in LePen's rhetoric on immigrant foreigners today are both about external boundaries and interior frontiers. Both discourses are permeated with images of purity, contamination, infiltration, and national decay. For both Martial and LePen, cultural identities refer to human natures and psychological propensities inimical to the identity of the French nation and a drain on the welfare state.[98]

On cultural hybridity and domestic subversions

These historically disparate discourses are striking in how similarly they encode métissage as a political danger predicated on the psychological liminality, mental instability, and economic vulnerability of culturally hybrid minorities.[99] But could we not re-present these discourses by turning them on their heads, by unpacking what the weakness of métissage was supposed to entail? Recast, these discourses may be more about the fear of empowerment, not about marginality at all; about groups that straddled and disrupted cleanly marked social divides and whose diverse membership exposed the arbitrary logic by which the categories of control were made.[100] These discourses are not unlike those about Indische women that, in disparaging their impoverished and hybrid Dutch and non-European tastes, eclipsed the more compelling reality that they could "sometimes pass between ethnic communities, cross lines drawn by color and caste and enter slots for which they had no birthright, depending on their alliance with men."[101] The final clause is critical because through these varied sexual contracts citizenship rights were accorded and métis identities were contested and remade.[102] The management of sexuality, parenting, and morality were at the heart of the late imperial project. Cohabitation, prostitution, and legally recognized mixed marriages slotted women, men, and their progeny differently on the social and moral landscape of colonial society. These sexual contracts were buttressed by pedagogic, medical, and legal evaluations that shaped the boundaries of European membership and the interior frontiers of the colonial state.

Métissage was first a name and then made a thing. It was so heavily politicized because it threatened both to destabilize national identity and the Manichean categories of ruler and ruled. The cultural density of class, gender, and national issues that it invoked converged in a grid of transgressions which tapped into metropolitan and colonial politics at the same time. The sexual affront that it represented challenged middle-class family order and racial frontiers, norms of childrearing and conjugal patriarchy, and made it increasingly difficult to distinguish between true

nationals and their sullied, pseudo-compatriots. The issue of fraudulent recognition could be viewed in a similar light. Poor white men and native women who
arranged legal recognition of their own children or those of others, defied the
authority of the state by using the legal system to grant Dutch and French citizenship to a younger generation.[103]

The turn of the century represents one major break point in the nature of
colonial morality and in national projects. In both the Indies and Indochina, a new
humanitarian liberal concern for mass education and representation was coupled
with newly recast social prescriptions for maintaining separatist and exclusionary
cultural conventions regarding how, where, and with whom European colonials
should live. Virtually all of these differentiating practices were worked through a
psychologizing and naturalizing impulse that embedded gender inequalities, sexual
privilege, class priorities, and racial superiority in a tangled political field. Colonial
liberalism in its nationalist cast opened the possibilities of representation for some
while it set out moral prescriptions and affixed psychological attributes which
partially closed those possibilities down.

But the exclusionary strategies of the colonial state were not meted out to a
passive population, nor is it clear that many of those who inhabited the borderlands of European colonial communities sought inclusion within them. At the core
of the métis problem were cultural contestations of gender and class that made
these "laboratories of modernity" unwieldy sites of engineering.[104] The experiments
were reworked by their subjects, not least of all by women who refused to give
"up" their children to charitable institutions for European training and by others
who chose cohabitation (not concubinage) over marriage. Women and men who
lived culturally hybrid lifestyles intercepted nationalist and racist visions. Without
romanticizing their impoverishment, we might consider the possibility that their
choices expressed a domestic subversion, a rejection of the terms of the civilizing
mission. For those who did not adhere to European bourgeois prescripts, cultural
hybridity may have affirmed their own new measures of civility.

Notes

1   Uday Mehta outlines some features of this relationship in "Liberal Strategies of
    Exclusion," *Politics and Society*, 18:(4) (1990), 427–54. He cogently argues for
    the more radical claim that the theoretical underpinnings of liberalism are exclu-
    sionary and cannot be explained as "an episodic compromise with the practical
    constraints of implementation" (p. 429).

2   Cochinchine's European population only increased from 594 in 1864 to 3,000
    by 1900 (Charles Meyer, *De Français en Indochine, 1860–1910*. 70 (Paris:
    Hachette, 1985]). By 1914 only 149 planters qualified as electors in the Chamber
    of Agriculture of Tonkin and Annam; on Java alone there were several thou-
    sand (John Laffey. "Racism in Tonkin before 1914," *French Colonial Studies*, no.
    1 [1977], 65–81). In 1900 approximately 91,000 persons were classified as
    European in the Indies. As late as 1931 there were just under 10,500 French
    civilians in Indochina, when the Indies census counted 244,000 Europeans for
    the same year (see A. van Marle, "De groep der Europeanen in Nederlands-
    Indie, iets over ontstaan en groei," *Indonesie*, 5:5 (1952), 490; and Gilles de

Gante, *La population française au Tonkin entre 1931 et 1938*, 23 [Mémoire de Maitrise, Université de Provence], 1981.

3 See Jean Taylor's subtle gendered analysis of the mestizo features of colonial culture in the Netherlands Indies *(The Social World of Batavia* [Madison: University of Winconsin Press, 1983]). The term *Indisch* is difficult to translate. According to Taylor, it is a cultural marker of a person who "partook of Mestizo culture in marriage, practice, habit and loyalty" (p. xx). It is most often used in contrast to the life style and values of the Dutch *totok* population comprised of Hollanders born and bred in Europe who refused such cultural accommodations and retained a distinct distance from inlander (native) customs and social practice. Thus, for example, the European *blivjers* (those who stayed in the Indies) were commonly referred to as Indisch as opposed to *vertrekkers* (those Europeans who treated their residence in the Indies as a temporary assignment away from their native metropolitan homes).

4 See Martin Lewis, "One Hundred Million Frenchmen: The 'Assimilation' Theory in French Colonial Policy," *Comparative Studies in Society and History*. 3:4 (1961), 129–51. While the social positioning of Eurasians in India is often contrasted to that in the Indies, there are striking similarities in their changing and contra- dictory legal and social status in the late nineteenth century. See Mark Naidis, "British Attitudes toward the Anglo-lndians," *South Atlantic Quarterly*, LXII:3 (Summer 1963), 407–22; and Noel Gist and Roy Wright, *Marginality and Identity: Anglo-Indians as a Racially-Mixed Minority in India*, especially 7–20 (Leiden, 1973).

5 For an extended discussion of the politics of degeneracy and the eugenics of empire, see my "Carnal Knowledge and Imperial Power: The Politics of Race and Sexual Morality in Colonial Asia" in *Gender at the Crossroads: Feminist Anthropology in the Post-Modern Era*, 51–101, Micaela di Leonardo, ed. (University of California Press, 1991).

6 In the following section I draw on Etienne Balibar's discussion of this concept in "Fichte et la Frontière Intérieure: A Propos des *Discours a la nation allemande,* "*Les Cahiers de Fontenay, 58/59* (June 1990).

7 Fichte quoted in Balibar, "Fichte et la Frontière Intérieure," 4.

8 See my "Carnal Knowledge and Imperial Power" on métissage and contamina- tion. Also see Andre-Pierre Taguieff's *La Force du Préjugé* (1987), in which he discusses "la hantisse due métissage" and argues that the métis problem is not a question of mixed-blood but a question of the indeterminate "social identity" which métissage implies (p. 345).

9 This is not to suggest that the French and Dutch rejection of métis as a legal category owed the same trajectory or occurred in the same way. As I later show, the legal status of métis children with unknown parents was still a subject of French juridical debate in the 1930s in a discourse in which race and upbringing were offered as two alternative criteria for judging whether a métis child should be granted the rights of a *citoyen*. See Jacques Mazet, *La condition juridique des métis dans les possession françaises* (Paris: Domat-Montchresiten, 1932).

10 Paul Rich, *Race and Empire in British Politics* (Cambridge: Cambridge University Press, 1986), argues that the anti-black riots in Liverpool and Cardiff in 1919 represented "the extension of rising colonial nationalism into the heart of the British metropolis itself at a time when nationalist ferment was being expressed in many parts of the empire" (p. 122).

11 The profusion of French juridical tracts in the 1930s debating whether métis

should be made a separate legal category (distinct from European and *indigène)* and what were the political effects of doing so were forged in the tense environment in which Vietnamese nationalists were making their opposition most strongly felt. See David Marr's two important studies of the Vietnamese nationalist movements, *Vietnamese Anticolonialism, 1885–1925* (Berkeley: California Press, 1971) and *Vietnamese Tradition on Trial. 1920–1945* (Berkeley: California Press, 1981). It is noteworthy that Marr makes no reference to the métis problem (generally or as it related to citizenship, immigration and education) in either text.

12 This is not to suggest, however, that the battles for legal reform regarding, for example, paternity suits, illegitimate children, and family law waged by jurists, feminists, and religious organizations in the Netherlands and the Indies at the turn of the century were animated by the same political projects or fears; on the contrary, in the colonies, the social menace of illegitimate children, as we shall see, was not only about future criminals and prostitutes but also about mixed-blood criminals and prostitutes, about European paternity, and native mothers – and thus about the moral landscape of race and the protection of European men by the Dutch colonial state. For contrasting discourses on paternity suits in the Indies and Holland, compare Selma Sevenhuijsen's comprehensive study of this political debate *(De Orde van het Vaderschap: Politieke debatten over ongehuwd moederschap, afstamming en huwelijk in Nederland 1870–1900* [Amsterdam: Stichting Beheer IISG. 1987]) to R. Kleyn's "Onderzock nar het vaderschap" *(Het Recht in Nederlandsch-Indie,* 67 [1896], 130–50).

13 See Mary Poovey's *Uneven Developments: The Ideological Work of Gender in Mid-Victorian England* (Chicago: Chicago University Press, 1988).

14 Benedict Anderson, *Imagined Communities,* 136 (London: Verso, 1983).

15 Archives d'Outre-Mer, Protectorat de l'Annam et du Tonkin, no. 1506, 17 December 1898.

16 See Archives d'Outre Mer, December 1898, No. 39127, Report from Monsieur E. Issaud, Procureur-Général to the Résident Superieure in Tonkon at Hanoi.

17 Relations immorales qui ont pu exister entre le détenue et celui qui s'est declaré son père" (Archives d'Outre Mer [hereafter, AOM], Fonds Amiraux, No. 1792, 12 December 1898).

18 AOM, Aix-en-Provence, No. 1792, 12 December 1898. Report of M. Villemont, Procureur in Haiphong, to the Procureur-Général, Head of the Judicial Service in Hanoi.

19 According to the procureur-général, Raoul Abor, these fraudulent acknowledgments were threatening to submerge the French element by a deluge of naturalized natives (see Raoul Abor, *Des Reconnaisances Frauduleuses d'Enfants Naturels en Indochine,* 25 [Hanoi: Imprimerie Tonkinoise, 1917]).

20 George Mosse, *Nationalism and Sexuality* (Madison: University of Wisconsin Press, 1985).

21 John Boswell's *The Kindness of Strangers: The Abandonment of Children in Western Europe from Late Antiquity to the* Renaissance (New York: Pantheon, 1988). According to Boswell, this relinquishment might occur by "leaving them somewhere, selling them, or legally consigning authority to some other person or institution" (p. 24). As we shall see, abandonment in colonial practice did not fit this definition at all.

22 See Jacques Donzelot's *The Policing of* Families, 29.

23 I do not use this term in the sense employed by Orlando Patterson with regard to slavery but to suggest the definitive exile from European society which abandonment implied.

24 AOM, Amiraux 7701, 1899, Statute of the "Société de protection et d'éducation des Jeunes Métis Français de la Cohcinchine et du Cambodge."

25 AOM, No. 164, 11 May 1904 (my emphasis).

26 AOM, 13 November 1903.

27 Letter from the Administrative Resident in Bac-giang to the Résident Superieure in Hanoi.

28 AOM, Letter (No. 151) to the Governor-General in Hanoi from Monsieur Paris, the President of the Société de Protection et d'Education des Jeunes Métis Française abandonnés, 29 February 1904. This concern over the entrapment of European young women in the colonies coincides with the concurrent campaigns against the white slave trade in Europe (see Frank Mort, *Dangerous Sexualities: Medico-Moral Politics in England Since 1830*, 126–7 [London: Routledge and Kegan Paul, 1987]).

29 For such recommendations, see A. Brou, "Le métis franco annamite," *Revue Indochinois* (July 1907), 897–908; Douchet, *Métis et congaies d'Indochine* (Hanoi, 1928); Jacques Mazet, *La conditions juridique des métis* (Paris: Domat-Montchrestien 1932); Philippe Gossard, *Études sur le métissage principalement en A.O.F.* (Paris: Les Presses Modernes, 1934).

30 Etats-Generaux du Feminisme, *Exposition Coloniale Internationale de Paris 1931, rapport général présenté par le Gouverneur Général Olivier*, 139 (Paris: Imprimerie Nationale, 1931).

31 AOM, Amiraux 7701, *Report on Métis in the Dutch East Indies* (1901).

32 "Courte notice sur les métis d'Extreme Orient et en particulier sur ceux de l'Indochine," Firmin Jacques Montagne, AOM, Amiraux 1669 (1903), 1896–1909.

33 The fact that the issue of poor whites loomed large on a diverse number of colonial landscapes at this time, in part, may derive from the fact that white poverty itself was coming to be perceived in metropole and colony in new ways. In Calcutta nearly one-fourth of the Anglo-Indian community in the late nineteenth century was on poor relief (N. Gist and R. Wright, *Marginality and Identity: Anglo-Indians as a Racially Mixed Minority in India,* 16 [Leiden: Brill, 1973]). Colin Bundy argues for South Africa that white poverty was redefined "as a social problem to be tackled by state action rather than as a phenomenon of individual failure to be assuaged by charity" (p. 104). In the Indies, this reassignment of poor relief from civic to state responsibility was hotly contested and never really made.

34 *Rapport der Pauperisme-Commissie* (Batavia: Landsdrukkerij, 1902); *Uitkomsten der Pauperisme-Enquete: Algemeen Verslag* (Batavia: Landsdrukkerij, 1902); *Het Pauperisme onder de Europeanen in Nederlandsch-Indie,* Parts 3, 5 (Batavia: Landsdrukkerij, 1901); *Uitkomsten der Pauperisme-Enquete: Gewestelijke Verslagen* (Batavia: Landsdrukkerij, 1901); *De Staatsarmenzorg voor Europeanen in Nederlandsch-Indie* (Batavia: Landsdrukkerij, 1901).

35 See Petrus Blumberger's *De Indo-Europeesche Beweging in Nederlandsch-Indie,* 26 Harlem: Tjeenk Willink, 1939).

36 See J. M. Coetzee, *White Writing: On the Culture of Letters in South Africa* (New Haven: Yale University Press, 1988), in which he argues that the British railed

against Boer idleness precisely because they refused the possibility that an alternative, native milieu may have been preferred by some European men and have held a real attraction.

37 AOM, Archives Centrales de l'Indochine, nos. 9147, 9273, 7770, 4680.

38 *Encyclopedie van Nederlandsch-Indie* (1919), 367.

39 In 1900, an educational survey carried out in Dutch elementary schools in the Indies among 1,500 students found that only 29 per cent of those with European legal standing knew some Dutch and more than 40 per cent did not know any (Paul van der Veur, "Cultural Aspects of the Eurasian Community in Indonesian Colonial Society," *Indonesia*, no. 6 (1968), 45.

40 See Dr. I. J. Brugmans, *Geschiedenis van het onderwijs in Nederlandsch-Indie* (Batavia: Walters, 1938).

41 See J. F. Kohlbrugge, "Prostitutie in Nederlandsch-Indie," *Indisch Genootschap*. 19 February 1901, 26–28.

42 See n.a., "Ons Pauperisme," *Mededeelingen der Vereeniging "Soeria Soemirat,"* no. 2 (1892), 8. One proof of the falsity of the claim was that these fathers often conferred upon these children "repulsive and obscene" names frequently enough that a government ruling stipulated that no family name could be given that "could humiliate the child" (G. H. Koster, "Aangenomen Kinderen en Staatsblad Europeanen," *De Amsterdammer,* 15 July 1922).

43 Letter from the Administrative Resident in Bac-giang to the Resident Superieure, Hanoi, AOM, No. 164, 11 May 1904.

44 See Jacques Mazet, *La Condition Juridique de Métis* (Paris: Domat-Montchrestien, 1932) and Douchet *Métis et congaies d'Indochine.*

45 Kohlbrugge, "Prostitutie in Nederlandsch-Indie," 23.

46 See Linda Gordon's discussion of this issue for early twentieth-century America in *Heroes of Their Own Lives: The Politics and History of Family Violence* (New York: Vintage, 1988).

47 See Mazet, *La Condition Juridique de Métis,* 37, 42.

48 Questions about the legal status of métis and the political consequences of that decision were not confined to the French alone. The International Colonial Institute in Brussels created by Joseph Chailley-Bert in 1893 engaged this question in at least three of its international meetings in 1911, 1920, and 1924. See *Comptes Rendus de l'institut Colonial International* (Bruxelles: Bibliotheque Coloniale Internationale, 1911, 1920, 1924).

49 Mazet, *La Condition Jurdique de Métis,* 114.

50 Ibid., 80.

51 Ibid., 90.

52 Statue of the "Societé de protection des enfants métis," 18 May 1904, Article 37.

53 "In de beschaafd wereld, niemand zonder staatsverband mag zijn" (K. H. Beyen, *Het Nederlanderschap in verband met het international recht* [Utrecht, 1890]), quoted in J.A. Nederburgh, *Wet en Adat,* 83 [Batavia: Kolff and Co., 1898]). The word *staatsverband* literally means "relationship to the state." Nederburgh distinguishes it from nationality and defines it as "the tie that exists between the state and each of its members, the membership of the state" (p. 91). Dutch scholars of colonial history say the term is rarely used but connotes citizenship.

54 Ibid., 87–88.

55 Ibid., 87.

56 See Willem Wertheim's incisive review of Prof. R. D. Kollewijn's *Intergentiel Recht, Indonesie,* 19 (1956), 169–73. Nederburgh's name comes up in this critique of Kottewijn, whose liberal rhetoric and opposition to such conservatives as Nederburgh belied the fact that he praised the virtues of the Indies mixed-marriage legislation of 1898, despite the racist principles that underwrote It.

57 Nederburgh, *Wet en Adat,* 88.

58 Ibid., 90.

59 Kooreman 1906.

60 Ibid.

61 See my "Rethinking Colonial Categories: European Communities and the Boundaries of Rule," *Comparative Studies in Society and History,* 31:1 (1989), 134–61; and "Carnal Knowledge and Imperial Power."

62 W. E. van Maszenbroek, *De Historische Ontwikkeling van de Staatrechtelijke Indeeling der Bevolking van Nederlandsch-Indie* 70 (Wageningen: Veenam, 1934).

63 See W. F. Prins, "De Bevolkingsgroepen in het Nederlandsch-Indische Recht," *Kolonlal Studien,* 17 (1933), 652–88. especially 677.

64 Ibid., 677; Van Marle, "De groep der Europeanen in Nederlands," *Indonesie,* 5:2 (1951), 110.

65 See William Mastenbroek, *De Historische Ontwikkeling van de Staatsrechtelijke Indeeling der Bevolking van Nederlandsch-Indie,* 87.

66 See Karen Offen's "Depopulation, Nationalism and Feminism in Fin-de-Siècle France," *American Historical Review,* 89:3 (1984), 648–76.

67 The following discussion is based on several documents that I will abbreviate in referring to in the section below as follows: *Verslag van het Verhandelde in de Bijeenkomsten der Nederlandsch-Indische Juristen-Vereeninging* on 25, 27, and 29 June 1887 in Batavia [hereafter, JV]; "Voldoet de wetgeving betreffende huwelijken tusschen personen behoorende tot de beide staatkundige categorien der Nederlandsch Indische bevolking (die der Europeanen en met hen, en die der Inlanders en met hen gelijkgestelden) aan de maatschappelijke behoefte? Zoo neen, welke wijzigingen zijn noodig? (1887) [hereafter, VW]; J. A. Nederburgh, *Gemengde Huwelijken, Staatsblad 1898, No. 158: Officiele Bescheiden met Eenige Aanteekeningen* [hereafter, GH].

68 Werhein, *Intergentiel Recht.*

69 The term mixed marriages (*gemengde huwelijken*) had two distinct but overlapping meanings in the Indies at the turn of the century. Common usage defined it as referring to contracts between a man and a woman of different racial origin; the state defined it as "a marriage between persons who were subject to different laws in the Netherlands Indies" with no reference to race. The distinction is significant for at least two reasons: (1) because the designations of legal standing as inlander versus European cut across the racial spectrum, with generations of mixed bloods falling on different sides of this divide and (2) because adat (customary) and Dutch law followed different rulings with respect to the marriage contract, divorce, inheritance, and child custody.

70 Although the hierarchies of gender and race of Indies colonial society in part account for the fact that in 1895 more than half of the European men in the Indies still lived with native women outside of marriage, this may only tell one part of the story. The juridical debates on legal reform of mixed marriages suggest that there were women who chose cohabitation over legal marriage. At the very least, this suggests that concubinage may not have been an appropriate

term for some of these arrangements, nor does it necessarily reflect what options women may have perceived in these arrangements.

71 W. F. Prins, "De bevolkingsgroepen in het Nederlandsch-Indische recht," *Koloniale Studien*, 17, 665. That some women chose cohabitation over legal mixed marriages is rarely addressed in the colonial or secondary literature on the assumption that all forms of cohabitation could be subsumed by the term concubinage, signaling the moral degradation of a "kept woman" that the latter term implies. References in these legal debates to the fact that some women chose not to marry suggests that this issue needs further investigation.

72 Nederburgh, *GH*, 17.

73 As the chairman of the commission poignantly illustrated, a woman with native legal standing could be arrested for wearing European attire at the very moment she emerged from the building in which she had just married a European. Nor could a European man and his wife of native standing take the short boat trip from Soerabaya to Madura without prior permission of the authorities since sea passage for natives was forbidden by law (*JV*, 29–30).

74 Nederburgh, *GH*, 20.

75 Ibid., 13.

76 Ibid., 13.

77 *JV*, 39.

78 *Idem*.

79 Ibid., 51.

80 Ibid., 40. The arguments presented over the mixed-marriage ruling are much more numerous and elaborate than this short account suggests. There were indeed those such as Abendanon (the lawyer friend of Kartini), whose proposals raised yet a whole different set of options than those offered in these accounts. He argued that both man and woman should be given European status, except in those cases in which a native man preferred to retain his rights under adat law. Abendanon also singlehandedly countered the claim that any European woman who chose to marry a native man was already debased, arguing that there were many Dutch girls in the Netherlands for whom this was not the case. But these arguments were incidental to the main thrust of the debate and had little sway in the final analysis.

81 Nederburgh, *GM*, 64.

82 See A. van Marle's "De Groep der Europeanen in Nederlands-Indie, iets over ontstaan en groei," *Indonesie*. 5:3 (1952), 322, 328. Van Marle suggests that the much larger number of illiterate women of European standing in central Java and the Moluccas compared to the rest of the Indies indicates that the number of mixed marriages in these regions was particularly high (p. 330). But this was not the case everywhere. In East Java, European men acknowledged more of their métis children but continued to cohabit with the native mothers of their children outside of marriage (p. 495).

83 Mevrouw Douaire Klerck, *Eenige Beschouwingen over Oost-Indische Toestanden*, 3–19 (Amsterdam: Versluys, 1898).

84 S. J. Ratu-Langie, *Sarekat Islam,* 21 (Baarn: Hollandia Drukkerij, 1913).

85 A woman who had contracted a mixed marriage could, upon divorce or death of her husband, declare her desire to reinstate her original nationality as long as she did so within a certain time. However, a native woman who married a European man and subsequently married and divorced a man of non-European

status could not recoup her European status.

86 Ernest Rodenwalt, "Eugenetische Problemen in Nederlandsch-Indie," *Ons Nages-lacht*, 1–8 (1928).

87 Johan Winsemius, *Nieuw-Guinee als kolonisatie-gebied voor Europeanen en van Indo-Europeanen*, 227 (Ph.D. Disser., Faculty of Medicine, University of Amsterdam, 1936).

88 Jacques van Doorn emphasizes the dualistic policy on poverty in the 1930s in "Armoede en Dualistisch Beleid" (unpublished); I would refer to it as a three-tiered policy, not a dualistic one.

89 J. Th. Petrus Blumberger, *De Indo-Europeesche Beweging in Nederlandsch-Indie*, 5 Haarlem: Tjeenk Willink, 1939).

90 See Paul van der Veur's "The Eurasians of Indonesia: A Problem and Challenge in Colonial History. "*Journal of Southeast Asian History*. 9:2 (September 1966), 191–207, and his "Cultural Aspects of the Eurasian Community in Indonesian Colonial Society," *Indonesia*, 6 (October 1968), 38–53.

91 On the various currents of Eurasian political activity, see Paul W. van der Veur's "The Eurasians of Indonesia: A Problem and Challenge in Colonial History," On the importance of Indo individuals in the early Malay press and nationalist move-ment, see Takashi Shiraishi's *An Age in Motion: Popular Radicalism in Java, 1912–1926*, especially 37, 58–59 (Ithaca: Cornell University Press. 1990). Neither account addresses the class differences within Eurasian groups and where their distinct allegiances lay.

92 Blumberger, *De Indo-Europeesche Beweging*, 50.

93 According to the historian, Rudolph Mrazek, the early silent rejection of the Indo-European community from the Indonesian nationalist project turned explicit under Soekarno in the mid-1920s, when Indo-Europeans were categorically barred from membership in nationalist political organizations. Mrazek suggests that this silence among Dutch-educated nationalist leaders on the Indo question should be understood as a response from their own cultural formation and iden-tification as cultural hybrids themselves (personal communication).

94 This issue of rootlessness is most subtly analyzed in contemporary contexts. Liisa Malkki explores the meanings attached to displacement and uprootedness in the national order of things "National Geographic: The Rooting of Peoples and the Territorialization of National Identity among Scholars and Refugees," *Cultural Anthropology* (1992). André-Pierre Taguieff examines LePen's nationalist rhetoric on the dangers of the rootlessness of immigrant workers in France. See Pierre-André Taguieff's excellent analysis of LePen's rhetoric in "The Doctrine of the National Front in France (1972–1989)," in *New Political Science,* no. 16/17, 29–70.

95 See A. Braconier, "Het Pauperisme onder de in Ned. Oost-Indie levende Europeanen," *Nederlandsch-Indie,* no. 1 (1917), 291–300, at 293.

96 Enquete sur Métissage, AOM, Amiraux 53.50.6.

97 René Martial, *Les Métis*, 58 (Paris: Flammarion. 1942).

98 See Taguieff, "The Doctrine of the National Front".

99 On the recent British discourse on Britishness and the cultural threat of Islam to that identity, see Talal Asad's rich analysis in "Multiculturalism and British Identity in the Wake of the Rushdie Affair," *Politics and Society*, 18:4 (December 1990), 455–80.

100 Hazel Carby ("Lynching, Empire and Sexuality," *Critical Enquiry,* 12:1 (1985), 262–77) argues that Afro-American women intellectuals at the turn of the

century focused on the métis figure because it both enabled an exploration and expressed the relations between the races, because it demythologized concepts of pure blood and pure race while debunking any proposition of degeneracy through amalgamation. Such black women writers as Pauline Hopkins embraced the mulatto to counter the official script that miscegenation was not the inmost desire of the nonwhite peoples but the result of white rape (p. 274). In both the Indies and the United States at the same time, the figure of the Indo-mulatto looms large in both dominant and subaltern literary production, serving to convey strategic social dilemmas and political messages. It is not surprising, then, that the portrayal of the Indo in fiction was widely discussed in the Indies and metropolitan press by many more than those who were interested in literary style alone.

101   Taylor, *The Social World of Batavia*, 155.
102   Carole Pateman argues that the sexual contract is fundamental to the functioning of European civil society, in that the principle of patriarchal right defines the social contract between men, and the individual and citizen as male *(The Sexual Contract* [Stanford: Stanford University Press, 1988])*.
103   I thank Luise White for pressing me to think out this point.
104   Gwendolyn Wright, "Tradition in the Service of Modernity: Architecture and Urbanism in Colonial Policy, 1900–1930," *Journal of Modern History*, 59 (June 1987), 291–316, at 297.

Chapter 24

Homi K. Bhabha

'RACE' TIME AND THE REVISION OF MODERNITY

'Dirty nigger!' Or simply, Look, a Negro!'

Frantz Fanon, *The Fact of Blackness*

I

WHENEVER THESE WORDS ARE SAID in anger or in hate, whether of the Jew in that *estaminet* in Antwerp, or of the Palestinian on the West Bank, or the Zairian student eking out a wretched existence selling fake fetishes on the Left Bank; whether they are said of the body of woman or the man of colour; whether they are quasi-officially spoken in South Africa or officially prohibited in London or New York, but inscribed nevertheless in the severe staging of the statistics of educational performance and crime, visa violations, immigration irregularities; whenever 'Dirty nigger!' or, 'Look, a Negro!' is not said at all, but you can see it in a gaze, or hear it in the solecism of a still silence; whenever and wherever I am when I hear a racist, or catch his look, I am reminded of Fanon's evocatory essay 'The Fact of Blackness' and its unforgettable opening lines.[1]

I want to start by returning to that essay, to explore only one scene in its remarkable staging, Fanon's phenomenological performance of what it means to be *not only a nigger* but a member of the marginalized, the displaced, the diasporic. To be amongst those whose very presence is both 'overlooked' – in the double sense of social surveillance and psychic disavowal – and, at the same time, over-determined – psychically projected made stereotypical and symptomatic. Despite its very specific location a Martinican subjected to the racist gaze on a street corner in Lyons – I claim a generality for Fanon's argument because he talks not simply of the historicity of the black man, as much as he writes in 'The Fact of Blackness' about the temporality of modernity within which the figure of the 'human' comes to be *authorized*. It is Fanon's temporality of emergence – his sense of the *belatedness of the black man* – that does not simply make the question of ontology inappropriate for black. identity, but somehow *impossible* for the very understanding of humanity in the world of modernity:

> You come too late, much too late, there will always be a world – a white world between you and us. (My emphasis)

It is the opposition to the ontology of that white world – to its assumed hierarchical forms of rationality and universality – that Fanon turns in a performance that is iterative and interrogative – a repetition that is initiatory, instating a differential history that will not return to the power of the Same. Between *you and us* Fanon opens up an enunciative space that does not simply contradict the metaphysical ideas of progress or racism or rationality; he distantiates them by 'repeating' these ideas, makes them uncanny by displacing them in a number of culturally contradictory and discursively estranged locations.

What Fanon shows up is the liminality of those Ideas – their ethnocentric margin – by revealing the *historicity* of its most universal symbol – Man. From the perspective of a postcolonial 'belatedness', Fanon disturbs the *punctum* of man as the signifying, subjectifying category of Western culture, as a unifying reference of ethical value. Fanon performs the desire of the colonized to identify with the humanistic, enlightenment ideal of Man: 'all I wanted was to be a man among other men. I wanted to come lithe and young into a world that was ours and build it together.' Then, in a catachrestic reversal he shows how, despite the pedagogies of human history, the performative discourse of the liberal West, its quotidian conversation and comments, reveal the cultural supremacy and racial typology upon which the universalism of Man is founded. 'But of course, come in, sir, there is no colour prejudice among us. . . . Quite, the Negro is a man like ourselves. . . . It is not because he is black that he is less intelligent than we are.'

Fanon uses the fact of blackness, of belatedness, to destroy the binary structure of power and identity: the imperative that 'the Black man must be Black; he must be Black in relation to the white man.' Elsewhere he has written: 'The Black man is not. [caesura] Any more than the white man' (my interpolation). Fanon's discourse of the 'human' emerges from that temporal break or caesura effected in the contuinist, progressivist myth of Man. He too speaks from the signifying timelag of cultural difference that I have been attempting to develop as a structure for the representation of subaltern and postcolonial agency. Fanon writes from that temporal caesura, the time-lag of cultural difference, in a space between the symbolization of the social and the 'sign' of its representation of subjects and agencies. Fanon destroys two time schemes in which the historicity of the human is thought. He rejects the 'belatedness' of the black man because it is only the opposite of the framing of the white man as universal, normative – *the white sky all around me:* the black man refuses to occupy the past of which the white man is the future. But Fanon also refuses the Hegelian-Marxist dialectical schema whereby the black man is part of a transcendental sublation: a minor term in a dialectic that will emerge into a more equitable universality. Fanon, I believe, suggests another time, another space.

It is a space of being that is wrought from the interruptive, interrogative, tragic experience of blackness, of discrimination, of despair. It is the apprehension of the social and psychic question of 'origin' – and its erasure – in a negative side that 'draws its worth from an almost substantive absoluteness . . . [which has to be] ignorant of the essences and determinations of its being . . . an absolute density . . . an abolition of the ego by desire'. What may seem primordial or timeless is, I believe, a moment of a kind of 'projective past' whose history and signification I shall attempt to explore here. It is a mode of 'negativity' that makes the enunciatory present of modernity disjunctive. It opens up a time-lag at the point at which we speak of humanity through its differentiations – gender, race, class – that mark an excessive marginality of modernity. It is the enigma of this form of temporality which emerges from what Du Bois also called the 'swift and low of human doing',[2] to face Progress with some unanswerable questions, and suggest some answers of its own.

In destroying the 'ontology of man' Fanon suggests that 'there is not merely one Negro, there are *Negroes*'. This is emphatically not a post-modern celebration of pluralistic identities. As my argument will make clear, for me the project of modernity is itself rendered so contradictory and unresolved through the insertion of the 'time-lag' in which colonial and postcolonial moments emerge as sign and history, that I am sceptical of those transitions to postmodernity in Western academic writings which theorize the experience of this 'new historicity' through the appropriation of a 'Third World' metaphor; 'the First World . . . in a peculiar dialectical reversal, begins to touch some features of third-world experience. . . . The United States is . . . the biggest third-world country because of unemployment, nonproduction, etc.'[3]

Fanon's sense of social contingency and indeterminacy, made from the perspective of a postcolonial time-lag, is not a celebration of fragmentation, *bricolage,* pastiche or the 'simulacrum'. It is a vision of social contraction and cultural difference – as the disjunctive space of modernity – that is best seen in a fragment of a poem he cites towards the end of 'The Fact of Blackness':

> As the contradiction among the features
> creates the harmony of the face
> we proclaim the oneness of the suffering
> and the revolt.

II

The discourse of race that I am trying to develop displays the *problem of the ambivalent temporality of modernity* that is often overlooked in the more 'spatial', traditions of some aspects of postmodern theory.[4] Under the rubric 'the discourse of modernity', I do not intend to reduce a complex and diverse historical moment, with varied national genealogies and different institutional practices, into a singular shibboleth – be it the 'idea' of Reason, Historicism, Progress – for the critical convenience of postmodern literary theory. My interest in the question of modernity resides in the influential discussion generated by the work of Habermas,

Foucault, Lyotard and Lefort, amongst many others, that has generated a critical discourse around historical modernity as an epistemological structure.[5] To put it succinctly, the question of ethical and cultural judgement, central to the processes of subject formation and the objectification of social knowledge, is challenged at its 'cognitivist' core. Habermas characterizes it as a form of Occidental self-understanding that enacts a cognitive reductionism in the relation of the human being to the social world:

> Ontologically the world is reduced to a world of entities *as a whole* (as the totality of objects . . .); epistemologically, our relationship to that world is reduced to the capacity of know[ing] . . . states of affairs . . . in a purposive-rational fashion; semantically it is reduced to fact-stating discourse in which assertoric sentences are used.[6] (My emphasis)

Although this may be a stark presentation of the problem, it highlights the fact that the challenge to such a 'cognitivist' consciousness displaces the problem of truth or meaning from the disciplinary confines of epistemology – the problem of the referential as 'objectivity' reflected in that celebrated Rortyesque trope, the mirror of nature. What results could be figuratively described as a preoccupation not simply with the reflection in the glass – the idea or concept in itself – but with the frameworks of meaning as they are revealed in what Derrida has called the 'supplementary necessity of a parergon'. That is the performative, living description of the *writing* of a concept or theory, 'a relation to the history of its writing and the writing of its history also'.[7]

If we take even the most cursory view of influential postmodern perspectives, we find that there is an increasing *narrativization* of the question of social ethics and subject formation. Whether it is in the conversational procedures and 'final vocabularies' of liberal ironists like Richard Rorty, or the 'moral fictions' of Alisdair Macintyre that are the sustaining myths 'after virtue'; whether it is the *petits récits* and *phrases* that remain from the fall-out of the grand narratives of modernity in Lyotard; or the projective but ideal speech community that is rescued *within* modernity by Habermas in his concept of communicative reason that is expressed in its pragmatic logic or argument and a 'decentred' understanding of the world: what we encounter in all these accounts are proposals for what is considered to be the essential gesture of Western modernity, an 'ethics of self-construction' – or, as Mladan Dolar cogently describes it:

> What makes this attitude typical of modernity is the constant reconstruction and the reinvention of the self. . . . The subject and the present it belongs to have no objective status, they have to be perpetually (re)constructed.[8]

I want to ask whether this synchronous constancy of reconstruction and reinvention of the subject does not assume a cultural temporality that may not be universalist in its epistemological moment of judgement, but may, indeed, be ethnocentric in its construction of cultural 'difference'. It is certainly true, as Robert Young argues, that the inscription of alterity within the self can allow for a new relation to ethics';[9] but does that *necessarily* entail the more general case argued by Dolar, that 'the persisting split [of the subject] is the condition of freedom'?

If so, how do we specify the historical conditions and theoretical configurations of 'splitting' in political situations of 'unfreedom' – in the colonial and postcolonial margins of modernity? I am persuaded that it is the catachrestic postcolonial agency of 'seizing the value-coding' – as Gayatri Spivak has argued – that opens up an interruptive time-lag in the 'progressive' myth of modernity, and enables the diasporic and the postcolonial to be represented. But this makes it all the more crucial to specify the discursive and historical temporality that interrupts the enunciative 'present' in which the self-inventions of modernity take place. And it is this 'taking place' of modernity, this insistent and incipient *spatial* metaphor in which the social relations of modernity are conceived, that introduces a temporality of the 'synchronous' in the structure of the 'splitting' of modernity. It is this 'synchronous and spatial' representation of cultural difference that must be reworked as a framework for cultural otherness *within* the general dialectic of doubling that postmodernism proposes. Otherwise we are likely to find ourselves beached amidst Jameson's 'cognitive mappings' of the Third World, which might work for the Bonaventura Hotel in Los Angeles, but will leave you somewhat eyeless in Gaza.[10] Or if, like Terry Eagleton, your taste is more 'other worldly' than Third World, you will find yourself somewhat dismissive of the 'real' history of the 'other' – women, foreigners, homosexuals, the natives of Ireland – on the basis of 'certain styles, values, life-experiences which can be appealed to now as a form of political critique' because 'the fundamental political question is that of demanding an equal right with others of what one might become, not of assuming some fully-fashioned identity which is merely repressed.'[11]

It is to establish a *sign* of *the present,* of modernity, that is not that 'now' of transparent immediacy, and to found a form of social individuation where communality is *not predicated on a transcendent becoming*, that I want to pose my questions of a contra-modernity: what is modernity in those colonial conditions where its imposition is itself the denial of historical freedom, civic autonomy and the 'ethical' choice of refashioning?

III

I am posing these questions from within the problematic of modernity because of a shift within contemporary critical traditions of postcolonial writing. There is no longer an influential separatist emphasis on simply elaborating an anti-imperialist or black nationalist tradition 'in itself'. There is an attempt to interrupt the Western discourses of modernity through these displacing, interrogative subaltern or post-slavery narratives and the critical–theoretical perspectives they engender. For example, Houston Baker's reading of the modernity of the Harlem Renaissance strategically elaborates a 'deformation of mastery', a vernacularism, based on the enunciation of the subject as 'never a simple coming into being, but a release from being possessed'.[12] The revision of Western modernism, he suggests, requires both the linguistic investiture of the subject and a practice of diasporic performance that is metaphorical. The 'public culture' project that Carol Breckenridge and Arjun

Appadurai have initiated focuses on the transnational dissemination of cultural modernity. What becomes properly urgent for them is that the 'simultaneous' global locations of such a modernity should not lose sense of the conflictual, contra-dictory locations of those cultural practices and products that follow the 'unequal development' of the tracks of international or multinational capital. Any trans-national cultural study must 'translate', each time locally and specifically, what decentres and subverts this transnational globality, so that it does not become enthralled by the new global technologies of ideological transmission and cultural consumption.[13] Paul Gilroy proposes a form of populist modernism to compre-hend both the aesthetic and political transformation of European philosophy and letters by black writers, but also to make sense of the secular and spiritual *popular* forms – music and dance – that have handled the anxieties and dilemmas involved in a response to the *flux of modern life'*.[14]

The power of the postcolonial translation of modernity rests in its *permative, deformative* structure that does not simply revalue the contents of a cultural tradi-tion, or transpose values 'cross-culturally'. The cultural inheritance of slavery or colonialism is brought *before* modernity *not* to resolve its historic differences into a new totality, nor to forego its traditions. It is to introduce another locus of inscription and intervention, another hybrid, 'inappropriate' enunciative site, through that temporal split – or time-lag – that I have opened up [. . .] for the signification of postcolonial agency. Differences in culture and power are consti-tuted through the social conditions of enunciation: the temporal caesura, *which is also the historically tranformative moment*, when a lagged space opens up *in*-between the *inter*subjective 'reality of signs . . . deprived of subjectivity' and the historical development of the subject in the order of social symbols.[15] This transvaluation of the symbolic structure of the cultural sign is absolutely necessary so that in the renaming of modernity there may ensue that process of the active agency of trans-lation – the moment of 'making a name for oneself' that emerges through 'the undecidabiity . . . [at work] in a struggle for the proper name within a scene of genealogical indebtedness'.[16] Without such a reinscription of the sign itself – without a transformation of the site of *enunciation* – there is the danger that the mimetic contents of a discourse will conceal the fact that the hegemonic struc-tures of power are maintained in a position of authority through a *shift in vocabulary* in the position of authority. There is for instance a kinship between the norma-tive paradigms of colonial anthropology and the contemporary discourse of aid and development agencies. The 'transfer of technology' has not resulted in the transfer of power or the displacement of a neo-colonial tradition of political control through philanthropy – a celebrated missionary position.

What is the struggle of translation in the name of modernity? How do we catachrestically seize the genealogy of modernity and open it to the postcolonial translation? The 'value' of modernity is not located, a priori, in the passive fact of an epochal event or idea – of progress, civility, the law – but has to be negoti-ated *within* the 'enunciative' present of the discourse. The brilliance of Claude Lefort's account of the genesis of ideology in modern societies is to suggest that the representation of the rule, or the discourse of generality that symbolizes authority, is ambivalent because it is split off from its effective operation.[17] The *new or the contemporary* appear through the splitting of modernity as event and enunciation, the epochal and the everyday. Modernity as a *sign* of the present emerges in that process of splitting, that *lag,* that gives the practice of everyday life its consistency as *being contemporary.* It is because the present has the value of a 'sign', that modernity is iterative; a continual questioning of the conditions of existence; making problematic its own discourse not simply 'as ideas' but as the position and status of the locus of social utterance.

IV

'It is not enough . . . to follow the teleological thread that makes progress possible; one must isolate, within the history [of modernity], an event that will have the value of a sign.'[18] In his reading of Kant's *Was ist Aufklärung?* Foucault suggests that the sign of modernity is a form of decipherment whose value must be sought in *petits récits,* imperceptible events, in signs apparently *without* meaning and value – empty and excentric – in events that are outside the 'great events' of history.

The sign of history does not consist in an essence of the event itself, nor exclusively in the *immediate consciousness* of its agents and actors, but in its form as a *spectacle*; spectacle that signifies *because of* the distanciation and displacement between the event and those who are its spectators. The indeterminacy of modernity, where the struggle of translation takes place, is not simply around the ideas of progress or truth. Modernity, I suggest, is about the historical construction of a specific position of historical enunciation and address. It privileges those who 'bear witness', those who are 'subjected', or in the Fanonian sense with which I began, historically displaced. It gives them a representative position through the spatial distance, or the *time-lag* between the Great Event and its circulation as a historical sign of the 'people'; or an 'epoch' that constitutes the memory and the moral of the event *as a narrative,* a disposition to cultural communality, a form of social and psychic identification. The discursive address of modernity – its structure of authority – decentres the Great Event, and speaks from that moment of 'imperceptibility', the supplementary space 'outside' or uncannily beside (*abseits*).

Through Kant, Foucault traces 'the ontology of the present' to the exemplary event of the French Revolution and it is there that he stages his sign of modernity. But it is the spatial dimension of distance – *the perspectival distance from which the spectacle is seen* – that installs a cultural homogeneity into the sign of modernity. Foucault introduces a Eurocentric perspective at the point at which modernity installs a 'moral disposition in mankind'. The Eurocentricity of Foucault's theory of cultural difference is revealed in his insistent spatializing of the time of modernity. Avoiding the problems of the sovereign subject and linear causality, he nonetheless falls prey to the notion of the 'cultural' as a social formation whose discursive doubleness – the transcendental and empirical dialectic – is contained in a temporal frame that makes differences repetitively 'contemporaneous', regimes of sense-as-synchronous. It is a kind of cultural 'contradictoriness' that always presupposes a correlative spacing. Foucault's *spatial distancing* seals the sign of modernity in 1789 into a 'correlative', overlapping temporality. Progress brings together the three moments of the sign as:

> a *signum rememorativum*, for it reveals that disposition [of progress] which
> has been present from the beginning; it is a *signum demonstrativum* because
> it demonstrates the present efficacity of this disposition; and it is also
> *signum prognosticum* for, although the Revolution may have certain ques-
> tionable results, one cannot forget the disposition [of modernity] that
> is revealed through it.[19]

What if the effects of 'certain questionable results' of the Revolution create
a disjunction, between the *signum demonstrativum* and the *signum prognosticum*? What
if in the geopolitical space of the colony genealogically (in Foucault's sense) related
to the Western metropolis, the symbol of the Revolution is partially visible as an
unforgettable, tantalizing promise – a *pedagogy* of the values of modernity – while
the 'present efficacy' of the sign of everyday life – its *political performativity*– repeats
the archaic aristocratic racism of the *ancien régime*?

The ethnocentric limitations of Foucault's spatial sign of modernity become
immediately apparent if we take our stand, in the immediate postrevolutionary
period, in San Domingo with the Black Jacobins, rather than Paris. What if the
'distance' that constitutes the meaning of the Revolution as sign, the *signifying lag*
between event and enunciation, stretches not across the Place de la Bastille or the
rue des Blancs-Monteaux, but spans the temporal difference of the colonial space?
What if we heard the 'moral disposition of mankind' uttered by Toussaint
L'Ouverture for whom, as C. L. R. James so vividly recalls, the signs of modernity, 'liberty, equality, fraternity . . . what the French Revolution signified, was
perpetually on his lips, in his correspondence, in his private conversations.'[20] What
do we make of the figure of Toussaint – James invokes Phèdre, Ahab, Hamlet –
at the moment when he grasps the tragic lesson that the moral, *modern* disposition
of mankind, enshrined in the sign of the Revolution, only fuels the archaic racial
factor in the society of slavery? What do we learn from that split consciousness,
that 'colonial' disjunction of modern times and colonial and slave histories, where
the reinvention of the self and the remaking of the social are strictly out of joint?

These are the issues of the catachrestic, postcolonial translation of modernity.
They force us to introduce the question of subaltern agency, into the question of
modernity: what is this 'now' of modernity? Who defines this present from which
we speak? This leads to a more challenging question: *what is the desire of this repeated
demand to modernize? Why does it insist, so compulsively, on its contemporaneous reality,
its spatial dimension, its spectatorial distance?* What happens to the sign of modernity
in those repressive places like San Domingo where progress is only heard (of) and
not 'seen', is that it reveals the problem of the disjunctive moment of its utterance: the space which enables a postcolonial contra-modernity to emerge. For the
discourse of modernity is *signified* from the time-lag, or temporal caesura, that
emerges in the tension between the epochal 'event' of modernity as the symbol
of the continuity of progress, and the interruptive temporality of the sign of the
present, the contingency of modern times that Habermas has aptly described as
its 'forward gropings and shocking encounters'.[21]

In this 'time' of repetition there circulates a contingent tension within modernity: a tension between the *pedagogy* of the symbols of progress, historicism,
modernization, homogeneous empty time, the narcissism of organic culture, the

onanistic search for the origins of race, and what I shall call the 'sign of the present': the performativity of discursive practice, the *récits* of the everyday, the repetition of the empirical, the ethics of self-enactment, the iterative signs that mark the non-synchronic *passages* of time in the archives of the 'new'. This is the space in which the question of modernity *emerges as a form of interrogation*: what do I belong to in this present? In what terms do I identify with the 'we', the intersubjective realm of society? This process cannot be represented in the binary relation of archaism/modernity, inside/outside, past/present, because these questions block off the forward drive or teleology of modernity. They suggest that what is read as the 'futurity' of the modern, its ineluctable progress, its cultural hierarchies, may be an 'excess' a disturbing alterity, a process of the marginalization of the symbols of modernity.

Time-lag is not a circulation of nullity, the endless slippage of the signifier or the theoretical anarchy of aporia. It is a concept that does not collude with current fashions for claiming the heterogeneity of ever-increasing 'causes', multiplicities of subject positions, endless supplies of subversive 'specificities', 'localities', 'terri-tories'. The problem of the articulation of cultural difference is not the problem of free-wheeling pragmatist pluralism or the 'diversity' of the many; it is the problem of the not-one, the minus in the origin and repetition of cultural signs in a doubling that will not be sublated into a similitude. What is *in* modernity *more* than modernity is this signifying 'cut' or temporal break: it cuts into the plen-itudinous notion of Culture splendidly reflected in the mirror of human nature; equally it halts the endless signification of difference. The process I have described as the sign of the present – *within modernity* – erases and interrogates those ethno-centric forms of cultural modernity that 'contemporize' cultural difference: it opposes both cultural pluralism with its spurious egalitarianism – different cultures in the same time ('The Magicians of the Earth', Pompidou Centre, Paris, 1989) – or cultural relativism – different cultural temporalities in the same 'universal' space 'The Primitivism Show', MOMA, New York, 1984)

V

This caesura in the narrative of modernity reveals something of what de Certeau has famously described as the non-place from which all historiographical operation starts, the lag which all histories must encounter in order to make a beginning.[22] For the emergence of modernity – as an ideology of *beginning, modernity as the new* – the template of this 'non-place' becomes the colonial space. It signifies this in a double way. The colonial space is the *terra incognita* or the *terra nulla*, the empty or wasted land whose history has to be begun, whose archives must be filled out; whose future progress must be secured in modernity. But the colonial space also stands for the *despotic* time of the Orient that becomes a great problem for the definition of modernity and its inscription of the history of the colonized from the perspective of the West. Despotic time, as Althusser has brilliantly described it, is 'space without places, time without duration'.[23] In that double-figure which haunted the moment of the enlightenment in its relation to the *otherness* of the Other, you can see the historical formation of the time-lag of modernity. And lest it be said that this disjunctive present of modernity is merely my theoretical abstraction, let me also remind you that a similar, signifying caesura occurs within the invention of progress in the 'long imperialist nineteenth century'. At the midpoint of the century questions concerning the 'origin of races' provided modernity with an ontology of its present and a justification of cultural hierarchy within the West and in the East. In the structure of the discourse, however, there was a recurrent ambivalence between the developmental, organic notion of cultural and racial 'indigenism' as the justification of supremacy, and the notion of evolution as abrupt cultural transition, discontinuous progress, the periodic eruption of invading tribes from somewhere mysterious in Asia, as the guarantee of progress.[24]

The 'subalterns and ex-slaves', who now seize the spectacular event of modernity do so in a catachrestic gesture of reinscribing modernity's 'caesura' and using it to transform the locus of thought and writing in their postcolonial critique. Listen to the ironic naming, the interrogative repetitions, of the critical terms themselves: black 'vernacularism' repeats the minor term used to designate the language of the native and the housebound slave to make demotic the grander narratives of progress. Black 'expressivism' reverses the stereotypical affectivity and sensuality of the stereotype to suggest that 'rationalities are produced *endlessly*' in populist modernism.[25] New ethnicity' is used by Stuart Hall in the black British context to create a discourse of cultural difference that marks ethnicity as the struggle against ethnicist 'fixing' and in favour of a wider minority discourse that represents sexuality and class. Cornel West's genealogical materialist view of race and Afro-American oppression is, he writes, 'both continuous and discontinuous with the Marxist tradition; and shares an equally contingent relation to Nietzsche and Foucault.'[26] More recently, he has constructed a prophetic pragmatic tradition from William James, Niebuhr and Du Bois suggesting that 'it is possible to be a prophetic pragmatist and belong to different political movements, e.g. feminist, Black, chicano, socialist, left-liberal ones.'[27] The Indian historian Gyan Prakash, in an essay on postorientalist histories of the Third World, claims that:

> it is difficult to overlook the fact that . . . third world voices . . . speak within and to discourses familiar to the 'West'. . . . The Third World, far from being confined to its assigned space, has penetrated the inner sanctum of the 'First World', in the process of being 'Third Worlded' – arousing, inciting, and affiliating with the subordinated others in the First World . . . to connect with minority voices.[28]

The intervention of postcolonial or black critique is aimed at transforming the conditions of enunciation at the level of the sign – where the intersubjective realm is constituted – not simply setting up new symbols of identity, new 'positive' images' that fuel an unreflective 'identity politics'. The challenge to modernity comes in redefining the signifying relation to a disjunctive 'present': staging the past as *symbol*, myth, memory, history, the ancestral – but a past whose iterative *value as sign* reinscribes the 'lessons of the past' into the very textuality of the present that determines both the identification with, and the interrogation of, modernity: what Is the 'we' that defines the prerogative of my present? The possibility of inciting cultural translations across minority discourses arises because of the disjunctive present of modernity. It ensures that what *seems* the 'same' within cultures is negotiated in the time-lag of the 'sign' which constitutes the intersubjective, social realm. Because that lag is indeed the very structure of difference and splitting within the discourse of modernity, turning it into a performative process, then each repetition of the sign of modernity is different, specific to its historical and cultural conditions of enunciation.

This process is most clearly apparent in the work of those 'postmodern' writers who, in pushing the paradoxes of modernity to its limits, reveal the margins of the West.[29] From the postcolonial perspective we can only assume a disjunctive and displaced relation to these works; we cannot accept them until we subject them to a *lagging*: both in the temporal sense of postcolonial agency with which you are now (over)familiar, and in the obscurer sense in which, in the early days of settler colonization, to be lagged was to be transported to the colonies for penal servitude!

In Foucault's Introduction to the *History of Sexuality*, racism emerges in the nineteenth century in the form of an historical retroversion that Foucault finally disavows. In the 'modern' shift of power from the juridical politics of death to the biopolitics of life, race produces a historical temporality of interference, overlapping, and the displacement of sexuality. It is, for Foucault, the great historical irony of modernity that the Hitlerite annihilation of the Jews was carried out in the name of the archaic, premodern signs of race and sanguinity – the oneiric exaltation of blood, death, skin – rather than through the politics of sexuality. What is profoundly revealing is Foucault's complicity with the logic of the 'contemporaneous' within Western modernity. Characterizing the 'symbolics of blood' as being retroverse, Foucault disavows the time-lag of race as the sign of cultural difference and its mode of repetition.

The *temporal* disjunction that the 'modern' question of race would introduce into the discourse of disciplinary and pastoral power is disallowed because of Foucault's spatial critique: 'we must conceptualize the deployment of sexuality on the basis of the techniques of power that are *contemporary* with it' (my emphasis).[30] However subversive 'blood' and race may be they are in the last analysis merely an 'historical retroversion'. Elsewhere Foucault directly links the 'flamboyant rationality' of Social Darwinism to Nazi Ideology, entirely ignoring colonial societies which were the proving grounds for Social Darwinist administrative discourses all through the nineteenth and early twentieth centuries.[31]

If Foucault normalizes the time-lagged, 'retroverse' sign of race, Benedict Anderson places the 'modern' dreams of racism 'outside history' altogether. For Foucault race and blood interfere with modern sexuality. For Anderson racism has its origins in antique ideologies of class that belong to the aristocratic 'pre-history' of the modern nation. Race represents an archaic ahistorical moment outside the 'modernity' of the imagined community: 'nationalism thinks in historical destinies, while racism dreams of eternal contaminations . . . outside history.'[32] Foucault's spatial notion of the conceptual contemporaneity of power-as-sexuality limits him from seeing the double and overdetermined structure of race and sexuality that has a long history in the *peuplement* (politics of settlement) of colonial societies; for Anderson the 'modern' anomaly of racism finds its historical modularity, and its fantasmatic scenario, in the colonial space which is a belated and hybrid attempt to 'weld together dynastic legitimacy and national community. . . to shore up domestic aristocratic bastions'.[33]

The racism of colonial empires is then part of an archaic acting out, a dream-text of a form of historical retroversion that 'appeared to confirm on a global, modern stage antique conceptions of power and privilege'.[34] What could have been a way of understanding the limits of Western imperialist ideas of progress within the genealogy of a 'colonial metropolis' – a hybridizing of the Western nation – is quickly disavowed in the language of the *opéra bouffe* as a grimly amusing *tableau vivant* of 'the [colonial] bourgeois gentilhomme speaking poetry against a backcloth of spacious mansions and gardens filled with mimosa and bougainvillea'.[35] It is in that 'weld' of the colonial site as, contradictorily, both 'dynastic and national', that the modernity of Western national society is confronted by its colonial double. Such a moment of temporal disjunction, which would be crucial for understanding the colonial history of contemporary metropolitan racism in the West, is placed 'outside history'. It is obscured by Anderson's espousal of 'a simultaneity across homogeneous empty time' as the modal narrative of the imagined community. It is this kind of evasion, I think, that makes Partha Chatterjee, the Indian 'subaltern' scholar, suggest, from a different perspective, that Anderson 'seals up his theme with a sociological determinism . . . without noticing the twists and turns, the suppressed possibilities, the contradictions still unresolved'.[36]

These accounts of the modernity of power and national community become strangely symptomatic at the point at which they create a rhetoric of 'retroversion' for the emergence of racism. In placing the representations of race 'outside' modernity, in the space of historical retroversion, Foucault reinforces his 'correlative spacing' by relegating the social fantasy of racism to an archaic daydream, Anderson further universalizes his homogeneous empty time of the 'modern' social imaginary. Hidden in the disavowing narrative of historical retroversion and its archaism, is a notion of the time-lag that displaces Foucault's spatial analytic of modernity and Anderson's homogeneous temporality of the modern nation. In order to extract the one from the other we have to see how they form a double boundary: rather like the more general intervention and seizure of the history of modernity that has been attempted by postcolonial critics.

Retroversion and archaic doubling, attributed to the ideological 'contents' of racism, do not remain at the ideational or pedagogical level of the discourse. Their inscription of a structure of retroaction returns to disrupt the enunciative function of this discourse and produce a different 'value' of the sign and time of race and modernity. At the level of content the archaism and fantasy of racism is represented as 'ahistorical', outside the progressive myth of modernity. This is an attempt, I would argue, to universalize the spatial fantasy of modern cultural communities as living their history 'contemporaneously', in a 'homogeneous empty time' of the People-as-One that finally deprives minorities of those marginal, liminal spaces from which they can intervene in the unifying and totalizing *myths* of the national culture.

However, each time such a homogeneity of cultural identification is established there is a marked disturbance of temporality in the *writing of modernity*. For Foucault it is the awareness that retroversion of race or sanguinity haunts and doubles the contemporary analytic of power and sexuality and may be subversive of it: we may need to think the disciplinary powers of race as sexuality in a hybrid cultural formation that will not be contained within Foucault's logic of the contemporary. Anderson goes further in acknowledging that colonial racism introduces an awkward weld, a strange historical 'suture' in the narrative of the nation's *modernity*. The archaism of colonial racism, as a form of cultural signification (rather than simply an ideological content), reactivates nothing less than the 'primal scene' of the modern Western nation: that is, the problematic historical transition between dynastic, lineage societies and horizontal, homogeneous secular communities. What Anderson designates as racism's 'timelessness', its location 'outside history' is in fact that form of time-lag, a mode of repetition and reinscription, that *performs* the ambivalent historical temporality of modern national cultures – the *aporetic coexistence*, within the cultural history of the *modern* imagined community, of both the dynastic, hierarchical, prefigurative 'medieval' traditions (the past), and the secular, homogeneous, synchronous cross-time of modernity (the present). Anderson resists a reading of the modern nation that suggests – in an iterative time-lag – that the hybridity of the colonial space may provide a pertinent problematic within which to write the history of the 'postmodern' national formations of the West.

To take this perspective would mean that we see 'racism' not simply as a hangover from archaic conceptions of the aristocracy, but as part of the historical traditions of civic and liberal humanism that create ideological matrices of national aspiration, together with their concepts of 'a people' and its imagined community. Such a privileging of ambivalence in the social imaginaries of nation*ness*, and its forms of collective affiliation, would enable us to understand the coeval, often *incommensurable* tension between the influence of traditional 'ethnicist' identifications that coexist with contemporary secular, modernizing aspirations. The enunciative 'present' of modernity, that I am proposing, would provide a political space to articulate and negotiate such culturally hybrid social identities. Questions of cultural difference would not be dismissed – with a barely concealed racism – as atavistic tribal instincts that afflict Irish Catholics in Belfast or 'Muslim fundamentalists' in Bradford. It is precisely such unresolved, transitional moments within the disjunctive present of modernity that are then projected into a time of historical retroversion or an inassimilable place outside history.

The *history* of modernity's antique dreams is to be found in the *writing out* of the colonial and postcolonial moment. In resisting these attempts to normalize the time-lagged colonial moment, we may provide a *genealogy* for postmodernity that is at least as important as the 'aporetic' history of the Sublime or the nightmare of rationality in Auschwitz. For colonial and postcolonial texts do not merely tell the modern history of 'unequal development' or evoke memories of underdevelopment. I have tried to suggest that they provide modernity with a modular moment of *enunciation:* the locus and locution of cultures caught in the transitional and disjunctive temporalities of modernity. What is in modernity *more* than modernity is the disjunctive 'postcolonial' time and space that makes its presence felt *at the level of enunciation*. It figures, in an influential contemporary fictional instance, as the contingent margin between Toni Morrison's indeterminate moment of the 'not-there' – a 'black' space that she distinguishes from the Western sense of synchronous tradition – which then turns into the 'first stroke' of slave rememory, the *time* of communality and the narrative of a history of slavery. This translation of the meaning of time into the discourse of space; this catachrestic seizure of the signifying 'caesura' of modernity's presence and *present;* this insistence that power must be thought in the hybridity of race and sexuality; that nation must be reconceived liminally as the dynastic-in-the-democratic, race-difference doubling and splitting the teleology of class-consciousness: it is through these iterative interrogations and *historical initiations* that the cultural location of modernity shifts to the post-colonial site. [. . .]

Notes

1   All citations from Fanon In the following pages come from 'The Fact of Blackness', in *Black Skin, White* Masks, Foreword by H. Bhabha (London: Pluto, 1986). pp. 109–40.

2   W. B. Du Bois, *The Souls of Black Folk* (New York: Signet Classics, 1982), p. 275.

3   'A conversation with Fredric Jameson', in A. Ross (ed.) *Universal Abandon: The Politics of Postmodernism* (Edinburgh: Edinburgh University Press, 1988), p. 17.

4   See my reading of Renan in *The Location of Culture,* Chapter 8, 'DissemiNation'.

5   Each of these writers has addressed the problem of modernity in a number of works so that selection becomes invidious. However, some of the most directly relevant are the following: J. Habermas, *The Philosophical Discourse of Modernity* (Cambridge: Polity Press, 1990), esp. chs 11 and 12; M. Foucault, *The History of Sexuality. Volume One: An Introduction* (London: Allen Lane, 1979); see also his 'The art of telling the truth', in L. D. Kritzman (ed.), *Politics, Philosophy and Culture* (New York Routledge, 1990); J.-F. Lyotard, *The Differend* (Minneapolis: University of Minnesota Press, 1988); C. Lefort, *The Political Forms of Modern Society*, J. B. Thompson (ed.) (Cambridge: Polity Press), especially Part II, 'History, ideology and the social imaginary'.

6   Habermas, *The Philosophical Discourse of Modernity,* p 311.

7   J. Derrida, *The Post Card: From Socrates to Freud and Beyond,* A. Bass (trans.) (Chicago: Chicago University Press, 1987), pp 303–4.

8   M. Dolar, *The Legacy of the Enlightenment: Foucault and Lacan*, unpublished manuscript.

9   R. J. C. Young, *White Mythologies: Writing, History and the West* (London: Routledge, 1990), pp. 16-17. Young argues a convincing case against the Eurocentrism of historicism through his exposition of a number of 'totalizing' historical doctrines, particular in the Marxist tradition, while demonstrating at the same time that the spatializing anti-historicismn of Foucault remains equally Eurocentric.

10   Cf. Young, *White Mythologies*, pp. 116–17.

11   T. Eagleton, *The Ideology of the Aesthetic* (Oxford: Blackwell, 1990), p. 414.

12   H. A. Baker, Jr, *Modernism and the Harlem Renaissance* (Chicago: Chicago University Press, 1987), p. 56.

13   C. Breckenridge and A. Appadurai, *The Situation of Public Culture*, unpublished manuscript. For the general elaboration of this thesis see various issues of *Public Culture: Bulletin of the Project for Transnational Cultural Studies* (University of Pennsylvania).

14   P. Gilroy, 'One nation under a groove', in D. T. Goldberg (ed.) *Anatomy of Racism* (Minneapolis: University of Minnesota Press, 1990), p. 280.

15   Although I introduce the term 'time-lag' more specifically in *The Location of Culture*, Chapters 8 and 9, it is a structure of the 'splitting' of colonial discourse that I have been elaborating and illustrating – without giving it a name – from my very earliest essays.

16   J. Derrida, 'Des Tours de Babel', in *Difference in Translation*, J. F. Graham (ed.) (Ithaca: Cornell University Press, 1985), p. 174.

17   Lefort, *The Political Forms of Modern Society*, p. 212.

18   Foucault, 'The art of telling the truth', p. 90.

19   Ibid., p. 93.

20   C. L. R. James, *The Black Jacobins* (London: Allison and Busby, 1980), pp. 290–1.

21   J. Habermas, 'Modernity: an incomplete project', in H. Foster (ed.) *Postmodern Culture* (London: Pluto, 1985).

22   M. de Certeau, 'The historiographical operation', in his *The Writing of History*, T. Conley (trans.) (New York: Columbia University Press, 1988), p. 91.

23   L. Althusser, *Montesquieu, Rousseau, Marx* (London: Verso, 1972), p. 78.

24   P. J. Bowler, *The Invention of Progress* (Oxford: Blackwell, 1990), ch. 4.

25   Gilroy, 'One nation under a groove', p. 278.

26   C. West, 'Race and social theory: towards a genealogical materialist analysis', in M. Davis, M. Marable, F. Pfeil and M. Sprinker (eds) *Towards a Rainbow Socialism* (London: Verso, 1987), pp. 86 ff.

27   C. West, *The American Evasion of Philosophy* (London: Macmillan, 1990), pp. 232–3.

28   G. Prakash, 'Post-orientalist third-world histories', *Comparative Studies in Society and History*, vol. 32, no. 2 (April 1990), p. 403.

29   Robert Young, in *White Mythologies*, also suggests, in keeping with my argument that the colonial and postcolonial moment is the liminal point, or the limit-text, of the holistic demands of historicism.

30   Foucault, *The History of Sexuality*, p. 150.

31   M. Foucault, *Foucault Live*, J. Johnstone and S. Lotringer (trans.) (New York: Semiotext(e), 1989), p. 269.

32   B. Anderson, *Imagined Communities* (London: Verso, 1983), p. 136.

33   Ibid., p. 137.

34   Ibid.

35   Ibid.

36   P. Chatterjee, *Nationalist Thought and the Colonial World* (London: Zed, 1986), pp. 21–2.

PART FIVE

Feminism, difference and identity

INTRODUCTION

AN IMPORTANT FEATURE OF DEBATES on race and racism over
the past two decades has been the development of what some writers have
defined as a gendered perspective on race and racism. We have discussed the broad
contours of this transformation in the Introduction and a number of the papers in
earlier parts of the Reader, particularly in Part Four, have touched upon the
growing emphasis on linking the analysis of racism to questions of gender and
sexuality. In this part we have included a group of extracts that explore this dimension in depth, focusing specifically on those writers whose work has been influential
in shaping the contours of academic and public debates about this issue.

The first two extracts are from works by two influential black feminists, bell
hooks and Hazel Carby, that have done much to influence debate on both sides of
the Atlantic about this issue. Interestingly enough, both of these influential texts
were written in the early 1980s and were part of a critical engagement by black
and minority feminists with what they saw as some of the limitations of white
feminist discourses. At the time most feminist publications were practically all-
white publications and their content dealt almost exclusively with white women in
the United States or in Europe. One consequence of this situation was that for
many feminist theorists writing at this time all men were equivalent oppressors
and all family structures were bastions of patriarchy. As hooks and Carby argue,
however, for many black feminists this was perceived to be a position that took
little account of the specific aspects of the experience of black communities and
of the history of slavery or racial discrimination. A recurrent refrain in Carby's
contribution, which led to intense debate at the time, was on the need for white
feminists to show a critical awareness of the role that racism played in shaping

the everyday lives of both black and white women and to explore the need to include the experiences of minority women within the conceptual frameworks that they were using. Although it is clear that the tenor of the public debates within feminism and in academia about these issues has moved on in the period since these contributions were first published, we have included them here in order to highlight the terms within which debates about this issue were framed as late as the 1980s.

In the two decades since the original publication of hooks and Carby's interventions there has been a rapid expansion of scholarship in this field, and there is an identifiable sub-field of black feminist theorising that has come to the fore in recent years. One of the key contributors to this work is the American sociologist Patricia Hill Collins, and the extract from her work that we include here is symptomatic of the concerns to be found in her work and that of others. A particular feature of Collins's argument is the need to explore the intersections between gender, race and class in structuring the position of African-American women. Another recurrent theme in her work is the need to situate the position of African-American women in relation to family structures, churches, and other community organisations in order to gain a fuller understanding of the way they are positioned within specific communities and localities. She also emphasises the need to understand that the conditions of black women's oppression are specific and complex, and that it is therefore important to seek particularised methodologies that might reveal the ways in which that oppression is experienced.

Another influential contributor to theorising in this field is Patricia Williams, whose book *The Alchemy of Race and Rights* attracted much attention when it was published in the early 1990s. Written in a style that is both personal and analytical at the same time Williams eschews much of the jargon of academic feminist writing in this field and adopts a discursive essay form. At its broadest level Williams's work explores the changing experiences of black American women and how their everyday lives continue to be shaped by race, class, gender and other social relations. The extract we have included here gives a flavour of the way Williams seeks to explore the changing boundaries of race and gender in contemporary America, and provides a fascinating insight into the ways in which these issues are talked about in the academic milieu of which she is a part.

The extract from Avtar Brah takes up the issue of how to theorise ideas about difference and diversity in relation to questions of race and gender. Drawing on debates that have become a recurrent theme among black and white feminists in both Britain and America, Brah seeks to show that there is a need for theorising on race and gender to open up new ways to understand the complex variety of subject positions that are occupied by different groups of women in contemporary societies. Her argument links up with the debates about 'new ethnicities' that have been initiated by Stuart Hall among others. But it also seeks to go beyond what she sees as the limitations of current debates in feminist circles about race and gender.

The extract from Ruth Frankenberg reflects another important trend in this field, namely the attempt to use insights derived from the study of the social construction of whiteness to explore the position of white women in American society and other parts of the West. Frankenberg's account of this question is framed by her in-depth life history interviews with white women and by her attempt to provide a broader framework as to how issues of race and gender are talked about by these women. There has been an explosion of theorising about 'whiteness' in recent years (see Part Six and Guide to Further Reading) but what is particularly important about Frankenberg's analysis is the way she seeks to situate her work within a life history approach in order to uncover what she sees as the complexities of the relationship between racial and gender relations in the contemporary environment.

The final extract by Barbara Christian is more squarely concerned with the dilemmas posed by the integration of black feminist perspectives within the boundaries of the academy. Christian's account is written from the angle of somebody who is both a black feminist and part of the academy in the United States and reflects on the division that she saw emerging between black writers and white theorists, particularly in the field of literary theory. Precisely because this is a reflexive piece that addresses issues at the core of academic practice it helps to situate some of the broader theoretical preoccupations covered in other readings in a more grounded fashion.

KEY QUESTIONS

- How has the analysis of race and racism been influenced by debates about gender, sexuality and masculinity?
- What does Ruth Frankenberg mean when she says that 'race shapes white women's lives'.
- Discuss Patricia Hill Collins's analysis of the intersections of race, class and gender in structuring the position of women in African-American communities.
- In what sense have we seen the emergence of a distinctive 'black feminism' in the present environment? What are the main distinguishing features of this approach and what does it have to tell us about the changing nature of contemporary racisms?
- Is Hazel Carby right to argue that in contemporary debates 'terms like women, gender, and sexuality have a decorative function only'. How can this situation be changed?

bell hooks

RACISM AND FEMINISM
The issue of accountability

A MERICAN WOMEN OF ALL RACES are socialized to think of racism solely in the context of race hatred. Specifically in the case of black and white people, the term racism is usually seen as synonymous with discrimination or prejudice against black people by white people. For most women, the first knowledge of racism as institutionalized oppression is engendered either by direct personal experience or through information gleaned from conversations, books, television, or movies. Consequently, the American woman's understanding of racism as a political tool of colonialism and imperialism is severely limited. To experience the pain of race hatred or to witness that pain is not to understand its origin, evolution, or impact on world history. The inability of American women to understand racism in the context of American politics is not due to any inherent deficiency in woman's psyche. It merely reflects the extent of our victimization.

No history books used in public schools informed us about racial imperialism. Instead we were given romantic notions of the "new world," the "American dream," America as the great melting pot where all races come together as one. We were taught that Columbus *discovered* America; that "Indians" were scalphunters, killers of innocent women and children; that black people were enslaved because of the biblical curse of Ham, that God "himself" had decreed they would be hewers of wood, tillers of the field, and bringers of water. No one talked of Africa as the cradle of civilization, of the African and Asian people who came to America before Columbus. No one mentioned mass murders of Native Americans as genocide, or the rape of Native American and African women as terrorism. No one discussed slavery as a foundation for the growth of capitalism. No one described the forced breeding of white wives to increase the white population as sexist oppression.

I am a black woman. I attended all-black public schools. I grew up in the south where all around me was the fact of racial discrimination, hatred, and forced segregation. Yet my education as to the politics of race in American society was not that different from that of white female students I met in integrated high schools, in college, or in various women's groups. The majority of us understood racism as a social evil perpetuated by prejudiced white people that could be overcome through bonding between blacks and liberal whites, through militant protest, changing of laws or racial integration. Higher educational institutions did nothing to increase our limited understanding of racism as a political ideology. Instead professors systematically denied us truth, teaching us to accept racial polarity in the form of white supremacy and sexual polarity in the form of male dominance.

American women have been socialized, even brainwashed, to accept a version of American history that was created to uphold and maintain racial imperialism in the form of white supremacy and sexual imperialism in the form of patriarchy. One measure of the success of such indoctrination is that we perpetuate both consciously and unconsciously the very evils that oppress us. I am certain that the black female sixth grade teacher who taught us history, who taught us to identify with the American government, who loved those students who could best recite the pledge of allegiance to the American flag was not aware of the contradiction; that we should love this government that segregated us, that failed to send schools with all black students supplies that went to schools with only white pupils. Unknowingly she implanted in our psyches a seed of the racial imperialism that would keep us forever in bondage. For how does one overthrow, change, or even challenge a system that you have been taught to admire, to love, to believe in? Her innocence does not change the reality that she was teaching black children to embrace the very system that oppressed us, that she encouraged us to support it, to stand in awe of it, to die for it.

That American women, irrespective of their education, economic status, or racial identification, have undergone years of sexist and racist socialization that has taught us to blindly trust our knowledge of history and its effect on present reality, even though that knowledge has been formed and shaped by an oppressive system, is nowhere more evident than in the recent feminist movement. The group of college-educated white middle and upper class women who came together to organize a women's movement brought a new energy to the concept of women's rights in America. They were not merely advocating social equality with men. They demanded a transformation of society, a revolution, a change in the American social structure. Yet as they attempted to take feminism beyond the realm of radical rhetoric and into the realm of American life, they revealed that they had not changed, had not undone the sexist and racist brainwashing that had taught them to regard women unlike themselves as Others. Consequently, the Sisterhood they talked about has not become a reality, and the women's movement they envisioned would have a transformative effect on American culture his not emerged. Instead, the hierarchical pattern of race and sex relationships already established in American society merely took a different form under "feminism": the form of women being classed as an oppressed group under affirmative action programs further perpetuating the myth that the social status of all women in America is the same; the form of women's studies programs being established with all-white faculty teaching literature almost exclusively by white women about white women and frequently from racist perspectives; the form of white women writing books that purport to be about the experience of American women when in fact they concentrate solely on the experience of white women; and finally the form of endless argument and debate as to whether or not racism was a feminist issue.

If the white women who organized the contemporary movement toward feminism were at all remotely aware of racial politics in American history, they would have known that overcoming barriers that separate women from one another would entail confronting the reality of racism, and not just racism as a general evil in society but the race hatred they might harbor in their own psyches. Despite the predominance of patriarchal rule in American society, America was colonized on a racially imperialistic base and not on a sexually imperialistic base. No degree of patriarchal bonding between white male colonizers and Native American men overshadowed white racial imperialism. Racism took precedence over sexual alliances in both the white world's interaction with Native Americans and African Americans, just as racism overshadowed any bonding between black women and white women on the basis of sex. Tunisian writer Albert Memmi emphasizes in *The Colonizer and the Colonized* the impact of racism as a tool of imperialism:

> Racism appears . . . not as an incidental detail, but as a con-substantial part of colonialism. It is the highest expression of the colonial system and one of the most significant features of the colonialist. Not only does it establish a (fundamental discrimination between colonizer and colonized, a sine qua non of colonial life, but it also lays the foundation for the immutability of this life.

While those feminists who argue that sexual imperialism is more endemic to all societies than racial imperialism are probably correct, American society is one in which racial imperialism supersedes sexual imperialism.

In America, the social status of black and white women has never been the same. In 19th and early 20th century America, few if any similarities could be found between the life experiences of the two female groups. Although they were both subject to sexist victimization, as victims of racism black women were subjected to oppressions no white woman was forced to endure. In fact, white racial imperialism granted all white women, however victimized by sexist oppression they might be, the right to assume the role of oppressor in relationship to black women and black men. From the onset of the contemporary move toward feminist revolution, white female organizers attempted to minimize their position in the racial caste hierarchy of American society. In their efforts to disassociate themselves from white men (to deny connections based on shared racial caste), white women involved in the move toward feminism have charged that racism is endemic to white male patriarchy and have argued that they cannot be held responsible for racist oppression. Commenting on the issue of white female accountability in her essay "'Disloyal to Civilization': Feminism, Racism, and Gynephobia," radical feminist Adrienne Rich contends:

> If Black and White feminists are going to speak of female account-ability, I believe the word racism must be seized, grasped in our bare hands, ripped out of the sterile or defensive consciousness in which it so often grows, and transplanted so that it can yield new insights for

our lives and our movement. An analysis that places the guilt for active domination, physical and institutional violence, and the justifications embedded in myth and language, on white women not only compounds false consciousness; it allows us all to deny or neglect the charged connection among black and white women from the historical conditions of slavery on, and it impedes any real discussion of women's instrumentality in a system which oppresses all women and in which hatred of women is also embedded in myth, folklore, and language.

No reader of Rich's essay could doubt that she is concerned that women who are committed to feminism work to overcome barriers that separate black and white women. However, she fails to understand that from a black female perspective, if white women are denying the existence of black women, writing "feminist" scholarship as if black women are not a part of the collective group American women, or discriminating against black women, then it matters less that North America was colonized by white patriarchal *men* who institutionalized a racially imperialistic social order than that white women who purport to be feminists support and actively perpetuate anti-black racism.

To black women the issue is not whether white women are more or less racist than white men, but that they are racist. If women committed to feminist revolution, be they black or white, are to achieve any understanding of the "charged connections" between white women and black women, we must first be willing to examine woman's relationship to society, to race, and to American culture as it is and not as we would ideally have it be. That means confronting the reality of white female racism. Sexist discrimination has prevented white women from assuming the dominant role in the perpetuation of white racial imperialism, but it has not prevented white women from absorbing, supporting, and advocating racist ideology or acting individually as racist oppressors in various spheres of American life.

Every women's movement in America from its earliest origin to the present day has been built on a racist foundation – a fact which in no way invalidates feminism as a political ideology. The racial apartheid social structure that characterized 19th and early 20th century American life was mirrored in the women's rights movement. The first white women's rights advocates were never seeking social equality for all women; they were seeking social equality for white women. Because many 19th century white women's rights advocates were also active in the abolitionist movement, it is often assumed they were anti-racist. Historiographers and especially recent feminist writing have created a version of American history in which white women's rights advocates are presented as champions of oppressed black people. This fierce romanticism has informed most studies of the abolitionist movement. In contemporary times there is a general tendency to equate abolitionism with a repudiation of racism. In actuality, most white abolitionists, male and female, though vehement in their anti-slavery protest, were totally opposed to granting social equality to black people. Joel Kovel, in his study *White Racism: A Psychohistory,* emphasizes that the "actual aim of the reform movement, so nobly and bravely begun, was not the liberation of the black, but the fortification of the white, conscience and all."

It is a commonly accepted belief that white female reformist empathy with the oppressed black slave, coupled with her recognition that she was powerless to end slavery, led to the development of a feminist consciousness and feminist revolt. Contemporary historiographers and in particular white female scholars accept the theory that the white women's rights advocates' feelings of solidarity with black slaves were an indication that they were anti-racist and were supportive of social equality of blacks. It is this glorification of the role white women played that leads Adrienne Rich to assert:

> . . . It is important for white feminists to remember that – despite lack of constitutional citizenship, educational deprivation, economic bondage to men, laws and customs forbidding women to speak in public or to disobey fathers, husbands, and brothers – our white foresisters have, in Lillian Smith's words, repeatedly been "disloyal to civilization" and have "smelled death in the word 'segregation'," often defying patri- archy for the first time, not on their own behalf but for the sake of black men, women, and children. We have a strong anti-racist female tradition despite all efforts by the white patriarchy to polarize its creature-objects, creating dichotomies of privilege and caste, skin color, and age and condition of servitude.

There is little historical evidence to document Rich's assertion that white women as a collective group or white women's rights advocates are part of an anti-racist tradition. When white women reformers in the 1830s chose to work to free the slave, they were motivated by religious sentiment. They attacked slavery, not racism. The basis of their attack was moral reform. That they were not demanding social equality for black people is an indication that they remained committed to white racist supremacy despite their anti-slavery work. While they strongly advo- cated an end to slavery, they never advocated a change in the racial hierarchy that allowed their caste status to be higher than that of black women or men. In fact, they wanted that hierarchy to be maintained. Consequently, the white women's rights movement which had a lukewarm beginning in earlier reform activities emerged in full force in the wake of efforts to gain rights for black people precisely because white women wanted to see no change in the social status of blacks until they were assured that their demands for more rights were met.

[. . .] At the beginning of the 20th century, white women suffragists were eager to advance their own cause at the expense of black people. In 1903 at the National American Woman's Suffrage Convention held in New Orleans, a southern suffragist urged the enfranchisement of white women on the grounds that it "would insure immediate and durable white supremacy." Historian Rosalyn Terborg-Penn discusses white female support of white supremacy in her essay "Discrimination Against Afro-American Women in the Woman's Movement 1830–1920":

> As early as the 1890s, Susan B. Anthony realized the potential to the woman suffrage cause in wooing southern white women. She chose expedience over loyalty and justice when she asked veteran feminist supporter Frederick Douglass not to attend the National American Woman Suffrage Association convention scheduled in Atlanta. . . .

During the National American Woman Suffrage Association meeting of 1903 in New Orleans, the *Times Democrat* assailed the association because of its negative attitude on the question of black women and the suffrage for them. In a prepared statement signed by Susan B. Anthony, Carrie C. Catt, Anna Howard Shaw, Kate N. Gordon, Alice Stone Blackwell, Harriet Taylor Upton, Laura Clay, and Mary Coggeshall, the board of officers of the NAWSA endorsed the organization's states' rights position, which was tantamount to an endorsement of white supremacy in most states, particularly in the south.

Racism within the women's rights movement did not emerge simply as a response to the issue of suffrage; it was a dominant force in all reform groups with white female members. Terborg-Penn contends:

> Discrimination against Afro-American women reformers was the rule rather than the exception within the woman's rights movement from the 1830s to 1920. Although white feminists Susan B. Anthony, Lucy Stone, and some others encouraged black women to join the struggle against sexism during the nineteenth century, antebellum reformers who were involved with women's abolitionist groups as well as women's rights organizations actively discriminated against black women.

In their efforts to prove that solidarity existed between 19th century black and white female reformers, contemporary women activists often cite the presence of Sojourner Truth at Women's Rights conventions to support their argument that white female suffragists were anti-racist. But on every occasion Sojourner Truth spoke, groups of white women protested. In *The Betrayal of the Negro,* Rayford Logan writes:

> When the General Federation of Women's Clubs was faced with the question of the color line at the turn of the century, Southern clubs threatened to secede. One of the first expressions of the adamant opposition to the admission of colored clubs was disclosed by the Chicago *Tribune* and the *Examiner* during the great festival of fraternization at the Atlanta Exposition, the Encampment of the GAR in Louisville, and the dedication of the Chickamauga battlefield. . . . The Georgia Women's Press Club felt so strongly on the subject that members were in favor of withdrawing from the Federation if colored women were admitted there. Miss Corinne Stocker, a member of the Managing Board of the Georgia Women's Press Club and one of the editors of the *Atlanta Journal*, stated on September 19: "In this matter the Southern women are not narrow-minded or bigoted, but they simply cannot recognize the colored women socially. . . . At the same time we feel that the South is the colored woman's best friend."

Southern white women's club members were most vehement in their opposition to black women joining their ranks, but northern white women also supported racial segregation. The issue of whether black women would be able to participate in the women's club movement on an equal footing with white women came to a head in Milwaukee at the General Federation of Women's Clubs conference when the question was raised as to whether black feminist Mary Church Terrell, then president of the National Association of Colored Women, would be allowed to offer greetings, and whether Josephine Ruffin, who represented the black organization the New Era Club, would be recognized. In both cases white women's racism carried the day. In an interview in the Chicago *Tribune*, the president of the federation, Mrs. Lowe, was asked to comment on the refusal to acknowledge black female participants like Josephine Ruffin, and she responded: "Mrs. Ruffin belongs among her own people. Among them she would be a leader and could do much good, but among us she can create nothing but trouble." Rayford Logan comments on the fact that white women like Mrs. Lowe had no objection to black women trying to improve their lot; they simply felt that racial apartheid should be maintained. Writing of Mrs. Lowe's attitude toward black women, Logan comments:

> Mrs. Lowe had assisted in establishing kindergartens for colored children in the South, and the colored women in charge of them were all her good friends. She associated with them in a business way, but, of course they would not think of sitting beside her at a convention. Negroes were "a race by themselves, and among themselves they can accomplish much, assisted by us and by the federation, which is ever ready to do all in its power to help them." If Mrs. Ruffin were the "cultured lady every one says she is, she should put her education and her talents to good uses as a colored woman among colored women."

Anti-black feelings among white female club members were much stronger than anti-black sentiment among white male club members. One white male wrote a letter to the Chicago *Tribune* in which he stated:

> Here we have the spectacle of educated, refined, and Christian women who have been protesting and laboring for years against the unjust discrimination practiced against them by men, now getting together and the first shot out of their reticules is fired at one of their own because she is black, no other reason or pretence of reason.

Prejudices white women activists felt toward black women were far more intense than their prejudices toward black men. As Rosalyn Penn states in her essay, black men were more accepted in white reform circles than black women. Negative attitudes toward black women were the result of prevailing racist sexist stereotypes that portrayed black women as morally impure. Many white women felt that their status as ladies would be undermined were they to associate with black women. No such moral stigma was attached to black men. Black male leaders like Frederick Douglass, James Forten, Henry Garnett and others were occasionally welcome in white social circles. White women activists who would not have considered dining in the company of black men welcomed individual black men to their family tables.

[. . .] Relationships between white and black women were charged by tensions and conflicts in the early part of the 20th century. The women's rights movement had not drawn black and white women close together. Instead, it exposed the fact that white women were not willing to relinquish their support of white supremacy to support the interests of all women. Racism in the women's rights movement and in the work arena was a constant reminder to black women of the distances that separated the two experiences, distances that white women did not want bridged. When the contemporary movement toward feminism began, white women organizers did not address the issue of conflict between black and white women. Their rhetoric of sisterhood and solidarity suggested that women in America were able to bond across both class and race boundaries – but no such coming together had actually occurred. The structure of the contemporary women's movement was no different from that of the earlier women's rights movement. Like their predecessors, the white women who initiated the women's movement launched their efforts in the wake of the 60s black liberation movement. As if history were repeating itself, they also began to make synonymous their social status and the social status of black people. And it was in the context of endless comparisons of the plight of "women" and "blacks" that they revealed their racism. In most cases, this racism was an unconscious, unacknowledged aspect of their thought, suppressed by their narcissism – a narcissism which so blinded them that they would not admit two obvious facts: one, that in a capitalist, racist, imperialist state there is no one social status women share as a collective group; and second, that the social status of white women in America has never been like that of black women or men.

When the women's movement began in the late 60s, it was evident that the white women who dominated the movement felt it was "their" movement, that is the medium through which a white woman would voice her grievances to society. Not only did white women act as if feminist ideology existed solely to serve their own interests because they were able to draw public attention to feminist concerns. They were unwilling to acknowledge that non-white women were part of the collective group women in American society. They urged black women to join "their" movement or in some cases the women's movement, but in dialogues and writings, their attitudes toward black women were both racist and sexist. Their racism did not assume the form of overt expressions of hatred; it was far more subtle. It took the form of simply ignoring the existence of black women or writing about them using common sexist and racist stereotypes. From Betty Friedan's *The Feminine Mystique* to Barbara Berg's *The Remembered Gate* and on to more recent publications like *Capitalist Patriarchy and the Case for Socialist Feminism,* edited by Zillah Eisenstein, most white female writers who considered themselves feminist revealed in their writing that they had been socialized to accept and perpetuate racist ideology.

In most of their writing, the white American woman's experience is made synonymous with *the* American woman's experience. While it is in no way racist for any author to write a book exclusively about white women, it is fundamentally racist for books to be published that focus solely on the American white woman's experience in which that experience is assumed to be *the* American woman's experience. For example, in the course of research for this book, I sought to find information about the life of free and slave black women in colonial America. I saw listed in a bibliography Julia Cherry Spruill's work *Women's Life and Work in the Southern Colonies,* which was first published in 1938 and then again in 1972. At the Sisterhood bookstore in Los Angeles I found the book and read a blurb on the back which had been written especially for the new edition:

> One of the classic works in American social history, *Women's Life and Work in the Southern Colonies* is the first comprehensive study of the daily life and status of women in southern colonial America. Julia Cherry Spruill researched colonial newspapers, court records, and manuscript material of every kind, drawing on archives and libraries from Boston to Savannah. The resulting book was, in the words of Arthur Schlesinger, Sr., "a model of research and exposition, an important contribution to American social history to which students will constantly turn."
>
> The topics include women's function in the settlement of the colonies; their homes, domestic occupation, and social life; the aims and methods of their education; their role in government and business affairs outside the home; and the manner in which they were regarded by the law and by society in general. Out of a wealth of documentation, and often from the words of colonial people themselves, a vivid and surprising picture – one that had never been seen before – emerges of the many different aspects of these women's lives.

I expected to find in Spruill's work information about various groups of women in American society. I found instead that it was another work solely about white women and that both the title and blurb were misleading. A more accurate title would have been *White Women's Life and Work in the Southern Colonies.* Certainly, if I or any author sent a manuscript to an American publisher that focused exclusively on the life and work of black women in the south, also called *Women's Life and Work in the Southern Colonies* the title would be automatically deemed misleading and unacceptable. The force that allows white feminist authors to make no reference to racial identity in their books about "women" that are in actuality about white women is the same one that would compel any author writing exclusively on black women to refer explicitly to their racial identity. That force is racism. In a racially imperialist nation such as ours, it is the dominant race that reserves for itself the luxury of dismissing racial identity while the oppressed race is made daily aware of their racial identity. It is the dominant race that can make it seem that their experience is representative.

In America, white racist ideology has always allowed white women to assume that the word woman is synonymous with white woman, for women of other races are always perceived as Others, as de-humanized beings who do not fall under the heading woman. White feminists who claimed to be politically astute showed themselves to be unconscious of the way their use of language suggested they did not recognize the existence of black women. They impressed upon the American public their sense that the word "woman" meant white woman by drawing endless analogies between "women" and "blacks." Examples of such analogies abound in almost every feminist work. In a collection of essays published in 1975 titled *Women: A Feminist Perspective,* an essay by Helen Hacker is included called "Women as a Minority Group" which is a good example of the way white women have used comparisons between "women" and "blacks" to exclude black women and to deflect attention away from their own racial caste status. Hacker writes:

> The relation between women and Negroes is historical, as well as analogical. In the seventeenth century the legal status of Negro servants was borrowed from that of women and children, who were under the patria potestas, and until the Civil War there was considerable cooperation between the Abolitionists and woman suffrage movement.

Clearly Hacker is referring solely to white women. An even more glaring example of the white feminist comparison between "blacks" and "women" occurs in Catherine Stimpson's essay " 'Thy Neighbor's Wife, Thy Neighbor's Servants': Women's Liberation and Black Civil Rights." She writes:

> The development of an industrial economy, as Myrdal points out, has not brought about the integration of women and blacks into the adult male culture. Women have not found a satisfactory way to bear children and to work. Blacks have not destroyed the hard doctrine of their unassimilability. What the economy gives both women and blacks are menial labor, low pay, and few promotions. White male workers hate both groups, for their competition threatens wages and their possible job equality, let alone superiority, threatens nothing less than the very nature of things. The tasks of women and blacks are usually grueling, repetitive, slogging, and dirty. . . .

Throughout Stimpson's essay she makes woman synonymous with white women and black synonymous with black men.

[. . .] Whenever black women tried to express to white women their ideas about white female racism or their sense that the women who were at the forefront of the movement were not oppressed women they were told that "oppression cannot be measured." White female emphasis on "common oppression" in their appeals to black women to join the movement further alienated many black women. Because so many of the white women in the movement were employers of non-white and white domestics, their rhetoric of common oppression was experienced by black women as an assault, an expression of the bourgeois woman's insensitivity and lack of concern for the lower class woman's position in society.

Underlying the assertion of common oppression was a patronizing attitude toward black women. White women were assuming that all they had to do was express a desire for sisterhood, or a desire to have black women join their groups, and black women would be overjoyed. They saw themselves as acting in a generous, open, non-racist manner and were shocked that black women responded to their overtures with anger and outrage. They could not see that their generosity was

directed at themselves, that it was self-centered and motivated by their own opportunistic desires.

Despite the reality that white upper and middle class women in America suffer
from sexist discrimination and sexist abuse, they are not as a group as oppressed
as *poor* white, or black, or yellow women. Their unwillingness to distinguish
between various degrees of discrimination or oppression caused black women to
see them as enemies. As many upper and middle class white feminists who suffer
least from sexist oppression were attempting to focus all attention on themselves,
it follows that they would not accept an analysis of woman's lot in America
which argued that not all women are equally oppressed because some women are
able to use their class, race and educational privilege to effectively resist sexist
oppression.

Initially, class privilege was not discussed by white women in the women's
movement. They wanted to project an image of themselves as victims and that
could not be done by drawing attention to their class. In fact, the contemporary
women's movement was extremely class bound. As a group, white participants
did not denounce capitalism. They chose to define liberation using the terms of
white capitalist patriarchy, equating liberation with gaining economic status and
money power. Like all good capitalists, they proclaimed work as the key to liberation. This emphasis on work was yet another indication of the extent to which
the white female liberationists' perception of reality was totally narcissistic, classist,
and racist. Implicit in the assertion that work was the key to women's liberation
was a refusal to acknowledge the reality that, for masses of American working
class women, working for pay neither liberated them from sexist oppression nor
allowed them to gain any measure of economic independence. In *Liberating Feminism,*
Benjamin Barber's critique of the women's movement, he comments on the white
middle and upper class women's liberationist focus on work:

> Work clearly means something very different to women in search of
> an escape from leisure than it has to most of the human race for most
> of history. For a few lucky men, for far fewer women, work has occa-
> sionally been a source of meaning and creativity. But for most of the
> rest it remains even now forced drudgery in front of the ploughs,
> machines, words or numbers – pushing products, pushing switches,
> pushing papers to eke out the wherewithal of material existence.
>
> . . . To be able to work and to have work are two different matters.
> I suspect, however, that few liberationist women are to be found
> working as menials and unskilled laborers simply in order to occupy
> their time and identify with the power structure. For status and power
> are not conferred by work per se, but by certain kinds of work gener-
> ally reserved to the middle and upper classes. . . . As Studs Terkel
> shows in *Working,* most workers find jobs dull, oppressive, frustrating
> and alienating – very much what women find housewifery.

When white women's liberationists emphasized work as a path to liberation,
they did not concentrate their attention on those women who are most exploited
in the American labor force. Had they emphasized the plight of working class

women, attention would have shifted away from the college-educated suburban housewife who wanted entrance into the middle and upper class work force. Had attention been focused on women who were already working and who were exploited as cheap surplus labor in American society, it would have de-romanticized the middle class white woman's quest for "meaningful" employment. While it does not in any way diminish the importance of women resisting sexist oppression by entering the labor force, work has not been a liberating force for masses of American women. And for some time now, sexism has not prevented them from being in the work force. White middle and upper class women like those described in Betty Friedan's *The Feminine Mystique* were housewives not because sexism would have prevented them from being in the paid labor force, but because they had willingly embraced the notion that it was better to be a housewife than to be a worker. The racism and classism of white women's liberationists was most apparent whenever they discussed work as the liberating force for women. In such discussions it was always the middle class "housewife" who was depicted as the victim of sexist oppression and not the poor black and non-black women who are most exploited by American economics.

[. . .] Feminism as a political ideology advocating social equality for all women was and is acceptable to many black women. They rejected the women's movement when it became apparent that middle and upper class college-educated white women who were its majority participants were determined to shape the movement so that it would serve their own opportunistic ends. While the established definition of feminism is the theory of the political, economic, and social equality of the sexes, white women liberationists used the power granted them by virtue of their being members of the dominant race in American society to interpret feminism in such a way that it was no longer relevant to all women. And it seemed incredible to black women that they were being asked to support a movement whose majority participants were eager to maintain race and class hierarchies between women.

Black women who participated in women's groups, lectures, and meetings initially trusted the sincerity of white female participants. Like 19th century black women's rights advocates, they assumed that any women's movement would address issues relevant to all women and that racism would be automatically cited as a force that had divided women, that would have to be reckoned with for true Sisterhood to emerge, and also that no radical revolutionary women's movement could take place until women as a group were joined in political solidarity. Although contemporary black women were mindful of the prevalence of white female racism, they believed it could be confronted and changed

As they participated in the women's movement they found, in their dialogues with white women in women's groups, in women's studies classes, at conferences, that their trust was betrayed. They found that white women had appropriated feminism to advance their own cause, i.e., their desire to enter the mainstream of American capitalism. They were told that white women were in the majority and that they had the power to decide which issues would be considered "feminist" issues. White women liberationists decided that the way to confront racism was to speak out in consciousness-raising groups about their racist upbringings, to encourage black women to join their cause, to make sure they hired one non-white woman in "their" women's studies program, or to invite one non-white woman to speak on a discussion panel at "their" conference.

When black women involved with women's liberation attempted to discuss racism, many white women responded by angrily stating: "We won't be guilt-tripped." For them the dialogue ceased. Others seemed to relish admitting that they were racist but felt that admitting verbally to being racist was tantamount to changing their racist values. For the most part, white women refused to listen when black women explained that what they expected was not verbal admissions of guilt but conscious gestures and acts that would show that white women liberationists were anti-racist and attempting to overcome their racism. The issue of racism within the women's movement would never have been raised had white women shown in their writings and speeches that they were in fact "liberated" from racism.

As concerned black and white individuals tried to stress the importance to the women's movement of confronting and changing racist attitudes because such sentiments threatened to undermine the movement, they met with resistance from those white women who saw feminism solely as a vehicle to enhance their own individual, opportunistic ends. Conservative, reactionary white women, who increasingly represented a large majority of the participants, were outspoken in their pronouncements that the issue of racism should not be considered worthy of attention. They did not want the issue of racism raised because they did not want to deflect attention away from their projection of the white woman as "good," i.e., non-racist victim, and the white man as "bad," i.e., racist oppressor. For them to have acknowledged woman's active complicity in the perpetuation of imperialism, colonialism, racism, or sexism would have made the issue of women's liberation far more complex. To those who saw feminism solely as a way to demand entrance into the white male power structure, it simplified matters to make all men oppressors and all women victims.

[. . .] The emergence of black feminist groups led to a greater polarization of black and white women's liberationists. Instead of bonding on the basis of shared understanding of woman's varied collective and individual plight in society, they acted as if the distance separating their experiences from one another could not be bridged by knowledge or understanding. Rather than black women attacking the white female attempt to present them as an Other, an unknown, unfathomable element, they acted as if they were an Other. Many black women found an affirmation and support of their concern with feminism in all-black groups that they had not experienced in women's groups dominated by white women; this has been one of the positive features of black women's groups. However, all women should experience in racially mixed groups affirmation and support. Racism is the barrier that prevents positive communication and it is not eliminated or challenged by separation. White women supported the formation of separate groups because it confirmed their preconceived racist–sexist notion that no connection existed between their experiences and those of black women. Separate groups meant they would not be asked to concern themselves with race or racism. While black women condemned the anti-black racism of white women, the mounting animosity between the two groups gave rise to overt expression of their anti-white racism. Many black women who had never participated in the women's movement saw the formation of separate black groups as confirmation of their belief that no alliance could ever take place between black and white women. To express their anger and rage at white women, they evoked the negative stereotypical image of the white woman as a passive, parasitic, privileged being living off the labor of others as a way to mock and ridicule the white women liberationists.

[. . .] Animosity between black and white women's liberationists was not due solely to disagreement over racism within the women's movement; it was the end result of years of jealousy, envy, competition, and anger between the two groups. Conflict between black and white women did not begin with the 20th century women's movement. It began during slavery. The social status of white women in America has to a large extent been determined by white people's relationship to black people. It was the enslavement of African people in colonized America that marked the beginning of a change in the social status of white women. Prior to slavery, patriarchal law decreed white women were lowly inferior beings, the subordinate group in society. The subjugation of black people allowed them to vacate their despised position and assume the role of a superior.

Consequently, it can be easily argued that even though white men institutionalized slavery, white women were its most immediate beneficiaries. Slavery in no way altered the hierarchical social status of the white male but it created a new status for the white female. The only way that her new status could be maintained was through the constant assertion of her superiority over the black woman and man. All too often colonial white women, particularly those who were slave mistresses, chose to differentiate their status from the slave's by treating the slave in a brutal and cruel manner. It was in her relationship to the black female slave that the white woman could best assert her power. Individual black slave women were quick to learn that sex-role differentiation did not mean that the white mistress was not to be regarded as an authority figure. Because they had been socialized via patriarchy to respect male authority and resent female authority, black women were reluctant to acknowledge the "power" of the white mistress. When the enslaved black woman expressed contempt and disregard for white female authority, the white mistress often resorted to brutal punishment to assert her authority. But even brutal punishment could not change the fact that black women were not inclined to regard the white female with the awe and respect they showed to the white male.

By flaunting their sexual lust for the bodies of black women and their preference for them as sexual partners, white men successfully pitted white women and enslaved black women against one another. In most instances, the white mistress did not envy the black female slave her role as sexual object; she feared only that her newly acquired social status might be threatened by white male sexual interaction with black women. His sexual involvement with black women (even if that involvement was rape) in effect reminded the white female of her subordinate position in relationship to him. For he could exercise his power as racial imperialist and sexual imperialist to rape or seduce black women, while white women were not free to rape or seduce black men without fear of punishment. Though the white female might condemn the actions of a white male who chose to interact sexually with black female slaves, she was unable to dictate to him proper behavior. Nor could she retaliate by engaging in sexual relationships with enslaved or free black men. Not surprisingly, she directed her anger and rage at the enslaved black women. In those cases where emotional ties developed between white men and black female slaves, white mistresses would go to great lengths to punish the female. Severe beatings were the method most white women used to punish black female slaves. Often in a jealous rage a mistress might use disfigurement to punish a lusted-after black female slave. The mistress might cut off her breast, blind an eye, or cut off another body part. Such treatment naturally caused hostility between white women and enslaved black women. To the enslaved black woman, the white mistress living in relative comfort was the representative symbol of white womanhood. She was both envied and despised – envied for her material comfort, despised because she felt little concern or compassion for the slave woman's lot. Since the white woman's privileged social status could only exist if a group of women were present to assume the lowly position she had abdicated, it follows that black and white women would be at odds with one another. If the white woman struggled to change the lot of the black slave woman, her own social position on the race-sex hierarchy would be altered.

Manumission did not bring an end to conflicts between black and white women; it heightened them. To maintain the apartheid structure slavery had institutionalized, white colonizers, male and female, created a variety of myths and stereotypes to differentiate the status of black women from that of white women. White racists and even some black people who had absorbed the colonizer's mentality depicted the white woman as a symbol of perfect womanhood and encouraged black women to strive to attain such perfection by using the white female as her model. The jealousy and envy of white women that had erupted in the black woman's consciousness during slavery was deliberately encouraged by the dominant white culture. Advertisements, newspaper articles, books, etc. were constant reminders to black women of the difference between their social status and that of white women, and they bitterly resented it. Nowhere was this dichotomy as clearly demonstrated as in the materially privileged white household where the black female domestic worked as an employee of the white family. In these relationships, black women workers were exploited to enhance the social standing of white families. In the white community, employing domestic help was a sign of material privilege and the person who directly benefited from a servant's work was the white woman, since without the servant she would have performed domestic chores. Not surprisingly, the black female domestic tended to see the white female as her "boss," her oppressor, not the white male whose earnings usually paid her wage.

[. . .] Resolution of the conflict between black and white women cannot begin until all women acknowledge that a feminist movement which is both racist and classist is a mere sham, a cover-up for women's continued bondage to materialist patriarchal principles, and passive acceptance of the status quo. The sisterhood that is necessary for the making of feminist revolution can be achieved only when all women disengage themselves from the hostility, jealousy, and competition with one another that has kept us vulnerable, weak, and unable to envision new realities. That sisterhood cannot be forged by the mere saying of words. It is the outcome of continued growth and change. It is a goal to be reached, a process of becoming. The process begins with action, with the individual woman's refusal to accept any set of myths, stereotypes, and false assumptions that deny the shared commonness of her human experience; that deny her capacity to experience the Unity of all life; that deny her capacity to bridge gaps created by racism, sexism, or classism; that deny her ability to change. The process begins with the individual woman's acceptance that American women, without exception, are socialized to be racist, classist, and sexist, in varying degrees, and that labeling ourselves feminists does not change the fact that we must consciously work to rid ourselves of the legacy of negative socialization.

If women want a feminist revolution – ours is a world that is crying out for feminist revolution – then we must assume responsibility for drawing women together in political solidarity. That means we must assume responsibility for eliminating all the forces that divide women. Racism is one such force. Women, all women, are accountable for racism continuing to divide us. Our willingness to assume responsibility for the elimination of racism need not be engendered by feelings of guilt, moral responsibility, victimization, or rage. It can spring from a heartfelt desire for sisterhood and the personal, intellectual realization that racism among women undermines the potential radicalism of feminism. It can spring from our knowledge that racism is an obstacle in our path that must be removed. More obstacles are created if we simply engage in endless debate as to who put it there.

Select references

Barber, Benjamin, *Liberating Feminism*. New York: Delta, 1976.

Berg, Barbara, *The Remembered Gate: Origins of American Feminism*. New York: Oxford University Press, 1979.

Douglass, Frederick, *Narrative of the Life of Frederick Douglass*. Edited by Benjamin Quarles. Cambridge, Mass.: Belknap Press, 1969.

Eisenstein, Zillah, ed.,*Capitalist Patriarchy and the Case for Socialist Feminism*. New York: Monthly Review Press, 1979.

Logan, Rayford, *The Betrayal of the Negro*. New York: Collier, 1954.

Spruill, Julia, *Women's Life and Work in the Southern Colonies*. New York: W. W. Norton, [1938] 1972.

Chapter 26

Hazel V. Carby

WHITE WOMAN LISTEN!
Black feminism and the boundaries
of sisterhood

I'm leaving evidence. And you got to leave evidence too. And your children got to leave evidence. . . . They burned all the documents. . . . We got to burn out what they put in our minds, like you burn out a wound. Except we got to keep what we need to bear witness. That scar that's left to bear witness. We got to keep it as visible as our blood.[1]

THE BLACK WOMEN'S CRITIQUE of *his*tory has not only involved us in coming to terms with 'absences'; we have also been outraged by the ways in which it has made us visible, when it has chosen to see us. *His*tory has constructed our sexuality and our femininity as deviating from those qualities with which white women, as the prize objects of the Western world, have been endowed. We have also been defined in less than human terms.[2] Our continuing struggle with *his*tory began with its 'discovery' of us. However, this chapter will be concerned with herstory rather than *his*tory. We wish to address questions to the feminist theories which have been developed during the last decade; a decade in which black women have been fighting, in the streets, in the schools, through the courts, inside and outside the wage relation. The significance of these struggles ought to inform the writing of the herstory of women in Britain. It is fundamental to the development of a feminist theory and practice that is meaningful for black women. We cannot hope to reconstitute ourselves in all our absences, or to rectify the ill-conceived presences that invade herstory from *his*tory, but we do wish to bear witness to our own herstories. The connections between these and the herstories of white women will be made and remade in struggle. Black women have come from Africa, Asia and the Caribbean and we cannot do justice to all their herstories in a single chapter. Neither can we represent the voices of all black women in Britain, our herstories are too numerous and too varied. What we will do is to offer ways in which the 'triple' oppression of gender, race and class can be understood, in their specificity, and also as they determine the lives of black women.

Much contemporary debate has posed the question of the relation between race and gender, in terms which attempt to parallel race and gender divisions. It can be argued that as processes, racism and sexism are similar. Ideologically for example, they both construct common sense through reference to 'natural' and 'biological' differences. It has also been argued that the categories of race and gender are both socially constructed and that, therefore, they have little internal coherence as concepts. Furthermore, it is possible to parallel racialized and gendered divisions in the sense that the possibilities of amelioration through legislation appear to be equally ineffectual in both cases. Michèle Barrett, however, has pointed out that it is not possible to argue for parallels because as soon as historical analysis is made, it becomes obvious that the institutions which have to be analysed are different, as are the forms of analysis needed.[3] We would agree that the construction of such parallels is fruitless and often proves to be little more than a mere academic exercise; but there are other reasons for our dismissal of these kinds of debate. The experience of black women does not enter the parameters of parallelism. The fact that black women are subject to the *simultaneous* oppression of patriarchy, class and 'race' is the prime reason for not employing parallels that render their position and experience not only marginal but also invisible.

In arguing that most contemporary feminist theory does not begin to adequately account for the experience of black women we also have to acknowledge that it is not a simple question of their absence, consequently the task is not one of rendering their visibility. On the contrary we will have to argue that the process of accounting for their historical and contemporary position does, in itself, challenge the use of some of the central categories and assumptions of recent mainstream feminist thought. We can point to no single source for our oppression. When white feminists emphasize patriarchy alone, we want to redefine the term and make it a more complex concept. Racism ensures that black men do not have the same relations to patriarchal/capitalist hierarchies as white men.

[. . .] It is only in the writings by black feminists that we can find attempts to theorize the interconnection of class gender and race as it occurs in our lives and it has only been in the autonomous organizations of black women that we have been able to express and act upon the experiences consequent upon these determinants. Many black women had been alienated by the non-recognition of their lives, experiences and herstories in the WLM. Black feminists have been, and are still, demanding that the existence of racism must be acknowledged as a structuring feature of our relationships with white women. Both white feminist theory and practice have to recognize that white women stand in a power relation as oppressors of black women. This compromises any feminist theory and practice founded on the notion of simple equality.

Three concepts which are central to feminist theory become problematic in their application to black women's lives: 'the family', 'patriarchy' and 'reproduction'. When used they are placed in a context of the herstory of white (frequently middle-class) women and become contradictory when applied to the lives and experiences of black women.

[. . .] The use of the concept of 'dependency', is also a problem for black feminists. It has been argued that this concept provides the link between the 'material organisation of the household, and the ideology of femininity'. How then can we account for situations in which black women may be heads of households, or where, because of an economic system which structures high black male unemployment, they are not financially dependent upon a black man? This condition exists in both colonial and metropolitan situations. Ideologies of black female domesticity and motherhood have been constructed, through their employment (or chattel position) as domestics and surrogate mothers to white families rather than in relation to their own families. West Indian women still migrate to the United States and Canada as domestics and in Britain are seen to be suitable as office cleaners, National Health Service domestics, etc. In colonial situations Asian women have frequently been forced into prostitution to sexually service the white male invaders, whether in the form of armies of occupation or employees and guests of multinational corporations. How then, in view of all this, can it be argued that black male dominance exists in the same forms as white male dominance? Systems of slavery, colonialism, imperialism, have systematically denied positions in the white male hierarchy to black men and have used specific forms of terror to oppress them.

Black family structures have been seen as pathological by the state and are in the process of being constructed as pathological within white feminist theory. Here, ironically, the Western nuclear family structure and related ideologies of 'romantic love' formed under capitalism, are seen as more 'progressive' than black family structures.

[. . .] Too often concepts of historical progress are invoked by the left and feminists alike, to create a sliding scale of 'civilized liberties'. When barbarous sexual practices are to be described the 'Third World' is placed on display and compared to the 'First World' which is seen as more 'enlightened' or 'progressive'. The metropolitan centres of the West define the questions to be asked of other social systems and, at the same time, provide the measure against which all 'foreign' practices are gauged. In a peculiar combination of Marxism and feminism, capitalism becomes the vehicle for reforms which allow for progress towards the emancipation of women. The 'Third World', on the other hand, is viewed as retaining pre-capitalist forms expressed at the cultural level by traditions which are more oppressive to women.

[. . .] It can be seen from this brief discussion of the use of the concept 'the family' that the terms 'patriarchy' and 'reproduction' also become more complex in their application. It bears repetition that black men have not held the same patriarchal positions of power that the white males have established. Michèle Barrett argues that the term patriarchy has lost all analytic or explanatory power and has been reduced to a synonym for male dominance. She tries therefore to limit its use to a specific type of male dominance that could be located historically.

> I would not . . . want to argue that the concept of patriarchy should
> be jettisoned. I would favour retaining it for use in contexts where
> male domination is expressed through the power of the father over
> women and over younger men. . . . Hence I would argue for a more

precise and specific use of the concept of patriarchy, rather than one which expands it to cover all expressions of male domination and thereby attempts to construe a descriptive term as a systemic explanatory theory.[4]

Barrett is not thinking of capitalist social organization. But if we try to apply this more 'classic' and limited definition of patriarchy to the slave systems of the Americas and the Caribbean, we find that even this refined use of the concept cannot adequately account for the fact that both slaves and manumitted males did not have this type of patriarchal power. Alternatively, if we take patriarchy and apply it to various colonial situations it is equally unsatisfactory because it is unable to explain why black males have not enjoyed the benefits of white patriarchy. There are very obvious power structures in both colonial and slave social formations and they are predominantly patriarchal. However, the historically specific forms of racism force us to modify or alter the application of the term 'patriarchy' to black men. Black women have been dominated 'patriarchally' in different ways by men of different 'colours'.

In questioning the application of the concepts of 'the family' and 'patriarchy' we also need to problematize the use of the concept of 'reproduction'. In using this concept in relation to the domestic labour of black women we find that in spite of its apparent simplicity it must be dismantled. What does the concept of reproduction mean in a situation where black women have done domestic labour outside of their own homes in the servicing of white families? In this example they lie outside of the industrial wage relation but in a situation where they are providing for the reproduction of black labour in their own domestic sphere, simultaneously ensuring the reproduction of white labour power in the 'white' household. The concept, in fact, is unable to explain exactly what the relations are that need to be revealed. What needs to be understood is, first, precisely *how* the black woman's role in a rural, industrial or domestic labour force affects the construction of ideologies of black female sexuality which are different from, and often constructed in opposition to, white female sexuality; and second, how this role relates to the black woman's struggle for control over her own sexuality.

If we examine the recent herstory of women in post-war Britain we can see the ways in which the inclusion of black women creates problems for hasty generalization. In pointing to the contradiction between 'home-making as a career' and the campaign to recruit women into the labour force during post-war reconstruction, Elizabeth Wilson fails to perceive migration of black women to Britain as the solution to these contradictory needs. The Economic Survey for 1947 is cited as an example of the ways in which women were seen to form 'the only large reserve of labour left', yet, as we know, there was a rather large pool of labour in the colonies that had been mobilized previously to fight in World War II. The industries that the survey listed as in dire need of labour included those that were filled by both male and female black workers, though Elizabeth Wilson does not differentiate them.

> The survey gave a list of the industries and services where labour was most urgently required. The boot and shoe industry, clothing, textiles,

iron and steel, all require female workers, as did hospitals, domestic
service, transport, and the women's land army. There was also a shortage of shorthand typists, and a dire shortage of nurses and midwives.[5]

This tells us nothing about why black women were recruited more heavily into
some of these areas than others; perhaps we are given a clue when the author goes
on to point out that women were welcomed into the labour force in a 'circumscribed way'.

as temporary workers at a period of crisis, as part-time workers, and
as not disturbing the traditional division of labour in industry along sex
lines – the Survey reflected the view which was still dominant, that
married women would not naturally wish to work.[6]

Not all black women were subject to this process: Afro-Caribbean women, for
example, were encouraged and chose to come to Britain precisely to work.
Ideologically they were seen as 'naturally' suitable for the lowest paid, most menial
jobs. Elizabeth Wilson goes on to explain that 'work and marriage were still understood as alternatives . . . two kinds of women . . . a wife and a mother or a single
career woman'. Yet black women bridged this division. They were viewed simultaneously as workers and as wives and mothers. Elizabeth Wilson stresses that the
post-war debate over the entry of women into the labour force occurred within
the parameters of the question of possible effects on family life. She argues that
'wives and mothers were granted entry into paid work only so long as this did
not harm the family'. Yet women from Britain's reserve army of labour in the
colonies were recruited into the labour force far beyond any such considerations.
Rather than a concern to protect or preserve the black family in Britain, the state
reproduced common-sense notions of its inherent pathology: black women were
seen to fail as mothers precisely because of their position as workers.

One important struggle, rooted in these different ideological mechanisms,
which determine racially differentiated representations of gender, has been the
black woman's battle to gain control over her own sexuality in the face of racist
experimentation with the contraceptive Depo-Provera and enforced sterilizations.[7]

It is not just our herstory before we came to Britain that has been ignored by
white feminists, our experiences and struggles here have also been ignored. These
struggles and experiences, because they have been structured by racism, have been
different to those of white women. Black feminists decry the non-recognition of
the specificities of black women's sexuality and femininity, both in the ways these
are constructed and also as they are addressed through practices which oppress
black women in a gender-specific but nonetheless racist way.

This non-recognition is typified by a very interesting article on women in Third
World manufacturing by Diane Elson and Ruth Pearson. In analysing the employment of Third World women in world market factories they quote from an
investment brochure designed to attract foreign firms:

The manual dexterity of the oriental female is famous the world over.
Her hands are small and she works fast with extreme care. Who, there-

> fore, could be better qualified by *nature and inheritance* to contribute to
> the efficiency of a bench-assembly production line than the oriental
> girl?[8] (original emphasis)

The authors, however, analyse only the naturalization of gender and ignore the
specificity signalled by the inclusion of the adjective 'oriental', as if it didn't matter.
The fact that the sexuality of the 'oriental' woman is being differentiated, is not
commented upon and remains implicit rather than explicit as in the following
remarks.

> It is in the context of the subordination of women as a gender that we
> must analyse the supposed docility, subservience and consequent
> suitability for tedious, monotonous work of young women in the Third
> World.[9]

In concentrating an analysis upon gender only, Elson and Pearson do not see the
relation between the situation they are examining in the periphery and the women
who have migrated to the metropole. This last description is part of the common-
sense racism that we have described as being applied to Asian women in Britain
to channel them into 'tedious, monotonous work'. Elson and Pearson discuss this
ascription of docility and passivity and compare it to Frantz Fanon's analysis of
colonized people, without putting together the ways in which the women who are
their objects of study have been oppressed not by gender subordination alone but
also by colonization. The 'oriental' sexuality referred to in the advertising brochure
is one of many constructions of exotic sexual dexterity promised to Western male
tourists to South East Asia. This ideology of 'Eastern promise' links the material
practice of the move from the bench – making microchips – to the bed, in which
multinational corporate executives are serviced by prostitutes. This transition is
described by Elson and Pearson but not understood as a process which illustrates
an example of racially demarcated patriarchal power.

> If a woman loses her job in a world market factory after she has re-
> shaped her life on the basis of a wage income, the only way she may
> have of surviving is by selling her body. There are reports from
> South Korea, for instance, that many former electronics workers have
> no alternative but to become prostitutes. . . . A growing market for
> such services is provided by the way in which the tourist industry has
> developed, especially in South East Asia.[10]

The photographs accompanying the article are of anonymous black women. This
anonymity and the tendency to generalize into meaninglessness, the oppression of
an amorphous category called 'Third World women', are symptomatic of the ways
in which the specificity of our experiences and oppression are subsumed under
inapplicable concepts and theories. Black feminists in the US have complained of
the ignorance, in the white women's movement, of black women's lives.

> The force that allows white feminist authors to make no reference to
> racial identity in their books about 'women' that are in actuality about
> white women, is the same one that would compel any author writing
> exclusively on black women to refer explicitly to their racial identity.
> That force is racism. . . . It is the dominant race that can make it seem
> that their experience is representative.[11]

In Britain too it is as if we don't exist.

There is a growing body of black feminist criticism of white feminist theory
and practice, for its incipient racism and lack of relevance to black women's lives.[12]
The dialogues that have been attempted[13] have concentrated more upon visible,
empirical differences that affect black and white women's lives than upon developing a feminist theoretical approach that would enable a feminist understanding
of the basis of these differences. The accusation that racism in the women's movement acted so as to exclude the participation of black women, has led to an
explosion of debate in the USA.

> from a black female perspective, if white women are denying the exis-
> tence of black women, writing 'feminist' scholarship as if black women
> are not a part of the collective group American women, or discrimi-
> nating against black women, then it matters less that North America
> was colonised by white patriarchal *men* who institutionalised a racially
> imperialist social order, than that white women who purport to be
> feminists support and actively perpetuate anti-black racism.[14]

What little reaction there has been in Britain has been more akin to lighting a
damp squib, than an explosion. US black feminist criticism has no more been
listened to than indigenous black feminist criticism. Yet, bell hooks's powerful
critique has considerable relevance to British feminists. White women in the British
WLM are extraordinarily reluctant to see themselves in the situations of being
oppressors, as they feel that this will be at the expense of concentrating upon
being oppressed. Consequently the involvement of British women in imperialism
and colonialism is repressed and the benefits that they – as whites – gained from
the oppression of black people ignored. Forms of imperialism are simply identified as aspects of an all embracing patriarchy rather than as sets of social relations
in which white women hold positions of power by virtue of their 'race'.

> Had feminists chosen to make explicit comparisons between . . . the
> status of black women and white women, it would have been more
> than obvious that the two groups do not share an identical oppression.
> It would have been obvious that similarities between the status of
> women under patriarchy and that of any slave or colonized person
> do not necessarily exist in a society that is both racially and sexually
> imperialistic. In such a society, the woman who is seen as inferior
> because of her sex can also be seen as superior because of her race,
> even in relationship to men of another race.[15]

The benefits of a white skin did not just apply to a handful of cotton, tea or sugar plantation mistresses; all women in Britain benefited – in varying degrees – from the economic exploitation of the colonies. The pro-imperialist attitudes of many nineteenth- and early-twentieth-century feminists and suffragists have yet to be acknowledged for their racist implications. However, apart from this herstorical work, the exploration of contemporary racism within the white feminist movement in Britain has yet to begin.

Feminist theory in Britain is almost wholly Eurocentric and, when it is not ignoring the experience of black women 'at home', it is trundling 'Third World women' onto the stage only to perform as victims of 'barbarous', 'primitive' practices in 'barbarous', 'primitive' societies.

It should be noted that much feminist work suffers from the assumption that it is only through the development of a Western-style industrial capitalism and the resultant entry of women into waged labour that the potential for the liberation of women can increase. For example, foot-binding, clitoridectomy, female 'circumcision' and other forms of mutilation of the female body have been described as 'feudal residues', existing in economically 'backward' or 'underdeveloped' nations (i.e. not the industrialized West). Arranged marriages, polygamy and these forms of mutilation are linked in reductionist ways to a lack of technological development. [. . .]

Constructing alternatives

It should be an imperative for feminist herstory and theory to avoid reproducing the structural inequalities that exist between the 'metropoles' and the 'peripheries', and within the 'metropoles' between black and white women, in the form of inappropriate polarizations between the 'First' and 'Third World', developed/ underdeveloped or advanced/backward. We have already argued that the generalizations made about women's lives across societies in the African and Asian continents, would be thought intolerable if applied to the lives of white women in Europe or North America. These are some of the reasons why concepts which allow for specificity, whilst at the same time providing cross-cultural reference points – not based in assumptions of inferiority – are urgently needed in feminist work. The work of Gayle Rubin and her use of discrete 'sex/gender systems' appears to provide such a potential, particularly in the possibility of applying the concept within as well as between societies. With regard to the problems with the concept of patriarchy discussed above, she has made the following assessment:

> The term 'patriarchy' was introduced to distinguish the forces maintaining sexism from other social forces, such as capitalism. But the use of 'patriarchy' obscures other distinctions.[16]

In arguing for an alternative formulation Gayle Rubin stresses the importance of maintaining, a distinction between the human capacity and necessity to create a sexual world, and the empirically oppressive ways in which sexual worlds have been organized. Patriarchy subsumes both meanings into the same term. Sex/gender system, on the other hand, is a neutral term which refers to the domain and indicates that oppression is not inevitable in that domain, but is the product of the specific social relations which organize it.[17]

This concept of sex/gender systems offers the opportunity to be historically and culturally specific but also points to the position of relative autonomy of the sexual realm. It enables the subordination of women to be seen as a 'product of the relationships by which sex and gender are organized and produced'.[18] Thus, in order to account for the development of specific forms of sex/gender systems, reference must be made not only to the mode of production but also to the complex totality of specific social formations within which each system develops. Gayle Rubin argues that kinship relations are visible, empirical forms of sex/gender systems. Kinship relations here is not limited to biological relatives but is rather a 'system of categories and statuses which often contradict actual genetic relationships'.

What are commonly referred to as 'arranged marriages' can, then, be viewed as the way in which a particular sex/gender system organizes the 'exchange of women'. Similarly, transformations of sex/gender systems brought about by colonial oppression, and the changes in kinship patterns which result from migration, must be assessed on their own terms, not just in comparative relation to other sex/gender systems. In this way patterns of subordination of women can be understood historically, rather than being dismissed as the inevitable product of pathological family structures.

[. . .] We need to counteract the tendency to reduce sex oppression to a mere 'reflex of 'economic forces'[19] whilst at the same time recognizing that:

> sexual systems cannot, in the final analysis, be understood in complete isolation. A full-bodied analysis of women in a single society, or through out history, must take everything into account: the evolution of commodity forms in women, systems of land tenure, political arrangements, subsistence technology, etc.[20]

We can begin to see how these elements come together to affect the lives of black women under colonial oppression in ways that transform the sex/gender systems which they live but that are also shaped by the sex/gender system of the colonizers. If we examine changes in land distribution we can see how capitalist notions of the private ownership of land (a primarily economic division) and ideas of male dominance (from the sex/gender system) work together against the colonized.

> Another problem affecting women's agricultural work is that as land ownership shifts from the collective 'land-use rights' of traditional village life, in which women shared in the distribution of land, to the European concept of private ownership, it is usually only the men who

have the necessary cash to pay for it (by virtue of their cash-cropping income). In addition, some men traditionally 'owned' the land, while women 'owned' the crops as in the Cameroons in West Africa. As land becomes increasingly scarce, men begin to rent and sell 'their' land, leaving women with no recourse but to pay for land or stop their agricultural work.[21]

It is impossible to argue that colonialism left pre-capitalist or feudal forms of organization untouched. If we look at the West Indies we can see that patterns of migration, for both men and women, have followed the dictates of capital.

When men migrated from the islands for work in plantations or building the Panama canal, women migrated from rural to urban areas. Both have migrated to labour in the 'core' capitalist nations. Domestic, marginal or temporary service work has sometimes been viewed as a great 'opportunity' for West Indian women to transform their lives. But as Shirley-Ann Hussein has shown,

> Take the case of the domestic workers. A development institution should be involved in more than placing these women in domestic jobs as this makes no dent in the society. It merely rearranges the same order. Domestic labour will have to be done away with in any serious attempt at social and economic reorganisation.[22]

If, however, imperialism and colonialism have ensured the existence of a world market it still remains necessary to explain how it is in the interests of capitalism to maintain social relations of production that are non-capitalist – that is, forms that could not be described as feudal because that means pre-capitalist, but which are also not organized around the wage relation. If we return to the example of changes in ownership of land and in agricultural production, outlined above, it can be argued that:

> the agricultural division of labor in the periphery – with male semi-proletarians and female agriculturalists – contributes to the maintenance of a low value of labor power for peripheral capital accumulation through the production of subsistence foodstuffs by the noncapitalist mode of production for the reproduction and maintenance of the labor force.[23]

In other words the work that the women do is a force which helps to keep wages low. To relegate 'women of colour' in the periphery to the position of being the victims of feudal relations is to aid in the masking of colonial relations of oppression. These relations of imperialism should not be denied. Truly feminist herstory should be able to acknowledge that:

> Women's economic participation in the periphery of the world capitalist system, just as within center economies, has been conditioned by the requirements of capital accumulation . . . (but) the economic participation of women in the Third World differs significantly from

women's economic participation within the center of the world capitalist system.[24]

Black women have been at the forefront of rebellions against land seizures and struggle over the rights of access to land in Africa, Latin America and the Caribbean. Adequate herstories of their roles in many of these uprisings remain to be written. The role of West Indian women in the rebellions preceding and during the disturbances in Jamaica in 1938, for example, though known to be significant has still not been thoroughly described. White feminist herstorians are therefore mistaken when they portray black women as passive recipients of colonial oppression. As Gail Omvedt has shown in her book *We Will Smash This Prison,* women in India have a long and complex herstory of fighting oppression both in and out of the wage relation. It is clear that many women coming from India to Britain have a shared herstory of struggle, whether in rural areas as agricultural labourers or in urban districts as municipal employees. The organized struggles of Asian women in Britain need to be viewed in the light of this herstory. Their industrial battles, and struggles against immigration policy and practice, articulate the triple oppression of race, gender and class that have been present since the dawn of imperialist domination.

In concentrating solely upon the isolated position of white women in the Western nuclear family structure, feminist theory has necessarily neglected the very strong female support networks that exist in many black sex/gender systems. These have often been transformed by the march of technological 'progress' intended to relieve black women from aspects of their labour.

> Throughout Africa, the digging of village wells has saved women enormous amounts of time which they formerly spent trekking long distances to obtain water. But it has often simultaneously destroyed their only chance to get together and share information and experiences. Technological advances such as household appliances do not free women from domestic drudgery in any society.[26]

Leghorn and Parker, in *Women's Worth,* attempt to create new categories to describe, in general terms, the diversity of male power across societies. Whilst they warn against the rigid application of these categories – few countries fit exactly the category applied to them – the work does represent an attempt to move away from Euro-American racist assumptions of superiority whether political, cultural or economic. The three classifications that they introduce are 'minimal', 'token' and 'negotiating power' societies. Interestingly, from the black women's point of view, the most salient factor in the categorization of a country has

> usually been that of women's networks, because it is the existence, building or dissolution of these networks that determines women's status and potential for change in all areas of their lives.[27]

These categories cut through the usual divisions of First/Third World, advanced/
dependent, industrial/non-industrial in an attempt to find a mechanism that would
'free' thinking from these definitions. Space will not allow for a critical assessment of all three categories but it can be said that their application of 'negotiating
power' does recognize as important the 'traditional' women's organizations to be
found in West Africa, and described [. . .] in relation to the Igbo. Leghorn and
Parker are careful to stress that 'negotiating power' is limited to the possibilities
of negotiating, it is not an absolute category of power that is held *over* men by
women. The two examples of societies given in their book, where women hold
this negotiating position are the Ewe, in West Africa, and the Iroquois. Both of
course, are also examples where contact with the whites has been for the worse.
Many of the Ewe female institutions disintegrated under colonialism whilst the
institutions that afforded Iroquois women power were destroyed by European
intrusion. In contrast to feminist work that focuses upon the lack of technology
and household mechanical aids in the lives of these women, Leghorn and Parker
concentrate upon the aspects of labour that bring women together. Of the Ewe
they note:

> Women often work together in their own fields, or as family members
> preparing meals together, village women meeting at the stream to do
> the wash, or family, friends and neighbours, walking five to fifteen
> miles a day to market together, sitting near each other in the market,
> and setting the day's prices together. They share childcare, news, and
> looking after each other's market stalls. In addition to making the time
> more pleasant, this shared work enables women to share information
> and in fact serves as an integral and vital part of the village communi-
> cations system. Consequently, they have a tremendous sense of
> solidarity when it comes to working in their collective interest.[28]

It is important not to romanticize the existence of such female support networks
but they do provide a startling contrast to the isolated position of women in the
Euro-American nuclear family structure.

In Britain, strong female support networks continue in both West Indian and
Asian sex/gender systems, though these are ignored by sociological studies of
migrant black women. This is not to say that these systems remain unchanged with
migration. New circumstances require adaptation and new survival strategies have
to be found.

> Even childcare in a metropolitan area is a big problem. If you live in
> a village in an extended family, you know that if your child's outside
> somewhere, someone will be looking out for her. If your child is out
> on the street and your neighbour down the road sees your child in
> some mess, that woman is going to take responsibility of dealing with
> that child. But in Brooklyn or in London, you're stuck in that apart-
> ment. You're there with that kid, you can't expect that child to be out
> on the street and be taken care of. You know the day care situation is
> lousy, you're not in that extended family, so you have a big problem

on your hands. So when they talk about the reduction of house-work, we know by now that that's a lie.[29]

However, the transformations that occur are not merely adaptive, neither is the black family destroyed in the process of change. Female networks mean that black women are key figures in the development of survival strategies, both in the past, through periods of slavery and colonialism, and now, facing a racist and authoritarian state.

> There is considerable evidence that women – and families – do not . . . simply accept the isolation, loss of status, and cultural devaluation involved in the migration. Networks are re-formed, if need be with non-kin or on the basis of an extended definition of kinship, by strong, active, and resourceful women. . . . Cultures of resistance are not simple adaptive mechanisms; they embody important alternative ways of organizing production and reproduction and value systems critical of the oppressor. Recognition of the special position of families in these cultures and social structures can lead to new forms of struggle, new goals.[30]

In arguing that feminism must take account of the lives, herstories and experiences of black women we are not advocating that teams of white feminists should descend upon Brixton, Southall, Bristol or Liverpool to take black women as objects of study in modes of resistance. We don't need that kind of intrusion on top of all the other information-gathering forces that the state has mobilized in the interest of 'race relations'. White women have been used against black women in this way before and feminists must learn from history. After the Igbo riots [. . .], two women anthropologists were sent by the British to 'study the causes of the riot and to uncover the organisational base that permitted such spontaneity and solidarity among the women'.[31] The WLM, however, does need to listen to the work of black feminists and to take account of autonomous organizations like OWAAD (Organisation of Women of Asian and African Descent) who are helping to articulate the ways in which we are oppressed as black women.

In addition to this it is very important that white women in the women's movement examine the ways in which racism excludes many black women and prevents them from unconditionally aligning themselves with white women. Instead of taking black women as the objects of their research, white feminist researchers should try to uncover the gender-specific mechanisms of racism amongst white women. This more than any other factor disrupts the recognition of common interests of sisterhood.

In *Finding a Voice* by Amrit Wilson, Asian women describe many instances of racial oppression at work from white women. Asian women

> are paid low salaries and everything is worse for them, they have to face the insults of supervisors. These supervisors are all English women. The trouble is that in Britain our women are expected to behave like servants and we are not used to behaving like servants and we can't. But if we behave normally . . . the supervisors start shouting and harassing us. . . . They complain about us Indians to the manager.[32]

Black women do not want to be grafted onto 'feminism' in a tokenistic manner as colourful diversions to 'real' problems. Feminism has to be transformed if it is to address us. Neither do we wish our words to be misused in generalities as if what each one of us utters represents the total experience of all black women. Audre Lourde's address to Mary Daly is perhaps the best conclusion.

> I ask that you be aware of how this serves the destructive forces of racism and separation between women – the assumption that the herstory and myth of white women is the legitimate and sole herstory and myth of all women to call for power and background, and that non-white women and our herstories are note-worthy only as decorations, or examples of female victimisation. I ask that you be aware of the effect that this dismissal has upon the community of black women, and how it devalues your own words. . . . When patriarchy dismisses us, it encourages our murders. When radical lesbian feminist theory dismisses us, it encourages its own demise. This dismissal stands as a real block to communication between us. This block makes it far easier to turn away from you completely than attempt to understand the thinking behind your choices. Should the next step be war between us, or separation? Assimilation within a sole Western-European herstory is not acceptable.[33]

In other words, of white feminists we must ask, what exactly do you mean when you say 'WE'??

Notes and references

1   Gayle Jones, *Corregidora* (Random House 1975), pp. 14, 72.
2   Winthrop Jordan, *White Over Black* (Penguin 1969), pp. 238, 495, 500.
3   My thanks to Michèle Barrett who, in a talk given at the Social Science Research Council's Research Unit on Ethnic Relations, helped to clarify many of these attempted parallels.
4   Michèle Barrett, *Women's Oppression Today* (Verso 1980).
5   Elizabeth Wilson, *Only Halfway to Paradise: Women in Postwar Britain 1945–1968* (Tavistock 1980), pp. 43–4.
6   ibid.
7   OWAAD, *Forward*, no. 2 (1979).
8   Diane Elson and Ruth Pearson, 'Nimble fingers make cheap workers: an analysis of women's employment in Third World export manufacturing', *Feminist Review*, no. 7 (Spring 1981), p. 93.
9   ibid., p. 95.
10 ibid.
11 bell hooks, *Ain't I a Woman* (South End Press 1981), p. 138.
12 Much of this critical work has been written in America but is applicable to the WLM in Britain. Apart from the books cited in this chapter, interested readers should look out for essays and articles by Gloria Joseph, Audre Lorde, Barbara Smith and Gloria Watkins that represent a range of black feminist thought. In

Britain, the very existence of the feminist Organisation of Women of Asian and African Descent (OWAAD) is a concrete expression of black feminists critical distance from 'white' feminism. See also: Valerie Amos and Pratibha Parmar, 'Resistances and responses: black girls in Britain', in A. McRobbie and T. McCabe (eds), *Feminism For Girls: An Adventure Story* (Routledge and Kegan Paul 1982), who criticize the WLM for its irrelevance to the lives of black girls in Britain.

13   See: Gloria Joseph and Jill Lewis, *Common Differences: Conflicts in Black and White Feminist Perspectives* (Anchor 1981), for an attempt at a dialogue that shows just how difficult it is to maintain.

14   bell hooks, *Ain't I a Woman* (South End Press 1981), pp. 123–4.

15   ibid., p. 141

16   Gayle Rubin, 'The traffic in women: notes on the political economy of sex', in R. Reiter (ed.) *Toward an Anthropology of Women* (Monthly Review Press 1975), p. 167.

17   ibid., p. 168.

18   ibid., p. 177.

19   Gayle Rubin, 'The traffic in women: notes on the political economy of sex', in R. Reiter (ed.) *Toward an Anthropology of Women* (Monthly Review Press 1975), p. 203.

20   ibid., p. 209.

21   Lisa Leghorn and Katherine Parker, *Women's Worth, Sexual Economics and the World of Women* (Routledge and Kegan Paul 1981), p. 45.

22   Shirley-Ann Hussein, 'Four views on women in the struggle', in *Caribbean Women in the Struggle*, p. 29; quoted in Leghorn and Parker, p. 52.

23   Carmen Diane Deere, 'Rural women's subsistence production', in Robin Cohen *et al.* (eds), *Peasants and Proletarians: The Struggles of Third World Women Workers* (Monthly Review 1979), p. 143.

24   ibid., p. 133.

25   Gail Omvedt, *We Will Smash this Prison* (Zed Press 1980).

26   Lisa Leghorn and Katherine Parker, *Women's Worth, Sexual Economics and the World of Women* (Routledge and Kegan Paul 1981), p. 55.

27   ibid., p. 60.

28   ibid., p. 88.

29   Margaret Prescod-Roberts and Norma Steele, *Black Women: Bringing it all Back Home* (Falling Wall Press 1980), p. 28.

30   Mina Davis Caufield, 'Cultures of resistance', in *Socialist Revolution,* 20, vol. 4, no. 2, October 1974, pp. 81, 84.

31   Leis, 'Women in groups', quoted in Mina Davis Caufield, ibid.

32   Amrit Wilson, *Finding a Voice: Asian Women in Britain* (Virago 1978), p. 122.

33   Audre Lorde, 'An open letter of Mary Daly', in Moraga and Anzaldúa (eds), *This Bridge Called My Back: Writings by Radical Women of Color* (Persephone Press 1981), p. 96.

Chapter 27

Patricia Hill Collins

BLACK FEMINIST THOUGHT

WIDELY USED YET RARELY DEFINED, Black feminist thought encompasses diverse and contradictory meanings. Two interrelated tensions highlight issues in defining Black feminist thought. The first concerns the thorny question of who can be a Black feminist. One current response, explicit in Patricia Bell Scott's (1982b) "Selected Bibliography on Black Feminism," classifies all African-American women, regardless of the content of our ideas, as Black feminists. From this perspective, living as Black women provides experiences to stimulate a Black feminist consciousness. Yet indiscriminately labeling all Black women in this way simultaneously conflates the terms *woman* and *feminist* and identifies being of African descent – a questionable biological category – as being the sole determinant of a Black feminist consciousness. As Cheryl Clarke points out, "I criticized Scott. Some of the women she cited as 'black feminist' were clearly not feminist at the time they wrote their books and still are not to this day" (1983, 94).

The term *Black feminist* has also been used to apply to selected African-Americans – primarily women – who possess some version of a feminist consciousness. Beverly Guy-Sheftall (1986) contends that both men and women can be "Black feminists" and names Frederick Douglass and William E. B. DuBois as prominent examples of Black male feminists. Guy-Sheftall also identifies some distinguishing features of Black feminist ideas: namely, that Black women's experiences with both racial and gender oppression result in needs and problems distinct from white women and Black men, and that Black women must struggle for equality both as women and as African-Americans. Guy-Sheftall's definition is helpful in that its use of ideological criteria fosters a definition of Black feminist thought that encompasses both experiences and ideas. In other words, she suggests that experiences gained from living as African-American women stimulate a Black feminist sensibility. But her definition is simultaneously troublesome because it makes the biological category of Blackness the prerequisite for possessing such thought. Furthermore, it does not explain why these particular ideological criteria and not others are the distinguishing ones.

The term Black feminist has also been used to describe selected African–American women who possess some version of a feminist consciousness (Beale 1970; hooks 1981; Barbara Smith 1983; White 1984). This usage of the term yields the most restrictive notion of who can be a Black feminist. The ground-breaking Combahee River Collective (1982) document, "A Black Feminist Statement," implicitly relies on this definition. The Collective claims that "as Black women we find any type of biological determinism a particularly dangerous and reactionary basis upon which to build a politic" (p.17). But in spite of this statement, by implying that only African-American women can be Black feminists, they require a biological prerequisite for race and gender consciousness. The Collective also offers its own ideological criteria for identifying Black feminist ideas. In contrast to Beverly Guy-Sheftall, the Collective places a stronger emphasis on capitalism as a source of Black women's oppression and on political activism as a distinguishing feature of Black feminism.

Biologically deterministic criteria for the term *black* and the accompanying assumption that being of African descent somehow produces a certain consciousness or perspective are inherent in these definitions. By presenting race as being fixed and immutable – something rooted in nature – these approaches mask the historical construction of racial categories, the shifting meaning of race, and the crucial role of politics and ideology in shaping conceptions of race (Gould 1981; Omi and Winant 1986). In contrast, much greater variation is afforded the term feminist. Feminists are seen as ranging from biologically determined – as is the case in radical feminist thought, which argues that only women can be feminist – to notions of feminists as individuals who have undergone some type of political transformation theoretically achievable by anyone.

Though the term Black feminist could also be used to describe any individual who embraces Black feminist ideas, the separation of biology from ideology required for this usage is rarely seen in the works of Black women intellectuals. Sometimes the contradictions among these competing definitions can be so great that Black women writers use all simultaneously. Consider the following passage from Deborah McDowell's essay "New Directions for Black Feminist Criticism":

> I use the term here simply to refer to Black female critics who analyze the works of Black female writers from a feminist political perspective. But the term can also apply to any criticism written by a Black woman regardless of her subject or perspective – a book written by a male from a feminist or political perspective, a book written by a Black woman or about Black women authors in general, or any writings by women.
>
> (1985, 191)

While McDowell implies that elite white men could be "black feminists," she is clearly unwilling to state so categorically. From McDowell's perspective, whites and Black men who embrace a specific political perspective, and Black women regardless of political perspective, could all potentially be deemed Black feminist critics.

The ambiguity surrounding current perspectives on who can be a Black feminist is directly tied to a second definitional tension in Black feminist thought: the question of what constitutes Black feminism. The range of assumptions concerning the relationship between ideas and their advocates as illustrated in the works of Patricia Bell Scott, Beverly Guy-Sheftall, the Combahee River Collective, and Deborah McDowell leads to problems in defining Black feminist theory itself. Once a person is labeled a "Black feminist," then ideas forwarded by that individual often become defined as Black feminist thought. This practice accounts for neither changes in the thinking of an individual nor differences among Black feminist theorists.

A definition of Black feminist thought is needed that avoids the materialist position that being Black and/or female generates certain experiences that automatically determine variants of a Black and/or feminist consciousness. Claims that Black feminist thought is the exclusive province of African-American women, regardless of the experiences and worldview of such women, typify this position. But a definition of Black feminist thought must also avoid the idealist position that ideas can be evaluated in isolation from the groups that create them. Definitions claiming that anyone can produce and develop Black feminist thought risk obscuring the special angle of vision that Black women bring to the knowledge production process.

The dimensions of a black women's standpoint

Developing adequate definitions of Black feminist thought involves facing this complex nexus of relationships among biological classification, the social construction of race and gender as categories of analysis, the material conditions accompanying these changing social constructions, and Black women's consciousness about these themes. One way of addressing the definitional tensions in Black feminist thought is to specify the relationship between a Black women's standpoint – those experiences and ideas shared by African-American women that provide a unique angle of vision on self, community, and society – and theories that interpret these experiences.[1] I suggest that Black feminist thought consists of specialized knowledge created by African-American women which clarifies a standpoint of and for Black women. In other words, Black feminist thought encompasses theoretical interpretations of Black women's reality by those who live it.

This definition does not mean that all African-American women generate such thought or that other groups do not play a critical role in its production. Before exploring the contours and implications of this working definition, understanding five key dimension of a Black women's standpoint is essential.

The core themes of a black women's standpoint

All African-American women share the common experience of being Black women in a society that denigrates women of African descent. This commonality of experience suggests that certain characteristic themes will be prominent in a Black women's standpoint. For example, one core theme is a legacy of struggle. Katie Cannon observes, "throughout the history of the United States, the interrelationship of white supremacy and male superiority, has characterized the Black woman's reality as a situation of struggle – a struggle to survive in two contradictory worlds simultaneously, one white, privileged, and oppressive, the other black, exploited, and oppressed" (1985, 30). Black women's vulnerability to assaults in the workplace, on the street, and at home has stimulated Black women's independence and self-reliance.

In spite of differences created by historical era, age, social class, sexual orientation, or ethnicity, the legacy of struggle against racism and sexism is a common thread binding African-American women. Anna Julia Cooper, a nineteenth-century Black woman intellectual, describes Black women's vulnerability to sexual violence:

> I would beg . . . to add my plea for the *Colored Girls* of the South – that large, bright, promising fatally beautiful class . . . so full of promise and possibilities, yet so sure of destruction; often without a father to whom they dare apply the loving term, often without a stronger brother to espouse their cause and defend their honor with his life's blood; in the midst of pitfalls and snares, waylaid by the lower classes of white men, with no shelter, no protection.
>
> (Cooper 1892, 240)

Yet during this period Black women struggled and built a powerful club movement and numerous community organizations (Giddings 1984, 1988; Gilkes 1985).

Age offers little protection from this legacy of struggle. Far too many young Black girls inhabit hazardous and hostile environments. In 1975 I received an essay entitled "My World" from Sandra, a sixth-grade student who was a resident of one of the most dangerous public housing projects in Boston. Sandra wrote, "My world is full of people getting rape. People shooting one another. Kids and grownups fighting over girlsfriends. And people without jobs who can't afford to get a education so they can get a job . . . winos on the streets raping and killing little girls." Her words poignantly express a growing Black feminist sensibility that she may be victimized by racism and poverty. They also reveal her awareness that she is vulnerable to rape as a gender-specific form of sexual violence. In spite of her feelings about her community, Sandra not only walked the streets daily but managed safely to deliver three younger siblings to school. In doing so she participated in a Black women's legacy of struggle.

This legacy of struggle constitutes one of several core themes of a Black women's standpoint. Efforts to reclaim the Black feminist intellectual tradition are revealing Black women's longstanding attention to a series of core themes first recorded by Maria W. Stewart (Richardson 1987). Stewart's treatment of the interlocking nature of race, gender, and class oppression, her call for replacing denigrated images of Black womanhood with self-defined images, her belief in Black women's activism as mothers, teachers, and Black community leaders, and her sensitivity to sexual politics are all core themes advanced by a variety of Black feminist intellectuals.

Variation of responses to core themes

The existence of core themes does not mean that African-American women respond to these themes in the same way. Diversity among Black women produces different concrete experiences that in turn shape various reactions to the core themes. For example, when faced with stereotypical controlling images of Black women, some women – such as Sojourner Truth – demand, "ain't I a woman?" By deconstructing the conceptual apparatus of the dominant group, they invoke a Black women's legacy of struggle. In contrast, other women internalize the controlling images and come to believe that they are the stereotypes (Brown-Collins and Sussewell 1986).

A variety of factors explain the diversity of responses. For example although all African-American women encounter racism, social class differences among African-American women influence how racism is experienced. A young manager who graduated with honors from the University of Maryland describes the specific form racism can take for middle-class Blacks. Before flying to Cleveland to explain a marketing plan for her company, her manager made her go over it three or four times in front of him so that she would not forget *her* marketing plan. Then he explained how to check luggage at an airport and how to reclaim it. "I just sat at lunch listening to this man talking to me like I was a monkey who could remember but couldn't think," the Black female manager recalled. When she had had enough, she responded, "I asked him if he wanted to tie my money up in a handkerchief and put a note on me saying that I was an employee of this company. In case I got lost I would be picked up by Traveler's Aid, and Traveler's Aid would send me back" (Davis and Watson 1985, 86). Most middle-class Black women do not encounter such blatant incidents, but many working-class Blacks do. For both groups the racist belief that African-Americans are less intelligent than whites remains strong.

Sexual orientation provides another key factor. Black lesbians have identified homophobia in general and the issues they face living as Black lesbians in homophobic communities as being a major influence on their angle of vision on everyday events (Shockley 1974; Lorde 1982, 1984; Clarke et al. 1983; Barbara Smith 1983). Beverly Smith describes how being a lesbian affected her perceptions of the wedding of one of her closest friends: "God, I wish I had one friend here. Someone who knew me and would understand how I, feel. I am masquerading as a nice, straight, middle-class Black 'girl'" (1983, 172). While the majority of those attending the wedding saw only a festive event, Beverly Smith felt that her friend was being sent into a form of bondage.

Other factors such as ethnicity, region of the country, urbanization, and age combine to produce a web of experiences shaping diversity among African-American women. As a result, it is more accurate to discuss a Black *women's* standpoint than a Black *woman's* standpoint.

The interdependence of experience and consciousness

Black women's work and family experiences and grounding in traditional African-American culture suggest that African-American women as a group experience a world different from that of those who are not Black and female. Moreover, these concrete experiences can stimulate a distinctive Black feminist consciousness concerning that material reality.[2] Being Black and female may expose African-American women to certain common experiences, which in turn may predispose us to a distinctive group consciousness, but it in no way guarantees that such a consciousness will develop among all women or that it will be articulated as such by the group.

Many African-American women have grasped this connection between what one does and how one thinks. Hannah Nelson, an elderly Black domestic worker, discusses how work shapes the perspectives of African-American and white women: "Since I have to work, I don't really have to worry about most of the things that most of the white women I have worked for are worrying about. And if these women did their own work, they would think just like I do – about this, anyway" (Gwaltney 1980, 4). Ruth Shays, a Black inner-city resident, points out how variations in men's and women's experiences lead to differences in perspective. "The mind of the man and the mind of the woman is the same" she notes "'but this business of living makes women use their minds in ways that men don' even have to think about" (Gwaltney 1980, 33).

This connection between experience and consciousness that shapes the everyday lives of all African-American women pervades the works of Black women activists and scholars. In her autobiography, Ida B. Wells describes how the lynching of her friends had such an impact on her worldview that she subsequently devoted much of her life to the antilynching cause (Duster 1970). Sociologist Joyce Ladner's (1972) *Tomorrow's Tomorrow,* a ground-breaking study of Black female adolescence, emerged from her discomfort with the disparity between the teachings of mainstream scholarship and her experiences as a young Black woman in the South. Similarly, the transformed consciousness experienced by Janie, the light-skinned heroine of Zora Neale Hurston's (1937) classic *Their Eyes Were Watching God,* from obedient granddaughter and wife to a self-defined African-American woman, can be directly traced to her experiences with each of her three husbands. In one scene Janie's second husband, angry because she served him a dinner of scorched rice, underdone fish, and soggy bread, hits her. That incident stimulates Janie to stand "where he left her for unmeasured time" and think. Her thinking leads to the recognition that "her image of Jody tumbled down and shattered . . . she had an inside and an outside now and suddenly she knew how not to mix them" (p. 63).

Consciousness and the struggle for a self-defined standpoint

African-American women as a group may have experiences that provide us with a unique angle of vision. But expressing a collective, self-defined Black feminist consciousness is problematic precisely because dominant groups have a vested interest in suppressing such thought.[3] As Hannah Nelson notes, "I have grown to womanhood in a world where the saner you are, the madder you are made to appear" (Gwaltney 1980, 7). Ms. Nelson realizes that those who control the schools, media, and other cultural institutions of society prevail in establishing their viewpoint as superior to others.

An oppressed group's experiences may put its members in a position to see things differently, but their lack of control over the ideological apparatuses of society makes expressing a self-defined standpoint more difficult. Elderly domestic worker Rosa Wakefield assesses how the standpoints of the powerful and those who serve them diverge:

> If you eats these dinners and don't cook 'em, if you wears these clothes and don't buy or iron them, then you might start thinking that the good fairy or some spirit did all that. . . . Black folks don't have no time to be thinking like that. . . . But when you don't have any-thing else to do, you can think like that. It's bad for your mind, though.
>
> (Gwaltney 1980 88)

Ms. Wakefield has a self-defined perspective growing from her experiences that enables her to reject the standpoint of more powerful groups. And yet ideas like hers are typically suppressed by dominant groups. Groups unequal in power are correspondingly unequal in their ability to make their standpoint known to them-selves and others.

Individual African-American women have long displayed varying types of consciousness regarding our shared angle of vision. By aggregating and articulat-ing these individual expressions of consciousness, a collective, focused group consciousness becomes possible. Black women's ability to forge these individual, unarticulated, yet potentially powerful expressions of everyday consciousness into an articulated, self-defined, collective standpoint is key to Black women's survival. As Audre Lorde points out, "it is axiomatic that if we do not define ourselves for ourselves, we will be defined by others – for their use and to our detriment" (1984, 45).

One fundamental feature of this struggle for a self-defined standpoint involves tapping sources of everyday, unarticulated consciousness that have traditionally been denigrated in white, male-controlled institutions. For Black women, the struggle involves embracing a consciousness that is simultaneously Afrocentric and feminist. What does this mean?

Research in African-American Studies suggests that an Afrocentric worldview exists which is distinct from and in many ways opposed to a Eurocentric world-view (Okanlawon 1972; Asante 1987; Myers 1988). Standard scholarly social constructions of blackness and race define these concepts as being either reflec-tions of quantifiable, biological differences among humans or residual categories that emerged in response to institutionalized racism (Lyman 1972; Bash 1979; Gould 1981; Omi and Winant 1986). In contrast, even though it often relies on biological notions of the "race," Afrocentric scholarship suggests that "blackness" and Afrocentricity reflect longstanding belief systems among African peoples (Diop 1974; Richards 1980; Asante 1987). While Black people were forced to adapt these Afrocentric belief systems in the face of different institutional arrange-ments of white domination, the continuation of an Afrocentric worldview has been fundamental to African-Americans' resistance to racial oppression (Smitherman 1977; Webber 1978; Sobel 1979; Thompson 1983). In other words, being Black encompasses *both* experiencing white domination *and* individual and group valuation of an independent, long-standing Afrocentric consciousness.

African-American women draw on this Afrocentric worldview to cope with racial oppression. But far too often Black women's Afrocentric consciousness remains unarticulated and not fully developed into a self-defined standpoint. In societies that denigrate African ideas and peoples, the process of valuing an Afrocentric worldview is the result of self-conscious struggle.

Similar concerns can be raised about the issue of what constitutes feminist ideas (Eisenstein 1983; Jaggar 1983). Being a biological female does not mean that one's ideas are automatically feminist. Self-conscious struggle is needed in order to reject patriarchal perceptions of women and to value women's ideas and actions. The fact that more women than men identify themselves as feminists reflects women's greater experience with the negative consequences of gender oppression. Becoming a feminist is routinely described by women (and men) as a process of transformation, of struggling to develop new interpretations of familiar realities.

The struggles of women from different racial/ethnic groups and those of women and men within African-American communities to articulate self-defined standpoints represent similar yet distinct processes. While race and gender are both socially constructed categories, constructions of gender rest on clearer biological criteria than do constructions of race. Classifying African-Americans into specious racial categories is considerably more difficult than noting the clear biological differences distinguishing females from males (Patterson 1982). But though united by biological sex, women do not form the same type of group as do African-Americans, Jews, native Americans, Vietnamese, or other groups with distinct histories, geographic origins, cultures, and social institutions. The absence of an identifiable tradition uniting women does not mean that women are characterized more by differences than by similarities. Women do share common experiences, but the experiences are not generally the same type as those affecting racial and ethnic groups (King 1988). Thus while expressions of race and gender are both socially constructed, they are not constructed in the same way. The struggle for an Afrocentric feminist consciousness requires embracing both an Afrocentric worldview and a feminist sensibility and using both to forge a self-defined standpoint.[4] [. . .]

Who can be a Black feminist? : The centrality of Black women intellectuals to the production of Black feminist thought

I aim to develop a definition of Black feminist thought that relies exclusively neither on a materialist analysis – one whereby all African-American women by virtue of biology become automatically registered as "authentic Black feminists" – nor on an idealist analysis whereby the background, worldview, and interests of the thinker are deemed irrelevant in assessing his or her ideas. Resolving the tension between these two extremes involves reassessing the centrality Black women intellectuals assume in producing Black feminist thought. It also requires examining the importance of coalitions with Black men, white women, people of color, and other groups with distinctive standpoints. Such coalitions are essential in order to foster other groups' contributions as critics, teachers, advocates, and disseminators of a self-defined Afrocentric feminist standpoint.

Black women's concrete experiences as members of specific race, class, and gender groups as well as our concrete historical situations necessarily play significant roles in our perspectives on the world. No standpoint is neutral because no individual or group exists unembedded in the world. Knowledge is gained not by solitary individuals but by Black women as socially constituted members of a group (Narayan 1989). These factors all frame the definitional tensions in Black feminist thought.

Black women intellectuals are central to Black feminist thought for several reasons. First, our experiences as African-American women provide us with a unique standpoint on Black womanhood unavailable to other groups. It is more likely for Black women as members of an oppressed group to have critical insights into the condition of our own oppression than it is for those who live outside those structures. One of the characters in Frances Ellen Watkins Harper's 1892 novel, *Iola Leroy*, expresses this belief in the special vision of those who have experienced oppression:

> Miss Leroy, out of the race must come its own thinkers and writers. Authors belonging to the white race have written good books, for which I am deeply grateful, but it seems to be almost impossible for a white man to put himself completely in our place. No man can feel the iron which enters another man's soul.
>
> (Carby 1987, 62)

Only African-American women occupy this center and can "feel the iron" that enters Black women's souls, because we are the only group that has experienced race, gender, and class oppression as Black women experience them. The importance of Black women's leadership in producing Black feminist thought does not mean that others cannot participate. It does mean that the primary responsibility for defining one's own reality lies with the people who live that reality, who actually have those experiences.

Second, Black women intellectuals provide unique leadership for Black women's empowerment and resistance. In discussing Black women's involvement in the feminist movement, Sheila Radford-Hill points out the connections among self-definition, empowerment, and taking actions in one's own behalf:

> Black women now realize that part of the problem within the movement was our insistence that white women do for/with us what we must do for/with ourselves: namely, frame our own social action around our own agenda for change. . . . Critical to this discussion is the right to organize on one's own behalf. . . . Criticism by black feminists must reaffirm this principle.
>
> (1986, 162)

Black feminist thought cannot challenge race, gender, and class oppression without empowering African-American women. "Oppressed people resist by identifying themselves as subjects, by defining their reality, shaping their new identity, naming their history, telling their story," notes bell hooks (1989, 43). Because self-definition is key to individual and group empowerment, using an epistemology that cedes the power of self-definition to other groups, no matter how well-meaning, in essence perpetuates Black women's subordination. As Black feminist sociologist Deborah K. King succinctly states, "Black feminism asserts self-determination as essential" (1988, 72).

Stressing the importance of Black women's centrality to Black feminist thought does not mean that all African-American women exert this leadership. While being an African-American woman generally provides the experiential base for an Afrocentric feminist consciousness, these same conditions suppress its articulation. It is not acquired as a finished product but must continually develop in relation to changing conditions.

Bonnie Johnson emphasizes the importance of self-definition. In her critique of Patricia Bell Scott's bibliography on Black feminism, she challenges both Scott's categorization of all works by Black women as being Black feminist and Scott's identification of a wide range of African-American women as Black feminists: "Whether I think they're feminists is irrelevant. *They* would not call themselves feminist" (Clarke et al. 1983, 94). As Patrice L. Dickerson contends, "a person comes into being and knows herself by her achievements, and through her efforts to become and know herself, she achieves" (personal correspondence 1988). Here is the heart of the matter. An Afrocentric feminist consciousness constantly emerges and is part of a self-conscious struggle to merge thought and action.

Third, Black women intellectuals are central in the production of Black feminist thought because we alone can create the group autonomy that must precede effective coalitions with other groups. This autonomy is quite distinct from separatist positions whereby Black women withdraw from other groups and engage in exclusionary politics. In her introduction to *Home Girls, A Black Feminist Anthology*, Barbara Smith describes this difference: "Autonomy and separatism are fundamentally different. Whereas autonomy comes from a position of strength, separatism comes from a position of fear. When we're truly autonomous we can deal with other kinds of people, a multiplicity of issues, and with difference, because we have formed a solid base of strength" (1983, xl). Black women intellectuals who articulate an autonomous, self-defined standpoint are in a position to examine the usefulness of coalitions with other groups, both scholarly and activist, in order to develop new models for social change. However, autonomy to develop a self-defined, independent analysis does not mean that Black feminist thought has relevance only for African-American women or that we must confine ourselves to analyzing our own experiences. As Sonia Sanchez points out, "I've always known that if you write from a black experience, you're writing from a universal experience as well . . . I know you don't have to whitewash yourself to be universal" (in Tate 1983, 142).

While Black feminist thought may originate with Black feminist intellectuals, it cannot flourish isolated from the experiences and ideas of other groups. The dilemma is that Black women intellectuals must place our own experiences and consciousness at the center of any serious efforts to develop Black feminist thought yet not have that thought become separatist and exclusionary. bell hooks offers a solution to this problem by suggesting that we shift from statements such as "I am a feminist" to those such as "I advocate feminism." Such an approach could "serve as a way women who are concerned about feminism as well as other political movements could express their support while avoiding linguistic structures that give primacy to one particular group" (1984, 30).

By advocating, refining, and disseminating Black feminist thought, other groups – such as Black men, white women, white men, and other people of color – further its development. Black women can produce an attenuated version of Black feminist thought separated from other groups. Other groups cannot produce Black feminist thought without African-American women. Such groups can, however, develop self-defined knowledge reflecting their own standpoints. But the full actualization of Black feminist thought requires a collaborative enterprise with Black women at the center of a community based on coalitions among autonomous groups [. . .]

What constitutes black feminism? The recurring humanist vision

A wide range of African-American women intellectuals have advanced the view that Black women's struggles are part of a wider struggle for human dignity and empowerment. In an 1893 speech to women, Anna Julia Cooper cogently expressed this alternative worldview:

> We take our stand on the solidarity of humanity, the oneness of life, and the unnaturalness and injustice of all special favoritisms, whether of sex, race, country, or condition. . . . The colored woman feels that woman's cause is one and universal; and that . . . not till race, color, sex, and condition are seen as accidents, and not the substance of life; not till the universal title of humanity to life, liberty, and the pursuit of happiness is conceded to be inalienable to all; not till then is woman's lesson taught and woman's cause won – not the white woman's nor the black woman's, not the red woman's but the cause of every man and of every woman who has writhed silently under a mighty wrong.
> Loewenberg and Bogin 1976, 330–31)

Like Cooper, many African-American women intellectuals embrace this perspective regardless of particular political solutions we propose, our fields of study, or our historical periods. Whether we advocate working through separate Black women's organizations, becoming part of women's organizations, working within existing political structures, or supporting Black community institutions, African-American women intellectuals repeatedly identify political actions such as these as a *means* for human empowerment rather than ends in and of themselves. Thus the primary guiding principle of Black feminism is a recurring humanist vision (Steady 1981, 1987).

Alice Walker's preference for the term *womanist*, a term she describes as "womanist is to feminist as purple is to lavender," addresses this notion of the

BLACK FEMINIST THOUGHT 415

solidarity of humanity. To Walker, one is "womanist" when one is "committed to the survival and wholeness of entire people, male and female." A womanist is "not a separatist, except periodically for health" and is "traditionally universalist, as is 'Mama, why are we brown, pink, and yellow, and our cousins are white, beige, and black?' Ans.: 'Well, you know the colored race is just like a flower garden, with every color flower represented'" (1983, xi). By redefining all people as "people of color," Walker universalizes what are typically seen as individual struggles while simultaneously allowing space for autonomous movements of self-determination.

In assessing the sexism of the Black nationalist movement of the 1960s, Black feminist lawyer Pauli Murray identifies the dangers inherent in separatism as opposed to autonomy, and also echoes Cooper's concern with the solidarity of humanity:

> The lesson of history that all human rights are indivisible and that the failure to adhere to this principle jeopardizes the rights of all is particularly applicable here. A built-in hazard of an aggressive ethnocentric movement which disregards the interests of other disadvantaged groups is that it will become parochial and ultimately self-defeating in the face of hostile reactions, dwindling allies, and mounting frustrations. . . . Only a broad movement for human rights can prevent the Black Revolution from becoming isolated and can insure ultimate success.
> (Murray 1970, 102)

Without a commitment to human solidarity, suggests Murray, any political movement – whether nationalist, feminist or antielitist – may be doomed to ultimate failure.

bell hook's analysis of feminism adds another critical dimension that must be considered: namely, the necessity of self-conscious struggle against a more generalized ideology of domination:

> To me feminism is not simply a struggle to end male chauvinism or a movement to ensure that women will have equal rights with men; it is a commitment to eradicating the ideology of domination that permeates Western culture on various levels – sex, race, and class, to name a few – and a commitment to reorganizing U.S. society so that the self-development of people can take precedence over imperialism, economic expansion, and material desires.
> (hooks 1981, 194)

Former assemblywoman Shirley Chisholm also points to the need for self-conscious struggle against the stereotypes buttressing ideologies of domination. In "working toward our own freedom, we can help others work free from the traps of their stereotypes" she notes. "In the end, antiblack, antifemale, and all forms of discrimination are equivalent to the same thing – antihumanism. . . . We must reject not only the stereotypes that others have of us but also those we have of ourselves and others" (1970, 181).

This humanist vision is also reflected in the growing prominence of international issues and global concerns in the works of contemporary African-American women intellectuals (Lindsay 1980; Steady 1981, 1987). Economists Margaret Simms and Julianne Malveaux's 1986 edited volume, *Slipping through the Cracks: The Status of Black Women,* contains articles on Black women in Tanzania, Jamaica, and South Africa. Angela Davis devotes an entire section of her 1989 book, *Women, Culture, and Politics,* to international affairs and includes essays on Winnie Mandela and on women in Egypt. June Jordan's 1985 volume, *On Call,* includes essays on South Africa, Nicaragua, and the Bahamas. Alice Walker writes compellingly of the types of links these and other Black women intellectuals see between African-American women's issues and those of other groups: "To me, Central America is one large plantation; and I see the people's struggle to be free as a slave revolt" (1988, 177).

The words and actions of Black women intellectuals from different historical times and addressing markedly different audiences resonate with a strikingly similar theme of the oneness of all human life. Perhaps the most succinct version of the humanist vision in Black feminist thought is offered by Fannie Lou Hamer, the daughter of sharecroppers, and a Mississippi civil rights activist. While sitting on her porch, Ms. Hamer observed "Ain' no such thing as I can hate anybody and hope to see God's face" (Jordan 1981, xi).

Taken together, the ideas of Anna Julia Cooper, Pauli Murray, bell hooks, Alice Walker, Fannie Lou Hamer, and other Black women intellectuals too numerous to mention suggest a powerful answer to the question "What is Black feminism?" Inherent in their words and deeds is a definition of Black feminism as a process of self-conscious struggle that empowers women and men to actualize a humanist vision of community.

Notes

1   For discussions of the concept of standpoint, see Hartsock (1983a, 1983b), Jaggar (1983), and Smith (1987). Even though I use standpoint epistemologies as an organizing concept in this volume, they remain controversial. For a helpful critique of standpoint epistemologies, see Harding (1986). Haraway's (1988) reformulation of standpoint epistemologies approximates my use here.

2   Scott (1985) defines consciousness as the symbols, norms, and ideological forms people create to give meaning to their acts. For de Lauretis (1986), consciousness is a process, a "particular configuration of subjectivity . . . produced at the intersection of meaning with experience . . . Consciousness is grounded in personal history, and self and identity are understood within particular cultural contexts. Consciousness. . . is never fixed, never attained once and for all, because discursive boundaries change with historical conditions" (p. 8).

3   The presence of a Black women's culture of resistance (Terborg-Penn 1986; Dodson and Gilkes 1987) that is both Afrocentric and feminist challenges two prevailing interpretations of the consciousness of oppressed groups. One approach claims that subordinate groups identify with the powerful and have no valid independent interpretation of their own oppression. The second assumes the oppressed are less human than their rulers, and are therefore less capable

of interpreting their own experiences (Rollins 1985; Scott 1985). Both approaches see any independent consciousness expressed by oppressed groups as being either not of their own making or inferior to that of the dominant group. More important, both explanations suggest that the alleged lack of political activism on the part of oppressed groups stems from their flawed consciousness of their own subordination.

4   Even though I will continue to use the term *Afrocentric feminist thought* inter-changeably with the phrase *Black feminist thought*, I think they are conceptually distinct.

5   My use of the term *humanist* grows from an Afrocentric historical context distinct from that criticized by Western feminists. I use the term to tap an Afrocentric humanism as cited by West (1977–78), Asante (1987) and Turner (1984) and as part of the Black theological tradition (Mitchell and Lewter 1986; Cannon 1988). See Harris (1981) for a discussion of the humanist tradition in the works of three Black women writers. See Richards (1990) for a discussion of African–American spirituality, a key dimension of Afrocentric humanism. Novelist Margaret Walker offers one of the clearest discussions of Black humanism. Walker claims:. "I think it is more important now to emphasize humanism in a technological age than ever before, because it is only in terms of humanism that society can redeem itself. I believe that mankind is only one race – the human race. There are many strands in the family of man – many races. The world has yet to learn to appreciate the deep reservoirs of humanism in all races, and particularly in the Black race" (Rowell 1975, 12).

References

Asante, Molefi Kete. 1987. *The Afrocentric Idea*. Philadelphia: Temple University Press.

Bash, Harry H. 1979. *Sociology, Race and Ethnicity*. New York: Gordon and Breach.

Beale, Frances. 1970 "Double Jeopardy: To Be Black and Female." In *The Black Woman: An Anthology*, edited by Toni Cade (Bambara), 90–100, New York: Signet.

Brown-Collins, Alice, and Deborah Ridley Sussewell. 1986. "The Afro-American Women's Emerging Selves" *Journal of Black Psychology* 13(1): 1–11.

Cannon, Katie G. 1985. "The Emergence of a Black Feminist Consciousness." In *Feminist Interpretations of the Bible*, edited by Letty M. Russell, 30–40, Philadelphia: Westminster Press.

——. 1988. *Black Womanist Ethics*. Atlanta: Scholars Press.

Carby, Hazel. 1987. *Reconstructing Womanhood: The Emergence of the Afro-American Woman Novelist*. New York: Oxford.

Chisholm, Shirley. 1970. *Unbought and Unbossed*. New York: Avon.

Clarke, Cheryl. 1983. "The Failure to Transform: Homophobia in the Black Community." In *Home Girls: A Black Feminist Anthology*, edited by Barbara Smith, 197–208. New York: Kitchen Table Press.

——, Jewell L. Gomez, Evelyn Hammonds, Bonnie Johnson, and Linda Powell. 1983. "Conversations and Questions: Black Woman on Black Women Writers." *Conditions: Nine* 3 (3): 88–137.

The Combahee River Collective. 1982. "A Black Feminist Statement." In *But Some of Us Are Brave*, edited by Gloria T. Hull, Patricia Bell Scott, and Barbara Smith, 13–22, Old Westbury, NY: Feminist Press.

Cooper, Anna Julia. 1892. *A Voice from the South: By a Black Woman of the South*. Xenia, OH: Aldine Printing House.

Davis, Angela Y. 1981. *Women, Race and Class*. New York: Random House.

——. 1989. *Women, Culture and Politics*. New York: Random House.

Davis, George and Glegg Watson. 1985. *Black Life in Corporate America*. New York: Anchor.

de Lauretis, Teresa. 1986. "Feminist Studies/Critical Studies: Issues, Terms and Contexts." In *Feminist Studies/Critical Studies*, edited by Teresa de Lauretis, 1–19. Bloomington: Indiana University Press.

Diop, Cheikh. 1974. *The African Origin of Civilization: Myth or Reality*. New York: L. Hill.

Dodson, Jualyne E., and Cheryl Townsend Gilkes. 1987. "Something Within: Social Change and Collective Endurance in the Sacred World of Black Christian Women." In *Women and Religion in America, Volume 3: 1900–1968*, edited by Rosemary Reuther and R. Keller, 80–130. New York: Harper and Row.

Duster, Alfreda M., ed. 1970. *Crusade for Justice: The Autobiography of Ida B. Wells*. Chicago: University of Chicago Press.

Eisenstein, Hester. 1983. *Contemporary Feminist Thought*. Boston: G. K. Hall.

Giddings, Paula. 1984. *When and Where I Enter . . . The Impact of Black Women on Race and Sex in America*. New York: William Morrow.

——. 1988. *In Search of Sisterhood: Delta Sigma Theta and the Challenge of the Black Sorority Movement*. New York: William Morrow.

Gilkes, Cheryl Townsend. 1985. " 'Together and in Harness': Women's Traditions in the Sanctified Church." *Signs* 10(4): 678–99.

Gould, Stephen Jay. 1981. *The Mismeasure of Man*. New York: W. W. Norton.

Guy-Sheftall, Beverly. 1986. "Remembering Sojourner Truth: On Black Feminism." *Catalyst* (Fall): 54–57.

Gwaltney, John Langston. 1980. *Drylongso, A Self-Portrait of Black America*. New York: Vintage.

Haraway, Donna. 1988. "Situated Knowledges: The Science Question in Feminism and the Privilege of Partial Perspective." *Feminist Studies* 14(3): 575–99.

Harding, Sandra. 1986. *The Science Question in Feminism*, Ithaca, NY: Cornell University Press.

Harris, Trudier. 1981. "Three Black Women Writers and Humanism: A Folk Perspective." In *Black American Literature and Humanism*, edited by R. Baxter Miller, 50–74. Lexington: University of Kentucky Press.

Hartsock, Nancy M. 1983a. "The Feminist Standpoint: Developing the Ground for a Specifically Feminist Historical Materialism." In *Discovering Reality*, edited by Sandra Harding and Merrill B. Hintikka, 283–310. Boston: D. Reidel.

——. 1983b. *Money, Sex and Power*. Boston: Northeastern University Press.

hooks, bell. 1981. *Ain't I a Woman: Black Women and Feminism*. Boston: South End Press.

——. 1984. *From Margin to Center*. Boston: South End Press.

——. 1989. *Talking Back: Thinking Feminist, Thinking Black*. Boston: South End Press.

Hurston, Zora Neale. [1937] 1969. *Their Eyes Were Watching God*. Greenwich, CT: Fawcett.

Jaggar, Alison M. 1983. *Feminist Politics and Human Nature*. Totawa, NJ: Rowman & Allanheld.

Jordan, June. 1981. *Civil Wars*. Boston: Beacon.

——. 1985. *On Call*. Boston: South End Press.

King, Deborah K. 1988. "Multiple Jeopardy, Multiple Consciousness: The Context of a Black Feminist Ideology." *Signs* 14(1): 42–72.

Ladner, Joyce. 1972. *Tomorrow's Tomorrow*. Garden City, NY: Doubleday.

Lindsay, Beverly, ed. 1980. *Comparative Perspectives of Third World Women: The Impact of Race, Sex and Class*. New York: Praeger.

Loewenberg, Bert J., and Ruth Bogin, eds. 1976. *Black Women in Nineteenth-Century American Life*. University Park: Pennsylvania State University Press.

Lorde, Audre. 1982. *Zami, A New Spelling of My Name*. Trumansberg, NY: The Crossing Press.

——. 1984. *Sister Outsider*. Trumansberg, NY: The Crossing Press.

Lyman, Stanford M. 1972. *The Black American in Sociological Thought: A Failure of Perspective*. New York: Capricorn.

McDowell, Deborah E. 1985. "New Directions for Black Feminist Criticism." In *The New Feminist Criticism*, edited by Elaine Showalter, 186–99, New York: Pantheon.

Mitchell, Henry H., and Nicholas Cooper Lewter. 1986. *Soul Theology: The Heart of American Black Culture*. San Francisco: Harper & Row.

Murray, Pauli. 1970. "The Liberation of Black Women." In *Voices of the New Feminism*, edited by Mary Lou Thompson, 87–102. Boston: Beacon.

Myers, Linda James. 1988. *Understanding an Afrocentric World View: Introduction to an Optimal Psychology*. Dubuque, IA: Kendall/Hunt.

Narayan, Uma. 1989. "The Project of Feminist Epistemology: Perspectives from a Nonwestern Feminist." In *Gender/Body/Knowledge: Feminist Reconstructions of Being and Knowing*, edited by Alison M. Jaggar and Susan R. Bordo, 256–69, New Brunswick, NJ: Rutgers University Press.

Okanlawon, Alexander. 1972. "Africanism – A Synthesis of the African World-View." *Black World* 21(9): 40–44, 92–97.

Omi, Michael, and Howard Winant, 1986. *Racial Formation in the United States: From the 1960s to the 1980s*. New York: Routledge & Kegan Paul.

Patterson, Orlando. 1982. *Slavery and Social Death*. Cambridge, MA: Harvard University Press.

Radford-Hill, Sheila. 1986. "Considering Feminism as a Model for Social Change." In *Feminist Studies/Critical Studies*, edited by Teresa de Lauretis, 157–72. Bloomington: Indiana University Press.

Richards, Dona. 1980. "European Mythology: The Ideology of 'Progress.'" In *Contemporary Black Thought*, edited by Molefi Kete Asante and Abdulai Sa. Vandi, 59–79. Beverly Hills, CA: Sage.

——. 1990. "The Implications of African-American Spirituality." In *African Culture: The Rhythms of Unity*, edited by Molefi Kete Asante and Kariamu Welsh Asante, 207–31, Trenton, NJ: Africa World Press.

Richardson, Marilyn, ed. 1987. *Maria W. Stewart, America's First Black Woman Political Writer*. Bloomington: Indiana University Press.

Ritchie, Beth. 1985. "Battered Black Women: A Challenge for the Black Community." *Black Scholar* 16: 40–44.

Rollins, Judith. 1985. *Between Women, Domestics and Their Employers*. Philadelphia: Temple University Press.

Rowell, Charles H. 1975. "An Interview with Margaret Walker." *Black World* 25(2): 4–17.

Scott, James C. 1985. *Weapons of the Weak: Everyday Forms of Peasant Resistance*. New

Haven, CT: Yale University Press.

Scott, Patricia Bell. 1982a. "Debunking Sapphire: Toward a Non-Racist and Non-Sexist Social Science." in *But Some of Us Are Brave*, edited by Gloria T. Hull, Patricia Bell Scott, and Barbara Smith, 85–92. Old Westbury, NY: Feminist Press.

——. 1982b. "Selected Bibliography on Black Feminism." In *But Some of Us Are Brave*, edited by Gloria T. Hull, Patricia Bell Scott, and Barbara Smith, 23–36. Old Westbury, NY: Feminist Press.

Shockley, Ann Allen. 1974. *Loving Her*. Hallahassee, FL: Naiad Press.

Simms, Margaret C. and Julianne Malveaux, eds. 1986. *Slipping through the Cracks: The Status of Black Women*. New Brunswick, NJ: Transaction.

Smith, Barbara. 1983. "Introduction." In *Home Girls: A Black Feminist Anthology*, edited by Barbara Smith, xix–lvi. New York: Kitchen Table Press.

Smith, Beverly. 1983. "The Wedding." In *Home Girls: A Black Feminist Anthology*, edited by Barbara Smith, 171–76. New York: Kitchen Table Press.

Smith, Dorothy. 1987. *The Everyday World as Problematic*. Boston: Northeastern University Press.

Smitherman, Geneva. 1977. *Talkin and Testifyin: The Language of Black America*. Boston: Houghton Mifflin.

Sobel, Mechal. 1979. *Trabelin' On: The Slave Journey to an Afro-Baptist Faith*. Princeton: Princeton University Press.

Steady, Filomina Chioma. 1981. "The Black Woman Cross-Culturally: An Overview." In *The Black Woman Cross-Culturally*, edited by Filomina Chioma Steady, 7–42. Cambridge, MA: Schenkman.

——. 1987. "African Feminism: A Worldwide Perspective." In *Women in Africa and the African Diaspora*, edited by Rosalyn Terborg-Penn, Sharon Harley, and Andrea Benton Rushing, 3–24. Washington, DC: Howard University Press.

Tate, Claudia, ed. 1983. *Black Women Writers at Work*. New York: Continuum Publishing.

Terborg-Penn, Rosalyn. 1986. "Black Women in Resistance: A Cross-Cultural Perspective." In *In Resistance: Studies in African, Caribbean and Afro-American History*, edited by Gary Y. Okhiro, 188–209. Amherst: University of Massachusetts Press.

Thompson, Robert Farris. 1983. *Flash of the Spirit: African and Afro-American Art and Philosophy*. New York: Vintage.

Walker, Alice. 1983. *In Search of Our Mothers' Gardens*. New York: Harcourt Brace Jovanovich.

——. 1988. *Living by the Word*. New York: Harcourt Brace Jovanovich.

Webber, Thomas L. 1978. *Deep Like the Rivers*. New York: W. W. Norton.

West, Cornel. 1977–78. "Philosophy and the Afro-American Experience." *Philosophical Forum* 9(2–3): 117–48.

White, E. Frances. 1984. "Listening to the Voices of Black Feminism." *Radical America* 18(2–3): 7–25.

Chapter 28

Patricia J. Williams

RACE AND RIGHTS

A T A F A C U L T Y M E E T I N G O N C E, I raised several issues: racism among my students, my difficulty in dealing with it by myself, and my need for the support of colleagues. I was told by a white professor that "we" should be able to "break the anxiety by just laughing about it." Another nodded in agreement and added that "the key is not to take this sort of thing too seriously."

Sometime after that, the *New York Times* ran a story about the arrest of one hundred parole violators who had been lured to a brunch with promises of free tickets to a Washington Redskins–Cincinnati Bengals football game: "The suspects reported to the Washington Convention Center after receiving a letter saying they had won the tickets from a cable television company, which had been set up as part of the police operation."[1] That evening, the televised news accounts of this story were infinitely more graphic. They showed one hundred black men entering a hall dressed for a party, some in tuxedos, some with fresh shiny perms, some with flowers in their lapels, some clearly hungry and there for the promised food, some dressed in the outfits of anticipatory football spectators, in raccoon coats and duckbill hats that said "Redskins." One hundred black men rolling up the escalators to the convention hall were greeted by smiling white (undercover) masters of ceremony, popping flashbulbs, lots of cameras, and pretty white women in skimpy costumes. Everyone smiled and laughed, like children at a birthday party. Everyone looked as though they were about the business of having a good time together. We saw the one hundred black men being rounded up by a swarm of white men, white women (also undercover agents) dressed as cheerleaders bouncing up and down on the side, a policeman dressed as a chicken with an automatic hidden in the lining, a SWAT team dressed in guerrilla-warfare green bursting in with weapons drawn.

My faculty colleagues have urged me not to give the voices of racism "so much power." Laughter is the way to disempower the forces of evil, I am told. But is it the racism I am disempowering if I laugh? Wouldn't this betray the deadly seri-ousness of it all? Laughing purposefully at what is hurtful seems somehow related to a first lesson in the skill of staged humiliation. Racism will thus be reduced to fantasy, a slapstick vaunting of good over evil – except that it is real. The cultural image of favored step-siblings laughing and pointing at such stupidity, at the sheer disingenuousness of bad children falling for the promise that they will get gifts, of even daring to imagine that they will get wonderful gifts too . . . if I laugh, don't I risk becoming that or, worse, a caricature of that image, that glossy marketing of despair?

Those who compose the fringe of society have always been the acceptable scapegoats, the butt of jokes, and the favored whipping boys. It resembles the pattern within psychotic families where one child is set up as "sick" and absorbs the whole family's destructiveness. The child may indeed be sick in unsociably visible and dramatically destructive ways, but the family is unhealthy in its conspiracy not to see in themselves the emanation of such sickness. The child becomes the public mirror of quietly enacted personality slaughter. Resistance to seeing the full reality is played out in the heaving of blame and, most cowardly of all, in disempowering others and ourselves by making fun of serious issues. The alternative (and infinitely more difficult) course is to face the interconnectedness, the enmeshed pattern of public dismissiveness and private humiliation, of private crimes and publicly righteous wrongs, of individual disappointments and national tragedies.

In sum, I see the problem at hand not as one of *my* giving racism too much power, but of how we may all give more power to the voices that racism suppresses.

I am attending a conference called The Sounds of Silence. The topic of the day is the social construction of race and gender and oppression. People hurl heavy names at one another: Hegel, Foucault, Adorno. The discussion is interesting, but the undercurrent is dialectical war; there are lots of authority-bullets whizzing through the air.

I think: my raciality is socially constructed, and I experience it as such. I feel my blackself as an eddy of conflicted meanings – and meaninglessness – in which my self can get lost, in which agency and consent are tumbled in constant motion. This sense of motion, the constant windy sound of manipulation whistling in my ears, is a reminder of society's constant construction of my blackness.

Somewhere at the center, my heart gets lost. I transfigure the undesirability of my racial ambiguity into the necessity of deference, the accommodation of condescension. It is very painful when I permit myself to see all this. I shield myself from it wherever possible. Indeed, at the conference it feels too dangerous to say any of this aloud, so I continue to muse to myself, pretending to doze. I am awakened suddenly to a still and deadly serious room: someone has asked me to comment on the rape of black women and the death of our children.

Caught with my guard down, I finesse the question with statistics and forgotten words. What actually comes to my mind, however, is a tragically powerful embod-iment of my ambiguous, tenuous, social positioning: the case of Tawana Brawley, a fifteen-year-old black girl from Wappinger Falls, New York. In late November 1987, after a four-day disappearance, she was found in a vacant lot, clothed only in a shirt and a plastic garbage bag into which she had apparently crawled; she was in a dazed state, not responding to noise, cold, or ammonia; there was urine-soaked cotton stuffed in her nose and ears; her hair had been chopped off; there were cigarette burns over a third of her body; "KKK" and "Nigger" had been inscribed on her torso; her body was smeared with dog feces.[2] This much is certain, "certain" because there were objective third persons to testify as to her condition in that foundling state (and independent "objective" testimony is apparently what is required before experience gets to be labeled truth) although even this much certainty was persistently recast as nothing-at-all in the subsequent months. By September the *New York Times* was reporting that "her ears and nose were *protected* by cotton wads"; that it was not her *own* hair that was cut, but hair extensions "woven into her own short hair" that had either been torn or cut out; that only her clothes and not her body had been burned; that, from the moment she was found, "*seemingly* dazed and degraded, [she] assumed the mantle of victim"; and that her dazed condition was "ephemeral" because, in the emergency room, after resisting efforts to pull open her eyes, "Dr. Pena concluded that Tawana was not unconscious and was aware of what was going on around her . . . In a moment of quiet drama, Dr. Pena confronted Miss Brawley: 'I know you can hear me so open your eyes,' she commanded. Tawana opened her eyes and was able to move them in all directions by following Pena's finger."[3]

This much is certainly worth the conviction that Tawana Brawley has been the victim of some unspeakable crime. No matter how she got there. No matter who did it to her – and even if she did it to herself. Her condition was clearly the expression of some crime against her, some tremendous violence, some great violation that challenges comprehension. And it is this much that I grieve about. The rest of the story is lost, or irrelevant in the worst of all possible ways.

But there is a second version of the story. On July 14, 1988, New York State Attorney General Robert Adams stated that "there may not have been any crime committed here."[4] A local television call-in poll showed that the vast majority of New Yorkers – the vast majority of any potential jury pool, in other words – agreed with him. Most people felt either that if she were raped it was "consensual" (as cruel an oxymoron that ever was) or that she "did it to herself" (as if self-mutilation and attempted suicide are free-enterprise, private matters of no social consequence with reference to which the concern of others is an invasion of privacy). It was a surprise to no one, therefore, when a New York grand jury concluded that Tawana Brawley had made the whole thing up.[5]

When Tawana Brawley was finally able to tell her story – she remained curled in fetal position for several days after she was found – she indicated that she had been kidnapped and raped by six white men:

> Nodding or shaking her head to questions . . . Miss Brawley gave contradictory answers. She indicated that she had been subjected to acts of oral sex, and after first indicating she had not been raped, she suggested she had been assaulted by three white men . . . Asked who assaulted her, she grabbed the silver badge on his uniform but did not respond when he asked if the badge she saw was like this. He then gave her his notebook and she wrote "white cop." Asked where, she wrote "woods."

He then asked her if she had been raped, and she wrote: "a lot" and drew an arrow to "white cop" . . . This response was the closest Miss Brawley ever came to asserting to authorities that she had been raped; her family and advisers, however, asserted many times that she was raped, sodomized and subjected to other abuse.[6]

The white men she implicated included the district attorney of Wappinger Falls, a highway patrolman, and a local police officer. This accusation was not only the first but also the last public statement Tawana Brawley ever made. (One may well question why she, a minor and a rape victim, was ever put in the position of making public statements at all. One might also inquire why the Child Protective Services Agency, which is supposed to intervene in such cases, did not.[7])

What replaced Tawana's story was a thunderous amount of media brouhaha, public offerings of a thousand and one other stories, fables, legends, and myths. A sampling of these enticing distractions includes:

- Tawana's mother, Glenda Brawley, who fled to the sanctuary of a church to avoid arrest for failing to testify before a grand jury and to protest the failure of the same grand jury to subpoena the men named by her daughter.
- Tawana's stepfather, from whom she had allegedly run away on prior occasions; by whom she had allegedly been beaten many times before – once even in a police station, in the presence of officers before they had a chance to intervene; and who served seven years for manslaughter in the death of his first wife, whom he stabbed fourteen times and, while awaiting trial for that much, then shot and killed.
- Tawana's boyfriend, who was serving time on drug charges in an upstate facility and whom she had gone to visit shortly before her disappearance.
- Tawana's lawyers, civil-rights activists Alton Maddox and C. Vernon Mason, who advised their client not to cooperate with investigating authorities until an independent prosecutor was appointed to handle the case.
- Tawana's spiritual counselor, the Reverend Al Sharpton, described variously as a "minister without a congregation" ("Mr. Sharpton, who is still a member of the Washington Temple Church of God in Christ, does not serve as the pastor of any church. 'My total time is civil rights,' he said. 'It's kind of hard to do both.'"[8]) and as an informer for the FBI ("The Rev. Al Sharpton, a Brooklyn minister who has organized civil disobedience demonstrations and has frequently criticized the city's predominantly white political leadership, assisted law-enforcement officials in at least one recent criminal investigation of black community groups, Government sources said. He also allowed investigators to wiretap a telephone in his home, the sources said."[9]). Al Sharpton, a man who had a "long and well-publicized history of involvement in the wiretapping of civil rights leaders, yet *mirabile dictu* a sudden but "trusted adviser" to the Brawley family. Al Sharpton, tumbling off the stage in a bout of fisticuffs with Roy Innis on the Morton Downey television show, brought to you Live! from the Apollo Theater.[10] Al Sharpton, railing against the court order holding Glenda Brawley in contempt, saying to the television cameras, "Their arms are too short to box with God."

It was Al Sharpton who proceeded to weave the story where Tawana left off. It was he who proceeded, on the Phil Donahue show, to implicate the Irish Republican Army, a man with a missing finger, and the Mafia. And it was he who spirited Tawana Brawley off into hiding, shortly after the police officer she had implicated in her rape committed suicide.

More hiding. As if it were a reenactment of her kidnap, a re-reenactment of her disappearing into the middle of her own case. It was like watching the Pied Piper of Harlem, this slowly replayed television spectacle of her being led off by the hand, put in a car, and driven to "a secret location"; a dance into thin air that could be accounted for by nothing less than sheer enchantment. I had a terrible premonition, as I watched, that Tawana Brawley would never be heard from again.

She has not been heard from again. From time to time there are missives from her advisers to the world: Tawana is adjusting well to her new school; Tawana wants to be a model; Tawana approves of the actions of her advisers; and, most poignantly, Tawana is "depressed," so her advisers are throwing her a party.

But the stories in the newspapers are no longer about Tawana anyway. They are all about black manhood and white justice; a contest of wills between her attorneys, the black community, and the New York state prosecutor's office. Since Tawana's statement implicated a prosecutor, one issue was the propriety of her case's being handled through the usual channels, rather than setting up a special unit to handle this and other allegations of racial violence. But even this issue was not able to hold center stage with all the thunder and smoke of raucous male outcry, curdling warrior accusations, the flash of political swords and shields — typified by Governor Cuomo's gratuitous offer to talk to Tawana personally; by Al Sharpton's particularly gratuitous statement that Tawana might show up at her mother's contempt hearing because "most children want to be in court to say good-bye to their mothers before they go to jail"[11]; by Phil Donahue's interview with Glenda Brawley, which he began with "No one wants to jump on your bones and suggest that you are not an honorable person but . . ."; by the enlistment of the support of Louis Farrakhan and a good deal of antisemitic insinuation; by the mishandling and loss of key evidence by investigating authorities; by the commissioning of a so-called Black Army to encircle Glenda Brawley on the courthouse steps; by the refusal of the New York attorney general's office to take seriously the request for an independent prosecutor; and by the testimony of an associate of Sharpton's, a former police officer named Perry McKinnon, that Mason, Maddox, and Sharpton did not believe Tawana's story. (On television I hear this story reported in at least three different forms: [McKinnon says Tawana lied; McKinnon says Sharpton lied about believing Tawana's story; McKinnon says that Mason and Maddox made up the whole thing in order to advance their own political careers. Like a contest, or a lottery with some drunken, solomonic gameshow host at the helm, the truth gets sorted out by a call-in poll. Channel 7, the local ABC affiliate, puts the issue to its viewers: Do you believe Sharpton? Or do you believe McKinnon? I forgot to listen to the eleven o'clock news, when the winner and the weather were to have been announced.)

To me, the most ironic thing about this whole bad business — as well as the thread of wisdom that runs at the heart of the decision not to have Tawana Brawley testify — is that were she to have come out of hiding and pursued trial in the conventional manner, she would no doubt have undergone exactly what she did undergo, in the courts and in the media. Without her, the script unfolded at a particularly abstract and fantastical level, but the story would be the same: wild black girl who loves to lie, who is no innocent (in New York television news-casters inadvertently, but repeatedly, referred to her as the "defendant") and whose wiles are the downfall of innocent, jaded, desperate white men; this whore-lette, the symbolic consort of rapacious, saber-rattling, buffoonish black men asserting their manhood, whether her jailbird boyfriend, her smooth-headed FBI drugbuster informant of a spiritual adviser; or her grandstanding, unethically boisterous so-called lawyers who have yet to establish "a *single* cognizable legal claim."[12]

Tawana's terrible story has every black woman's worst fears and experiences wrapped into it. Few will believe a black woman who has been raped by a white man. In one of the more appallingly straightforward statements to this effect, Pete Hamill, while excoriating the "racist hustlers" Sharpton, Mason, and Maddox for talking "about 'whites' as if they were a monolith" asked: "After Tawana Brawley, who will believe the next black woman who says she was raped by white men? Or the one after her?"[13] A slightly more highbrow version of the same sentiment was put forth in a *New York Times* editorial: "How can anyone know the depths of cynicism and distrust engendered by an escapade like this? Ask the next black person who is truly victimized – and meets skepticism and disbelief. Ask the next skeptic, white or black."[14]

If anyone believes that some white man even wanted her, no one will believe that she is not a whore. (White women are prostitutes; black women are whores. White women sell themselves, in implied Dickensian fashion, because they are jaded and desperate; black women *whore* as a way of being, as an innateness of sootiness and contamination, as a sticky-sweet inherency of black womanhood persistently imaged as overripe fruit – so they whore, according to this fantasy-script, as easily as they will cut your throat or slit open said deep sweet fruit, spitting out afterwards a predictable stream of blood and seeds and casual curses.) Black women whore because it is sensual and lazy and vengeful. How can such a one be raped? Or so the story goes.

It is no easier when a black woman is raped by a black man (many of the newspapers have spun eager nets of suspicion around Tawana's stepfather[15] or a boyfriend). Black-on-black rape is not merely the violation of one woman by one man; it is a sociological event, a circus of stereotypification.[16] It is a contest between the universalized black man and the lusty black female. The intimacy of rape becomes a public display, full of passion, pain and gutsy blues.

Tawana Brawley herself remains absent from all this. She is a shape, a hollow, an emptiness at the center. Joy Kogawa's "white sound":

> There is a silence that cannot speak.
> There is a silence that will not speak.
> Beneath the grass the speaking dreams and beneath the dreams is a
> sensate sea. The speech that frees comes forth from that amniotic deep.
> To attend its voice, I can hear it say, is to embrace its absence. I fail
> the task. The word is stone.[17]

There is no respect or wonder for her silence. The world that created her oppression now literally countenances it, filling the void of her suffering with sacrilegious noise, clashing color, serial tableaux of lurid possibility. Truth, like a fad, takes on life of its own, independent of action and limited only by the imagination of self-proclaimed visionaries; untruth becomes truth through belief, and disbelief untruths the truth. The world turns upside-down; the quiet, terrible, nearly invisible story of her suffering may never emerge from the clamor that overtook the quest for "what happened" and polarized it into the bizarre and undecideable litigation of "something happened" versus "nothing happened."

In the face of all this, there is some part of me that wanted this child to stay in hiding, some part of me that understands the instinct to bury her rather than expound. Exposure is the equivalent of metarape, as hiding with Al Sharpton is the equivalent of metakidnap. It feels as if there are no other options than hiding or exposing. There is danger everywhere for her, no shelter, no protection. There is no medicine circle for her, no healing society, no stable place to testify and be heard, in the unburdening of one heart.

There are three enduring pictures I have of Tawana Brawley. The first is drawn from the images that both signaled and sensationalized the public controversy: the "television cameras invading the Brawley home to zoom in for a close-up of Tawana lying on a couch, looking brutalized, disoriented, almost comatose." And the pictures that were either leaked or "escaped" from the attorney general's office, the "police-evidence photographs showing Tawana Brawley as she looked when she was first brought by ambulance to a hospital following her rape: unconscious, dirty, half-naked, a 'censorship band' on the pictures covering only the nipples on her otherwise exposed breasts."[18] Her body so open and public; her eyes closed, her face shuttered, her head turned always away from the cameras.

The second image I carry of her is the widely circulated picture of her standing just behind Al Sharpton as he spoke for her. It is an image retained from innumerable photographs, taken from every angle and published over and over again, for months, everywhere: Al Sharpton with his mouth open, the perpetually open mouth. Tawana standing in his shadow clothed in silence, obedient and attentive, patient, wide-eyed, and unremittingly passive.

The third image is one described by a student of mine. At the height of the controversy, Tawana attended a comedy show at the Apollo Theater in Harlem. One of the comedians called attention to her presence in the audience and, in a parody of the federal antisex and antidrug campaigns, advised her to "just say no next time." As the audience roared with merriment and the spotlight played on her, Tawana threw back her head and laughed along with the crowd. She opened her mouth and laughed, in false witness of this cruel joke. It is the only image I have of Tawana with her mouth open – caught in a position of compromise, of satisfying the pleasure and expectations of others, trapped in the pornography of living out other people's fantasy.

I also take away three images of the men in whose shadow Tawana always stood. The first, and just plain weirdest, is that of Al Sharpton boxing with Roy Innis on the ultraconservative and ultrapsychotic Morton Downey show:

> Conservative black leader Roy Innis toppled Tawana Brawley adviser
> Al Sharpton while taping a TV program on black leadership, and the
> two civil rights gadflies vowed yesterday to settle their dispute in a
> boxing ring . . . "He tried to 'Bogart' me in the middle of my state-
> ment," said Innis . . . "I said no dice . . . We stood up and the body
> language was not good. So I acted to protect myself. I pushed him and
> he went down" . . . As the rotund preacher tumbled backward, Downey
> and several bodyguards jumped between the pair. Neither man was
> hurt . . . Sharpton said he hoped boxing promoter Don King would
> help organize a Sharpton–Innis charity boxing match . . . but said he
> would promote it himself if necessary . . . "The best part is that we
> will be giving a very positive lesson" to young black people in this city
> about conflicting resolution – but not on the street with guns and
> knives," Innis said. "It will be an honest, clean and honorable contest."[19]

The second image I have is of heavyweight champion Mike Tyson, whose own tumultuous home life was momentarily overshadowed when, with a great deal of public ceremony, he presented Tawana with a gold Rolex watch and ringside tickets for his next match. Yet there was an odd intersection in the Brawley and Tyson stories: in the contemporaneous coverage of the marital spats between Tyson and his wife, actress Robin Givens – and in the face of uncontested allegations that Tyson used his lethal million-dollar fists to beat her up – it was somehow Givens and her mother, like Tawana and hers, who became everyone's favorite despised object in supermarket-checkout conversation.[20] Tyson's image as a big harmless puppy whose uncontrolled paws were only a feature of his exuberant lovability found ultimate and ironic expression, as cultured in the media, with his visit and gifts to the Brawley family.

The last image is one I saw in the newspaper shortly after the grand-jury report had been published, of Louis Farrakhan, unkindly captured with his mouth wide open. The story says that Tawana Brawley has surfaced from her long silence and

> expressed a desire to become a Muslim and will receive a new Muslim
> name . . . Mr. Farrakhan [leader of the Nation of Islam] . . . told an
> audience of 10,000 on Sunday that he . . . rejected the grand jury's
> findings, and he vowed vengeance on those who, he said, had attacked
> the girl. "You raped my daughter and I will kill you and dismember
> your body and feed it to the fowl of the air."[21]

The photo also shows Tawana, standing just behind Farrakhan. She is wrapped and turbanned in white, the image of chastity, of rigid propriety, of womanhood's submission to rule and ritual in a world where obedience is an unendingly compli- cated affair. There is a prayerful expression on her face. Her eyes are unreadable, and her mouth is closed.

Notes and references

1   "Police, Marshals and Chicken Lure Fugitives into Custody," *New York Times*, December 16, 1985, p. B17.

2   E. Diamond, "The Brawley Fiasco," *New York Magazine*, July 18, 1988, p. 22.

3   "Evidence Points to Deceit by Brawley," *New York Times*, September 27, 1988, p. A1, italics added.

4   M. Cottman, "Abrams' Brawley Update: There Might Be No Crime," *New York Newsday*, July 15, 1988, p. 5.

5   Robert McFadden, "Brawley Made Up Story of Assault, Grand Jury Finds," *New York Times*, October 7, 1988, p. 1.

6   *New York Times,* September 27, 1988, p. A1.

7   "What first signalled to me that a Black girl was about to become a public victim was hearing the *name* of an alleged rape victim – Tawana Brawley – given on a local radio news show. Since when does the press give the name of any rape victim, much less one who is underage? Obviously when the victim is Black, and thus not worthy of the same respect and protection that would be given a white child." Audrey Edwards, "The Rape of Tawana Brawley," *Essence*, November 1988, p. 80.

As NAACP attorney Conrad Lynn observed, "State law provides that if a child appears to have been sexually molested, then the Child Protective Services Agency is supposed to take jurisdiction and custody of that child. Now, Tawana Brawley was 15 at the time of the incident. If that had been done, as I proposed early on, the agency would have given her psychiatric attention and preserved evidence, if there were evidence . . . But there was a state decision that the agency shouldn't be involved." Editorial, "What happened to Tawana Brawley's Case – and to Attitudes about Race and Justice," *New York Times*, October 9, 1988, p. E8.

8   E. R. Shipp, "A Flamboyant Leader of Protests," *New York Times*, January 21, 1988, p. B6.

9   M. A. Farber, "Protest Figure Reported To Be a U.S. Informant," *New York Times*, January 21, 1988, p. B1. "Mr. Sharpton said that he – not investigators – had put a recording device on his phone, but only to serve as a 'hot line' for people turning in crack dealers" (p. B6).

10   "Roy Innis Pushes Al Sharpton: Fracas at 'Downey Show' Taping: Boxing Match Planned," *Washington Post*, August 11, 1988, p. D4.

11   A. Bollinger, "Tawana's Mom to Get 'Black Army' Escort," *New York Post*, June 3,1988, p. 7

12   Howard Kurtz, "New York Moves Against Brawley Lawyers," *Washington Post*, October 7, 1988, p. A1.

13   Pete Hamill, "Black Media Should Tell the Truth" *New York Post*, September 29, 1988, p. 5.

14   "The Victims of the Brawley Case," *New York Times*, September 28, 1988, p. A22.

15   "One witness said Mr. King 'would watch her exercise' and talked to the girl 'in a real sexual way,' sometimes describing her as a 'fine fox'" *New York Times*, September 27, 1988, p. A16.

16   "Then it was off to the airport cafeteria for a strategy session and some cheeseburgers with advisers Alton Maddox, C. Vernon Mason and the Rev. Al Sharpton.

'The fat one, he ate the most,' said Carmen, the cashier. 'He and the skinny one [an aide] bought about $50 or $60 of cheeseburgers, orange juice, chocolate cake, pasta salad and pie,' she added." J. Nolan, "Traveling Circus Has 'Em Rollin' in Aisles," *New York Post*, September 29, 1988, p. 4.

17   Joy Kogawa, *Obasan* (Boston: David Godine, 1981), p. 1.

18   Edwards, "The Rape of Tawana Brawley," p. 80.

19   *Washington Post*, August 11, 1988, p. D4.

20   Under the caption "Robin Givens: Waiter, A Tonic with Slime for the Lady," even *Ms* magazine wrote: "We sympathized with the fights. We understood the divorce. But this crazy libel suit we don't get. Was it his personality and his pecs, or did you just want the bucks all along?" E. Combs and M. Suh, "Women Who Made Us Cringe," *Ms*, January–February 1989, p. 96.

21   "Brawley to Get Muslim Name," *New York Times*, October 11, 1988, p. B3.

Chapter 29

Avtar Brah

DIFFERENCE, DIVERSITY, DIFFERENTIATION
Processes of racialisation and gender

DIFFERENCE, DIVERSITY, PLURALISM, HYBRIDITY — these are some of the most debated and contested terms of our time. Questions of difference are at the heart of many discussions within contemporary feminisms. In the field of education in Britain, questions of identity and community continue to dominate debates surrounding multiculturalism and anti-racism. In this chapter, I consider how these themes might help us to understand the racialisation of gender. However often the concept is exposed as vacuous, 'race' still acts as an apparently ineradicable marker of social difference. What makes it possible for the category to act in this way? What is the nature of social and cultural differences and what gives them their force? How does 'racial' difference then connect to difference and antagonisms organised around other markers, like 'gender' or 'class'? Such questions are important because they can help to explain people's tenacious investment in notions of identity, community and tradition.

One recurrent problem in this area is essentialism: that is, a notion of ultimate essence that transcends historical and cultural boundaries. Here I argue against an essentialist concept of difference while simultaneously problematising the issue of 'essentialism'. At what point, and in what ways, for example, does the specificity of a particular social experience become an expression of essentialism? In reviewing feminist debates, I suggest that black and white feminism should not be seen as essentially fixed oppositional categories but rather as historically contingent fields of contestation within discursive and material practices in a post-colonial society. In similar vein, I shall be arguing that analysis of the interconnections between racism, class, gender and sexuality must take account of the positionality of different racisms with respect to one another. Overall, I underline the importance of a macro-analysis that studies the inter-relationships between various forms of social differentiation empirically and historically, but without necessarily deriving them all from a single determining instance. In other words, I shall also be trying to avoid the danger of 'reductionism'.

The article is divided into three parts. In the first, I address the various notions of 'difference' that have emerged in recent discussions of how extensively the term 'black' can be used to define the experience of African-Caribbean and south Asian groups in post-war Britain. The second section is concerned with the ways in which issues of 'difference' have been framed with respect to racism within feminist theory and practice. My primary focus here is on the ongoing debate in Britain. I conclude with a brief examination of some conceptual categories used in the theorisation of 'difference' and suggest that greater clarity in how we conceptualise 'difference' may aid in developing sharper political strategies for social justice.

What's in a name? What's in a colour?

Over the past few years the usage of the term 'black' to refer to people of African-Caribbean and south Asian descent in Britain has been the subject of considerable controversy. It is relevant to address some of these arguments as they often centre around notions of difference.

The African-Caribbean and south Asian people who migrated to Britain in the post-war period found themselves occupying a broadly similar structural position within British society, as workers performing predominantly unskilled or semi-skilled jobs on the lowest rungs of the economy. Although the ideologies which racialised them were not identical in content there were similarities in their encounters with racism in arenas such as the workplace, the education system, the housing market and the health services. Their 'non-whiteness' was a common referent within the racism confronting them. These groups were then commonly described in popular, political and academic discourses as 'coloured people'. This was not a simple descriptive term. It had been the colonial code for a relationship of domination and subordination between the coloniser and colonised. Now the code was reworked and reconstituted in and through a variety of political, cultural and economic processes in post-war Britain.

The term 'black' was adopted by the emerging coalitions amongst African-Caribbean and south Asian organisations and activists in the late 1960s and 1970s. They were influenced by the way that the Black Power movement in the USA, which had turned the concept of Black on its head, divested it of its pejorative connotations in racialised discourses, and transformed it into a confident expression of an assertive group identity. The Black Power movement urged black Americans to construe the black community not as a matter of geography but rather in terms of the global African diaspora. Eschewing 'chromatism' – the basis of differentiation amongst blacks according to lighter or darker tone of skin – 'black' became a political colour to be worn with pride against colour-based racisms. The African-Caribbean and south Asian activists in Britain borrowed the term from the Black Power movement to foster a rejection of chromatism amongst those defined as 'coloured people' in Britain.

The politics of solidarity between African-Caribbean and south Asian activists of the period were also influenced by the history of anti-colonial struggles in Africa,

Asia and the Caribbean. The fusion of these two influences in the formation of a project concerned to address the social condition of post-colonial subjects in the heart of the British metropolis meant that the concept of black has been associated with rather distinctive and somewhat different meanings in Britain as compared with the USA.

Recently British usage of the term 'black' has been criticised by commentators like Hazareesingh (1986) and Modood (1988). They argue that the 'black' in Black Power ideology referred specifically to the historical experience of people of sub-Saharan African descent, and was designed to create a positive political and cultural identity amongst black Americans. When used in relation to south Asians the concept is *de facto* emptied of those specific cultural meanings associated with phrases such as 'black music'. The concept can incorporate south Asians in a political sense only, and they therefore conclude that it denies Asian cultural identity. Clearly there is some force in this argument. It is certainly the case, as we have already noted, that the Black Power movement's mobilisation of the term 'black' was an attempt at reclaiming an African heritage that had been denied to black Americans by racism. But, as a historically specific political project located in the socio-political and economic dynamics in the USA, the Black Power ideology did not simply reclaim a pre-given ancestral past. In that very process, it also constructed a particular version of this heritage. Given that cultural processes are dynamic, and the process of claiming is itself mediated, the term 'black' does not have to be construed in essentialist terms. It can have different political and cultural meanings in different contexts. Its specific meaning in post-war Britain cannot be taken to have denied cultural differences between African, Caribbean and south Asian people when cultural difference was not the organising principle within this discourse or political practice. The concrete political struggles in which the new meaning was grounded acknowledged cultural differences but sought to accomplish political unity against racism. In any case, the issue of cultural difference cannot be posed purely in terms of differences between south Asian and African–Caribbean cultures. There are, for example, many differences between African and Caribbean cultures (which also include cultures of people of south Asian descent). Cultures in the diasporas always have their own specificity. In other words, even when the use of the 'black' is restricted to sub-Saharan Africa and its diasporas, it can be said, within the parameters of the terms set by the critics, to deny the cultural specificities of these diverse groups.

A second criticism of the ways in which 'black' has been employed in Britain has been that the concept is meaningless since many south Asians do not define themselves as black, and many African-Caribbeans do not recognise them as such. This assertion hinges partly on the criterion of numbers, but without providing supporting numerical evidence. In my own research I have found that south Asians will frequently describe themselves as 'kale' (black) when discussing issues of racism. But since the whole social being of south Asian and African-Caribbean peoples is not constituted only by the experience of racism, they have many other identifications based on, for example, religion, language and political affiliation. Moreover, as many demonstrations and campaigns show, the concept of black was mobilised as part of a set of constitutive ideas and principles to promote collective action. As a social movement, black activism has aimed to generate solidarity;

it has not necessarily assumed that all members of the diverse black communities inevitably identify with the concept in its British usage.

Another area of contention has centred on the distribution of resources by the state to different categories of consumers. It is argued that the term 'black' serves to conceal the cultural needs of groups other than those of African-Caribbean origin. This particular critique is often steeped in 'ethnicism'. Ethnicism, I would suggest, defines the experience of racialised groups primarily in 'culturalist' terms: that is it posits 'ethnic difference' as the primary modality around which social life is constituted and experienced. Cultural needs are defined largely as independent of other social experiences centred around class, gender, racism or sexuality. This means that a group identified as culturally different is assumed to be internally homogeneous, when this is patently not the case. The 'housing needs' of a working-class Asian living in overcrowded conditions on a housing estate, for instance, cannot be the same as those of a middle-class Asian living in a semi-detached house in suburbia. In other words, ethnicist discourses seek to impose stereotypic notions of 'common cultural need' upon heterogeneous groups with diverse social aspirations and interests. They often fail to address the relationship between 'difference' and the social relations of power in which it may be inscribed. It is clearly important that the state should be sensitive to the plurality of needs amongst its citizens. But we need to be attentive to the ways in which 'needs' are socially constructed and represented in various discourses.

[. . .] The main point I wish to stress through this foray into the debate surrounding the use of 'black' in Britain is to highlight how difference is constructed within these competing discourses. That is, the usage of 'black', 'Indian' or 'Asian' is determined not so much by the nature of its referent, but by its semiotic function within different discourses. These various meanings signal differing political strategies and outcomes. They mobilise different sets of cultural or political identities, and set limits to where the boundaries of a 'community' are established. This debate has to an extent been echoed within feminism. And it is against this general background that I turn to issues of 'difference' within feminism.

Is sisterhood global?

In 1985 I attended the International Women's Conference in Nairobi. It was a gathering of over 10,000 women from over 150 countries. There we were all gathered together as women to address questions of our universal subordination as a 'second sex', yet the most striking aspect of this conference was the heterogeneity of our social condition. The issues raised by the different groups of women present at the conference, especially those from the Third World, served to underline the fact that issues affecting women cannot be analysed in isolation from the national and international context of inequality (Brah 1988; Mohanty 1988).

Our gender is constituted and represented differently according to our differential location within the global relations of power. Our insertion into these global relations of power is realised through a myriad of economic, political and ideological processes. Within these structures of social relations we do not exist simply as women but as differentiated categories such as working-class women, peasant

women, migrant women. Each description references a specificity of social condition. And real lives are forged out of a complex articulation of these dimensions.
As is currently being increasingly recognised in feminist theory and practice, woman
is not a unitary category. Yet, this does not mean that the noun 'woman' is meaningless. It too has its own specificity constituted within and through historically
specific configurations of gender relations. But in different womanhoods the noun
is only meaningful – indeed only exists – with reference to a fusion of adjectives
which symbolise particular historical trajectories, material circumstances and
cultural experiences. Difference in this sense is a difference of social condition. At
this level of analysis the focus is on the social construction of different categories
of women within the broader structural and ideological processes within societies.
No claims are made that an individual category is internally homogeneous.
Working-class women, for instance, comprise very diverse groups of people both
within and between societies. Class position signals certain commonalities of location within the social structure, but class articulates with other axes of
differentiation such as racism, heterosexism or caste in delineating the precise social
position of specific categories of women.

The primary objective of feminism has been to change the social relations of
power embedded within gender. Since gender inequalities pervade all spheres of
life, feminist strategies have involved a challenge to women's subordinated position within both state institutions and civil society. The driving force behind feminist
theory and practice in the post-war period has been its commitment to eradicate
inequalities arising from a notion of sexual difference inherent in biologically deterministic theories which explain women's position in society as a result of innate
differences. Despite evidence that sex differences in cognitive behaviour among
infants are slight, and the psychological similarity between men and women is very
high, research to establish innate differences continues unabated (Segal 1990; Rose,
Kamin and Lewontin 1984). Feminists do not, of course, ignore women's biology,
but they challenge ideologies which construct and represent women's subordination as resulting from their biological capacities.

The ways in which questions of biology are addressed and taken account of
vary within different feminisms. Radical feminist accounts, for example, tend to
identify women's biologically-based subordination as the fundamental basis of
gender inequality. The relations of power between men and women are seen as
the primary dynamic of women's oppression almost to the exclusion of other determinants such as class and racism. Radical feminist perspectives often represent
women's procreative abilities as an indicator of certain psychological qualities which
are uniquely and universally female. These qualities are assumed to have been
undermined through patriarchal domination and thus have to be rediscovered and
reclaimed. They may often celebrate sexual difference in the form of presumed
unique female attributes and qualities. It has been argued that whilst repudiating
biological determinism embedded within patriarchal discourses, some versions of
radical feminism in turn construct a trans-historical notion of essential femaleness
in need of rescuing and recapturing beyond patriarchal relations (Weedon 1987;
Segal 1987; Spellman 1988).

Socialist feminism, on the other hand, has been based on the assumption that
human nature is not essential but is socially produced. The meaning of what it is

to be a woman – biologically, socially, culturally and psychically – is considered to be historically variable. Socialist feminism has mounted a powerful critique of those materialist perspectives which prioritise class, neglect the social consequences of the sexual division of labour, privilege heterosexuality and pay scant attentions to the social mechanisms which prevent women from attaining economic, political and social equality. This strand of feminism distances itself from the radical feminist emphasis on power relations between the sexes as the almost exclusive determinant of women's subordination.

On the whole, and especially until very recently, western feminist perspectives of whatever kind have paid little attention to the processes of racialisation of gender, class or sexuality. Processes of racialisation are, of course, historically specific, and different groups have been racialised differently under varying circumstances, and on the basis of different signifiers of 'difference'. Each racism has a particular history. It arose from a particular set of economic, political and cultural circumstances, has been reproduced through specific mechanisms, and has found different expression in different societies. Anti-black racism, anti-Irish racism, anti-Jewish racism, anti-Arab racism, different varieties of orientalisms: all have distinctive features.

The specific histories of these various racisms place them in particular relationship to each other. For example, there are several similarities in the social experience of the Irish and black groups in Britain. Both sets of people have a history of being colonised by Britain, their migration patterns to Britain share common features, both groups occupy a predominantly working-class position within the British class structure, and they both have been subjected to racism. But anti-black and anti-Irish racism situate these groups differently within British society. As white Europeans, the great majority of Irish people are placed in a dominant position *vis-à-vis* black people in and through the discourses of anti-black racism, even when the two groups may share a similar class location. In other words, we assume different subject positions within various racisms. Analysis of the interconnections between racism, class, gender and sexuality must take account of the positionality of different racisms with respect to one another.

A second example may illustrate the above point further. African-Caribbean and south Asian communities have developed differing responses to racism because their experiences of racism, though similar in many ways, have not been identical (Brah and Deem 1986). State policies have impacted differently on these communities. African-Caribbean communities have mobilised far more around their collective experience of the criminal justice system, particularly the police and the courts, whereas Asian groups have been much more actively involved in defending communities against violent racial attacks, racial harassment on housing estates, and in organising campaigns against deportations and other issues arising from the effects of immigration laws. The stereotypic representations of African-Caribbean and south Asian communities have also been substantially different. The gendered discourses of the 'nigger' and the 'Paki' in post-war Britain represent distinctive ideologies, yet they are two strands of a common racism structured around colour/phenotype/culture as signifiers of superiority and inferiority in post-colonial Britain. This means that African-Caribbean, south Asian and white groups are relationally positioned within these structures of representation. By their behaviour and actions they may reinforce these structures or alternatively they may assume a political practice which challenges these different strands of anti-black racism.

There is a tendency in Britain to see racism as 'something to do with the presence of black people'. But it is important to stress that both black and white people experience their gender, class and sexuality through 'race'. Racialisation of white subjectivity is often not manifestly apparent to white groups because 'white' is a signifier of dominance, but this renders the racialisation process no less significant. We need to analyse the processes which construct us as 'white female', 'black female', 'white male', 'black male' etc. We need to examine how and why the meanings of these words change from plain descriptions to hierarchically organised categories under given economic, political and social circumstances.

Black feminism, white feminism

During the 1970s there was a lack of much serious and sustained engagement with issues of gendered exploitation of post-colonial labour in the British metropolis, racism within state policies and cultural practices, the racialisation of black and white subjectivity in the specific context of a period following the loss of empire, and the particularities of black women's oppression within feminist theory and practice. This played an important part in the formation of black feminist organisations as distinct from the 'white' Women's Liberation Movement. These organisations emerged against the background of a deepening economic and political crisis and an increasing entrenchment of racism. The 1970s was a period when the Powellism of the 1960s came to suffuse the social fabric, and was gradually consolidated and transmuted into Thatcherism in the 1980s. The black communities were involved in a wide variety of political activity throughout the decade. There were major industrial strikes of which several were led by women. The Black Trade Union Solidarity Movement was formed to deal with racism in employment and trade unions. There were massive campaigns against immigration control, fascist violence, racist attacks on person and property, modes of policing that resulted in the harassment of black people, and against the criminalisation of black communities. There were many self-help projects concerned with educational, welfare and cultural activities. Black women were involved in all these activities, but the formation of autonomous black women's groups in the late 1970s injected a new dimension into the political scene.

The specific priorities of local black women's organisations, a number of which combined to form a national body – the Organisation of Women of Asian and African Descent (OWAAD), varied to an extent according to the exigencies of the local context. But the overall aim was to challenge the specific forms of oppression faced by the different categories of black women. The commitment to forging unity between African, Caribbean and Asian women demanded sustained attempts to analyse, understand and work with commonalities as well as heterogeneity of experience. It called for an interrogation of the role of colonialism and imperialism and that of contemporary economic, political and ideological processes in sustaining particular social divisions within these groups. It required black women to be sensitive to one another's cultural specificities while constructing common political strategies to confront sexism, racism and class inequality. This was no easy task, and it is a testimony to the political commitment and vision of the women involved that this project thrived for many years, and some of the local groups have survived the divisive impact of ethnicism and remain active today (Bryan, Dadzie and Scafe 1985; Brixton Black Women's Group 1984).

The demise of OWAAD as a national organisation in the early 1980s was precipitated by a number of factors. Many such divisive tendencies have been paralleled in the women's movement as a whole. The organisations affiliated to OWAAD shared its broad aims but there were political differences amongst women on various issues. There was general agreement that racism was crucial in structuring our oppression in Britain, but we differed in our analysis of racism and its links with class and other modes of inequality. For some women racism was an autonomous structure of oppression and had to be tackled as such; for others it was inextricably connected with class and other axes of social division. There were also differences in perspectives between feminists and non-feminists in OWAAD. For the latter, an emphasis on sexism was a diversion from the struggle against racism. The devaluation of black cultures by the onslaughts of racism meant that for some women the priority was to 'reclaim' these cultural sites and to situate themselves 'as women' within them. Whilst this was an important project there was, at times, more than a hint of idealising a lost past. Other women argued that, whilst the empowering aspects of culture did need to be affirmed and validated, it was equally important to examine how culture is also a terrain on which women's oppression is produced and reproduced. The problem of male violence against women and children, the unequal sexual division of labour in the household, questions of dowry and forced marriages, clitoridectomy, heterosexism and the suppression of lesbian sexualities: all these were issues demanding immediate attention. Although most women in OWAAD did recognise the importance of these issues, there were nonetheless major differences about priorities and political strategies to deal with them.

Alongside these tendencies there was an emerging emphasis within the women's movement as a whole on identity politics. Instead of embarking on the complex but necessary task of sifting out the specificities of particular oppressions, identifying their similarities or connections with other oppressions, and building a politics of solidarity, some women were beginning to differentiate these specificities into hierarchies of oppression. The mere act of naming oneself as a member of an oppressed group was assumed to vest one with moral authority. Multiple oppressions came to be regarded not in terms of their patterns of articulation/interconnections – but rather as separate elements that could be added in a linear fashion, so that the more oppressions a woman could list the greater her claims to occupy a higher moral ground. Assertions about authenticity of personal experience could be presented as if they were an unproblematic guide to an understanding of processes of subordination and domination. Declarations concerning self-righteous political correctness sometimes came to substitute for careful political analysis (Adams 1989; Ardill and O'Sullivan 1986).

Despite the fragmentation of the women's movement, black women in Britain have continued to raise critical questions about feminist theory and practice. As a result of our location within diasporas formed by the history of slavery, colonialism and imperialism black feminists have consistently argued against parochialism and stressed the need for a feminism sensitive to the international social relations of power (Carby 1982; Parmar 1982; Feminist Review 1984; Brah and Minhas 1985; Brah 1987; Phoenix 1987; Grewal, Kay, Landor, Lewis and Parmar 1988; Mama 1989; Lewis 1990). Hazel Carby's article 'White Woman Listen!', for instance, presents a critique of such key feminist concepts as 'patriarchy', 'the family' and 'reproduction'. She criticises feminist perspectives which use notions of 'feudal residues' and 'traditionalism' to create sliding scales of 'civilised liberties', with the 'Third World' seen at one end of the scale and the supposedly progressive 'First World' at the other. She provides several illustrations of how a certain type of western feminism can serve to reproduce rather than challenge the categories through which 'the west' constructs and represents itself as superior to its 'others'.

These critiques have generated some critical self-reflection on the part of white feminist writers. Barrett and McIntosh (1985), for example, have attempted to reassess their earlier work. They acknowledge the limitations of the concept of patriarchy as unambiguous and invariable male dominance undifferentiated by class or racism, but wish to retain the notion of 'patriarchal' as signifying how 'particular social relations combine a public dimension of power, exploitation or status with a dimension of personal servility' (p.39). Having made this point, they fail to explore in any systematic way how and why the concept of the 'patriarchal' helps us to engage with the interconnections between gender, class and racism. The mere substitution of the concept of patriarchy by patriarchal relations will not by itself deal with the charges of ahistoricism, universalism or essentialism that have been levelled at the former (although, as Walby (1990) argues, it is possible to provide historicised accounts of patriarchy). As a response to recent reconceptualisations of patriarchy, Joan Acker suggests that it might be more appropriate to shift 'the theoretical object from patriarchy to gender, which we can define briefly as structural, relational, and symbolic differentiations between women and men' (Acker 1989: 238). She remains cautious about this shift, however, as 'gender', according to her, lacks the critical political sharpness of 'patriarchy' and could much more easily be co-opted and neutralised within 'mainstream' theory.

Patriarchal relations are a specific form of gender relations in which women inhabit a subordinated position. In theory, at least it should be possible to envisage a social context in which gender relations are not associated with inequality between the sexes *qua* women and men. I would argue in favour of retaining the concept of 'patriarchal' without necessarily subscribing to the concept of 'patriarchy' – whether historicised or not – because I hold serious reservations about the analytic or political utility of maintaining system boundaries between 'patriarchy' and the particular socio-economic and political formation (e.g. capitalism or state socialism) with which it articulates. The issue is not whether patriarchal relations predate capitalism or state socialism, for they patently do, but how they are manifested within these systems in the context of a history of colonialism and imperialism in different parts of the globe. Structures of class, racism, gender and sexuality cannot be treated as 'independent variables' because the oppression of each is inscribed within the other – is constituted by and is constituted of the other.

Acknowledging the black feminist critique, Barrett and McIntosh stress the need to analyse the ideological construction of white femininity through racism. This in my view is essential since there is still a tendency to address questions of inequality through a focus on the victims of inequality. Discussions around feminism and racism often centre around the oppression of black women rather than exploring how both black and white women's gender is constructed through class and racism. This means that white women's 'privileged position' within racialised discourses (even when they may share a class position with black women) fails to be adequately theorised, and processes of domination remain invisible. The representation of white women as 'the moral guardians of a superior race', for instance, serves to homogenise white women's sexuality at the same time as it fractures it across class in that the white working-class woman, although also presented as 'carrier of the race', is simultaneously constructed as prone to 'degeneracy' because of her class background. Here we see how class contradictions may be worked through and 'resolved' ideologically within the racialised structuration of gender.

Barrett and McIntosh's article generated considerable debate (Ramazanoglu, Kazi, Lees and Safia-Mirza in *Feminist Review*, 22, 1986; Bhavnani and Coulson 1986). Whilst acknowledging the importance of the reassessment of a part of their work by two prominent white feminists, the critics argued that their methods of re-examination failed to provide the possibility of radical transformation of previous analysis, thus leaving the ways in which 'race' features within social reproduction largely untheorised. Although Barrett and McIntosh note that socialists are divided as to whether the social divisions associated with ethnicity and racism should be seen as absolutely autonomous of social class, as reducible to social class, or as having historical origins but articulating now with the divisions of class in capitalist society (p.38), they do not signal their own analytical preference on these issues. This is a surprising silence in an article whose aim is to advance our understanding of conceptual and theoretical concerns in the field.

I would argue that racism is neither reducible to social class or gender nor wholly autonomous. Racisms have variable historical origins but they articulate with patriarchal class structures in specific ways under given historical conditions. Racisms have independent effectivity but to suggest this is not the same as saying, as Caroline Ramazanoglu (1989) does, that racism is an 'independent form of domination'. The search for grand theories specifying the interconnections between racism, gender and class has been less than productive. They are best construed as historically contingent and context-specific relationships. Hence, we can focus on a given context and differentiate between the demarcation of a category as an object of social discourse, as an analytical category, and as a subject of political mobilisation without making assumptions about their permanence or stability across time and space. This means that 'white' feminism or 'black' feminism in Britain are not essentialist categories but rather they are fields of contestation inscribed within discursive and material processes and practices in a post-colonial terrain. They represent struggles over political frameworks for analysis; the meanings of theoretical concepts; the relationship between theory, practice and subjective experiences; and over political priorities and modes of mobilisations, but they should not, in my view, be understood as locating 'white' and 'black' women as 'essentially' fixed oppositional categories.

More recent contributions to the debate make the point that irrespective of the intentions of the authors, anti-racist feminist discourses of the late 1970s and 1980s did not always facilitate political mobilisation. Knowles and Mercer (1990), for example, take the position that Carby's and Bourne's emphasis on the inscription of racism and gender inequality within processes of capitalism, colonialism and patriarchal social systems produced functionalist arguments – that sexism and racism were inherent within these systems and served the needs of these systems to perpetuate themselves. They believe that this approach demanded nothing short of an all-embracing struggle against these 'isms' that thereby undermined more localised, small-scale political responses. Their own method of dealing with this is to suggest that racism and sexism be 'viewed as a series of effects which do not have a single cause'. I would accept the arguments that the level of abstraction at which categories such as 'capitalism' or 'patriarchal relations' are delineated does not provide straightforward guidelines for concrete strategy and action, and also that racism and sexism are not monocausal phenomena. Nonetheless, I am not sure how treating racism and sexism as a 'series of effects' provides any clearer guidelines for political response. The same 'effect' may be interpreted from a variety of political positions, and lead to quite different strategies for action. Taking up a specific political position means that one is making certain assumptions about the nature of the various processes that underline a social phenomenon of which a particular event may be an effect. A focus only on 'effects' may render invisible the workings of such ideological and material processes, thereby hindering our understanding of the complex basis of inequalities. Although crucial in mobilising specific constituencies the single-issue struggles as ends in themselves may delimit wider-ranging challenges to social inequalities. The language of 'effects' in any case assumes the existence of some causes. The main issue is not whether we should jettison macro-level analysis of gender or racism in relation to capitalism, colonialism or state socialism in favour of empirically grounded analysis of the concrete manifestations of racism in a given local situation, but how each is overdetermined by, and also helps to determine, the others.

I share Knowles and Mercer's reservations about analytical and political perspectives in which social inequality comes to be personified in the bodies of the dominant social groups – white people, men, or heterosexual individuals in relation to racism, sexism or heterosexism – but we cannot ignore the social relations of power that inscribe such differentiations. Members of dominant groups do occupy privileged positions within political and material practices that attend these social divisions, although the precise interplay of this power in specific institutions or in interpersonal relations cannot be stipulated in advance, may be contradictory and can be challenged. [. . .]

Difference, what difference?

It is evident that the concept of difference is associated with different meanings in different discourses. But how are we to understand 'difference'? A detailed discussion of this topic is beyond the scope of this chapter but I would like to suggest four ways in which difference may be conceptualised and addressed.

Difference as experience

Experience has been a key concept within feminism. Women's movements have aimed to give a collective voice to women's personal experiences of social and psychic forces that constitute the 'female' into the 'woman'. The everyday of the social relations of gender – ranging from housework and child care, low-paid employment and economic dependency to sexual violence and women's exclusion from key centres of political and cultural power – have all been given a new significance through feminism as they have been brought out of the realm of the 'taken for granted' to be interrogated and challenged. The personal with its profoundly concrete yet elusive qualities, and its manifold contradictions, acquired new meanings in the slogan 'the personal is political' as consciousness-raising groups provided the forums for exploring individual experiences, personal feelings and women's own understandings of their daily lives.

The limitations of the consciousness-raising method (empowering though it was for some women) as a strategy for systematically challenging the structures of gender inequality have been widely acknowledged. Nonetheless there was at least an implicit recognition in this mode of working that experience did not transparently reflect reality, but instead it was a constellation of mediated relationships, a site of contradictions to be addressed collectively. This insight is quite often missing from current discussions about differences between women where difference and experience are used primarily as a 'commonsensical term' (Barrett 1987). Hence, the need to re-emphasise a notion of experience not as unmediated guide to 'truth' but as a practice of making sense, both symbolically and narratively; as struggle over material conditions and over meaning.

Difference as social relation

The emphasis here is on social relations at the level of the social structure. A group usually mobilises the concept of difference in this sense of a social relation when addressing the structural, political and historical basis of the commonality of its experience. Experience is understood here primarily in terms of collective histories.

In practice, the everyday of lived experience and experience as a social relation do not exist in mutually exclusive spaces. For example, if we speak of 'north African women in France', we are, on the one hand, referring to the social relations of gendered post-coloniality in France. On the other hand, we are also making a statement about the everyday experience of this post-coloniality on the part of such women, although we cannot specify, in advance, the particularity of individual women's lives or how they interpret and define this experience. In both instances, the question of how difference is defined remains paramount. Are perceptions of difference in a given context a basis of affirming diversity or a mechanism for exclusionary and discriminatory practices? Do discourses of difference legitimise progressive or oppressive state policies and practices? How are different categories of women represented within such discourses? How do the women themselves construct or represent the specificity of their experience? Under what circumstances does 'difference' become the basis of asserting a collective identity?

Difference as subjectivity

Issues of difference have been central to theoretical debates around subjectivity. A key question facing us is: how are racialised subjects formed? But the question of racialisation of subjectivity has not yet received much attention within feminist theory, which has been preoccupied primarily with the status of 'sexual difference' in the formation of subjectivity. Feminists have turned to psychoanalysis (notably its post-structuralist and object-relations variants) and to forms of deconstructionist thought to understand the processes of identity formation.

With the growing awareness that women's innermost emotions, feelings, desires and fantasies with their multiple contradictions could not be understood purely in terms of the imperatives of the social institutions and the forces of male domination, feminists have approached psychoanalysis for a more complex account of the trials and tribulations of psychic life. Dissatisfied with the social conditioning approaches to women's psychology, some feminists have looked to Lacan's rereading of Freud for a non-reductive understanding of subjectivity. Post-structuralist accounts have proved attractive to feminism, for they seek to problematise 'sexual difference': sexual difference is something to be explained rather than assumed. Subjectivity is seen as neither unified nor fixed – rather it is something that is constantly in progress. Compelling arguments have been made in favour of the importance of psychoanalysis for feminism against those critics who assume that the notion of a fragmented sexual identity constantly in process is at odds with the feminist project of constructing oppositional consciousness through collective action (cf. Rose 1986; Penley 1989; Minsky 1990).

These arguments are convincing, but certain issues still need to be addressed. The enormous contribution of individuals such as Fanon notwithstanding, much work is yet to be undertaken on the subject of how the racialised 'other' is constituted in the psychic domain. How is post-colonial gendered and racialised subjectivity to be analysed? Does the privileging of 'sexual difference' and early childhood in psychoanalysis limit its explanatory value in helping understand psychic dimensions of social phenomena such as racism? How do the 'symbolic order' and the social order articulate in the formation of the subject? In other words, how is the link between social and psychic reality to be theorised? There is also the issue of how certain psychoanalytical discourses are themselves implicated in the inscription of racism (Dalal 1988).

Difference as identity

Our struggles over meaning are also our struggles over different modes of being: different identities (Minh-ha 1989). Identity is never a fixed core. On the other hand, changing identities do assume specific, concrete patterns, as in a kaleidoscope, against particular sets of historical and social circumstances. Our cultural identities are simultaneously our cultures in process but they acquire specific meanings in a given context. Social phenomena such as racism seek to fix and naturalise 'difference' and create impervious boundaries between groups. The modalities of difference inscribed within the particularities of our personal and collective historical, cultural and political experience – our ethnicities – can interrogate and challenge the strangulating imagination of racism, but the task is a complex one, for ethnicities are liable to be appropriated by racism as signifiers of permanent boundaries. Hence, the 'Englishness' of a particular class can come to represent itself via racism as 'Britishness' against those ethnicities that it subordinates – such as those of the Irish, Scottish, Welsh, black British, or the ethnicities of the formerly colonised world. But, as I noted earlier, 'white'/European ethnicities are subordinated differently from non-white, non-European ethnicities.

It should be possible through political practice to retrieve ethnicity from racialised nationalist discourses so that it can be manifested as a non-essentialist horizontality rather than hierarchically organised difference. As Stuart Hall says:

> The fact that this grounding of ethnicity in difference was deployed, in the discourse of racism, as a means of disavowing the realities of racism and repression does not mean that we can permit the term to be permanently colonised. That appropriation will have to be contested, the term disarticulated from its position in the discourse of 'multi-culturalism' and transcoded, just as we previously had to recuperate the term 'black', from its place in a system of negative equivalences
>
> Hall 1988: 27

But the project is always beset with difficulties. Since ethnicities are always gendered they construct sexual difference in specific ways. The appropriation of a particular ethnicity cannot be assumed necessarily to involve challenging gender inequalities unless this is undertaken as a conscious objective. Indeed, the reverse may be the case. Similarly, depending upon the context, ethnicities may legitimise class or caste divisions by proclaiming and stressing only the unity of an otherwise heterogeneous group.

So how can we claim ethnicities that do not reinforce inequalities? The project is complex but broadly will entail a variety of concrete practices at the economic, political and cultural level designed to undermine the relations of power that underlie these inequalities. There will be the need to remain vigilant of the circumstances under which affirmation of a particular collective experience becomes an essentialist assertion of difference. This problem may arise not only in relation to dominant ethnicities but also dominated ethnicities. In their struggle against the hegemonic, universalising imperatives of the former, the latter may also take recourse to constructing essentialist differences. This can be especially problematic for women if the cultural values that the groups in question excavate, recast, and reconstruct are those that underscore women's subordination.

Although I have argued against essentialism, it is not easy to deal with this problem. In their need to create new political identities, dominated groups will often appeal to bonds of common cultural experience in order to mobilise their constituency. In so doing they may assert a seemingly essentialist difference. Spivak (1987) and Fuss (1989) have argued in favour of such a 'strategic essentialism'. They believe that the 'risk' of essentialism may be worth taking if framed from the vantage point of a dominated subject position. This will remain problematic if a challenge to one form of oppression leads to the reinforcement of another.

It may be over-ambitious, but it is imperative that we do not compartmentalise oppressions, but instead formulate strategies for challenging all oppressions on the basis of an understanding of how they interconnect and articulate.

References

Acker, J. (1989) 'The Problem with Patriarchy', *Sociology*, 23, 2: 325–40

Adams, M. L. (1989) 'Identity Politics', *Feminist Review* 31: 22–34

Ardill, S. and O'Sullivan, S. (1986) 'Upsetting an Applecart: Difference, Desire and Lesbian Sadomasochism', *Feminist Review*, 23: 31–57

Barrett, M. (1987) 'The Concept of Difference', *Feminist Review*, 26: 29–43

Barrett, M. and McIntosh, M. (1985) 'Ethnocentrism and Socialist-Feminist Theory', *Feminist Review*, 20: 23–49

Bhavnani, K. K. and Coulson, M. (1986) 'Transforming Socialist Feminism: The Challenge of Racism,' *Feminist Review*, 23: 81–92

Brah, A. (1987) 'Women of South Asian Origin in Britain: Issues and Concerns', *South Asia Research* 7, 1: 39–55

—— (1988) 'A Journey to Nairobi', in S. Grewal et al. (eds) *Charting the Journey*, London, Sheba

Brah, A. and Deem, R. (1986) 'Towards Anti-Sexist and Anti-Racist Schooling', *Critical Social Policy*, 16: 65–79

Brah, A. and Minhas, R. (1985) 'Structural Racism or Cultural Difference: Schooling for Asian Girls', in G. Weiner (ed), *Just A Bunch of Girls*, Milton Keynes, Open University Press

Bryan, B., Dadzie, S. and Scafe, S. (1985) *Heart of the Race*, London, Virago Press

Carby, H. (1982) 'White Woman Listen! Black Feminism and Boundaries of Sisterhood', in CCCS, *The Empire Strikes Back*, London, Hutchinson

Dalal, F. (1988) 'The Racism of Jung', *Race and Class*, 29, 3: 1–23

Feminist Review (1984) 'Many Voices, One Chant: Black Feminist Perspectives', *Feminist Review*, 17, Special Issue

—— (1986) 'Feedback: Feminism and Racism', *Feminist Review*, 22: 82–105

Fuss, D. (1989) *Essentially Speaking*, London, Routledge

Grewal, S., Kay, J., Landor, L., Lewis, G. and Parmar, P. (1988) *Charting The Journey*, London, Sheba

Hall, S. (1988) 'New Ethnicities', in *ICA Documents: Black Film British Cinema*, London, ICA

Hazareesingh, S. (1986) 'Racism and Cultural Identity: An Indian Perspective', *Dragons Teeth*, Issue 24

Knowles, C. and Mercer, S. (1990) 'Feminism and Anti-Racism', in A. X. Cambridge and S. Feuchtwang (eds), *Anti-racist Strategies*, Aldershot, Avebury

Lewis, G. (1990) 'Audre Lorde: Vignettes and Mental Conversations', *Feminist Review*, 34: 100–15

Mama, A. (1989) 'Violence against Black Women: Gender, Race, and State Responses', *Feminist Review*, 32: 30–48

Minh-ha, T. (1989) *Women, Native, Other: Writing Post Coloniality and Feminism*, Bloomington, Indiana University Press

Minsky, R. (1990) '"The Trouble is It's Ahistorical": The Problem of the Unconscious in Modern Feminist Theory', *Feminist Review*, 36: 4–15

Modood, T. (1988) '"Black" Racial Equality and Asian Identity', *New Community*, 14, 3: 397–404

Mohanty, C. T. (1988) 'Under Western Eyes: Feminist Scholarship and Colonial Discourses', *Feminist Review*, 30: 61–89

Parmar, P. (1982) 'Gender, Race and Class: Asian Women in Resistance' , in CCCS, *The Empire Strikes Back*, London, Hutchinson

Penley, C. (1989) *The Future of an Illusion: Film, Feminism and Psychoanalysis*, London, Routledge

Phoenix, A. (1987) 'Theories of Gender and Black Families', in Weiner, G. and Arnot, M. (eds) *Gender Under Scrutiny*, London: Hutchinson

Ramazanoglu, C. (1989) *Feminism and the Contradictions of Oppression*, London, Routledge

Rose, J. (1986) *Sexuality in the Field of Vision*, London, Verso

Rose, S., Kamin, J. and Lewontin, R. C. (1984) *Not In Our Genes*, Harmondsworth, Pelican

Segal, L. (1987) *Is The Future Female?* London, Virago Press

—— (1990) *Slow Motion: Changing Masculinities, Changing Men*, London, Virago Press

Spellman, E. V. (1988) *Inessential Woman: Problems of Exclusion in Feminist Thought*, London, Women's Press

Spivak, G. (1987) *In Other Worlds: Essays in Cultural Politics*, London, Methuen

Walby, S. (1990) *Theorizing Patriarchy*, Oxford, Basil Blackwell

Weedon, C. (1987) *Feminist Practice and Poststructuralist Theory*, Oxford, Basil Blackwell

Chapter 30

Ruth Frankenberg

WHITE WOMEN, RACE MATTERS
The social construction of whiteness

MY ARGUMENT IN THIS BOOK is that race shapes white women's lives. In the same way that both men's and women's lives are shaped by their gender, and that both heterosexual and lesbian women's experiences in the world are marked by their sexuality, white people *and* people of color live racially structured lives. In other words, any system of differentiation shapes those on whom it bestows privilege as well as those it oppresses. White people are "raced," just as men are "gendered." And in a social context where white people have too often viewed themselves as nonracial or racially neutral, it is crucial to look at the "racialness" of white experience. Through life history interviews, the book examines white women's places in the racial structure of the United States at the end of the twentieth century and views white women's lives as sites both for the reproduction of racism and for challenges to it.

If race shapes white women's lives, the cumulative name that I have given to that shape is "whiteness." Whiteness, I will argue in the pages that follow, has a set of linked dimensions. First, whiteness is a location of structural advantage, of race privilege. Second, it is a "standpoint," a place from which white people look at ourselves, at others, and at society.[1] Third, "whiteness" refers to a set of cultural practices that are usually unmarked and unnamed. This book seeks to begin exploring, mapping, and examining the terrain of whiteness.

There are two analytic dimensions to the book. In beginning to research the significance of race in white women's lives, I expected to learn about, and document, the daily experience of racial structuring and the ways race privilege might be crosscut by other axes of difference and inequality: class, culture, ethnicity, gender, and sexuality. From there, I hoped to comprehend how that daily experience shapes white women's perceptions of the significance of race in the social structure as a whole. As my work proceeded, however, a second dimension of analysis became equally significant, for it became clear that, as much as white women are located in – and speak from – physical environments shaped by race, we are also located in, and perceive our environments by means of, a set of discourses on race, culture, and society whose history spans this century and, beyond it, the broader sweep of Western expansion and colonialism.[2]

The material and discursive dimensions of whiteness are always, in practice, interconnected. Discursive repertoires may reinforce, contradict, conceal, explain, or "explain away" the materiality or the history of a given situation. Their interconnection, rather than material life alone, is in fact what generates "experience"; and, given this, the "experience" of living as a white woman in the United States is continually being transformed. Analytically, chapters of the book at times foreground that which is clearly concrete, tangible, and material about white women's experience of race – childhood, interracial relationships, political activism. At other times my focus is on issues of discourse – the meaning and apparent emptiness of "white" as a cultural identity; the political contexts, strengths, and limitations of different ways of "thinking through race"; the persistence of a discourse against interracial relationships.

Points of origin

This book emerged out of the 1980s, the decade in which white feminist women like myself could no longer fail to notice the critique of white feminist racism by feminist/radical women of color (a critique that had, in fact, marked the entire "second wave" of feminism).[3] More specifically, the research project had as its inception my own passage through that decade, and my own despair over the confused mess that white feminist women's response to charges of racism had collectively become by 1983–84. At worst – and it appeared from where I was standing that "worst" was much of the time – it seemed as though we white feminists had a limited repertoire of responses when we were charged with racism: confusion over accusations of racism; guilt over racism; anger over repeated criticism; dismissal; stasis. Feminist/radical women of color would also, it seemed, go through phases: anger over racism; efforts to communicate with white women about racism, despite it; frustration; and the temptation (acted upon temporarily or permanently) to withdraw from multiracial work.

Sites of productive multiracial feminist dialogue and activity existed, but they were few and far between.[4] Too often, I witnessed situations in which, as predominantly white feminist workplaces, classrooms, or organizations tried to move to more multiracial formats or agendas, the desire to work together rapidly deteriorated into painful, ugly processes in which racial tension and conflict actually seemed to get worse rather than better as the months went by. There were, it appeared, multiple ways in which the racism of the wider culture was simply being replayed in feminist locations.

Increasingly, this generated for me a sense of contradiction, a need to know more. As a white feminist, I knew that I had not previously known I was "being racist" and that I had never set out to "be racist." I also knew that these desires and intentions had had little effect on outcomes. I, as a coauthor, in however modest a way, of feminist agendas and discourse, was at best failing to challenge racism and, at worst, aiding and abetting it. How had feminism, a movement that, to my knowledge, intended to support and benefit all women, turned out not to be doing so?

In the early 1980s, I found myself straddling two sides of a "race line." On the one hand, I spent time sitting with white feminist university friends (roughly my age, roughly my class), at times in discussion groups and at other times more informally, as we struggled to make sense of the "racism question." The issue was anything but trivial to us. For one thing, it was startling in its implication that we were about to lose our newly found grip on the reins of liberation. (My friends and I were mostly socialist feminists. I, for one, liked the idea that, as women – apparently racially undefined – we had a distinctively radical purview of society, premised in part upon our status as structurally oppressed in relation to men – again apparently racially undefined. We were, however, analytically honest enough to realize that analyses such as that proposed by the Combahee River Collective, pointing to the structural subordination of women of color, and the potentially radical standpoint arising out of that position, changed all that!)[5] Because we were basically well-meaning individuals, the idea of being part of the problem of racism (something I had associated with extremists or institutions but not with myself) was genuinely shocking to us. And the issue was also terrifying, in the sense that we constantly felt that at any second we might err again with respect to racism, that we didn't know the rules and therefore didn't know how to prevent that happening. There was, perhaps, a way racism was disembodied in our discussions, sometimes an issue of standpoint, sometimes one of etiquette, and definitely an issue that provoked the intense frustration that came of not being able to "get it," or to "get it right."

Meanwhile, I was also spending a great deal of time with a friendship/support network of working-class women of color and white women, some of whom I had also first met through the university. These women were mainly parents (I was not), as well as older, poorer, and positioned very differently than I in the relations of racism in the United States. As I sat with them and traveled their daily pathways – thanks to an unexpectedly profound connection to one woman in particular – an inventory of meanings of racism, of racist behaviors began, de facto, to accumulate in my consciousness. In part, the inventory felt necessary to my ability to cope in those gatherings without offending anyone, but in part my friend made it her business to educate me. I learned by proximity what it means to navigate through a largely hostile terrain, to deal with institutions that do not operate by one's own logic nor in one's interests, and to need those institutions to function in one's favor if one is to survive, let alone to achieve. I realized for almost the first time in my life the gulf of experience and meaning between individuals differentially positioned in relation to systems of domination, and the profundity of cultural difference. (I say *almost* the first time because the culture shock of moving to the United States from Britain at the age of twenty-one had opened my eyes to the latter.)

Uniting the divergent experiences of being both a part of that network and a graduate student was, and remains, beyond my capability. In any case, doing so, and especially conveying the experiences of women of color, in general or in particular, is not my goal in any direct way.[6] More relevant here is the multifaceted impact of both affiliations, and their disjunction, on my own under-standing of racism and on the genesis of this project. When my white sisters and I struggled to comprehend a situation we did not understand and had not meant to create, critical questions for me were: How did this happen? How did we get into this mess? What do "they" mean when they tell us white feminism is racist? Translated into research, the same questions looked something like this:

- (How) does racism shape white women's lives?
- What are the social processes through which white women are created as social actors primed to reproduce racism within the feminist movement?
- (How) can white women's lives become sites of resistance to the reproduc-tion of racism?

Socialist feminism had also given me an analytical commitment to three axioms: first, that in "societies structured in dominance"[7] we, as feminists, must always remember that we act from within the social relations and subject positions we seek to change; second, that experience constructs identity; and, third, that there is a direct relationship between "experience" and "worldview" or "standpoint" such that any system of domination can be seen most clearly from the subject positions of those oppressed by it. As the project developed, applying those axioms to posi-tions of privilege or domination, or to subjects simultaneously privileged and oppressed, required me to complicate the second and third of these axioms. The first remained not only intact but even more challenging than it had appeared at the outset.

From the network predominantly made up of women of color, of which I was in some way a part, I carried into the research three realizations: first, that there is frequently a gulf of experience of racism between white people and people of color; second, that white women might have a range of awareness in relation to racism, with greater awareness based on, among other things, their long-term connectedness to communities of color (I did not, I should perhaps clarify, include myself in the latter category at that time); third, that there *is* a cultural/racial specificity to white people, at times more obvious to people who are not white than to white individuals.

What's in a name?

When I began work on this book, I described it as one that would examine the relationship between white women and racism. In the years between then and now, I have added another conceptualization of it, one that perhaps overlaps, without displacing, my earlier description. For I now also describe this book as a study of the social construction of whiteness.

Calling the project a study of white women and racism marked out the set of concerns that motivated me to begin it, namely, emphasizing that racism was and is something that shapes white women's lives, rather than something that people of color have to live and deal with in a way that bears no relationship or rele-vance to the lives of white people. For when white people – and I was especially concerned about white feminists, since the project had its origins in the feminist movement – look at racism, we tend to view it as an issue that people of color face and have to struggle with, but not as an issue that generally involves or implicates us. Viewing racism in this way has serious consequences for how white women look at racism, and for how antiracist work might be framed. With this view, white women can see antiracist work as an act of compassion for an "other," an optional, extra project, but not one intimately and organically linked to our own lives. Racism can, in short, be conceived as something external to us rather than as a system that shapes our daily experiences and sense of self.

The "and" in "white women and racism" implies, but does not really define, a link between the two terms. The need to speak of whiteness further specifies what is at stake in speaking of racism in relation to white people. To speak of "the social construction of whiteness" asserts that there are locations, discourses, and material relations to which the term "whiteness" applies. I argue in this book that whiteness refers to a set of locations that are historically, socially, politically, and culturally produced and, moreover, are intrinsically linked to unfolding relations of domination. Naming "whiteness" displaces it from the unmarked, unnamed status that is itself an effect of its dominance. Among the effects on white people both of race privilege and of the dominance of whiteness are their seeming normativity, their structured invisibility. This normativity is, however, unevenly effective. I will explore and seek to explain the invisibility and modes of visibility of racism, race difference, and whiteness. To look at the social construction of whiteness, then, is to look head-on at a site of dominance. (And it may be more difficult for white people to say "Whiteness has nothing to do with me – I'm not white" than to say "Race has nothing to do with me – I'm not racist.") To speak of whiteness is, I think, to assign *everyone* a place in the relations of racism. It is to emphasize that dealing with racism is not merely an option for white people – that, rather, racism shapes white people's lives and identities in a way that is inseparable from other facets of daily life.

To name whiteness also broadens the focus of my study, first because it makes room for the linkage of white subjects to histories not encompassed by, but connected to, that of racism: histories of colonialism and imperialism, and, secondarily, histories of assimilationism in the United States. Second, it allows me to view certain practices and subject positions as racialized (that is, structured by relations of race, usually alongside other structuring principles) rather than necessarily racist – although whiteness is for the most part racialized in the context of racism. Third, by examining and naming the terrain of whiteness, it may, I think, be possible to generate or work toward antiracist forms of whiteness, or at least toward antiracist strategies for reworking the terrain of whiteness.

Several distinct but, I believe, compatible theoretical and methodological orientations have been distilled into my approach. First, I share in a feminist commitment to drawing on women's daily lives as a resource for analyzing society. Second, I also share what is, in a sense, the converse of that commitment (and also an approach adopted by feminists): the belief that women's daily life experiences can only be adequately understood by "mapping" them onto broader social processes. Third, then, in order to better comprehend the social processes involved in the construction of whiteness, I have drawn on both theoretical and substantive analyses of race, racism, and colonialism in the United States and beyond.

Feminism: personal, political, theoretical

My decision, in 1984, to begin to explore whiteness through white women's life histories drew on a strong current of feminist thought that has used accounts of women's experience as ground for the construction and critique of theory and strategy. Since the consciousness-raising groups of the late 1960s, feminists have transformed accounts of personal experience into politicized and theorized terrain.[8] Through this process, the private, the daily, and the apparently trivial in women's activities came to be understood as shared rather than individual experiences, and as socially and politically constructed. The personal, in short, became political.

In addition to anchoring theories of gender and of society in general, women's accounts of personal experience have served as leverage points from which to criticize canons, whether of social theory or of political movements' agendas for change. During the "second wave" of feminism, from the late 1960s to the present, this kind of critique has challenged at least two canons that are especially relevant here. First, white feminists and feminist/radical women of color have criticized the lack of attention to gender domination – and effective male-centredness – of left and anti-racist movements. Second, feminist/radical women of color have challenged feminisms dominated by white-centered accounts of female experience. As women activists of a range of racial identities criticized theory based on male standpoints, it became clear that such standpoints obscured or ignored female subordination. And again, as women of color challenged white feminist accounts of "women's place" in society, the partiality of those accounts became visible.

Theorizing "from experience" rested on several key epistemological claims that, over time, became staples of feminist "common sense." The first of these was a critique of "objectivity" or "distance" as the best stances from which to generate knowledge. For, feminists argued, there is a link between where one stands in society and what one perceives. In addition, this epistemological stance made another, stronger claim: that the oppressed can see with the greatest clarity not only their own position but also that of the oppressor/privileged, and indeed the shape of social systems as a whole.[9]

To theorize "from experience" is thus to propose that there is no firm separation to be drawn between woman as member of society and woman as thinker, theorist, or activist. And therefore, as became clear in the context of a critique of white feminist racism, there are multiple problems in attempting (by default) to use white women's lives as a resource for analyzing gender domination in its entirety. Through the 1980s and into the present, work predominantly by women of color has been transforming feminist analysis, drawing attention to the white-centredness, and more generally the false universalizing claims, of much feminist discourse.[10] Ethnocentrism based on the racial specificity of white women's lives, it was pointed out, limits feminist analysis and strategy in relation to issues such as the family[11] and reproductive rights.[12] In the realm of theory, women of color were the first to advance frameworks for understanding the intersection in women's lives of gender, sexuality, race, and class[13] as well as visions and concepts of multiracial coalition work.[14]

The issue here was not only that white women's daily experiences *differed* from those of our sisters of color. If that had been the case, simply adding more accounts by women from a variety of racial locations would have resolved the problem. Instead, it became clear that white feminist women accounting for our experience were missing its "racialness" and that we were not seeing what was going on around us: in other words, we lacked an awareness of how our positions in society were constructed in relation to those of women – and men – of color.

One of my concerns, as I looked at white women's lives through a specifically racial lens, was, as a result, trying to comprehend those lacunae in perception. I needed to understand not only how race is lived, but also how it is seen – or more often, in my immediate political and social networks, *not* seen. In 1983 (before beginning the interviews for this book) I argued that the extent to which white women were "missing" or "not getting" the significance of race in either our or anyone else's experience had everything to do with standpoint: because we were race privileged, I argued, we were not in a structural position to see the effects of racism on our lives, nor the significance of race in the shaping of U.S. society.[15]

But by themselves, the material, daily relations of race cannot adequately explain whether, when, and in what terms white women perceive race as structuring either their own or anyone else's experience. The "dailiness" of racial separation and the inescapability of whiteness as a position of relative privilege cannot explain the *content* of white women's descriptions of others and of themselves – the ways, for example, masculinity and femininity are divided in racial and cultural terms. Similarly, they cannot explain why some white women learn or contest explicitly racist attitudes from childhood onward, while for others racial inequality is, in the words of one of the women I interviewed, "a reality enjoyed, but not acknowledged, a privilege lived in, but unknown."

Through the second half of the 1980s, several ongoing areas of feminist work were critical as I interviewed white women and analyzed their narratives. First, feminist scholars, mainly women of color, engaged in the painstaking work of refracting gender through the lenses of race and culture: examining, for example, how constructions of womanhood have always been racially and culturally marked and, in a racist society, even racially exclusive.[16] This work of rigorous specification exposes the universalism of the second wave of feminism as largely false – and calls, I suggest, for the reciprocal specification of *white* womanhood.[17] Second, feminists of all racial groups (but, as noted earlier, in a process initiated by women of color) made richer and more complex our theorizations of subjectivity and of society in general. Thus, for example, theorists described the "simultaneity" of the impact of race, class, and gender in shaping the lives of women of color[18] (and, I would add, white women too) and emphasized that subjectivity is "[displaced] across a multiplicity of discourses"[19] rather than produced out of the single axis of gender domination or the twin poles of capitalism and patriarchy. Third, more complex views of the subject produced correspondingly complex epistemologies, understood as emerging out of multifaceted political locations.[20]

While feminist women of color have worked to specify their histories and the contemporary shape of their lives in gendered and racial terms, however, a corresponding particularism has too often been lacking on the part of white feminist women. Thus, as white feminists participate alongside women of color in developing new theoretical articulations of "difference" and the "multiplicity" of women's experiences, there is, I fear, a danger that while increasingly theorists of color speak from concrete conceptualizations of what that multiplicity means to them, for white women visions of "difference" and "multiplicity" may remain abstract.

There are critical exceptions here. In a productive approach to questions about white women and racism, some white feminists began in the late 1970s and 1980s to examine through autobiography the ways race privilege and racism have shaped their own lives.[21] Thus, as these women and others like them continue to articulate feminist practice, they do so with a more multifaceted understanding of the social forces that made them who they are.

My study, and the exploration of white women's life histories upon which this book is based, share these women's commitment to careful and detailed analysis of how racism enters and shapes white women's lives, and to making more visible how our lives are embedded in a range of histories, political struggles, and social forces. My assumption here is one I've held since I first came to politics in the 1970s: that knowledge about a situation is a critical tool in dismantling it.

[. . .] The majority of the women I interviewed for this study did not consider themselves particularly interested in the racial order, or especially implicated in racism. All of them, however, said a great deal that was relevant to both. Successive chapters of this book have traveled the terrain of whiteness as material, cultural, and subjective location, exploring childhood, interracial relationships, discursive repertoires on race, and constructions of culture and identity. This process has, I hope, rendered more explicit and complex the meaning – or better, meanings – of whiteness in the contemporary United States. I have attempted to mark out the historical and contemporary conditions, material and discursive, that define and limit it. Through reading white women's life histories, I have examined the ways in which region, class, generation, and ethnicity further subdivide the terrain of lived experiences of whiteness. I have also indicated in preliminary ways how gender and sexuality may intersect with whiteness. In addition to marking out the limits and the "givenness" of whiteness, I have argued that the women I interviewed actively negotiated it. I have explored in detail the forms and content of that negotiation process.

Whiteness changes over time and space and is in no way a transhistorical essence. Rather, as I have argued, it is a complexly constructed product of local, regional, national, and global relations, past and present. Thus, the range of possible ways of living whiteness, for an individual white woman in a particular time and place, is delimited by the relations of racism *at that moment and in that place*. And if whiteness varies spatially and temporally, it is also a relational category, one that is coconstructed with a range of other racial and cultural categories, with class and with gender. This coconstruction is, however, fundamentally asymmetrical, for the term "whiteness" signals the production and reproduction of dominance rather than subordination, normativity rather than marginality, and privilege rather than disadvantage.[22]

In this text, the coconstruction of gender and whiteness were most visible in the arena of interracial sexuality and relationships. There, I argued, first, that the discourse against interracial relationships entails specifically racialized constructions of white femininity in relation to racialized masculinities. Second, I suggested that white women and men were placed, respectively, as victim and rescuer in the discourse against interracial sexuality, vis-à-vis the supposed sexual threat posed by men of color toward white women. Third, and in a sense exceeding the terms of the discourse against interracial sexuality, I suggested that white heterosexual women's choices of primary partners at times involved negotiations over preferred modes of living out femininity and living with men. Fourth, I argued that both heterosexual and lesbian white women's strategies for coping with the burdens that racism placed on interracial couples seemed at times to be distinctively "female" ones.

To speak about the intersections of femininity or femaleness and whiteness in the context of sexuality and partnerships is, however, only the beginning of the story. A range of further questions, most of which are beyond the scope of this study, present themselves. One set of questions concerns childhood. Here one might ask, for example, whether white boys and white girls use their environments in different ways. Were this so, boys might have different contexts from girls in which to interact with boys and girls, or men and women, of color. In relation to the fearful response of many white girls to peers of color, one can also ask whether white boys and white girls are socialized differently with regard to racial Others and hence whether white boys might be more hostile than fearful in interracial situations. (In fact, this difference, if it did exist, would be partly explicable in the context of the discourse on interracial sexuality just discussed.) Here I am, of course, speculating, for questions of this kind would have to be addressed in the context of a study that included both women and men.

How does the interweaving of material and discursive limitation, "local" variation, ascription, agency, and self-consciousness translate into individual trajectories through and within whiteness? On one level, it is impractical to unravel these strands, since they are lived, second by second, as interwoven. However, it is also possible analytically – if artificially – to separate these strands and place them on a continuum of fixity and mutability. And it is also, I suggest, necessary to do so, for such an exercise might expose more clearly the points of pressure, of potential challenge to racial domination.

[. . .] White women also inhabited as given a universe of discourses on race, on whiteness, on racial Others, and on racism, each of which could be identified temporally and spatially in terms of their emergence, but that coexisted in the present in uneven and complex ways. The key discursive repertoires in question here were, first, modes of naming culture and difference associated with west European colonial expansion; second, elements of "essentialist" racism again linked to European colonialism but also critical as rationale for Anglo settler colonialism and segregationism in what is now the USA; third, "assimilationist" or later "color- and power-evasive" strategies for thinking through race first articulated in the early decades of this century; and, fourth, what I have called "race-cognizant" repertoires that emerged in the latter half of the twentieth century and were linked both to U.S. liberation movements and to broader global struggles for decolonization. For the most part, I have argued, a color- and power-evasive repertoire was dominant, at least as a public language of race, in the times and places at which these interviews took place. Nonetheless, elements of the other repertoires were also in play.

This discursive environment was given, then, according to a complex logic and temporality. For I have argued that these white women lived, negotiated, appropriated, and rejected, at some times more consciously and intentionally than at others, the entire array of discursive repertoires. It was possible to identify individual trajectories of change with respect to discursive repertoires, which themselves mapped onto much broader social processes, both national and regional. Individual women at times self-consciously deployed one discursive repertoire against another (color evasiveness against essentialist racism, race cognizance against color evasiveness), and at other times appeared simultaneously caught within and critical of specific elements of one or another. In these ways, discourse was "given" and yet more fluid than the material relations of race. In ways that defied dualistic analysis, the women were apparently both self-conscious about the discursive history of race and not conscious of it; apparently both capable and not capable of changing their discursive repertoires.

In arguing that race shapes white women's lives, then, I am making a claim with two linked dimensions. First, white women's lives are marked by their diverse locations in the materiality of the racial order. But, second, white women's senses of self, other, identity, and worldview are also racialized, for they emerged here as repositories of the key elements of the history of the idea of race, in the United States and beyond. The white subject and the white imaginary thus by no means confine themselves to the present in their construction, but rather draw, consciously and unconsciously, on moments in the racial order long past in material terms.

[. . .] Attention to the construction of white "experience" is important, both to transforming the meaning of whiteness and to transforming the relations of race in general. This is crucial in a social context in which the racial order is normalized and rationalized rather than upheld by coercion alone. Analyzing the connections between white daily lives and discursive orders may help make visible the processes by which the stability of whiteness — as location of privilege, as culturally normative space, and as standpoint — is secured and reproduced. In this context, reconceptualizing histories and refiguring racialized landscapes are political acts in themselves.

Analyzing the construction of whiteness is important as a means of reconceptualizing the grounds on which white activists participate in antiracist work. In that regard, this book may help generate a checklist of existing conceptualizations of both whiteness and racism and the potential strengths and weaknesses of each. I have, for example, criticized the "power-evasive" view that reduces racism to individual, intentional acts. Not only does that view distract white people's attention from the results of individual actions, it also evades a much broader range of historical and contemporary processes through which the racial order is maintained. Again, I have criticized conceptions of white complicity with racism that deploy as metaphor colonialism or neocolonialism but do not trace in practical terms the real and varying relationships of white people to either project. Operating as, in a sense, secularized metaphors for "sin" and "evil," such conceptions are in fact simultaneously reductive and excessive, and actually have the potential to disempower and short-circuit white antiracism. By contrast, I have argued here that white complicity with racism should be understood — and challenged — in the complex, multifaceted terms in which it operates.

Examining the coconstruction of whiteness and other racial identities is useful because it may help lead white activists (and also, for that matter, activists of color) away from the incorporation of "old" discursive elements into "new" strategies. I have, for example, argued that we need to displace the colonial construction of whiteness as an "empty" cultural space, in part by refiguring it as constructed and dominant rather than as norm. Without reconceptualizing culture, we run the risk of reifying and dehistoricizing *all* cultural practices, valorizing or romanticizing some while discounting others as not cultural at all. But a dualistic framework is retained, for example, in new curricular programs that include attention to nondominant cultures but do not simultaneously reconceptualize or reexamine the status, content, and formation of whiteness. Similarly, references to women of color, but not white women, as "racial-ethnic women," implicitly suggest that race does *not* shape white identities or experience.

Beyond a point, however, the reinterpretation of white women's experience and the historicizing of whiteness are simply retellings of the same tale. Analysis of the place of whiteness in the racial order can and should be, rather than an end in itself, only one part of a much broader process of social change leveled both at the material relations of race and at discursive repertoires. It is not, in any case, realistic or meaningful to reconceptualize whiteness outside of racial domination when, in practical terms, whiteness still confers race privilege. It would be similarly naive to imagine that political will alone might bring about the kinds of shifts necessary to challenge those discourses that most effectively stabilize the racial order.

Ultimately, the process of altering present and future meanings of whiteness is inextricably connected to that of altering the meanings of other, coconstructed racial and cultural identities. That process is in turn linked to the effort to transform the racial order in both material and discursive terms and to alter, perhaps, more than anything, the distribution of power. Clearly, that project is not individual but collective. Nor does it rest with white activists alone, so much as with collective actions by people from a range of locations in the racial order.

Notes

1   Following Nancy Hartsock, "The Feminist Standpoint: Developing the Ground for a Specifically Feminist Historical Materialism," in *Discovering Reality*, ed. Sandra Harding and Merrill B. Hintikka (Dordrecht: D. Riedel, 1983), 283–310, the word "standpoint" has two linked meanings. The first is the perspective that arises out of a class's or gender's received and unanalyzed engagement with its material environment, perceived through the worldview of the dominant group. The second is the self-conscious perspective on self and society that arises out of a class (or gender) grouping's critical apprehension of itself and its location in relation to the system it inhabits. With respect to gender, Hartsock styles the former "women's standpoint" and the latter "feminist standpoint." No such distinction is currently available for my purposes. In referring here to whiteness as a standpoint, I intend, loosely, an analogy with Hartsock's "women's standpoint." The most appropriate analogy for Hartsock's "feminist standpoint" would

be "white antiracist standpoint." At points in this book, I and some interviewees articulate elements of a white antiracist standpoint. Finally, it should be emphasized that the analogy is by no means perfect, since both "feminist" and "proletarian" standpoints refer to the self-conscious engagements of oppressed groups with their own positioning, whereas, of course, a "white antiracist standpoint" refers to self-conscious and self-critical engagement with a *dominant* position in the racial order.

2   "Discourses" may be understood in this book as historically constituted bodies of ideas providing conceptual frameworks for individuals, made material in the design and creation of institutions and shaping daily practices, interpersonal interactions, and social relations. "Western" is capitalized here to draw attention to its status as a discursive rather than a geographical construct. In the geographical sense, "west" is of course a relative term (tied to "east," "north," and "south," as well as to a particular point in space from which a given calculation emanates). But "west," *in* the West, tends to be understood to refer to the capitalist European countries, North America, Australia, New Zealand, and, on occasion, Japan(!). Discursively, too, "West" and "Western" are relational terms, constructed out of opposition to non-Western Others or "Orientals." Westernness implies a particular, dominative relationship to power, colonial expansion, a belonging to center rather than margin in a global capitalist system, and a privileged relationship to institutions – be they academic or oriented to mass communication – for the production of knowledge. Not all people in the (pseudogeographical) West/west are, within the terms of a discourse on West-non-West, Westerners. This is because the cultural content of Westernness draws on Christian, rationalist, north and west European customs and patterns of thought and because, discursively, Westernness is racially exclusive and tends to mean only Caucasian. Thus, for example, Ward Churchill, in describing the stages of European colonization of Native Americans, remarks that, "In the beginning, troops arrive to butcher the indigenous population. Later, the 'savages' are seen as worthy of being 'educated' and 'civilized' to white, *Western* standards, dealing a devastating blow to the cultures possessed by the survivors of the slaughter." Ward Churchill, *Fantasies of the Master Race: Literature, Cinema and the Colonization of American Indians*, ed. Annette Jaimes (Monroe, Maine: Common Courage Press, 1992), 264 (emphasis mine).

3   I use "second wave" to refer to feminism from the late 1960s to the present. "Third wave" has at times been used to characterize, optimistically, the emergence of distinctively multiracial feminisms through the 1980s.

4   Examples of the published record of Black–white feminist dialogue in particular are Tia Cross, Frieda Klein, Barbara Smith, and Beverley Smith, "Face-to-Face, Day-to-Day: Racism CR [Consciousness Raising]," *Heresies* 3: 3, 66–67; Elly Bulkin, Minnie Bruce Pratt, and Barbara Smith, *Yours in Struggle: Three Feminist Perspectives on Anti-Semitism and Racism* (Brooklyn, N.Y.: Long Haul Press, 1984; Ithaca, N.Y.: Firebrand, 1988); Gloria I. Joseph and Jill Lewis, *Common Differences: Conflicts in Black and White Feminist Perspectives* (Garden City, N.Y.: Anchor, 1981). See also Chandra Talpade Mohanty, Ann Russo, and Lourdes Torres, eds., *Third World Women and the Politics of Feminism* (Bloomington: Indiana University Press, 1991), ix, for reference to the conference Common Differences: Third World Women and Feminist Perspectives, University of Illinois, Urbana-Champaign, April 1983.

5   Combahee River Collective, "A Black Feminist Statement," in *Capitalist Patriarchy and the Case for Socialist Feminism*, ed. Zillah R. Eisenstein (New York: Monthly Review Press, 1979), 362–72. The statement argues for the need to analyze U.S. society in terms of four interlocking axes of oppression based on race, class, gender, and sexuality. It also articulates an identity politics that linked the positioning of Black women who are targets of all four systems of domination with a unique purview and political agency.

6   In fact, bell hooks and Chela Sandoval, two women I met at that time at the University of California, Santa Cruz, have written precisely about the political and strategic implications for women of color of their positioning within webs of power and systems of domination. Both of these women have been critical to my thinking about racism, and Sandoval's work has been crucial to my thinking about power and political strategy. bell hooks, *Ain't I a Woman? Black Women and Feminism* (Boston: South End Press, 1981); *Feminist Theory: From Margin to Center* (Boston: South End Press, 1984); *Talking Back: Thinking Feminist, Thinking Black* (Boston: South End Press, 1989). Chela Sandoval, "The Struggle Within: Women respond to Racism – Report on the National Women's Studies Conference, Storrs Connecticut" (Oakland, California: Occasional Paper, Center for Third World Organizing, 1982) (revised version of this paper is published in *Making Face, Making Soul, Haciendo Caras: Creative and Critical Perspectives by Women of Color*, ed. Gloria Anzaldúa, [San Francisco: Aunt Lute, 1990], 55–71); "U.S. Third World Feminism: The Theory and Method of Oppositional Consciousness in the Postmodern World," *Genders* 10 (Spring 1991): 1–24.

7   I owe this term to Stuart Hall, "Race, Articulation, and Societies Structured in Dominance," in *UNESCO: Sociological Theories, Race and Colonialism* (Paris: UNESCO Press, 1980), 305–45.

8   For accounts of the uses and effectiveness of consciousness raising in the second wave of feminism, see Anna Coote and Beatrix Campbell, *Sweet Freedom: The Struggle for Women's Liberation* (London: Picador, 1982); Alice Echols, *Daring to Be Bad: Radical Feminism in America, 1967–75* (Minneapolis: University of Minnesota Press, 1989); Katie King, "The Situation of Lesbianism as Magical Sign: Contests for Meaning in the U.S. Women's Movement, 1968–72," *Communications* 9 (1986): 65–91.

9   From a white feminist perspective, the clearest articulation of this position is Hartsock, "The Feminist Standpoint." Articulations of a similar epistemological stance by U.S. women of color include Combahee River Collective," A Black Feminist Statement"; Aida Hurtado, "Relating to Privilege: Seduction and Rejection in the Subordination of White Women and Women of Color," *Signs* 14, no. 4 (1989): 833–55; and Patricia Hill Collins, "The Social Construction of Black Feminist Thought," *Signs* 14, no. 4 (1989): 745–73.

10   A key text here is Cherríe Moraga and Gloria Anzaldúa, eds., *This Bridge Called My Back: Writings by Radical Women of Color* (Watertown, Mass.: Persephone, 1981; New York: Kitchen Table Women of Color Press, 1983).

11   Among others, see Hazel Carby, "White Woman Listen! Black Feminism and the Boundaries of Sisterhood," Center for Contemporary Cultural Studies, *The Empire Strikes Back: Race and Racism in '70s Britain* (London: Hutchinson, 1981), 212–35; Kum Kum Bhavnani and Margaret Coulson, "Transforming Socialist Feminism: The Challenge of Racism," *Feminist Review* 23 (Summer 1986): 81–92.

12   See, for example, Angela Y. Davis, *Women, Race and Class* (New York: Random House, 1981), 202–21.

13   The founding text here is, I believe, the Combahee River Collective's "A Black Feminist Statement."

14   For example, Bernice Johnson Reagon, "Coalition Politics: Turning the Century," in *Home Girls: A Black Feminist Anthology*, ed. Barbara Smith (New York: Kitchen Table Women of Color Press, 1983), 356–69; Cherríe Moraga and Gloria Anzaldúa's concept of "El Mundo Zurdo/The Left Handed World," *This Bridge Called My Back*, 195–96.

15   Ruth Frankenberg, "Different Perspectives: Interweaving Theory and Practice in Women's Work," qualifying essay, Board of Studies in the History of Consciousness, University of California, Santa Cruz, 1983.

16   Among such developments, Chicana scholars have examined how the figure of La Malinche constructs Chicana femininity (for example, Norma Alarcon, "Chicana's Feminist Literature: A Revision Through Malintzin/or Malintzin: Putting Flesh Back on the Object," Moraga and Anzaldúa. *This Bridge Called My Back*, 182–90. Similarly, Hortense Spillers builds on the work of African–American historians to show how, given the material conditions of Black women's lives, they were "excluded" from racially dominant notions of femininity, "Mama's Baby, Papa's Maybe: An American Grammar book," *Diacritics*, Summer 1987: 65–81. Rayna Green, in "The Pocahontas Perplex: The Image of Indian Women in American Culture," in *Unequal Sisters*, ed. Ellen Carol DuBois and Vicki L. Ruiz (New York: Routledge, 1990), 15–21, analyzes the ideological construction of the figure of Native American women within a colonial matrix.

17   Such work has been undertaken by, for example, Gloria I. Joseph and Jill Lewis, *Common Differences*, who examine the differences in perspective, experience, and sense of self between white and Black women; Vron Ware, *Beyond the Pale: White Women, Racism and History* (London: Verso, 1992), who articulates in particular the place of white womanhood in the discursive economies of racism and imperialism; and Teresa L. Amott and Julie A. Matthaei, R*ace, Gender, and Work: A Multicultural History of Women in the United States* (Boston: South End Press, 1991), who by juxtaposing and contrasting the histories of U.S. women across racial and ethnic lines enable greater attention to the specification of gender by race and class.

18   Patricia Zavella, "The Problematic Relationship of Feminism and Chicana Studies," *Women's Studies* 17 (1988): 123–34.

19   Norma Alarcon, "The Theoretical Subjects of *This Bridge Called My Back* and Anglo-American Feminism," in *Haciendo Caras*, ed. Anzaldúa, 356–69.

20   Chandra Talpade Mohanty, "Feminist Encounters: Locating the Politics of Experience," *Copyright* 1, no. 1 (1984); Donna J. Haraway, "Situated Knowledges: The Science Question and the Privilege of Partial Perspective," in Donna J. Haraway, *Simians, Cyborgs and Women: The Reinvention of Nature* (New York: Routledge, 1991), 183–202.

21   Foremost in this regard were Elly Bulkin ("Hard Ground: Jewish Identity, Racism and Anti-Semitism") and Minnie Bruce Pratt ("Identity: Skin, Blood, Heart") in Bulkin, Pratt, and Smith, *Yours in Struggle*, 89–228 and 9–64; Mab Segrest, *My Mama's Dead Squirrel: Lesbian Essays on Southern Culture* (Ithaca, N.Y.: Firebrand, 1985); Adrienne Rich, "Disloyal to Civilization: Feminism, Racism, Gynephobia," in Adrienne Rich, *On Lies, Secrets and Silence: Selected Prose, 1966–1978* (New

York: Norton, 1979), 275–310; and Adrienne Rich, "Notes Toward a Politics of Location," in Adrienne Rich, *Blood, Bread and Poetry: Selected Prose, 1979–1985* (New York: Norton, 1986), 210–31.

22   As I have repeatedly emphasized, this does not mean that all white individuals have absolute privilege, any more than all male individuals have absolute privilege. Rather, it means that individuals whose ascribed characteristics include whiteness (or maleness) will find the benefits of that ascription accruing to them.

Chapter 31

Barbara Christian

BLACK FEMINISM AND THE ACADEMY[1]

WHEN I WAS ASKED TO SPEAK at this conference on "Feminisms in the Twenty-first Century," at first I chose a topic that asked the question whether feminism in America is still largely conceived of as a white movement by most American institutions. Despite the impact the Anita Hill/Clarence Thomas hearings had on feminism in this country, I was amazed that when the media focused its attention on the women's movement as it did in 1992, it still featured primarily white women as its major spokespersons. For example, *Time Magazine* in 1992 featured on its oh-too-predictable March cover, Gloria Steinem and Susan Faludi, representing two generations of the second wave of feminism.[2] Even *The Atlantic*, by featuring Wendy Kaminer's "Feminism's Identity Crisis," got into the fray, perhaps because of first lady (a title I hate) Hillary Clinton's media profile. But while Wendy Kaminer's clearly conservative (backlash) piece did mention the white feminist theorist Carol Gilligan's work, it did not indicate that African-American women scholars had contributed anything of worth to American feminism(s).[3] Apparently Wendy Kaminer still thinks that feminism is a strictly-white upper-class phenomenon emanating from prestigious universities such as Harvard.

So much for media writers. As I thought about the concerns of this conference, however, who my likely audience would be – that of the smarter and purer folk in the academy where I am situated – I decided it would be more appropriate, more honest for me to assess my own site, hence the title of this exploration, "Diminishing Returns: Can Black Feminism(s) Survive the Academy?" [original title].

I hope it is clear to everyone here that black feminisms have existed for a long time – that since the nineteenth century, black women such as activist Sojourner Truth, poet Frances Harper, and educator Anna Julia Cooper had articulated a position that stressed the interrelatedness of racism, sexism, and classism as central to this society's structure. I name these women's primary commitments because I want us all to be clear that African-American feminists have operated in many arenas, a fact that gets left out in cultural histories, even on the left.[4] Radical Black women such as turn-of-the-century feminist Ida B. Wells' hard-hitting journalistic pieces about lynchings demonstrate how racism and sexism are not separate entities, but are interdependent modes of domination which affect us all, for contrary to much contemporary white feminist theorizing, racism often expresses itself in sexist terms and sexism in racist terms. Works on African-American women are not just examples of some cultural nationalist problem, but rather a mirror image of this country's inability to deal with its hierarchical inequities. Too often race issues are seen as the "problems" of blacks and people of color, gender issues as the "problems" of women.

Contemporary black feminists have continued and developed their foremothers' tradition – especially in the literature they have produced – in which they have claimed themselves as subjects. Scholar Deborah King put it this way in her essay, "Multiple Jeopardies, Multiple Consciousness": "A black feminist ideology fundamentally challenges the interstructure of the oppressions of racism, sexism, and classism both in the dominant society and within movements for liberation."[5]

I hope it is clear also that the second wave of black feminist thought and practice did not originate or does not now reside primarily in the academy despite all the hoopla about political correctness. Rather, its roots were in popular movements, in the civil rights, black power, and women's movements of the 1960s and early 1970s as exemplified by the many voices of black women collected in Toni Cade's edition of *The Black Woman* (1970). Black feminist thought and practice is very much alive outside the academy, whether its proponents use that label or not, although I could not prove that since most studies conducted by American white women demonstrate the incidence of feminism among American women without taking into account in any real way the ways in which African-American women might frame that concept quite differently. Some African-American women call themselves womanists, the word coined by writer Alice Walker to distinguish themselves and their specific perspective from white feminists. Other African-American women, like many of their women of color and white counterparts, may not call themselves feminists or even womanists, yet practice the tenets that that point of view signifies.[6]

As was true of the black women's rights movement of the nineteenth century, contemporary black feminisms have been articulated in many arenas, an important one being the literature of African-American women such as Alice Walker, Audre Lorde, Toni Morrison, and June Jordan. As I have already noted in my essay, "But What Do We Think We're Doing Anyway? The State of Black Feminist Criticism(s) or My Version of a Little bit of History,"[7] in the seventies, the academy scarcely acknowledged the existence of black women in major knowledge areas such as literature or history, nor had a black feminist inquiry been initially central to the establishment of African-American and women's studies in the academy. For much of that decade, the subject of race was usually associated with men and the subject of gender with white women for even the most astute intellectuals. The few black women scholars who existed in the university often fell between the cracks or just managed to straddle the apparently divided terrains of race and gender.

By the early eighties, however, scholars had established a small but influential place in the academy for black women's studies, mostly as a result of the intensity and quality of African-American women's literature and scholarship. A few of us were able to excavate the neglected histories and literatures of African-American women, to articulate the interrelatedness of race, class, and gender as the core of a black feminist inquiry, and to critique the male bias of race analysis and the white bias of gender studies. The number and quality of these studies are too vast for me to cite in this essay. Suffice it to say that black feminist inquiry in all of the major disciplines of the university as well as in interdisciplinary areas, such as women's studies, African-American studies, and diaspora studies, has been substantive. As well, in collaboration with other women of color, in anthologies such as *This Bridge Called My Back* and *Making Face, Making Soul*, African-American women writers and scholars have challenged the concept of a universalized woman. As a result, the editors of the book *Feminist Theory in Practice and Process*, a collection of essays published in the women's studies journal *Signs* during the decade of the 1980s, could note "the shift away from an undifferentiated concept of woman," in recent feminist theorizing:

> Just as one of the first acts in the development of a feminist theory was to reject the standpoint and experiences of white men as normative, so too, one of the first acts in developing black feminist theory has been to reject the perspectives of white women as normative, focusing instead on the concrete everyday experiences of black women as the basis for theory making.[8]

Black feminist inquiry also has had a major effect on the study of race, so that male African-American studies specialists increasingly include African-American women in their studies – to the extent that some of the major scholars in the area of African-American women's literature are African-American men. Some African-American women critics have noticed that contemporary societal institutions still tend to choose African-American men over African-American women to be the "real" experts and spokesmen when it comes to critiquing the relationship between race and gender, again reflecting the hierarchical structure of our society in which men are always better than women.[9]

Fortunately, some male scholars are beginning to explore the other side of African-American women's studies, that constructions of masculinity in relation to race are often camouflaged in our society. Major contemporary African-American male writers such as John Wideman and Clarence Major credit African-American women's intellectual questionings in the 1970s with opening spaces for them to investigate themselves as men in relationships with family and female and male lovers, as opposed to the white/black border wars, relegated to black male writers of the past. Such an anthology is Joseph Beane's *Brother to Brother*. Some of my graduate students are engaged in this endeavor. An important anthology called *The African-American Black Male, His Person, Status and Family*, edited by Richard Myers and Jacob Gorden, which places the intersection of race and gender in relation to men, is about to be published. As well, major intellectuals such as Cornel West and Manning Marable have used black feminist ideological positions in their analyses of black community contexts, and possibilities for liberation.[10]

African diasporic and postcolonial feminist studies also have developed in the last decade. Because of its marginality in US studies and its long tradition of subjugation to colonial/racial points of view that extend even beyond the celebration of left male critics' idealization of male Caribbean writer Frantz Fanon's writings, this field has understood the importance of one of the first tenets of black feminist scholarship – that of intervention and change. Postcolonial scholar Chandra Mohanty has pointed out that feminist scholarship:

> is not the mere production of knowledge about a certain subject. It is a political praxis which counters and resists the totalizing imperative of age-old "legitimate" and "scientific" bodies of knowledge.[11]

Critiques originating in black feminist thought, then, have had a sure effect on the restructuring of traditional disciplines. Positioned at the vortex of so many discourses that seem to be vying with one another for centrality, black feminist critics have had to rethink traditional constructs in the academy and the world. Many of my sister/colleagues, as well as graduate students with whom I work, have often asked ourselves the question, "To whom do I belong? Black studies? Women's studies? A specific discipline such as English or sociology?" Black feminist scholar Patricia Hill Collins recalls that she:

> found [her] training as a social scientist inadequate to the task of studying the subjugated knowledge of a black woman's standpoint. This is because subordinate groups have long had to use alternate ways to create independent self-definitions and self-valuations and to rearticulate them through our own specialists.[12]

In creating alternate systems, black feminist critics have helped to validate the necessity for interdisciplinary approaches, such as those of cultural studies as well as the possibility of redefining the very concept of what it means to be an intellectual, since so many of our thinkers have resided outside the academy or even outside traditional black institutions.

But not only has black feminist inquiry critiqued the race bias of white feminisms, the gender bias of race matters, the usually neglected subject of class, the too-rigid boundaries of academic systems, it exists also for itself. In other words, black feminist thought is not only a critique of other systems that is at the service of "the real" points of view, it is also a distinctive, one is tempted to say, a coherent perspective which places black women, including those from the rest of this hemisphere and Africa, at the center of its inquiry. That distinctiveness is obvious especially in the literature that African-American women have produced during the last two decades in which I would insist they have been major theorizers about gender, race, class, and sexual preference. Toni Morrison's receipt of the 1993 Nobel Prize for Literature – the first time a black woman, and an African-American – has been so honored is a sign that African-American women finally are being perceived as intellectuals within their own right, nationally and internationally. Increasingly, black feminist thought is also being articulated in critical works such as bell hooks' *Talking Back: Thinking Feminist, Thinking Black*; Patricia Hill Collins' *Black Feminist*

Thought; and anthologies such as *Home Girls*, edited by Barbara Smith; *Wild Women in the Whirlwind*, edited by Braxton and McLaughlin; and *Changing Our Own Words*, edited by Cheryl Wall.

Without question, as the applications to the Ph.D. Program in ethnic studies at my university indicate, more and more students are studying African-American women's thought, especially in the area of literature. I, for example, now find myself, as I am sure most of my sister/colleagues do, "an academic mother to more children than I could have possibly imagined, and to types of children beyond my conjuring . . . at a time when my white counterparts are already academic grandmothers."[13]

Clearly black feminisms no longer are completely absent in the academy and have had some effect on the ways in which we think about the intersections of race, gender, and class, as well as the accomplishments and thought of black women. And yet – I have entitled this essay "Diminishing Returns: Can Black Feminisms Survive the Academy?" for, though there have been some advances, they have been achieved at much cost and have not really changed the landscape or the population of the academy. What central problems do black women and, therefore, black feminisms face in the academy in the last decade of this century?

One especially important dilemma we face is who black feminist academics of the future will be. My experience during the last few years is that although African-American women's thought and literature, and intersections of race, class, gender, and even sexual preference are being focused on by some graduate students, few of them are black women or men. Of course, not all black women in the academy do feminist scholarship, nor is all black feminist scholarship done by black women. Yet, although black women are not all the same, they do bring a certain urgency to this area of study precisely because it affects them directly and emanates from their personal and historical contexts since black feminist thought, for them, is not only and primarily an artifact to be studied. It would be a tremendous loss, a distinct irony, if some version of black feminist inquiry exists in the academy to which black women are not major contributors.

My experience that there are few African-Americans entering graduate school, is verified by statistics. In 1991, according to *The Journal of Blacks in Higher Education*, only 2.3 per cent of the Ph.D.s in all academic disciplines awarded in this country went to blacks, a percentage far below that of Ph.D.s awarded in the 1970s to blacks, such as myself. There was a slight gain in overall black graduate enrollments in the late 1980s, but progress occurred mostly at professional schools such as business, law, and medicine. The *Journal* also included a survey of the status of African-Americans on the faculties of American colleges and universities. Although there were gains in the 1970s, there was a slowdown, then an abrupt drop during the Reagan/Bush years of the percentage of blacks at predominantly white institutions. The *Journal* points out that roughly half of the 19,000 black professors in the United States teach at the predominantly black colleges and universities – that is, one hundred colleges as opposed to the 3,000 "historically white" colleges and universities.[14] Even then, only 2.5 per cent of all professors in the country, 4.2 per cent of associate professors, 6.0 per cent of assistant professors, and 6.7 per cent of instructors were black.[15] How are African-American women faring? In 1987, African-American women received 54 per cent of the doctoral degrees awarded blacks, that is 2 per cent of the doctorates awarded that year. In 1985, 0.6 per cent of all full professors were black women, 1.4 per cent were associate professors, 2.5 per cent were assistant professors, and 3.2 per cent were instructors.[16]

Even I, suspicious of numbers and statistical studies, could see that the situation for African-American women graduate students and faculty is dismal. While I could have some measure of pride in the fact that such a small percentage of black feminist academics had had such a significant impact on intellectual inquiry in the 1970s and 1980s, any optimism I have about our situation was greatly outweighed by the reality of the minuscule number of black women entering the academy. Why are African-Americans, and especially women, not going into academic areas at a time when issues of race and gender have become increasingly acknowledged as central to intellectual inquiry?

I recall the many students I've worked with, very bright, intellectually oriented, and interested in graduate study, who decided to go into business, law, or medicine. I think about the many African-American students who didn't have the opportunity to make such a choice since they had not finished high school or did not have *access* even to the knowledge about these choices. For them, making it big in music or sports continues to be their only option out of poverty or the violence of an early death.

Some of us African-American academics have focused much of our attention on those students who manage to graduate from high school. I've learned in my 20 years at University of California, Berkeley, that students of color who supposedly could not succeed in college often did very well when they learned about, were inspired by, the possibilities that other students had taken for granted from the time they were born. Still, many of those students, though interested in pursuing graduate study, moved into more "practical" areas such as the professional schools, community activism, and journalism. They felt, for some reason, that life in the academy would be unrewarding. While life in the professions might be difficult, at least they could make some money and pay back the debts their education incurred, even as they might be able possibly to affect our contemporary society.

As I was working on this essay, a new volume was published, exploring specifically the issue of black women faculties' survival in white universities. Called *Spirit, Space and Survival: African-American Women in (White) Academe*, this anthology, a collection of black women's voices from inside the academy, voices concerns that we black women faculty talk about when we see each other at conferences, usually the only time we do see each other since so many of us are the only black woman, or one of a few at our respective universities. In fact this volume grew out of such a meeting at a conference. The editors, Joy James and Ruth Farmer, say that the objective of the volume is to examine the voices of African-American women "struggling with Eurocentric disciplines, students, faculty and administrators in predominantly white institutions." Most African-American women faculty, they inform us, are at the bottom of the academic hierarchy and, even in comparison to the fewer black male academics, are paid less, have higher workloads, and get fewer returns. For most African-American academics, research and writing does not come easy, beleaguered as they are by demands within their institutions as well as in their families and communities, demands that they feel they must meet if they are to fulfill their many roles in their diverse communities.

I am aware of how better off African-American women are in the academy than they are in many sectors of our community. After all, we have the possibility of doing work we like to do, an opportunity that probably only 2 per cent of the planet has got. Still it is important that we raise our voices about the inequities we face in our terrain and how it affects our daily lives, for our "complaints" nuance a site of possible resistance.

In their introduction to their courageous volume, Joy James and Ruth Farmer remind us that African-American women academics work in environments which often are not only nonsupportive but, at times, outright hostile. They (we) are expected to perform mightily – with little reward – and to be grateful that we are allowed in the halls of learning. Overworked and underrecognized, we are forced to cope with office and university politics as well as the racism, sexism, and homophobia inherent in these environments and the larger society.[17]

Perhaps my students are smarter than I think. Salaries paid to business, law, and medical graduates are considerably more than those paid to nontenured, even tenured professors. For African-Americans, most of whom come from families who are struggling to survive, the issue of monetary returns is not a mercenary concern but a communal one. In addition, as Martin Anderson, as senior fellow at the Hoover Institution at Stanford University, has pointed out,

> the time necessary to earn a Ph.D. has gradually lengthened in recent years . . . that after receiving a bachelor's degree, the median time it takes to earn a Ph.D. is now 10.5 years. For women the median time to earn a Ph.D. has reached 12.5 years . . . the time it takes for black Americans to earn the Ph.D. stretches out to 14.9 years.[18]

Pursuing one's intellectual interests might seem frivolous to many African-American students, especially women, who are generally perceived as necessary contributors to their family and community's financial well-being.

In the essay "Balancing the Personal and the Profession," Adrienne Andrews extends the knowledge we have about African-American women academics by interviewing a number of black women faculty at different universities around the country about their lives. Inevitably she found they faced issues of concern to Euro-American women, but also issues specifically related to being black and female in the academic environment:

> [t]he issues they felt were the most pressing ones facing them as black women, were not only the impact of gender and salary discrimination based on male dominance in the profession, and struggling to get tenure, but racial discrimination and a type of role conflict and professional burnout that was compounded by the fact of race, as well.[19]

One respondent noted:

> Most women have family responsibilities, and when black women have family responsibilities, they're even more difficult for us than for the

white woman because for us many of us are the first, second generation at best. In university life . . .[20]

Other respondents described how the black woman professor is often called
upon to serve as mentor, mother, and counselor in addition to educator to African-
American students who experience the academy as a hostile and alien place and
that she often is expected to serve on committees to make certain the minority
and woman perspective are represented. Some of my sister/colleagues refuse to
be what they call "academic mules"; yet they are also aware that it is usually our
communities who lose if we do not attempt to fulfill the demands of our respective institutions.

Many of the women in this study also are struggling with the issue of finding
a suitable mate who could contend with a woman who has a doctorate, and whose
professional life would involve much of her time. The question as to whether the
feminist movement has negatively affected women's marital status or whether that
idea is a media hype is one that Susan Faludi explores in her book *Backlash*. The
situation in African-American communities perhaps might be different, an example
of how an important mainstream "theory" might take on different ramifications if
it is viewed from the point of view of African-Americans, and possibly other people
of colour. African-American men have been under severe attack from the judicial
system, levels of poverty that affect their ability to be breadwinners. I note that
in the last month, my local paper *The Oakland Tribune* ran a Sunday feature article
about the fact that one-third of African-American women in the ages from 18 to
50 who express heterosexual desires are not able to find a mate. Whether that
fact is true or not (I always doubt newspaper articles), the experiences of many
of my colleagues, as well as my own personal experience, indicate that African-
American women academics very often are single, or single mothers, with little
prospect of intragroup heterosexual relationships, if that is what they desire. As
well, African-American women academics, whether they are heterosexual or homo-
sexual, often are living in areas where there is no vibrant African-American presence
so that they suffer from cultural isolation.

But the problems of monetary returns, time concerns, probable work over-
load, and distorted personal relationships are not the only issues confronting an
African-American woman who might want to go into the academy. When *The
Journal of Blacks in Higher Education* asked black feminist scholar Professor Johnetta
Cole why there is a shortage of black professors, she not only cited these restraints
but also that:

> Many African-Americans entering the academy today do so because they
> have been lured by the promise of alternative models of research and
> action-oriented scholarship. . .[But] anything not fitting the traditional
> model is considered less than scholarly.[21]

While some African-American women are willing to endure financial and personal
lifestyle sacrifices because they love intellectual inquiry and understand its importance, some are deterred by the realization that they will likely have to do the
kind of work they want to do in a hostile environment, or they might have to

change their sense of themselves and the position from which they explore ideas if they are to succeed in the academy.

In her essay "Teaching Theory, Talking Community," Joy James, who teaches courses on African-American women in political movements in Women's Studies, University of Massachusetts–Amherst, passionately delineates this theoretical dilemma:

> If it is assumed that we only speak as "black" women – not as *women* – or "black" people – not as *human beings* – our stories and theorizing are considered irrelevant or not applicable to women or people in general; they are reduced to descriptions of a part rather than analyses of a whole (humanity).[22]

The way in which the writings of bell hooks are viewed by some white scholars, female and male, is one example of this reduction. While my graduate students use her work extensively and cite her quite extensively in their dissertations, while her books are widely used in sociology and literature classes as well as in women's studies and African-American studies class, I have heard many a white scholar, female and male, insist that hooks does not articulate theories. Rather she reacts to others' theories, uses inappropriate language, and has no scholarly methodology. I believe, although it is never really said, that her work is suspect because it is so popular. While I certainly do not agree with everything hooks has ever written, I consider her work to be an example of theorizing, of making connections between many different forms of intellectual discipline, as well as between the so-called popular cultural terrain and intellectual marketplaces. She has emphasized how she has consciously chosen to locate her work "in the margin." Not one "imposed by oppressive structures" but one she has chosen as a "site of resistance – as location of radical openness and possibility."[23]

Perhaps some academics' assessment of bell hooks and other black intellectuals has to do with another bias. Professor Andrew Hacker, the author of the much celebrated study *Two Nations: Separate, Hostile and Unequal*, believes that many black intellectuals "rely on more discursive modes of analysis as opposed to the more schematic linear method embodied in the multiple-choice matrix and – later on – the formats expected for academic research." Thus, "they are seen as failing to internalize and adapt to white mental ways," that is, of not assimilating intellectually.[24] Whether all African-American intellectuals can be so characterized is a question for debate. The point, however, that Hacker is making has more to do with the monolithic standard as to what "real" scholarship is and how it should be expressed.

Can one be a *successful* academic, artist, or writer and still be seen as an African-American woman? I recall the many times television and radio commentators stated, on the occasion of Toni Morrison's recent receipt of the Nobel Prize for Literature, that she was not *just* an African-American woman writer, she was a universal writer. I wrote a piece on Morrison's receipt of the Nobel Prize which emphasized that she wrote as an African-American woman writer. I got letters in response from white women readers who were upset that I had "limited" her by locating her in that tradition. In other words, if you're really good, you somehow are no longer an African-American woman. African-American writers have had to contend with such responses, ones that have "limited" their access to the literary establishments of the West and, thus, to other "Third World" countries whose educational systems take their cue from the West. Clearly, the literary tradition is surviving that assault, and I suspect that black feminism(s) in the academy will, too.

Besides, the point is, and it is an important point, that there is joy in struggle, a fact that a few genuinely wonderful students of mine, female and male, African-American, colored, and white, have understood and have demonstrated in their teaching, writing, and campus and community activism, thus regenerating these old bones of mine. We will survive in the academy.

Still, it is important that those of us who understand the importance of black feminist thought's role in the academy be clear about the dire situation that African-American women academics face; in other words, praxis is central to our survival. We need not only fancy treatises on *Beloved* or smart feminist theses that include black feminisms. We need nuts and bolts action. We need to ask questions that at first glance may seem to have nothing to do with scholarship but are central to our survival. For example, how many African-American women and men graduate students are there at my institution? Can we conceive of the idea that oftentimes their projects and the ways in which they pursue them might be incomprehensible to our sense of what scholarly enterprises should be about? Can we think about how narrowly defined our own definition of scholarship might be? Do we really subscribe to the idea that feminist scholarship should be interventionist, should change our view of society, and therefore of our site, the university?

I fear that if we do not engage these issues, potential black feminist scholars, faced with diminishing returns, may have to reconsider whether the academy is a suitable site for them or whether more gains in scholarship and intellectual inquiry may lie elsewhere. If that occurs, the academy will be the loser.

Notes and references

1   This paper was originally written for a conference entitled "Figuring Feminism at the Fin-de-Siècle," sponsored by Scripps College Humanities Institute and the Claremont Graduate Humanities Center, to be published by Stanford University Press, edited by Kari Weil.

2   See "The Backlash Debate," *Time*, 139, 10 (March 9, 1992), pp. 50–7. Also see "'I'm Not a Feminist, But . . .'," *San Francisco Chronicle*, *This World* section (February 23, 1992), pp. 7, 9–11.

3   Wendy Kaminer "Feminism's Identity Crisis," *The Atlantic*, 272, 4 (October 1993), pp. 51–68. Even Susan Faludi's more respectable study, *Backlash* (New York: Crown, 1991) does not pay much attention to African-American women's contributions to the development of feminist concepts.

4   See Paula Giddings' *When and Where I Enter* (New York: W. Morrow, 1984), a marvelous historical study of African-American women except that it gives short shrift to the women involved in cultural transformation, such as Frances Harper.

5   Deborah King, "Multiple Jeopardy, Multiple Consciousness: The Context of a Black Feminist Ideology," in *Feminist Theory in Practice and Process*, eds Micheline R. Malson, Jean F. O'Barr, Sarah Westphal-Wihl, and Mary Wyer (Chicago: The University of Chicago Press, 1989), p. 105.

6   For a popular view of the way in which most white women in this country do not call themselves feminist, while a good proportion of them believe in and/or practice its basis tenets, take a look at Wendy Kaminer's quite conservative article in *The Atlantic*, October 1993. See also Susan Faludi's *Backlash*.

7   Barbara T. Christian, "What Do We Think We're Doing," in Changing Our Own Words: Essays on Criticism, Theory and Writing by Black Women, ed. Cheryl Wall (New Brunswick, NJ: Rutgers University Press, 1991), pp. 58–74.

8   "Introduction," to *Feminist Theory in Practice and Process*, eds Micheline R. Malson, Jean F. O'Barr, Sarah Westphal-Wihl and Mary Wyer (Chicago: University of Chicago Press, 1989).

9   See Barbara T. Christian et al. "Conference Call," *Differences*, 2 (Fall, 1990), pp. 52–108. For a comprehensive and brilliant analysis on this issue published after I completed this essay, see Ann duCille, "The Occult of True Black Womanhood: Critical Demeanor and Black Feminist Studies," *Signs: Journal of Women in Culture and Society*, 19, 3 (Spring 1994), pp. 591–629.

10   See Patricia Hill Collins, *Black Feminist Thought: Knowledge, Consciousness and the Politics of Empowerment* (Boston: Unwin Hyman Publishers, 1990).

11   Chandra Talpade Mohanty, "Under Western Eyes: Feminist Scholarship and Colonial Discourses," *Boundary* 2, 12, 3 (1984), pp. 333–58.

12   Patricia Hill Collins, *Black Feminist Thought*, p. 202.

13   Barbara T. Christian, "Polylogue on Feminism and the Institution," *Differences: A Journal of Feminist Cultural Studies*, 2 (Fall 1990), p. 57.

14   Andrew Hacker, "Why the Shortage of Black Professors?," *The Journal of Blacks in Higher Education*, 1, 1 (Autumn 1993), p. 32.

15   *The Journal of Blacks in Higher Education*, 1, 1 (Autumn 1993), pp. 23–5.

16   "Introduction," *Spirit, Space and Survival: African-American Women in (White) Academe*, eds Joy James and Ruth Farmer (New York: Routledge, 1993), p. 2.

17   Ibid., p. 3.

18   Martin Anderson in "Why the Shortage of Black Professors?," *The Journal of Blacks in Higher Education*, 1 (Autumn 1992), p. 34.

19   Adrienne Andrews, "Balancing the Personal and the Professional," *Spirit, Space and Survival*, p. 183. See also: Yolanda Moses' study, *Black Women in Academia: Issues and Status* (Baltimore: Project on the Status of Education of Women, August 1989).

20   Ibid., p. 190.

21   Johnetta B. Cole, "Why the Shortage of Black Professors?," *The Journal of Blacks in Higher Education*, 1, 1 (Autumn 1993), p. 30.

22   Joy James, "Teaching Theory, Talking Community," *Spirit, Space and Survival*, p. 121.

23   bell hooks, *Yearning: Race, Gender and Cultural Politics* (Boston: South End Press, 1990), p. 153.

24   Andrew Hacker, "Why the Shortage of Black Professors?," p. 33.

PART SIX

Changing boundaries and spaces

INTRODUCTION

THE FOCUS OF THE MATERIAL INCLUDED in the preceding Parts
has been largely, though not exclusively, on the elaboration of key theoretical
and conceptual debates about race and racism. Within the limitations of one volume
we have attempted to be as open as we could be to the inclusion of extracts from
the major authors who have helped to shape in one way or another the course of
academic debate in this field over the years, though we are aware that there is
also much that cannot be fitted into the specific parameters of this Reader (but
see the Guide to Further Reading for an indication of key texts in relation to each
Part). In doing so we have also sought to give a flavour of the passion and political feeling that questions about race and racism are bound to give rise to in one
way or another. Much of the most intense debate in this field has been focused
on how to conceptualise the boundaries of race and racism, particularly in an
environment that is rapidly changing. This is the dimension that we turn to in this
Part, where we shift focus somewhat by bringing together a series of extracts that
raise questions that are likely to be the subject of extensive debate and scholarship in the years to come.

   This Part opens with a paper from the work of Gargi Bhattacharyya, who is
one of the younger generation of black British cultural theorists. In this extract
she is specifically concerned with questions about the intersection between race
and gender, and she writes from the perspective of somebody working within higher
education in Britain and of being one of the few 'race ladies' in that field. Written
in a deliberately ironic style and a narrative form that eschews broad theorisation
Bhattacharyya's account is a timely reminder of the limits and contradictions of

what it means to teach race in the academy and raises important questions about pedagogical practice as well as theory.

This is followed by an extract from Paul Gilroy, who is one of the most original contemporary theorists in this field. Gilroy takes up a question that has been the focus of much of his influential oeuvre, namely the changing patterns of identity formation within the African diaspora in a context of social change and transformation that characterises the everyday realities within which diasporic communities live and interact with other social groups. This is an issue that has been at the heart of much of the more recent theorising in this field both in the United States and in Europe and raises important questions about the complex forms that diasporic identification often takes among particular communities and groups within them. The arguments developed by Gilroy also link up with some of the key contributions to be found in Parts Four and Five and it may be useful to explore some of these linkages in thinking through the implications of his analysis for future research.

A related set of questions is taken up by Kobena Mercer, who provides an insightful account of the changing patterns of identity politics within the context of increasing social and cultural diversity. Linking his analysis to broader debates about postmodernism Mercer is particularly concerned with analysing the contradictions within identity politics, and he seeks to situate the preoccupation with both identity and diversity in the new social and cultural politics that have emerged in contemporary societies.

The next two extracts take up a somewhat different area of concern, namely the changing morphology of race, ethnicity and identity in contemporary societies. The question of identity is perhaps the main arena around which many of the recent debates on race and racism have been constructed. As a keyword in contemporary social theory identity has taken on many different connotations, and it is often seen as symptomatic of the postmodern predicament of contemporary politics. But it is also clear that different meanings have been attached to the very idea of identity. Michael Keith's contribution, for example, reflects an important aspect of these recent debates, in that he seeks to explore the contested ways in which politicised claims to authenticity are being articulated in the mixed urban environments that make up inner city neighbourhoods in places such as London. Keith's account is particularly interesting because of the way he seeks to link wider theoretical concerns to an analysis of everyday political mobilisations about race and ethnicity in a particular local environment.

Richard Dyer's contribution takes up the issue of how constructions of 'whiteness' play an important role in the development of racial categories and images in popular cultural forms. Dyer is particularly concerned to show that whiteness is constructed around a number of potentially contradictory identities, which battle within us for allegiance: as men or women, black or white, straight or gay. He is also interested in the ways in which racial discourses are often concerned as much with policing the boundaries of whiteness as with the articulation of ideas about the 'other'.

The extracts from Kimberlé Crenshaw and Stephen Steinberg shift the focus from theory to the level of political institutions and ideas. From rather different angles they take up questions at the heart of the changing politics of race in the United States of America and the impact of state policies aimed at ameliorating the effects of racism. Both authors focus on the diverse initiatives and programmes that were brought into existence by the racial conflicts in the 1950s and 1960s in the United States. Crenshaw's analysis, which is part of what is called 'critical race theory' in the US, seeks to challenge conceptions of anti-discrimination policies that do not take fully into account the complex linkages between race, class and gender in structuring the everyday experiences of African–Americans in the period since the 1960s. Crenshaw's contribution is followed by Stephen Steinberg, who is one of the most astute and vocal critics of what he sees as a 'retreat from racial justice' in the period since the 1980s. Steinberg's analysis focuses on the ways in which the political and social discourses of both the Conservative Right and of Liberals can be seen as representing a retreat from the promise of reform and action to tackle the root causes of racial inequality in the United States that was much in evidence in the aftermath of the Civil Rights Movement. Both of these extracts highlight important conceptual issues as to the way we can attempt to understand the impact of political institutions on questions of racial inequality and exclusion.

The final group of three extracts can all be seen as exploratory and suggestive of issues that are likely to be the focus of more scholarship and research in the future. The extract from Chetan Bhatt bears on a facet of contemporary racism that is little known and ignored in the mainstream literature on race and racism, namely the emergency of discourses about race in the language of nationalist movements such as those represented by Hindu nationalism. Bhatt's analysis is particularly pertinent in the context of growing support in countries such as India and elsewhere for nationalist and religious movements that articulate what he calls 'indigenist neoracism' among other elements of their philosophies. Drawing on research on religious movements in India as well as the Indian diaspora, Bhatt's analysis is suggestive of the need for more attention to this dimension of contemporary racism. Much of the focus of research and scholarship on race and racism has been on the 'west' and this is reflected in this Reader, but there is clearly a need to broaden our focus if we are to understand the articulation of forms of racial discourse that are rooted in other geographical spaces.

The complex forms of narratives and claims that have become an integral element of contemporary debates about race and nation are explored from an innovative angle by the Slovakian social theorist and psychoanalyst Slavoj Žižek. Utilising arguments derived from the recent experience of the former Yugoslavia, as well as other eastern European societies, Žižek seeks to show what the reassertion of rootedness and fixed national identities means in terms of the construction of ideas about identity and culture. Drawing on psychoanalytic theory as much as social theorising, he is particularly concerned with what ideas about 'belonging' and 'nationhood' mean in environments that are increasingly global and yet also centred on assertions about who belongs to particular nation states and geographical boundaries. Although much of his analysis is very abstract, Žižek deals with the need to explore in more detail the psychosocial spaces in which ideas about race and nation play an important role.

The concluding extract by Anthony Appiah can usefully be seen as a kind of conclusion to the Reader as a whole. Appiah's nuanced exploration of the dilemmas faced in thinking about the boundaries of racial identification was written as part of a dialogue between himself and the political theorist Amy Gutmann. But in many ways it can be seen as neatly capturing dilemmas that are at the heart of contemporary debates about the changing boundaries of racial identity. What is particularly interesting about Appiah's account is the way he does not lose sight of the need to situate the new patterns of identity formation that characterise contemporary societies against the background of historical trends and processes. In this he reminds us that we need to know as much about where racial ideas come from as we do about where they are going at the present time.

KEY QUESTIONS

- Gargi Bhattacharyya argues: 'Being one kind of woman didn't mean that you were automatically connected to all other kinds'. What are the implications of this argument for the analysis of race and gender?
- What processes can help us to understand what Stephen Steinberg has called the 'retreat from racial justice' in American society?
- Kimberlé Crenshaw argues that there is a need to reconceptualise race 'as a coalition between men and women of colour'. What are the consequences of this approach for anti-racist politics?
- Paul Gilroy has argued: 'The idea of a common, invariant racial identity capable of linking divergent black experiences across different spaces and times has been fatally undermined'. What are the implications of this argument for the analysis of racial and other forms of identity in contemporary societies?
- Explore the ways in which the study of whiteness helps to develop the analysis of racism in contemporary societies.
- What does Chetan Bhatt mean when he argues that with the resurgence of ethnic, nationalist and religious movements we have seen the articulation of an 'indigenist neoracism'?
- W. E. B. Du Bois argued that 'the problem of the twentieth century is the problem of the color line'. What significance will the 'color line' have in the twenty-first century?

Chapter 32

Gargi Bhattacharyya

BLACK SKIN/WHITE BOARDS
Learning to be the 'race' lady in British higher education

I'VE BEEN THINKING ABOUT this paper for a long time – too long to remember its original focus or intended purpose. Now it will have to serve as part of my ongoing academic diary – the trials of your first year of teaching. Because of this it is probably informed by new lecturer anxieties – am I doing this right? What is it I'm doing anyway? But it's also informed by the bizarre boundary-crossing of the black woman teaching in British higher education – a relatively new ball-game, and certainly a new ball-game for me.

This is an oh-so-tentative initial excursion into what might be going on here.

I teach English Literature – which means, amongst other things, that I have an investment in trying to learn things from stories.[1] This is an attempt to think through some of the possible narratives for the scenario of black skin in front of whiteboard, to try out some stories about 'race' and contemporary higher education.

I'm trying to unlearn polemic, for a whole set of reasons, which I can't help but defend polemically. I've been schooled in the model of academia which thinks that scholarship is like activism, that politics is what makes book-reading socially valuable rather than embarrassing and self-indulgent. The informing principle is that some knowledges can make people free – and that this is the test of true and useful knowledge.

Some scholarship is not political enough – these bookreaders haven't got enlightened consciousnesses or can't connect their work convincingly to the real world of relevance – and this stuff is largely a waste of time. Instead, the business of learning can redeem itself from the guilt of its privilege only by continually restating the greater importance of the political, by saying again and again that the real work must go on elsewhere. Reading books is supposed to help you know which elsewhere to travel to.

Recently I've loosened up enough to be able to poke fun at this a little – I'm not quite so awed by the sacred status of the political. *But*, this is still the model of schooling which I believe in, the one I use to legitimate my own work to myself. Trying to unlearn polemic is part of an attempt to unpack what is difficult or untenable about this position.

Polemic assumes that you already have a position that you're certain of, and that your engagement with other people should be a selling of this point of view. The polemicist doesn't have anything to learn from their interlocutor, because they know it already. Instead, it's worth talking in order to spread the good word of your political vision, so that your enlightenment can be shared. What I'm having trouble with is sustaining the pretence that I am one of the enlightened. This might mean that I need to meet a really good polemicist and learn the certainties of a new argument. Or it might mean that the polemical model of academic engagement doesn't leave much room for feeling doubtful. My polemical point against polemic is that a way of operating that silences uncertainty makes it hard to ever learn anything new. A worst case scenario of this would mean that we all die stupid, while making self-righteous speeches to each other. Because I'm afraid of this, this is a piece about things I'm not sure about. I don't have a line to sell. Instead, this is an exercise in thinking through options and possibilities.

I've been thinking about trying to do the right thing, and of the difficulty of knowing what this thing might be. I feel uncomfortable with the assumption that teachers of the humanities must necessarily be doing this right thing – with the idea that the humanities lecturer is a classroom revolutionary dispensing the tools of emancipation. In this model, people who work in certain sectors of H.E. already know what doing the right thing is, and the only thing which stops them from it is the incursion of an unhelpful management or government or market. Political good-sense is demonstrated by the demand to carry on as you are, to be left to do what you (or your kind) have always done.

In this climate there doesn't seem to be much room to consider those old debates about education and reproduction theory, to think about education as an arm of the state, and the state as, if not a function of economy, at least as tied to some economic imperative. Instead, in a defensive gesture, we return to arguing that education – old-style liberal education based around small groups and personal contact and individual growth – must be an unambiguously good thing, and that this is what should be defended without question. I can see that this is an understandable response to difficult times – but I'm not convinced that it stands up to scrutiny. It may be the case that it is important to retain that model of equality of distribution – so that if we think of education as a commodity which will in turn enhance the commodity value of its possessor, we might try to ensure that everyone gets an equal shot at this. What it pains me to lose is that other model which tries to understand what it means to teach people to be better commodities, not as a way of trashing schooling, but as an attempt to make it better.

My anxiety is that if you perceive yourself to be perpetually on the defensive, battling to maintain the place you have, no-one has much energy for the indulgences of self-criticism. And that indulgence might be necessary to any attempt to teach critique, rather than the deference of gratitude. If you think that teaching is about opening avenues which might lead to freedom, then it's difficult not to operate on the assumption that the people you teach are lucky to have you, and that appreciation should encourage diligence and obedience. Being the right-on teacher, both in course content and in teaching method, might be a way of wrapping yourself in authority even more securely. If you are teaching people how to be free, then their resistances must be their problem, shortcomings which the student brings with them.

What I'm saying is that sometimes it might be important to think of education as something other than a gift. Sometimes getting educated means learning what education cannot do. This is one of the uncertain points which interests me – the point at which an honest attempt at political education must talk about what is not possible.

The rest of this piece tries to present some ways of thinking about this – some possible storylines. I'm very much talking about 'race', but I think the difficulties arise in all those well-meaning attempts to teach people how to lead better lives. I think I'm running at two things – how you analyse the processes of education and how you might operate within these processes as a teacher. What you can know and what you can do, perhaps – of course the two are all jumbled up together, but it might help to know that I'm interested in both.

The title. Clearly the title is a too obvious and too childish reference to Fanon – but it made me giggle. I can use this echo of Fanon because Fanon is echoing all over the place already. The joke works because of certain developments in the study of 'race' in certain quarters. Fanon becomes a key text for examining the psychological experience of blackness – I can amuse myself with this reference because of the establishment of a whole arena in which these things are discussed, because Fanon can be something like canonical for some people now.

However, as well as to get a cheap laugh, I also want to rework Fanon to think about a different setting for blackness. The original work examines attempts to disguise or deny – for Fanon dark skin is a wound which must be come to terms with. What I'm talking about is a situation in which the pain associated with dark skin means that some people can wear their skin for a living. This isn't what Fanon is talking about. He writes, "The colonized is elevated above his jungle status in proportion to this adoption of the mother country's cultural standards. He becomes whiter as he renounces his blackness, his jungle".[2]

What if elevation depends upon some retention of jungle status? In the scenario that I am thinking of the black skin is not covered by a white mask – it is staged more starkly against the background of the whiteboard. In our racially tense moment, the institution of higher education desires and requires a certain amount of this conspicuously staged blackness. The black teacher is invited to wear a version of jungle status as an entry into the mother country's cultural standards, as a way of being professional and respectable. Here I want to use the Fanon of *Black skin, white masks* as one way of thinking about this paradoxical bargain, partly because this work has been chosen already by black academics in this country.

Early in the work Fanon paraphrases a Professor D. Westermann to state, "The Negroes' inferiority complex is particularly intensified among the most educated, who must struggle with it unceasingly".

It's the people who try to lose the jungle who feel most marked by the jungle – the attempt to cross boundaries which confirms how unpassable these boundaries are. It's those who are pushed right up against the limit of the racial divide who feel their blackness most acutely and woundingly – this is the argument.

Whether or not it is true, this idea can give us a possible handle on the position of the black academic – and perhaps an indication of why Fanon becomes *the* text for cultural inquiry about 'race' in this country. In the situation described, the experience of blackness intensifies with proximity to whiteness, in both physical and cultural terms.

For the black person who becomes so educated that they become an educator, the beauty of this theory is that it makes their existence into the focus of analysis – this position of anxiety becomes the place to look if you want to understand the meanings of 'race'. Fanon's model allows the black academic to refuse the constraining demand that they be typical, that they stand in as an example of their racial group, with this example serving as a means of analysing the whole. The mixture of education and blackness is not typical, and this untypicality has its own set of effects. Fanon says this, and yet, even as he extricates the educated black person from the awkwardness of being seen as representative of their race, he reinstates their position as the one of analytic privilege. Education gives us, not the most typical experience of blackness, but the most intense – what it means to be black is most sharply delineated at this point, right up against the background of whiteness.

What I want to suggest is that this is an attempt to read the educated black person as a symptom of other structures. Instead of standing in as a metonym for their people, here the physically conspicuous symptom of the black body in the British academy calls for a different type of reading for its significance to become apparent. It is still the position of the educated black person which merits analysis, but now because they make manifest an informing paradox of our racial times, rather than because they can speak for and provide an example of the absent black masses. In this model, the black teacher does not need to look for legitimation in some place beyond the academy, does not have to reform themselves anxiously as authentic native of the real world of oppression. Instead, the black teacher as black teacher becomes the exemplary educational text, the visible symptom which illuminates the whole hidden structure of 'race'. Here being anomalous is what makes the black teacher informative.

This is one possible story – that the oddness of some situations is what makes them illuminating and educational.

Next story.

One of the books I've managed to finish reading in my too-busy first year of employment is *The Alchemy of Race and Rights* by Patricia J. Williams – the diary of a law professor who is African-American and female.[3]

Her writing is difficult and charming, all theory and poetry and anecdote, with some talk about clothes thrown in – and, in my head, I've been using her as a private argument for staying in academia. She also, helpfully and thankfully, writes about the strangeness of teaching for some sorts of people.

One of the pieces she writes is about the oddness of her institutional role ["Crimes without Passion (some impersonal notes about personal politics")]. This piece starts out with a story about a weeping first-year student who has been called an 'activist' by the school administrator for complaining about the racism of a law exam in which *Othello* is used as the example of a murder-case. The model answer gives points for ability to "individualize the test" of provocation by recognizing that "a rough untutored Moor might understandably be deceived by the wiles of a more sophisticated European".

I was interested in this immediately – look, here was proof that stories had some effect in society, that literary education meant something in the wider world, and that what this something was needed to be understood. One of my earliest assignments in my new job had been to discuss E. D. Hirsch's ideas of cultural literacy with a group of third-year students. Hirsch suggests that not being able to swap the short-hand of terms like 'Othello' results in social disenfranchisement for some people, and an emasculated culture for the nation. I had tried to extend this argument to suggest that you might have to be literate in the languages of racism in order to critique them, but that it might be impossible to distinguish an attempt to teach this literacy from another repetition of old-style racism. I'm sure this only served to confirm my status as crazy-lady. This is something like the point Williams ends up making – that some educational projects just end up seeming bizarre in our historical moment.

A little like my reading of Fanon, Williams describes the anomaly of minority educational achievement – of participating in education when marked by outsiderdom.

> A few exceptionally strong people, usually reinforced by an alternative sense of community, can just ignore it and carry on, despite the lack of that part of education which flows from full participation, perhaps thus resulting in a brand of knowledge that is more abstract than relational.

Her suggestion is that you miss out on half the business of education if you are socially ostracised – if you find yourself amongst people who don't want to deal with you, then productive interchange is hard to achieve. Dark-skinned people who live in places where you are penalised for having a dark skin can succeed in the unfriendly context of formal education by taking their strength from elsewhere and learning to study alone – this doesn't mean that you can't have educational success (although the implication is that it means this for most people), but it might mean that you end up with a different sort of education. More floating concept than concrete interaction, perhaps.

I've been thinking about this suggestion in relation to the role of the black teacher. If suffering on account of racism makes you into an abstract thinker, does that limit your chances of being a communicative teacher? What happens if we start to think of the experience of victimage as a drawback even in the survivor, rather than as a source of enabling insight? I don't want to suggest that colleges should go back to only employing old white guys. What I do want to do is get to the point where we can think that even if me and my student have suffered similar hard times due to our skin, this might not help either of us negotiate the teaching and learning scenario. Yet even while thinking this still try to understand what difference my skin does make here.

One version of the black teacher as an unquestionably good thing works on the assumption that the teacher's bad experiences will aid communication with students. Being a victim is what makes you a certain sort of good teacher here.

I still want to believe that there is an element of truth in this – but I also know that this isn't a sufficiently full account of what can go on.

What makes me grateful about Patricia Williams' work is her acknowledgement that you can't always know how to do the right thing. Not out of personal laziness or evil, but because sometimes no right thing is apparent in that time and place. She tells a story about how bad her student evaluations are.

> Two students come to visit me in the wake of the evaluations, my scores having been published in the student newspaper. They think that the response has to do with race and gender, and with the perceived preposterousness of the authority that I, as the first black woman ever to have taught at this particular institution, symbolically and imagistically bring to bear in and out of the classroom. Breaking out of this, they say, is something we all suffer as pawns in a hierarchy, but it is particularly aggravated in the confusing, oxymoronic hierarchic symbology of me as black female law professor.
>
> That, I tell them in a grateful swell of unscholarly emotionalism, feels like truth to me.

The value of the black teacher as anti-racist gesture derives from the understanding gained from experience – knowing about being a victim is what qualifies you for this pedagogical project. The minority teacher is supposed to have a certain amount of pain. That's how you know they're in a minority that counts. However, unlike other kinds of qualification, the minority-status of the teacher never gets to the point of final assessment – you don't finish the course and get the certificate. The identities which the teacher brings, as well as being sources of additional insight, will continue to be subject to difficulty and confusion, both inside and outside the classroom, for everyone concerned, both teacher and pupil.

Patricia Williams is suggesting that some bodies (black, female) have more trouble wearing the authority of teacher – that it is difficult to think of the teacher as at once Ms. Marginal-Minority and Dr Academic/Institutional Power. Even if you can understand how both these things are in operation in the same time and place, negotiating these simultaneous identities is hard work for everyone. Even as the black teacher is wheeled on as some institutional response to a whole set of racial difficulties, presented as a fixing gesture, a whole new set of problems is called into play.

This is another possible story – not one which contradicts the one I extract from Fanon, but one which does suggest that the confusions caused by the oxymoron of black female teacher might not be immediately educational.

Let's go back to thinking about doing the right thing.

I've been looking at the beginning of a Spivak essay called "French Feminism Revisited: Ethics and Politics" – it's in a collection called *Feminists Theorize the Political*, so it's framed as a response to that demand.[4] This is the paragraph which I have been thinking about,

> Texts open when you talk to groups of others, which often turn out to be classes, public audiences. Yet these openings are not beginnings,

for the staging of each such talking is secured by politics; classes at least by the individualism and competition of the academy 'at its best', public lectures by the politics of funding and the thematics of travel and lodging; the gender, race and class politics of custodial staff in both arenas. No attempt such as ours can begin without a grounding mistake, cutting off the space where theory is persistently normed by politics.

I have been both troubled and intrigued by this suggestion. I understand that the event of academic interchange is enabled by a whole material and social structure which is not acknowledged at the point of utterance – that the academic address pretends to be the point where business starts in a way which disregards all the other business which must go on for that point to be reached. What I can't understand is why this should be a *necessary* grounding mistake.

I'm taking grounding mistake to mean an enabling misapprehension in this context – knowledge production stages itself as enquiry by disregarding its more material formation and function. Not talking about some things is what allows you to start talking about others, but this start is shaped by these things that aren't mentioned. The start of the talk isn't the start of the process, but, for our ways of trying to learn things, it's important to act as if this is the start.

Enquiry depends upon some notion of a fresh start, of this being a new ballgame in which new possibilities will become apparent. If instead of this we start to say that the moment of academic utterance is the product of something like a hierarchy of exploitation between different fractions of wage labour, even perhaps that its primary function is to demonstrate this differential, to be an empty (or might as well be empty) marker of privilege, then the openings promised by enquiry start to close down. If you start to suggest that the moment of academic utterance can occur only as an indication of the deals that have been cut between various structures of power, that study depends upon what bargains can be struck at any historical moment, then the academic event starts to seem too determined for the longed-for openings of enquiry to be available. For these reasons, the academy behaves like the ungrateful children it houses, and pretends not to know its origins while still cashing the cheques.

I take this to be what Spivak is talking about when she describes the grounding mistake of theoretical endeavour. What I'm unclear about is what sort of term "grounding mistake" is here. If a grounding mistake is the misnaming which you must do to start doing – if this is a mistake which enables certain kinds of activity, not just helps them run more smoothly, but allows them to happen in the first place – then what happens when you expose your own grounding mistake, when you acknowledge what makes you? If the grounding mistake is *necessary*, how did you ever manage to make it visible? Are all acts of enquiry in the academy based on this grounding mistake, even enquiries into the nature of the grounding mistake? Why is it that knowing something which you're not supposed to know makes no difference here? As you can see, I'm very confused by this. But my suspicion is that this set of untenable arguments is some sort of lesson about political education, and that it might tell me something about being the 'race' lady.

In this story, the well-meaning teacher with a political conscience should acknowledge the ugly things which make the space of education possible. This gesture is necessarily paradoxical (or hypocritical, depending on how you feel), because it also is enabled by that same ugliness. Learning the critique doesn't alter the practice, not because people aren't trying, but because this critique doesn't offer that possibility. This story suggests that political education must demonstrate what education cannot do – that any attempt to teach in good faith should tell people about this informing and inescapable principle of bad faith.

One of the many stories which I have been brooding about is a story which happened to me. At other times I've tried to warn against this falling into confessional mode for the markedly 'marginal' academic. Narratives of experience are too seductive for both speaker and listener, promising access to authority to one and access to authenticity to the other. What is lost in this mutual pleasuring is the chance of dialogue – and this doesn't seem any good for those of us in the talking-game. Particularly if interchange, the opening of possibility, is meant to be how knowledge is made. If saying how you feel becomes the first and last word in any argument, then its difficult to see what you gain by studying or chatting. I've been trying to unlearn the ambiguous privilege of speaking with the legitimation of being Ms. Multiple-Minority – but, at the same time, my work is becoming increasingly conversational. What I want to argue is that the story I'm going to tell is useful as a way of thinking about 'race', gender and teaching – the story is instructive rather than how I feel about it. However, even as I argue this, I know that how I feel has come into the choosing and narrating of this story, and that its potentially instructive nature is vouched for by my Ms. Minority status, whether I like it or not. What I'm hoping is that this story will dramatise some of what is going on here.

As part of my contract of employment I am obliged to attend a day of first-aid training – this is compulsory for all employees of my institution. The training days are scattered throughout the year, and across various sites (we are spread between several towns). The chances are that you won't know most of the other people on your training day – at mine there was only one person to whom I'd spoken before.

The training day is supposed to prepare you to deal with a whole range of possible emergencies requiring first-aid. Much of this was instruction in judging a situation – how you understand what's going on from only looking. We were given tips on how to read the state of the body by its outward manifestations. You look at what you can see as a way of understanding what can't be seen.

I was pleased with this model of enquiry – it echoed the educational models with which I was familiar. Reading was about plotting what was immediately apparent, the visible, the surface, as a way of gaining access to significances which were not readily available. Here was a nice reminder of where all those varieties of symptomatic reading which I had been taught got their metaphors of learning from. The literary educations which I'd been brought up on regarded writing as the corporeal outer shell of some hidden meaning which was inside or elsewhere. I was used to thinking that reading books was like watching bodies for clues. It was somehow reassuring to be told that diagnosing the state of an unfamiliar body was also like reading a book, this thing which I knew something about.

One of the catastrophic possibilities for which we were being prepared was some unlucky soul having a heart-attack in front of us. The person leading the workshop was a white woman in her later-middle years – she asked us what someone who was having a heart attack might do. Some of us dutifully mimed a heart attack victim clutching their chest in pain. "Yes" said Mrs First-Aid, "They might clutch their chest", and she mirrored the gestures of the audience.

Mmm, I thought – learning to read gestures by mimicking them, by anticipating the gestures of the teacher and mimicking the gesture of authority which has not yet been staged – what sort of model of instruction is this? Is making yourself symptomatic a method of working back to the important meanings – so that by mimicking the symptom which veils and makes manifest the places where things are really happening, you make it seem as if you secretly hold this originary meaning. Here the real secret is that you don't have a secret – that you mimic the gesture of at once showing and hiding without having anything to show or hide.

Now I wonder if this is another instance of academia's grounding mistakes. If perhaps academic life operates by everyone mimicking the symptoms of an authority which is not held within the realms of academia, so that making yourself into an exemplary symptom is what is symptomatic about this kind of business. I wonder if learning the gestures, the turn of your head, the pitch of your voice, is in fact the only way of teaching an approximation to academic authority. A book-based version of charm school. Whether or not this is the case, it still makes me watch my mouth and my posture.

Having confirmed the importance of interpreting gesture in any process of diagnosis, our instructor tried to chivvy some more participation out of us. "What else? How else might they look?" Our lessons were very much concerned with gleaning information from what could be seen. "Well", she said, "they might change colour, they might go pale". This idea of bodies changing colour before your eyes set all sorts of bells ringing for me, in both celebration and warning. I understood that the lesson was that when physical attributes become uncertain and changeable, catastrophe may be striking. "What about black people?" said the woman, "How can you tell when they go pale?" Everyone there was white apart from me – and I seemed like the youngest, which changed what went on. The woman looked over to me and asked me to come up to the front of the group "dear".

"Now, she's not very black", the woman carried on addressing the rest of the group. I was still trying to hold my own, so I laughed back "But I am in attitude" – but the woman was too enmeshed in the imperatives of her own pedagogical project to be distracted. "Now, she's not very black, but if we had a West Indian here you'd see what I meant. In fact, when you've been working with black people for as long as I have you can see when they change colour. But in case you're not sure, I'm going to show you how to tell". I was expecting trouble, so I waited. What she asked me to do was to pull out my lower lip, so that the audience could see the inside texture of my mouth. She did the same with her mouth, and we stood side by side, displaying our inner lips. She continued her commentary, "See, they're both pink. If you need to know if they've lost their colour, that's how to tell". Then I sat down and we moved on to the next lesson.

At the time, this whole incident made me laugh – not least because I didn't want to seem weak or over-sensitive. Later it unfortunately made me weep, and became the incident through which I made sense of my work situation. I do think that there are things which are potentially illuminating about this story – as well as being bizarre and frightening – and that is what I'd like to think about here.

Firstly, there is the unreadability of the black body. The black body is so starkly and conspicuously different in its physicality, that it becomes impossible to judge variations within this category. This doesn't exactly mean that black bodies are unreadable – it's difficult to think of another category of bodies which is so much the constant subject of interpretation – but it does mean that the black body calls a different way of reading into play. There isn't any point perusing the black body for symptoms if the only symptom you can see is its blackness. If you can only take the black body itself as a symptom, then your diagnosis can't be about the state of that body. When the black body is the symptom the disease we are looking for is the one which has caused this symptom to come into view. One way of reading Fanon might give us a clue how to do this, a way of coming to understand a structure by looking closely at its anomalies. This might also involve foregrounding the role of some of what Spivak categorises under the term "grounding mistake" – that whole mish-mash of forces which throws up certain speakers in certain places. This shift in focus is the negative lesson of a first-aid which can only see blackness when it looks at some kinds of body.

The first-aid trainer, unsurprisingly, did not adopt this suggested model of reading. Her task was not to chart the significance of the black body in the terrain of higher education (that's more like my task), but to somehow make the black body more like the white ones which she knew how to read. The way she did this was to resort to the old 'we're all the same under the skin' line – backed up by a racist's need for proof of this. In this process, my body served as the exemplary text of blackness, despite her disappointment that I was 'not very black'. I stood in as a typical example, the part that could represent the entire frightening whole of the Earth's dark-skinned population. Mrs First-Aid stood in as the control of white normality.

I take this to be the most familiar model of the benefits of the black teacher – their educational mileage is seen to derive from being a representative of their race. This way of thinking about the position of the black teacher tends to fall into the difficulties demonstrated on the first-aid day. The exemplary text of the teacher, who is at once anomalous boundary-pusher and typical example, can be made sense of only against the background of a normative whiteness. In this framework whiteness too easily becomes once again the model of human value – in relation to which blackness must be proved to be less monstrous than you expect. There is a considerable pressure for the black teacher to display the pink under-the-skinness of their open mouth as proof of the humanity of their people, but of course this kind of spectacle of proof hurtles back into monstrousness. Displaying your inner lip can only highlight your distance from whiteness.

As this is the case, the only option is to teach as a monster, to display yourself as unworkable anomaly. This might be a way of being honest about the limitations of education and the contradictions which can't be resolved for us in this time and place. The model of the monster retains the status of Fanon's illuminating anomaly and the wounds of Williams' victim of history, while also containing the guilty and frightening power of the wielder of educational privilege. However much I want to be the good chocolate fairy, everybody's sweet dream of equal opportunities, monster seems like a much more accurate description of what I do.

The only trouble with this is that it makes us all feel bad. Everything remains painful, nothing ever seems to get fixed. Instead of the pleasure of self-righteousness, new discomforts appear to unnerve us. The attempts to make things better, to save something worthwhile from education, reveal previously unnoticed difficulties. Sometimes it seems as if trying to do the right thing creates more bad feeling than carrying on as before. Everyone feels stressed and nothing feels right. Living with the discomforts of these inadequate compromises is what we are left with. But maybe that's just the way it has to be.

Later

I don't teach 'English Literature' any more – now I teach the even more mysterious entity, 'Cultural Studies'. For me this has meant keeping a lot of the strategies of reading I knew from before, but dumping the books. Instead, I find that in my new place of work all kinds of things can stand in as an illuminating text for the skilled reader, including the everyday experience of first-aid courses.

I like my first-aid story because of all the tasty teaching issues it stages – the ambiguous role of black person in British higher education as both authority and specimen and how difficult it is for anyone, performer or audience, to resist that positioning; the assumptions about how we can gather knowledge from a mysterious material world; the spectacle of education at its most insensitive. The story dramatises a lot of those difficult contradictory themes which characterise much well-meaning academic work nowadays – it stages the perils of token representation and the temptation toward too-easy identification while showing why we cannot help but fall into those traps. The story shows how sometimes knowing better doesn't make it better and that critique doesn't always change the situation. This is the kind of demonstration I want from education right now – a better indication of what can't happen yet, so that we can all concentrate our energies on the things which could happen soon.

In the places where I work impatience can make people too certain too soon. Lots of shouted accusations and demands for immediate action. I know that we are all hungry for progress, but it feels dangerous to forget the repercussions of our fixing gestures. Most people I know are so exhausted from making space for the 'race' lady that they have no energy to consider what she is supposed to *do*. For them it is enough for her to just *be*. But, of course, just being quickly becomes spectacle, and around come the stories again. I am as trapped in this cycle as anyone – so I am concentrating on stories which show how this happens, trying to get a handle on this tangled dynamic which I am living. Don't listen if you hope to be moved by my honesty (who says I'm not a liar? do you really believe everything you read?) – instead, listen if you want to think about why our choices as teachers and learners are so constrained.

Notes and references

1   This is a previous job at another (unnamed) institution. I now teach Cultural Studies, whatever that may be.
2   Frantz Fanon, *Black Skin, White Masks* (London: Paladin, 1970): 14.
3   Patricia J. Williams, *The Alchemy of Race and Rights* (Cambridge, Massachusetts: Harvard University Press, 1991).
4   *Feminists Theorize the Political*, eds., Judith Butler and Joan W. Scott (London and New York: Routledge, 1992).

Chapter 33

Paul Gilroy

THE DIALECTICS OF DIASPORA
IDENTIFICATION

[. . .]

THE SUBJECT OF THIS PAPER is culture and resistance and I want
to begin by asking you to consider how resistance itself is to be understood.
I think that our recent political history, as people in but not necessarily of the
modern, Western world, a history which involved processes of political organization that are explicitly transcultural and international in nature, demands that we
consider this question very carefully. What is being resisted and by what means?
Slavery? Capitalism? Coerced industrialization? Racial terror? Or ethnocentrism
and European solipsism? How are the discontinuous, plural histories of diaspora
resistance to be *thought*, to be theorized by those who have experienced the consequences of racial domination?

In this paper, I want to look specifically at the positions of the nation-state,
and the idea of nationality in accounts of black resistance and black culture, particularly music. Towards the end, I will also use a brief discussion of black music
to ask implicit questions about the tendencies towards ethnocentrism and
ethnic absolutism of black cultural theory. The problem of weighing the claims of
national identity against other contrasting varieties of subjectivity and identification has a special place in the intellectual history of blacks in the West. W. E. B.
Du Bois's concept of 'double consciousness'[1] is only the best-known resolution of
a familiar problem which points towards the core dynamic of racial oppression as
well as the fundamental antinomy of diaspora blacks. How has this doubleness,
what Richard Wright calls the 'dreadful objectivity'[2] which flows from being both
inside and outside the West, affected the conduct of political movements against
racial oppression and towards black autonomy? Can the inescapable pluralities
involved in the movements of black peoples, in Africa and in exile, ever be synchronized? How would these struggles be periodized in relation to modernity: the

fatal intermediation of capitalism, industrialization and a new conception of political democracy? Does even posing these questions in this way signify nothing except
the reluctant intellectual affiliation of diaspora blacks to an approach which attempts
a premature totalization of our infinite struggles, an approach which has deep roots
within the ambiguous intellectual traditions of the European enlightenment?

In my view, the problematic intellectual heritage of Euro-American modernity still determines the manner in which nationality is understood within black
political discourse. In particular, it conditions the continuing aspiration to acquire
a supposedly authentic, natural and stable identity. This identity is the premise of
a thinking 'racial' self that is both socialized and unified by its connection with
other kindred souls encountered usually, though not always, within the fortified
frontiers of those discrete ethnic cultures which also happen to coincide with the
contours of a sovereign nation-state that guarantees their continuity. Consider for
a moment the looseness with which the term 'black nationalism' is used both
by its advocates and by sceptics. Why is a more refined political language for
dealing with these crucial issues of identity, kinship and affiliation such a long time
coming?

This area of difficulty has recently become associated with a second, namely
the over-integrated conceptions of culture which mean that black political struggles are construed as somehow automatically *expressive* of the national or ethnic
differences with which they are articulated. This over-integrated sense of cultural
and ethnic particularity is very popular today and blacks do not monopolize it. It
masks the arbitrariness of its own political choices in the morally charged language
of ethnic absolutism and this poses significant dangers because it overlooks the
development of political ideology and ignores the restless, recombinant qualities
of our affirmative political cultures. The critical political project forged in the
journey from slave ship to citizenship is in danger of being wrecked by the seemingly insoluble conflict between two distinct but currently symbiotic perspectives
which can be loosely identified as the essentialist and the pluralist standpoints.

The antagonistic relationship between these outlooks is especially intense in
discussions of black art and cultural criticism. The essentialist view comes in gender-
specific forms, but has often been characterized by an archaic pan-Africanism that,
in Britain at least, is now politically inert. In the newer garb of Africentricity it
has still proved unable to specify precisely where the highly prized but doggedly
evasive essence of black artistic sensibility is currently located. This perspective
sees the black artist as a potential leader. It is often allied to a realist approach to
aesthetics which minimizes the substantive political and philosophical issues involved
in the processes of artistic representation. Its absolutist conception of ethnic cultures
can be identified by the way in which it registers uncomprehending disappointment with the actual cultural choices and patterns of the mass of black people in
this country. It looks for an artistic practice that can disabuse them of the illusions
into which they have been seduced by their condition of exile. The community is
felt to be on the wrong road and it is the artist's job to give them a new direction, first by recovering and then by donating the racial awareness that the masses
seem to lack.

This perspective currently confronts a pluralistic position which affirms blackness as an open signifier and seeks to celebrate complex representations of a black

particularity that is *internally* divided: by class, sexuality, gender, age and political consciousness. There is no unitary idea of black community here and the authoritarian tendencies of those who would 'police' black cultural expression in the name of their own particular history or priorities are rightly repudiated. Essentialism is replaced by a libertarian alternative: the saturnalia which attends 'the dissolution of the essential black subject'. Here, the polyphonic qualities of black cultural expression form the main aesthetic consideration and there is often an uneasy but exhilarating fusion of 'modernist' and populist techniques and styles. From this perspective, the cultural achievements of popular black cultural forms like music are a constant source of inspiration and are prized for their implicit warning against the pitfalls of artistic conceit. The difficulty with this second tendency is that, in leaving racial essentialism behind by viewing 'race' itself as a social and cultural construction, it has been insufficiently alive to the lingering power of specifically 'racial' forms of power and subordination. Each outlook attempts to compensate for the obvious weaknesses in the other camp but so far there has been little open and explicit debate between them.

This conflict, initially formulated in debates over black aesthetics and cultural production, is valuable as a preliminary guide to some of the dilemmas faced by cultural and intellectual *historians* of the African diaspora. The problems it raises become acute, particularly for those who seek to comprehend cultural developments and political resistances which have had scant regard for either modern borders or pre-modern frontiers. At its worst, the lazy, casual invocation of cultural insiderism which characterizes the essentialist view is nothing more than a melancholy symptom of the growing cleavages *within* the black communities. There, uneasy spokespeople of the black middle classes – some of them professional cultural commentators, artists, writers, painters and film-makers as well as career politicians – have fabricated a volkish political outlook as an expression of their own contradictory position. Although the 'neo' is never satisfactorily explained, this is often presented as a neo-nationalism. It incorporates meditation on the special needs and desires of the relatively privileged castes within black communities, but its most consistent trademark is the persistent mystification of that group's increasingly problematic relationships with the black poor who, after all, supply them with a dubious entitlement to speak on behalf of black people in general.

The idea of blacks as a 'national' or proto-national group with its own hermetically enclosed culture plays a key role in this mystification and, though seldom overtly named, the misplaced idea of a 'national interest' gets invoked here as a means to silence dissent and censor political debate.

These problems take on a specific aspect in Britain, which still lacks anything that can credibly be called a black bourgeoisie. However, they are not confined to this country and they cannot be overlooked. The idea of nationality and the assumptions of cultural absolutism come together in various other ways.[3] For example, the archaeology of black critical knowledges in which we are engaged, currently involves the construction of canons which seems to be proceeding on an exclusively *national* basis – Afro-American, Anglophone Caribbean and so on. (This is not just my oblique answer to the pressure to produce an equivalent inventory of black English or British cultural forms and expressions.) If it seems indelicate to ask whom the formation of such canons might serve, then the related question of where the impulse to formalize and codify elements of our cultural heritage in this particular pattern comes from may be a better one with which to commence.

The historiography of canon formation raises interesting issues for the intellectual historian in and of itself. But if the way that these issues occur around the question of the canon appears too obscure, similar problems are also evident in recent debates over hip-hop culture, the powerful expressive medium of America's urban black poor. Rap is a hybrid form rooted in the syncretic social relations of the South Bronx where Jamaican sound-system culture, transplanted during the 1970s, put down new roots and in conjunction with specific technological innovations, set in train a process that was to transform black America's sense of itself and a large portion of the popular music industry as well. How does a form which flaunts and glories in its own malleability as well as its transnational character become interpreted as an expression of some authentic Afro-American essence? Why is rap discussed as if it sprang intact from the entrails of the blues?[4] What is it about Afro-America's writing elite which means that they need to claim this diasporic cultural form in such an assertively nationalist way?[5] Hip-hop culture has recently provided the raw material for a bitter contest between black vernacular expression and repressive censorship of artistic work. This has thrown some black commentators into a quandary which they resolve by invoking the rhetoric of cultural insiderism and drawing the distinctive cloak of ethnicity even more tightly around their shoulders. It is striking, for example, that apologists for the woman-hating antics of the 2 Live Crew have been so far unconcerned that the vernacular tradition they desire to affirm has its own record of reflection on the specific ethical obligations and political responsibilities which constitute the unique burden of the black artist. This may have generational, even authoritarian, implications because the 'racial' community is always a source of constraint as well as a source of support and protection for its artists and intellectuals but, leaving the question of misogyny aside for a moment, to collude in the belief that black vernacular is *nothing* more than a playfully parodic cavalcade of Rabelaisian subversion decisively weakens the positions of the artist, the critical commentator[6] and the community as a whole. What is more significant is surely the failure of either academic or journalistic commentary on black popular music in America to develop a reflexive political aesthetics capable of distinguishing the 2 Live Crew and their ilk from their equally 'authentic' but possibly more compelling and certainly more constructive peers.[7] I am not suggesting that the self-conscious racial pedagogy of artists like KRS1, The Poor Righteous Teachers, Lakim Shabazz or The X Clan can be straightforwardly counterposed against the carefully calculated affirmative nihilism of Ice Cube, Above The Law and Compton's Most Wanted. The different styles and political perspectives expressed within the music are linked both by the bonds of a stylized but aggressively masculinist discourse and by formal borrowings from the linguistic innovations to Jamaica's distinct traditions of 'kinetic orality'.[8] The debt to Caribbean forms is more openly acknowledged in the ludic Afrocentrisms of The Jungle Brothers, De La Soul and A Tribe Called Quest, which may represent a third alternative – in its respectful and egalitarian representation of women and in its ambivalent relationship to America. This stimulating and innovative work operates a rather different conception of black authenticity which effectively contrasts the local (black nationalism) with the global (black internationalism) and Americanism with Ethiopianism. It is important to emphasize that all three strands within hip-hop contribute to a folk-cultural constellation where neither the political compass of weary leftism nor the shiny navigational instruments of premature black post-modernism[9] in aesthetics offer very much that is useful.

An additional, and possibly more profound, area of political difficulty comes into view where the voguish language of absolute cultural difference I have described provides an embarrassing link between the practice of blacks who comprehend racial politics through it and the activities of their foresworn opponents – the racist New Right – who approach the complex dynamics of race, nationality and ethnicity through a similar set of precise, culturalist equations. [. . .]

[. . .] I want to make all these abstract and difficult points more concrete and accessible by turning to some of the lessons to be learned from considering the musical traditions of blacks in the West. The history and significance of these musics are consistently overlooked by black writers for two reasons: first, because they escape the frameworks of national or ethnocentric analysis, and second, because talking seriously about the politics and aesthetics of black vernacular cultures demands a confrontation with the order of 'intra-racial' differences. These may be to do with class, gender, sexuality or other factors, but they provide severe embarrassment to the rhetoric of racial and cultural homogeneity. As these internal divisions have grown, the price of that embarrassment has been an aching silence.

To break that silence, I want to examine the role of black musical expression in reproducing what Zygmunt Bauman has called a distinctive 'counter culture of modernity'. The shifting relationship of music-making to other modes of black cultural expression requires a much more sustained treatment that I can give it here. However, I want to use a brief consideration of black musical development to move our critical thoughts beyond an understanding of cultural processes which, as I have already suggested, is currently torn between seeing them as either the expression of an essential, unchanging, sovereign racial self or as the effluent from a constituted subjectivity that emerges contingently from the endless play of racial signification conceived solely in terms of the inappropriate model which *textuality* provides. The vitality and complexity of this musical culture offers a means to get beyond the related oppositions between essentialists and pluralists on the one hand and between tradition, modernity and post-modernity on the other.

Black music's obstinate and consistent commitment to the idea of a better future is a puzzle to which our enforced separation from literacy and the compensatory refinement of musical art supplies less than half an answer. The power of music in developing our struggles by communicating information, organizing consciousness and testing out, deploying or amplifying the forms of subjectivity which are required by political agency – individual and collective, defensive and transformational – demands attention to both the formal attributes of this tradition of expression and its distinctive *moral* basis. The formal qualities of this music are becoming better known,[10] so I shall concentrate here on the moral aspects and in particular on the disjunction between the ethical value of the music and its ethnic significance.

In the simplest possible terms, by posing the world as it is against the world as the racially subordinated would like it to be, this musical culture supplies a great deal of the courage required to go on living in the present. It is both produced by and expressive of that 'transvaluation of all values' precipitated by the history of racial terror in the new world. It contains a theodicy but moves beyond theodicy because the profane dimensions of that racial terror made theodicy impossible.[11]

I have considered its distinctive critique of capitalist social relations elsewhere.[12] Here, because I want to suggest that its critical edge includes but also surpasses anti-capitalism, I want to draw out some of its inner philosophical dynamics and place emphasis on the connection between its normative character and its utopian aspirations. These are interrelated and even inseparable from each other and from the critique of racial capitalism.[13] Comprehending them requires us to link together analysis of the lyrical content and the forms of musical expression as well as the often hidden social relations in which these deeply encoded oppositional practices are created and consumed. The issue of normative content focuses attention on what might be called the politics of fulfilment:[14] the notion that a future society will be able to realize the social and political promise that present society has left unaccomplished. Reflecting the primary semantic position of the Bible, this is primarily a discursive mode of communication. Though by no means literal, it relates mainly to what is said, shouted, screamed or sung. The issue of utopia is more complex not least because it strives continually to move beyond the grasp of the merely linguistic, textual or discursive. It references what, following Seyla Benhabib's suggestive lead, I propose to call the politics of transfiguration. This emphasizes the emergence of qualitatively new desires, social relations and modes of association within the racial community of interpretation and resistance *and* between that group and its erstwhile oppressors. It points specifically to the forma-tion of a community of needs and solidarity which is magically made audible in the music itself and palpable in the social relations of its cultural consumption and reproduction.

The politics of fulfilment practiced by the descendants of slaves demands that bourgeois civil society lives up to the promises of its own rhetoric and offers a means whereby demands for justice, rational organization of the productive processes, etc., can be expressed. It is immanent within modernity and is no less a valuable element of modernity's counter-discourse for being so consistently ignored. Created under the nose of the overseer, the utopian desires which fuel the politics of transfiguration must be invoked by other deliberately opaque means. This politics exists on a lower frequency where it is played, danced and acted, as well as sung about, because words, even words stretched by melisma and supple-mented or mutated by the screams which still index the conspicuous power of the slave sublime, will never be enough to communicate its unsayable claims to truth. The wilfully damaged signs which betray the utopian politics of transfiguration therefore partially transcend modernity. This is not a counter-discourse but a counter-culture that defiantly constructs its own critical, intellectual and moral genealogy anew in a partially hidden public sphere of its own. The politics of trans-figuration therefore reveals the internal problems in the concept of modernity. The bounds of politics are extended precisely because this tradition of expression refuses to accept that the political is a readily separable domain. Its basic desire is to conjure up and enact the new modes of friendship, happiness and solidarity that are consequent on the overcoming of the racial oppression on which modernity and the duality of rational Western progress as excessive barbarity relied. Thus the vernacular arts of the children of slaves give rise to a verdict on the role of art which is strikingly in harmony with Adorno's reflections on the dynamics of European artistic expression in the wake of Auschwitz:

> Art's Utopia, the counterfactual yet-to-come, is draped in black. It goes on being a recollection of the possible with a critical edge against the real; it is a kind of imaginary restitution of that catastrophe, which is world history; it is a freedom which did not pass under the spell of necessity and which may well not come to pass ever at all.[15]

These sibling dimensions of black sensibility, the politics of fulfilment and the politics of transfiguration, are not coextensive. There are significant tensions between them but they are closely associated in the vernacular cultures of the diaspora. They can also be used to reflect the doubleness with which I began and which is often argued to be our constitutive experience in the modern world: in the West but not of it. The politics of fulfilment is content to play occidental rationality at its own game. It necessitates a hermeneutic orientation which can assimilate the semiotic, verbal and textual. The politics of transfiguration strives in pursuit of the sublime, struggling to repeat the unrepeatable, to present the unpresentable. Its rather different hermeneutic focus pushes towards the mimetic, dramatic and performative.

It seems especially significant that the cultural traditions which these musics allow us to map out, do not seek to exclude problems of inequality or to make racial justice an exclusively abstract matter. Their grounded ethics offers, among other things, a continuous commentary on the systematic and pervasive relations of domination that supply its conditions of existence. Their grounded aesthetics is never separated off into an autonomous realm where familiar political rules cannot be applied and where, as Salman Rushdie puts it, 'the little room of literature' can continue to enjoy its special privileges as a heroic resource for the well-heeled adversaries of liberal capitalism.[16]

I am proposing then, that we re-read and rethink this tradition of cultural expression not simply as a succession of literary tropes and genres, but as a philosophical discourse which refuses the modern, occidental separation of ethics and aesthetics, culture and politics. The traditional teaching of ethics and politics – practical philosophy – came to an end some time ago, even if its death agonies were prolonged. This tradition had maintained the idea that a good life for the individual and the problem of the best social and political order for the collectivity could be discerned by rational means. Although it is seldom acknowledged even now, this tradition lost its exclusive claim to rationality, in part, through the way that slavery became internal to Western civilization and through the obvious complicity which both plantation slavery and colonial regimes revealed between rationality and the practice of racial terror.

Not perceiving its residual condition, blacks in the West eavesdropped on and then took over a fundamental question from that tradition. Their progress from the status of slaves to the status of citizens led them to enquire into what the best possible forms of social and political existence might be. The memory of slavery, actively preserved as a living, intellectual resource in their expressive political culture, helped them to generate a new set of answers to this enquiry. They had to fight – often through the invocation of spirituality – to hold on to the unity of ethics and politics sundered from each other by modernity's insistence that the true, the good and the beautiful had distinct origins and belong to different domains of knowledge. First, slavery itself and then their memory of it induced many of them to query the foundational moves of modern philosophy and social thought whether they came from the natural-rights theorists who sought to distinguish between the spheres of morality and legality, the idealists who wanted to eman-cipate politics from morals so that it could become a sphere of strategic action, or the political economists of the bourgeoisie who first formulated the separation of economic activity from both ethics and politics. The brutal excess of the slave plantation supplied a set of moral and political responses to each of these attempts.

The history of black music enables us to trace something of the means through which the unity of ethics and politics has been reproduced as a form of folk know-ledge. This sub-culture often appears to be the intuitive expression of some racial essence but is in fact an elementary historical acquisition produced from the viscera of an alternative tradition of cultural and political expression which considers the world critically from the point of view of its emancipatory transformation. In the future, it will become a place which is capable of satisfying the (redefined) needs of human beings that will emerge once the violence – epistemic and concrete – of racial typology is at an end. Reason is thus reunited with the happiness and freedom of individuals and the reign of justice within the collectivity.

I have already implied that there is a degree of convergence here with other projects towards a critical theory of society, particularly Marxism. However, where lived crisis and systemic crisis come together, Marxism allocates priority to the latter while the memory of slavery insists on the priority of the former. Their convergence is also undercut by the simple fact that in the critical tradition of blacks in the West, social self-creation through labour is not the core of emanci-patory hopes. For the descendants of slaves, work signifies only servitude, misery and subordination. Artistic expression, expanded beyond recognition from the grudging gifts offered by the masters as a token substitute for freedom from bondage, therefore becomes the means towards both individual self-fashioning and communal liberation. Poiesis and poetics begin to coexist in novel forms – auto-biographical writing, special and uniquely creative ways of manipulating spoken language and, above all, the music.

Antiphony (call and response) is the principal formal feature of these musical traditions. It reaches out beyond music into other modes of cultural expression, supplying, along with improvisation, montage and dramaturgy, the hermeneutic keys to the full medley of black artistic practices from kinesics to rhetoric. The intense and often bitter dialogues, which make the black arts movement move, offer a small reminder that there is a 'democratic' moment enshrined in the prac-tice of antiphony which anticipates new, non-dominating social relationships. Lines between self and other are blurred and special forms of pleasure are created as a result. Ellison's famous observation on the inner dynamics of jazz uses visual art as its central analogy and can be extended beyond the specific context it was written to illuminate:

> There is in this a cruel contradiction implicit in the art form itself. For true jazz is an art of individual assertion within and against the group. Each true jazz moment . . . springs from a contest in which the artist challenges all the rest; each solo flight, or improvisation, represents (like the canvasses of a painter) a definition of his identity: as individual, as member of the collectivity and as a link in the chain of tradition. Thus because jazz finds its very life in improvisation upon traditional materials, the jazz man must lose his identity even as he finds it. . .[17]

By way of a conclusion, I want to illustrate these arguments further by very briefly bringing forward two concrete historical instances in which the musical traditions of the black Atlantic world acquired a special political valency. These examples are simultaneously both national, in that they had a direct impact on British politics, and diasporic, in that they tell us something fundamental about the limit of that national perspective. They are not, of course, the only examples I could have chosen. They have been selected somewhat at random, although the fact that they span a century will, I hope, be taken as preliminary evidence for the existence of fractal[18] patterns of cultural and political affiliation which will need further elaboration and detailed critical consideration. Both, in rather different ways, reflect the special position of Britain within the black Atlantic world, standing at the apex of the semi-triangular structure which saw commodities and people shipped to and fro across the ocean.

The first relates to the visits by the Fisk University Jubilee Singers[19] to England, Ireland, Wales and Scotland in the early 1870s under the philanthropic patronage of the Earl of Shaftesbury. The Fisk Singers have a profound historical importance because they were the first group to perform spirituals on a public platform, offering this form of black music as mass entertainment.[20] Their success is especially significant amidst the changed cultural and ideological circumstances that attended the 're-making' of the English working class in the era of imperialism.[21] In explicit opposition to minstrelsy, which was becoming an established element in popular culture by this time,[22] the Fisk Singers constructed an aura of seriousness and projected the memory of slavery outwards as the means to make their musical performances intelligible and pleasurable. The choir had taken to the road seven years after the founding of their Alma Mater to raise funds. They produced books to supplement the income from their concert performances and these volumes ran to over 60,000 copies sold between 1877 and the end of the century. Interestingly, these publications included a general historical account of Fisk and its struggles, some unusual autobiographical statements from the members of the ensemble and the music and lyrics of between 104 and 139 songs from their extensive repertoire. In my opinion, this unusual combination of communicative modes and genres is especially important for anyone seeking to locate the origins of the polyphonic montage technique developed by Du Bois in *The Souls of Black Folk*.

The Fisk Singers' text describes Queen Victoria listening to 'John Brown's body' 'with manifest pleasure', the Prince of Wales requesting 'No More Auction Block for Me' and the choir being waited upon by Mr and Mrs Gladstone after their servants had been dismissed.[23] These images are important, although the choir's performances to enormous working-class audiences in British cities may be more significant for contemporary anti-racism struggling to escape the strictures of its own apparent novelty. It is clear that for their liberal patrons, the music and song of the Fisk Singers offered an opportunity to feel closer to God while the memory of slavery, recovered by their performances, entrenched the feelings of moral rectitude which flowed from the commitment to political reform for which the imagery of elevation from slavery was emblematic long after emancipation. The Fisk Singers' music can be shown to have articulated what Du Bois calls 'the articulate message of the slave to the world' into British culture and society at several distinct and class-specific points. The spirituals enforced the patrician moral concerns of Shaftesbury and Gladstone but also introduced a specific moral sensibility into the lives of the lower orders who, it would appear, began to create Jubilee choirs of their own.[24]

My second example of diasporic cultural innovation is contemporary, although it relates to the song 'I'm So Proud', originally written and performed by the Chicagoan vocal trio The Impressions at the peak of their artistic and commercial success in the mid-1960s. The Impressions' 1960s hits like 'Gypsy Woman', 'Grow Closer Together', 'Minstrel and Queen' and 'People Get Ready' were extremely popular among blacks in Britain and in the Caribbean. In Jamaica, the male vocal trio format popularized by the band inaugurated a distinct genre within the vernacular musical form which would eventually be marketed internationally as reggae.[25] The Wailers were only one of many groups that patterned themselves on The Impressions and strove to match the singing of the Americans for harmonic texture, emotional dynamics and black metaphysical grace. A new version of The Impressions' hit 'I'm So Proud' has recently topped the reggae charts in Britain. Re-titled 'Proud of Mandela', it was performed by the toaster Macka B and the Lovers' Rock singer Kofi who had produced her own version of the tune itself, patterned on another soft soul version issued by the American singer Deniece Williams in 1983.

I want to make no special claims for the formal, musical merits of this particular record, but I think that it is exemplary in that it brings Africa, America, Europe and the Caribbean seamlessly together. It was produced in Britain by the children of Caribbean and African settlers from raw materials supplied by black Chicago but filtered through Kingstonian sensibility in order to pay tribute to a black hero whose global significance lies beyond his partial South African citizenship and the impossible national identity which goes with it. The very least that this music and its history can offer us today is an analogy for comprehending the lines of affiliation and association which take the idea of the diaspora beyond its symbolic status as the fragmentary opposite of an imputed racial essence. Foregrounding the role of music allows us to see England, or perhaps London, as an important junction point on the web of black Atlantic political culture: a place where, by virtue of local factors like the informality of racial segregation, the configuration of class relations and the contingency of linguistic convergences of global phenomena such as anti-colonial and emancipationist political formations are still being sustained, reproduced and amplified.

Notes and references

I have taken the title of this essay directly from lyrics written and performed by Rakim (W. Griffin). In his recordings with his sometimes partner Eric B, Rakim has persistently returned to the problem of diasporic identification and the connected issue of the relationship between local and global components of blackness. His 'I Know You got Soul' (1987) was received as a classic recording in London's soul underground, and since then he has produced what I regard as the most complex and exciting poetry to emerge from the hip-hop movement. The dread recording which directly inspired the production of this essay is called 'The Ghetto' and is included on the MCA (1990) album 'Let the Rhythm Hit 'Em'. I wish to thank my children for tolerating the repeated playing of this cut at bone-breaking volume, Vron Ware for her insight and bell hooks for the transatlantic dialogue which has helped me to frame this piece of work.

1   W. E. B. Du Bois, *The Souls of Black Folk* (1903) reprinted Bantam, New York, 1989. See also the discussion of this in ch. 4 of my book *The Black Atlantic*.

2   This phrase is taken from Wright's novel *The Outsider*, Harper and Row, New York, 1965. In his book of essays, *White Man Listen!*, Anchor Books, New York, 1964, he employs the phrase 'dual existence' to map the same terrain.

3   Etienne Balibar and Immanuel Wallerstein, *Race, Nation, Class*, Verso, London, 1991.

4   Nelson George, *The Death of Rhythm and Blues*, Omnibus, London, 1988.

5   I should emphasize that it is the assimilation of these cultural forms to an unthinking notion of nationality which is the object of my critique here. Of course, certain cultural forms become articulated with sets of social and political forces over long periods of time. These forms may be played with and lived with as though they were 'natural' emblems of racial and ethnic particularity. This may even be an essential defensive attribute of the interpretive communities involved. However, the notion of nationality cannot be borrowed as a ready-made means to make sense of the special dynamics of this process.

6   Henry Louis Gates jnr, 'Rap Music: Don't knock it if you're not onto its "lies"', *Herald Tribune*, 20 June 1990.

7   I am prepared to defer to black Americans who argue that it is probably necessary to be both defenders and critics of the 2 Live Crew. However, watching the MTV video of their hit single, 'Banned in the USA', I found it difficult to accept the way in which the powerful visual legacy of the black movement of the 1950s and 1960s had been appropriated and made over so that it became readily and unproblematically continuous with the group's own brand of American patriotism.

8   Cornel West, 'Black Culture and Postmodernism' in B. Kruger and P. Mariani (eds), *Re-Making History*, Dia Foundation, Bay Press, Seattle, 1989.

9   Trey Ellis's famous piece on the new black aesthetic in a recent issue of *Callaloo* exemplifies the perils of this casual, 'anything goes' post-modernism for the black arts movement. It was striking how, for example, profound questions of class antagonism within the black communities were conjured out of sight. Apart from his conflation of forms which are not merely different but actively oppose one another, Ellis does not seriously consider the notion that the NBA might have a very particular and highly class-specific articulation within a small and isolated

segment of the black middle class which struggles with its own dependency on the cultural lifeblood of the black poor.

10 Anthony Jackson's dazzling exposition of James Jamerson's bass style is, in my view, indicative of the type of detailed critical work which needs to be done on the form and dynamics of black musical creativity. His remarks on Jamerson's use of harmonic and rhythmic ambiguity and selective employment of dissonance were especially helpful. To say that the book from which it is taken has been geared to the needs of the performing musician rather than the cultural historian is to indict the current state of cultural history rather than the work of Jackson and his collaborator, Dr Licks. See 'An Appreciation of the Style' in Dr Licks (ed.) *Standing in the Shadows of Motown*, Hal Leonard, Detroit, 1989.

11 I am thinking here both of Wright's tantalizing discussion of 'The Dozens' in the essay on the 'Literary Tradition of the Negro in the United States' in *White Man Listen!* and also of Levinas's remarks on useless suffering in another context: 'useless and unjustifiable suffering [is] exposed and displayed . . . without any shadow of consoling theodicy' (see 'Useless Suffering' in R. Bernasconi and D. Wood (eds), *The Provocation of Levinas*, Routledge, London, 1988). Jon Michael Spencer's thoughtful but fervently Christian discussion of what he calls the Theodicy of the Blues is also relevant here. See *The Theology of American Popular Music*, a special issue of *Black Sacred Music*, vol. 3, no. 2, Fall 1989 (Duke University Press). I do not have space to develop my critique of Spencer here.

12 *There Ain't No Black in the Union Jack: The Cultural Politics of Race and Nation*, Hutchinson, London, 1987, ch. 5.

13 Cedric Robinson, *Black Marxism*, Zed Press, London, 1982.

14 This concept and its pairing with the politics of transfiguration have been adapted from Seyla Benhabib's inspiring book *Critique, Norm and Utopia*, Columbia University Press, New York, 1987.

15 *Aesthetic Theory*, Routledge, London, p. 196.

16 Salman Rushdie, *Is Nothing Sacred?* The Herbert Read Memorial Lecture 1990, Granta, Cambridge.

17 Ralph Ellison, *Shadow and Act*, Random House, New York, 1964, p. 234. There are in Ellison's remarks the components of a definitive response to the position of Adorno in 'Uber Jazz'; see also Susan Buck Morss, *The Origin of Negative Dialectics*, Free Press, New York pp. 108–10.

18 I am thinking of fractal geometry as an analogy here because it allows for the possibility that a line of infinite length can enclose a finite area. The opposition between totality and infinity is thus recast in a striking image of the scope for agency in restricted conditions.

19 The radical historian Peter Linebaugh has recently discussed the etymology of the word 'jubilee' and some of the political discourses that surround it: 'Jubilating', *Midnight Notes*, Fall 1990. Reviews of the singers' performances in England can be found in *East Anglian Daily Times*, 21 November 1874 and the *Surrey Advertiser*, 5 December 1874.

20 John M. MacKenzie (ed.), *Imperialism and Popular Culture*, Manchester University Press, 1986.

21 Gareth Stedman Jones, 'Working-class Culture and Working-class Politics in London 1870–1900: Notes on the remaking of a working class' in *Languages of Class*, Cambridge University Press, Cambridge, 1983.

22 An 'Eva Gets Well' version of *Uncle Tom's Cabin* was doing excellent business

on the London stage in 1878. See also Robert C. Toll, *Blacking Up: The Minstrel Show in Nineteenth Century America*, Oxford University Press, Oxford, 1974; Barry Anthony, 'Early Nigger Minstrel Acts in Britain', *Music Hall*, vol. 12, April 1980; and Josephine Wright, 'Orpheus Myron McAdoo', *Black Perspective in Music*, vol. 4, no. 3, Fall 1976.

23   These events are described in Gladstone's diaries for 14 and 29 July 1873. Apart from the singers' own text, there is a lengthy discussion of these events in the New York *Independent*, 21 August 1873. See also Ella Sheppard Moore, 'Historical Sketch of The Jubilee Singers', *Fisk University News*, October 1911, p. 42.

24   In his essay on the Fisk Singers in Britain, Doug Seroff cites the example of the East London Jubilee Singers of Hackney Juvenile Mission, a 'ragged school' formed after an inspirational visit by the Fisk Singers to Hackney in June 1873. John Newman, the manager of the Mission, 'felt that such singing from the soul should not be forgotten, and speedily set to work to teach the children of the Mission the songs the Jubilee singers had sung'; see R. Lotz and I. Pegg (eds), *Under the Imperial Carpet: Essays in Black History 1780–1950*, Rabbit Press, Crawley, 1986. Listening recently to my 7-year-old son's primary school singing 'Oh Freedom' in furtherance of the multicultural and anti-racist educational policies of the Borough of Islington was confirmation that slave songs are still being sung in inner London schools in the 1990s.

25   The phenomenon of Jamaican male vocal trios is discussed by Randall Grass, 'Iron Sharpen Iron: The great Jamaican harmony trios' in P. Simon (ed.), *Reggae International*, Thames & Hudson, London, 1983. Key exponents of this particular art would be The Heptones, The Paragons, The Gaylads, The Meditations, The Itals, Carlton and The Shoes, Justice Hines and The Dominoes, Toots and The Maytals, Yabby Yu and The Prophets, The Gladiators, The Melodians, The Ethiopians, The Cables, The Tamlins, The Congoes, The Mighty Diamonds, The Abyssinians, Black Uhuru, Israel Vibration and, of course, The Wailers, whose Neville O'Reilly/Bunny Livingstone/Bunny Wailer does the best Curtis Mayfield impersonation of the lot.

Chapter 34

Kobena Mercer

IDENTITY AND DIVERSITY IN POSTMODERN POLITICS

JUST NOW EVERYBODY WANTS to talk about identity. As a keyword in contemporary politics it has taken on so many different connotations that sometimes it is obvious that people are not even talking about the same thing. One thing at least is clear – identity only becomes an issue when it is in crisis, when something assumed to be fixed, coherent and stable is displaced by the experience of doubt and uncertainty. From this angle, the eagerness to talk about identity is symptomatic of the postmodern predicament of contemporary politics.

The salient ambiguity of the word itself draws attention to the breakup of the traditional vocabulary of Left, Right and Center. Our conventional maps are no longer adequate to the territory, as the political landscape has been radically restructured over the last decade by the hegemony of the New Right. Hence, in no uncertain terms, the 'identity crisis' of the Left. After ten years of Thatcherism, the attitudes, assumptions and institutions of the British Left have been systematically demoralized, disorganized and disaggregated. Neoliberal hegemony has helped to transform the political terrain to the point where the figurative meaning of the Left/Right dichotomy has been totally reversed. This was always a metaphor for the opposition between progressive and reactionary forces, derived in fact from the seating arrangements of the General Assemblies after the French Revolution. But today the word 'revolution' sounds vaguely embarrassing when it comes out of the mouths of people on the Left: it only sounds as if it means what it says when uttered in the mouths of the radicalized Right. In the modern period, the Left anticipated the future with optimism, confident that socialism would irreversibly change the world. Today such epic beliefs seem to be disappearing into the grand museum, as it is the postmodern Right that wants to 'revolutionize' the entire society and remake our future in its own millennial image of neoliberal market freedom.

The identity crisis of the Left is underlined not only by the defeat experienced by trade unions and other organizations that make up the labor movement, but above all by the inability of the Labour Party to articulate an effective 'opposition.' Even so, the problem goes beyond the official theater of parliamentary democracy. The classical Marxist view of the industrial working classes as the privileged agent of revolutionary historical change has been undermined and discredited from below by the emergence of numerous social movements – feminisms, black struggles, national liberation, antinuclear and ecology movements – that have also reshaped and redefined the sphere of politics. The ambiguity of 'identity' serves in this regard as a way of acknowledging the presence of new social actors and new political subjects – women, black people, lesbian and gay communities, youth – whose aspirations do not neatly fit into the traditional Left/Right dichotomy. However I am not sure that 'identity' is what these movements share in common: on the contrary, within and between the various new movements that have arisen in postwar, Western, capitalist democracies, what is asserted is an emphasis on 'difference.' In a sense, the 'newness' of these struggles consists precisely in the fact that such differences cannot be coded or programmed into the same old formula of Left, Right and Center. The proliferation of differences is highly ambivalent, as it relativizes the Big Picture and weakens the totalizing universalist truth claims of ideologies like Marxism, thus demanding acknowledgment of the *plural* sources of oppression, unhappiness and antagonism in contemporary capitalist societies.

On the other hand, the downside of such diversification and fragmentation is the awareness that there is no necessary relationship between the new social movements and the traditional labor movement, or to put it another way, it cannot be taken for granted that there is common cause in the project of creating a socialist society. This question arises with a double sense of urgency, not only because it has become difficult to imagine what a socialist society looks like as something 'totally' different from any other type of society, but because the new social subjects have no necessary belonging on either side of the distinction between progressive and reactionary politics, which is to say they could go either way.

Difference and division

I want to examine the unwieldy relationship between the Left and the new social movements because they both share problems made symptomatic in terms of 'identity,' and yet there is no vocabulary in which to conduct a mutual dialogue on the possibility of alliances or coalitions around a common project, which is the starting point for any potentially hegemonic project. This dilemma was forcefully brought to light in the experiments in municipal socialism led by the Greater London Council (GLC) and other metropolitan local authorities in Britain in the early to mid-1980s. Such initiatives mobilized popular enthusiasm for socialist politics, but now that the whole experience is a fast-fading memory, what is mostly remembered is the mess created by the microantagonisms that erupted precisely in the relationship between the traditional Left and the political movements articulated around race, gender, ethnicity and sexuality.

The scenario of fragmentation that emerged was further dramatized by the conflictual differences within and between the new social movements themselves. The tabloid discourse of 'Loony Leftism' picked up on this state of affairs and created a reactive populist parody to which the Labour leadership readily capitulated. In the aftermath of a local campaign for 'Positive Images' of lesbians and gays in Haringey schools in 1987, the Labour Party disassociated itself from the GLC's somewhat ragged rainbow coalition with the dismissive and divisive remark that 'the lesbian and gay issue is costing us dear among the pensioners.' The so-called 'London factor' was held to be responsible for yet another electoral defeat, but in the search for something to blame, Labour not only rationalized its unwillingness to construct new alliances, but helped pave the way for the hateful, authoritarian logic of Clause 28. Why could Labour not articulate pensioners *and* lesbians and gays within the same discourse? Was it not conceivable that pensioners and lesbians and gay men might even have a common interest in constructing an alternative to the unremitting 'new reality' of Thatcherite Britain?

What was important and exciting about the GLC in that briefly optimistic moment around 1983 was precisely the attempt to find forms of democratic representation and participation that would be responsive to the diversity of social identities active in the contemporary polity. Looking back, was it any wonder the experiment failed given that *this was the first time it had ever been contemplated*? The question of alliances between the labor movement, the Left and the various new social movements arose in the 1970s in trade union strikes, single-issue protest campaigns, localized community action and cultural mobilizations such as Rock Against Racism. While these experiences helped to create a fragile network of association either in the workplace or in civil society, the GLC experiment attempted to remobilize alliances around a socialist program *within* the institutional spaces of the local state. The shift was important because of the symbolic and material resources invested in local government as an apparatus of the state, but by the same token it proved impossible to translate the connections between the various elements once they were 'inside' the bureaucratic machinery of 'representative democracy.'

The Labour Left administration of the 1981 to 1986 GLC was the first of its kind to take the demands of the new movements seriously and to go beyond the tokenistic management of noisy 'minorities.' Conversely, this was the first time many community-based activists had operated within the framework of officialdom, whereas their previous extraparliamentary 'autonomy' made them skeptical of having anything to do with it. What happened when the two came face to face was that expectations about equal participation and representation were converted into sectional demands and competing claims about the legitimation of different needs. The possibility of coalition building was preempted by the competitive dynamic of who would have priority access to resources.

The worst aspects of the new social movements emerged in a rhetoric of 'identity politics' based on an essentialist notion of a fixed hierarchy of racial, sexual or gendered oppressions. By playing off each other to establish who was more authentically oppressed than whom, the residual separatist tendencies of the autonomous movements played into the normative calculation of 'disadvantage' inscribed in welfare statism. For their part, the generation of New Left activists who became the managers of state bureaucracy could only take over, rather than transform, the traditional top-down conception of meeting needs. Hence official rhetoric acknowledged diversity in a discourse of 'race, class and gender,' which became the policy repertoire in which each element was juggled about and administered according to expediency, patronage and good old Labourite pragmatism. The rationing of meager resources became a means of regulating and controlling 'difference' because, as the various actors perceived it, one group's loss was another group's gain. In this zero-sum game the only tangible consequence of diversity was dividedness.

[. . .] Like 'identity,' difference, diversity and fragmentation are keywords in the postmodern vocabulary, where they are saturated with groovy connotations. But it should be clear that there is nothing particularly groovy about the postmodern condition at all. As a best-seller ideology in artistic and intellectual circles, the postmodern paradigm has already been and gone, but as a pervasive sensibility in everyday life its smelly ideological effect lingers on. Postmodernism means many different things to many different people, but the key motifs of displacement, decentering and disenchantment have a specific resonance and relevance for the Left and new social movements after the demoralizing decade of Thatcherism.

In philosophical terms, postmodernism has been discussed as a weakening, fading or relativization of the absolutist or universalist values of the Western Enlightenment. The master narratives are collapsing, which is to say we no longer have the confidence to invest belief in the foundational myths of inevitable human rationality or social progress. Certain intellectuals, however (like Baudrillard), are apt to exaggerate the effect in a rather stupefied apocalyptic manner simply because they can no longer adopt the universalist postures they once did. Just like the organized Left, a whole generation of postwar intellectuals have been thrown into identity crisis as philosophies of Marxism and Modernism have begun to lose their adversarial aura. The loss of faith in the idea of a cultural avant-garde parallels the crisis of credulity in now-discredited notions of political vanguardism or 'scientific socialism.' But the narcissistic pathos expressed within the prevailing postmodern ideology obscures the more generalized effect of decentering acknowledged in common sense. Everybody intuitively knows that everyday life is so complex that no singular belief system or Big Story can hope to explain it all. We don't need another hero. But we do need to make sense of the experiences that characterize postmodern structures of feeling.

In sociological terms, this means a recognition of the fragmentation of traditional sources of authority and identity, the displacement of collective sources of membership and belonging, such as 'class' and 'community,' that help to construct political loyalties, affinities and identifications. One does not need to invoke the outmoded base/superstructure metaphor to acknowledge the impact of deterritorialized and decentralized forms of production in late-modern capitalism. While certain structures associated with the highly centralized logic of mass production and mass consumption give way to more flexible transnational arrangements that undermine the boundaries of the sovereign nation-state, other boundaries become more rigid, such as those that exclude the late-modern underclass from participation in free-market choices — 'you can have anything you want, but you better not take it from me.'[1] The New Right is not at the origin of these changes, but its brutalizing reassertion of competitive individualism and archaic 'Little Englandism' has hegemonized the commonsense terms in which the British are invited to make sense of and live through the vertiginous experience of displacement and decentering that these processes entail. It is here that we arrive at the political terms of postmodernism, in the sense that Thatcherism represents a new type of hegemony which has totally displaced the mythical 'Center' of the postwar social democratic consensus.

Identity is a key motif of post-consensus politics because the postwar vocabulary of Left, Right and Center, in which individual and collective subjects identified their loyalties and commitments, has been shot to pieces. The decentering of the social-democratic consensus, which was historically constructed around the axioms of welfare-state capitalism, was partly the result of its own internal economic and political contradictions. But, as Stuart Hall's analyses (1988) of Thatcherism have shown, it was the neoliberal agenda of 'free market and strong state' (Gamble, 1988), crystallized in the mid-1970s, that took the lead in answering the task of constructing a new form of popular consent by creating a new form of governmentality – 'authoritarian populism.'[2] If one identifies 1968 as the turning point in the deepening crisis of social-democratic consensus, it can be said that it was the New Right, not the New Left or the new social movements, that won out historically. It is precisely for this reason that we need to undertake an archaeology of the recent past, in which the problematic relationship between the Left and the new social movements developed.

Children of the revolution

> And my brother's back at home, with his Beatles and his Stones,
> We never got it off on that revolution stuff, What a drag, Too many snags.
> *All the Young Dudes*[3]

One way of clarifying what is at stake in the postmodern is to point out that the grammatical prefix 'post' simply means that the noun it predicates is 'past.' The ubiquitous prefix thus suggests a generalized mood or sensibility which problematizes perceptions of the past in relation to the contemporary horizon from which we imagine the future. Jacques Donzelot has characterized this as a new 'apprehension of time' resulting from the exhaustion of the rationalist myth of progress: new future or no future, adapt or die, that is how it feels, especially on the Left and among the oppositional movements that once thought that time was on our side. In this sense, as a shift in popular memory that results in a changed disposition towards the past, one recognizes that the cultural forms of postmodernism – the pervasive *mode retro*, nostalgia and recycling aesthetic, or the prevalence of pastiche and parody – are implicated in a logic that problematizes the recent past by creating ironic distance between 'then' and 'now.' The sixties and seventies are effectively historicized in much the same way as historians treat 'the twenties' or 'the forties.' What happened the day before yesterday now looks like it happened a long time ago, and sometimes it looks as if it never happened at all. While ex-leftist intellectuals are eager to repudiate and renounce the radical political fantasies of '1968,' a more generalized process of erasure and effacement is at work, selectively wiping out certain traces of the recent past sedimented in common sense by the progressive gains of the 1960s.

Taking this analysis a step further, Lawrence Grossberg (1988) has suggested a reading of this postmodern sensibility as a crucial resource for the hegemony of the New Right. Neoconservatism dominates our ability to imagine the future by performing on the postmodern 'frontier effect' in popular memory. Although Grossberg's analysis is addressed to the experience of Reaganism in the United States, it pertains to the British experience, because he argues that the sense of disillusionment with the radical aspirations of the sixties is central to the mobilization of popular support for the neoliberal programme of restructuring state and civil society in the present:

> If the state hegemonic project of the New Right entails deconstructing the postwar social democratic consensus, its cultural hegemonic project entails disarticulating the central relationship between the national identity, a specific set of generational histories, and the equation of the national-popular with postwar youth culture.
>
> (Grossberg, 1988: 52)

One has only to recall those images of Harold Wilson and the Beatles (fresh from Buckingham Palace with their OBEs) to appreciate the resonance of the equation between postwar modernization in Western capitalist democracies and the cultural presence of a new social subject, the teenager. In this equation 'youth' came to embody the promise of modernity within the ethos of social democracy. Grossberg argues that the repudiation of capitalist modernization within the youth counter-cultures of the late 1960s marked the cutoff point or threshold of dissensus against the Center. The neoconservative onslaught against 'the sixties' has since become a crucial component in winning consent for neoliberal democracy, or, as Conservative minister Francis Pym once put it, 'I think public expectations are too high. We have an end to the language of the Sixties. Today we have got to rid ourselves of these outlooks and look at economic and social matters in a new light.'[5]

During its period of opposition in the 1970s, Thatcherism mobilized a frontier effect which polarized the political field into two antagonistic positions. Labourism was identified with the interventionist state, while the Tories positioned themselves 'out there' with the people, against the state, to recruit support for a market-led definition of freedom detached from the welfarist conception of equality.[6] Since 1979 the Tories have never stopped using the state to pursue monetarist economic policies, but as an ideology that has now achieved considerable 'leadership' in official institutions and popular common sense, Thatcherism seeks to maintain its sources of support by playing on the binary polarity in which the Left is identified with the past and the Right monopolizes the imaginary horizon of the future. There can be no return to the bad old days of dissensus, which is to say that in popular consciousness the possibility of a future for socialism is rendered 'unthinkable' because the prevailing image of the Left is fixed in 'the winter of discontent' of 1979, a vestige of the past which occasionally flickers up in television documentaries.

The 'active forgetting' of the recent past is further underlined by Thatcherite identity politics, in which 'Little Englandism,' the peculiarly English combination of racism, nationalism and populism, becomes the predominant framework of the imagined community in which the 'collective will' is constructed – 'it's great to be Great again,' as the 1987 Tory election slogan put it. The Falklands War and Royal Weddings, Victorian values and Raj nostalgia movies are all recycled in the Great British heritage industry, and not just for the benefit of Japanese or American tourists either. Workers in Sunderland or Derbyshire know that their futures might well depend on decisions taken in Tokyo or Chicago, but the British do not like to think of themselves as a Third World nation run on a service economy. So the nation is enjoined to travel back to the future in a rewriting of history which leapfrogs over the recent past in order to retrieve an entirely fictional image of systemic 'national-popular' unity based on the retrieval and recycling of the wretched age of Empire.

Dick Hebdige (1987) has called this 'digging for Britain,' in that historicity and popular conceptions of the past have become a key site in which the changed circumstances of the present are apprehended and defined. One only has to consider the retrieval of historical *counter*memory in black pop culture (where the 'cut 'n' mix' aesthetic informs the narration of stories precisely hidden from history in dominant discourses of the past) to recognize the sources of popular resistance to the postmodern frontier effect, something underlined in a recent comment by the pop group Tears for Fears:

> The Tories are renowned for evoking memories of the Victorian era 'cos it falls in line with their paternalistic morality. What I wanted to do was bring back memories of that era when Britain was 'great' – the era of Harold Wilson, The Beatles, the red London bus, Twiggy and the mini. . . . There was a time when it was okay to be idealistic or, dare I say it, spiritual. And I wanted to jog everybody's memory.[7]

A few years ago Judith Williamson rightly criticized a simple-minded left-wing populism which merely imitated and capitulated to neoconservative definitions of popularity, and indeed one might also note a tendency towards culturalism or 'cultural substitutionism,' among Left intelligensia for whom 'postmodernism' just means going to the shops.[8] In one sense this is symptomatic of the Left's deeply demoralizing experience of being actively disarticulated as a result of the post-modern frontier effect. The withdrawal and retreat into culturalism further underlines another ironic twist of the Thatcher decade, as cultural studies has been appropriated into a knowledge-producing apparatus that services the reproduction of hyperconsumption in the culture industry.

These indicative signs of the times underscore the identity crisis of the Left, but the *contradictoriness* of the postmodern requires a *relational* emphasis, because what is experienced as the loss of identity and authority in some quarters is also an empowering experience which affirms the identities and experiences of others *for precisely the same reasons*. The 1980s have seen a significant renewal and revitalization of black politics. Whether this has occurred despite Thatcherism or because of it, issues of race and ethnicity have been irrevocably inscribed on the national political agenda, a process which represents a considerable advance on the previous decades. Indeed, if I think about the intensity of all those discussions about 'the definition of black' which occurred in the post-1981 scenario after the 'inner-city' riots, the experience of decentering has been highly empowering, as it has also articulated an experience of demarginalization, in which new forms of collective subjectivity and imagined community have been mobilized by various political and cultural activities.

What was so important about the demand for 'black representation' that could be heard in Britain in the early 1980s was an extension of radical democracy in which a marginalized and subordinate group affirmed and asserted their political rights to representation. The shift from 'ethnic minority' to 'black' registered in the language of political discourse, demonstrated a process in which the objects of racist ideology reconstituted themselves as subjects of social, cultural and political change, actively making history, albeit under circumstances not of their own choosing. A minority is literally a minor, not simply the abject and dependent childlike figure necessary for the legitimation of paternalistic ideologies of assimilation and integration, but a social subject that is *in-fans*, without a voice, debarred and disenfranchised from access to political representation in a liberal or social democracy.

The rearticulation of black as a political rather than racial category among Asian, Caribbean and African peoples, originating from a variety of ethnic backgrounds and sharing common experiences of British racism, thus created a new form of symbolic unity out of the signifiers of racial difference. For over four centuries the sign /black/ had nothing but negative connotations, as it signified racialized identities within Manichaean dualism, an absolute division between 'the West' and 'the rest' in which the identity of the black subject was negated as Other, ugly and ultimately unhuman. The decentering of 'Man,' the centered subject of Western liberal humanism, is nothing if not a good thing, as it has radically demonstrated the coercive force and power implicated in the worldly construction of the Western rational *cogito* – the subject of logocentrism and all the other 'centrisms' that construct its representations of reality. Western 'Man' consisted of a subject whose identity and subjectivity depended on the negation, exclusion and denial of Others. Women, children, slaves, criminals, madmen and savages were all alike in as much as their otherness affirmed 'his' identity as the universal norm represented in the category 'human.' Indeed, if the period after the modern is when the Others of modernity talk back, what is revealed is the fictional character of Western universality, as the subject who arrogated the power to speak on behalf of humanity was nothing but a minority himself – the hegemonic, white, male, bourgeois subject whose sovereign, centered identity depended on the 'othering' of subordinate class, racial, gendered and sexual subjects who were thereby excluded from the category 'human' and marginalized from democratic rights to political subjectivity. [. . .]

1968: What did you do in the war?

Chantal Mouffe (1988) has brought such critical tasks into focus by calling for the 'institutionalization of a true pluralism' on the Left which recognizes and respects the diversified character of political struggles which have radicalized democracy in postwar capitalist societies. By grounding her analysis of 'new demo-cratic struggles' in terms of a view which emphasizes the processes that enable or prevent the extension of the subversive logic of democratic 'equality,' Mouffe argues that:

> The progressive character of a struggle does not depend on its place of origin . . . but rather on its link with other struggles. The longer the chain of equivalences set up between the defence of the rights of one group and those of other groups, the deeper will be the democratization process and the more difficult it will be to neutralize certain struggles or make them serve the ends of the Right. The concept of solidarity can be used to form such a chain of demo-cratic equivalences.
>
> (Mouffe, 1988: 100)

Laclau's metaphorical concept of frontier effects (1977) refers precisely to the formation of imaginary unities and political solidarities, crystallized out of numerous microalliances or systems of equivalence that polarize the political field into demo-cratic antagonism. The 'us and them' logic of authoritarian populism, and the paranoid policing of the 'enemy within' articulated by Thatcherite ideology repre-sent one such frontier effect that has hegemonized popular consciousness in the present. But to understand the effectiveness of this right-wing closure (which largely explains why the Left is so defeated and demoralized) we have to grasp the rever-sals by which the New Right disarticulated and rearticulated the emancipatory identifications which the new social movements opened up against the 'Center' by inaugurating the democratic revolutions of the 1960s.

   As Mouffe notes, forms of oppression and inequality based on racism and patri-archy predate industrial capitalism, but the contradictory development of democracy within the universalized commodification of social relations in the postwar period was one of the key conditions by which the demand for equality was radicalized in the politics of feminism and black struggles. Just like women, the colonized participated equally in the war effort against facism, and in this respect were interpellated as 'equal' in one set of discourses, while the terms of social democratic consensus repositioned them – in the labor process, in the polit-ical process, in social relations – once more as 'unequal.' Mouffe argues that this contradictory interpellation created the conditions for new forms of democratic antagonism, not because people 'naturally' aspire towards freedom, equality and solidarity, but because such values were placed at the center of social and polit-ical life by social democracy, which nevertheless denied access to such values to its subordinate subjects and marginalized citizenry. It is from this perspective that 'we can see the widening of social conflict as the extension of the democratic revolution into more and more spheres of social life' (1988: 100). It seems to me that a historical reading of this concrete conjuncture would reveal the *privileged metaphor of 'race'* within the radicalization of the postmodern democratic imaginary.

At one level this is acknowledged globally in the geopolitical metaphor of First, Second and Third Worlds. In the context of the Cold War, whose 'Iron Curtain' polarized two rival superpowers, the assertion of US hegemony in a new phase of multinational capitalism required the presence of the underdeveloped world to stabilize and reproduce the logic of modernization necessary to the existence of the overdeveloped world. But politically speaking, the Third World was brought into existence by the anticolonial struggles of the colonized, by the historical presence of subjects who were formerly objects of imperialism. In such movements as Pan-Africanism or Gandhi's non-violent mobilization on the Indian subcontinent, localized regional, ethnic and 'tribal' identities were hegemonized by revolutionary nationalisms. Western forms of nationhood were appropriated and articulated with 'syncretic' traditionalism and indigenous 'folklore' to encode the demand of new collective historical subjects for democratic self-determination, liberation and independence. In Kwame Nkrumah's speculations about the existence of an 'African personality,' and in Frantz Fanon's diagnosis of the political unconscious of colonialism (and the psychic reality of its 'superiority/inferiority' complex as constitutive of white/black subjectivities), what we see is not the description of preexisting, already formed identities, but intellectual reflection on the transformative practices, made possible by new democratic antagonisms, that were bringing new forms of postcolonial subjectivity into being.[9] Aside from the chain of equivalence constructed within anticolonial movements for national liberation, we also see an extension of the same process within the metropolitan First World in terms of the radicalized demand for autonomy.

The Afro-American civil rights movement in the United States during the 1950s and early 1960s acted as the catalyst in which the radical democratic chain of equivalence reconstituted political subjects across the metaphorical boundary of racial difference itself. On the one hand, this unfolded internally as a radicalization of subaltern racial identity inscribed in the transition from 'Negro' to 'Black.' The reformist character of Martin Luther King's leadership, through which the demand for equal citizenship rights was articulated, was transformed in the Northern urban setting by nationalist ideologies, such as those advocated by Malcolm X, to extend beyond legal and social rights into an existential affirmation of a negated subjectivity (exactly that which was designated under erasure as simply 'X'). This resulted in the mid-1960s in the highly volatile and indeterminate metaphor of 'Black Power.' As Manning Marable (1984) has pointed out, this rallying cry was articulated into right-wing positions (and even President Nixon became an advocate, as he endorsed it as a form of black capitalism), as well as the left-wing positions associated with the Black Panther Party and its charismatic leadership which, for a brief moment around the late 1960s, became a counterhegemonic subject capable of leading and directing a range of positions into the chain of radical democratic equivalence.

One of the factors behind this process lay in the transracial identifications by which the codified symbols and imaginary metaphors of 'black liberation' were taken up, translated and rearticulated among postwar generations of white youth.

Among student activists, within the bohemian 'underground,' within second-wave feminism, and in the nascent gay and lesbian liberation movement, the signs and signifiers of radical blackness were appropriated into a chain of equivalences that empowered subordinate identities within *white* society. Of course, this most often took a cultural rather than conventionally political form of solidarity. The mass diffusion of black expressive culture through the pop and rock music industry played a key role in the dissemination of such imaginary modes of alternative iden-tification, culminating in the 1969 Woodstock Festival, where the predominantly white, middle-class youth who gathered there thought they constituted a nation within the nation, a new imagined community. In psychedelic Britain this was the imaginary space in which representations of an 'alternative society' were constructed. Here we see the vicissitudes of ambivalence, inversion and othering in the political identifications made possible by the cultural forms of antagonism which articulated the extension of the radical democratic chain of equivalences. At its liminal point, whiteness was emptied out in a direct imitation of empowered black subjectivity, such as when the activist John Sinclair formed the short-lived White Panther Party in the United States in 1968.[10]

Some of the contradictions inherent in the unfolding of this system of equiv-alences became apparent both at the frontier with the 'law and order' state (which effectively wiped out and repressed the guerrilla strategies of the far Left), and within the counterculture itself, where the masculinist character of its antiauthor-itarianism was contested by women and gay men. But it was precisely in this respect that the radicalization of sexual politics from 1970 onwards derived signif-icant momentum from imaginary equivalences with black struggles, as 'black pride' and 'brotherhood' acted as metonymic leverage for the affirmation of 'gay pride' and the assertion that 'sisterhood is strength.' Finally, although it should be pointed out that such radicalization also affected the increasing militancy of the labor move-ment in the early 1970s (as shown in the miners' strike of 1973), in the context of the polyvocal anticonsensus populism of the period it was ultimately the New Right, and not the New Left nor the new social movements, that got hold of what the Situationists used to call 'the reversible connecting factor' (Debord, 1981).

The metaphor of 'race' was privileged in the sense that it was also crucial to the emergence of a neoconservative populism which, in Britain, was forcefully articulated in 1968 by the dramatic interventions of Enoch Powell. Volosinov noted that 'the social multi-accentuality of the sign . . . has two faces, like Janus,' and that 'this inner dialectic quality of the sign comes out into the open only in times of social crises or revolutionary changes,' because 'in ordinary circumstances . . . the ideological sign in an established dominant ideology . . . always tries to stabi-lize the dialectical flux' (Volosinov, 1973: 23–24). In his political speeches on race and nation, culminating in the 'Enemies Within' speech in 1970, Powell encoded the dialectical flux of the crisis of authority into a populist chain of equivalences in which issues of race and immigration opened up a broader ideological attack against the Centre, radically destabilizing the values of social democracy. As an advocate of free-market capitalism, and a staunch defender of the primacy of the nation-state in politics, Enoch Powell prefigured and helped pave the way for the logic of authoritarian populism we now know as Thatcherism.[11] But what also needs acknowledging is the fact that the three lines of force which divided the field of political antagonism between the new social movements, the New Left and the New Right were all implicated in the *same* struggle over the 'communifying' logic of democratic equivalences, set in motion by the decentering of the consensual Center. What is at issue in our understanding of the moment of 1968 is how these three nuclei of political identification competed for the collective will of society. Contrary to the impression given by academic deconstructionists, the moment of indeterminacy, undecidability and ambivalence is never a neutral or purely textual affair – it is when politics is experienced at its most intense.

As someone who was eight years old in 1968, I have no direct experience, memory or investment on which to draw, as more recent dates like 1977 or 1981 punctuate more formative experiences in the political consciousness of my generation. Yet precisely as a textual construction in popular memory, '1968' has an affective resonance that I feel needs to be defended and conserved against the 'active forgetting' which the contemporary postmodern frontier effect encourages. What is demanded by the shift in popular memory is not a history that aims to 'articulate the past the way it really was,' but a mode of storytelling which, in Walter Benjamin's (1973) phrase, aims to 'seize hold of a memory as it flashes up at a moment of danger.' In lieu of a concrete historical account of the postmodern crisis of social democracy (which should be backdated to the period between 1956 and 1968), my sketch of radical democratic equivalences is really only an inventory arising out of my own formation growing up in the aftermath of the post-'68 conjuncture. Nevertheless, by asking 'whatever happened to the empowering identifications of the sixties?' we might arrive at a clearer understanding of why the 1980s have been so awful.

Between the fragments: citizenship in a decentred society

> We no longer regard ourselves as the successive incarnations of the absolute spirit – Science, Class, Party – but as the poor men and women who think and act in a present which is always transient and limited; but that same limitation is the condition of our strength – we can be ourselves and regard ourselves as constructors of the world only insofar as the gods have died. There is no longer a logos.
>
> (Ernesto Laclau, 1988: 21)

> Our diversity is a strength: let's value it.
>
> (Mobil Corporation advertising logo)[12]

Ten years ago such narrative strategies informed the counterhistory undertaken by the influential socialist-feminist text, *Beyond the Fragments* (Rowbotham, Wainwright, Segal, 1979). Taking stock of the uneven development of a dialogue between the male-dominated Left and the 1970s women's liberation movement, it emphasized the important differences between the organizational form of political parties and the participatory politics of social movements such as feminism. Sheila Rowbotham's nuanced account of the political culture of sectarianism on the British Left – dominated by macho dogmatism and the authoritative stance of Leninist vanguard leadership – drew attention to the 'emotionally terrorizing morality' (*ibid*.: 126) of having to be 'politically correct' in order to lay claim to the identity of being a 'true' socialist. Considering the transformative impact of various feminisms over the past two decades, it seems to me that the contrasting decline of the organized Left can be accounted for by just such unpleasant behaviors concerning the policing of one's 'correct' credentials. Such attitudes also contribute to the widespread apathy and boredom inspired by conventional Left/Right politics today. In the wake of heroic models of modernist commitment, the withdrawal of affective involvement from formal politics, like the decline of the public sphere itself, underlines postmodern indifference and the privatization of political passions (the so-called 'crisis of caring') as much as it underpins the rise of 'conviction politics' and all sorts of fundamentalism which speak in the name of the silent majorities.

So where is the passion that was once invested in the Left? Such passion certainly exists, as has been seen in the system of equivalences unfolding in the ex-Communist world as a result of glasnost and perestroika. Gramsci argued for a symbolic view of politics and power, as his conception of the party as a 'modern prince' was based on the argument that all forms of living practice necessarily produce *myth*, which is

> expressed neither in the form of a cold utopia nor as learned theorizing, but rather by a creation of concrete phantasy which acts on a dispersed and shattered people to arouse and organize its collective will.
>
> (Gramsci, 1971: 126)

The New Right has certainly heeded such Gramscian advice: since 1968 the 'concrete phantasy' that has aroused and organized the collective will of the British people has been hegemonized and directed by the bifurcated neoconservative vision of shrinking freedom and deepening inequalities. The myth of a socialist society, on the other hand, for so long institutionalized in the image of the 'caring' welfare state, is tattered, torn and untenable. Moreover, the prospects for reconstruction look bleak, as the organized Left – what is left of it – has shown no sign of being able to grasp the imaginary and symbolic dimensions of hegemonic strategy. Even when sections of the British Left have mobilized an alternative populism against the Tories, as occurred in the GLC experience (borrowing 'rainbow coalition' imagery from Jesse Jackson's Democratic campaigns in the US), the 'thinkability' of new alliances has been undermined from within by the conservative traditionalism of the Left, as well as by the essentialist tendencies of 'identity politics' on the part of the new movements.

Since the 1950s, the new social movements have autonomously constructed diverse political myths and fantasies which have not only empowered people in their everyday lives, but which have thereby enriched and expanded the horizon of popular politics. But in the plurality of particularisms, what can also be seen at the outer limits of the new diversified and decentred public sphere is the paradoxical replication of an authoritarian desire for a center. The Left's sectarian or doctrinaire anxiety over the 'correct' interpretation of the master thinkers Marx,

Lenin and Trotsky is reproduced at a subjective level in the new movements by the ethical imperative of 'authenticity,' expressed in the righteous rhetoric of being 'ideologically right-on.' The moral masochism that informs the attitude policing and credibility inspection routines so characteristic of the separatist tendencies of some of the autonomous movements reproduces the monological and puritanical conception of agency found in Marxist economism and class essentialism. The search for an authentic, essential 'self' in adversarial ideologies such as black cultural nationalism or lesbian–feminist separatism, to cite just two examples, often replays the vanguardist notion that there can be only *one* privileged agent of social and historical change. However tactically necessary in the 'war-of-maneuver' against white/male supremacist ideologies, the consequences of such separatism is self-defeating, as it mimics the authoritarian power to which it is initially opposed by simply inverting the binarism of discourses that legitimate domination. In any case, such fixed beliefs in immutable identity within the new antagonisms of race, gender, ethnicity and sexuality have been called into question by the pluralization effect that occurs in the encounter between the different movements – something that has become more progressively pronounced in the 1980s. The emergence of black women as a distinct 'class' or group in politics, for example, has relativized radical feminist notions of 'global sisterhood' by raising issues of racial and ethnic oppression that cut across experiences of power and powerlessness among women. By the same logic, black feminist positions disrupt complacent notions of a homogeneous and self-identical 'black community' by highlighting gender antagonisms and the divisive consequences of masculinist rhetoric in black political strategies (see Barbara Smith, 1983; Amos, Lewis, Mama and Parmar, 1984; hooks, 1989).

Essentialist notions of identity and subjectivity surface in the vortex of this bewildering experience of difference because of the absence of a common idea of what diversity really means for the multitude of subjects who are deeply unhappy with, and antagonistic towards, New Right hegemony. One appreciates the awfulness of this condition (which marks out the historic failure of the Left) by recognizing that the only available ideology which has taken diversity seriously is the social-democratic discourse on 'multiculturalism,' which enjoys little credibility among both racists and antiracists, Left and Right alike. But insofar as the British Left evacuates and abandons the terrain, it is colonized by the Right, and monocultural essentialism is mobilized in the defence of 'our way of life' to deny the very existence of diversity and difference.

Beyond the Fragments was influential (and informed the GLC's project of participatory democracy) because it recognized the diverse sources of antagonism in capitalist society: as Hilary Wainwright said, 'it is precisely the connections between these sources of oppression, both through the state and through the organization of production and culture, that makes a piecemeal solution impossible' (1979, *op. cit.*: 4). But in the scenario of further fragmentation and detotalization that has characterized the 1980s, who really has the confidence to assume that there is such a transcendental realm of the 'beyond'? Should we not begin again by relativizing the perspective to examine the contradictions that characterize the complex relations 'between'? This would mean deepening and extending the analysis of the interdependency of culture and politics in the process by which men and women 'acquire consciousnessness through social relations.' It would also entail a more detailed understanding of the salient differences and similarities between political parties and social movements. Alain Touraine has remarked that 'the labour movement, whose power is frequently invoked to underscore the weakness of the new social movements, is not really a wholly social movement' (1988: 131), because it has confined itself to class contradictions at the expense of other social antagonisms that do not arise directly out of the conflict of capital and labor. However, to understand the combined and uneven development of potentially counter-hegemonic forces, it is the very dichotomy between the state and civil society that also needs to be reformulated.

First, because it obscures the double-edged situation whereby the incorporation and neutralization of the industrial labor movement (in corporatism, bureaucracy and other forms of state mediation) is paralleled by the cultural appropriation and commodification of the new movements in the marketplace, where many radical slogans (such as 'the personal is political') have been hijacked, objectified and sold back to us an ever-widening range of 'life-style' options for those who can afford to pay. Yet, just as the welfare state did deliver limited gains by extending citizenship rights from the legal and political to the social arena, the new movements have had significant impact on personal relations and lived experience precisely through the diffusion of their ideologies in the commodified forms of the cultural marketplace.

Second, the concrete problems of political representation that came to light in the GLC experiment demonstrated that the distinction between state formation and the public sphere is not an impassable or absolute boundary, but nevertheless a boundary through which it is difficult simply to translate correspondences from one to the other. Paul Gilroy's (1987: 114–152) reading of the 'success' of the Rock Against Racism campaign in civil society in the 1970s, and the 'failure' of top-down bureaucratic methods of municipal antiracism in the 1980s, highlights the degree of incommensurability between the two. But because the analysis remains within the state/civil society dichotomy it describes, it does not identify the pragmatic points of entry from which to conduct or prefigure counter-hegemonic strategy 'in and against' the state. Given the legacy of statism within the British labor movement, one cannot evade the task of conceptualizing the necessary transformation of the state and its role in socialist strategy.

The official discourse of antiracism failed precisely because it imposed a one-dimensional view of racial antagonism in practices such as 'racism awareness training,' which simply reinforced existing relations of minority representation. Problems of tokenism – in which the one black person on the committee or in the organization is positioned, or rather burdened, with the role of a 'representative' who 'speaks for' the entire community – were left intact. Black subjects historically marginalized from political representation by exclusionary practices reproduced within the Left were legitimately angry. But the encoding of such anger often took the displaced form of 'guilt-tripping' in which potential allies were paralyzed by the sins of their past. While activists recognized the untenable innocence of conciliatory liberal pluralism, but without a common set of terms in which to openly share criticism and disagreements, alliance-building was inhibited by the fear of being seen to be 'incorrect' or not 'ideologically right-on.' Rather than learn from the educative value of active mistakes and errors, action was inhibited by a dogmatic discourse of antiracism which merely disguised the guilt, anger and resentment that gave urgency to issues of race and racism. In my view solidarity does not mean that everyone thinks in the same way; it begins when people have the confidence to disagree over issues of fundamental importance precisely because they 'care' about constructing common ground. It is around such passions encountered in the pluralized and diversified forms of contemporary democracy that the issue of alliances needs to be rethought, through an expanded and thoroughly modernized conception of citizenship.

The concept of citizenship is crucial because it operates in the hinge that articulates civil society and the state in an open-ended or indeterminate relationship. In the modern period, somewhere between 1880 and 1920, the industrial labor movement contested the narrow range of citizenship rights of 'the people' within liberal democracy. The gradual enfranchisement of excluded and marginalized subjects, as the result of class struggles in relation to the state, constituted the form of government defined after 1945 as social democracy. In the postindustrial word, however, the democratic image of 'the people' has been radically pluralized and hybridised by the proliferation of new antagonisms, and by the presence of a diversity of social subjects whose needs and interests can no longer be programmed around the limited citizenship rights inscribed in the welfare state. Yet neoliberal democracy – the freedom and inequality pursued by the New Right – threatens to erode and reduce even such minimal rights by prioritizing the market over society as the ultimate site upon which basic needs and rights are guaranteed only by individual initiative. As Margaret Thatcher told us, 'there is no such thing as society, only individual men and women and families.'

The prospects for a radical renewal of the 'myth' of a socialist society cannot lie in the revival or recycling of Labourite welfare statism, although the defence of minimal civil rights to employment, housing, health care, education and freedom of association has never been more necessary than it is now. Is it possible to envisage a minimalist state capable of guaranteeing such basic rights of citizenship against the structured inequalities produced by free-market forces? John Keane and others have argued that only a new constitutional settlement around an expanded conception of democratic citizenship can make socialism thinkable again.[13] Some sections of the Left in Britain, like *Marxism Today* magazine, would have us believe that the process of rethinking is already underway. But I have yet to hear the chorus of a genuinely plural discourse of the Left which actually acknowledges the sheer difficulty of living with difference.

The postimperial decline of British manufacturing was once explained as a consequence of the uniquely British resistance to postwar modernization. Politically, the British Left still resists and retreats from the democratic task that confronts it, namely to thoroughly modernize its conception of what a socialist society could and should be. To date there has been very little sustained analysis of what went wrong in the GLC,[14] and such 'active forgetting,' of course, serves the purpose of the Tories quite nicely. If, however, as Stuart Hall has remarked, the noise produced in its attempt to find new forms of democratic representation and participation 'is the positive sound of a real, as opposed to phoney and pacified democracy at work . . . a positive recognition of the necessary tension between civil society and the state' (1988: 235), then instead of withdrawing into quiet conformity, the Left has to recognize that it is being called upon to actively enjoy and encourage such noise if it is to arouse and organize a popular counter-hegemonic conception of radical democracy in a plural society. If this is what 'socialist pluralism in a real democracy will be like,' we cannot go back to the future, so bring the noise.

Notes

1   'Welcome to the Jungle,' from Guns 'N Roses, *Appetite for Destruction*, Geffen Records, 1988.

2   See, also, Claus Offe, *Contradictions of the Welfare State* (London: Hutchinson, 1984).

3   Written by David Bowie (1972), performed by Mott the Hoople, *Mott the Hoople Greatest Hits*, CBS Records, 1976.

4   Jacques Donzelot, 'The Apprehension of Time,' in Don Barry and Stephen Mueke, eds., *The Apprehension of Time* (Sydney: Local Consumption Publications, 1988).

5   Cited in Jon Savage, 'Do You Know How to Pony? The Messianic Intensity of the Sixties,' (1982) reprinted in Angela McRobbie, ed., *Zoot Suits and Second-Hand Dresses: An Anthology of Fashion and Music* (London: Macmillan, 1989), 121.

6   Stuart Hall, 'Popular Democratic vs. Authoritarian Populism: Two Ways of Taking Democracy Seriously,' (1980) in Hall (1988); the concept of frontier effects is originally developed in Ernesto Laclau (1977).

7   *Melody Maker* (August 19, 1989), 41.

8   Judith Williamson, 'The Problem with Being Popular,' *New Socialist* (September 1986).

9   See Kwame Nkrumah, *I Speak of Freedom: An African Ideology* (London: Heineman, 1961); and Frantz Fanon, 1970 [1952] and 1967 [1961].

10 The White Panther manifesto, the 'Woodstock Nation,' and other documents from the countercultures in Britain, Europe and the United States are collected in Peter Stansill and David Zane Mairowitz, eds., *BAMN (By Any Means Necessary): Outlaw Manifestoes and other Ephemera, 1965–1970* (Harmondsworth: Penguin 1971). On the 'alternative society' in Britain, see David Widgery, *The Left in Britain, 1956–1968* (Harmondsworth: Penguin, 1976). On feminist and gay equivalences, see Robin Morgan, 'Goodbye to All That,' in *BAMN*; and Aubrey Walter, ed., *Come Together: The Years of Gay Liberation, 1970–1973* (London: Gay Mens Press, 1980).

11 Key speeches of the 1960s are gathered in Enoch Powell, *Freedom and Reality* (Farnham: Elliot Right Way Books, 1969); see also, John Elliot, ed., *Powell and the 1970 Election* (Farnham, Elliot Right Way Books, 1970); and for a Marxist account, see Tom Nairn, *The Break-Up of Britain: Crisis and Neo-Nationalism*, (London: New Left Books, 1981), especially chapter six, 'English Nationalism: The Case of Enoch Powell.'

12 Advertisement in *Black Enterprise* magazine (January–February 1989).

13 See John Keane, ed., *Democracy and Civil Society* (London: Verso, 1988).

14 An important exception is Franco Bianchini, 'GLC RIP: Cultural Policies in London, 1981–1986,' *New Formations*, 1 (Spring 1987).

References

Amos, Valerie, Gail Lewis, Amina Mama, Pratibha Parmar, eds. (1984) 'Many Voices, One Chant,' *Feminist Review*, 17.

Benjamin, Walter (1973 [1940]) 'Theses, on the Philosophy of History,' *Illuminations*, London: Fontana.

Debord, Guy (1981 [1959]) 'Detournment as Negation and Prelude,' in Knabb, ed. *Situationist International Anthology*, Berkeley: Bureau of Public Secrets.

Gamble, Andrew (1988) *The Free Economy and the Strong State: The Politics of Thatcherism*, London: Macmillan.

Gilroy, Paul (1987) *There Ain't No Black in the Union Jack: The Cultural Politics of Race and Nation*, London: Hutchinson.

Gramsci, Antonio (1971 [1930]) *Selections from the Prison Notebooks*, London: Lawrence & Wishart.

Grossberg, Lawrence (1988) *It's a Sin: Essays on Postmodernism, Politics and Culture*, Sydney: Power Institute.

Hall, Stuart (1988) *The Hard Road to Renewal: Thatcherism and the Crisis of the Left*, London: Verso.

Hebdige, Dick (1987) 'Digging for Britain: an Excavation in Seven Parts,' in *The British Edge*, Boston: Institute of Contemporary Arts.

hooks, bell (1989) *Talking Back: Thinking Feminist, Thinking Black*, London: Sheba Feminist Publishers.

Laclau, Ernesto (1977) *Politics and Ideology in Marxist Theory*, London: New Left Books.

——(1990[1988]) 'Building a New Left' [interview] *Strategies*, 1, reprinted in *New Reflections on the Revolution of Our Time*.

——and Chantal Mouffe (1985) *Hegemony and Socialist Strategy: Towards a Radical Democratic Politics*, London: Verso.

Marable, Manning (1984) *Race, Reform and Rebellion: The Second Reconstruction of Black America, 1945–1982*, London: Macmillan.

Mouffe, Chantal (1988) 'Hegemony and New Political Subjects: Towards a New Concept of Democracy,' in Cary Nelson and Lawrence Grossberg, eds. *Marxism and the Interpretation of Culture*, London: Macmillan.

Rowbotham, Sheila, Hilary Wainwright, Lynne Segal (1979) *Beyond the Fragments: Feminism and the Making of Socialism*, London: Merlin.

Smith, Barbara, ed. (1983) *Home Girls: A Black Feminist Anthology*, New York: Kitchen Table/Women of Color Press.

Touraine, Alain (1988) *The Return of the Actor: Social Theory in Post-Industrial Society*, Minneapolis: University of Minnesota Press.

Volosinov, V. N. (1973 [1929]) *Marxism and the Philosophy of Language*, Cambridge: Harvard University Press.

Chapter 35

Michael Keith

IDENTITY AND THE SPACES
OF AUTHENTICITY

Introduction

THIS ARTICLE IS IN ONE SENSE about the manner in which contemporary racist and racialised mobilisation draws on a sense of authenticity. It is also an attempt to link the emergence and strengthening of place-based identities to the contexts in which authenticity is invoked to trump or to close particular academic, cultural and political debates.

Being 'of' a place is in part about the authority such status bestows. Rarely is this authority more marked by the conflation of race and belonging than it is in the East End of London, an area that has for so long exemplified both the appalling privations and intense forms of local solidarity characteristic of the capitalist city of modernity, in this case most commonly articulated through the globally renowned frame of reference of 'the eastender'. Likewise, this particular part of London has become over the last century and more both an object of extreme forms of sociological scrutiny and the cherished subject of a particularly intense form of urban identification. Being an eastender invokes a notion of a placed identity. More pointedly it provides an organising theme for stories of race and place that parade a series of British miniatures of the proud nation-state, from the visits to the area by the Queen during the German blitz in the 1940s through to the election of London's first local authority extreme right (fascist) councillor in 1993.

In a not dissimilar fashion the street also provides an organising theme for a particular genre of tales of the city, again foregrounding a sense of placed authenticity. It is a frame of reference that appears so out of kilter with contemporary academic fashion and yet remains at the heart of the popular understandings of everyday life that emerge most stridently in political debate but no less problematically in our representations of knowledge production and aesthetic judgement.

Between the lines of this article is just the slightest suggestion that such a notion of authenticity, so dangerous in most of its forms, can not be as easily discredited as some might believe. The tentative suggestion of such a possibility emerges from a consideration of the streets of the contemporary East End.

Sometimes I think that all politics in the East End are about authenticity. Veering between wanting none of the sectarian spectacle this creates and standing back in respect at the sincerity with which such claims are made, the garrulous rush to stake bids in the auction of authenticity can surely only be understood by reference both to outstanding expressions of communal solidarity and singularly frightening manifestations of mutual intolerance that the area is famous for.

Quite clearly on some levels this is nothing particular to one part of one city in the decaying metropolitan heartland of old capitalism. The right to make claims on behalf of one of many imagined communities, the right to articulate demands for jobs, for welfare and for houses – in short the representation of genuine political subjects – is the very stuff of social theory and political action. More often than not such claims to be heard contain within them, either explicitly or implicitly, reference to a place. Such locations may draw on the full vocabulary of urbanism to authenticate claims of knowledge, of aesthetics and of ethical judgement: from the Clapham Omnibus to the Bonaventure Hotel. And among these spatial reference points the street has historically occupied a privileged position in the cities of modernity.

There is a narrative structure through which the street itself may signify authenticity. Immersion in the street generates its own way of knowing the city, the politics of the street can connote both populism and transgression, whilst as the site of a celebrated vernacular aesthetic, street culture readily stands for the contemporary, truly 'where it's at'.

In this paper I want to work through three instances in which the street has been used as an organising trope in the fields of art, knowledge production and popular protest, to make sense of the multi-racial and multi-racist place that is the contemporary East End of London.[1]

In the last two years Tower Hamlets has witnessed the first election of a British National Party (fascist) councillor in Britain, an upsurge in popular protest, a mass mobilisation of young people, drawn in the main from second generation Bengali households, clashes between young people and the police and a savage 300 per cent increase in racial attacks, exemplified in the beating of Quddus Ali which was so severe that it left him in a coma and near death for three months.

In part this piece was written from a strong personal belief that it is as obscene to divorce this grim and steady rise in brutal racist violence and populist racist culture from the mutating political economies which have produced the economic space of the East End as it is to reduce such racist cultural forms to the status of mere effects of these sea changes. I am trying to argue that it is through a sophisticated vocabulary of urbanism that we can link the contemporary cultural studies invocations of spatiality with political economies of the production of space in order to take apart some of the most horrific forms of racism in the 1990s, something that is the object of endless popular interest and the subject of appalling institutional indifference and complicit political inaction. It is precisely this process of the production of urban spaces that is surely central both to the return to spatiality so salient to contemporary social theory and to a rejection of any simplistic opposition between 'real' and imagined or metaphoric spaces of identity.

Street aesthetics and street identity

The first case is that of an exhibition that took place at the Whitechapel Gallery from 14 February to 29 March 1992.[2] The exhibition was of the work of the New York based, Chilean photographer, Alfredo Jaar, as part of his broader project of 'a new cartography' examining the relationships 'between the developed and developing world' (Whitechapel Art Gallery flier, 1992). In a central piece of the exhibition Jaar had worked with Gayatri Chakravorty Spivak to produce a site specific multi-media installation 'inspired by the Bangladeshi community living in east London'.

Just before the exhibition Jaar and Spivak talked about their work at the ICA. For a long time Jaar's work has focused fascinatingly on the interplay of place naming and the politics of identity, using 'a spare honed aesthetic practice to provide visibility and space to sites and people in crisis' (Philips in *Republica de Chile Pasaporte*, an exhibition catalogue). Together they wanted to make of the grand institution of the Whitechapel Gallery a truly public space that was open to all, a site specific installation that in the words of John Bird, the author of the exhibition guide, 'raises the possibility of an aesthetic dimension that can contribute to change across the terrain of the social formation'.[3] Somebody asks them at the ICA, 'Why do you want to come to London to do this work?' They reply that they do not find the question either interesting or relevant, it is just not an issue.

The installation is titled 'Two or three things I imagine about them', consciously drawing on Godard's *Deux ou trois choses que je sais d'elle* (*Two or three things I know about her*). It has three main elements and an introductory 'framing' of video and water.

The first element consists of two neon lights, legible only in their reflection in the mirrors placed alongside them. One says, 'What is it to make the street visible?', the other 'What is it to make the visible visible?' The second element involves some images of young girls skipping, while on the floor nearby about twenty speakers give a hubbub of street noise, talking and shouting, many voices, mostly speaking Sylheti, Bengali and English. Thirdly a series of light boxes, with cropped fragmentary images of glamorous young Bengali women diagonally traverses the space of the gallery at ceiling level, with selective quotes from a sweat shop manager placed across them. The quotes include comments such as 'They are all unskilled and illiterate'. 'The £20 a week they earn just helps the family', and 'We are all a big family here'. All of this is introduced by a large video screen with a looped film which partly features Spivak talking to 'local people' but consists mainly of an image of her in a soliloquy addressed to the camera. The latter appears on screen as a talking head that is upside down; to see it the right way up it is necessary to look in the pool of water in front of the screen. Spivak intones:

How to make the street visible. How to learn to see differently. To learn to see differently is to see with the back, to learn to see differently is to see well in front. To learn to see differently is to see broader. . . . To learn to see differently. You are innocent, they are not? They are innocent, you are not? To see is to see differently. To learn to see differently. Seeing differently. Is it to make the street visible? To see and to make visible. What is it to see? What then is to make visible? Who are they? Who makes visible? Who sees? How do we see? How do we make the street visible? (*in a louder voice*) How to make the street visible?

The installation was clearly very clever, highlighting the practices of representation, the aesthetics of the gaze, the fragile play between representation and (in)visibility. It was exciting in the manner in which the standard conventions and protocols of the art gallery exhibition were transgressed. Deliberately enigmatic, the installation simultaneously tried to highlight the exploitation of the local rag trade,[4] the absences and silences of practices of representation and also a more optimistic invocation of the possibility of the public spaces that find their exemplary form in the streets of the modern city. In the terms of John Bird's introduction to the installation:

> On the street is where we negotiate the complexities of cultural differences made deceptively familiar through the repetitive encounters of daily life, at one moment made to feel our singularity, at another to sense our otherness fragmenting in the fleeting connections of community and dependency expressed in the glance or gesture that bridges a gap, dissolves a boundary, initiates a dialogue.
>
> (Bird, 1992)

But the exhibition itself prompted a considerable furore. A group of young women from a local school objected both to the way their images were cropped in the light boxes and the matching of them with the quotes from the sweatshop owner, prompting protests at the gallery itself. They suggested that as successful sixth formers in what is, in terms of educational qualifications, the most successful school in Tower Hamlets, they were ill served by the portrayals of themselves as victims of the exploitation of the rag trade. The installation had failed to capture the dynamics of the contemporary lives of young Bengali women, reproducing the stereotypes of victimhood in the photographic vocabulary of the fashion shot. The length of time Spivak had dedicated to putting the piece together and finding out about the local streets was criticised in public, an exchange took place in the British press, and a well known black artist withdrew from a public talk about the exhibition at the gallery.

In one sense such a minor controversy might seem unremarkable. Yet even in its marginality the installation is in some important ways almost paradigmatic. Challenging the exoticisation of ethnicity in an informed manner, problematising the gaze of the urban spectator, the installation surely contained precisely the sort of street aesthetic that must lie at the heart of a radical multi-culturalism in its appeal to a contingent and ambivalent invocation of public space. The street was simultaneously celebrated for its potential and debunked for its romanticised associations. And in the gap that was generated by this contradiction the metaphoric power of the street escaped the canny ironies of the curators through their failure to capture sensitively the politics and poetics of articulation. Ultimately, the representational space of the gallery was transgressed more symbolically than practically, failing to take along with it the audiences who came to see the installation, not to mention those whose images constituted it.[5]

Ultimately the weakest link was the framing of the installation, the immediate presentation of Spivak herself at the very foreground of the exhibition space. It is surely part of the ambivalence around which the whole installation was structured that whilst we were expected to gain knowledge by looking into the pool of water and seeing Spivak the right way up, the narcissistic conceit produced an effect where cursory observation suggested that most spectators looked at the inverted image on the screen whilst Spivak appeared to be looking at her own reflection on the water. Hybridising myth, the Delphic Oracle plays Narcissus. But if the Narcissus myth teaches us anything it is surely that this is not always the best way to look at things at all.[6]

Street walkers

The second case I want to reference is a particular instance of the spatial practice of walking and knowing the street, a specific invocation of the claims to knowledge that are made when 'botanising the asphalt'. On 10 September 1993, shortly after the particularly brutal attack on Quddus Ali, and after clashes between police and a crowd that was mostly young, male and Bengali had broken out around a vigil outside the London Hospital where he lay in a coma, Brick Lane was attacked by a group of fascist sympathisers who ran down the street throwing bricks through the windows of restaurants, daubing racist graffiti and assaulting people on the street.[7] This occurred in spite of the fact that the area was saturated with police patrolling the area at the time, one van in particular had been on a small circuit that included Brick Lane itself for many hours and several young Bengali men had been picked up by the police. Into the early hours of the morning an impromptu march took place of between 50 and 200 which went straight to another main area of Bangladeshi settlement around Canon Street Road, protesting at the outrage.[8] The following night several gatherings of local people took place, still furious at the previous night's events.

On Brick Lane groups of people, black and white, milled around in a scene palpably expectant and fractious. One meeting in a community hall I witnessed was particularly tense with a large crowd of extremely angry local people, mostly young, disgusted by the incursion that had been made on the symbolic heart of the Bengali community of Tower Hamlets, mad at the police for their perceived complicity. After the meeting I went with friends into one of the pubs just off Brick Lane, which had itself had its windows bricked as part of the revenge actions on more than 15 public houses that had followed the Quddus Ali attack. And into the pub walked a man in deer stalker and overcoat, his pipe making up the full

Sherlock Holmes set, the simulacrum of an English eccentric, a walking guide with 20 American tourists in tow giving one of the many Ripper tours of Whitechapel, revealing the inscribed knowledges of the Victorian East End through the street walk, a performance flaneurie that re-enacted the serial murders and assaults.

On one level this appeared surreal, on another obscene. The place itself was staged as Jack's East End, the tour proceeded blithely unaware that there was anything beyond the ordinary going on; the American tourists were more concerned that they might be ripped off by the taxi drivers that arrived at the pub to pick them up than they were by the hidden possibility that they could be caught in the middle of an urban uprising. And the authority of the guide remained, unquestioned and unquestionable, resting on his navigation of the street; an insider position that cast him as the fount of local knowledge.

Seemingly only a single bizarre event, the incident is more typical than it might appear. The rich history of the Whitechapel area leads to a cluster of different tour guides working the area: Jack the Ripper tours, Jewish tours, Kray gangster tours, Huguenot tours; the street walk on each occasion renders visible particular genres of spatialised knowledges. The tour itself becomes the medium through which the identity of the place is revealed, the knowledge production process replicated through the individuals making the tour. In this way the knowledge production process of the flaneur is mimed for the benefit of the contemporary tourist; but is it rendered inauthentic in doing so?

Paradoxically, it has always been the unknowability and the illegibility of the urban that privileges the episteme of the street.[9] Knowing that nobody knows, or ever can know completely, places the spatial practice of the walk above the meta-narrative certainties of the plan, the scheme, the totalising schema of the panoramic view. But such a valorisation can become the guarantee of parochialism – both a licence to stroll and to gaze and a limit to the scientific value of botanised asphalt. It is also a privilege that is not open to all equally. The very act of walking prefigures seeing which prefigures viewing which prefigures a particular form of knowledge production,[10] which was gendered as a dominantly male preserve, the classic modern public, but was also contested by women in the spaces of modernity.[11]

As a site that can be viewed only through a privileged gaze, the street becomes a field of the visible with its own implicit rules of knowledge production. It is in such representational spaces that post-structuralist critiques of the totalising narratives of social justice derive from the epistemological violence that works through logics of identity that harden soft borders – inside-outside, me-you, black-white, self-other, the clichéd binaries of the enlightenment imagination.

But the street is also simultaneously dangerous and desirable, the site and material cause of inter-community violence and the condition of possibility of inter-cultural identification. The street is not a space which is necessarily signified but it can be a medium through which particular cultural forms are expressed.

There is a moment here when behind the romance there is a nuanced understanding of the public sphere which offers the possibilities of a transformative politics and a situated notion of identity formation and knowledge production. A positively understood invocation of urbanism has to be about opening oneself up to difference (Young, 1990). The creation of a political space, a social space and a cultural space where the boundary stalking logics of identification are overturned, where uncertainty and unpredictability provide the conditions of possibility for the mutations, hybridity and combinations that define how newness comes into the world – these are all definitive features of the lived city just as the roots of demo-cracy and citizenship are part of the city's history.[12] But such spaces can never be assumed, we have always to map the political economies of the production of city spaces whose cartography may exceed and escape the desires of their designers. In this sense such a public sphere cannot and must not be normalised by casual reference to a street that may be scored with 18th century roots and 20th century taboos. The 'public' is always, almost self-evidently, marked by traces of its historicity and spatiality.

In this context the relationship between flaneurie and epistemology is neither straightforward nor consistent. In most representations of the flaneur the individual walks through the urban environment finding 'himself' as 'he' reads and relates 'his' way through the great city. The frequently implicit masculinity of this subject position has prompted criticisms of the failure to acknowledge the gendering of both the right of the gaze and the practices of visual pleasure itself (Mulvey, 1989; Pollock, 1988; Wolff, 1989). Modernist cities were in part structured by gendering processes that in part defined the public/private distinction while at times both the city generally and the streets specifically, represented as feminine, were frequently eroticised through the processes of exploration and capture of the soft city (Davidoff and Hall, 1987). More recently the nuances of these gendering processes have been disputed in the assertion that the flaneur might be seen as androgynous (Wilson, 1991) or else that a more historically inflected study reveals that spaces of the city were contested terrains open to selective appropriation by women (Walkowitz, 1992).

At other times it is the process of immersion that is celebrated as axiomatic of the constraints of knowledge production, the poets of the street contrasted to the will to power implicit in the aerial view of the urban plan.

Certainly the processing of knowing the city through becoming lost in its streets, espoused by Walter Benjamin, is far more complicated than some cele-brants of flaneurie have subsequently suggested,[13] but we can still suggest that the links between walking, seeing, knowing and writing do create their own epistemic genealogy.

From Benjamin for the purposes of this article it is necessary only to stress that there is a misreading of his work, increasingly common in some forms of urban studies, in which the ambivalence of his positioning becomes apparent. Whilst keen to stress the value of losing himself in the city, the process of street walking was always a process of doubling: on the one hand the precariousness of the flaneur losing himself (sic) in the crowd always leads to an immersion in the street but also, through immersion in the crowd, to an identification with and fetishisation of the commodity. So that the flaneur, once confronted with the department store, finds that 'he roamed through the labyrinth of merchandise as he had once roamed through the labyrinth of the city' (Benjamin in *Charles Baudelaire: A Lyric Poet in the Era of High Capitalism*). Making contradictory sense of oneself in the street is about locating the body in the possibly incommensurable matrices of economy and culture.[14]

What Benjamin clearly never accepts is that the walk involves the sovereign subject moving through space. His is no situationist drive through the unknown city. To understand the episteme of the flaneur it is firstly essential to reject the notion of the individual body penetrating the spaces of the city. Mapping and walking instead prefigures and is prefigured by the process of identity formation. As an interior the street is a constitutive feature of the walker, be it the flaneur as tour guide, rebel or even white male academic.

What I want to reject is the dualism that is so central to Lewis Mumford's great work, *The City in History*, through which he contrasts the urban as container with the urban as movement. The corporeal walker through urban space is always rhizomatically linked to the streets through which that body inscribes their route (Deleuze and Guattari, 1987). If we return to the scene just off Brick Lane the relationship between the character who returns again and again to the Ripper and the resident who walks the same streets is one of degree rather than one of kind.

So there are two points to be made here. First, the street is not the point at which immersion detaches the body from the matrices of political economy. It is, certainly for Benjamin, a point at which the flaneur and the commodity become subjects created by geography. Secondly, street knowledge is not hermetically sealed, in fact quite the opposite, it is always part of the collapse of inside and outside.[15] Acknowledged as such, heterotopic public space is defined by and defines a street where it is possible to go out in public and meet strangers.

It is surely in this way that the hermetically sealed inside of community politics is unlocked whilst at the same time the spatial practices through which particular places are inscribed differently by different spatialities and historicities are preserved. This sort of cognitive mapping is in part about the prioritisation of 'routes over roots' (Chambers, 1990), partly about placing all people on the net of humanity. But it is also valorising some claims to place over others, not a strategically essential moment of identification as much as a topography of authority claims which says, in a moment, that this person's claim to this place at this time for these reasons is superior to that other person's. Such valorisation has to be of the moment, in a context. It is always precarious, invariably open to questioning; in short, a form of synchronic authenticity.

In part we answer critiques of essentialism with a call to focus on the process of making which is about the inscriptions of both commodity flows and personal and collective agency. The street is just one modality through which these inscriptions are made visible. In such circumstances the bizarre spectacle of the guided tour has a place in the East End alongside the symbolic marches of protest that have been the first resort for communities besieged by the violent spectre of racism. We always have to map out where they are coming from and where they are going to.

Bluntly, it is on the street where it is possible to 'come to see with eyes of those who come from a special place', where emotional relations are based on actions shared rather than states of being and where public life can disrupt and transgress destructive *gemeinschaft*.[16] But it is never easy, never innocent of the inscriptions of time and space which the street itself represents and realises in the body of the individual flaneur.

Street politics: heroes and villains

Articulated as politics the street is 'where it's at', it is everything the ivory tower is not[17] – which is why it is perhaps so much loved by academics. Here we find a generic narrative form that is not so much about making the street visible as about making the barricades visible, the intoxicating rush of ethical certainty, social justice in a spatially corporeal form.

But what kind of a vicarious experience is this? And who is to man these barricades, for let us make it clear that manning is the operative term here. The third case I want briefly to examine relates to the proliferation of political mobilisations that developed in Tower Hamlets from late 1993 onwards. These have been both national and local. While the national anti-racist organisations have, once again, looked to make Tower Hamlets a battlefield for the fight against Nazism, there has also been a mushroom growth of movements among local people, both men and women, to combat the growth of racism. In particular there has been the clear politicisation and large scale mobilisation of local young Bengalis, demonstrated in vigils to show respect to victims of racist attacks, in marches through and laying symbolic claim to the area, in benefits to raise money and in the defence campaigns to protect those arrested in the struggle. Such mobilisations have become the subject of intense press and media attention; featuring on several documentary programmes, detailed journalistic essays and on the cover of a variety of journals, 'the youth' heralded as new political subjects of the East End.

I want to distinguish between two strands in this revolutionary story. The first is judgmental. There is no way in this paper that I am attempting to evaluate, undermine or underestimate the remarkable patterns of politicisation that are taking place among second generation Bengalis in London. This is no ethnographic analysis of the experiences of young Bengali men and women. That is only one element of the mosaic that is East End life. I am, however, trying to comment on the racialised configuration of the whole mosaic. It is a configuration that reveals the East End as both lived and signified, an exemplary urbanism in which places are both the conditions of possibility and the expressive modality of identities.

But how are such identifications represented? I think it is important to understand the narrative tropes which make such stories comprehensible and the moments of slippage which characterise populist racist sentiment. There is a barely hidden genealogy here of place and identity, normatively construed. The street is not innocent of racialised meaning. The black body is interpellated through the street. It was after all Lord Scarman who so egregiously talked about 'West Indian' people as a people of the street. Here we have the corollary of Fanon's 'look a Negro',[18] a successful racist placing of the body of the other in the field of vision.

We know these stories. They appeal to a knowledge that predates the moment the camera shutter closed. They place race in the field of vision in a way in which sense becomes self-evident. It is possible to examine news cuttings of recent coverage of the protest of Bengali communities and recognise a photographic vocabulary of another time. The placing of non-white masculinity on the street is a constitutive feature of the process of race formation and the manner in which racialised identities are linked to processes of criminalisation (Keith, 1993, Chapter

12). Images of young men, aggressively looking into the camera, evoke a host of not only histories of black looks (bell hooks, 1992) but also common sense geographies of racism. These images work because we the viewer know what they mean, two or three things we know about the racialised masculinity of the dangerous street.[19]

There is another story here. On the covers of the anti-racist journals *Socialist Review*, *Searchlight* and *CARF*, young Bengali men appear as transgressive heroes, their defiance celebrated in their claiming of the streets of the East End. But is it possible to look at such valorised exhibitions of masculine force and then at the criminalising gaze of the mainstream press and say that they are unrelated? Is it really coincidence that the lineaments of racist culture share so much in common with the rhetorics of revolutionary action?

Now this is undoubtedly a complex story. The subject positions of oppression are regularly taken on board as the vessels that secure movements of resistance – from pejorative black to politically black, from pejorative queer to queer politics – the categories are inverted to be mocked and subverted in the mimesis of the mirror dance.[20] And in the multitude of debates and actions the gendering of the public sphere of political action as a constitutive feature of the interpellation of Asian masculinity within both liberal and conservative stories of white anti-racist is far too complex for simplistic analysis.

But there is also a sense in which the liberal white left themselves, in desperate search for the transformative political subject, will cast young Bengali men as the teleological delivery boys; and as Stuart Hall pointed out in a not dissimilar context in 1981, the streets will not only stage glorious insurrection they will also witness the fact that it is upon young male Bengali heads that the fully armed apparatus of the state will fall; it is they who will be attacked on the streets at the vigil for Quddus Ali outside the London Hospital, and they who will be confronted by and confront the BNP gangs who increasingly conspire to roam the streets of Tower Hamlets to go Paki-bashing. Street politics is easy for the absent.

Three-way street

I think what the three examples share is the foregrounding of place and authenticity, which misleadingly conveys the authentic aesthetic, the authentic episteme, the authentic political subject. Place, specifically the street itself, serves as rhetorical backbone rather than as a medium of articulation through which beauty, truth and politics are mixed together and hybridised. It is possible to take the three examples in turn to see how this 'cross dressing' takes place.

In the Whitechapel gallery accidentally orientalist fragments of eroticised glamour, boxed up and packaged, together with the disembodied murmuring of the chaotic public, are all framed by the arcane image of wisdom and insiderdom reflected in the pool of water. Narcissus lives.

In the pastiche detective figure of Sherlock Holmes, the walkers who desire the otherness of difference, eroticising street life, are seduced by the aesthetically captivating nature of experience. This allows them to read themselves into the illegibility of the great city and then rationalises this triumph of being over becoming by writing the street, by translating the gaze into the script, the privileged view into the written word, through a claim to knowledge – 'to have been there'.

And in the media coverage of 'youth movements' the subjectification of the transformative agent valorises street politics as ethical action and revels in the connotative dreams of St Petersburg, Paris and the barricades. Through such evocative slippage a project is validated – the political is defined as the moment of contestation[21] and action validates the epistemological frame through which such contestation is known. And more than anything else there is the spectacle consumed – mass insurrection on the TV screens, heroes framed in the photographers' lenses nourishing the utopian romance in the eroticised imaginary.

In each case 'the street' is more than a stage on which authority claims are made; it is a constitutive feature of the authority itself, something that I want to go on to argue can only be addressed by unpacking the spatialities that such claims invariably invoke. These spatialities are themselves conditions of possibility which demand a more sophisticated and contingent notion of both politics and social justice than we are normally ready to develop; something that I believe can be addressed by a project of radical contextualisation.

Radical contextualisation

Is beauty truth, truth beauty? Are fact and value so distinct? The clichéd questions that are no more easily resolved now than two thousand years ago in part reveal the artifice of the moments of identity production, knowledge production and political judgement that I have just described. But they do share some important features. In each case the spatiality of the street is both the condition of possibility through which claims of authenticity are staked and also a sign of empirical specificity that is silenced as soon as it is voiced precisely because geographical traces may play to the audience as the stigmata of relativism.

Yet surely in each case the claims, mediated as they are by this silenced spatiality, are all contingently valid just as they are contingently fraudulent. As Martin Luther King said, 'the riot is the voice of the unheard'. But equally when 'shouts in the street' turn into the brutal vocabulary of racial battering and ethnic cleansing then we find the moment when Rousseau turns into Robespierre.[22] Likewise, identifying with otherness must surely depend upon both the representational spaces through which it occurs and also the mapping of such spaces into the political economy of the city, whilst the eroticisation of the street is surely on its own free of necessary morality.

In part this is no more than saying – *pace* Habermas – that the classic notions of public space filled by universals and individuals must be replaced with a more nuanced version that acknowledges both individual rights of humanity and communal or collective rights that reflect inscribed structures of power. This is a proposition outlined in Iris Marion Young's demands for an understanding of heterotopic public space. However, it is also a way of suggesting that an understanding of social justice must always revolve around a politics of articulation, contingent epistemologies and situated aesthetics; a set of practices that has elsewhere been described as radical contextualisation (see in particular Laclau, 1990, but also Keith and Pile, 1994).

The project of radical contextualisation is at one and the same time straightforward and arcane. Straightforwardly many of the old binaries are subverted because neither abstraction nor empiricism (in knowledge production), neither theory nor practice (in political action), neither universalism nor relativism (in aesthetic judgements) can resolve any of Kant's three fundamental questions of philosophy – what do I know, what should I do, what do I want. The answers to all such questions depend on abolishing the *a priori* and spelling out of the grounds on which they are made, accepting that the traces of historicity and spatiality are always a constitutive feature of the processes of subject and object formation.

But the confusion between ethics, epistemology and identity is not just one of plurality. At one level I think it important to find a vocabulary that indicts the Jaar/Spivak installation as fascinating but fraudulent, that ties the revolutionary plaudits to their prefiguring of racism, and renders the walker as always problematic.

Through radical contextualisation it is possible to foreground both the dead ends of standpoint epistemology and the false promises of universalism. It is possible to cherish the public spaces of modernity without romanticising them. Third space, liminal space, the privileged margin – all open up the moment of identification as a moment of uncertainty. Reassuring narratives of time are dislocated by the uncertainties of the spatial. Acknowledged as such, heterotopic public space is defined by and defines a street where it is possible to go out in public and meet strangers.

But the project of radical contextualisation is also about acknowledging the contingency of all identities, affirming that the traces of historicity and spatiality are inscribed not just by presence but also by absence, by a lack as much as a plenitude. Within this heterotopic public space, claims of authenticity and redress are not just grounded; they are also constituted by their historicity and spatiality in what Homi Bhabha, drawing on Benjamin, describes as 'a dialectic of cultural negation as negotiation':

> Community is the antagonist supplement of modernity: in the metropolitan space it is the territory of the minority, threatening the claims of civility; in the transnational word it becomes the border-problem of the diasporic, the migrant, the refugee. Binary divisions of social space neglect the profound temporal disjunction – the translational time and space – through which minority communities negotiate their collective identifications. For what is at issue in the discourse of minorities is the creation of agency through incommensurable (not simply multiple) positions. Is there a poetics of the interstitial community? How does it name itself, author its agency?[23]

It is this incommensurability that arises from and constitutes the spatialities of subjectification that work through and on 'the street'. It is out of the incommensurability of different spatialities that both the spaces of resistance emerge as social practice and the moments of utopianism can insert themselves as political projects of discursive closure.

The spaces of the street are, in other words and a familiar language, contra-dictory.[24] And a language of contradiction usefully returns us to the agenda of political economy, not in search of Hegelian resolution but for bearings. Paul Gilroy has recently argued forcefully that 'the problem with the cultural left' is that they have never been cultural enough. It is worth echoing this with the comment that cultural politics without political economy will be equally rudderless.

The power of a focus on the practices and processes of production of both culture and class, of moralities, identities and knowledges, is to place the stress on becoming rather than being. It is to open up politics without reducing it to either economistic caricature or cultural self-indulgence. Invariably this must involve foregrounding the influences of time and space through either radical contextualisation or something that would look much like it. Moments of productive cultural syncretism, fusion and hybridity take place not just in any place nor in some rarefied, abstract liminal space or third space or marginal space. They are realised through particular articulations of spatiality just as those spatialities are a constructive feature of their formation. The street is frequently one such articulation and it is as such that we can celebrate the 'shouts of the street' (see Berman, 1982, Part V). For where is the place at which 'communality is not based on a transcendent becoming' (Bhabha, 1994, p. 241) if it is not the street, if it is not a celebration of the places where one can go out in public and meet strangers.

The street is both a state of consciousness and a locus of meaning, a way of thinking about the world and a semiotic source of dramaturgical keys and cues. As such it is an exemplary case of the sites of the urban, a particularly powerful illustration of the manner in which a vocabulary of the city renders the social visible.

In one sense we clearly have to do away with authenticity, to understand the lie that is at the heart of the term. But in another it is equally the case that the rights of local people to speak out against property capital valorise a particular understanding of authenticity; the rights of British black communities to represent themselves in the anti-racist movement valorise a particular understanding of authenticity; the right of the Bengali community to defend itself against racist attacks acknowledges a territorial authenticity and the political moment at which the democratic act is legitimated with a vote valorises a particular understanding of the authenticity of the 'real me'.

It is from such articulated speaking positions, in such explicit spaces of repre-sentation, and at particular historically contingent moments that a politics of authenticity will continue to find a new place on progressive left politics. Diachronically, we know that authenticity has no place but if we freeze the moving film momentarily, in particular places at particular times, the authentic can be voiced synchronically, an appeal that is of the moment, directed to particular audiences and justified by specific ends. This is not so much an instance of the strategic essentialism favoured by Spivak and others as much as the 'true lies' described by Fanon.[25]

Authenticity is a true lie of political action, a strategy but not a goal. What we are currently seeing in the East End of London and in so many other places where authenticity underscores the very vocabulary of popular politics is what happens when such a strategy becomes mistaken for a goal in and of itself. There are echoes of Los Angeles on the streets of London that can not be reduced to naïve descriptions of globalisation and localisation. In such situations the message is clear for both contemporary politics and the spaces of identity formation, in the words of the Tower Hamlets 9 campaign,[26] 'No Justice, No Peace'.

Notes

1   The area referenced in this paper is a small patch of East London, bounded by the Highway in the South, Bethnal Green Road in the North, Spitalfields market in the West and by Burdett Road in the East. London's own Ellis Island, it is an area that has been inscribed with the presence of Huguenot, Jewish, African, Afro-Caribbean, Irish, Somali migrants along with countless other dispossessed and displaced minorities, tracked, traced and explored by generations of urban explorers, spectators, philanthropists, walkers and academics.

2   In the three cases I am trying to follow Stallybrass and Whyte's (1986) contention that 'what is socially peripheral is so frequently symbolically central'.

3   Bird (1992) in the guide to the exhibition. There was no conventional catalogue as such for the exhibition but instead a commentary by John Bird, three of Jaar's maps in his 'new cartography' and an essay on Jaar's work by Patricia C. Philips inside a replica Chilean passport. It is this 'package' that is referred to below as 'the catalogue'.

4   An article from the journal *Capital and Class* almost ten years before was pointed to in the gallery for 'background reading.'

5   Paradoxically, given the fuss that the exhibition prompted, the accompanying essay by John Bird in the exhibition 'catalogue', which in the main gives a valuable theoretical frame of reference for the installation, closes with a quote from Spivak: 'It's all very well to theorise cultural practices and institutions as potential sites for discursive intervention into the construction of social meaning, but this has also to take account of discrepant audiences, different agendas and modalities of resistance – of the necessity of 'doing our homework properly'. It is surely around precisely this notion of doing 'one's homework' properly that the installation, provoking though it was, ultimately failed.

6   Taken one way the image of Spivak and the pool of water was a clever and very witty way of ironising some of the debates around masculinism, narcissism and the lust for knowledge; and in particular the feminist cut on these debates (see Mitchell, 1974; Rose, 1986; Irigaray, 1985, all in marked contrast to Lasch, 1978).

7   Brick Lane lies at the heart of Spitalfields and is dominated by small Bengali businesses, particularly restaurants and shops. It is also the site of a mosque in an old Jewish synagogue. In many ways it is the symbolic heart of Bengali settlement in Britain.

8   It is important to stress that in this and the subsequent example there is no attempt here to provide an authoritative account of these events or represent the perceptions or feelings of the Bengali community at this time. For such accounts see the bulletins produced by Tower Hamlets Against Racism, Tower

Hamlets Anti-Racist Committee and the interview with Kumar Murshid in *Regenerating Cities* (1994), number 6. It is instead the case that I am trying to work through how these and other practices are 'placed' within the racialised frame of everyday life in the East End.

9   It is surely no coincidence that a postmodern displacement of metanarrative certainty with little narratives and local knowledges has found a narrative echo in the renewed fascination with the personal memoir, the wanderings of the contemporary flaneur – Davis and Rieff in Los Angeles, Wright, Sinclair and Wilson in London. There are also epistemological equivalents of such developments that might owe their lineage principally to the urban mythologies of Roland Barthes, tracing the indeterminacy of the signs of the streets and the celebrations of the poets of the street by Michel de Certeau. For such a valorisation see for instance Deutsche (1991). However, it is surely paradoxically the case that such privileging renders the two perspectives meaningful only in relation to each other, each presumes the other, if only through absence.

10   It is perhaps symptomatic that the recent fascination with the flaneur at times slips into an equivalence between flaneurie, sociological observation and post-structural epistemological paradigms. See for example the attempt to represent Benjamin as a sociologist by Frisby (1994).

11   Heron (1994). See also how Judith Walkowitz (1992) has described the manner in which the changing configuration of late Victorian capitalism 'rendered the streets of London an enigmatic and contested site for class and gender encounters'. Walkowitz usefully problematises the multiplicity of feminine gazes in the 19th century city.

12   This is not to say that these properties are necessary properties of an essential urban – only that vocabularies of urbanism are constitutive organising principles of them (see Keith and Cross, 1993).

13   As John Rignall (1989) has pointed out Benjamin himself was not consistent; on the one hand Benjamin's flaneur, who revels in the gaze, never really challenges the idea that to see is to know, indeed 'the transformation of the street into a kind of interior is one of the ways in which he makes the alien urban world bearably familiar . . . the flaneur also combines the casual eye of the stroller with the purposeful gaze of the detective. His vision is thus both widely ranging and deeply penetrating at the same time'. However the flaneur's position remains a precarious one, not because of a crisis of aesthetics, but because with the changing form of the capitalist city he (sic), through immersion, becomes identified with the commodity caught in the maelstrom of the capitalist urban. Consequently 'the narrator has come finally to admit that the heart of the world cannot be known' (p. 119), pointing a way to the crisis of the realist narrative form.

14   In losing oneself on the streets only to find oneself and an identity within the matrices of contemporary capitalism Benjamin's uncertain flaneur predates Jameson's project of 'cognitive mapping' and in his doubt pre-empts Jameson's notion of 'incommensurability-vision'.

15   There is one caveat here. On the one hand the more optimistic characterisations of cross-cultural identification disrupt the metanarrative certainties of history with a spatially nuanced vocabulary – space subverts time, geography is the modality through which third space is articulated. On the other hand, celebrations of the city, be it the city as lived or the city as signed, tend to slide

towards an assessment of the immanent properties of the essential urban, something that is not suggested here.

16   These are the central values at the heart of Sennett's (1977) analysis.

17   One striking example of this particular representation was seen in the title given to a recent edition of the journal *Race and Class* – 'Black America: the Street and the Campus' (*Race and Class*, (1993) 35 (1: July-September)), an explicit contrast easily slipping into an implicit binary opposition.

18   Fanon's opening of *Black Skin, White Masks* captures the subjectification of the black body through the white gaze. Taken together with his axiomatic notion that 'the black man's souls is a white man's artefact' and the memorably epigrammatic comment that 'The Black man is not. Any more than the white man' (Fanon, 1967). Fanon's work has become increasingly important in cultural studies projects that trace back the construction of processes of racialisation to the social context in which the formative experiences of identification and identity formation take place. It is this taking place element of this process that makes an understanding of the spatialities of a sophisticated urbanism indispensable to anti-racist theory and practice.

19   In discussing the framing of images of the beating of Rodney King, Judith Butler has made precisely this point forcefully with the comment that 'The visual field is not neutral to the question of race; it is itself a racialised formation, an episteme, hegemonic and forceful' (1993, p. 17).

20   The most impressive exposition of this is surely to be found in Michael Taussig (1987), developed theoretically in his more recent *Mimesis and Alterity* (1993).

21   See for instance how Laclau (1990) defines the political in terms of contestable practices.

22   It is precisely this sort of slippage that lies at the heart of Berman (1971).

23   H. Bhabha (1994), pp. 228, 231. It is perhaps not insignificant that the demands to speak to the authenticity of territory is not equivalent across the range of the new cultural politics of difference. For example the nuances of sexualised and gendered territorial authenticity contrast strikingly with those of race and class.

24   Although Bhabha himself talks about 'the contradictory and ambivalent space of enunciation' (1994, p. 37) he appears reluctant to tie this in to sophisticated understandings of political economy. Powerfully exposing the narrative form through which Frederic Jameson ultimately resorts to the optical ontology of class categories to enable him to 'see to the bottom of the stream' and resolve the problems of 'incommensurability vision' (1994, pp. 216–24) Bhabha remains reluctant to examine the imbrication of class and culture, always preferring to cite colonialism without ever representing colonialism itself as a productive system, a silence that is surely a weakness of much post-colonial cultural studies. See for instance Ashcroft *et al.* (1993).

25   Where representation necessarily misrepresents we find the political moment when the strategic nature of closure is revealed. Such closures are moments in a politics of articulation, an echo of something Fanon reflected on while listening to the radio in the midst of anti-colonial war. Feuchtwang writes: 'The Arabic channel was of course jammed. But the scraps of sound had an exaggerated effect. Like rumours, they were constructively heard, and listening to them became an act of participation in revolutionary victories which might never have occurred. To quote Fanon, 'the radio receiver guaranteed this true lie,' (Feuchtwang, 1990).

26   The Tower Hamlets 9 are nine Bengali youths arrested at the vigil outside London Hospital for Quddus Ali. The Tower Hamlets 9 Defence Campaign has been set up by local young people in Tower Hamlets to campaign on their behalf: contributions to TH9 Defence Campaign, PO Box 273, London E7.

References

Ashcroft, B., G. Griffiths and H. Tiffin (eds) (1993) *The Post-colonial Studies Reader*, London: Routledge.

Berman, M. (1971) *The Politics of Authenticity: Radical Individualism and the Emergence of Modern Society*, London: Allen and Unwin.

—— (1982) *All That is Solid Melts into Air*, London: Verso.

Bhabha, H. (1994) *The Location of Culture*, London: Routledge.

Bird, J. (1992) 'Alfredo Jaar: Two or Three Things I Imagine about Them', an essay from the 1992 exhibition, London: Whitechapel Art Gallery.

Butler, J. (1993) 'Endangered/Endangering Schematic Racism and White Paranoia', in R. Gooding-Williams (ed.) *Reading Rodney King, Reading Urban Uprising*, London: Routledge.

Chambers, I. (1990) *Border Dialogues*, London: Routledge.

Davidoff, L. and C. Hall (1987) *Family Fortunes: Men and Women of the English Middle Class, 1780–1850*, London: Hutchinson.

Davis, M. (1990) *City of Quartz: Excavating the Future in Los Angeles*, London: Verso.

Deleuze, G. and F. Guattari (1987) *A Thousand Plateaus Capitalism and Schizophrenia*, London: Athlone Press.

Deutsche, R. (1991) 'Boys Town', *Environment and Planning D: Society and Space*, 9: 5–30.

Fanon, F. (1967) *Black Skin, White Masks*, London: Pluto.

Feuchtwang, S. (1985) 'Fanon's Politics of Culture: the Colonial Situation and its Extension', *Economy and Society*, 14 (4): 450–73.

Frisby, D. (1994) 'The Flaneur in Social Theory', in K. Tester (ed.) *The Flaneur*, London: Routledge.

Heron, L. (ed.) (1994) *Streets of Desire*, London: Virago.

hooks, bell (1992) *Black Looks: Race and Representation*, London: Turnaround.

Irigaray, L. (1985) *Speculum of the Other Woman*, Ithaca: Cornell University Press.

Keith, M. (1993) *Race, Riots and Policing: Lore and Disorder in a Multi-racist Society*, London: UCL Press.

Keith, M. and M. Cross (1993) *Racism, the City and the State*, London: Routledge.

Keith, M. and S. Pile (1994) 'The Politics of Place', in M. Keith and S. Pile (eds) *Place and the Politics of Identity*, London: Routledge.

Laclau, E. (1990) *New Reflections on the Revolution for Our Time*, London: Verso.

Lasch, C. (1978) *The Culture of Narcissism: American Life in an Age of Diminishing Expectations*, New York: Norton.

Mitchell, J. (1974) *Feminism and Psychoanalysis*, London: Allen Lane.

Mulvey, L. (1989) *Visual and Other Pleasures: Language, Discourse, Society*, London: Macmillan.

Phillips, P.C. (1992) 'Republica de Chile: Pasaporte', an essay from the 1992 exhibition, London Whitechapel Art Gallery.

Pollock, G. (1988) *Vision and Difference: Feminism, Feminity and the Histories of Art*, London: Routledge.

Race and Class (1993) 'Black America: the Street and the Campus', 35 (1).

Rieff, D. (1991) *Los Angeles: Capital of The Third World*, London: Phoenix.

Rignall, J. (1989) 'Benjamin's Flaneur and the Problem of Realism', in A. Benjamin (ed.) *The Problems of Modernity: Adorno and Benjamin*, London: Routledge.

Rose, J. (1986) *Sexuality in the Field of Vision*, London: Verso.

Sennett, R. (1977) *The Fall of Public Man*, London: Faber and Faber.

Sinclair, I. (1995) *Downriver*, New York: Vintage.

——(1994) *Radon Daughters: a Voyage Between Art and Terror, from the Mound of Whitechapel to the Limestone Pavements of the Burren*, London: Cape.

Stallybrass, P. and A. Whyte (1986) *The Politics and Poetics of Transgression*, London: Methuen.

Taussig, M. (1993) *Mimesis and Alterity: a Particular History of the Senses*, London: Routledge.

——(1987) *Shamanism, Colonialism and the Wild Man*, Chicago: University of Chicago Press.

Walkowitz, J. (1992) *City of Dreadful Delight: Narratives of Sexual Danger in Late-Victorian London*, London: Virago.

Wilson, E. (1991) *Sphinx in the City: Urban Life, the Control of Disorder and Women*, London: Virago.

Wolff, J. (1989) 'The Invisible Flaneuse: Women and the Literature of Modernity', in A. Benjamin (ed.) *The Problems of Modernity: Adorno and Benjamin*, London: Routledge.

Wright, P. (1991) *A Journey Through Ruins: The Last Days of London*, London: Radius.

Young, I.M. (1990) 'The Ideal of Community and the Politics of Difference', in L.J. Nicholson (ed.) *Feminism/Postmodernism*, London: Routledge.

Chapter 36

Richard Dyer

THE MATTER OF WHITENESS

R ACIAL[1] IMAGERY IS CENTRAL to the organisation of the modern world. At what cost regions and countries export their goods, whose voices are listened to at international gatherings, who bombs and who is bombed, who gets what jobs, housing, access to health care and education, what cultural activities are subsidised and sold, in what terms they are validated – these are all largely inextricable from racial imagery. The myriad minute decisions that constitute the practices of the world are at every point informed by judgements about people's capacities and worth, judgements based on what they look like, where they come from, how they speak, even what they eat, that is, racial judgements. Race is not the only factor governing these things and people of goodwill everywhere struggle to overcome the prejudices and barriers of race, but it is never not a factor, never not in play. And since race in itself – insofar as it is anything in itself – refers to some intrinsically insignificant geographical/physical differences between people, it is the imagery of race that is in play.

There has been an enormous amount of analysis of racial imagery in the past decades, ranging from studies of images of, say, blacks or American Indians in the media to the construction of the fetish of the racial Other in the texts of colonialism and post-colonialism. Yet until recently a notable absence from such work has been the study of images of white people. Indeed, to say that one is interested in race has come to mean that one is interested in any racial imagery other than that of white people. Yet race is not only attributable to people who are not white, nor is imagery of non-white people the only racial imagery.

[. . .] There is no more powerful position than that of being 'just' human. The claim to power is the claim to speak for the commonality of humanity. Raced people can't do that – they can only speak for their race.[2] But non-raced people can, for they do not represent the interests of a race. The point of seeing the racing of whites is to dislodge them/us from the position of power, with all the inequities, oppression, privileges and sufferings in its train, dislodging them/us by undercutting the authority with which they/we speak and act in and on the world.

The sense of whites as non-raced is most evident in the absence of reference to whiteness in the habitual speech and writing of white people in the West. We (whites) will speak of, say, the blackness or Chineseness of friends, neighbours, colleagues, customers or clients, and it may be in the most genuinely friendly and accepting manner, but we don't mention the whiteness of the white people we know. An old-style white comedian will often start a joke: 'There's this bloke walking down the street and he meets this black geezer', never thinking to race the bloke as well as the geezer. Synopses in listings of films on TV, where wordage is tight, none the less squander words with things like: 'Comedy in which a cop and his black sidekick investigate a robbery', 'Skinhead Johnny and his Asian lover Omar set up a launderette', 'Feature film from a promising Native American director' and so on. Since all white people in the West do this all the time, it would be individious to quote actual examples, and so I shall confine myself to one from my own writing. In an article on lesbian and gay stereotypes (Dyer 1993b), I discuss the fact that there can be variations on a type such as the queen or dyke. In the illustrations which accompany this point, I compare a 'fashion queen' from the film *Irene* with a 'black queen' from *Car Wash* – the former, white image is not raced, whereas all the variation of the latter is reduced to his race. Moreover, this is the only non-white image referred to in the article, which does not however point out that all the other images discussed are white. In this, as in the other white examples in this paragraph, the fashion queen is, racially speaking, taken as being just human.

This assumption that white people are just people, which is not far off saying that whites are people whereas other colours are something else, is endemic to white culture. Some of the sharpest criticism of it has been aimed at those who would think themselves the least racist or white supremacist. bell hooks, for instance, has noted how amazed and angry white liberals become when attention is drawn to their whiteness, when they are seen by non-white people as white.

> Often their rage erupts because they believe that all ways of looking that highlight difference subvert the liberal belief in a universal subjectivity (we are all just people) that they think will make racism disappear. They have a deep emotional investment in the myth of 'sameness', even as their actions reflect the primacy of whiteness as a sign informing who they are and how they think.
>
> (hooks 1992: 167)

Similarly, Hazel Carby discusses the use of black texts in white classrooms, under the sign of multiculturalism, in a way that winds up focusing 'on the complexity of response in the (white) reader/student's construction of self in relation to a (black) perceived "other"'. We should, she argues, recognise that 'everyone in this social order has been constructed in our political imagination as a racialised subject' and thus that we should consider whiteness as well as blackness, in order 'to make visible what is rendered invisible when viewed as the normative state of existence:

the (white) point in space from which we tend to identify difference' (Carby 1992: 193).

The invisibility of whiteness as a racial position in white (which is to say dominant) discourse is of a piece with its ubiquity. When I said above that this book wasn't merely seeking to fill a gap in the analysis of racial imagery, I reproduced the idea that there is no discussion of white people. In fact for most of the time white people speak about nothing but white people, it's just that we couch it in terms of 'people' in general. Research – into books, museums, the press, advertising, films, television, software – repeatedly shows that in Western representation whites are overwhelmingly and disproportionately predominant, have the central and elaborated roles, and above all are placed as the norm, the ordinary, the standard.[3] Whites are everywhere in representation. Yet precisely because of this and their placing as norm they seem not to be represented to themselves *as* whites but as people who are variously gendered, classed, sexualised and abled. At the level of racial representation, in other words, whites are not of a certain race, they're just the human race.

We are often told that we are living now in a world of multiple identities, of hybridity, of decentredness and fragmentation. The old illusory unified identities of class, gender, race, sexuality are breaking up; someone may be black *and* gay *and* middle class *and* female; we may be bi-, poly- or non-sexual, of mixed race, indeterminate gender and heaven knows what class. Yet we have not yet reached a situation in which white people and white cultural agendas are no longer in the ascendant. The media, politics, education are still in the hands of white people, still speak for whites while claiming – and sometimes sincerely aiming – to speak for humanity. Against the flowering of a myriad postmodern voices, we must also see the countervailing tendency towards a homogenisation of world culture, in the continued dominance of US news dissemination, popular TV programmes and Hollywood movies. Postmodern multiculturalism may have genuinely opened up a space for the voices of the other, challenging the authority of the white West (cf. Owens 1983), but it may also simultaneously function as a side-show for white people who look on with delight at all the differences that surround them.[4] We may be on our way to genuine hybridity, multiplicity without (white) hegemony, and it may be where we want to get to – but we aren't there yet, and we won't get there until we see whiteness, see its power, its particularity and limitedness, put it in its place and end its rule. This is why studying whiteness matters.

It is studying whiteness *qua* whiteness. Attention is sometimes paid to 'white ethnicity' (e.g. Alba 1990), but this always means an identity based on cultural origins such as British, Italian or Polish, or Catholic or Jewish, or Polish–American, Irish–American, Catholic–American and so on. These however are variations on white ethnicity (though, as I suggest below, some are more securely white than others), and the examination of them tends to lead away from a consideration of whiteness itself. John Ibson (1981), in a discussion of research on white US ethnicity, concludes that being, say, Polish, Catholic or Irish may not be as important to white Americans as some might wish. But being white is. [. . .] White people need to learn to see themselves as white, to see their particularity. In other words, whiteness needs to be made strange.

There is a political need to do this, but there are also problematic political feelings attendant on it, which need to be briefly signalled in order to be guarded against. The first of these is the green light problem. Writing about whiteness gives white people the go-ahead to write and talk about what in any case we have always talked about: ourselves. In, at any rate, intellectual and educational life in the West in recent years there have been challenges to the dominance of white concerns and a concomitant move towards inclusion of non-white cultures and issues. Putting whiteness on the agenda now might permit a sigh of relief that we white people don't after all any longer have to take on all this non-white stuff.

Related to this is the problem of 'me-too-ism', a feeling that, amid all this (*all* this?) attention being given to non-white subjects, white people are being left out. One version of this is simply the desire to have attention paid to one, which for whites is really only the wish to have all the attention once again. Another is the sense that being white is no great advantage, what with being so uptight, out of touch with our bodies, burdened with responsibilities we didn't ask for. Poor us. A third variant is the notion of white men, specifically, as a new victim group, oppressed by the gigantic strides taken by affirmative action policies, can't get jobs, can't keep women, a view identified and thus hardened up by a *Newsweek* cover story on 5 September 1993 on white male paranoia.

The green light and me-too-ism echo the reaction of some men to feminism. There is a lesson here. My blood runs cold at the thought that talking about whiteness could lead to the development of something called 'White Studies', that studying whiteness might become part of what Mike Phillips suspects is 'a new assertiveness . . . amounting to a statement of "white ethnicity", the acceptable face of white nationalism' (1993: 30)[5] or what Philip Norman (1992) identifies as a 1990s fascist chic observable in Calvin Klein and Häagen-Dazs ads as well as the rise of neo-fascist parties in Europe and North America. I dread to think that paying attention to whiteness might lead to white people saying they need to get in touch with their whiteness, that we might end up with the white equivalent of 'Iron John' and co, the 'men's movement' embrace of hairiness replaced with strangled vowels and rigid salutes. The point of looking at whiteness is to dislodge it from its centrality and authority, not to reinstate it (and much less, to make a show of reinstating it, when, like male power, it doesn't actually need reinstating).

A third problem about talking about whiteness is guilt. The kind of white people who are going to talk about being white, apart from conscious racists who have always done so, are liable to be those sensitised to racism and the history of what white people have done to non-white peoples. Accepting ourselves as white and knowing that history, we are likely to feel overwhelmed with guilt at what we have done and are still doing.[6] Guilt tends to be a blocking emotion. One wants to acknowledge so much how awful white people have been that one may never get around to examining what exactly they have been, and in particular, how exactly their image has been constructed, its complexities and contradictions. This problem – common to all 'images of' analyses – is a special temptation for white people. We may lacerate ourselves with admission of our guilt, but that bears witness to the fineness of a moral spirit that can feel such guilt – the display of our guilt is our calvary.[7]

A political problem of a different order has to do with what term to use to refer to (images of) people who are not white. In most contexts, one would not want to make such sweeping reference to so generalised a category, but in the present context of trying to see the specificity of whiteness it is sometimes neces- sary. I have opted for the term non-white. This is problematic because of its negativity, as if people who are not white only have identity by virtue of what they are not; it is not a term that I would want to see used in other contexts. However, the two common alternatives pose greater problems for my purposes. 'Black', the term preferred by many theorists and activists, has two drawbacks. First, it excludes a huge range of people who are neither white nor black, Asians, Native Americans (North and South), Chicanos, Jews and so on. Second, it rein- forces the dichotomy of black : white that underpins racial thought but which it should be our aim to dislodge. Black is a privileged term in the construction of white racial imagery and I shall examine it as such, but where I need to see whiteness in relation to all peoples who are not white, 'black' will not do. The other option would be 'people of colour', the preferred US term (though with little currency in Britain). While I have always appreciated this term's generosity, including in it all those people that 'black' excludes, it none the less reiterates the notion that some people have colour and others, whites, do not. We need to recognise white as a colour too, and just one among many, and we cannot do that if we keep using a term that reserves colour for anyone other than white people. Reluctantly, I am forced back on 'non-white'.

Politics also inform more evidently methodological questions. When I first started thinking about studying the representation of whiteness, I soon realised that what one could not do was the kind of taxonomy of typifications that had been done for non-white peoples. One cannot come up with a limited range of endlessly repeated images, because the privilege of being white in white culture is not to be subjected to stereotyping in relation to one's whiteness. White people are stereotyped in terms of gender, nation, class, sexuality, ability and so on, but the overt point of such typification is gender, nation, etc. Whiteness generally colonises the stereotypical definition of all social categories other than those of race. To be normal, even to be normally deviant (queer, crippled),[8] is to be white. White people in their whiteness, however, are imaged as individual and/or endlessly diverse, complex and changing. There are also gradations of whiteness: some people are whiter than others. Latins, the Irish and Jews, for instance, are rather less securely white than Anglos, Teutons and Nordics; indeed, if Jews are white at all, it is only Ashkenazi Jews, since the Holocaust, in a few places.

The individuated, multifarious and graded character of white representation does not mean that white culture has succeeded in imagining in white people the plenitude of human potential and is only at fault for denying this representational range to non-white people. There is a specificity to white representation, but it does not reside in a set of stereotypes so much as in narrative structural positions, rhetorical tropes and habits of perception. The same is true of all representation – the taxonomic study of stereotypes was only ever an initial step in the study of non-white representation. However, stereotyping – complex and contradictory though it is (cf. Perkins 1979, Bhabha 1983, Dyer 1993a) – does characterise the representation of subordinated social groups and is one of the means by which they are categorised and kept in their place, whereas white people in white culture are given the illusion of their own infinite variety.

[. . .] Equally, given the variety of whiteness, I have sometimes thought that what I am really writing about is the whiteness of the English, Anglo-Saxons or North Europeans (and their descendants), that this whiteness would be unrecognisable to Southern or Eastern Europeans (and their descendants). For much of the past two centuries, North European whiteness has been hegemonic within a whiteness that has none the less been assumed to include Southern and Eastern European peoples (albeit sometimes grudgingly within Europe[9] and less assuredly without it, in, for instance, the Latin diaspora of the Americas). It is this overarching hegemonic whiteness which concerns me, one to which Northern Europeans most easily lay claim but which is not to be conflated with distinctive North European identities.

As others have found, it often seems that the only way to see the structures, tropes and perceptual habits of whiteness, to see past the illusion of infinite variety, to recognise white *qua* white, is when non-white (and above all black) people are also represented. My initial stab at the topic of whiteness (Dyer 1988) approached it through three films which were centrally about white–black interactions, and my account [. . .] of how I may have got thinking about the topic at all also empha-sises the role of non-white people in my life. Similarly, Toni Morrison in her study of whiteness in American literature, *Playing in the Dark* (1992), focuses on the centrality, indeed inescapability, of black representation to the construction of white identity, a perception shared by the very influential work of Edward Saïd (1978) on the West's construction of an 'Orient' by means of which to make sense of itself. This is more than saying that one can only really see the specificity of one's culture by realising that it could be otherwise, in itself an unobjection-able human process. What the work of Morrison, Saïd *et al.* suggests is that white discourse implacably reduces the non-white subject to being a function of the white subject, not allowing her/him space or autonomy, permitting neither the recog-nition of similarities nor the acceptance of differences except as a means for knowing the white self. This cultural process justifies the emphasis, in work on the repre-sentation of white people, on the role of images of non-white people in it.

Yet this emphasis has also worried me, writing from a white position. If I continue to see whiteness only in texts in which there are also non-white people, am I not reproducing the relegation of non-white people to the function of enabling me to understand myself? Do I not do analytically what the texts themselves do? Moreover, while this is certainly the usual function of black images in white texts,[10] to focus exclusively on those texts that are 'about' racial difference and interac-tion risks giving the impression that whiteness is only white, or only matters, when it is explicitly set against non-white, whereas whiteness reproduces itself as white-ness in all texts all of the time. As a product of enterprise and imperialism, whiteness is of course always already predicated on racial difference, interaction and domination, but that is true of all texts, not just those that take such matters as their explicit subject matter. Similarly, [. . .] there is implicit racial resonance to the idea, endemic to the representation of white heterosexuality, of sexual desire as itself dark [. . .]. The point is to see the specificity of whiteness, even when the text itself is not trying to show it to you, doesn't even know that it is there to be shown.[11] I do make reference to non-white in my analyses in order to clarify the specificity of white and I do look at texts with implicit (the peplum) or explicit (*The Jewel in the Crown*) colonial structures, since colonialism is one of the elements that subtends the construction of white identity. But I have eschewed a focus on non-white characters as projections of white imaginings, as the Other to the white person who is really the latter's unknown or forbidden self. This function, as the work of Morrison and others makes abundantly clear, is indeed characteristic of white culture, but it is not the whole story and may reinforce the notion that whiteness is only racial when it is 'marked' by the presence of the truly raced, that is, non-white subject.

[. . .] White identity is founded on compelling paradoxes: a vividly corporeal cosmology that most values transcendence of the body; a notion of being at once a sort of race and the human race, an individual and a universal subject; a commitment to heterosexuality that, for whiteness to be affirmed, entails men fighting against sexual desires and women having none; a stress on the display of spirit while maintaining a position of invisibility; in short, a need always to be everything and nothing, literally overwhelmingly present and yet apparently absent, both alive and dead. Paradoxes are fascinating, endlessly drawing us back to them, either in awe at their unfathomability or else out of a wish to fathom them. Paradoxes provide the instabilities that generate stories, millions of engrossing attempts to find resolution. The dynamism of white instability, especially in its claims to universality, is also what entices those outside to seek to cross its borders and those inside to aspire ever upwards within it. Thus it is that the paradoxes and instabilities of whiteness also constitute its flexibility and productivity, in short, its representational power.

Notes

1   I use the terms 'race' and 'racial' in this opening section in the most common though problematic sense, referring to supposedly visibly differentiable, supposedly discrete social groupings.

2   In their discussion of the extraordinarily successful TV sitcom about a middle-class African-American family, *The Cosby Show*, Sut Jhally and Justin Lewis note the way that viewers repeatedly recognise the characters' blackness but also feel that 'you just think of them as people', in other words that they don't only speak for their race. Jhally and Lewis argue that this is achieved by the way the family conforms to 'the everyday, generic world of white television' (1992: 100), an essentially middle-class world. The family is 'ordinary' *despite* being black; because it is upwardly mobile, it can be accepted as 'ordinary', in a way that marginalises most actual African-Americans. If the realities of African-American experience were included, then the characters would not be perceived as 'just people'.

3   See, for instance, Bogle 1973, Hartmann and Husband 1974, Troyna 1981, MacDonald 1983, Wilson and Gutiérez 1985, van Dijk 1987, Jhally and Lewis 1992 (58ff.), Ross 1995. The research findings are generally cast the other way round, in terms of non-white under-representation, textual marginalisation and positioning as deviant or a problem. Recent research in the US does suggest that

African-Americans (but not other racially marginalised groups) have become more represented in the media, even in excess of their proportion of the population. However, this number still falls off if one focuses on central characters.

4   *The Crying Game* (GB 1992) seems to me to be an example of this. It explores, with fascination and generosity, the hybrid and fluid nature of identity: gender, race, national belonging, sexuality. Yet all of this revolves around a bemused but ultimately unchallenged straight white man – it reinscribes the position of those at the intersection of heterosexuality, maleness and whiteness as that of the one group which does not need to be hybrid and fluid.

5   He makes this point in the context of both a TV documentary about D. W. Griffith and an article by me on Lillian Gish; though I think it is inaccurate to call the latter a 'celebration' (as opposed to a recognition) of the whiteness of her stardom, the general tenor of his remarks is salutary.

6   Pascal Bruckner discusses liberal guilt and 'Third Worldism' in his *Le sanglot de l'homme blanc* (The White Man's Tears) (1983).

7   Alastair Bonnett makes a related point about the discourse of blame in recent studies of whiteness by white people.

> [A]lthough whiteness is subjected to a barrage of unsentimental critique, it emerges from this process as an omnipresent and all-powerful historical force. Whiteness is seen to be responsible for the failure of socialism to develop in America, for racism, for the impoverishment of humanity. With this 'blame' comes a new kind of centring: Whiteness, and White people, are turned into the key agents of historical change, the shapers of contemporary America.
>
> (Bonnett 1996: 153)

8   On the whiteness of queers see Hart 1994, and of disabled people see Cumberbatch and Negrine 1992: 74. Paul Darke argues (in a personal communication) that the overwhelming prevalence of whites in the representation of disability is due not only to the assumption of white as a human norm but to two other factors specific to disability – that it is to be imagined as 'the worst quality of life on earth', which must be most tragic for the most privileged, and that in the overriding representation of whites as individuals, the fact of the social construction of disability is hidden.

9   A schoolboy phrase I remember being taught was that 'wogs begin at Calais'; even the French were not white enough for little Englanders. ('Wog' is British slang for 'nigger'.)

10   An insight explored in a film context in Cameron Bailey's analysis of *Something Wild* (USA 1986), where non-white culture is used as a marker of authenticity and wildness that will give vitality and essence to the garish emptiness of middle-American mass culture, to the point that the 'wild' white woman (played by Melanie Griffiths) who distracts the hero (Jeff Daniels) from the straight and narrow is entirely coded in terms of black culture (Bailey 1988).

11   Lynda Hart's discussion (1994: 104–23) of *Attack of the 50-Ft Woman* and *Single White Female* is an example of an analysis in these terms that I read too late to integrate into the discussion.

References

Alba, Richard D. (1990) *Ethnic Identity: The Transformation of White America*, New Haven: Yale University Press.

Bailey, Cameron (1988) 'Nigger/Lover: the Thin Sheen of Race in *Something Wild*', *Screen* 29(4): 28–40.

Bhabha, Homi (1983) 'The Other Question: the Stereotype and Colonial Discourse', *Screen* 24(6): 18–36.

Bogle, Donald (1973) *Toms, Coons, Mulattoes, Mammies and Bucks: An Interpretive History of Blacks in American Films*, New York: Viking Press.

Bonnett, Alistair (1996) '"White Studies": The Problems and Projects of a New Research Agenda', *Theory, Culture and Society* 13(2): 145–55.

Carby, Hazel V. (1992) 'The Multicultural Wars' in Dent, Gina (ed.) *Black Popular Culture*, Seattle: Bay Press, 187–99.

Cumberbatch, Guy and Negrine, Ralph (1992) *Images of Disability on Television*, London: Routledge.

Dyer, Richard (1988) 'White', *Screen* 29(4): 44–65. (Reprinted in Dyer 1993a: 141–63.)

Dyer, Richard (1993a) *The Matter of Images: Essays on Representations*, London: Routledge.

Dyer, Richard (1993b) 'Seen To Be Believed: Problems in the Representation of Gay People as Typical' in Dyer 1993a: 19–51.

Hart, Lynda (1994) *Fatal Women: Lesbian Sexuality and the Mark of Aggression*, London: Routledge.

Hartmann, Paul and Husband, Charles (1974) *Racism and the Mass Media*, London: Davis-Poynter.

hooks, bell (1992) 'Madonna: Plantation Mistress or Soul Sister?' and 'Representations of Whiteness in the Black Imagination', in *Black Looks: Race and Representation*, Boston: South End Press, 157–64, 165–78.

Ibson, John (1981) 'Virgin Land or Virgin Mary? Studying the Ethnicity of White Americans', *American Quarterly* 33(3): 284–308.

Jhally, Sut and Lewis, Justin (1992) *Enlightened Racism: 'The Cosby Show', Audiences and the Myth of the American Dream*, Boulder: Westview Press.

MacDonald, J. F. (1983) *Blacks and White TV: Afro-Americans in Television since 1948*, Chicago: Nelson-Hall.

Morrison, Toni (1992) *Playing in the Dark: Whiteness and the Literary Imagination*, Cambridge, MA: Harvard University Press.

Norman, Philip (1992) 'The Shock of the Neo', *Weekend Guardian* 30–31 May: 4–6.

Owens, Craig (1983) 'The Discourse of Others: Feminists and Postmodernism' in Foster, Hal (ed.) *The Anti-Aesthetic: Essays on Postmodern Culture*, Port Townsend WA: Bay Press, 57–82.

Perkins, T. E. (1979) 'Rethinking Stereotypes' in Barrett, Michèle, Corrigan, Philip, Kuhn, Annette and Wolff, Janet (eds) *Ideology and Cultural Production*, London: Croom Helm, 135–59.

Phillips, Mike (1993) 'White Heroes in the Hall of Fame', *Black Film Bulletin* 1(4): 30.

Ross, Karen (1995) *Black and White Media*, Oxford: Polity.

Saïd, Edward (1978) *Orientalism*, London: Routledge & Kegan Paul.

Troyna, Barry (1981) 'Images of Race and Racist Images in the British News Media' in Halloran, J. D. (ed.) *Mass Media and Mass Communications*, Leicester: Leicester University Press.

van Dijk, T.A. (1987) *Communicating Racism*, London: Sage.

Wilson, C. J. and Gutiérrez, F. (1985) *Minorities and Media*, Beverley Hills: Sage.

Chapter 37

Kimberlé Williams Crenshaw

RACE, REFORM, AND RETRENCHMENT
Transformation and legitimation in antidiscrimination law

[. . .]

I**N 1984, PRESIDENT RONALD REAGAN** signed a bill that created the Martin Luther King, Jr. Federal Holiday Commission.[1] The commission was charged with the responsibility of issuing guidelines for states and localities to follow in preparing their observances of King's birthday. The commission's task would not be easy. Although King's birthday had come to symbolize the massive social movement that grew out of African-Americans' efforts to end the long history of racial oppression in America,[2] the first official observance of the holiday would take place in the face of at least two disturbing obstacles: first, a constant, if not increasing, socioeconomic disparity between the races,[3] and second, a hostile administration devoted to changing the path of civil rights reforms which many believe responsible for most of the movement's progress.[4]

The commission, though, was presented with a more essential difficulty: a focus on the continuing disparities between blacks and whites might call not for celebration but for strident criticism of America's failure to make good on its promise of racial equality. Yet such criticism would overlook the progress that has been made, progress that the holiday itself represents. The commission apparently resolved this dilemma by calling for a celebration of progress toward racial equality while urging continued commitment to this ideal. This effort to reconcile the celebration of an ideal with conditions that bespeak its continuing denial was given the ironic, but altogether appropriate title "Living the Dream."[5] The "Living the Dream" directive aptly illustrates Derrick Bell's observation that "[m]ost Americans, black and white, view the civil rights crusade as a long, slow, but always upward pull that must, given the basic precepts of the country and the commitment of its people to equality and liberty, eventually end in the full enjoyment by blacks of all rights and privileges of citizenship enjoyed by whites."[6]

[. . .] Throughout American history, the subordination of blacks was rationalized by a series of stereotypes and beliefs that made their conditions appear logical and natural. Historically, white supremacy has been premised upon various political, scientific, and religious theories, each of which relies on racial characterizations and stereotypes about blacks which have coalesced into an extensive legitimating ideology. Today, it is probably not controversial to say that these stereotypes were developed primarily to rationalize the oppression of blacks. What is overlooked, however, is the extent to which these stereotypes serve a hegemonic function by perpetuating a mythology about both blacks and whites even today, reinforcing an illusion of a white community that cuts across ethnic, gender, and class lines.

[. . .] Racism does not support the dominant order simply because all whites want to maintain their privilege at the expense of blacks, or because blacks sometimes serve as convenient political scapegoats; rather, the very existence of a clearly subordinated Other group is contrasted with the norm in a way that reinforces identification with the dominant group. Racism helps to create an illusion of unity through the oppositional force of a symbolic "other."[7] The establishment of an Other creates a bond, a burgeoning common identity of all nonstigmatized parties – whose identity and interests are defined in opposition to the other.

According to the philosophy of Jacques Derrida, a structure of polarized categories is characteristic of Western thought:

> Western thought . . . has always been structured in terms of dichotomies or polarities: good vs. evil, being vs. nothingness, presence vs. absence, truth vs. error, identity vs. difference, mind vs. matter, man vs. woman, soul vs. body, life vs. death, nature vs. culture, speech vs. writing. These polar opposite do not, however, stand as independent and equal entities. The second term in each pair is considered the negative, corrupt, undesirable version of the first, a fall away from it. . . . In other words, the two terms are not simply opposed in their meanings, but are arranged in a hierarchical order which gives the first term priority. . . .[8]

Racist ideology replicates this pattern of arranging oppositional categories in a hierarchical order; historically, whites have represented the dominant element in the antinomy, while blacks came to be seen as separate and subordinate. This hierarchy is reflected in the list on p. 551; note how each traditional negative image of blacks correlates with a counterimage of whites (see Table).

The oppositional dynamic exemplified in this list was created and maintained through an elaborate and systematic process. Laws and customs helped to create "races" out of a broad range of human traits. In the process of creating races, the categories came to be filled with meaning: whites were characterized one way and associated with normatively positive characteristics, whereas blacks were characterized another way and became associated with the subordinate, even aberrational characteristics. The operation of this dynamic, along with the important political role of racial oppositionalism, can be illustrated through a few brief historical references.

Edmund Morgan provides vivid illustration of how slaveholders from the seventeenth century onward created and politicized racial categories in order to maintain the support of nonslaveholding whites. Morgan recounts how the planters "lump[ed] Indians, mulattoes, and Negroes in a single slave class," and how these categories became "an essential, if unacknowledged, ingredient of the republican ideology that enabled Virginians to lead the nation."[9] Having accepted a common interest with slaveholders in keeping blacks subordinated, even those whites who had material reasons to object to the dominance of the slaveholding class could challenge the regime only so far. The power of race-consciousness convinced whites to support a system that was opposed to their own economic interests. As George Fredrickson put it, "racial privilege could and did serve as a compensation for class disadvantage."[10]

Domination through race-consciousness continued throughout the post-Reconstruction period. Historian C. Vann Woodward has argued that the ruling plantocracy was able to undermine the progressive accomplishments of the Populist movement by stirring up antiblack sentiment among poor whites farmers; racism was articulated as the "broader ground for a new democracy."[11] As racism formed the new base for a broader notion of democracy, class differences were mediated through reference to a racial community of equality.[12] A tragic example of the success of such race-conscious political manipulation is the career of Tom Watson, the leader of the progressive Populist movement of the 1890s. Watson, in his attempts to educate the masses of poor farmers about the destructive role of race-based politics, repeatedly told black and white audiences: "You are made to hate each other because upon that hatred is rested the keystone of the arch of financial despotism which enslaves you both. You are deceived and blinded that you may not see how this race antagonism perpetuates a monetary system which beggars you both."[13] Yet by 1906, Watson had joined the movement to disenfranchise blacks; according to Woodward, Watson had "persuaded himself that only after the Negro was eliminated from politics could Populist principles gain a hearing. In other words, the white men would have to unite before they could divide."[14]

White race-consciousness also played a role in the nascent labor movement in the North. Labor historian Herbert Hill has demonstrated that unions of virtually all trades excluded black workers from their ranks and often entirely barred black employment in certain fields. Immigrant labor unions were particularly adamant about keeping out black workers; indeed, it was precisely in order to assimilate

Historical oppositional dualities

WHITE IMAGES	BLACK IMAGES
industrious	lazy
intelligent	unintelligent
moral	immoral
knowledgeable	ignorant
enabling culture	disabling culture
law-abiding	criminal
responsible	shiftless
virtuous/pious	lascivious

into the American mainstream that immigrant laborers adopted these exclusionary policies.[15]

The political and ideological role that race-consciousness continues to play is suggested by racial polarization in contemporary presidential politics. Several political commentators have suggested that many whites supported Ronald Reagan in the belief that he would correct a perceived policy imbalance that unjustly benefited blacks, and some argue further that Reagan made a direct racist appeal to white voters. . . . Reagan received nearly 70 percent of the white vote, whereas 90 percent of black voters cast their ballots for Mondale. Similarly, the vast majority of blacks – 82 percent – disapproved of Reagan's performance, whereas only 32 percent of whites did.

Even the Democratic party, which has traditionally relied on blacks as its most loyal constituency, has responded to this apparent racial polarization by seeking to distance itself from black interests. Although some have argued that the racial polarization demonstrated in the 1984 election does not represent a trend of white defections from the Democratic party, it is significant that, whatever the cause of the party's inability to attract white votes, Democratic leaders have expressed a willingness to moderate the party's stand on key racial issues in an effort to recapture the white vote.[16]

[. . .] Prior to the civil rights reforms, blacks were formally subordinated by the state. Blacks experienced being the "other" in two aspects of oppression, which I shall designate as symbolic and material.[17] Symbolic subordination refers to the formal denial of social and political equality to all blacks, regardless of their accomplishments. Segregation and other forms of social exclusion – separate restrooms, drinking fountains, entrances, parks, cemeteries, and dining facilities – reinforced a racist ideology that blacks were simply inferior to whites and were therefore not included in the vision of America as a community of equals.

Material subordination, on the other hand, refers to the ways that discrimination and exclusion economically subordinated blacks to whites and subordinated the life chances of blacks to those of whites on almost every level. This subordination occurs when blacks are paid less for the same work, when segregation limits access to decent housing, and where poverty, anxiety, poor health care, and crime create a life expectancy for blacks that is five to six years shorter than for whites.

Symbolic subordination often created material disadvantage by reinforcing race-consciousness in everything from employment to education. In fact, symbolic and material subordination were generally not thought of separately: separate facilities were usually inferior facilities, and limited job categorization almost invariably brought lower pay and harder work. Despite the pervasiveness of racism, however, there existed even before the civil rights movement a class of blacks who were educationally, economically, and professionally equal – if not superior – to many whites; yet even these blacks suffered social and political exclusion as well.

It is also significant that not all separation resulted in inferior institutions. School segregation – although often presented as the epitome of symbolic and material subordination – did not always bring about inferior education. It is not separation per se that made segregation subordinating; rather, this result is more properly attributable to the fact that it was enforced and supported by state power, and accompanied by the explicit belief in African-American inferiority.[18]

The response to the civil rights movement was the removal of most formal barriers and symbolic manifestations of subordination. Thus, "whites only" notices and other obvious indicators of the social policy of racial subordination disappeared – at least in the public sphere. The disappearance of these symbols of subordination reflected the acceptance of the rhetoric of formal equality, signaling the demise of white supremacy rhetoric as expressing America's normative vision. In other words, it could no longer be said that blacks were not included as equals in the American political vision.

Removal of these public manifestations of subordination was a significant gain for all blacks, although some benefited more than others. The eradication of formal barriers meant more to those whose oppression was primarily symbolic than to those who suffered lasting material disadvantage. Yet despite these disparate results, it would be absurd to suggest that no benefits came from these formal reforms, especially in regard to racial policies, such as segregation, that were partly material but largely symbolic. Thus, to say that the reforms were "merely symbolic" is to say a great deal: these legal reforms and the formal extension of "citizenship" were large achievements precisely because much of what characterized black oppression was symbolic and formal.

Yet the attainment of formal equality is not the end of the story. Racial hierarchy cannot be cured by the move to facial race-neutrality in the laws that structure the economic, political, and social lives of black people. White race-consciousness, in a new but nonetheless virulent form, plays an important, perhaps crucial, role in the new regime that has legitimated the deteriorating day-to-day material conditions of the majority of blacks.

The end of Jim Crow has been accompanied by the demise of an explicit ideology of white supremacy. The white norm, however, has not disappeared; it has only been submerged in popular consciousness. It continues in an unspoken form as a statement of the positive social norm, legitimating the continuing domination of those who do not meet it. Nor have the negative stereotypes associated with blacks been eradicated. The rationalizations once used to legitimate black subordination based on a belief in racial inferiority have now been reemployed to legitimate the domination of blacks through reference to an assumed cultural inferiority.

Thomas Sowell, for example, suggests that underclass blacks are economically depressed because they have not adopted the values of hard work and discipline. He further implies that blacks have not pursued the need to attain skills and marketable education, and have not learned to make the sacrifices necessary for success. Instead, he charges, blacks view demands for special treatment as a means for achieving what other groups have achieved through hard work and the abandonment of racial politics.

Sowell applies the same stereotypes to the mass of blacks that white supremacists had applied in the past, but bases these modern stereotypes on notions of "culture" rather than genetics. Sowell characterizes underclass blacks as victims of self-imposed ignorance, lack of direction, and poor work attitudes: culture, not race, now accounts for this Otherness. Except for vestigial pockets of historical racism, any possible connection between past racial subordination and the present situation has been severed by the formal repudiation of the old race-conscious policies. The same dualities that historically have been used to legitimate racial subordination in the name of genetic inferiority have now been adopted by Sowell as a means for explaining the subordinated status of blacks today in terms of cultural inferiority.[19]

Moreover, Sowell's explanation of blacks' subordinated status also illustrates the treatment of the now-unspoken white stereotypes as the positive social norm. His assertion that the absence of certain attributes accounts for the continued subordination of blacks implies that it is the presence of these attributes that explains the continued advantage of whites. The only difference between this argument and the older oppositional dynamic is this: whereas the latter explained black subordination through reference to the ideology of white supremacy, the former explains black subordination through reference to an unspoken social norm. That norm – although no longer explicitly white supremacist – nevertheless, remains a white norm.

White race-consciousness, which includes the modern belief in cultural inferiority, furthers black subordination by justifying all the forms of unofficial racial discrimination, injury, and neglect that flourish in a society only formally dedicated to equality. Indeed, in ways more subtle, white race-consciousness reinforces and is reinforced by the myth of equal opportunity which explains and justifies broader class hierarchies.

Race-consciousness also reinforces whites' sense that American society truly is meritocratic, and thus it helps to prevent them from questioning the basic legitimacy of the free market. Believing both that blacks are inferior and that the economy impartially rewards the superior over the inferior, whites see that most blacks are indeed worse off than whites are, which reinforces their sense that the market is operating "fairly and impartially"; those who logically should be on the bottom are on the bottom. This strengthening of whites' belief in the system in turn reinforces their beliefs that blacks are indeed inferior. After all, equal opportunity is the rule, and the market is an impartial judge; if blacks are on the bottom, it must reflect their relative inferiority. Racist ideology thus operates in conjunction with the class components of legal ideology to reinforce the status quo, both in terms of class and race.

To bring a fundamental challenge to the way things are, whites would have to question not just their own subordinate status but also both the economic and the racial myths that justify the status quo. Racism, combined with equal opportunity mythology, provides a rationalization for racial oppression, making it difficult for whites to see the black situation as illegitimate or unnecessary. If whites believe that blacks, because they are unambitious or inferior, get what they deserve, it becomes that much harder to convince whites that something is wrong with the entire system. Similarly, a challenge to the legitimacy of continued racial inequality would force whites to confront myths about equality of opportunity which justify for them whatever measure of economic success they may have attained.

[. . .] Rights discourse provided the ideological mechanisms through which the conflicts of federalism, the power of the presidency, and the legitimacy of the courts could be orchestrated against Jim Crow. Movement leaders used these tactics to force open a conflict between whites, which eventually benefited black people. Casting racial issues in the moral and legal rights rhetoric of the prevailing ideology helped to create the political controversy without which the state's coercive function would not have been enlisted to aid blacks.

Merely critiquing the ideology from without or making demands in language outside the rights discourse would have accomplished little. Rather, blacks gained by using a powerful combination of direct action, mass protest, and individual acts of resistance, along with appeals, both to public opinion and to the court, that were couched in the language of the prevailing legal consciousness. The result was a series of ideological and political crises in which civil rights activists and lawyers induced the federal government to aid blacks and triggered efforts to legitimate and reinforce the authority of the law in ways that benefited blacks. Merely insisting that blacks be integrated or speaking in the language of "needs" would have endangered the lives of those who were already taking risks – and with no reasonable chance of success. President Eisenhower, for example, would not have sent federal troops to Little Rock simply at the behest of protesters demanding that black schoolchildren receive an equal education. Instead, the successful manipulation of legal rhetoric led to a crisis of federal power that ultimately benefited blacks.

Some critics of legal reform movements seem to overlook the fact that state power has made a significant difference – sometimes between life and death – in the efforts of black people to transform their world. Attempts to harness the power of the state through the appropriate rhetorical and legal incantations should be appreciated as intensely powerful and calculated political acts. In the context of white supremacy, engaging in rights discourse should be seen as an act of self-defense. This was particularly true once the movement had mobilized people to challenge the system of oppression, because the state could not assume a position of neutrality regarding black people; either the coercive mechanism of the state had to be used to support white supremacy, or it had to be used to dismantle it. We know now, with hindsight, that it did both.[20]

Blacks did use rights rhetoric to mobilize state power to their benefit against symbolic oppression through formal inequality and, to some extent, against material deprivation in the form of private, informal exclusion of the middle class from jobs and housing. Yet today the same legal reforms play a role in providing an ideological framework that makes the present conditions facing underclass blacks appear fair and reasonable. However, the eradication of barriers has created a new dilemma for those victims of racial oppression who are not in a position to benefit from the move to formal equality. The race neutrality of the legal system creates the illusion that racism is no longer the primary factor responsible for the condition of the black underclass; instead, as we have seen, class disparities appear to be the consequence of individual and group merit within a supposed system of equal opportunity. Moreover, the fact that some blacks are economically successful gives credence both to the assertion that opportunities exist and to the backlash attitude that blacks have "gotten too far." Psychologically, for blacks who have not made it, the lack of an explanation for their underclass status may result in self-blame and other self-destructive attitudes.

Another consequence of the formal reforms may be the loss of collectivity among blacks. The removal of formal barriers created new opportunities for some blacks which were not shared by various other classes of African-Americans; as blacks moved into different spheres, the experience of being black in America became fragmented and multifaceted, and the different contexts presented opportunities to experience racism in different ways. The social, economic, and even residential distance between the various classes may complicate efforts to unite behind issues as a racial group. Although "whites only" signs may have been crude and debilitating, they at least presented a readily discernible target around which to organize. Now, the targets are obscure and diffuse, and this difference may create doubt among some blacks as to whether there is enough similarity between their own life experiences and those of other blacks to warrant collective political action.

Formal equality significantly transformed the black experience in America. With society's embrace of formal equality came the eradication of symbolic domination and the suppression of white supremacy as the norm of society. Future generations of black Americans would no longer be explicitly regarded as America's second-class citizens. Yet the transformation of the oppositional dynamic – achieved through the suppression of racial norms and stereotypes, and the recasting of racial inferiority into assumptions of cultural inferiority – creates several difficulties for the civil rights constituency. The removal of formal barriers, although symbolically significant to all and materially significant to some, will do little to alter the hierarchical relationship between blacks and whites until the way in which white race-consciousness perpetuates norms that legitimate black subordination is revealed. This is not to say that white norms alone account for the conditions of the black underclass; it is, instead, an acknowledgement that until the distinct racial nature of class ideology is itself revealed and debunked, nothing can be done about the underlying structural problems that account for the disparities. The narrow focus of racial exclusion – that is, the belief that racial exclusion is illegitimate only where the "whites only" signs are explicit – coupled with strong assumptions about equal opportunity, makes it difficult to move the discussion of racism beyond the societal self-satisfaction engendered by the appearance of neutral norms and formal inclusion.

[. . .] For blacks, the task at hand is to devise ways to wage ideological and political struggle while minimizing the costs of engaging in an inherently legitimating discourse. A clearer understanding of the space we occupy in the American political consciousness is a necessary prerequisite to the development of pragmatic strategies for political and economic survival. In this regard, the most serious challenge for blacks is to minimize the political and cultural cost of engaging in an inevitably co-optive process in order to secure material benefits. Because our present predicament gives us few options, we must create conditions for the maintenance of a distinct political thought that is informed by the actual conditions of black people. Unlike the civil rights vision, this new approach should not be defined and thereby limited by the possibilities of dominant political discourse; rather, it should maintain a distinctly progressive outlook that focuses on the needs of the African-American community.

Notes and references

1   Act of Aug. 27, 1984, Pub. L. No. 98–399, 98 Stat. 1473. President Reagan's
     signing is reported in 20 *Weekly Comp. Pres. Doc.* 1192 (Sept. 3, 1984).

2   I shall use "African-American" and "black" interchangeably. . . . The naming of
     Americans of African descent has had political overtones throughout history. See
     W. E. B. Du Bois, 2 *The Seventh Son*, 12–13 (1971) (arguing that the "N" in
     Negro was always capitalized until, in defense of slavery, the use of the lower
     case "N" became the custom in "recognition" of Blacks' status as property; that
     the usage was defended as a "description of the color of a people"; and that the
     capitalization of other ethnic and national origin designations made the failure
     to capitalize "Negro" an insult). "African-American" is now preferred by some
     because it is both culturally more specific and historically more expansive than
     the traditional terms that narrowly categorize us as America's Other. . . .

3   Continuing disparities exist between African-Americans and whites in virtually
     every measurable category. In 1986, the African-American poverty rate stood
     at 31 percent, compared with 11 percent for whites; see Williams, "Urban
     League Says Blacks Suffered Loss over Decade," *New York Times*, Jan. 15, 1988,
     A10:1. "[B]lack median income is 57 percent that of whites, a decline of about
     four percentage points since the early 1970's"; Bernstein, "20 Years After the
     Kerner Report: Three Societies, All Separate," *New York Times*, Feb. 29, 1988,
     B8:2. Between 1981 and 1985, black unemployment averaged 17 percent,
     compared to 7.3 percent for whites; see National Urban League, *The State of
     Black America 1986*, 15 (1986). In 1986, approximately 44 percent of all black
     children lived in poverty; see Lauter and May, "A Saga of Triumph, a Return
     to Poverty: Black Middle Class Has Grown but Poor Multiply," *Los Angeles Times*,
     April 2, 1988, 1. 16:1. Blacks comprise 60 percent of the urban underclass in
     the United States; *id*. at 16:3.

     The African-American socioeconomic position in American society has actu-
     ally declined in the last two decades. Average annual family income for
     African-Americans dropped 9 percent from the seventies to the eighties, see
     Williams, *supra*, A10:1. Since 1969, the proportion of black men between 25
     and 55 earning less than $5000 a year rose from 8 to 20 percent, see Lauter
     and May, *supra*. African-American enrollment in universities and colleges is also
     on the decline; see Williams, *supra*, A10:2.

     The decline in the African-American socioeconomic position has been paral-
     leled by an increase in overt racial hostility. See generally U.S. Commission on
     Civil Rights, *Intimidation and Violence: Racial and Religious Bigotry in America* (1983).
     In addition to well-publicized incidents of racial violence like the Howard Beach
     attack . . . and the lynching of Michael Donald, . . . racial unrest has risen
     dramatically on university campuses; see Wilkerson, "Campus Blacks Feel
     Racism's Nuances," *New York Times*, April 17, 1988, 1.1:3.

     For a comprehensive analysis of the conditions afflicting the black urban under-
     class, see W. Wilson, *The Truly Disadvantaged: The Inner City, the Underclass, and
     Public Policy* (1987).

4   The principal civil rights reforms are the Civil Rights Act of 1964, Pub. L. No.
     88–352,. 78 Stat. 243 (codified as amended at 42 U.S.C. ss 2000(e)–2000(h)(6)
     (1982)); the Voting Rights Act of 1965, Pub. L. No. 89–110, 79 Stat. 437
     (codified as amended at 42 U.S.C. ss 1971–1974 (1982)); U.S/CONST. amends.

XIII–XV; 42 U.S.C. ss 1981, 1983, 1985 (1982); Exec. Order No. 11,246, 3 C.F.R. 339 (1964–1965 comp.); and the Equal Employment Opportunity Commission regulations, 29 C.F.R. ss 1600–1691 (1987).

See ACLU, *In Contempt of Congress and the Courts – The Reagan Civil Rights Record* (1984); Chambers, "Racial Justice in the 1980's," 8 *Campbell L. Rev.*, 29, 31–34 (1985); Devins, "Closing the Classroom Door to Civil Rights," 11 *Hum. Rts.*, 26 (1984); Selig, "The Reagan Justice Department and Civil Rights: What Went Wrong," 1985 *U. Ill. L. Rev.*, 785; Wolvovitz and Lobel, "The Enforcement of Civil Rights Statutes: The Reagan Administration's Record," 9 *Black L.J.*, 252 (1986); see also Hernandez, Weiss, and Smith, "How Different Is the World of 1984 from the World of 1964?," 37 *Rutgers L. Rev.*, 755, 757–60 (1985).

Some scholars have been critical of the overall development of civil rights law over the past decade, positing that we have reached the end of the "Second Reconstruction"; see generally D. Bell, *And We Are Not Saved* (1987); Bell, "The Supreme Court, 1984 Term – Foreword: The Civil Rights Chronicles," 99 *Harv. L. Rev.*, 4 (1985).

5   Martin Luther King, Jr., Federal Holiday Commission, *Living the Dream* (1986).

6   D. Bell, *Race, Racism and American Law* (2nd ed. 1981).

7   The notion of blacks as a subordinated Other in Western culture has been a major theme in scholarship exploring the cultural and sociological structure of racism. See Trost, "Western Metaphysical Dualism as an Element in Racism," in J. Hodge, D. Struckmann, and L. Trost, eds., *Cultural Bases of Racism and Group Oppression* 49 (1975) (arguing that black and white are seen as paired antinomies, and that there is a hierarchy within the antinomies, with Caucasians and Western culture constituting the preferred or higher antinomy). Frantz Fanon has summarized the attitude of the West toward blackness as a projection of Western anxiety concerning the Other in terms of skin color: "In Europe, the black man is the symbol of Evil. . . . The torturer is the black man, Satan is black, one talks of shadow, when one is dirty one is black – whether one is thinking of physical dirtiness or moral dirtiness. It would be astonishing, if the trouble were taken to bring them all together, to see the vast number of expressions that make the black man the equivalent of sin. In Europe, whether concretely or symbolically, the black man stands for the bad side of the character. As long as one cannot understand this fact one is doomed to talk in circles about the 'black problem.' Blackness, darkness, shadow, shades, night, the labyrinths of the earth, abysmal depths, blacken someone's reputation; and on the other side, the bright look of innocence, the white dove of peace, magical, heavenly light"; F. Fanon, *Black Skins, White Masks*, 188–89 (1967); see S. Gilman, *Difference and Pathology: Stereotypes of Sexuality, Race, and Sadness*, 30 (1985) (arguing that the notion that "blacks are the antithesis of the mirage of whiteness, the ideal of European aesthetic values, strikes the reader as an extension of some 'real,' perceived difference to which the qualities of 'good' and 'bad' have been erroneously applied. But the very concept of color is a quality of Otherness, not of reality."); Isaacs, "Blackness and Whiteness," *Encounter*, 8 (Aug. 1963); see also W. Jordan, *White Over Black: American Attitudes Toward the Negro, 1650–1712* (1968) (discussing how sixteenth- and seventeenth-century English writers used the concept that blacks were the Europeans' polar opposites in order to establish an elaborate hierarchy to classify other colored people in the

world). Others who have used the concept of Otherness as a framework for examining black/white relations include C. Degler, *Neither Black Nor White: Slavery and Race Relations in Brazil and The United States* (1971), and Copeland, "The Negro as a Contrast Conception," in E. Thompson, ed., *Race Relations and the Race Problem: A Definition and An Analysis*, 152–79 (1939).

8   J. Derrida, *Dissemination*, viii, trans. B. Johnson (1981) (emphasis is original).

9   E. Morgan, *American Slavery – American Freedom*, 386 (1975).

10 G. Fredrickson, *White Supremacy: A Comparative Study in American and South African History*, (1981).

11 C. Vann Woodward, *The Strange Career of Jim Crow*, 76 (1958).

12 One might argue that the fact that many poor whites were simultaneously disenfranchised cuts against the idea that racist ideology was the glue that organized and held whites together across class lines. In reality, the ability to exclude lower-class whites was achieved politically, via racist rhetoric.

13 *Id*. at 44–45.

14 *Id*. at 73–74.

15 "The historical record reveals that the embrace of white supremacy as ideology and as practice was a strategy for assimilation by European working class immigrants, the white ethnics who were to constitute a major part of the membership and leadership of organized labor in the United States"; . . . Hill, "Race and Ethnicity in Organized Labor: The Historical Sources of Restrictions to Affirmative Action," *J. Intergroup Rel.*, 6 (winter 1984). Even today, unions that are supposed to represent the "consciousness of the working class" often still fail to represent the interests of the black American worker. For an account of the racist history of the AFL-CIO, see Hill, "The AFL-CIO and the Black Worker: Twenty-Five Years After the Merger," *J. Intergroup Rel.*, 5 (Sept. 1982).

16 This effort to minimize black influence reflects what Derrick Bell, Jr., has called the principle of "involuntary sacrifice"; see D. Bell, *Race, Racism, and American Law*, U 1.8, at 29–30. . . . Bell asserts that throughout American history, Black interests have been sacrificed when necessary to reestablish the bonds of the white community, "so that identifiably different groups of whites may settle a dispute and establish or reestablish their relationship"; *id*. at 30.

17 These two manifestations of racial subordination are not mutually exclusive. In fact, it only makes sense to separate various aspects of racial oppression in this post-civil rights era in order to understand how the movement changed some social norms and reinforced others. Most blacks probably did not experience or perceive their oppression as reflecting two separate structures.

18 Socially, many blacks lived in a society comparable in many ways to that of the white elites. Hardly strangers to debutante balls, country clubs, and vacations abroad, these blacks lived lives of which many whites only dreamed. Nevertheless, despite their material wealth, upper-middle-class blacks were still members of a subordinated group. Where rights and privileges were distributed on the basis of race, even a distinguished African-American had to take a back seat to each white – no matter how poor, ignorant, or uneducated the white might be.

19 Sowell exemplifies what may be the worst development of the civil rights movement – that some blacks who have benefited the most from the formal gestures of equality now identify with those who attempt to affirm the legitimacy of oppressing other blacks. Clearly, this legitimation and desertion by

some blacks has been politically damaging and may undermine future efforts to organize.

20   Consider, for example, the possible police responses to students who violated local ordinances by sitting in at segregated lunch counters and demanding service. Government officials could have ordered the students arrested, thereby upholding the segregation policy, or they could have ignored them, which would have incidentally supported the students' efforts. Both tactics were followed throughout the course of the movement. Because officials sometimes had a degree of choice in the matter, and courts had the ultimate power to review the legitimacy of the laws and the officials' actions, black protesters' use of rights rhetoric can be seen as an effort to defend themselves against arrest or conviction for violating the norms of white supremacy.

Chapter 38

Stephen Steinberg

AMERICA AGAIN AT
THE CROSSROADS

WHEN THIS NATION'S FOUNDING FATHERS betrayed the noble principles enshrined in the Declaration of Independence and the Constitution, and surrendered to temptation and greed by sanctioning the slave trade, they placed the nation on a calamitous path of racial division and conflict that continues down to the present. Yet the thirteen decades since the abolition of slavery are littered with lost opportunities – golden moments when the nation could have severed this historical chain, but either failed to do so or did not go far enough in eradicating the legacy of slavery.

The first lost opportunity, of course, was the failure of Reconstruction. The Thirteenth, Fourteenth, and Fifteenth Amendments to the Constitution elevated blacks to full citizenship, and ushered in a period of biracial democracy in which blacks voted, held office, and, despite a general pattern of social segregation, enjoyed a modicum of civil equality.[1] However, these gains were tenuous and short-lived. As W.E.B. Du Bois wrote in his 1935 study *Black Reconstruction in America*: "The slave went free; stood a brief moment in the sun; then moved back again toward slavery."[2]

Had the promise of Reconstruction been kept, then this would have obviated the need for a civil rights revolution a century later. Nor can blame for the failure of Reconstruction be placed wholly on the South. As Neil McMillen writes in his history of Jim Crow in Mississippi: "Without the ready acquiescence of northern white sentiment, the national Republican party, and the three branches of the federal government, blacks could not have been driven from politics in any state."[3] Indeed, Northern acquiescence to black disfranchisement persisted until 1965, when Congress, under unrelenting pressure from the black protest movement, passed the Voting Rights Act. During the preceding century, however, even anti-lynching legislation was beyond the pale of political possibility.

The failure of Reconstruction goes beyond the subversion of the Reconstruction amendments. After two centuries of slavery, the bestowal of political rights on blacks scarcely began to address the needs of an expropriated people. Genuine reconstruction would have included a massive redistribution of land, as envisioned by a few "radical" Republicans. Not only would this have placed freedmen on a path toward self-sufficiency, but it also would have secured their newly won political rights as well. As Thaddeus Stevens commented when he submitted his proposal for a land redistribution to Congress in 1865: "How can republican institutions, free schools, free churches, free social intercourse exist in a mingled community of nabobs and serfs?"[4]

Indeed, "forty acres and a mule" epitomized the dream of blacks at the end of the Civil War. This was a dream unfulfilled, however. The legislation establishing the Freedmen's Bureau in March 1865 had provided for the distribution of land confiscated from Confederate soldiers and their supporters, but within months President Johnson ordered that the land be returned to its former owners. Most blacks ended up working as sharecroppers or tenant farmers, a system that amounted to a form of debt servitude that restricted the freedoms of workers and kept them tied to the land. As Myrdal lamented in *An American Dilemma*: "The story of the Negro in agriculture would have been a rather different one if the Negro farmer had greater opportunity to establish himself as an independent owner."[5]

The subjugation of the South's black population was so complete that we can only imagine how the course of race history might have been altered if white America had delivered on the promise of "forty acres and a mule." One historical example provides a glimpse into the future that never was: the so-called "exoduster movement." This involved a migration of tens of thousands of Southern blacks to Kansas in the spring of 1879. Kansas was only one of a number of emigration schemes that were explored by blacks desperate to escape the tightening noose of racial oppression. Emissaries had gone as far away as Haiti, Canada, and even Liberia. Kansas emerged as an option because it was in need of settlers, and the abolitionist Republicans who ruled the state accepted blacks on a parity with whites.[6] Word of "cheap land in Kansas" spread like wildfire throughout the South, with the help of blacks working on steamboats and railroads.

As the migration gained momentum, it assumed messianic overtones. Migrants, who were called "exodusters," saw themselves as fleeing Egypt for the Promised Land. The leader of the movement, "Pap" Singleton, was dubbed the Father of the Exodus and the Moses of the Colored People. In some respects the story parallels the one told by Leon Uris in *Exodus*. The land available for black settlement had been passed over during the westward migration because of the dearth of water. Lacking trees and shelter, settlers were forced to live in dugouts gouged out of the arid soil. Many gave up in frustration and resumed their northward migration. However, several "colonies" were established that eventually developed into flourishing agricultural communities, replete with churches, newspapers, hotels, businesses, and all of the other accouterments and amenities of a Midwestern town.

Like the rest of rural America, the black towns were hard hit by the Depression and the Dust Bowl, and most of the residents dispersed to cities in the North and West. However, one community, Nicodemus, still exists, a living symbol of "what might have been" if blacks had been masters of their own destiny.

I stumbled upon Nicodemus in 1975 while doing research on the impact of European immigration on African Americans. The research began with the naive question: why did so few blacks migrate to the Northern cities that offered opportunity to millions of immigrants at the turn of the century? The social science literature was of little help. In *An American Dilemma*, for example, Gunnar Myrdal puzzled about why so few blacks migrated to the North and West, conceding that this was "a mystery."[7] Historians, for their part, are so riveted on chronicling "what happened" that they tend to ignore non-events – in this case, the *non-migration* of blacks to the North during this period.[8] Nor in 1975 were there any major studies of the exoduster movement.[9] I found one nugget of information in the Kansas volume of the Federal Writer's Project that described Nicodemus as the "last survivor of Kansas' three colonies settled by the exodusters." I decided to go see for myself.[10]

On my first field trip to Nicodemus I interviewed two women: Hattie Burney and Ola Scruggs Wilson, both octagenarians who had been schoolteachers to generations of Nicodemus's youth. They were repositories of memory, and filled my notebook with stories about life on the prairie where they battled droughts, dust storms, rattlesnakes, and fierce winters; gave birth to children with the help of midwives; and, despite the many privations, cultivated a singular grace and sophistication. Mrs. Burney's eyes filled with tears as she recalled what breakfast was like, with her eight siblings encircling the breakfast table, and the overpowering sense of gratitude that they felt for their father who, despite hardships, had provided them with their daily bread. She also loaned me a manuscript that her father had written late in his life. It was a history of Nicodemus that traced its origins and development, and celebrated its triumph over adversity.

Mrs. Wilson, who prided herself as Nicodemus's historian, rebuffed some of my questions, accusing me of "stealing her thunder." Like all historians, she jealously guarded her sources. But she did tell me about the racism in the surrounding communities, and how Nicodemus was crippled when the decision was made to run the railroad through the neighboring town of Bogue. She also described her mother's joy upon learning of her freedom. I was struck by the ease with which Mrs. Wilson invoked the word "master." For me this word had a cold abstract meaning. But here was a woman, only a generation removed from slavery, for whom the word was replete with deep personal significance. And here I was, conversing with someone whose *mother* had been a slave. It was a chilling reminder of how proximate slavery is to the present.

I returned to Nicodemus a year later for the annual Homecoming. Originally it was called "Emancipation Day," but the event was later redefined as a homecoming. Between four and five hundred descendants return every August for a week of festivities. The community boasts of a judge in Denver, an assistant attorney general in Colorado, and a big-league football player, but aside from these success stories, most of Nicodemus's progeny seem to have "made it" in various walks of life. They returned to Nicodemus in late-model cars, with a sense of pride, both of their shared origins and of their second lives in the diaspora. To be sure, Nicodemus is a historical anomaly, but it signifies "what might have been" – if more blacks had been able to escape the yoke of Southern oppression, if they had been free to own land and develop their own communities, if Reconstruction had not wound up a broken promise.

A second lost opportunity spans the period between 1880 and 1924, the years of the last great wave of European immigration. With the notable exception of Eastern European Jews, these immigrants – like blacks – generally came from peasant origins and had high rates of illiteracy. They were a surplus rural population drawn to America primarily by the prospect of jobs in its burgeoning industries. Between 1880 and 1920 some 24 million immigrants arrived. At the beginning of this period – 1880 – the entire African-American population totaled only 6.6 million, 90 percent of whom lived in the South. Despite the "Great Migration" during the First World War, 85 percent of blacks still lived in the South in 1920. The chief reason so few migrated North should have been obvious. A color line, maintained by employers and workers alike, barred blacks from virtually the entire industrial sector. This simple truth may have eluded Myrdal, but it is clearly enunciated in a 1944 book by an obscure black scholar, John G. Van Deusen, who wrote:

> Regardless of qualifications, most Northern Negroes at this time found themselves forced into domestic and personal service or restricted to odd jobs at unskilled labor. History does not show many peoples who have migrated because of persecution alone. The Negro is not dissimilar to others, and where no economic base was assured, he preferred to endure those ills he had rather than fly to others he knew not of.[11]

In the categorical exclusion of blacks from the industrial work force, the nation missed a unique opportunity to incorporate blacks into the mainstream of the economy at a time when there was rapid growth and a dire shortage of labor. Needless to say, Europe's "wretched refuse" were hardly embraced as racial kin. They, too, were regarded as pariahs, feared and despised for their ethnic peculiarities, and ruthlessly exploited. Nativists of various stripes were determined to make Americans of them. But this is precisely the point: as whites they could be naturalized and assimilated into the body politic. In the final analysis immigration policy and employment practices were predicated on the racist assumption that even the most reprobate Europeans were preferable to African-Americans.

A third lost opportunity came with the Second World War, when powerful forces for racial change were set into motion. On the level of ideology, the war against fascism served as a backlight on America's own racist and fascist tendencies. The contradiction of drafting blacks into a Jim Crow army to fight for American democracy could no longer be patched over, and A. Philip Randolph launched a "double-V campaign," standing for victory abroad *and* at home. Expectations ran high among blacks and whites alike that blacks would be rewarded for their patriotism. With characteristic optimism, Myrdal wrote: "There is bound to be a redefinition of the Negro's status in America as a result of this War."[12]

No less important were the economic and demographic changes wrought by the war. Rapid growth, combined with the mobilization of the armed forces, generated a need for black labor. A million and a half black workers were part of the war-production work force alone, and the income of black workers increased twice as fast as that of whites. The opening up of the Northern labor markets to blacks stimulated the migration of Southern blacks. Between 1940 and 1950 net migration reached an all-time high of 1.6 million.

The ancillary effects of these changes were far-reaching. Blacks developed large and cohesive communities in major Northern cities. Membership in the NAACP mushroomed to 85,000.[13] Northern residence translated into greater political leverage, evident in the fact that black voters provided the margin of victory in the election of Truman in 1948. For the first time blacks consolidated the economic and institutional base from which they could mount resistance to white oppression.[14]

The momentum was quickly blunted, however. The Fair Employment Practices Commission that Roosevelt established during the war in order to forestall Randolph's march on Washington was a feeble organization with a skeletal staff and no enforcement powers. Even so, it was embroiled in controversy from the outset, and after a Southern filibuster in 1946 the agency was dismantled. Here was an early portent that the federal government would not be a champion of black rights during the postwar period. Black soldiers returning home had to accept the bitter fact that victory had been secured on one front only. For African-Americans the return to normalcy – the hallmark of the 1950s – meant a return to second-class citizenship.

The fourth lost opportunity has been the [. . .] failure to follow through on the momentous changes wrung out of white society by the civil rights movement. The passage of civil rights legislation in 1964 and 1965 was a monumental achievement. In securing civil rights for African-Americans, they signified the end to official racism. Of paramount importance, the state of terror, so graphically documented in *An American Dilemma*, was brought to an end. Segregation in public accommodations, long the trademark of the Southern way of life, virtually disappeared. Eventually blacks derived benefits from the franchise, at least in municipalities with a black population majority.[15] After much foot-dragging and circumvention, school desegregation was implemented throughout the South, even more successfully than in the North. By the standard of what preceded it, the post-civil rights era amounted to a great social metamorphosis.

On the other hand, to paraphrase James Baldwin, the crimes of the past cannot be used to gloss over the inequities of the present. The appropriate benchmark for assessing progress is not how much worse things were as we move closer to slavery, but rather, how much blacks continue to lag behind whites in terms of major social indicators. When these comparisons are made, a far less sanguine picture emerges – one of persistent and even widening gaps between blacks and whites in incomes and living standards.[16]

In their totality these four lost opportunities represent the greatest failure of American democracy: to come to terms with the legacy of slavery. Moreover, this failure occurred during the most expansive and prosperous period in its history, the century after slavery when the United States emerged as an industrial monolith, providing opportunity to tens of millions of immigrants, and boasting the highest standard of living in the world. Here, then, is the present conundrum: If the United States failed to come to terms with the legacy of slavery in an era of empire, what can we hope for in an era of decline?

That is to say, if the nation failed to incorporate African-Americans into the economic mainstream during a century marked by overall growth and prosperity, what can we hope for at a time when real wages are declining and the nation's overall level of prosperity and standard of living are undergoing a secular decline? If white America turned a deaf ear to black demands in the halcyon days of "the affluent society," how will it respond in a time of national hand-wringing over "the end of the American dream" and "the fall of the middle class?"[17] What will the nation have to offer African-Americans who were never included in the American dream and who never made it to the middle class?

The answers are becoming painfully obvious. In the first place, the number of blacks below the official poverty line (currently $14,763 for an urban family of four) has steadily *increased* over the past two decades – from 7.5 million in 1970 to 8.6 million in 1980, to 9.8 million in 1990, to 10.9 million in 1993. Today blacks, who are 12 percent of the population, account for 29 percent of the poor, the same proportion as in 1960.[18] Even these figures underestimate the extent to which poverty is concentrated among blacks. Nearly half of all black children under age eighteen are being raised in families below the poverty line, as compared to 16 percent of whites.[19] Poverty among blacks is also far more likely to be long-term. One study devised a measure of "persistent poverty," which applied to households that were below the official poverty level in at least eight of the ten years under examination. It found that persistent poverty was more than seven times as prevalent among urban blacks as among the rest of the urban population.[20] Another recent study found that blacks account for 58 percent of the "severely distressed" in ninety-five major cities.[21]

[. . .] The nation's failure, even at propitious moments in its history, to come to terms with its legacy of slavery has always had regressive implications for race and politics alike. As Eric Foner wrote at the conclusion of *Reconstruction*:

> If racism contributed to the undoing of Reconstruction, by the same token Reconstruction's demise and the emergence of blacks as a disenfranchised class of dependent laborers greatly facilitated racism's further spread, until by the twentieth century it had become more deeply embedded in the nation's culture and politics than at any time since the beginning of the antislavery crusade and perhaps in our entire history. The removal of a significant portion of the nation's laboring population from public life shifted the center of gravity of American politics to the right, complicating the tasks of reformers for generations to come.[22]

In much the same way, the failure of the Second Reconstruction, as the civil rights revolution has been called, to remedy the deep-seated inequalities between blacks and whites has engendered both racism and reaction, each feeding on the other.

This is the context for the recent recrudescence of scientific racism, in the form of Richard Herrnstein and Charles Murray's *The Bell Curve*.[23] This retrograde book represents the apogee of the backlash, the culmination of forces of retreat that have been building for three decades, fueled not only by the agents of racism and reaction, but also by the white liberals and black conservatives who have made the fatal mistake of shifting the focus of blame away from societal institutions onto the individuals and groups who have been cast to the fringes of the social order. As Adolph Reed has written: "We can trace Murray's legitimacy directly to the spinelessness, opportunism and racial bad faith of the liberals in the social-policy establishment. . . . Many of those objecting to Herrnstein and Murray's racism embrace positions that are almost indistinguishable, except for the resort to biology."[24]

One would think from the extraordinary attention that has been showered on *The Bell Curve* that the book offered something new to the debate over inequality. Notwithstanding all the cybernetics that the authors bring to bear – a daunting array of statistics and graphs – the book's major tenets are only a rarefied version of arguments that began with the development of IQ testing early in this century: that there is a unitary thing called intelligence, that it exists independently of environmental influences and can be accurately measured by conventional IQ tests, that the source of intelligence is in the gene and is therefore a matter of biological inheritance, and that some groups – notably African-Americans – have lower average intelligence and this genetic deficit explains why they occupy the lowest strata of society. Far from new, this timeworn model had long ago been relinquished to the trashbin of history, and perhaps would have remained there if not for the persistence and largess of the Pioneer Fund, an ultrarightist foundation that was founded by eugenicists in the 1930s and has subsidized much of the research that forms the basis for *The Bell Curve*.[25]

The question that needs to be addressed, therefore, is: Why now? What accounts for the book's publication by a major publishing house, and its extraordinary reception in the mass media? *The New York Times Magazine* christened the publication with a cover story under the title "Daring Research or 'Social Science Pornography'?" *Newsweek* and *Time* followed with feature stories. *The New Republic* printed a lengthy excerpt, along with an apologia from the editors explaining why such a reversion to scientific racism should appear on the pages of an ostensibly liberal journal.[26] Thanks to this media blitz, augmented with appearances by Charles Murray on numerous television programs, *The Bell Curve* rapidly climbed to second place on the *New York Times* Best Seller List. Against this background, it behooves us to ask: What is it about this book and the times that make them "right" for each other?

Biological determinism originally fell into disrepute not only because its knowledge-claims were debunked by the emerging social sciences, but also because the prevailing system of social relations was no longer conducive to maintaining a theory that defined social status as immutable and fixed. Notions of biological inferiority had been perfectly tailored to a caste-like society where, in the words of one anthropologist, "everyone is sentenced for life to a social cell shared by others of like birth, separated from and ranked relative to all other social cells."[27] In the twentieth century, however, the forces of industrialization, urbanization, and modernity transformed traditional society, and threw into question the ideological justifications of the old order, including the pseudo-scientific theories that consigned whole groups – racial minorities, women, and the poor – to permanent inferiority. Especially as these groups were elevated in status, it became increasingly difficult to maintain the postulates of biological determinism. To state the obvious, if this nation had followed through on the promise of the civil rights revolution, and enacted the changes that would have established a basic parity between blacks and whites in socioeconomic status and living standards, we would not today be debating whether black subordination is a product of genes.

Clearly, it is the existence of a "permanent underclass" that is sustaining the recrudescence of scientific racism. *The Bell Curve* comes on stream at a time when the American class system has become more static, when poverty is on the increase, when the gap between the haves and have-nots is growing wider, and when many of the middle rungs on the ladder of success have been eliminated, making it more difficult than ever to escape poverty.[28] For the black poor in particular, who must cope with the impediments of race as well as the disabilities of class, their situation is not far removed from one where "everyone is sentenced for life to a social cell shared by others of like birth." The significance of *The Bell Curve* is that it provides ideological justification for this rigidification of class lines. The book is driven by the same ideological agenda as Murray's previous work, *Losing Ground*, which argued that social programs to uplift the poor are futile and even counter-productive, in that they foster a welfare dependency that keeps their beneficiaries trapped in poverty. Thanks to his collaboration with Richard Herrnstein, Murray has added a biological twist to this argument. The underclass is destined by nature to remain on the tail end of the socioeconomic curve. Ameliorative social policy is destined to failure. We can only resign ourselves to the dictates of nature in the name of a perverse multiculturalism.

Yet it would be premature to conclude that *The Bell Curve* represents a decisive shift in the prevailing paradigm. For one thing, an avalanche of criticism was heaped on the book, even before it had been reviewed in scholarly journals. As Adolph Reed has noted, "Even illiberals like Pat Buchanan, John McLaughlin and Rush Limbaugh . . . are eloquently dissenting from Herrnstein and Murray's unsavory racial messages."[29] The same is true of a number of conservatives who participated in a symposium on *The Bell Curve* in *The National Review*.[30] The reason these conservatives do not want "to play the IQ card," as one put it, is not that they have seen the liberal light, but rather that they prefer the neoconservative model that traces inequality to aberrant values rather than defective genes. As far as they are concerned, Murray had it right the first time, and his fling into biology along with Herrnstein threatens to discredit the entire conservative paradigm. Besides, the idea that this is a nation where *everyone* can rise to the top – where people are judged by the content of their character – is the ideological linchpin of the American myth, irreconcilable with Herrnstein and Murray's conception of a Brave New World stratified by the content of one's germ plasm.

In the final analysis, *The Bell Curve* is flourishing on its notoriety, on its petulant flouting of ideas long considered taboo. In this sense the publication of the book, and the wide public discussion that has ensued, represents the triumph of the anti-PC campaign. Nevertheless, there is good reason to think that, like the earlier publications of William Shockley, Arthur Jensen, and Herrnstein himself, *The Bell Curve* is destined to collect layers of merciful dust on our bookshelves.

As Myrdal noted in *An American Dilemma*, periods of racial advance have typically been followed by periods of retreat, though "not as much ground was lost as had been won."[31] Race history, one might say, has observed the pattern of two steps forward and one step back. *The Bell Curve* represents that metaphoric step back. It leaves "America Again at the Crossroads" – the title that Myrdal chose for the concluding chapter of *An American Dilemma*. Indeed, this is the tragedy of history – that half a century later the nation finds itself again at the crossroads, still uncertain whether to take the road back to the benighted past, or to forge a new path leading to a historical reconciliation between the black and white citizens of this nation.

What will it take to move history forward again? Clearly, there is no return to the civil rights movement: it was the product of forces unique to that time, and it fulfilled its chief purpose, which was the passage of civil rights legislation that brought an end to Jim Crow. Indeed, this has been the quandary that has stymied the liberation movement ever since: how to develop a theory and praxis for attacking the institutionalized inequalities that constitute the enduring legacy of slavery. Given the recent ascendancy of the political right, based in large part on its cynical use of race and racism to launch an attack on the welfare state, it is difficult even to imagine a political scenario leading to the fulfillment of Martin Luther King's celebrated dream.

Yet the lesson of history is that the flame of liberation cannot be extinguished. Racial oppression has always originated at the top echelons of society, but the irrepressible forces for black liberation have always sprung from the bottom. Not from the political establishment – its leaders, the political parties, or the vaunted institutions of American democracy. Not from white liberals who have too often equivocated and temporized, offering little more than a kinder and gentler version of the racial status quo. Certainly not from some armchair theorist or policy maven who has lit on some hitherto elusive truth. Not even from the civil rights establishment that, despite valiant efforts, must settle for meager concessions extracted from white power structures.

To be sure, democratic institutions, liberals, scholars, and civil rights organizations may again serve as constructive agents for change, as they have in the past. However, the paramount truth is that this nation has never had the political will to address the legacy of slavery until forced by events to do so. As in the past, the catalyst for change will be "the mounting pressure" that emanates from those segments of black society that have little reason to acquiesce in the racial status quo. It has yet to be seen exactly what form resistance and protest will take. However, we can take comfort from Lerone Bennett's astute observation: "There has been . . . a Negro revolt in every decade of this century. Each revolt failed, only to emerge in the next decade on a higher level of development."[32]

Our nation has chosen to canonize the Martin Luther King who, in his celebrated "I Have a Dream" oration, projected a racial nirvana in some indefinite future. But let us also remember the King who in the same speech said: "The whirlwinds of revolt will continue to shake the foundations of our nation until the bright day of justice emerges."[33]

Notes and references

1   Eric Foner, *Reconstruction: America's Unfinished Revolution, 1863–1877* (New York: Harper & Row, 1988).

2   W. E. B. Du Bois, *Black Reconstruction* (New York: Harcourt, Brace, 1935), p. 30.

3   Neil R. McMillen, *Dark Journey: Black Mississippians in the Age of Jim Crow* (Urbana and Chicago: University of Illinois Press, 1989), p. 38.

4   Foner, *Reconstruction: America's Unfinished Revolution, 1863–1877*, p. 236.

5   Gunnar Myrdal, *An American Dilemma: The Negro Problem and Modern Democracy* (New York: Harper & Row, 1944), p. 237.

6   Nell Irvin Painter, *Exodusters* (New York: Knopf, 1977), p. 159.

7   Myrdal, *An American Dilemma*, pp. 189–90.

8   An exception is Peter Uhlenberg, "Noneconomic Determinants of Nonmigration: Sociological Considerations for Migration Theory," *Rural Sociology* 38 (Fall 1973): 296.

9   Nell Irvin Painter's excellent study, *Exodusters*, was published in 1977.

10 A second field trip involved oral histories and the production of a film under a grant from the Ethnic Heritage Studies Program of the Office of Education.

11 John G. Van Deusen, *The Black Man in White America* (Washington, D.C.: Associated Publishers, 1944), p. 30. See also Stephen Steinberg, *The Ethnic Myth* (Boston: Beacon Press, 1989), Chapter 7.

12 Myrdal, *An American Dilemma*, p. 997.

13 Ibid., p. 821.

14 Francis Fox Piven and Richard A. Cloward, *Poor People's Movements* (New York: Vintage Books, 1979), p. 205.

15 For an assessment of the impact of the civil rights movement on Southern blacks, see James Button, *Blacks and Social Change* (Princeton, N.J.: Princeton University Press, 1989).

16 For detailed analyses of income trends and related issues, see Gerald David Jaynes and Robin M. Williams, Jr., *A Common Destiny* (Washington, D.C.: National Academy Press, 1989), especially Chapter 6. See also Gerald David Jaynes, "The Labor Market Status of Black Americans: 1939–1985," *Journal of Economic Perspectives* (Fall 1990); 9–24; James P. Smith and Finis R. Welch, "Black Economic Progress After Myrdal," *Journal of Economic Literature* 27 (June 1989): 119–164; and Reynolds Farley, *Blacks and Whites: Narrowing the Gap?* (Cambridge, Mass.: Harvard University Press, 1984).

17 These themes are at the center of a number of recent works: Katherine S. Newman, *Falling from Grace: The Experience of Downward Mobility in the American Middle Class* (New York: Free Press, 1988); Michael W. Haga, *Is the American Dream Dying?* (Denver: Acclaim Publishing, 1994); Lillian B. Rubin, *Families in the Front Line* (New York: HarperCollins, 1994).

18 *Statistical Abstracts of the United States, 1994* (Washington, D.C.: Government Printing Office, 1994), p. 475; *Income, Poverty, and Valuation of Non-Cash Benefits*, Current Population Reports, series P-60, no. 188 (Washington, D.C.: Government Printing Office, 1993).

19 *Statistical Abstracts of the United States, 1994* (Washington, D.C.: Government Printing Office, 1994), p. 475.

20 The time period under examination was 1974–1983. Terry K. Adams, Greg J. Duncan, and Willard L. Rodgers, "The Persistence of Urban Poverty," in *Quiet Riots*, ed. Fred R. Harris and Roger W. Wilkins (New York: Pantheon, 1988), pp. 83–85. Another study reports that while 63 percent of whites who are in poverty are there for only one year, the figure for blacks is 48 percent. The percentage of those in poverty for seven years or more is 4 percent for whites, but 15 percent for blacks; Peter Gottschalk, Sara McLanahan, and Gary D. Sandefur, "The Dynamics and Intergenerational Transmission of Poverty and Welfare Participation," in *Confronting Poverty*, ed. Sheldon H. Danziger, Gary D. Sandefur, and Daniel H. Weinberg (Cambridge, Mass.: Harvard University Press, 1994), p. 94.

21 "The severely distressed" is a composite measure consisting of five factors: low education; single parenthood; poor work history; public assistance recipiency; and poverty. John D. Kasarda, "The Severely Distressed in Economically Transforming Cities," in *Drugs, Crime, and Social Isolation*, ed. Adele V. Harrell and George E. Peterson (Washington, D.C.: The Urban Institute Press, 1992), pp. 49–54.

22 Eric Foner, *Reconstruction: America's Unfinished Revolution, 1863–1877*, p. 604.

23 Richard J. Herrnstein and Charles Murray, *The Bell Curve: Intelligence and Class Structure in American Life* (New York: Free Press, 1994).

24 Adolph Reed, Jr., "Looking Backward," *The Nation* (November 28, 1994): 661–62.

25 According to Charles Lane, Herrnstein and Murray cite thirteen scholars who were beneficiaries of grants over the last two decades totalling over $4 million. Seventeen researchers cited in the bibliography have contributed to *Mankind Quarterly*, a neo-fascist journal that espouses the genetic superiority of the white race; "The Tainted Sources of 'The Bell Curve,'" *New York Review of Books* (December 1, 1994), p. 15. The role of the Pioneer Fund in underwriting research on race and IQ was also the subject of a report on ABC news with Peter Jennings, November 22, 1994.

26 Jason DeParle, "Daring Research or 'Social Science Pornography'?" *New York Times Magazine* (October 9, 1994): p. 48; "IQ: Is It Destiny?" *Newsweek* (October 24, 1994); Richard Lacayo, "For Whom the Bell Curves: A New Book Raises a Ruckus by Linking Intelligence to Genetics and Race," *Time* (October 24, 1994). Charles Murray and Richard J. Herrnstein, "Race, Genes and I.Q. – An Apologia," *The New Republic* (October 31, 1994): 27–37; the issue included responses from an array of critics.

27 Gerald D. Berryman, "Race, Caste, and Other Invidious Distinctions in Social Stratification," reprinted in *Majority and Minority*, ed. Norman R. Yetman (Boston: Allyn & Bacon, 1991), p. 22.

28 For recent documentation of the increase in the absolute and relative rates of poverty, and the growing gap between those at the top and those at the bottom of the income distribution, see Sheldon H. Danziger and Daniel H. Weinberg, "The Historical Record: Trends in Family Income, Inequality, and Poverty," in *Confronting Poverty*, ed. Sheldon H. Danziger, Gary D. Sandefur, and Daniel H. Weinberg, pp. 18–50.

29 Reed, "Looking Backward," p. 661.

30 "*The Bell Curve*: A Symposium," *The National Review* (December 5, 1994): 32–61.

31 Myrdal, *An American Dilemma*, p. 997.

32   Lerone Bennett, "Tea and Sympathy: Liberals and Other White Hopes," in Bennett, *The Negro Mood and Other Essays* (Chicago: Johnson Publications, 1963), p. 22.

33   Martin Luther King, Jr., *I Have a Dream: Writing and Speeches that Changed the World*, ed. James Melvin Washington (New York: HarperCollins, 1992), p. 103.

Chapter 39

Chetan Bhatt

THE LORE OF THE HOMELAND
Hindu nationalism and indigenist 'neoracism'

Introduction

CONVENTIONAL WESTERN PARADIGMS OF RACE and ethnic relations sociology, as well as the political practices of anti-racism, have undergone significant internal evaluation over the last decade. This has been partly the result of the political conflicts over varieties of authoritarian anti-racism and identity politics since the mid-1980s. Sociological paradigms around race and class have also been interrogated and developed in a number of feminist interventions over the same period (Solomos and Back 1996). Many of the recent debates on globalisation and European integration have shifted emphasis away from some of the more parochial aspects of ethnic and race relations sociology of the last two decades. However, perhaps the most significant challenge to the theorisation of 'race' or racism, the ethnographic assessment of minority communities or the policy framework of multicultural pluralism has been the rise since the mid-1980s of ethnic and cultural absolutist movements in South Asian communities in the UK. The impact of the Rushdie affair is well known, and established the vulnerable nature of the secularism that was inherent in the projects of 'Asian' or 'black' politics. The affair also exposed an absence in political sociology of a serious and sustained consideration of the specificity of the politics of the South Asian experience in the UK, especially in a way that did not reduce the latter to an ethnography of cultural habits or to 'black anti-racism'. If there has been a rapid, though uneven move away from the secular politics of black liberation and anti-racism towards issues of primarily religious and ethnic difference, it is still the case that 'race' has retained an importance for some black political formations. For example, a concept of 'race', and a claim about the value of 'racial' attributes is as important for some varieties of Afrocentricity as it is for the right-wing, neo-nazi and racist political formations that are animating contemporary European politics.

This essay explores the importance of 'race thinking' in the new Hindu author-itarian religious movements that are dominating both Indian politics and the Hindu diaspora. These movements are variously labelled 'Hindu nationalism', the sangh parivar,[1] the Hindutva movement or 'Hindu cultural nationalism'. Their partic-ular formations of 'race' may be very different from western scientific or cultural 'racial' paradigms. Because of the relative unfamiliarity within mainstream western sociology of South Asian politics and history, and in particular the substantive historical, political and cultural configurations of Hinduisms, the essay is broadly introductory. Much can be learned from the experience of religious and ethnic conflict in India during and since the colonial period. Many of the political languages of multiculturalism, secularism, diversity and discrimination that are important in the west have a longer pedigree in South Asian politics and admin-istration and indeed have been fundamental to (and fundamentally contested in various ways) in Indian politics. The depth of the debates in India about these matters can inform discussions of these issues in progressive British multicultural sociology and political theory. It also needs remembering that multiculturalist discourse itself arose in the period of colonial administrative theory and practice, especially in the New World, South Asia and central Africa. Many of its older languages survive in surprisingly similar forms in contemporary western race and ethnic relations theory.

The Hindutva movement condenses numerous themes about ethnogenesis, reli-gious authoritarianism, cultural absolutism, the nature of secular postcolonial citizenship, majority–minority relations, and 'racial' and ethnic hatred that often appear separately in other examples of contemporary religious and ethnic conflict. In this sense, Hindutva ideology can represent a universal example of the numerous directions that absolutist and totalitarian ideologies can travel in the late modern period. Similarly, in describing Hindutva ideology using conventional theoretical paradigms, none of the analytical concepts of 'race', racism, religion, ethnicity or culture on their own suffice, but all are deeply relevant in a combination that perhaps requires a new description, as perhaps do many other contemporary 'abso-lutist ideologies of indigenism'.

Hindutva ideology presents an highly overdetermined ontology of *ethnos* and *xenos*. There is, for example, a powerful hereditarian 'race concept' in Hindutva but this has little to do with western scientific racism proper. It is instead related to, and often indistinguishable from a separate hereditarian discourse of culture, religion and ethnicity. If the opposition between biology and culture has often been used to analytically situate western racisms, it is important to consider how 'culture' already contains powerful epistemic resources that can provide for a sentimentalist racism that is never obliged to take actual biology or science seriously but can still contain a hereditary or genetic core, the latter frequently articulated through primordial origin myths, and the tropes of breeding, cultivation, blood and lineage. This kind of 'racism'[2] is virtually definitive of Hindutva discourse (Jaffrelot 1995, Bhatt 1997). There is a different equally relevant Hindutva 'civilisational–nationalist' discourse that need not necessarily be hereditarian, but can conviningly be called 'racist', and in many ways presents a paradigmatic case of 'monocultural neoracism'. There is yet another purely 'metaphysical ethnology' that arises in Hindutva ideology (Bhatt 1999). In this sense, the Hindutva movement has created a distinctive ontology of selves and others that is not easily captured by many of the theoretical discourses typically used to analyse racism. We shall however see later that the relations between Hindutva and western 'race thinking' are historically closer and deeper than is usually imagined.

An assessment is presented below that some South Asian ideological formations have come close in form and content to versions of classical fascism and Nazism. This may seem a stark judgment, especially when applied to some of the political formations arising from minority communities who may already face structural discrimination or 'racial' inequality in the west. The ethical challenge is indeed to keep equally abreast of both issues in all their dense historical and social complexity and without reducing each to the other. In doing so, it is necessary to move away from a distinct 'metaphysics of innocence' (an explicit disavowal of the capacity for ethical judgement that travels beyond the rhetorical labour that is required to uphold the unity of one's ownmost identity or being), that accompanies much discussion of the victims of racism and discrimination and engage in a deeper and more reflexive consideration of the global and national processes of South Asian community formation and representation that by and large overwhelm the binary syntax of racism and anti-racism. Indeed, it is precisely the normative location of those communities within the nexus of British racial discourse (or sociological racialisation) that has prevented more comprehensive assessments of some of the far right-wing movements and networks that claim to represent those communities.

It finally needs emphasising that the discussion below is about Hindu nationalism, and not about vernacular, cultural, historical or ascetic forms of Hinduism, or their attendant beliefs and practices in South Asian communities. However, some general points about the relation between Hindutva and Hinduism are necessary. The Hindutva movement has attempted to blur the distinctions between its novel ideology and historical Hinduisms in general, and has mobilised various strategies of obfuscation and indigenist claims about incommensurability to achieve this. In doing so, the Hindutva movement reproduces a grand epistemology about Hinduism that fundamentally subverts the methods of history and historical sociology. In this view, Hinduism or its essence is in some fundamental way unchanging and primordial (Hindutva is indeed based on this 'essence'). The extraordinarily complex histories of sects, caste development and change, and the social, political and cultural processes that eventually led in the modern period to the idea of Hinduism are grossly simplified and reified – in essence, they are stagnated. The similarity with western thinking (for example, Marxism) about South Asian social formations during the colonial period is obvious. In this Hindutva conception, ideas such as brahminism, sanatana dharma ('the eternal religion') and so forth are detached from the historical processes in which they developed and mobilised as self-evident signifiers of a contemporary identity. In this sense, 'Hinduism' becomes an abstraction, an empty but normative signification of something that exists above and beyond the histories of societies and cultures. The temporal schemes of Hindu mythology are applied to contemporary histories (indeed, a realism is claimed for mythic temporalities). The Hindutva movement also supplies other grand linear historiographies, one of which, like James Mill, simply divides Indian history into ancient (Vedic–Aryan), medieval (Muslim–Mughal) and modern (colonial British) hermetic periods (Thapar 1996a). Much of the structure and power of Hindutva discourse is derived by intentionally blending (and confusing) mythic, archaeological, medieval, colonial and contemporary time, space and event.

A second aspect of Hindutva methodology has included reliance on some traditional Hindu conceptual schemes and tropes, especially, but not exclusively, selective components of brahminism. Within many forms of traditional Hinduism, its many texts, symbols, myths and iconography are subject to compounded and variant meanings. In the cultural ecology of traditional Hinduism, conceptions of mythic, historical and contemporary times and spaces can cohabit the same intellectual universe without contradiction. That these layered religious and secular concepts may be seen, from an external gaze, to accumulate epistemological or ontological anomalies is viewed as irrelevant to their purposes. This is a distinctive characteristic of many Hinduisms: though processes of accretion, conflict, epistemic breaks, interpolation, fabulations, refabulations and retellings, Hinduism invests its symbols (in the broadest sense) with a vast number of meanings that remain together in a shifting hermeneutic and semiotic alliance. This is a self-conscious process (rather than a consequence of linguistic theory) which is sometimes referred to as periphrasis, but in an important sense it is its opposite: a symbol is invested with a large number of mundane and metaphysical aspects that are known, in various hybrid, syncretistic ways by Hindus who may otherwise belong to differing sects.[3]

Hindutva exploits these characteristics around time, space, event, symbol and myth by appropriating the symbols of Hinduism and rearticulating their various layered cultural and religious meanings into a politically ordered, 'syndicated' and homogeneous Hinduism (Thapar 1991). This has also been identified as a key characteristic of the history of brahminism, which mobilised similar strategies to incorporate within itself, hegemonise, politically exploit or reach a complex syncretic negotiation with other movements, such as Buddhism, Jainism and the numerous bhakti (devotional) sects. Consequently, the Hindutva movement has been interpreted by some writers as a legacy of the same historical tendency within dominant forms of brahminism (Lele 1995). It certainly is the case that the Hindutva movement has been brahmin-led and dominated, and reliant on north-Indian brahminic metaphysics or ideals (such as the glorification of Vedic and Upanishadic religion and sanatana dharma) rather than other metaphysical narratives produced by other castes and sects, including dalit movements.

The Hindutva family

Hindu nationalism has a long and complex ideological history that owes much to the formation of, and indigenous Indian negotiation with, European Romantic and British colonial knowledges about Indian social formations, their cultural and epistemic products, their histories and their antiquity. In their paradoxical way, the antecedents of Hindu nationalism are located precisely in that period from the mid-eighteenth to the late-nineteenth-century Europe, and in that divergence between Enlightenment secular rationality and Romantic affective primordialism whose product was itself an unsettled 'secular nationalism', the latter phrase perhaps capturing a key instability within modernity.

However, the birth of contemporary Hindu nationalism is usually traced to, and just after, the inter-war period, from 1916–25, during which two organisations, the Hindu Mahasabha (The Great Assembly of Hindus) and its 'semi-rival', the Rashtriya Swayamsevak Sangh (RSS, the National Volunteer-Servers Organisation) were formed. Hindu nationalism's key, but by no means only ideologue was Vinayak Damodar Savarkar, an anti-colonial revolutionary hero and founder of the Mahasabha, who in 1923 presented the novel idea of hindutva, the essence or 'beingness' of a Hindu. Hindutva was a hereditarian conception, born from the time the intrepid Aryans entered India and whose 'blood commingled' with that of the original inhabitants of India.[4] For Savarkar, a Hindu could be defined as someone who considers India as their fatherland, motherland and holy-land and 'who inherits the blood of that race whose first discernible source could be traced back' to the Vedic Aryans (Savarkar 1989: 115).

Savarkar's formulation of Hindutva considerably influenced Keshav Baliram Hedgewar, the founder of the paramilitary Rashtriya Swayamsevak Sangh (RSS, formed in 1924) as well as Madhav Golwalkar, the RSS's second leader. Golwalkar extended strands of Hindutva to develop an extraordinarily modern, Nazi-like racial idea of Hinduness, most clearly elaborated in his *We – or our nationhood defined* (1939).[5] The RSS is the core ultra-nationalist organisation of the Hindutva movement and has about 2.5 million members in India. It has emphasised since its beginning a novel organisational method that owes practically nothing to Hindu traditions. This is the shaka, a regimented and regulated system of boy-scout discipline involving physical games and exercise, nationalist ideological inculcation and martial arts. The RSS recruits its members from among young and very young boys, reflecting a conscious 'catch them young' policy. It has a distinctive uniform based on the British colonial police uniform – khaki shorts, white shirt, black cap – which evokes variously both considerable amusement and fear. Its supreme emblem, 'the true preceptor', is the saffron flag. This is saluted as a symbol of the Hindu nation with a bodily gesture that cannot but invoke for an onlooker the period of the 1930s and 1940s in Germany. The RSS has developed several mantras that extol the glory of a united Hindu society or nation. It celebrates six main festivals (utsavs) a year, several of which are traditional Hindu festivals, but the traditional pedagogies of these festivals are heavily slanted towards the secular-nationalist concerns of the sangh: political unity and social cohesion among Hindus, a celebration of Hindu strength and nationhood, and worship of the nation and motherland. It would be extremely difficult to conceptualise the cultural, symbolic and ideological content of RSS philosophy as anything other than anti-traditional, especially its explicit secular deification of nation and nationalism. Its organisational structure is hierarchical, centralised and based on the principle of *ek chalak anuvartita* (devotion to the One Supreme Leader). An obsession with organisation and discipline sums up the RSS's quotidian philosophy. However, its wider aim is to literally take individual after individual 'and mould them for an organised national life'.

> The ultimate vision of our work, which has been the living inspiration
> for all our organisational efforts, is a perfectly organised state of our
> society wherein each individual has been moulded into a wider ideal

of Hindu manhood and made into the living limb of the corporate
personality of society.

(Golwalkar 1966: 61)

Deendayal Upadhyaya, an RSS member and one of the founders of the Jana Sangh
political party, precursor to the contemporary Bharatiya Janata Party (BJP) developed many of Savarkar's and Golwalkar's ideas into a simplistic corporatist social
and political philosophy, Integral Humanism, which became increasingly important from the mid-1960s. This defined an ideal social order as an organic unity
(based on *ekatmata*, 'the unifying principle' or 'oneness') in which *kama* ('desire',
especially bodily desire) and *artha* ('wealth', but including political and economic
instrumental need), are to be subsumed under the greater principle of *dharma*
('natural law', order and duty) for the ideal of *moksha* ('salvation' or liberation)
(Upadhyaya 1991). Integral Humanism now forms the main ideological plank of
the contemporary BJP and is based on a view of the ideal social formation as one
regulated by Hindu *dharma* (religion, ethical code) which is seen as transcendent
and prior to the exigencies of the state and civil society. As in Golwalkar's mystical
cultural nationalism, Upadhyaya's philosophy stresses the *a priori* nature of the
cultural–dharmic field which exists above and beyond the social and political histories of nations and societies and is indeed the condition for them. Integral Humanism
also emphasises an organicist view of the social formation and state–civil society
relations, the latter, and indeed all social relations, to be conceived of as non-
conflictual and non-contradictory if *dharmic* principles are followed.

The RSS created several other organisations of which the Vishwa Hindu
Parishad (VHP, World Hindu Council), formed in the 1960s and representing a
federation of Hindu religious leaders, and the BJP created in 1980 out of the RSS
remnants of the Jana Sangh, are the most important. From the 1960s onwards,
and especially from the early 1980s, one can speak of the formation of a mass
far-right-wing Hindu social movement which perhaps reached its peak in the
successful campaign to destroy the medieval Mughal mosque, the Babri masjid, in
1992. In 1998, the BJP formed India's government under a broad, shaky coalition
and entered the world's political stage by ordering the explosion of five nuclear
devices, including allegedly a thermonuclear device, at the Pokharan test site in
northern India.[6]

Aside from its political successes, the Hindutva movement has developed formidable, in several respects unique, cultural and ideological strategic practices in
Indian civil society that have not been matched by recent secular movements. The
emphasis on slow patient work in civil society should be noted, and indeed the
RSS often calls itself the largest voluntary organisation in the world. Its self-
conscious and deep cultural strategy attempts to intervene in the detail of the
ecology, vernacular practices and beliefs of everyday Hinduisms, to reconstitute
these into a new habitus, a way of practising and thinking about Hinduism and its
relation to the life-world that reappears as innate, natural and instinctive, despite
its historical newness and fabrication. The Vedas, Puranas and epics become
palimpsests, simplified icons of the new Hinduism. An attempt is made to rearticulate many vernacular Hinduisms, and their epics, myths or devotionalism into a
political (that is, a secular) idiom in a way that seeks to fundamentally alter the

cultural meanings and symbolic import of religious forms and artefacts. These 'neotraditional' methods aim to make their intended subjects not more religious but more political.

The complex and compounded histories of Hinduisms, Buddhism, Sikhism, Jainism and South Asian Islam over several millennia, as well as the complexities of the economic, social, political and cultural formations in the Indian sub-continent are shielded from followers in favour of a monologic view of history and of the social formation as an elementary, easily intelligible totality made up of just Hindus and just minorities, and the conflicts between the latter. The parameters of state or civil society are reduced to ones solely of religious belonging. Culture is a simple inventory of the cultural artefacts that tell stories of a golden age or a glorious and endless war. The familiar temporal scheme of many ethnic absolutist movements is also evident. 'Historicity', and 'a revenge against history' are customary tropes. History is typically imagined as commencing from an ancient primordial and sublime origin, a temporally illegible utopia that falters because of Hindu failure in faith, or external aggression or both. This is followed by a period of medieval (Muslim) or modern (British) degradation and oppression and a long unflinching war that drives time forward. The present dystopian moment is one of Hindu renewal and identity formation. Futurity is closed with the establishment of a perfected and powerful Hindu utopia.

War metaphors are central to the political language of the Hindutva movement. The movement has identified the domestic 'enemies' that have placed 'Hindu society under siege' – communism ('Soviet Imperialism'), western influences ('Christian' or 'Western Imperialism' or 'Macaulayism') and Muslims ('Islamic Imperialism'). India's Muslim population is already articulated as a minority that has been *appeased* for too long by previous governments. India's traditional military adversaries, the belligerent and aggressive Pakistan, as well as China, are joined by Bangladesh, the latter seen in Hindutva political language as a source of Islamic 'demographic aggression' against, and 'infiltration' of, India (because of Bangladeshi migration into India). The extremely volatile situation in Kashmir is already conceivable as a war by proxy.

The 'anti-imperialist' rhetoric of Hindu nationalism, as in many varieties of Islamism, is less to do with the history of British economic imperialism and political domination. Apart from its banning after the murder of Gandhi, and its paramilitary activities in the Punjab during Partition, the RSS was conspicuously absent from the Indian liberation movement that it now seeks to own. Its anti-imperialism is however related to a xenophobic religious–cultural indigenism that is to be cultivated against what are seen as foreign influences. It is also axiomatic that Hindu nationalism reduces all social identities and social, economic and political processes to bare religious signifiers – Hindu and Muslim/Christian, the former conceived of as tolerant, peaceful and inclusive of all Hindu sects, which are seen to include Buddhism, Jainism and Sikhism, and the latter as monolithic, intolerant and violent. This disembedding of complex major or quotidian social, cultural and political processes and identities into pure religious signifiers of self and other is a familiar authoritarian strategy in which the democratic ideals of people, citizenship and individual autonomy are reconstituted into antagonistic, permanently separate religious collectives (Panikkar 1997). It also raises a deeper question about why modern democracies tend to problematise minorities. Hindu nationalism also undertakes the familiar metaphoric substitution of the nation by the idea of the national, or social or human body; conversely minorities, especially Muslims, are seen as a polluting presence within that body. Consequently, Hindu nationalism is dangerously obsessed with Muslim demography, reproduction and fertility (see, for example, Lal 1990). Within the Hindutva repertoire of blood and belonging, Muslims are for the most part Hindus 'whose original Hindu blood has been unaffected by alien adulteration' but who have betrayed their original faith or were coerced into Islam, and now constitute the traitorous fifth column in the Hindu nation. This *ambiguity* about blood, allegiance and betrayal is suggestively primordial. It is also extremely similar to Serbian (and Croat) nationalist discourses about Bosnian, Croat or Albanian Muslims who have transgressed their 'original' Slavic or Croat 'blood heritage'.

'Global' Hindutva

A significant feature of Hindu nationalism has been its international network and form of organisation. The RSS and the VHP have established an organisational presence in over 150 countries, virtually everywhere that Hindus have settled because of indentured labour, migrant labour, economic migration, as refugees or through the more recent professional economic migration of NRIs (non-resident Indians) to the US and Canada. (In RSS hagiography, the first overseas *sangh shaka* was formed aboard a ship of South Asian migrants and labourers heading from Bombay to Kenya in 1946, and the first non-Indian *shaka* formed in Keyna the following year.) In the west, the RSS, the VHP and the supporters of the BJP are extremely (USA) or relatively (UK and Europe) well organised. However, the sociological features of Hindutva in Britain and the US are dissimilar, and related to the different processes of migration and settlement, as well as the different socio-economic characteristics of South Asian communities in the respective countries. US Hindutva is primarily organised through the VHP (the latter being perhaps the main RSS platform) and the Overseas Friends of the BJP (OFBJP). Its key feature is 'silicon Hindutva', the relatively large influence of Hindu nationalism and RSS–VHP ideology on professional, educated and relatively wealthy American NRIs and their families, especially physicists and computer scientists. Indeed, the key US Hindutva activists are natural scientists. Youth and children are involved in RSS activities through the distinctively American summer camp tradition or through various Hindu Students Councils at various US campuses. The US Hindutva phenomenon reflects a characteristic global process of ultra-nationalism by a relatively young community of professionals and students that has chosen to leave India, and yet supports financially the Hindutva movement 'at home' and attempts to dominate the representation of Hindus or India in the US media and within political fora. In both areas it has been very successful.

In the UK, the Hindutva movement, first organisationally established in 1973 (though it is claimed that the first *sangh shaka* was formed in the mid-1960s), has been subject to a longer more complex and varied process of South Asian community formation and settlement and the rise of communal-religious conflict in recent years. Both the RSS and the VHP are well established in the UK. Perhaps their most important events were the Virat Hindu Sammelan organised in Milton Keynes in 1989 and attended by some 50,000 Hindus, as well as their Hindu Sangam in Bradford in 1984. The RSS's current UK structure reflects the centralist structure of its Indian parent. This includes the idiosyncratic titles and tiers that RSS members and officers have: executives (*sanghchalak*), organisers (*karyawahas*), guides/intellectuals (*bauddhiks*), teachers (*mukya shikshaks*), probationary officers (*vistaraks*) and full-time officers (*pracharaks*). The RSS women's affiliate in the UK, the Rashtriya Sevika Samiti, has a parallel national structure. The RSS has branches across the UK, and several regional offices. It is organised by region (*vibhag*), city (*nagar*) and local branch (*shaka*) level. There are over 20 regular *shakas* as well as *sevika samitis* in London (mainly in west London, Brent, Newham and Essex). Organisationally, the RSS is strongest in the South East and Midlands, though with a strong presence in Bradford, Oldham, Manchester and Bolton. Attendance at its regular *shakas* is fairly low, ranging from 15 at a local *shaka* or *samiti* to 150 at a city level event involving both men and women. However, at public events, the RSS can muster a much larger attendance of local Hindus, invited Asian guests and other local dignitaries, the latter typically local councillors and officers. In some areas, the RSS has managed to cultivate extremely strong and regular associations with the local authority, the city council, education authorities or political parties. The National Hindu Students Federation (NHSF), which, like many of its US counterparts, uses a key RSS corporate slogan ('A vision in action') is still fairly small in comparison with other student bodies. It is dominated by RSS–Hindutva philosophy and several officers of its central executive are RSS members or younger RSS officers, including RSS *vistaraks*. It receives its instructions from the RSS and its main officers indeed meet at RSS head offices. Its political orientation can be gauged from the title of one of its leaflets – *The smokescreen of 'Asian Unity'* – *establishing a Hindu youth agenda* (NHSF 1996). During the campaigns in the mid-1990s by the National Union of Students against the activities of the fringe Islamic fundamentalist Hizb ut Tahrir, the NHSF joined Jewish and gay student groups in demanding its banning. A key claim in their national campaign against the 'religious persecution' of Hindu university students was the forced conversion to Islam of young Hindu women by the Hizb – a curious transplantation of an Indian VHP agenda onto UK campuses.

The political concerns of the RSS family in the UK and US have revolved around several main themes: the authoritarian policing of the popular representation of Hinduism; the organisational, cultural, historical and national representation of Hindu communities in official public and policy fora; the desecularisation of the languages of minority South Asian political negotiation; the assertion of one particular kind of militant Hindu identity with self-evident needs that have to be articulated, typically antagonistically in diverse political processes; and the mobilisation of community support for BJP–RSS–VHP ventures in India. The RSS has faced little sustained political opposition in the UK except for activities of the small South Asian secular left, some strands within the women's movement and, indirectly, by progressive and syncretic South Asian youth cultures whose transgressions, 'blasphemies' and 'sin' they increasingly seek to discipline, even though such semitic concepts are typically alien to Hinduisms. Hindu nationalist sensitivities about the representation of Hindu icons, texts, symbols and especially deities are particularly acute and it would not be surprising if the authoritarian surveillance of the representation of images, idols and text came to dominate much of their activism in the UK, just as it has with many Islamist groups. Indeed the equivalence and convergence in political activism and language between ostensibly adversarial fundamentalisms, Christian, Jewish, Islamic or Hindu, is a key sociological feature.

Cultural incommensurability and the field of intellectual production

One dominant aspect of the political projects of many fundamentalist movements is the claim that their conceptual and epistemic schemes are unique and not capable of translation and comprehension from a 'foreign' or 'western' gaze. These absolutist claims about cultural incommensurability are remarkably similar to those made within many recent western postmodern or postcolonial theoretical writings. Religious fundamentalism has indeed provided the empirical example for the most obscurantist varieties of cultural and epistemic relativism in some contemporary multicultural theory. However, it needs emphasising that apart from its many epistemological problems, claims about cultural incommensurability can never be self-evident but are an intrinsic part of the political strategy employed by fundamentalist movements to disavow the legitimacy of oppositional political critiques. The claim is made that reason and rationality, arbitrarily identified as 'western', cannot legitimately provide a foundation for the critique of Hindu nationalism since the latter, in the form of its metaphysical spirituality, exists prior to the emergence of reason itself (Bhatt 1997).

Cultural incommensurability and its sibling strategy, the self-conscious cultivation of epistemic vagueness in core political concepts, is a key tactic of the Hindutva movement. However, despite the consistent and vigorous claims of the Hindutva movement that concepts such as 'dharma' and 'rashtra' are untranslatable into western concepts of 'religion' and 'nation-state' or 'nationalism', many of the aims of Hindutva movement are based on very familiar modern-authoritarian political conceptions. The Hindutva movement is primarily a majoritarian movement that demands, to differing degrees, an exclusive Hindu rashtra or Hindu nation-state which provides the precepts for the obligations of citizenship for all those, including all minorities, who live within the national territory. A Hindu rashtra is frequently, though not always, conceived to be genuinely secular and reflecting simply the 'Hindu ethos', 'Hindu civilisation' or Hindu dharma that has moulded and shaped the lives of Hindus, Buddhists, Jains and Sikhs over a period seen to be commencing from some ineffable, primordial moment. In this register, Hindu dharma is presented as secular and non-discriminatory. Consequently, it is frequently claimed that Hinduism and the Hindu nation-state are the basis for a genuine secularism. The Indian Supreme Court in its wisdom indeed made the appalling judgement in the mid-1990s that Hindutva was, like Hinduism, intrinsically secular (M. Rama Jois 1996).

Dharma is a key trope in Hindu nationalist political language. Its meaning is held to be both ineffable and totalising and this is central to the manner of its use by the Hindutva movement. It is also monotonously claimed that dharma is unique and untranslatable from a foreign gaze. In many varieties of Hinduism, dharma has compounded meanings that include religion, religious law (as in jurisprudence), a religious code of conduct, way of life, an ethics, or more broadly the natural order of things, 'natural law', the righteous path, the following the ordinances of sacred revelation or tradition, 'the way things are' or 'the way things ought to be'. There are many sect and subcaste *dharmashastras*[7] ('law books') that can govern or inform the lives of Hindus to widely varying degrees. In the practical lives of Hindus, *dharma* is more mundane. In many (north Indian) Hindu sects or subcastes, *dharma* can define rules for, for example, caste mixing and marriage, birth and death rites, gender relations, food and the compulsion to respect one's parents. It is a fundamentally religious, typically ritualistic conception. However, in Hindu nationalism it is disingenuously claimed to be secular since *dharma* is held to be the basis for Hinduism's unique traditional tolerance and reverence for all paths towards the Ineffable. The typical religious source used by many secularists and Hindu nationalists alike, is Rig Veda 1:164:46 'It is of one existence that the sages speak in many ways.'[8] However, arguably, 'tolerance' was an attribute ascribed to Hinduism, and against Islam, in the modern colonial period, and was dependent on the reformative strands of modern Hinduism that eventually culminated in Gandhianism. Similarly, the ahistoricised conception of *dharma* promoted in Hindu nationalism is a distinctly brahminic one, the ideal of *sanatana dharma*, the eternal ethical order of things. These ideas of Hindu *dharma* are claimed to be unique, and Hinduism is held to be a unique code for human and natural existence that cannot be compared with other religious traditions. Hinduism in this view is a complete universal order for life,[9] whereas Christianity and Islam are simply religious ideologies.

Hinduism, in this sense, is articulated in the Hindutva movement as not a religion at all but an eternally valid ethical code, a distinct orientation to the temporal and spiritual world, the natural social and political order, the fulfilment of civilisation and a world-view for humankind. It cannot, therefore, be compared with or comprehended by external western or Islamic paradigms. If Hinduism (Hindu *dharma*) can be conceptualised not as a religion but as an incommensurable civilisational ethos, a further claim can be made that Hinduism is itself a tolerant genuinely secular way of being and not a religion as such. Descriptions such as fundamentalism, fascism, authoritarianism can be dismissed as western concepts that are inapplicable to Hinduism (see for example Goel 1994a, Frawley 1995a). Consequently, state and civil society can be *dharmic* and secular, even as all citizens can be compelled to live by Hindu *dharma* and love and adulation for the Hindu nation.

This kind of holistic revolutionary conservatism is not, however, simply the package of prejudice and exclusivist identity politics that emerges in its political languages. The Hindutva movement has cultivated its own 'field of intellectual production' (Bourdieu 1991). Whatever the critical rational evaluation of its intellectual content, Hindu nationalism is a deeply intellectual enterprise and it would be a fundamental error to reduce its intellectual and cultural strategy to 'chauvinism' or propaganda, or to reduce its political trajectory to only that of seeking elected power or political representation. In Hindu nationalism one can speak of the creation of a major revisionist project around nation, state, civil society, culture, religion, ethnicity, metaphysics and human origins. Its form is manifest in the now incalculably large body of literature produced or fundamentally influenced by far-right-wing Hindu nationalist ideologues. This has attempted to breach the boundaries and methods of research and verification within several intellectual disciplines, including social and cultural history, ancient and medieval history, archaeology, philosophy and metaphysics, anthropology, sociology, political science, religious studies, natural science and mathematics, education and peda-gogy, astronomy, linguistics, comparative philology and human geography. In the process the Hindutva movement has managed to carve out a characteristic intel-lectual field. This has a typically antagonistic conceptual border (anti-secular, anti-Muslim, anti-marxist, anti-western) that is necessary for its reproduction. Its intellectual content is reproduced by a relatively large and international orbit of writers and critics. Its political languages and academic-nationalist thematics are discrete, distinguishable, and broadly unified. Its intellectual disagreements occur within its own field and mutually reinforce the field itself, but much of the core and productive nationalist content and its 'thematic and lexical ramifications' are shared.

The long nineteenth century

The intellectual antecedents of both the Hindutva movement and of many modern Hinduisms are complex and related to several ideological currents, prominent from the mid-1850s that were concerned to re-present, and in many ways recreate Hinduism in relation to modern political and social systems during a period of colonial domination. There are several aspects of this complex and diverse period of the mid-nineteenth-century 'Hindu Renaissance' that are worth noting briefly because they have important contemporary resonances. This period can also be viewed as reconstructive of certain strands of especially, but not exclusively, elite, brahminic or higher-caste Hindu thinking. In the face of the challenge and ethical claims of colonial Christianity, several mostly elite organisations undertook the project of demonstrating the ethical content or superiority of an intellectual Hinduism that was concerned to shed what was perceived as its polytheism and idolatry and its backward practices regarding the status of women and the injus-tice of the caste system. Both the liberal Brahmo Samaj (1828) and the 'fundamentalist' Arya Samaj (1875) can be seen as representative of some of these strands.

As important was the necessity of negotiating with key political concepts that made a modernist Hinduism thinkable: nation, the people, citizenship, self-deter-mination, representation, equality, autonomy, state and civil society. Put differently, how could elite Hinduism reconstruct itself within the framework of modern procedural, bureaucratic, scientific and technical rationality? How could Hinduism simultaneously negotiate both secular rationality and affective nation-alism in a period of colonial and imperial domination? Perhaps the third important strand was an intense negotiation with, and recovery of, important philosophical aspects of Vedic and Upanishadic Hinduism, which elite Hinduism could use to develop an epistemic and ethical resource both for modernity and against western colonial modernity. A related and powerful syncretic current from within the nineteenth century 'Hindu Renaissance' that continued to resonate deeply in numerous, otherwise antagonistic conceptions of modern Hinduism in this century was the belief not only in the universality of Hinduism but of its relevance outside India. Hinduism was not necessarily superior to other religious or ideological systems, though that claim was (and is) enunciated often enough, but rather that its metaphysical resources and epistemic and ethical systems, especially those of tolerance, peace, pluralism, and organicist reverence for all of creation provided a foundational example for all other ideological and political systems. Hinduism's revelation was the *a priori* for all other religious systems. Hinduism in some fundamental way could not be compared to any other religion, just as India was a country unlike any other. In this register, deeply resonant in contemporary Hindutva movement, Hinduism was the seat of all religion and revelation, just as India was the cradle of all civilisation.

The aryas: philology and ethnology

Another important though often ambiguous strand emerged during the nineteenth century that was concerned with the recovery of the Hindu present by cultivating its primordial past. This was quite fundamentally reliant on the discoveries from the mid-eighteenth century of both British philology and Germany Indology. The contemporary Hindutva movement also closely follows the epistemic trajectory of early Indology, expressed through that early German love affair with India during the late eighteenth century, in the period during and after the French revolution. Charles Wilkins's translation of Sanskrit, and Sir William Jones's discovery in the 1780s of the philological similarities between Greek, Latin and archaic Sanskrit, and his discussions of the antiquity and perfection of the Sanskrit language and its grammar provided rich material for those who sought a new, non-Biblical, and importantly a non-Semitic, non-Hebraic origin for 'the obscurer portions' of European, especially German history and civilisation (Poliakov 1974). In Germany and to a lesser degree France, from the eighteenth century onwards, this became a major justification for the fascination with India.

Frederick Schlegel's *On the language and wisdom of the Indians* (Schlegel 1849), published in 1808, contained several key points that were to become so effective later: India received the primordial revelation (and, he added, the primordial errors); world civilisation emerged either from Indian migration out of India or from Indian influence; Greek, Latin, Hebraic and Arabic language and mythology are already both superseded and captured in Sanskrit and in the Vedic religion; Indian spiritual and mystical reverence for a 'northern place' was the basis for Indian outward migration, which led ultimately to the formation of the Teutonic races in northern Europe.[10]

For Schlegel the Teutons were descendants of the primordial Indians (for his brother August Wilhelm, Germany was the 'orient of Europe'). Similar themes were to differing degrees embraced by other writers. India was seen as the site of the first revelation (Herder) or civilisation (Kant, among numerous Enlightenment thinkers, including the encylopaedists). Hinduism's key concepts, such as 'metempsychosis' provided other writers with a 'pessimistic immortalism' which was contrasted with life-denying ethics of Judaeo-Christianity (Schopenhauer).

However, much of this 'arche-philology' became immensely complicated towards the late eighteenth century. Max Muller, the British-German Indologist, had in the mid-1800s argued comprehensively for the popularisation of 'the technical term, Aryan' to refer to the group of languages which Frederick Schlegel had earlier called 'Indo-Germanic' and Franz Bopp had called 'Indo-European' (various other names were popular in Britain, including 'Japhetic', 'Sanskritic' or 'Mediterranean'). 'Aryan', which was borrowed from the archaic Sanskrit *arya*[11] and the Zend Avestan *airya*, 'had the advantage of being short, and being of foreign origin lending itself more easily to any technical definition' (Muller 1881: 205). Muller also explicitly and often inadvertently created a convergence between the arya language and the arya people, itself reflective of a problematic disciplinary equivalence between comparative philology and ethnology that was to have such horrifying consequences in this century. Some of this was based on translations of the Rig Veda which, it was claimed, showed the Aryans as both a warrior race and one that was distinctly organised on racial-colour and 'nobility'[12] hierarchies (caste). The aryas, it was claimed, had a definitive xenology whose victims were the ('dark-skinned, stub-nosed') *dasyus*, *mlecchas* ('foreigners' or 'barbarians') and other non-*arya* speaking groups (Thapar 1996a).

The third, and perhaps consequential focus was on the origins of the Aryans. Schlegel's original lineage was increasingly modified (a project that continues to today) and the primordial Aryan homeland moved westwards and northwards out of India proper and settled variously in Persia, the Caucasus, the Russian steppe, 'Atlantis', Lithuania or the Balkans generally, the Mediterranean or Greece, Germany, Scandinavia, Eire and even the North Pole.[13] Max Muller, exasperated by many of these debates, retracted his earlier discussions of the Aryans as a racial rather than a linguistic group, and was eventually to conclude that the primordial Aryan linguistic homeland was 'somewhere in Asia' (Muller 1888: 127). However, Aryanist thinking had already travelled widely and by the mid 1800s in the hands of Joseph Arthur de Gobineau, became a fully-fledged theory of white Aryan-noble racial supremacy. In the case of Houston Stewart Chamberlain, Wagner and the Bayreuth Circle, it became a vicious anti-semitism (Mosse 1966), a refraction of an earlier metaphysics in which the Judeo-Christian and the Hindu–Buddhist were antagonistically polarised (Schopenhauer 1890).

Aryanism and Hindutva

The importance of Aryanism for the contemporary Hindutva movement has been highlighted by the Indian historian Romila Thapar (1996b). A distinctive variety of Aryanist thinking, often metonymically linked to a separate hereditarian discourse, aspects of which were already embedded in many varieties of Hinduism, became an important current from the late nineteenth century in colonial India itself. Hindu discussions about Aryan origins are probably best represented in the speeches and writings of the nationalist activist and spiritualist Aurobindo Ghose during the early part of this century. Aurobindo, a spiritual source of emulation for both the Hindutva movement and for some remarkably reactionary strands of a burgeoning 'New Age evolutionism' (Danino and Nahar 1996), stated that Aryans were autochthonous to India and the theory of an Aryan migration into or invasion of India was a British colonialist myth that sought to deny India's unique, superlative nature.

However, Hindutva appropriations of Aryanism only really became important after the 1930s. For the founders of the contemporary Hindutva movement, western Aryanism presented an obvious epistemic problem. The evidences of English and German comparative linguistics and Indology suggested Aryans entered from outside physical India, and hence the idea of an immemorial originary cultural hearth in which the physical land, culture and people intermingled to give rise to Hindu civilisation is already disturbed at its origin by a founding presence which is alien to the land. In the 1920s Savarkar indeed initially argued for a hybrid origin for Vedic civilisation: it was the mixture of the blood of the Aryans and the people they encountered that gave rise to Vedic–Hindu civilisation, though evidently only the Aryan blood was of any consequence. Savarkar articulated the birth of Vedic civilisation through a Lamarckian conception whereby the physical land and environment impressed upon, and was conversely affected by the Aryan people so as to instil a unique *hereditary* quality to land, culture and people. Savarkar provided an archetypal genealogy of cultural hearth and reverence for the land, imagined as the first and best land of the Aryans. The essence of Aryan culture was *hindutva*, the 'beingness' of a Hindu that defines a common nation (*rashtra*), race (*jati*) and civilisation (*sankskriti* culture). *Hindutva* is transmitted patrilineally by blood and apprehended by a *feeling*, a structure of emotion that makes a Hindu realise his or her true connection with the sublime civilisation of the Vedic Aryans (Savarkar [1923] 1989). Savarkar's powerful 'race concept' combines land, heredity, affect, an ancestral blood community, and an originary Vedism. But, at least in its earlier form, it still depended on an external invasive event.

In later Hindutva writers, just as in Aurobindo's writings, this hybrid, syncretic Aryan origin for Hinduism is simply rejected and, in a fundamentally instructive move, Schlegel's (and indeed the Enlightenment's) original thesis is resurrected. For Golwalkar, the RSS's second and perhaps most important 'Supreme Guide and Philosopher', the idea of an Aryan invasion of India was a product of colonialism, aimed to denigrate Hindus. Against this view, Golwalkar stated that Hindus had existed in India from time immemorial: 'Undoubtedly . . . we Hindus have been in undisputed and undisturbed possession of this land for over 8 or even 10 thousand years before the land was invaded by any foreign race'. (Golwalkar [1939] 1944)

From language to archaeology

If western speculations about Aryan origins and the popular view of the Aryans as a dynamic or conquering force were initially based on comparative philology and on certain translations of the Rig Veda, perhaps of greater importance was the insertion into this warrior-Aryan discourse of the discovery of a vast pre-Aryan civilisation in northern India in the early decades of this century. There has been considerable scholarly debate about the Indus Valley cultures and its peoples since the urban ruins of Harappa and Mohenjo Daro were discovered in the 1920s, and were followed by subsequent archaeological finds of numerous ancient towns in northern India and Pakistan. These discoveries demonstrated a considerably advanced urban civilisation, contemporaneous with the earliest world riverine civil-isations. The abandonment of these vast urban centres was explained by the British archaeologist Sir Mortimer Wheeler as being completed by a vicious, barbaric Aryan invasion from outside India (Wheeler 1963: 113–14). For many European adherents of some version of Aryanist thinking, the ruins of Mohenjo Daro provided conclusive evidence of a destructive warrior-Aryan invasion of India. It has however since been generally accepted that no such invasion occurred and indeed the pre-Aryan Indus valley civilisation may have declined well before Indo-Aryan speaking tribes migrated over an extremely long period into India and this resulted, through complex and syncretic processes, in what later became Vedic-Arya culture. It needs reiterating that virtually all scholars accept that the Harappan and Mohenjo Daro civilisations were not Aryan in language or culture. To suggest that 'the Harappans were Vedic' (Singh 1995) is pleading a special case for which there is neither strong nor irrefutable nor controvertible evidence (Mallory 1989). The Indus Valley civilisation threw up numerous conundrums, of which perhaps the most pertinent is its script which is still undeciphered and may well remain so in the absence of further archaeological discoveries that contain larger continuous examples of the script. Seals bearing motifs and writing from the ancient Indus Valley have also been discovered in other parts of the ancient world.

It is exactly around these issues the Hindutva movement and its western New Age[14] apologists have forcefully intervened over the last few years in an imposing revisionist project that has regenerated an epistemic obsession with primordial Aryanism in many Hindutva or Hinducentric circles (Gupta 1996, Singh 1995, Sethna 1989 and 1992, Talageri 1993a and 1993b, Rajaram 1995, Rajaram and Frawley 1997, Shendge 1996, Danino and Nahar 1996, Kak 1992a, 1989, Feuerstein, Kak and Frawley 1995). The rewriting of history, both medieval[15] and ancient, has become a dominant theme in the literary outpourings of the Hindutva movement, as well as of other Hinducentric efforts. The project appropriated by the Hindutva movement may well be dependent on a recent intellectual reassess-ment of India's and Pakistan's antiquity in which more recent archaeological and geographical discoveries might suggest that the Indus Valley civilisations were both more extensive and older than may have been assumed. However, the pace of actual archaeological scholarship, the possibilities of rethinking Indian antiquity against western colonial distortions, and the speculations and fancies of Hindu nationalists have become mixed up in these recent interventions. The Hindutva movement has instead attempted to set the agendas for debate and create 'commonsense' world-views about India's and Pakistan's antiquity that shortcut the methods of traditional scholarship, and which would have relied, in different circumstances, on a necessary mobilisation of the whole critical intellectual process itself.

It is in the interests of the Hindutva movement to claim, despite the archaeo-logical and linguistic evidence to the contrary, that the Indus Valley civilisation was Aryan in language, culture, ethnicity and 'nobility', Vedic in religion, and Sanskritic in civilisation. Several other consequences immediately follow, for such claims imply that Aryans were autochthonous and not usurpers, that a fundamen-tally Aryan civilisation was the first world civilisation, that all other civilisations were its direct or indirect products, that the differentiations between Indo-Aryan and other Indian languages are colonial racist fabrications, and that, instead, all Indian languages and cultural products are essentially derived from one ethnic, indigenous, non-invasive Aryan culture and civilisation. This, of course, also provides a far greater lineage for Hinduism, and confirms not only its primordial antiquity, but its superlative and original genesis in that first civilisational hearth, 'the best land of the Aryans'. The congruence of this Aryan 'prehistory' with that developed in early German orientalism, and its exact mirroring in the western racial Aryanism that animated the pre-Nazi and Nazi periods, is less important than the general Aryan primordialism that all these tendencies share.

Much of this unsettled Hindutva Aryanist thinking, which can itself be cloaked in volkish 'anti-racist' and 'anti-imperialist' rhetoric, illustrates how *varieties of Aryanism* are important to contemporary politics, and that Aryanism continues to be a resource for origin myths that are not completed by the kind of specifically western white Aryanism that dominated Europe, and especially Germany, earlier this century. In late modernity, authoritarian movements have arisen again that seek to ideologically combine an organic and holistic natural-social order, a purified nationality, a primeval mysticism, and a belief in a superlative civilisation that was created by an ancestral community of blood.

Notes

I would like to thank John Solomos, Jane Hindley and Parita Mukta for comments on an earlier draft.

1   Or just 'sangh', whose meaning sits suggestively between 'organisation' and 'society'.
2   The term 'racism' is used in describing aspects of Hindutva discourse throughout the essay despite its very different meanings in many contemporary western debates about 'race' and racism. This is acknowledged to be a deeply problematic area and its taxonomic difficulties are symptomatic of a wider epistemic shift that is necessary in thinking through a range of absolutist ideologies of primordial indigenism.
3   'Sect' is a misleading term in relation to branches of Hinduism, or varieties of Hindu belief and practice, but is used for convenience.
4   Savarkar's genesis of Hindutva is worth contrasting with, for example, Gobineau's or Houston Stewart Chamberlain's or Alfred Rosenberg's view of the racial degradation of the Aryans once their blood mixed with that of the original Indians.
5   It is likely that Golwalkar's *We. . .* was a paraphrasing of Savarkar's brother, Babarao's earlier work.
6   The appeal to religious sensibilities during the nuclear tests should be noted. The tests, like those undertaken in the 1970s, were conducted on Buddha purnima. The Vishwa Hindu Parishad has declared the test site holy and is planning to build there a temple to the Mother Goddess (*shaktipeeth*, a 'seat of strength') that symbolises India's resurgence as a nuclear power. 'We are no longer eunuchs', declared the Shiv Sena. Some parivar activists wanted to

distribute sand from the site throughout India as a religious symbol and offering, though this idea was abandoned because of possible harmful radiation. If the literal worship and deification of nuclear bombs whose only purpose is mass human destruction seems obscene, it also illustrates how far the contemporary representatives of Hinduism have travelled from Hinduism itself. The inevitable claim that nuclear weapons are traditional to Hinduism was also made: the fire god Agni in the Vedas was proof, it was said, that the ancient Hindus possessed nuclear bombs, *India Abroad* 22.5.98.

7   The *Manu Dharmashastra* is often held to be the archaic basis for many other (north Indian Hindu) *dharmic* regulations that may use, or oppose, its precepts. But the point is that *dharma* is an abstract term for an extremely widely varying series of caste or subcaste, sect and regional regulations.

8   The full verse (Griffith translation, 1896) is: 'They call him Indra, Mithra, Varuna, Agni, and he is heavenly nobly-winged Garutman. To what is One [Reality], sages give many a title [name]: they call it Agni, Yama, Matarisvan.'

9   This exact claim is, of course, also made in Islamist and other fundamentalist movements.

10   This critical idea of the mountainous cold north derived from an interpretation of the Rig Veda and the reverence with which the Aryans held mountains, possibly the Himalayas, has influenced numerous writers, up to the present period. Kant held this cradle to be Tibet, and later writers assumed the Caucasus. A north pole origin for the Aryans gained currency from various interpretations of the Rig Veda and was pronounced again this century by Tilak, a founder and leader of the Indian National Congress.

11   The word arya occurs over 30 times in the ancient Sanskrit Rig Veda, and may have been used in this and in the ancient Persian Zend Avesta as a description of self by the putative groups who composed the original versions of these texts. It is also used much more freely in later Indian Buddhist texts to describe a quality, usually considered to be 'noble'.

12   What it translated as 'nobility' or 'noble' in western thinking requires a much fuller discussion than can be provided here, especially because the western use of the concept of nobility has been so fundamentally important in the histories of 'race thinking'. Similarly, the ease with which aristocratic ideals, nobility, culture and hierarchy are translated into their archaic Hindu counterparts (and vice versa) require much further elaboration. 'Nobility' is also of considerable importance for Hindutva apologists for the caste system and for arya xenology.

13   Childe (1926) is an earlier overview, useful for illustrating both an abhorrence of racism and a warrior or dynamic quality to the Aryan. For the current state of debate on Aryan origins and homeland, see Mallory (1989). Renfrew (1987) is perhaps the main scholarly western advocate for an Indian Aryan homeland. The recent, numerous Indian and Hindutva contributions are discussed below, and tend to argue for an Aryan primordial homeland in *the east*, especially in northern- or central-eastern India.

14   The relation between some syncretic western spiritual movements and varieties of deep conservatism, including racism and racial Aryanism are considerable. The transmutation of some strands of the New Thought movement, and some strands of Theosophy in the earlier parts of this century into a specifically Aryan religion, Ariosophy, which formed the epistemic content for much of Nazism's natural religion has been brilliantly described by Goodrick-Clarke (1985). It is

important to note the marriage between far-right-wing Hindutva ideology and western New Ageism in the works of writers like David Frawley (1994, 1995a, 1995b) who is both a key apologist for the Hindutva movement and the author of various New Age books on Vedic astrology, oracles and yoga. Similarly, Subhash Kak a collaborator on a work that is both distinctively New Ageist and rehearses the Hindutva obsession with arya-Vedic primordialism (Feuerstein, Kak and Frawley 1995) is also an Hindu nationalist writer who has a substantial publications record on Aryans in *Mankind Quarterly*, perhaps the most important academic racist eugenicist journal in the west.

15 The revision of medieval Indian history is at least as important to the Hindutva project, and in many respects far more important for its immediate political purposes than the obsession with ancient India, but cannot be discussed here for reasons of space. However, it should be noted that historical revisionism around the medieval, especially Mughal period constitutes a monumental project for the Hindutva movement. This project is single-minded in its desire to demonstrate that the medieval period was one of Muslim religious conquest and oppression of non-aggressive and tolerant Hindus. Virtually everything disagreeable within Hinduism is traced to this period and viewed either as a consequence of Islamic rule or an intrinsic attribute of Islam that has polluted Hinduism. This includes caste and caste discrimination, tribe formation, purdah, harems, bonded labour systems, corruption, poverty, women's oppression, educational backwardness, obscurantism, alongside the more typical discussions of religious oppression of Hindus, genocide, minorityism, and so forth (Lal 1992, 1994, 1995, Rai 1993, 1994). Everything considered agreeable within Hinduism, especially wars that can be reinterpreted from the gaze of the present as simply 'heroic Hindu resistance against Muslim invaders' is celebrated within this historical revisionism. See Goel 1994a.

References

Bhatt, C. 1997. *Liberation and Purity*, London: UCL Press.

Bhatt, C. 1999. 'Ethnic absolutism and the authoritarian spirit', *Theory, Culture and Society*, 16(2).

Bourdieu, P. 1991. *The Political Ontology of Martin Heidegger*, Cambridge: Polity.

Childe, V.G. 1926. *The Aryans*, London: Kegan Paul.

Danino, M. and Nahar, S. 1996. *The Invasion That Never Was*, Mysore: Mira Aditi.

Dhavalikar, M.K. 1995. *Cultural Imperialism: Indus Civilisation in Western India*, New Delhi: Books and Books.

Feuerstein, G., Kak, S., and Frawley, D. 1995. *In Search of the Cradle of Civilisation*, Wheaton, Ill.: Quest.

Frawley, D. 1994. *The Myth of the Aryan Invasion of India*, New Delhi: Voice of India.

Frawley, D. 1995a. *Hinduism: the Eternal Tradition*, New Delhi: Voice of India.

Frawley, D. 1995b. *Arise Arjuna: Hinduism and the Modern World*, New Delhi: Voice of India.

Gautier, F. 1994. *The Wonder That Is India*, New Delhi: Voice of India.

Goel, S.R. [1983] 1994a. *Defence of Hindu Society*, New Delhi: Voice of India.

Goel, S.R. 1994b. *Heroic Hindu Resistance to Muslim Invaders*, New Delhi: Voice of India.

Golwalkar, M.S. [1939] 1944. *We, Or Our Nationhood Defined*, second edn., Nagpur: Bharat Publications.

Golwalkar, M.S. 1966. *Bunch of Thoughts*, Bangalore: Vikrama Prakashan.

Goodrick-Clarke, N. 1985. *The Occult Roots of Nazism*, New York: University Press.

Gupta, S.P. 1996. *The Indus-Saraswati Civilisation: Origins, Problems, Issues*, Delhi: Pratibha Prakashan.

Jaffrelot, C. 1995. 'The idea of the Hindu race' in P. Robb ed. *The Concept of Race in South Asia*, Delhi: Oxford University Press.

Jois, M.R. 1996. *Supreme Court Judgment on Hindutva: An Important Landmark*, New Delhi: Suruchi Prakashan.

Kak, S.C. 1989. 'Indus writing', *Mankind Quarterly* 30: 113–118.

Kak, S.C. 1992. 'The Indus tradition and the Indo-Aryans', *Mankind Quarterly 32*: 195–213.

Lal, K.S. 1990. *Indian Muslims – Who Are They?*, New Delhi: Voice of India.

Lal, K.S. 1992. *The Legacy of Muslim Rule in India*, New Delhi: Aditya Prakashan.

Lal, K.S. 1994. *Muslim Slave System in Medieval India*, New Delhi: Aditya Prakashan.

Lal, K.S. 1995. *Growth of Scheduled Tribes and Castes in Medieval India*, New Delhi: Voice of India.

Lele, J. 1995. *Hindutva: the Emergence of the Right*, Madras: Earthworm Books.

Mallory, J.P. 1989. *In Search of the Indo-Europeans: Language, Archaeology, Myth*, London: Thames & Hudson.

Mosse, G.L. 1966. *The Crisis of German Ideology*, London: Weidenfeld & Nicholson.

Muller, F.M. 1881. *Selected Essays on Language, Mythology and Religion*, vol I, London: Longmans, Green & Co.

Muller, F.M. 1888. *Biographies of Words and The Home of the Aryas*, London: Longmans, Green & Co.

Panikkar, K.N. 1997. *Communal Threat Secular Challenge*, Madras: Earthworm Books.

Poliakov, L. 1974. *The Aryan Myth: A History of Racist and Nationalist Ideas in Europe*, London: Chatto Heinemann.

Rai, B. 1993. *Demographic Aggression Against India*, Chandigarh: B.S. Publishers.

Rai, B. 1994. *Is India Going Islamic?*, Chandigarh: B.S. Publishers.

Rajaram, N.S. 1995. *The Politics of History: Aryan Invasion Theory and the Subversion of Scholarship*, New Delhi: Voice of India.

Rajaram, N.S. and Frawley, D. 1997. *Vedic Aryans and the Origins of Civilisation*, New Delhi: Voice of India.

Renfrew, C. 1987. *Archaeology and Language*, Cambridge: University Press.

Savarkar, V.D. [1923] 1989. *Hindutva – Who is a Hindu?* sixth edn., Bombay: Veer Savarkar Prakashan.

Schlegel, F. 1849. *Aesthetic and Miscellaneous Works*, London: Henry G. Bohn.

Schopenhauer, A. 1890. *Studies in Pessimism*, London: George Allen & Unwin.

Sethna, K.D. 1989. *Ancient India in a New Light*, New Delhi: Aditya.

Sethna, K.D. 1992. *The Problem of Aryan Origins From an Indian Point of View*, second edn. New Delhi: Aditya Prakashan.

Shendge, M.J. 1996. *The Aryas: Facts without Fancy or Fiction*, New Delhi: Abhinav.

Singh, B. 1995. *The Vedic Harappans*, New Delhi: Aditya Prakashan.

Solomos, J. and Back, L. 1996. *Racism and Society*, London: Macmillan.

Talageri, S.G. 1993a. *Aryan Invasion Theory and Indian Nationalism*, New Delhi: Voice of India.

Talageri, S.G. 1993b. *The Aryan Invasion Theory: A Reappraisal*, New Delhi: Aditya Prakashan.

Thapar, R. 1991. 'A historical perspective on the story of Rama' in S. Gopal ed. *The Anatomy of a Confrontation*, New Delhi: Penguin.

Thapar, R. 1996a. *Ancient Indian Social History: Some Interpretations*, London: Sangam.

Thapar, R. 1996b. 'The theory of Aryan race and India: history and politics', *Social Scientist* 24, 1–3, Jan–Mar.

Upadhyaya, D. 1991. *Ideology and Perception, Part II: Integral Humanism*, New Delhi: Suruchi Prakashan.

Wheeler, M. 1963. *Early India and Pakistan to Ashoka*, London: Thames & Hudson.

Chapter 40

Slavoj Žižek

ENJOY YOUR NATION AS YOURSELF!

WHY WAS THE WEST so fascinated by the disintegration of Communism in Eastern Europe? The answer seems obvious: what fascinated the Western gaze was the *reinvention of Democracy*. It is as if democracy, which in the West shows more and more signs of decay and crisis and is lost in bureaucratic routine and publicity-style election campaigns, is being rediscovered in Eastern Europe in all its freshness and novelty. The function of this fascination is thus purely ideological: in Eastern Europe, the West seeks for its own lost origins, its own lost original experience of "democratic invention." In other words, Eastern Europe functions for the West as its Ego Ideal (*Ich-Ideal*): the point from which West sees itself in a likeable, idealized form, as worthy of love. The real object of fascination for the West is thus the *gaze*, namely the supposedly naive gaze by means of which Eastern Europe stares back at the West, fascinated by its democracy. It is as if the Eastern Gaze is still able to perceive in Western societies its own *agalma*, the treasure that causes democratic enthusiasm and that the West has long ago lost the taste of.

The reality emerging now in Eastern Europe is, however, a disturbing distortion of this idyllic picture of the two mutually fascinated gazes: the gradual retreat of the liberal-democratic tendency in the face of the growth of corporate national populism which includes all its usual elements, from xenophobia to anti-Semitism. To explain this unexpected turn, we have to rethink the most elementary notions about national identification – and here, psychoanalysis can be of help.

The "theft of enjoyment"

The element which holds together a given community cannot be reduced to the point of symbolic identification: the bond linking together its members always implies a shared relationship toward a Thing, toward Enjoyment incarnated.[1] This relationship toward the Thing, structured by means of fantasies, is what is at stake when we speak of the menace to our "way of life" presented by the Other: it is what is threatened when, for example, a white Englishman is panicked because of the growing presence of "aliens." What he wants to defend at any price is *not* reducible to the so-called set of values that offer support to national identity. National identification is by definition sustained by a relationship toward the Nation qua Thing. This Nation-Thing is determined by a series of contradictory properties. It appears to us as "our Thing" (perhaps we could say *cosa nostra*), as something accessible only to us, as something "they," the others, cannot grasp; nonetheless it is something constantly menaced by "them." It appears as what gives plenitude and vivacity to our life, and yet the only way we can determine it is by resorting to different versions of the same empty tautology. All we can ultimately say about it is that the Thing is "itself," "the real Thing," "what it really is about," etc. If we are asked how we can recognize the presence of this Thing, the only consistent answer is that the Thing is present in that elusive entity called "our way of life." All we can do is enumerate disconnected fragments of the way our community organizes its feasts, its rituals of mating, its initiation ceremonies, in short, all the details by which is made visible the unique way a community *organizes its enjoyment*. Although the first, so to speak, automatic association that arises here is of course that of the reactionary sentimental *Blut und Boden*, we should not forget that such a reference to the "way of life" can also have a distinctive "leftist" connotation. Note George Orwell's essays from the war years, in which he attempted to define the contours of an English patriotism opposed to the official, stuffy imperialist version of it. His points of reference were precisely those details that characterize the "way of life" of the working class (the evening gathering in the local pub, etc.).[2]

It would, however, be erroneous simply to reduce the national Thing to the features composing a specific "way of life." The Thing is not directly a collection of these features; there is "something more" in it, something that *is present* in these features, that *appears* through them. Members of a community who partake in a given "way of life" *believe in their Thing*, where this belief has a reflexive structure proper to the intersubjective space: "I believe in the (national) Thing" equals "I believe that others (members of my community) believe in the Thing." The tautological character of the Thing – its semantic void which limits what we can say about the Thing to "It is the real Thing," etc. – is founded precisely in this paradoxical reflexive structure. The national Thing exists as long as members of the community believe in it; it is literally an effect of this belief in itself. The structure is here the same as that of the Holy Spirit in Christianity. The Holy Spirit *is* the community of believers in which Christ lives after his death: *to believe in Him equals believing in belief itself*, i.e., believing that I'm not alone, that I'm a member of the community of believers. I do not need any external proof or confirmation of the truth of my belief: by the mere act of my belief in others' belief, the Holy Spirit is here. In other words, the whole meaning of the Thing turns on the fact that "it means something" to people.

This paradoxical existence of an entity which "is" only insofar as subjects believe (in the other's belief) in its existence is the mode of being proper to ideological causes: the "normal" order of causality is here inverted, since it is the Cause itself which is produced by its effects (the ideological practices it animates). Significantly, it is precisely at this point that the difference between Lacan and "discursive idealism" emerges most forcefully: Lacan does not reduce the (national, etc.) Cause to a performative effect of the discursive practices that refer to it. The pure discursive effect does not have enough "substance" to compel the attraction proper to a Cause – and the Lacanian term for the strange "substance" which must be added so that a Cause obtains its positive ontological consistency, the only substance acknowledged by psychoanalysis, is of course *enjoyment* (as Lacan states it explicitly in *Encore*[3]). A nation *exists* only as long as its specific *enjoyment* continues to be materialized in a set of social practices and transmitted through national myths that structure these practices. To emphasize in a "deconstructionist" mode that Nation is not a biological or transhistorical fact but a contingent discursive construction, an overdetermined result of textual practices, is thus misleading: such an emphasis overlooks the remainder of some *real*, nondiscursive kernel of enjoyment which must be present for the Nation qua discursive entity-effect to achieve its ontological consistency.[4]

Nationalism thus presents a privileged domain of the eruption of enjoyment into the social field. The national Cause is ultimately nothing but the way subjects of a given ethnic community organize their enjoyment through national myths. What is therefore at stake in ethnic tensions is always the possession of the national Thing. We always impute to the "other" an excessive enjoyment: he wants to steal our enjoyment (by ruining our way of life) and/or he has access to some secret, perverse enjoyment. In short, what really bothers us about the "other" is the peculiar way he organizes his enjoyment, precisely the surplus, the "excess" that pertains to this way: the smell of "their" food, "their" noisy songs and dances, "their" strange manners, "their" attitude to work. To the racist, the "other" is either a workaholic stealing our jobs or an idler living on our labor, and it is quite amusing to notice the haste with which one passes from reproaching the other with a refusal to work to reproaching him for the theft of work. The basic paradox is that our Thing is conceived as something inaccessible to the other and at the same time threatened by him. [. . .]

Capitalism without capitalism

What sets in motion this logic of the "theft of enjoyment" is of course not immediate social reality – the reality of different ethnic communities living closely together – but the *inner antagonism inherent in the communities*. It is possible to have a multitude of ethnic communities living side by side without racial tensions (like the Amish and neighboring communities in Pennsylvania); on the other hand, one does not need a lot of "real" Jews to impute to them some mysterious enjoyment that threatens us (it is a well-known fact that in Nazi Germany, anti-Semitism was most ferocious in those parts where there were almost no Jews; in today's ex-East Germany, the anti-Semitic Skinheads outnumber Jews by ten to one). Our perception of "real" Jews is always mediated by a symbolic–ideological structure which tries to cope with social antagonism: the real "secret" of the Jew is our own antagonism. In today's America, for example, a role resembling that of the Jew is played more and more by the Japanese. Witness the obsession of the American media with the idea that Japanese don't know how to enjoy themselves. The reason for the growing Japanese economic superiority over the U.S.A. is located in the somewhat mysterious fact that the Japanese don't consume enough, that they accumulate too much wealth. If we look closely at the logic of this accusation, it soon becomes clear that what American "spontaneous" ideology really reproaches the Japanese for is not simply their inability to take pleasure but rather the fact that their very relationship between work and enjoyment is strangely distorted. *It is as if they find an enjoyment in their very renunciation of pleasure*, in their zeal, in their inability to "take it easy," relax, and enjoy – and it is this attitude which is perceived as a threat to American supremacy. Thus the American media report with such evident relief how Japanese are finally learning to consume, and why American TV depicts with such self-satisfaction Japanese tourists staring at the wonders of the American pleasure-industry: finally they are "becoming like us," learning our way of enjoying.

It is too easy to dispose of this problematic by pointing out that what we have here is simply the transposition, the ideological displacement, of the effective socioeconomic antagonisms of today's capitalism. The problem is that, while this is undoubtedly true, *it is precisely through such a displacement that desire is constituted*. What we gain by transposing the perception of inherent social antagonisms into the fascination with the Other (Jew, Japanese . . .) is the fantasy-organization of desire. The Lacanian thesis that enjoyment is ultimately always enjoyment of the Other, i.e., enjoyment supposed, imputed to the Other, and that, conversely, the hatred of the Other's enjoyment is always the hatred of one's own enjoyment, is perfectly exemplified by this logic of the "theft of enjoyment."[5] What are fantasies about the Other's special, excessive enjoyment – about the black's superior sexual potency and appetite, about the Jew's or Japanese's special relationship toward money and work – if not precisely *so many ways, for us, to organize our own enjoyment*? Do we not find enjoyment precisely in fantasizing about the Other's enjoyment, in this ambivalent attitude toward it? Do we not obtain satisfaction by means of the very supposition that the Other enjoys in a way inaccessible to us? Does not the Other's enjoyment exert such a powerful fascination because in it we represent to ourselves our own innermost relationship toward enjoyment? And, conversely, is the anti-Semitic capitalist's hatred of the Jew not the hatred of the excess that pertains to capitalism itself, i.e., of the excess produced by its inherent antagonistic nature? Is capitalism's hatred of the Jew not the hatred of its own innermost, essential feature? For this reason, it is not sufficient to point out how the racist's Other presents a threat to our identity. We should rather inverse this proposition: the fascinating image of the Other gives a body to our own innermost split, to what is "in us more than ourselves" and thus prevents us from achieving full identity with ourselves. *The hatred of the Other is the hatred of our own excess of enjoyment*.

The national Thing functions thus as a kind of *"particular Absolute"* resisting *universalization*, bestowing its special "tonality" upon every neutral, universal notion. It is for that reason that the eruption of the national Thing in all its violence has always taken by surprise the devotees of international solidarity. Perhaps the most traumatic case was the debacle of the international solidarity of the worker's movement in the face of "patriotic" euphoria at the outbreak of the First World War. Today, it is difficult to imagine what a traumatic shock it was for the leaders of all currents of social democracy, from Edouard Bernstein to Lenin, when the social-democratic parties of all countries (with the exception of the Bolsheviks in Russia and Serbia) gave way to chauvinist outbursts and "patriotically" stood behind "their" respective governments, oblivious of the proclaimed solidarity of the working class "without country." This shock, the *powerless fascination* felt by its participants, bears witness to an encounter with the Real of enjoyment. That is to say, the basic paradox is that these chauvinist outbursts of "patriotic feeling" were far from unexpected. Years before the actual outbreak of the war, social democracy alerted workers to how imperialist forces were preparing for a new world war, and warned them against yielding to "patriotic" chauvinism. Even at the very outbreak of the war, i.e., in the days following the Sarajevo assassination, the German social democrats cautioned workers that the ruling class would use the assassination as an excuse to declare war. Furthermore, the Socialist International adopted a formal resolution obliging all its members to vote against war credits in the case of war. With the outbreak of the war, international solidarity vanished into thin air. An anecdote about how this overnight reversal took Lenin by surprise is significant: when he saw the daily newspaper of German social democracy, announcing on its front page that the social-democratic deputies had voted for the war credits, he was at first convinced that this issue was fabricated by German police to lead workers astray! [. . .]

The blind spot of liberalism

Paradoxically, we could say that what Eastern Europe needs most now is *more alienation*: the establishment of an "alienated" State which would maintain its distance from the civil society, which would be "formal," "empty," i.e., which would not embody any particular ethnic community's dream (and thus keep the space open for them all). Is, then, the solution for Eastern Europe's present woes simply a larger dose of liberal democracy? The picture we have presented seems to point in this direction: Eastern Europe cannot start to live in peace and true pluralist democracy because of the specter of nationalism, i.e., because the disintegration of Communism opened up the space for the emergence of nationalist obsessions, provincialism, anti-Semitism, hatred of all that comes from abroad, ideology of a threat to the nation, antifeminism, and a postsocialist moral majority inclusive of a pro-life movement – in short, *enjoyment* in its entire "irrationality." Yet what is deeply suspicious about this attitude, about the attitude of an antinationalist, liberal Eastern European intellectual, is the already-mentioned obvious fascination exerted on him by nationalism: liberal intellectuals refuse it, mock it, laugh at it, yet at the same time stare at it with powerless fascination. The intellectual pleasure procured by denouncing nationalism is uncannily close to the satisfaction of successfully explaining one's own impotence and failure (which always was a trademark of a certain kind of Marxism). On another level, Western liberal intellectuals are often caught in a similar trap: the affirmation of their own autochthonous tradition is for them a red-neck horror, a site of populist proto-fascism (for example, in the U.S.A., the "backwardness" of the Polish, Italian, etc. communities, the alleged brood of "authoritarian personalities" and similar liberal scarecrows), whereas such intellectuals are at once ready to hail the autochtho-nous ethical communities *of the other* (African Americans, Puerto Ricans . . .). Enjoyment is good, on condition that it not be too close to us, on condition that it remain the *other's* enjoyment.

[. . .] What truly disturbs liberals is therefore *enjoyment* organized in the form of self-sufficient ethnic communities. It is against this background that we should consider the ambiguous consequences of the politics of school busing in the U.S.A., for example. Its principal aim, of course, was to surmount racist barriers: chil-dren from black communities would widen their cultural horizons by partaking in the white way of life, children from white communities would experience the nullity of racial prejudices by way of contacts with blacks, etc. Yet, inextricably, another logic was entwined in this project, especially where school busing was externally imposed by the "enlightened" state bureaucracy: to destroy the enjoy-ment of the closed ethnic communities by abrogating their boundaries. For this reason, school busing – insofar as it was experienced by the concerned commu-nities as imposed from outside – reinforced or to some extent even generated racism where previously there was a desire of an ethnic community to maintain the closure of its way of life, a desire which is *not* in itself "racist" (as liberals themselves admit through their fascination with exotic "modes of life" of others).[6] What one should do here is to call into question the entire theoretical apparatus that sustains this liberal attitude, up to its Frankfurt-school-psychoanalytical *pièce de résistance*, the theory of the so-called "authoritarian personality": the "authori-tarian personality" ultimately designates that form of subjectivity which "irrationally" insists on its specific way of life and, in the name of its self-enjoyment, resists liberal proofs of its supposed "true interests." The theory of the "authoritarian personality" is nothing but an expression of the ressentiment of the left-liberal intelligentsia apropos of the fact that the "non-enlightened" working classes were not prepared to accept its guidance: an expression of the intelligentsia's inability to offer a positive theory of this resistance.[7]

The impasses of school busing also enable us to delineate the inherent limita-tion of the liberal political ethic as it was articulated in John Rawls's theory of distributive justice.[8] That is to say, school busing fully meets the conditions of distributive justice (it stands the trial of what Rawls calls the "veil of ignorance"): it procures a more just distribution of social goods, it equalizes the chances for success of the individuals from different social strata, etc. Yet the paradox is that everyone, including those deemed to profit most by busing, somehow felt cheated and wronged – why? The dimension infringed upon was precisely that of *fantasy*. The Rawlsian liberal-democratic idea of distributive justice ultimately relies on "rational" individuals who are able to abstract their particular position of enunci-ation, to look upon themselves from a neutral place of pure "metalanguage" and thus perceive their "true interests." Such individuals are the supposed subjects of the social contract which establishes the coordinates of justice. What is thereby a priori left out of consideration is the fantasy-space within which a community organizes its "way of life" (its mode of enjoyment): within this space, what "we" desire is inextricably linked to (what we perceive as) the other's desire, so that what "we" desire may turn out to be the very destruction of our object of desire (if, in this way, we deal a blow to the other's desire). In other words, human desire, insofar as it is always-already mediated by fantasy, can never be grounded in (or translated back into) our "true interests": the ultimate assertion of our desire, sometimes the only way to assert its autonomy in the face of a "benevolent" other providing for our Good, is to act *against* our Good.[9]

Every "enlightened" political action legitimized by the reference to "true interests" encounters sooner or later the resistance of a particular fantasy-space: in the guise of the logic of "envy," of the "theft of enjoyment." Even such a clear-cut issue like the Moral Majority pro-life movement is in this respect more ambiguous than it may seem: one aspect of it is *also* the reaction to the endeavor of the "enlightened" upper-middle-class ideology to penetrate the lower-class community life. And, on another level, was not the same attitude at work in the uneasiness of the wide circle of English leftist-liberal intellectuals apropos of the great miner's strike in 1988 [sic]? One was quick to renounce the strike as "irrational," an "expression of an outdated working-class fundamentalism," etc.; while all this was undoubtedly true, the fact remains that this strike was also a desperate form of resistance from a certain traditional working-class way of life. As such, it was perhaps more 'postmodern,' on account of the very features perceived by its critics as "regressive," than the usual "enlightened" liberal-leftist criticism of it.[10]

The fear of "excessive" identification is therefore the fundamental feature of the late-capitalist ideology: the Enemy is the "fanatic" who "over-identifies" instead of maintaining a proper distance toward the dispersed plurality of subject-positions. In short: the elated "deconstructionist" logomachy focused on "essentialism" and "fixed identities" ultimately fights a straw-man. Far from containing any kind of subversive potentials, the dispersed, plural, constructed subject hailed by postmodern theory (the subject prone to particular, inconsistent modes of enjoyment, etc.) simply designates *the form of subjectivity that corresponds to late capitalism.* Perhaps the time has come to resuscitate the Marxian insight that Capital is the ultimate power of "deterritorialization" which undermines every fixed social identity, and to conceive of "late capitalism" as the epoch in which the traditional fixity of ideological positions (patriarchal authority, fixed sexual roles, etc.) becomes an obstacle to the unbridled commodification of everyday life.

[. . .] In the ethnic tensions emerging in Eastern Europe, the Western gaze upon the East encounters its own uncanny reverse usually qualified (and by the same token disqualified) as "fundamentalism": the end of cosmopolitanism, liberal democracy's impotence in the face of this return of tribalism. It is precisely here that, for the sake of democracy itself, one has to gather strength and repeat the exemplary heroical gesture of Freud, who answered the threat of Fascist anti-Semitism by depriving Jews of their founding father: *Moses and Monotheism* is Freud's answer to Nazism. What Freud did was therefore the exact opposite of Arnold Schoenberg, for example, who scornfully dismissed Nazi racism as a pale imitation of the self-comprehension of the Jews as the elected people: by way of an almost masochistic inversion, Freud targeted Jews themselves and endeavored to prove that their founding father, Moses, was Egyptian. Notwithstanding the historic (in)accuracy of this thesis, what really matters is its discursive strategy: to demonstrate that Jews are already in themselves "decentered," that their "originality" is a bricolage. The difficulty does not reside in Jews but in the transference of the anti-Semite who thinks that Jews "really possess it," *agalma*, the secret of their power: the anti-Semite is the one who "believes in the Jew," so the only way effectively to undermine anti-Semitism is to contend that *Jews do not possess "it."*[11]

In a similar move, one has to detect the flaw of liberal democracy which opens up a space for "fundamentalism." That is to say, there is ultimately only one question which confronts political philosophy today: is liberal democracy the ultimate horizon of our political practice, or is it possible effectively to comprise its inherent limitation? The standard neoconservative answer here is to bemoan the "lack of roots" that allegedly pertains to liberal democracy, to this kingdom of the Nietzschean "last man" where no place is left for ethical heroism, where we are more and more submerged in the idiotic routine of everyday life regulated by the pleasure-principle, etc.: within this perspective, "fundamentalism" is a simple reaction to this "loss of roots," a perverted, yet desperate search for new roots in an organic community. Yet this neoconservative answer falls short by failing to demonstrate how the very project of formal democracy, conceived in its philosophical founding gesture, opens up the space for "fundamentalism."

[. . .] This pathological "stain" also determines the deadlocks of today's liberal democracy. The problem with the liberal democracy is that a priori, for structural reasons, it cannot be universalized. Hegel said that the moment of victory of a political force is the very moment of its splitting: the triumphant liberal-democratic "new world order" is more and more marked by a frontier separating its "inside" from its "outside" – a frontier between those who manage to remain "within" (the "developed," those to whom the rules of human rights, social security, etc., apply) and the others, the excluded (the main concern of the "developed" apropos of them is to contain their explosive potential, even if the price to be paid for such containment is the neglect of elementary democratic principles).[12] This opposition, not the one between the capitalist and the socialist "bloc," is what defines the contemporary constellation: the "socialist" bloc was the true "third way," a desperate attempt at modernization outside the constraints of capitalism. What is effectively at stake in the present crisis of postsocialist states is precisely the struggle for one's place, now that the illusion of the "third way" has evaporated: who will be admitted "inside," integrated into the developed capitalist order, and who will remain excluded from it? Ex-Yugoslavia is perhaps the exemplary case: every actor in the bloody play of its disintegration endeavours to legitimize its place "inside" by presenting itself as the last bastion of European civilisation (the current ideological designation for the capitalist "inside") in the face of oriental barbarism. For the right-wing nationalist Austrians, this imaginary frontier is Karavanke, the mountain chain between Austria and Slovenia: beyond it, the rule of Slavic hordes begins. For the nationalist Slovenes, this frontier is the river Kolpa, separating Slovenia from Croatia: we are *Mitteleuropa*, while Croatians are already Balkan, involved in the irrational ethnic feuds which really do not concern us; we are on their side, we sympathize with them, yet in the same way one sympathizes with a third world victim of aggression. For Croatians, the crucial frontier, of course, is the one between them and Serbians, i.e., between the Western Catholic civilisation and the Eastern Orthodox collective spirit which cannot comprehend the values of Western individualism. Serbians, finally, conceive of themselves as the last line of defense of Christian Europe against the fundamentalist danger bodied forth by Muslim Albanians and Bosnians. (It should be clear, now, who, within the space of ex-Yugoslavia, effectively behaves in the civilized "European" way: those at the very bottom of this ladder, excluded from all – Albanians and Muslim Bosnians.) The traditional liberal opposition between "open" pluralist societies and "closed" nationalist–corporatist societies founded on the exclusion of the Other has thus to be brought to its point of self-reference: the liberal gaze itself functions according to the same logic, insofar as it is founded upon the exclusion of the Other to whom one attributes the fundamentalist nationalism, etc. On that account, events in ex-Yugoslavia exemplify perfectly the properly dialectical reversal: something which first appeared within the given set of circumstances as the most backward element, a left-over of the past, all of a sudden, with the shift in the general framework, emerges as the element of the future in the present context, as the premonition of what lies ahead. The outbursts of Balkan nationalism were first dismissed as the death throes of Communist totalitarianism disguised in new nationalist clothes, as a ridiculous anachronism that truly belongs to the nineteenth-century age of nation-states, not to our present era of multinationals and world integration; however, it suddenly became clear that the ethnic conflicts of ex-Yugoslavia offer the first clear taste of the twenty-first century, the prototype of the post-cold war armed conflicts.

This antagonistic splitting opens up the field for the Khmer Rouge, Sendero Luminoso, and other similar movements which seem to personify "radical Evil" in today's politics: if "fundamentalism" functions as a kind of "negative judgment" on liberal capitalism, as an inherent negation of the universalist claim of liberal capitalism, then movements such as Sendero Luminoso enact an "infinite judgment" on it. In his *Philosophy of Right*, Hegel conceives of the "rabble" (*Pöbel*) as a necessary product of the modern society: a nonintegrated segment in the legal order, prevented from partaking of its benefits, and for this very reason delivered from any responsibilities toward it – a necessary structural surplus excluded from the closed circuit of social edifice. It seems that only today, with the advent of late capitalism, has this notion of "rabble" achieved its adequate realization in social reality, through political forces which paradoxically unite the most radical indigenist antimodernism (the refusal of everything that defines modernity: market, money, individualism . . .) with the eminently modern project of effacing the entire symbolic tradition and beginning from a zero-point (in the case of Khmer Rouge, this meant abolishing the entire system of education and killing intellectuals). What, precisely, constitutes the "shining path" of the Senderistas if not the idea to reinscribe the construction of socialism within the frame of the return to the ancient Inca empire? The result of this desperate endeavour to surmount the antagonism between tradition and modernity is a double negation: a radically anti-capitalist movement (the refusal of integration into the world market) coupled with a systematic dissolution of all traditional hierarchical social links, beginning with the family (at the level of "micro-power," the Khmer Rouge regime functioned as an "anti-Oedipal" regime in its purest i.e., as the "dictature of adolescents," instigating them to denounce their parents). The truth articulated in the paradox of this double negation is that capitalism cannot reproduce itself without the support of the precapitalist forms of social links. In other words, far from presenting a case of exotic barbarism, the "radical Evil" of the Khmer Rouge and the Senderistas is conceivable only against the background of the constitutive antagonism of today's capitalism. There is more than a contingent idiosyncrasy in the fact that, in both cases, the leader of the movement is an intellectual well skilled in the subtleties of Western culture. (Prior to becoming a revolutionary, Pol Pot was a professor at a French lycée in Phnom Penh, known for his subtle readings of Rimbaud and Mallarmé; Abimael Guzman, "presidente Gonzalo," the leader of the Senderistas, is a philosophy professor whose preferred authors are Hegel and Heidegger and whose doctoral thesis was on Kant's theory of space.) For this reason, it is too simple to conceive of these movements as the last embodiment of the millenarist radicalism which structures social space as the exclusive antagonism between "us" and "them," allowing for no possible forms of mediation; instead, these movements represent a desperate attempt to avoid the imbalance constitutive of capitalism without seeking support in some previous tradition supposed to enable us mastery of this imbalance (the Islamic fundamentalism which remains within this logic is for that reason ultimately a perverted instrument of modernization). In other words, behind Sendero Luminoso's endeavor to erase an entire tradition and to begin from the zero-point in an act of creative sublimation, there is the correct insight into the complementary relationship of modernity and tradition: any true return to tradition is today a priori impossible, its role is simply to serve as a shock-absorber for the process of modernization.

The Khmer Rouge and the Senderistas therefore function as a kind of "infinite judgment" on late capitalism in the precise Kantian sense of the term: they are to be located in a third domain beyond the inherent antagonism that defines the late-capitalist dynamic (the antagonism between the modernist drive and the fundamentalist backlash), since they radically reject both poles of the opposition. As such, they are – to put it in Hegelese – an integral part of the notion of late capitalism: if one wants to comprise capitalism as a world-system, one must take into account its inherent negation, the "fundamentalism," as well as its absolute negation, the infinite judgment on it.

It is against this background that one must judge the significance of the renewed (symbolic and real) violence against "foreigners" in the developed Western countries. Apropos of the French Revolution, Kant wrote that its world-historical significance is not to be sought in what actually happened on the streets of Paris, but the enthusiasm this endeavor to realize freedom aroused in the educated, enlightened public: it may well be true that what actually took place in Paris was horrifying, that the most repulsive passions were let loose, yet the reverberations of these events within the enlightened public all around Europe bear witness not only to the possibility of freedom, but also to the very actuality of the tendency toward freedom qua anthropological fact.[13] The same step – the shift from the event's immediate reality to the modality of its inscription into the big Other epitomized by passive observers – is to be repeated apropos of the anti-immigrant violent outbursts in Germany in the summer of 1992 (in Rostock and other cities in the ex-East Germany): the true meaning of these events is to be sought in the fact that the neo-Nazi pogroms met with approval or at least "understanding" in the silent majority of observers – even some top Social Democratic politicians used them as an argument for reconsidering German liberal immigrant policies. This shift in the zeitgeist is where the real danger lurks: it prepares the ground for the possible hegemony of an ideology which perceives the presence of "aliens" as a threat to national identity, as the principal cause of antagonisms that divide the political body.

What we must be particularly attentive to is the difference between this "postmodern" racism which now rages around Europe and the traditional form of racism. The old racism was direct and raw – "they" (Jews, blacks, Arabs, Eastern Europeans . . .) are lazy, violent, plotting, eroding our national substance, etc., whereas the new racism is "reflected," as it were squared racism, which is why it can well assume the form of its opposite, of the fight *against* racism. Etienne Balibar hit the mark by baptizing it "metaracism."[14] How does a "postmodern" racist react to the outbursts in Rostock? He of course begins by expressing his horror and repulsion at the neo-Nazi violence, yet he is quick to add that these events, deplorable as they are, must be seen in their context: they are actually a perverted, distorted expression and effect of a true problem, namely that in contemporary Babilon the experience of belonging to a well-defined ethnic community which gives meaning to the individual's life is losing ground; in short, the true culprits are cosmopolitic universalists who, in the name of "multiculturalism," mix races and thereby set in motion natural self-defense mechanisms.[15] Apartheid is thus legitimized as the ultimate form of antiracism, as an endeavor to prevent racial tensions and conflicts. What we have here is a palpable example of what Lacan has in mind when he insists that "there is no metalanguage": the distance of metaracism toward racism is void; metaracism is racism pure and simple, all the more dangerous for posing as its opposite and advocating racist measures as the very form of fighting racism. [. . .]

Notes and references

1   For a detailed elaboration of this notion of the Thing see *The Ethics of Psychoanalysis, 1959–1960, The Seminar of Jacques Lacan*, book 7, ed. Jacques-Alain Miller (London: Routledge/Tavistock, 1992). What should be pointed out here is that enjoyment (*jouissance, Genuss*) is not to be equated with pleasure (Lust): enjoyment is precisely "Lust im Unlust"; it designates the paradoxical satisfaction procured by a painful encounter with a Thing that perturbs the equilibrium of the "pleasure principle." In other words, enjoyment is located "beyond the pleasure principle."

2   The way these fragments persist across ethnic barriers can be sometimes quite affecting, as, for example, with Robert Mugabe who, when asked by a journalist what was the most precious legacy of British colonialism to Zimbabwe, answered without hesitation: "Cricket" – a senselessly ritualized game, almost beyond the grasp of a Continental, in which the prescribed gestures (or, more precisely, gestures established by an unwritten tradition), the way to throw a ball, for example, appear grotesquely "dysfunctional."

3   See chapter 6 of Jacques Lacan, *Le Séminaire*, book 20: *Encore* (Paris: Editions du Seuil, 1966).

4   The fact that a subject fully "exists" only through enjoyment, i.e., the ultimate coincidence of "existence" and "enjoyment," was already indicated in Lacan's early seminars by the ambiguously traumatic status of existence: "By definition, there is something so improbable about all existence that one is in effect perpetually questioning oneself about its reality" (*The Seminar of Jacques Lacan*, book 2 [Cambridge: Cambridge University Press, 1988], p. 226). This proposition becomes much clearer if we simply replace "existence" by "enjoyment": "By definition, there is something so improbable about all enjoyment that one is in effect perpetually questioning oneself about its reality." The fundamental subjective position of a *hysteric* involves posing precisely such a question about his or her existence qua enjoyment, whereas a sadist *pervert* avoids this questioning by transposing the "pain of existence" onto the other (his victim).

5   Herein lies also Lacan's criticism of Hegel, of the Hegelian dialectic of lordship and bondage: contrary to Hegel's thesis that, by submitting himself to the lord, the bondsman renounces enjoyment, which thus remains reserved for the lord, Lacan claims that it is precisely enjoyment (and not the fear of death) which keeps the bondsman in servitude – enjoyment procured by the relationship toward the (hypothetical, presupposed) Master's enjoyment, by the expectation of enjoyment waiting for us at the moment of the Master's death, etc. Enjoyment is thus never immediate, it is always mediated by the presupposed enjoyment imputed to the Other; it is always enjoyment procured by the expectation of enjoyment, by the renunciation of enjoyment.

6   Consider the success of Peter Weir's thriller *Witness*, which mostly takes place in an Amish community: are not the Amish an exemplary case of a closed community which persists in its way of life, yet without falling prey to a paranoiac logic of the "theft of enjoyment"? In other words, the paradox of the Amish is that, while they live according to the highest standards of the Moral Majority, *they have absolutely nothing to do with the Moral Majority qua politico-ideological movement*, i.e., they are as far as possible from the Moral Majority's paranoiac logic of envy, of aggressive imposition of its standards onto others. And, incidentally, the fact that the most pathetic and effective scene of the film is the collective building of a new barn testifies again to what Fredric Jameson calls the "utopian" potential of the contemporary mass-culture.

7   As it was already noted by numerous critics, the theory of "authoritarian personality" is actually a foreign body within the Frankfurt-school theoretical edifice: it is based on presuppositions undermined by the Adorno–Horkheimer theory of late-capitalist subjectivity.

8   See John Rawls, *A Theory of Justice* (Cambridge: Harvard University Press, 1971).

9   The notion of fantasy thus designates the inherent limitation of distributive justice: although the other's interests are taken into account, *his fantasy is wronged*. In other words, when the trial by "veil of ignorance" tells me that, even if I were to occupy the lowest place in community, I would still accept my ethical choice, I move within my own fantasy-frame. *What if the "other" judges from within the frame of an absolutely incompatible fantasy?* For a more detailed Lacanian criticism of Rawls's theory of justice, see Renata Salecl, *The Spoils of Freedom* (London: Routledge, 1993).

10   The reverse of this resistance is a desire to maintain the "other" in its specific, limited form of (what our gaze perceives as) "authenticity." Let us mention the recent case of Peter Handke, who expressed doubts about Slovene independence,

claiming that the notion of Slovenia as an independent state is something imposed on Slovenes from outside, not part of the inherent logic of their national development. Handke's mother was Slovene and, within his artistic universe, Slovenia functions as a mythical point of reference, a kind of maternal paradise, a country where words still directly refer to objects, somehow miraculously bypassing commodification, where people are still organically rooted in their landscape, etc. (See his *Repetition* [*Wiederholung*].) What ultimately bothers him is therefore simply the fact that the actual Slovenia does not want to behave according to his private myth and thus disturbs the balance of his artistic universe.

11   See Sigmund Freud, "Moses and Monotheism," in *The Standard Edition of the Complete Psychological Works of Sigmund Freud* (London: Hogarth Press, 1953–74), vol. 23. And does not Lacan make the same gesture apropos of woman? "Woman's secret" is man's fantasy, which is why the only proper feminist gesture is to assert that woman qua real does not possess the mysterious X imputed to her by man – in short, "Woman doesn't exist."

12   This split is therefore *the very form of universality of the liberal democracy*: the liberal-democratic "new world order" affirms its universal scope by way of imposing this split as the determining antagonism, the structuring principle, of inter- and intranational relations. What we have here is an elementary case of the dialectic of identity and difference: the very *identity* of the liberal-democratic "order" consists in the *scissure* which separates its "inside" from its "outside."

13   Immanuel Kant, *The Conflict of the Faculties* (Lincoln: University of Nebraska Press, 1992), p. 153.

14   See Etienne Balibar, "Is There a 'Neo-Racism'?", in Etienne Balibar and Emmanuel Wallerstein, *Race, Nation, Class* (London: Verso Books, 1991).

15   Or, to quote from a recent letter to *Newsweek* magazine: "Maybe it's fundamentally unnatural for different races or ethnic groups to live together. . . . While no one can condone the attacks against foreigners in Germany, the Germans have every right to insist that their country remain ethnically German."

Chapter 41

K. Anthony Appiah

RACIAL IDENTITY AND RACIAL IDENTIFICATION

[. . .]

IF **WE FOLLOW THE BADGE** of color from "African" to "Negro" to "colored race" to "black" to "Afro-American" to "African-American" (and this ignores such fascinating detours as the route by way of "Afro-Saxon") we are thus tracing the history not only of a signifier, a label, but also a history of its effects. At any time in this history there was, within the American colonies and the United States that succeeded them, a massive consensus, both among those labeled black and among those labeled white, as to who, in their own communities, fell under which labels. (As immigration from China and other parts of the "Far East" occurred, an Oriental label came to have equal stability.) There was, no doubt, some "passing"; but the very concept of passing implies that, if the relevant fact about the ancestry of these individuals had become known, most people would have taken them to be traveling under the wrong badge.

The major North American exception was in southern Louisiana, where a different system in which an intermediary Creole group, neither white nor black, had social recognition; but *Plessy v. Fergusson* reflected the extent to which the Louisiana Purchase effectively brought even that state gradually into the American mainstream of racial classification. For in that case Homer Adolph Plessy – a Creole gentleman who could certainly have passed in most places for white – discovered in 1896, after a long process of appeal, that the Supreme Court of the United States proposed to treat him as a Negro and therefore recognize the State of Louisiana's right to keep him and his white fellow citizens "separate but equal."

The result is that there are at least three sociocultural objects in America – blacks, whites and Orientals – whose membership at any time is relatively, and increasingly, determinate. These objects are historical in this sense: to identify all the members of these American races over time, you cannot seek a single criterion that applies equally always; you can find the starting point for the race – the subcontinental source of the population of individuals that defines its initial membership – and then apply at each historical moment the criteria of inter-temporal continuity that apply at that moment to decide which individuals in the next generation count as belonging to the group. There is from the very begin-ning until the present, at the heart of the system, a simple rule that very few would dispute even today: where both parents are of a single race, the child is of the same race as the parents.

The criteria applicable at any time may leave vague boundaries. They certainly change, as the varying decisions about what proportion of African ancestry made one black or the current uncertainty as to how to assign the children of white-yellow "miscegenation" demonstrate. But they always definitely assign some people to the group and definitely rule out others; and for most of America's history the class of people about whom there was uncertainty (are the Florida Seminoles black or Indian?) was relatively small.[1]

Once the racial label is applied to people, ideas about what it refers to, ideas that may be much less consensual than the application of the label, come to have their social effects. But they have not only social effects but psychological ones as well; and they shape the ways people conceive of themselves and their projects. In particular, the labels can operate to shape what I want to call "identification": the process through which an individual intentionally shapes her projects – including her plans for her own life and her conception of the good – by reference to avail-able labels, available identities.

Identification is central to what Ian Hacking has called "making up people."[2] Drawing on a number of examples, but centrally homosexuality and multiple personality syndrome, he defends what he calls a "dynamic nominalism," which argues that "numerous kinds of human beings and human acts come into being hand in hand with our invention of the categories labeling them."[3] I have just artic-ulated a dynamic nominalism about a kind of person that is currently usually called "African-American."

Hacking reminds us of the philosophical truism, whose most influential formulation is in Elizabeth Anscombe's work on intention, that in intentional action people act "under descriptions"; that their actions are conceptually shaped. It follows, of course, that what people can do depends on what concepts they have available to them; and among the concepts that may shape one's action is the concept of a certain kind of person and the behavior appropriate to that kind.

Hacking offers as an example Sartre's brilliant evocation, in *Being and Nothingness*, of the Parisian *garçon de café*: "His movement is quick and forward, a little too precise, a little too rapid. He comes towards the patrons with a step a little too quick. He bends forward a little too eagerly, his eyes express an interest too solicitous for the order of the customer."[4] Hacking comments:

> Sartre's antihero chose to be a waiter. Evidently that was not a possible choice in other places, other times. There are servile people in most societies, and servants in many, but a waiter is something specific, and a *garçon de café* more specific. . . .

> As with almost every way in which it is possible to be a person, it
> is possible to be a *garçon de café* only at a certain time, in a certain
> place, in a certain social setting. The feudal serf putting food on my
> lady's table can no more choose to be a *garçon de café* than he can
> choose to be lord of the manor. But the impossibility is evidently of a
> different kind.[5]

The idea of the *garçon de café* lacks, so far as I can see, the sort of theoretical
commitments that are trailed by the idea of the black and the white, the homo-
sexual and the heterosexual. So it makes no sense to ask of someone who has a
job as a *garçon de café* whether that is what he really is. The point is not that we
do not have expectations of the *garçon de café*: that is why it is a recognizable identity. It is rather that those expectations are about the performance of the role;
they depend on our assumption of intentional conformity to those expectations.
As I spent some time arguing earlier, we *can* ask whether someone is really of a
black race, because the constitution of this identity is generally theoretically
committed: we expect people of a certain race to behave a certain way not simply
because they are conforming to the script for that identity, performing that role,
but because they have certain antecedent properties that are consequences of the
label's properly applying to them. It is because ascription of racial identities – the
process of applying the label to people, including ourselves – is based on more
than intentional identification that there can be a gap between what a person ascrip-
tively is and the racial identity he performs: it is this gap that makes passing
possible.

   Race is, in this way, like all the major forms of identification that are central
to contemporary identity politics: female and male; gay, lesbian, and straight;
black, white, yellow, red, and brown; Jewish-, Japanese-, and Korean-American;
even that most neglected of American identities, class. There is, in all of them, a
set of theoretically committed criteria for ascription, not all of which are held by
everybody, and which may not be consistent with one another even in the ascriptions of a single person; and there is then a process of identification in which the
label shapes the intentional acts of (some of) those who fall under it.

   It does not follow from the fact that identification shapes action, shapes life
plans, that the identification itself must be thought of as voluntary. I don't recall
ever choosing to identify as a male;[6] but being male has shaped many of my plans
and actions. In fact, where my ascriptive identity is one on which almost all my
fellow citizens agree, I am likely to have little sense of choice about whether the
identity is mine; though I *can* choose how central my identification with it will be
– choose, that is, how much I will organize my life around that identity. Thus if
I am among those (like the unhappily labeled "straight-acting gay men," or most
American Jews) who are able, if they choose, to escape ascription, I may choose
not to take up a gay or Jewish identity; though this will require concealing facts
about myself or my ancestry from others.

   If, on the other hand, I fall into the class of those for whom the consensus on
ascription is not clear – as among contemporary so-called biracials, or bisexuals,
or those many white Americans of multiple identifiable ethnic heritages[7] – I may
have a sense of identity options: but one way I may exercise them is by marking

myself ethnically (as when someone chooses to wear an Irish pin) so that others will then be more likely to ascribe that identity to me.

Differences among differences

Collective identities differ, of course, in lots of ways; the body is central to race, gender, and sexuality but not so central to class and ethnicity. And, to repeat an important point, racial identification is simply harder to resist than ethnic identification. The reason is twofold. First, racial ascription is more socially salient: unless you are morphologically atypical for your racial group, strangers, friends, officials are always aware of it in public and private contexts, always notice it, almost never let it slip from view. Second – and again both in intimate settings and in public space – race is taken by so many more people to be the basis for treating people differentially. (In this respect, Jewish identity in America strikes me as being a long way along a line toward African-American identity: there are ways of speaking and acting and looking – and it matters very little whether they are "really" mostly cultural or mostly genetic – that are associated with being Jewish; and there are many people, white and black, Jewish and Gentile, for whom this identity is a central force in shaping their responses to others.)

This much about identification said, we can see that Du Bois's analytical problem was, in effect, that he believed that for racial labeling of this sort to have the obvious real effects that it did have – among them, crucially, his own identification with other black people and with Africa – there must be some real essence that held the race together. Our account of the history of the label reveals that this is a mistake: once we focus, as Du Bois almost saw, on the racial badge – the signifier rather than the signified, the word rather than the concept – we see both that the effects of the labeling are powerful and real and that false ideas, muddle and mistake and mischief, played a central role in determining both how the label was applied and to what purposes.

This, I believe, is why Du Bois so often found himself reduced, in his attempts to define race, to occult forces: if you look for a shared essence you won't get anything, so you'll come to believe you've missed it, because it is super-subtle, difficult to experience or identify: in short, mysterious. But if, as I say, you understand the sociohistorical process of construction of the race, you'll see that the label works despite the absence of an essence.

Perhaps, then, we can allow that what Du Bois was after was the idea of racial identity, which I shall roughly define as a label, R, associated with *ascriptions* by most people (where ascription involves descriptive criteria for applying the label); and *identifications* by those that fall under it (where identification implies a shaping role for the label in the intentional acts of the possessors, so that they sometimes act *as an R*), where there is a history of associating possessors of the label with an inherited racial essence (even if some who use the label no longer believe in racial essences).

In fact, we might argue that racial identities could persist even if nobody believed in racial essences, provided both ascription and identification continue.

There will be some who will object to my account that it does not give racism a central place in defining racial identity: it is obvious, I think, from the history I have explored, that racism has been central to the development of race theory. In that sense racism has been part of the story all along. But you might give an account of racial identity in which you counted nothing as a racial essence unless it implied a hierarchy among the races;[8] or unless the label played a role in racist practices. I have some sympathy with the former strategy; it would fit easily into my basic picture. To the latter strategy, however, I make the philosopher's objection that it confuses logical and causal priority: I have no doubt that racial theories grew up, in part, as rationalizations for mistreating blacks, Jews, Chinese, and various others. But I think it is useful to reserve the concept of racism, as opposed to ethnocentrism or simply inhumanity, for practices in which a race concept plays a central role. And I doubt you can explain racism without first explaining the race concept.

I *am* in sympathy, however, with an animating impulse behind such proposals, which is to make sure that here in America we do not have discussions of race in which racism disappears from view. As I pointed out, racial identification is hard to resist in part because racial ascription by others is so insistent; and its effects – especially, but by no means exclusively, the racist ones – are so hard to escape. It is obvious, I think, that the persistence of racism means that racial ascriptions have negative consequences for some and positive consequences for others – creating, in particular, the white-skin privilege that it is so easy for people who have it to forget; and it is clear, too, that for those who suffer from the negative consequences, racial identification is a predictable response, especially where the project it suggests is that the victims of racism should join together to resist it. I shall return later to some of the important moral consequences of present racism and the legacy of racisms of the past.

But before I do, I want to offer some grounds for preferring the account of racial identity I have proposed, which places racial essences at its heart, over some newer accounts that see racial identity as a species of cultural identity.

[. . .] In the United States, not only ethnic but also racial boundaries are culturally marked. In *White Women, Race Matters: The Social Construction of Whiteness*,[9] Ruth Frankenberg records the anxiety of many white women who do not see themselves as white "ethnics" and worry, therefore, that they have no culture.[10] This is somewhat puzzling in people who live, as every normal human being does, in rich structures of knowledge, experience, value and meaning; through tastes and practices: it is perplexing, in short, in people with normal human lives. But the reason these women do not recognize that they have a culture is because none of these things that actually make up their cultural lives are marked as white, as belonging specially to them: and the things that *are* marked as white (racism, white privilege) are things they want to repudiate. Many African-Americans, on the other hand, have cultural lives in which the ways they eat, the churches they go to, the music they listen to, and the ways they speak *are* marked as black: their identities are marked by cultural differences.

I have insisted that African-Americans do not have a single culture, in the sense of shared language, values, practices, and meanings. But many people who think of races as groups defined by shared cultures, conceive that sharing in a different way. They understand black people as sharing black culture *by definition*: jazz or hip-hop belongs to an African-American, whether she likes it or knows anything about it, because it is culturally marked as black. Jazz belongs to a black person who knows nothing about it more fully or naturally that it does to a white jazzman. [. . .]

Identities and norms

I have been exploring these questions about culture in order to show how unsatisfactory an account of the significance of race that mistakes identity for culture can be. But if this is the wrong route from identity to moral and political concerns, is there a better way?

We need to go back to the analysis of racial identities. While the theories on which ascription is based need not themselves be normative, these identities come with normative as well as descriptive expectations; about which, once more, there may be both inconsistency in the thinking of the individuals and fairly widespread disagreement among them. There is, for example, a very wide range of opinions among American Jews as to what their being Jewish commits them; and while most Gentiles probably don't think about the matter very much, people often make remarks that suggest they admire the way in which, as they believe, Jews have "stuck together," an admiration that seems to presuppose the moral idea that it is, if not morally obligatory, then at least morally desirable, for those who share identities to take responsibility for each other. (Similar comments have been made increasingly often about Korean-Americans.)

We need, in short, to be clear that the relation between identities and moral life are complex. In the liberal tradition, to which I adhere, we see public morality as engaging each of us as individuals with our individual "identities": and we have the notion, which comes (as Charles Taylor has rightly argued[11]) from the ethics of authenticity, that, other things being equal, people have the right to be acknowledged publicly as what they already really are. It is because someone is already authentically Jewish or gay that we deny them something in requiring them to hide this fact, to "pass," as we say, for something that they are not. Charles Taylor has suggested that we call the political issues raised by this fact the politics of recognition: a politics that asks us to acknowledge socially and politically the authentic identities of others.

As has often been pointed out, however, the way much discussion of recognition proceeds is strangely at odds with the individualist thrust of talk of authenticity and identity. If what matters about me is my individual and authentic self, why is so much contemporary talk of identity about large categories – race, gender, ethnicity, nationality, sexuality – that seem so far from individual? What is the relation between this collective language and the individualist thrust of the modern notion of the self? How has social life come to be so bound up with an idea of identity that has deep roots in romanticism with its celebration of the individual over and against society?[12]

The connection between individual identity, on the one hand, and race and other collective identities, on the other, seems to be something like this: each person's individual identity is seen as having two major dimensions. There is a collective dimension, the intersection of her collective identities; and there is what I will call a personal dimension, consisting of other socially or morally important features of the person – intelligence, charm, wit, cupidity – that are not themselves the basis of forms of collective identity.

The distinction between these two dimensions of identity is, so to speak, a sociological rather than a logical distinction. In each dimension we are talking about properties that are important for social life. But only the collective identities count as social categories, kinds of person. There is a logical category but no social category of the witty, or the clever, or the charming, or the greedy: people who share these properties do not constitute a social group, in the relevant sense. The concept of authenticity is central to the connection between these two dimensions; and there is a problem in many current understandings of that relationship, a misunderstanding one can find, for example, in Charles Taylor's recent (brilliant) essay *Multiculturalism and the Politics of Recognition*. [. . .]

Beyond identity

The large collective identities that call for recognition come with notions of how a proper person of that kind behaves: it is not that there is *one* way that blacks should behave, but that there are proper black modes of behavior. These notions provide loose norms or models, which play a role in shaping the life plans of those who make these collective identities central to their individual identities; of the identifications of those who fly under these banners.[13] Collective identities, in short, provide what we might call scripts: narratives that people can use in shaping their life plans and in telling their life stories. In our society (though not, perhaps, in the England of Addison and Steele) being witty does not in this way suggest the life script of "the wit." And that is why what I called the personal dimensions of identity work differently from the collective ones.

This is not just a point about modern Westerners: cross-culturally it matters to people that their lives have a certain narrative unity; they want to be able to tell a story of their lives that makes sense. The story – my story – should cohere in the way appropriate by the standards made available in my culture to a person of my identity. In telling that story, how I fit into the wider story of various collectivities is, for most of us, important. It is not just gender identities that give shape (through, for example, rites of passage into woman- or manhood) to one's life: ethnic and national identities too fit each individual story into a larger narrative. And some of the most "individualist" of individuals value such things. Hobbes spoke of the desire for glory as one of the dominating impulses of human beings, one that was bound to make trouble for social life. But glory can consist in fitting and being seen to fit into a collective history: and so, in the name of glory, one can end up doing the most social things of all.

How does this general idea apply to our current situation in the multicultural West? We live in societies in which certain individuals have not been treated with equal dignity because they were, for example, women, homosexuals, blacks, Catholics. Because, as Taylor so persuasively argues, our identities are dialogically shaped, people who have these characteristics find them central – often, negatively central – to their identities. Nowadays there is a widespread agreement that the insults to their dignity and the limitations of their autonomy imposed in the name of these collective identities are seriously wrong. One form of healing of the self that those who have these identities participate in is learning to see these collective identities not as sources of limitation and insult but as a valuable part of what they centrally are. Because the ethics of authenticity requires us to express what we centrally are in our lives, they move next to the demand that they be recognized in social life as women, homosexuals, blacks, Catholics. Because there was no good reason to treat people of these sorts badly, and because the culture continues to provide degrading images of them nevertheless, they demand that we do cultural work to resist the stereotypes, to challenge the insults, to lift the restrictions.

These old restrictions suggested life scripts for the bearers of these identities, but they were negative ones. In order to construct a life with dignity, it seems natural to take the collective identity and construct positive life scripts instead.

An African-American after the Black Power movement takes the old script of self-hatred, the script in which he or she is a nigger, and works, in community with others, to construct a series of positive black life scripts. In these life scripts, being a Negro is recoded as being black: and this requires, among other things, refusing to assimilate to white norms of speech and behavior. And if one is to be black in a society that is racist then one has constantly to deal with assaults on one's dignity. In this context, insisting on the right to live a dignified life will not be enough. It will not even be enough to require that one be treated with equal dignity despite being black: for that will require a concession that being black counts naturally or to some degree against one's dignity. And so one will end up asking to be respected *as a black*.

I hope I seem sympathetic to this story. I *am* sympathetic. I see how the story goes. It may even be historically, strategically necessary for the story to go this way.[14] But I think we need to go on to the next necessary step, which is to ask whether the identities constructed in this way are ones we can all be happy with in the longer run. What demanding respect for people *as blacks* or *as gays* requires is that there be some scripts that go with being an African-American or having same-sex desires. There will be proper ways of being black and gay: there will be expectations to be met; demands will be made. It is at this point that someone who takes autonomy seriously will want to ask whether we have not replaced one kind of tyranny with another. If I had to choose between Uncle Tom and Black Power, I would, of course, choose the latter. But I would like not to have to choose. I would like other options. The politics of recognition requires that one's skin color, one's sexual body, should be politically acknowledged in ways that make it hard for those who want to treat their skin and their sexual body as personal dimensions of the self. And "personal" doesn't mean "secret" but "not too tightly scripted," "not too constrained by the demands and expectations of others."

In short, so it seems to me, those who see potential for conflict between individual freedom and the politics of identity are right. [. . .]

Notes and references

1   See Kevin Mulroy, *Freedom on the Border: The Seminole Maroons in Florida, the Indian Territory, Coahuila, and Texas* (Lubbock, Tex.: Texas Tech University Press, 1993).

2   Ian Hacking, "Making Up People" reprinted from *Reconstructing Individualism: Autonomy, Individuality and the Self in Western Thought*, ed. Thomas Heller, Morton Sousa, and David Wellbery (Stanford: Stanford University Press, 1986), in *Forms of Desire: Sexual Orientation and the Social Constructionist Controversy*, ed. Edward Stein (New York: Routledge, 1992), pp. 69–88 (page references are to this version).

3   Hacking, "Making Up People," p. 87.

4   Cited in ibid., p. 81.

5   Ibid., p. 82.

6   That I don't recall it doesn't *prove* that I didn't, of course.

7   See Mary C. Waters, *Ethnic Options: Choosing Identities in America* (Berkeley and Los Angeles: University of California Press, 1990).

8   This is the proposal of a paper on metaphysical racism by Berel Lang at the New School for Social Research seminar "Race and Philosophy" in October 1994, from which I learned much.

9   Ruth Frankenberg, *White Women, Race Matters: The Social Construction of Whiteness* (Minneapolis: University of Minnesota Press, 1993).

10 The discussion of this work is shaped by conversation with Larry Blum, Martha Minow, David Wilkins, and David Wong.

11 Charles Taylor, *Multiculturalism and "The Politics of Recognition."* With commentary by Amy Gutmann, ed., K. Anthony Appiah, Jürgen Habermas, Steven C. Rockefeller, Michael Walzer, and Susan Wolf (Princeton: Princeton University Press, 1994).

12 Taylor reminds us rightly of Trilling's profound contributions to our understanding of this history. I discuss Trilling's work in chap. 4 of *In My Father's House*.

13 I say "make" here not because I think there is always conscious attention to the shaping of life plans or a substantial experience of choice but because I want to stress the antiessentialist point that there are choices that can be made.

14 Compare what Sartre wrote in his "Orphée Noir," in *Anthologie de la Nouvelle Poésie Nègre et Malagache de Langue Française*, ed. L. S. Senghor, p. xiv. Sartre argued, in effect, that this move is a necessary step in a dialectical progression. In this passage he explicitly argues that what he calls an "antiracist racism" is a path to the "final unity . . . the abolition of differences of race."

Guide to further reading

We have selected the following texts as a guide in structuring further reading on the themes covered in this Reader as a whole as well as in specific Parts. We have aimed to suggest readings that provide a variety of conceptual perspectives as well as historical and empirical examples. The literature on each of the main Parts of this volume is rapidly expanding at the present time and the selections we have made are to some extent both personal and illustrative, rather than comprehensive. We hope, nevertheless, that they help to show the breadth of perspectives found in the main Parts of the Reader.

We have divided the recommendations for each Part into Key Texts and Background Reading and have added a short note on each to describe broadly what they seek to cover.

General readings

Key texts

Bulmer, M. and Solomos, J. (eds) (1999) *Ethnic and Racial Studies Today*, London: Routledge (an up-to-date collection of papers on a wide range of social science and humanities disciplines).

Cornell, S. and Hartman, D. (1998) *Ethnicity and Race: Making Identities in a Changing World*, Thousand Oaks, CA: Pine Forge Press (an overview of global trends and developments in this field).

Solomos, J. and Back, L. (1996) *Racism and Society*, Basingstoke: Macmillan (an analysis of contemporary theories and perspectives).

Background reading

Gates Jr, H. L. (ed.) (1986) *'Race', Writing and Difference*, Chicago: University of Chicago Press (an influential collection of papers written largely from a literary perspective).

Goldberg, D. T. (ed.) (1990) *Anatomy of Racism*, Minneapolis: University of Minnesota Press (a collection of papers that examine various kinds of racism from a theoretical and historical perspective).

Jones, S. (1996) *In the Blood: God, Genes and Destiny*, London: HarperCollins (a detailed examination of genetic research and its implications for research on issues such as race and ethnicity).

LaCapra, D. (ed.) (1991) *The Bounds of Race: Perspectives on Hegemony and Resistance*, Ithaca: Cornell University Press (a collection of papers that focuses on changing racial ideologies and resistance to racism).

Miles, R. (1989) *Racism*, London: Routledge (an attempt to develop a neo-Marxist analysis of racism as a social phenomenon).

Montagu, A. (1997) *Man's Most Dangerous Myth: The Fallacy of Race*, sixth edition, Walnut Creek CA: AltaMira Press (a new edition of a classic critique of the mythologies of race thinking).

Mosse, G. L. (1985) *Toward the Final Solution: A History of European Racism*, Madison: University of Wisconsin Press (an insightful historical analysis of the processes that shaped European racism, leading to the 'final solution').

Rex, J. and Mason, D. (eds) (1986) *Theories of Race and Ethnic Relations*, Cambridge: Cambridge University Press (an important collection of papers that provides an insight into key debates during the 1980s).

UNESCO (1980) *Sociological Theories: Race and Colonialism*, Paris: UNESCO (collection of papers that outline different theories of race and racism, including papers by Rex, Hall and Guillaumin).

Winant, H. (1994) *Racial Conditions: Politics, Theory, Comparisons*, Minneapolis: University of Minnesota Press (an attempt to link theoretical debates with a historical analysis).

Zack, N., Shrage, L. and Sartwell, C. (eds) (1998) *Race, Class, Gender and Sexuality: The Big Questions*, Cambridge, MA: Blackwell (a collection of papers that links the analysis of race to other social phenomena).

Part One: Origins and transformations

Key texts

Banton, M. (1998) *Racial Theories*, second edition, Cambridge: Cambridge University Press (a masterly overview of theoretical perspectives written from a historical perspective).

Gossett, T. F. (1997) *Race: The History of an Idea in America*, new edition, New York: Oxford University Press (a classic account of the development of racial thinking in America).

Gould, S. J. (1984) *The Mismeasure of Man*, London: Penguin (a study of the history and usages of scientific attempts to measure human intelligence, including a discussion of race and IQ).

Background reading

Banton, M. (1977) *The Idea of Race*, London: Tavistock (an account of the origins of ideas about race in European and American thought).

Baker, L. D. (1998) *From Savage to Negro: Anthropology and the Construction of Race, 1896–1954*, Berkeley: University of California Press (an exploration of changing ideas about race in American anthropology).

Barkan, E. (1992) *The Retreat of Scientific Racism*, Cambridge: Cambridge University Press (an insightful account of the move away from scientific racism).

Barzun, J. (1938) *Race: A Study in Modern Superstition*, London: Methuen (a classic attempt to undermine myths about race).

Benedict, R. (1943) *Race and Racism*, London: Routledge and Kegan Paul (an early attempt to provide arguments against racism, influenced by debates in American anthropology and the Nazi experience).

Cox, O. C. (1970) *Caste, Class and Race*, New York: Monthly Review Press (a classic attempt to write a history of racial domination from a Marxist perspective).

Gilman, S. L. (1985) *Difference and Pathology: Stereotypes of Sexuality, Race and Madness*, Ithaca: Cornell University Press (an innovative analysis of the use of race in the construction of stereotypes).

Hannaford, I. (1996) *Race: The History of an Idea in the West*, Baltimore: The Johns Hopkins University Press (an attempt to trace the history of thinking about race in Western thought).

Jahoda, G. (1999) *Images of Savages: Ancient Roots of Modern Prejudice in Western Culture*, London: Routledge (a historical analysis of how ideas and images about 'savages' developed in Western thought and influenced ideas about race).

Jordan, W. D. (1968) *White Over Black: American Attitudes Towards the Negro 1550–1812*, New York: W. W. Norton (a historical analysis of changing ideas about Africans from the early stages of European exploration to the eighteenth century).

Kohn, M. (1995) *The Race Gallery: The Return of Racial Science*, London: Jonathan Cape (an influential analysis of contemporary debates about race in scientific thought).

Lal, B. B. (1990) *The Romance of Culture in an Urban Civilization: Robert E. Park on race and ethnic relations in cities*, London: Routledge (an analysis of the theories of Robert Park about race and ethnicity in urban environments).

Montagu, A. (ed.) (1964) *The Concept of Race*, New York: Free Press (a classic collection of essays on the idea of race).

Pieterse, J. N. (1992) *White on Black: Images of Africa and Blacks in Western Popular Culture*, New Haven: Yale University Press (an account of the usages of images of Africa and blacks in popular cultural forms).

Roediger, D. R. (1991) *The Wages of Whiteness: Race and the Making of the American Working Class*, London: Verso (a historical account of the emergence and impact of white working class racism in America).

Snowden, F. M. Jr (1983) *Before Color Prejudice: The Ancient View of Blacks*, Cambridge, MA: Harvard University Press (a reconstruction of ancient ideas about blacks).

Stanfield II, J. H. (ed.) (1993) *A History of Race Relations Research: First Generation Recollections*, London: Sage (a collection of interesting biographical recollections of early American researchers on various aspects of race relations).

Stepan, N. (1982) *The Idea of Race in Science*, Basingstoke: Macmillan (an important analysis of the development of ideas about race in scientific discourses).

Todorov, T. (1993) *On Human Diversity: Nationalism, Racism and Exoticism in French*

Thought, Cambridge, MA: Harvard University Press (an account of ideas about race in French political and social thought).

Part Two: Sociology, race and social theory

Key texts

Goldberg, D. T. (1993) *Racist Culture*, Oxford: Blackwell (an influential analysis of race and racism that seeks to link theoretical analysis with an analysis of racist practices).

Miles, R. (1993) *Racism After 'Race Relations'*, London: Routledge (a collection of essays by an important contemporary theorist that provide an overview of key strands of his intellectual development).

Wieviorka, M. (1995) *The Arena of Racism*, London: Sage (an analysis of racism that draws on classical and contemporary European and American theories).

Background reading

Anthias, F. and Yuval-Davis, N. (1992) *Racialized Boundaries*, London: Routledge (an analysis of the construction of racial boundaries that emphasises links to gender, class and ethnicity).

Baker Jr. H. A., Diawara, M. and Lindeborg, R. H. (eds) (1996) *Black British Cultural Studies: A Reader*, Chicago: University of Chicago Press (a collection of essays about contemporary black British cultural studies, including papers by Hall, Gilroy and Carby).

Donald, J. and Rattansi, A. (eds) (1992) *'Race', Culture and Difference*, London: Sage (a collection of papers focusing on contemporary theories about race and cultural difference).

Eze, E. C. (ed.) (1997) *Race and the Enlightenment: A Reader*, Cambridge, MA: Blackwell (a collection of classical philosophical texts on race).

Gilroy, P. (1993) *The Black Atlantic: Modernity and Double Consciousness*, London: Verso (an influential reconstruction of the black diasporic experience from slavery to the present).

Guillaumin, C. (1995) *Racism, Sexism, Power and Ideology*, London: Routledge (a collection of essays that analyse the development of racism and sexism).

Malik, K. (1996) *The Meaning of Race: Race, History and Culture in Western Society*, London: Macmillan (an analysis of the relationship between ideas about race and post-enlightenment Western thought).

Marx, A. W. (1997) *Making Race and Nation: A Comparison of the United States, South Africa, and Brazil*, Cambridge: Cambridge University Press (a comparative analysis of the making of ideas about race and nation from the perspective of historical sociology).

Mills, C. W. (1997) *The Racial Contract*, Ithaca: Cornell University Press (an attempt to analyse ideas about race within contemporary philosophical terms).

Mostern, K. (1996) 'Three Theories of Race of W. E. B. Du Bois', *Cultural Critique* 34, 27–63 (an exploration of different ideas about race in the work of Du Bois).

Outlaw, Jr, L. T. (1996) *On Race and Philosophy*, New York: Routledge (a study of the relationship between race, philosophy and modernity).

Park, R. (1950) *Race and Culture*, New York: Free Press (a classic collection of papers by Robert Park that trace the development of his thinking on race relations from the early part of the twentieth century).

Reed Jr, A. L. (1997) *W. E. B. Du Bois and American Political Thought: Fabianism and the Color Line*, New York: Oxford University Press (an exploration of Du Bois's thinking on race, that suggests links to more contemporary debates).

Rex, J. (1983) *Race Relations in Sociological Theory*, second edition, London: Routledge and Kegan Paul (a classic attempt to outline a theoretical basis for the study of race relations).

Stanfield II, J. H. (1985) *Philanthropy and Jim Crow in American Social Science*, Westport: Greenwood Press (a study of the development of early research on race relations in America during the Jim Crow period).

Part Three: Racism and anti-semitism

Key texts

Arendt, H. (1973) *The Origins of Totalitarianism*, new edition, San Diego: Harcourt Brace (influential analysis of the historical basis of the historical origins of anti-semitism and its impact on Nazi thought).

Bauman, Z. (1989) *Modernity and the Holocaust*, Oxford: Blackwell (an account of the social and historical conditions that made the Holocaust possible).

Gilman, S. L. and Katz, S. T. (eds) (1991) *Anti-Semitism in Times of Crisis*, New York: New York University Press (a valuable collection of papers on the experience of anti-semitism in specific historical settings).

Background reading

Adam, H. (1996) 'Anti-Semitism and Anti-Black Racism: Nazi Germany and Apartheid South Africa', *Telos* 108: 25–46 (an exploration of similarities and differences between Nazi Germany and apartheid South Africa).

Adorno, T. W. and Horkheimer, M. (1986) *Dialectic of Enlightenment*, London: Verso (contains an insightful analysis of the origins of anti-semitism and its role under Nazism).

Berman, P. (1994) *Blacks and Jews: Alliances and Arguments*, New York: Delta (a collection of papers that discuss anti-semitism among African–Americans as well as a discussion of broader aspects of Black and Jewish relations in America).

Biale, D., Galchinsky, M. and Heschel, S. (eds) (1998) *Insider/Outside: American Jews and Multiculturalism*, Berkeley: University of California Press (a collection that focuses on the changing cultural and identity politics of American Jews).

Burleigh, M. (1996) 'A Political Economy of the Final Solution? Reflections on Modernity, Historians and the Holocaust', *Patterns of Prejudice* 30, 2: 29–41 (a critical analysis of current debates about the Holocaust).

Burleigh, M. and Wippermann, W. (1991) *The Racial State: Germany 1933–1945*, Cambridge: Cambridge University Press (a masterful overview of the institutions and mechanisms of extermination developed by the Nazi racial state).

Cheyette, B. (1993) *Constructions of 'the Jew' in English Literature and Society: Racial Representations, 1875–1945*, Cambridge: Cambridge University Press (an account of ideas about Jews, focusing on images in English literature from the late nine-teenth to the early twentieth century).

Cheyette, B. (ed.) (1996) *Between 'Race' and Culture: Representations of 'the Jew' in English and American Literature*, Stanford: Stanford University Press (a collection of papers that brings together recent English and American research on literary represen-tations of 'the Jew').

Cheyette, B. and Marcus, L. (eds) (1998) *Modernity, Culture and 'The Jew'*, Cambridge: Polity Press (an important collection of papers that explore representations of Jewishness from the angle of literary theory and cultural studies).

Cohn, N. (1970) *Warrant for Genocide: The Myth of the Jewish World-Conspiracy and the Protocols of the Elders of Zion*, Harmondsworth: Penguin (a classic account of the role of conspiracy theories in anti-semitic discourses).

Gay, P. (1978) *Freud, Jews and Germans: Masters and Victims in Modernist Culture*, Oxford: Oxford University Press (an insightful account of the changing images of Jews in German culture).

Geras, N. (1998) *The Contract of Mutual Indifference: Political Philosophy after the Holocaust*, London: Verso (an attempt to situate the relevance of the Holocaust in terms of contemporary intellectual and political developments).

Gilman, S. L. (1986) *Jewish Self-Hatred: Anti-Semitism and the Hidden Language of the Jews*, Baltimore: The Johns Hopkins University Press (an exploration of the notion of 'self-hatred' among Jews from a historical and contemporary perspective).

——(1991) *The Jew's Body*, New York: Routledge (an innovative account of the role of images about the body in discourses about Jews).

——(1996) *Smart Jews: The Construction of the Image of Jewish Superior Intelligence*, Lincoln: University of Nebraska Press (an exploration of ideas about Jews and intelli-gence in scientific thought and popular culture).

Goldberg, D. T. and Krausz, M. (eds) (1993) *Jewish Identity*, Philadelphia: Temple University Press (an exploration of the changing patterns of contemporary Jewish identity).

Goldhagen, D. J. (1996) *Hitler's Willing Executioners: Ordinary Germans and the Holocaust*, London: Little, Brown and Company (a controversial account of the role of anti-semitism in German society in shaping the Holocaust).

Hitler, A. (1992) *Mein Kampf*, London: Pimlico (contains a version of Hitler's thoughts about Jews, race and related issues).

Kushner, T. (1994) *The Holocaust and the Liberal Imagination*, Oxford: Blackwell (an exploration of political and social responses to the Holocaust from the 1930s onwards).

Mayer, A. J. (1990) *Why Did the Heavens Not Darken: The 'Final Solution' in History*, London: Verso (an analysis of the conditions that led to the final solution).

Mosse, G. L. (1971) *Germans and Jews*, London: Orbach and Chambers (contains an insightful account of the development of the changing images of Jews in German society).

Poliakov, L. (1974) *The History of Anti-Semitism*, 4 Volumes, London: Routledge and Kegan Paul (an exhaustive historical analysis of anti-semitism in different histor-ical settings).

Pulzer, P. (1988) *The Rise of Political Anti-Semitism in Germany and Austria*, London: Peter Halban (an exploration of the politicisation of anti-semitic thought and its impact on political culture).

Rose, P. L. (1990) *German Question/Jewish Question: Revolutionary Antisemitism in Germany from Kant to Wagner*, Princeton: Princeton University Press (an account of the links between anti-semitic thought and the development of German nationalism).

Sartre, J.-P. (1976) *Anti-Semite and Jew*, New York: Schocken Books (a classic attempt to construct a philosophical understanding of anti-semitism).

Todorov, T. (1999) *Facing the Extreme: Moral Life in the Concentration Camps*, London: Weidenfeld and Nicolson (an account of the moral significance of the Holocaust, including reflections on accounts by perpetrators and survivors, as well as wider philosophical issues).

Part Four: Colonialism, race and the Other

Key texts

Alexander, M. J. and Mohanty, C. T. (eds) (1997) *Feminist Genealogies, Colonial Legacies, Democratic Futures*, New York: Routledge (an important collection of papers that explore questions about race and gender in colonial and postcolonial situations).

Bhabha, H. (1994) *The Location of Culture*, London: Routledge (an influential collection of papers that explore various facets of Bhabha's theoretical model).

Stoler, A. L. (1995) *Race and the Education of Desire: Foucault's History of Sexuality and the Colonial Order of Things*, Durham NC: Duke University Press (an attempt to link Foucault's analysis of sexuality to an analysis of colonialism).

Background reading

Adas, M. (1989) *Machines as the Measure of Men: Science, Technology and Ideologies of Western Dominance*, Ithaca: Cornell University Press (an analysis of changing ideas about race and civilisation through the nineteenth and early twentieth centuries).

Appiah, K. A. (1992) *In My Father's House: Africa in the Philosophy of Culture*, London: Methuen (an exploration of questions about race and identity in Africa).

Apter, A. (1991) 'Herskovits's Heritage: Rethinking Syncretism in the African Diaspora', *Diaspora* 1, 3: 235–60 (an account of debates about syncretism and cultural forms in the African diaspora).

Brantlinger, P. (1988) *Rule of Darkness: British Literature and Imperialism 1830–1914*, Ithaca: Cornell University Press (explores the interrelationship between literature and imperialism).

Cesaire, A. (1972) *Discourse on Colonialism*, New York: Monthly Review Press (a classical exploration of the cultural and social impact of colonialism).

Coombes, A. (1994) *Reinventing Africa: Museums, Material Culture and Popular Imagination in Late Victorian and Edwardian England*, London: Yale University Press (an exploration of representations of Africa and Africans in museums and popular culture).

Dirks, N. B. (ed.) 1992 *Colonialism and Culture*, Ann Arbor: University of Michigan Press (a collection of historical papers on the cultural impact of colonialism).

Eze, E. C. (ed.) (1997) *Postcolonial African Philosophy: A Critical Reader*, Cambridge, MA: Blackwell (a collection of papers on current debates about postcolonial African philosophy).

Fuss, D. (1994) 'Interior Colonies: Frantz Fanon and the Politics of Identification', *Diacritics* 24, 2–3: 20–42 (a critical analysis of Fanon's account of processes of identity formation in colonial situations).

Diawara, M. (1998) *In Search of Africa*, Cambridge, MA: Harvard University Press (a biological narrative of the author's return to his native Guinea and exploration of everyday features of the postcolonial situation in West Africa).

Frantz Fanon (1986) *Black Skin, White Masks*, London: Pluto (a classic account of the psychological impact of colonialism).

Füredi, F. (1998) *The Silent War: Imperialism and the Changing Perception of Race*, London: Pluto Press (an analysis of the role of imperialism in shaping ideas about race).

Gordon, L. R. (1997) *Her Majesty's Other Children: Sketches of Racism from a Neocolonial Age*, Lanham, Maryland: Rowman and Littlefield (a collection of essays that explore historical and contemporary features of racism).

Greenblatt, S. (1991) *Marvelous Possessions: The Wonder of the New World*, Chicago: University of Chicago Press (an account of the impact of the discovery of the New World on images of other cultures).

Hobsbawm, E. (1987) *The Age of Empire 1875–1914*, London: Weidenfeld and Nicolson (an influential history of the high-point of European imperial expansion).

Hulme, P. (1986) *Colonial Encounters: Europe and the Native Caribbean*, London: Methuen (an analysis of the emergence of colonialism in the Caribbean).

Kiernan, V. G. (1969) *The Lords of Humankind: Black Man, Yellow Man, and White Man in the Age of Empire*, Harmondsworth: Penguin (a classic account of the articulation of changing ideas about race in the context of colonialism).

Lewis, R. (1996) *Gendering Orientalism: Race, Femininity and Representation*, London: Routledge (an analysis of the intersections between race and gender in orientalist discourses).

Low, G. C-L. (1996) *White Skins, Black Masks: Representation and Colonialism*, London: Routledge (a study of literary representations of colonialism, focusing on Haggard and Kipling).

Lowe, L. (1991) *Critical Terrains: French and British Orientalisms*, Ithaca: Cornell University Press (a comparative analysis of the changing images of race and the Other to be found in French and British orientalisms).

Mani, L. (1998) *Contentious Traditions: The Debate on Sati in Colonial India*, Berkeley: University of California Press (a detailed analysis of how colonial discourses constructed ideas of tradition in India).

Mannoni, O. (1964) *Prospero and Caliban: The Psychology of Colonization*, New York: Frederick A. Praeger (a classic account of the psychological impact of colonialism, based on a study of Madagascar).

Mbembe, A. (1992) 'The Banality of Power and the Aesthetics of Vulgarity in the Postcolony', *Public Culture* 4, 2: 1–30 (explores the role of power and force in postcolonial Africa).

Mudimbe, V. Y. (1994) *The Idea of Africa*, Bloomington: Indiana University Press (an account of ideas about Africa from ancient times to the present).

Nandy, A. (1988) *The Intimate Enemy: Loss and Recovery of Self Under Colonialism*, second edition, Delhi: Oxford University Press (a discussion of the impact of colonialism on ideas about self and other).

Padgen, A. (1995) *Lords of All the World: Ideologies of Empire in Spain, Britain and France c.1500–c.1800*, New Haven and London: Yale University Press (a comparative account of early ideologies of empire).

Parry, B. (1998) *Delusions and Discoveries: India in the British Imagination, 1880–1930*, new edition, London: Verso (an exploration of evolving British ideas about Indian culture and society).

Parsons, N. (1998) *King Khama, Emperor Joe and the Great White Queen: Victorian Britain Through African Eyes*, Chicago: University of Chicago Press (an innovative look at Victorian society through the eyes of Africans).

Pieterse, J. N. and Parekh, B. (eds) (1995) *The Decolonization of Imagination: Culture, Knowledge and Power*, London: Zed Books (an exploration of discourses of colonial domination and decolonisation).

Pratt, M. L. (1992) *Imperial Eyes: Travel Writing and Transculturation*, London: Routledge (a study that focuses on travel writings and how they constructed images of other people in the nineteenth and early twentieth centuries).

Ross, R. (ed.) (1982) *Racism and Colonialism*, The Hague: Martinus Nijhoff (an important collection of papers that explore the relationship between racism and colonialism).

Said, E. (1978) *Orientalism*, Harmondsworth: Penguin (the foundational statement of the orientalist thesis).

UNESCO (1977) *Race and Class in Post-Colonial Society*, Paris: UNESCO (a collection of papers that is focused on the relationship between class and race, particularly in the Caribbean and Latin America).

Williams, B. F. (ed.) (1996) *Women Out of Place: The Gender of Agency and the Race of Nationality*, New York: Routledge (a collection of papers that explore constructions of gender, race and nation).

Yegenoglu, M. (1998) *Colonial Fantasies: Towards a Feminist Reading of Orientalism*, Cambridge: Cambridge University Press (a feminist reading of the debates about orientalism).

Young, R. J. C. (1995) *Colonial Desire: Hybridity in Theory, Culture and Race*, London: Routledge (an influential analysis of changing ideas about race and hybridity from the nineteenth century onwards).

Part Five: Feminism, difference and identity

Key texts

Collins, P. H. (1990) *Black Feminist Thought*, London: Unwin Hyman (a critical analysis of the emergence of black feminism and its contribution to the understanding of the position of black women).

Mirza, H. S. (ed.) (1997) *Black British Feminism: A Reader*, London: Routledge (a collection of some important contributions to the development of black British feminism).

Williams, P. J. (1991) *The Alchemy of Race and Rights*, Cambridge, MA: Harvard University Press (an exploration of everyday experiences of race and gender in American Society).

Background reading

Bhattacharyya, G. (1998) *Tales of Dark-Skinned Women: Race, Gender and Global Culture*, London: UCL Press (a series of stories that explores the encounter between black women and the West).

Brody, J. D. (1998) *Impossible Purities: Blackness, Femininity, and Victorian Culture*, Durham NC: Duke University Press (a historical reconstruction of images of femininity and blackness in the Victorian imagination).

Bryan, B., Dadzie, S. and Scafe, S. (1985) *The Heart of the Race: Black Women's Lives in Britain*, London: Virago (an early attempt to explore the experiences of black women in contemporary Britain).

Carby, H. V. (1998) *Race Men*, Cambridge, Mass.: Harvard University Press (an innovative account of the articulation of ideas about black masculinity in American culture, with a focus on Du Bois and other important figures in black American history).

Christian, B. (1985) *Black Feminist Criticism: Perspectives on Black Women Writers*, New York: Pergamon Press (an important collection of papers on key black women writers).

Davis, A. Y. (1982) *Women, Race & Class*, London: The Women's Press (an influential early attempt to link the analysis of race with questions about class and gender).

Frankenberg, R. (1993) *White Women, Race Matters: The Social Construction of Whiteness*, London: Routledge (an investigation of the meanings of race and whiteness among a sample of white women in America).

Friedman, S. S. (1998) *Mappings: Feminism and the Cultural Geographies of Encounter*, Princeton: Princeton University Press (an argument that feminism needs to move beyond difference and become more transnational and heterogeneous).

Gates Jr. H. L. (ed.) *Reading Black, Reading Feminist: A Critical Anthology*, New York: Meridian (a collection of recent critical perspectives on black women's writing in America).

hooks, b. (1990) *Yearning: Race, Gender and Cultural Politics*, Boston: South End Press (an influential analysis of the new cultural politics of race and gender in America).

Ifekwunigwe, J. O. (1999) *Scattered Belongings: Cultural Paradoxes of 'Race', Nation and Gender*, London: Routledge (mixes biography and academic analysis to map the borders between race and gender in the contemporary environment).

James, J. (ed.) (1998) *The Angela Y. Davis Reader*, Oxford: Blackwell (a collection of Davis's writings on race, class and gender).

James, S. and Busia, A. (eds) (1993) *Theorizing Black Feminisms*, London: Routledge (a collection of papers on various aspects of contemporary black feminism).

Jarrett-Macauley, D. (ed.) (1996) *Reconstructing Womanhood, Reconstructing Feminism: Writings on Black Women*, London: Routledge (a collection of papers on debates within black British feminism).

Mama, A. (1995) *Beyond the Masks: Race, Gender and Subjectivity*, London: Routledge (an account of psychological discourses about race and Africans).

Mohanty, C. T., Russo, A., and Torres, L. (eds) (1991) *Third World Women and the Politics of Feminism*, Bloomington: Indiana University Press (an influential collection of papers that explore feminism from a third world perspective).

Mullings, L. (1997) *On Our Own Terms: Race, Class and Gender in the Lives of African American Women*, New York: Routledge (an analysis of the changing experiences of African–American women).

Nelson, D. D. (1998) *National Manhood: Capitalist Manhood and the Imagined Fraternity of White Men*, Durham NC: Duke University Press (a historical analysis of ideas about nation, race and gender in America).

Spivak, G. C. (1988) *In Other Worlds: Essays in Cultural Politics*, London: Routledge (a collection of influential essays, including Spivak's critical analysis of Western feminism).

——(1993) *Outside in the Teaching Machine*, New York: Routledge (a collection of essays, including questions of multiculturalism, postcolonialism and feminism).

Parker, A., Russo, M., Sommer, D., and Yaeger, P. (eds) (1992) *Nationalisms and Sexualities*, New York: Routledge (a collection of papers that explore the relationship between nationalism and sexuality in a variety of contexts).

Sudbury, J. (1998) *'Other Kinds of Dreams': Black Women's Organisations and the Politics of Transformation*, London: Routledge (an account of forms of self-organisation among black women in Britain).

Ware, V. (1992) *Beyond the Pale: White Women, Racism and History*, London: Verso (a historical treatment of the role of white women in relation to colonialism and racism).

Part Six: Changing boundaries and spaces

Key texts

Bhatt, C. (1997) *Liberation and Purity: Race, New Religious Movements and the Ethics of Postmodernity*, London: UCL Press (a suggestive account of the role of new religious movements and the changing boundaries of race and identity).

Frankenberg, R. (ed.) (1997) *Displacing Whiteness: Essays in Social and Cultural Criticism*, Durham NC: Duke University Press (a collection of papers on current debates about whiteness from a variety of historical and contemporary angles).

Papastergiadis, N. (1998) *Dialogues in the Diasporas: Essays and Conversations on Cultural Identity*, London: Rivers Oram Press (a collection of essays on diasporic cultural identities and ideas of globalisation and belonging).

Background reading

Allen, T. W. (1994) *The Invention of the White Race. Volume One: Racial Oppression and Social Control*, London: Verso (an analysis of the history of ideas about whiteness in America).

Appadurai, A. (1996) *Modernity at Large: Cultural Dimensions of Globalization*, Minneapolis: University of Minnesota Press (a collection of papers that explores the changing boundaries of globalisation and identity).

Appiah, K. A. and Gates Jr. H. L. (eds) (1995) *Identities*, Chicago: University of Chicago Press (a collection of papers on changing processes of identity formation in relation to race, ethnicity, gender and related issues).

Appiah, K. A. and Gutmann, A. (1996) *Color Conscious: The Political Morality of Race*, Princeton: Princeton University Press (a collection of essays in which the authors outline their understandings of race and multiculturalism in contemporary America).

Balibar, E. (1995) 'Ambiguous Universality', *Differences* 7, 1: 48–74 (explores the contested meanings of ideas about universalism and difference).

Balibar, E. and Wallerstein, I. (1991) *Race, Nation, Class: Ambiguous Identities*, London: Verso (a collection of papers in which the authors present their views on the relationship between race, nation and class).

Brah, A. (1996) *Cartographies of Diaspora: Contesting Identities*, London: Routledge (a collection of essays focusing on questions of diasporic culture and identity).

Calhoun, C. (ed.) (1994) *Social Theory and the Politics of Identity*, Oxford: Blackwell (a collection of essays on the politics of identity in the contemporary global environment).

Clifford, J. (1994) 'Diasporas', *Cultural Anthropology* 9, 3: 302–38 (an overview of the notion of diaspora).

Cohen, R. (1997) *Global Diasporas: An Introduction*, London: UCL Press (a systematic analysis of various diasporas and of their role in shaping global processes).

Connolly, W. E. (1995) *The Ethos of Pluralization*, Minneapolis: University of Minnesota Press (argues for a new political theory based on pluralism that can deal with issues such as multiculturalism and fundamentalism).

Delgado, R. and Stefancic, J. (eds) (1997) *Critical White Studies: Looking Behind the Mirror*, Philadelphia: Temple University Press (a comprehensive collection of historical and contemporary texts on various aspects of the construction of whiteness).

di Leonardo, M. (1998) *Exotics at Home: Anthropologies, Others, American Modernity*, Chicago: University of Chicago Press (outlines a critical analysis of anthropological treatments of foreign and domestic others, with a focus on anthropological discourses in America).

Goldberg, D. T. (ed.) (1994) *Multiculturalism: A Critical Reader*, Oxford: Blackwell (an important collection of papers that encompasses both the theory and the practice of multiculturalism).

Gordon, A. F. and Newfield, C. (1996) *Mapping Multiculturalism*, Minneapolis: University of Minnesota Press (an exploration of the different uses of the concept of multiculturalism, with a focus on intellectual debates and political trends).

Gutmann, A. (ed.) (1994) *Multiculturalism: Examining the Politics of Recognition*, Princeton: Princeton University Press (a collection of papers debating Charles Taylor's notion of the 'politics of recognition').

Hall, S. and du Gay, P. (eds) (1996) *Questions of Cultural Identity*, London: Sage (a collection of papers on the development of new forms of cultural identity).

Hannerz, U. (1996) *Transnational Connections: Culture, People, Places*, London: Routledge (explores the development of forms of transnationalism based on people, culture and movement).

Howe, S. (1998) *Afrocentrism: Mythical Pasts and Imagined Homes*, London: Verso (an important critique of the foundations of Afrocentrism).

JanMohamed, A. R. and Lloyd, D. (eds) (1990) *The Nature and Context of Minority Discourse*, New York: Oxford University Press (a collection of papers on the development of minority discourses and identity formation).

Kaplan, A. and Pease, D. E. (eds) (1993) *Cultures of United States Imperialism*, Durham NC: Duke University Press (brings together a number of papers that look at the role of ideas about nation and race in the context of globalisation).

Kymlicka, W. (1995) *Multicultural Citizenship: A Liberal Theory of Minority Rights*, Oxford: Oxford University Press (a discussion of the rights and status of minority cultures in multicultural societies).

Lemelle, S. and Kelley, R. D. G. (eds) (1994) *Imagining Home: Class, Culture and Nationalism in the African Diaspora*, London: Verso (a collection of papers on narratives of home and belonging in the African diaspora).

Lipsitz, G. (1998) *The Possessive Investment in Whiteness: How White People Profit from Identity Politics*, Philadelphia: Temple University Press (explores the values and meanings of whiteness in shaping politics, culture and public policy in American society).

Lowe, L. and Lloyd, D. (eds) (1997) *The Politics of Culture in the Shadow of Capital*, Durham, NC: Duke University Press (a collection of papers about the impact of cultural politics in diverse national and regional settings).

Rattansi, A. and Westwood, S. (eds) (1994) *Racism, Modernity and Identity: On the Western Front*, Cambridge: Polity Press (a collection of essays that provide an overview of recent debates about racism, modernity and postmodernism).

Roediger, D. R. (ed.) (1998) *Black on White: Black Writers on What it Means to be White*, New York: Schocken Books (a collection that focuses on how black writers have defined the meaning of whiteness).

Sollors, W. (1997) *Neither Black Nor White Yet Both: Thematic Explorations in Interracial Literature*, New York: Oxford University Press (a detailed analysis of interracial themes in literature and the visual arts, from the perspective of what this literature tells us about construction of race and of the categories 'black' and 'white').

Van Hear, N. (1998) *New Diasporas: The Mass Exodus, Dispersal and Regrouping of Migrant Communities*, London: UCL Press (an appraisal of the development of new forms of migration and dispersal in the current global environment).

West, C. (1993) *Race Matters*, Boston: Beacon Press (an influential essay on current dilemmas about race in America).

Willett, C. (ed.) (1998) *Theorizing Multiculturalism: A Guide to the Current Debate*, Oxford: Blackwell (a collection of papers on the philosophy and politics of multiculturalism).

Williams, P. J. (1997) *Seeing a Color-Blind Future: The Paradox of Race*, New York: The Noonday Press (a series of lectures that reflect on current dilemmas about racism and anti-racism).

Name index

Subject index

academy: black feminism and the 371, 462–71; race teaching 473–4

Adam, descendants of 52–3

Africa: apes and Negroes 42–3; European settlement 33; religion 38–40; women as universal dependants 307; women as victims of male violence 306; women's work 287–8, 297–9; *see also* South Africa

African-American: communities 370, 372; cultures 611–12; life-scripts 614; studies 464–6; women 406–16, 463–71

African-Caribbean: communities 436; women 393, 432

Africentricity 491

Afrocentric worldview 410–11

Alliance Israélite Universelle 199, 200

American Negro Academy 84–6

animal imagery 197, 274

anthropologists, anthropology 107, 117, 158, 162

anti-semitism: black 186; bourgeois 207; Eastern European 594, 596; elements of 206–11; extermination policy 219–23; issue 2; key questions 194; modern 224–7; myth and counter-myth 195–204; racism and 10–13; responses to 600–1; without Jews 194, 224, 596; *see also* Holocaust, Jews

apartheid 164, 166, 604, *see also* segregation

apes 42–3, 161–2

Arab: civilization 117; familial system 309

art: black 491; race groups 82; Whitechapel Gallery 523–5

Aryan: Aryanist thinking 586–9; languages 114–15, 586; races 114, 201, 586

Asian: groups 432; women 391, 394, 399, 401

authenticity: ethical imperative 516, 614; lie of 533–4; spaces of 521–34

Bemba marriage ritual 308–9

Bharatiya Janata Party (BJP) 578, 581

Bible creation story 52

biology: brain and skull size 98–9n, 156; feminist accounts 435; Moscow Declaration 120–1; popular belief 138; racist conceptions 119–20, 567–8; skin colour *see* colour

Birmingham: CCCS 7, 8, 16, 133–4; Handsworth study 5

black: anti-semitism 186; art 491; category 24, 510; cultural expression 491–9; diaspora 490–1, 494–5; educators 478–88; family structures 390, 391; femininity 272–6; feminism and the academy 462–71; feminist thought 369–70, 372, 404–16; franchise 561; identity 150–1, 230; masculinity 151–2; music 490, 493–4, 497–9; nationalism 491;